Depression: Theories and Treatments

PSYCHOLOGICAL, BIOLOGICAL, AND SOCIAL PERSPECTIVES

DEPRESSION
THEORIES AND TREATMENTS

Psychological, Biological, and Social Perspectives

ARTHUR SCHWARTZ

AND

RUTH M. SCHWARTZ

COLUMBIA UNIVERSITY PRESS *New York*

The logs in chapters 14 and 15 first appeared in Arthur Schwartz and Israel Goldiamond, *Social Casework: A Behavioral Approach* (New York: Columbia University Press, 1975). Table 3.1 has been reproduced from E. McGrath, G. P. Keita, B. R. Strickland, and N. F. Russo, eds., *Women and Depression: Risk Factors and Treatment Issues*, Final Report of the American Psychological Association's National Task Force on Women and Depression. Washington D.C.: American Psychological Association, 1990, p. 3. Copyright © 1990 by the American Psychological Association. Reprinted by permission of the APA. Neither the original nor this reproduction can be republished, photocopied, reprinted, or distributed in any form without the prior permission of the American Psychological Association.

Extended passages from the *Diagnostic and Statistical Manual of Mental Disorders* 3d ed., revised (Washington, D.C.: American Psychiatric Association, 1987) are printed by permission of the American Psychiatric Association.

The passage from *Movie Stars, Real People, and Me*, by Joshua Logan (New York: Bantam, 1978) is quoted by permission of Delacorte Press.

Columbia University Press
New York   Oxford
Copyright © 1993 Columbia University Press
All rights reserved

Library of Congress Cataloging-in-Publication Data

Schwartz, Arthur.
Depression : theories and treatments : psychological, biological, and social perspectives Arthur Schwartz and Ruth M. Schwartz.
p.   cm.
Includes bibliographical references and index.
ISBN 0–231–06818–2
1. Depression, Mental.   I. Schwartz, Ruth M.   II. Title.
[DNLM: 1. Depressive Disorder.   WM 171 S399d]
RC537.S395   1993
616.85'27—dc20
DNLM/DLC   92–49525
                CIP

Casebound editions of Columbia University Press books are printed on permanent and durable acid-free paper.

Book design by Jennifer Dossin

PRINTED IN THE UNITED STATES OF AMERICA

c 10 9 8 7 6 5 4 3 2 1

This book is dedicated to our children,
Elizabeth and David

CONTENTS

PART II
Biological Theories and Treatments of Depression

PART III
Psychological Theories and Treatments of Depression   171

PREFACE

There are increasing grounds for optimism in the treatment of the depressions because of the vast amount of research being conducted and the exciting, significant findings that are emerging. These findings are constantly expanding our already sizable and many-faceted body of knowledge.

Depression: Theories and Treatments is written primarily for the busy practitioner who does not have access to the diverse and often very technical professional journals that report on the many aspects of depression. It is also for the student who seeks a fair and understandable introduction to this complex problem area.

The book provides an overview of the major orientations to the currently most important theories and treatments of the depressions. We have reviewed and drawn from a large number of sources, and have tried to present the material directly, accurately, and concisely, with extensive notes and references for the reader who wishes more information on particular topics. We have emphasized the practical information that we think is important for the treatment of depressed clients and have provided case studies as well as a unified treatment model.

The lay reader will find this book useful in a number of ways. It should demystify both the biology and the psychology of the depressions and the various treatment options currently available, including the new—even experimental—approaches. The specific information provided about the treatment process should prove beneficial to a depressed individual who may be considering professional treatment. It will assist in choosing a therapist whose treatment approach is valid and viable, and it will help the depressed client know how to obtain *good* treatment and how to monitor this treatment.

The book should also provide valuable information for those who are involved with a depressed person—his or her support network or significant others—who must cope with the many ramifications of the illness, and be supportive of the client and be his or her advocate as required.

The reader will not need specialized knowledge and will not have to consult outside sources to understand the topics discussed in this book. We define all technical terms and include brief "minitutorials" for those who do not know—or do not remember—the principles underlying the various theories we cover for example in the areas of genetics, neurochemical and neuroendocrine function, sleep physiology, applied behavior analysis, and more.

ACKNOWLEDGMENTS

Many people have helped us in the long process of writing this book. We express our deepest gratitude to Louise Waller, former executive editor of the Columbia University Press, who suggested this book, encouraged us during the writing, and was most generous in her comments, criticisms, and constant support. Thank you, Louise.

During the writing of the book many colleagues and professionals took time from their busy teaching and research to read and comment upon various parts of the manuscript. They are, in alphabetical order: Dr. Joann A. Boughman, Department of Medical Genetics in Obstetrics-Gynecology of the School of Medicine, University of Maryland; Dr. Fred DiBlasio of the School of Social Work, University of Maryland; Dr. Mohyee E. Eldefrawi of the Department of Pharmacology of the School of Medicine, University of Maryland; Dr. Steven E. Hyman of the Molecular Neurobiology Laboratory, Massachusetts General Hospital and the Harvard Medical School; Dr. Stanley McCracken of the Anxiety and Depression Clinic, University of Chicago; Dr. Lisa Robinson-Glushakow of the School of Nursing of the University of Maryland; Dr. Stanley E. Weinstein, of the Department of Health and Mental Hygiene, State of Maryland; and Dr. Richard J. Wurtman, Department of Brain and Cognitive Sciences, Massachusetts Institute of Technology. We thank all these individuals for their unselfish help in assisting us to interpret some of this very technical material. We are also grateful to Marcia Ames for her careful editing of the sections on biology.

We are indebted to the many librarians and staff members of the Health Sciences Library of the University of Maryland at Baltimore who assisted us, particularly M. J. Tooey, who patiently explained electronic information retrieval, and Mary Ann Williams. The staff at the Psychiatry, Neuroscience Library at Johns Hopkins University, especially Jane Campbell, was also helpful and generous. Similarly, we thank the librarians of the Towson Library, Baltimore County, Maryland.

Many of our colleagues at the School of Social Work at the University of Maryland at Baltimore were supportive of our efforts. We especially thank Dr. Jesse J. Harris, dean, and Ms. Lily Gold, associate dean, for their encouragement and help.

We wish to thank Stephanie M. Czech and Tom Stevenson of the Illustrative Services, Office of Medical Education, University of Maryland at Baltimore, for creating the illustrations while under great pressure to meet our deadline. The staff of the Columbia University Press was also very helpful; we especially thank Gioia Stevens, our current editor; Matthew Weiland, who answered many questions; Leslie Bialler, who demystified the computer process; Anne McCoy, managing editor, who brought the book to publication; and Ron Harris, who edited the manuscript with exquisite care. Finally, we thank our children, Elizabeth and David, other members of our family (particularly Dr. Howard Fuerst, who regularly supplied us with his publications on depression), and our loyal friends for their unflagging encouragement, support, and patience with us while we were so often unavailable.

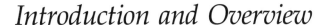

Introduction and Overview

Depression in the United States is widespread, some would say epidemic. It is so prevalent that the psychiatrist Gerald Klerman (1978) has justly called the time we are living in the "Age of Melancholy."

We shall not flood the reader with statistics. Yet even conservative estimates indicate that millions of people worldwide are depressed (Marsella et al. 1985:299). In the United States, it has been calculated that in any six-month period, 9.4 million people suffer from depression (Fink 1988). It is also likely that at least one in every twenty Americans, from the very young to the very old, will have a major depressive disorder sometime in his or her lifetime, and many others will experience depressions that do not reach clinical significance but that interfere with their functioning and cause untold suffering and pain.

Depression itself is not only widespread but also associated with many other psychological conditions, with many physical diseases, and most certainly, with social and external factors. Depression increases with poverty, unemployment, marital and family discord, emotional disturbances in both adults and children, the reverses that are sometimes experienced in life, and often—but not always—aging and disability. It appears in so many forms that it is more accurate to speak of the *depressions.*

Besides the serious emotional and social costs of depression, the economic costs are enormous. Acknowledging that their figures are estimates (which, if anything, underassess the costs), one study states the direct costs—including inpatient, outpatient, drugs, and other care costs—are over $2.1 billion a year. Indirect costs, including "total morbidity and mortality costs due to lost productivity" are over $14 billion, or an estimated total of over $16 billion a year. These figures are in 1980 dollars; costs have undoubtedly risen significantly since then (Stoudemire et al. 1986).

Many people who suffer from depression are not properly diagnosed and treated. Whether they go directly to mental health practitioners, physicians, the clergy, or others for help with problems ranging from feelings of sadness, hopelessness and despair, and even suicidal thoughts, to backache, sexual problems, fatigue, or vague aches and pains, they are not always diagnosed as depressed. In fact, no more than one-third of nonhospitalized people who have major depressions (serious depressions, which we shall define in chapter 3), receive mental health treatment, and from 50 to 70 percent of these people will return again and again to their physicians for medical treatments (Katon 1987). The general practitioner who cannot identify the patient's symptoms as depression may prescribe medication that, at best, may be inadequate. Even when the depression *is* diagnosed, medications are often prescribed incorrectly, owing to lack of expertise in a very complicated area.

All health professionals—counselors, doctors, ministers, nurses, occupational and physical therapists, psychiatrists, psychologists, social workers, and other human service workers—constantly deal with people suffering from some degree of depression. When depression is undiagnosed, or even when it is diagnosed but not treated properly, the patient may pay enormous psychological, physical, and economic costs. This is why an understanding of the many aspects of depression is a priority for all practitioners.

Although depression is common, even professionals are not united on defining what it is and, more important, on how to treat it. Debate continues on its nature, questioning if it is basically biological or psychological, as we shall explain. The question is extremely important, for the definition often determines the treatment. If a person with depression goes to a practitioner who believes that depression is essentially biological, then the treatment will usually be drugs or electroconvulsive therapy (mistakenly called shock therapy) or another somatic (body-related) intervention. If a depressed person goes to a practitioner who believes that depression is essentially psychological, then the treatment will probably be one of the "talking therapies."

An underlying thesis of this book is that the dichotomy of the biological versus the psychological is essentially artificial. This polarization, an either/or approach, is often responsible for inadequate therapy, sometimes with tragic results.

The Causes of Depression

■■ There are many theories about the causes of depression.
■■ Speaking broadly, they reflect the differences in viewing depression as primarily biological or primarily psychological—a restatement of the persisting issue of heredity versus environment or nature versus nurture.

The biological causes are thought to be (1) *heredity* (as described by the general term *genetic conditions*), which includes what individuals inherit directly, as well as the genetic transmission of vulnerability, and (2) *physiological disturbance,* which currently focuses on the body's neurochemical, endocrine, and limbic systems. Psychological causes are thought to include (1) *family origin* (or family transition), which focuses on the general area of personality and its development, and on particular consequences of child rearing (determinants include interactions between parents and child in matters of discipline and demonstration of caring, among other factors), and (2) *social influences,* a broad category covering the general area of social and cultural factors, such as poverty, segregation, and so on. Many theories of depression as well as treatments consider such factors as a patient's family circumstances, developmental history, and socialization process as central to assessment and treatment.

Stress is considered to be another cause of depression. In this context, it may refer to an upset in the emotional or physical equilibrium of an individual. For example, stress can result from physical illness; from the inability to cope with certain life events, such as separation and loss; and from significant changes, such as marriage, childbirth, and so on. Thus it can be viewed as primarily biological, primarily psychological, or a combination of the two. Stress may also trigger an episode of depression, especially in individuals who are vulnerable because of predisposing biological or social factors.

Although these various "causes" of depression are often categorized as internal or external, the actual picture is far from clear; these differences are obviously not so distinct in reality. We cannot overemphasize that each depressed individual is unique, and many different causative factors combine in varying amounts and are in constant flux, influencing and interacting with each other. We often cannot pinpoint the genesis of a problem, for even symptoms that seem to be the same may have completely different origins.

It is becoming increasingly apparent that there are many diverse aspects to depression. Just as medical and disease conditions are being viewed more and more within the framework of social systems, studies show that depression is expressed differently in various cultures and is affected by social systems such as the family, the society, the neighborhood, the tribe, and so forth (Kleinman and Good 1985; Marsella, Hirschfeld, and Katz 1987). Keyes (1985:316) speaks of hierarchies of analysis, from the biopsychosocial to the biobehavioral to the psychosocial to the microsocial and the macrosocial. Social systems and subsystems obviously are relevant to the etiology and the expression of depression, and we shall discuss the influence of these factors, where relevant. We elaborate on social factors in part 5.

Overview

■■ We intend this book to be a concise yet comprehensive guide
■■ to recognizing and treating the depressions. We present a
brief but inclusive overview of the various biological and psychological
theories of depression, the therapy models based on those theories, and
the evidence supporting their use. Rather than advocate either medication or psychotherapy, we encourage the appropriate use of each, separately or in combination, as dictated by the needs of the individual
case situation.

We present a summary of the latest evidence regarding the use of
medication and somatic therapies, the psychotherapies, and the combined approach of using both medications and psychotherapy together.
We hope to provide evidence to encourage the biologically oriented
therapist to consider increasing the use of "talking" therapy, when
appropriate, and we hope to provide guidelines to enable the psycho-
therapeutically oriented therapist to judge when consultations should
be sought to determine the possible need for medication.

We also try to help the reader understand how to access and utilize
the immense, growing, and sometimes contradictory literature on the
diagnosis and treatment of depression.

Organization

■■ In part 1 we examine the multifaceted nature of the depres-
■■ sions and the complexities of definition and assessment. We
discuss the various aspects of different kinds of depression. We discuss
how it is identified by its presenting symptoms and present the formal
classification of the depressions, as well as several alternative schemes.

In parts 2 and 3 we elaborate upon the biological and psychological
aspects of the depressions and relate them to the various interventions.
In part 4 we present our view of differential assessment in helping to
determine whether a talking therapy or a combination of talking and
somatic therapy is indicated. We then present a unified framework for
treating depression.

In part 5 we discuss some specific contemporary issues in depression, such as the relationship of gender to depression, the occurrence
of depression at various life stages (childhood, adolescence, and old
age) and in certain life situations (couple relationships, marriage, the
family), and sociocultural variations in the diagnosis and treatment of
depression, including depression in minority groups.

What Is Depression?

Depression has always been with us. Our human ancestors must certainly have experienced depression, just as such modern-day primates as baboons and chimpanzees seem to become depressed (Klerman 1987:3).

The clinical descriptions of depression, from Hippocrates to the present, have remained fairly consistent over the centuries. However, clinical explanations of depression have varied, as the result sometimes of scientific findings and sometimes of shifts in the dominance of theoretical models. This is important, for just as our views of causation have changed, so have our views on therapy.

We must define depression, for the definition often determines the treatment. Complicating any discussion of depression are the controversies over what it is. What do we mean when we speak of depression?

The Many Aspects of Depression

When we speak of depression we usually mean a disturbance in mood. This may range from the so-called normal and expected changes in mood to the depth of clinical depression.

Depression has other aspects. It has been observed as a reaction to certain substances, such as alcohol and other drugs. Depression may be seen as a way of life—a way of actively coping, albeit dysfunctionally. It can also be a combination of any or all of these factors, as well as a lawful, very understandable reaction to difficulties and setbacks that we experience in life. In fact, under certain conditions, something may be very wrong if we are *not* depressed.

Depression manifests itself in different ways in different people and, to complicate matters, often in different ways in the same person at different times in that person's life. It may be primary or secondary to physical and/or other emotional conditions. It can appear in ways that are obvious, or it can be hidden or masked.

Mood Change: Sadness or Depression

■■   We are all sad from time to time, and sometimes this sadness
■■   persists or deepens to the point where we are depressed.
There is a point—not entirely agreed upon, even by professionals—
where depression ceases to be in the normal range of emotions, where
one no longer is suffering merely from the blues or feeling down but is
either functioning with great pain and difficulty or not functioning at
all. This stage can be called clinical depression.

Common to all views of depression is the problem of differentiating
normal grief or sadness from clinical depression. Wender and Klein
(1981:45) emphasize that sadness differs from the feelings experienced
in some types of depression. In grief one feels an aching loss, whereas
in depression the mood is "colorless . . . [it] has been described as
painful anesthesia—painful because the patient remembers that life
used to be pleasurable, . . . anesthesia because of the general numb-
ness" (Wender and Klein 1981:45). The person may also feel helpless,
bored, indecisive, guilty, and unable to love.

The controversial psychiatrist Thomas Szasz (a critic of the concept
of mental illness), when teaching medical students about depression,
would first discuss the various symptoms and aspects of depression
and then write on the blackboard *unhappy person.* He would then challenge his students to differentiate between this unhappy person and a
depressive. This view of depression as merely unhappiness may be
questioned as being simplistic, but it does contain the proverbial grain
of truth. Szasz, in speaking against the view that depression is exclusively an illness, intended to illustrate that "unhappiness" can result
from reality factors as well as from mental illness.

Wender and Klein (1981:231) speak of "realistic unhappiness" in
people who are upset by circumstances: environments they cannot
change, avoid, or escape; personal situations, such as an unhappy
marriage or an unsatisfying job; or situational unhappiness from stresses
caused by life changes, such as new jobs, or developmental phases,
such as adolescence. They state that these stresses do cause suffering,
but in most persons the way they experience the distress differs primarily in quality, but also in degree, from what we call clinical depression.

Whybrow, Akiskal, and McKinney (1984:15) developed these guidelines to define depression:

1. There is a difference in the quality and the intensity of the mood
   that seems to permeate all aspects of the person and cannot be
   dispelled, and the person does not respond to comfort and support (reassurance).

2. There may not be any identifiable stimulus for the mood, or the reaction may be out of proportion to the stimulant.

3. The mood seems to have a life of its own; it persists autonomously. This is often seen as part of the qualitative difference between sadness and depression.

The formal criteria for differentiating between sadness and depression are given later in this section.

1

Defining Clinical Depression

The Basic Questions

■■ Beck (1967:3–4), in discussing the difficulties in defining
■■ depression, raised several succinct questions that are still
relevant. We have paraphrased and amplified them as follows:

1. Since we all suffer at times from periods of feeling blue, down, or sad, is what we call clinical depression an exaggeration of our normal moods, or is it a disease, with an etiology (a cause), a course, and an outcome?[1]
2. If it is a disease, is it a specific, clear-cut one, or is it, in Beck's words, a " 'wastebasket' category of diverse disorders"?
3. If it is not a disease, is depression a type of reaction?
4. Is depression caused primarily by psychological stress and conflict, or is it essentially a result of a biological dysfunctioning?

Disease or Reaction? The Kraepelinian Versus Meyerian View

■■ Discussion of the basic issues of depression as a disease or as
■■ a reaction reflects the Kraepelinian versus the Meyerian view.
The concept that depression is a disease, with an etiology, a course, and an outcome, is named after the famous European psychiatrist Emil Kraepelin, who first categorized the mental disorders. From the Kraepelinian perspective, the causes of depression are to be found primarily in biology, particularly in the areas of genetics and physiology. First, there is a biological (biochemical) disorder; the psychological aspects develop after the biological dysfunction. Since depression is a disease, the main treatments proposed are somatic.

For advocates of the opposing view, clinical depression is not a distinct disease but a continuation and deepening of normal feelings. To understand this concept, visualize a straight line with *normal* at the extreme left. Within this area are the temporary "blues" and the "feeling down" that we all experience. As we go along this line to the right, the quantity and quality of these "blue" or "down" feelings increase and become more severe, to the point where the feelings interfere with our functioning. This is *neurotic depression*. As we move further to the right the depression may last a long time, functioning is increasingly limited, and there may be delusions, hallucinations, and suicide attempts. This is *psychotic depression*. This view is associated mainly with the American psychiatrist Adolph Meyer and is called the *continuity hypothesis of depression* or the *Meyerian view of depression*. Depression is viewed primarily, although not exclusively, as a reaction and is believed to be predominantly psychological. First, there are psychological problems, then a reaction, and finally physiological effects. Proposed treatment is usually psychotherapy.

Exogenous and Endogenous Depression

■■ Depression has also been categorized as *exogenous* (external,
■■ or reactive) and *endogenous* (internal, or autonomous). These terms are no longer used in the American Psychiatric Association's *Diagnostic and Statistical Manual of Mental Disorders* (currently, the D.S.M.-III-R, 1987, which is discussed at length in chapter 3) or in other diagnostic schemes, yet they are still frequently encountered in practice and in some of the older writings.

The term *exogenous* (*exo*, "without"; *genes*, "body") was used to describe depressions thought to be generated by environmental matters, usually interpreted as psychological. *Endogenous* (*endo*, "within") referred to depressions that resulted from "internal" (which usually meant biological) causes. These are obviously simplifications, for depressions that are reactive to outside pressures can have physiological consequences, whereas depressions that are endogenous may be triggered by external stress. It was also formerly thought that medication for depression would be effective only for endogenous depressions. This is, as we shall see, an oversimplification.

The exogenous and endogenous categorizations of depression have caused considerable controversy in psychiatry. There is some support for an endogenous (i.e., biologically rooted) concept of depression (Leber, Beckham, and Danker-Brown 1985:348). However, some authorities—particularly those espousing biologically based views—question whether an environmental event could be strong enough, or toxic enough, to cause a major depression (Leber, Beckham, and Danker-Brown 1985:350). This particular set of polar terms may have outlived whatever usefulness it once had.

Vital and Nonvital Depression

■■ Somewhat paralleling the endogenous/exogenous split, but
■■ more descriptive, is the *vital/nonvital* dichotomy proposed by
Wender and Klein (1981) and Klein and Wender (1988). Their books
argue that psychiatric problems are basically biological problems. They
emphasize that the term *depression* is used to describe not one but three
major conditions. The first is "demoralization" (a usage obviously taken
from Frank [1961]): being overcome by feelings of "ineffectiveness and
helplessness" because of the rough times life sometimes gives us, such
as physical illness and psychological setbacks, accompanied by appre-
hensions of recurrences.

With the second type, *vital* or "physiological" depression, the depressed person has lost the ability to enjoy consummatory activities.
"To this depressive, food has come to taste like cardboard and sex
becomes a mechanical, pleasureless routine" (Wender and Klein 1981:43).

Vital depression, which used to be called melancholia, is usually self-
limiting. It may last from several months to a year and tends to recur,
with the same complaints characterizing future attacks of depression
(Wender and Klein 1981:46). Wender and Klein (1981:43) feel that vital
depression clearly has physiological causes and probably a very high
genetic "loading" (component). It is a common form of depression but
one that is frequently undiagnosed, which means that it often goes
untreated.

The third type is *nonvital* depression (or what used to be called
neurotic depression), the result of reactions to setbacks, disappointments, and losses. The nonvital depressive is overwhelmed by feelings
of being deprived of things he or she desires that will never be attaina-
ble, for the person does not believe that his or her efforts could improve
anything. This depressive may or may not have vegetative symptoms
(those affecting, arising from, or relating to bodily functions, such as
insomnia; vital depressives always have these symptoms) and usually
does not respond to somatic treatments such as antidepressant medication or electroconvulsive therapy (ECT). Unlike the vital depressives,
the nonvital depressive can enjoy consummatory events (such as sex,
eating, and so on), but the overwhelming feeling is one of blueness,
sadness, and unhappiness. In both demoralization and nonvital depressions the individuals can still feel pleasure and respond to encouragement, although they may not feel very motivated to attempt making
any improvements.

Wender and Klein think that even when this type of depression
occurs in reaction to an external event, such as a death or a job setback,

individuals can develop physiological changes. The researchers do not like the terms *reactive* or *endogenous* because they feel that these terms conceal the importance of physiology.

In assessing the nature of the depressive episode, Wender and Klein (1981:59) caution that *mild* should not be equated with *neurotic* (nonvital) depression. Reflecting their commitment to a biological point of view, they state that the "mild biologically depressed" are able to respond to medication but usually do not respond to positive changes in their life situations. However, depressions that are not attributable to "physiological shifts," whether mild or severe, do not generally respond to antidepressant medications.

This is a point of disagreement with other authorities, who hold that if the nonvital depression has lasted for some time—say, several months—there usually are physiological effects (e.g., the appearance or worsening of vegetative symptoms). The depressed person may very well respond to and receive "symptom comfort" from a drug, even though his or her life situation may not have improved. In this situation medication may be considered, but only as an adjunct to psychotherapy. The practitioner must carefully weigh whatever relief the nonvital depressives obtain from their vegetative symptoms against the real side effects of these potent medications. Clients who are not suffering from vegetative symptoms of depression usually are good candidates for psychotherapy (Rush 1986).

Bipolar and Unipolar Depression

The D.S.M.-III-R has divided the section on mood disorders into bipolar disorders and major depressions. A bipolar disorder is characterized by periods of both mania and depression, although some individuals experience mania alone. Mania, or manic episodes, are periods of extremely elevated moods; the person experiencing mania is "high." The episodes may be severe or mild. During manic episodes the person may speak rapidly and be in continual motion. He or she expresses grandiose ideas, sometimes characterized by delusions—a symptom that makes it hard to differentiate mania from schizophrenia. Hospitalized manics often appear to the staff never to sleep. (Although they may not seem to tire, they can exhaust others!) Manics are sometimes very creative people and can be appealing and convincing (Goodwin and Jamison 1990:332–337). They are frequently "big spenders," often stepping over the limits of their charge accounts. It is not unusual for manics to undertake enterprises involving large amounts of money they believe they possess but do not actually have.

As we shall discuss in chapter 10, many bipolar disorders are now treated effectively with lithium carbonate. There seems to be increasing, but not yet definitive, evidence that there are genetic factors in bipolar disorders.[2]

Unipolar disorders are depressions in which there is no indication of any form of mania or manic episodes. They comprise the overwhelming majority of cases of depression seen in clinical practice.

Primary and Secondary Depression

■■ The differentiation between depression as a primary or a
■■ secondary disorder is one that is valuable for the clinician. It avoids conjecture about causation and can include such distinctions as *reactive* or *endogenous* and *mild* or *severe*. It is not used in the current D.S.M.; it is a contribution of the "St. Louis Group," a research team at Washington University in Saint Louis (Goodwin and Guze 1989).

The diagnosis of primary affective disorder is used when an individual has had "no previous psychiatric disorder or else only episodes of depression or mania" (Goodwin and Guze 1989:4). This designation applies to either bipolar or unipolar conditions.

Secondary affective disorder "refers to patients with a preexisting psychiatric illness other than depression or mania" (Goodwin and Guze 1989:4). Depression can occur in conjunction with a number of conditions, such as obsessive compulsive disorder, phobias, panic disorders, drug and alcohol abuse, and other psychiatric states, including schizophrenia and organic brain disorders (Goodwin and Guze 1989:14).

Goodwin and Guze (1989:14–16) think that there are a number of important differences between primary and secondary disorders. One significant distinction is the assumption that the person with a primary affective disorder is "well" between episodes, whereas one with a secondary disorder is "not well"—that there is by definition a preexisting illness. There are also differences in prognosis. The researchers feel that, with the exception of people who suffer from alcoholism, clients diagnosed as having a primary affective disorder are at higher risk for suicide (Goodwin and Guze 1989:14).

Gold (1987a:242) states that the predominant treatments for primary affective disorder are psychotherapy, drugs, or a combination of these. The therapy should be supportive and not "insight-oriented" (*insight* generally refers to "awareness of the unconscious factors . . . [in] emotional conflict" [Thomas 1989:921]). In secondary affective disorders the concurrent primary disturbance must be treated along with the secondary depression (Goodwin and Guze 1989).

Depression as a Symptom of Physical Illness

■■
■■   Depression may also be secondary to a wide range of physical disorders. One authority cited research indicating that depression may be found in 5–30 percent of medically ill outpatients and 20 percent of medically ill inpatients (Kathol 1985:759). But it is often overlooked or undiagnosed, with the patient being treated only for what appears to be a physical illness. Sometimes the reverse is true—a physical illness is overlooked when a patient is seen to be depressed.

Gold, who calls himself a biopsychiatrist (one who advocates a medical model of psychiatry), suggested five possibilities for the interaction of physical and mental disorders, on which we shall elaborate (1987a:75–76; the headings are those used by Gold):

1. *Physical illness can intensify emotional disorders.* All illness subjects the individual to stress, and the more severe or more chronic the illness, the greater the stress. Relieving the physical illness may or may not relieve the distress of the emotional disorder, depending upon the state of the patient before the onset of the physical illness. Sometimes relapses of psychiatric conditions, or lack of response to psychiatric treatment, are really due to the lack of diagnosis or treatment of the physical illnesses (Lentz 1990). This is especially true when a chronic physical condition is accompanied by chronic pain (Roy, Thomas, and Matas 1984). For example, at least 24 percent of a sample of patients receiving dialysis treatment for end-stage renal disease fulfilled the diagnostic criteria for depression (Hinrichsen et al. 1989).

2. *Psychiatric symptoms can develop in reaction to a previously existing illness.* Many reactive depressions are responses to physical illness and pain. The feelings of helplessness often produced by physical illness may turn into feelings of hopelessness. The depression can appear at any time: before the diagnosis of the illness, during the treatment, after the completion of treatment, during recuperation, and on the anniversaries of the illness—first counted in months, then in years, depending on the illness. These depressions are associated with a wide range of conditions, from serious illnesses requiring major surgery to the lingering of a common cold. They include myocardial infarction (constriction or blockage of a coronary artery), gout, paraplegia, and other conditions resulting from traumatic bodily injury. For example, a study of 283 new patients admitted with myocardial infarction, interviewed eight to ten days after the attack showed that 45 percent filled the diagnostic criteria for depression, and 18 percent met the criteria for major depression. After three to four months, 33 percent met the criteria for depression.

Most of the major depressives had not returned to work three months after the attack (Schleifer et al. 1989).

Reactive depression may be overlooked during treatment of the physical illness, especially when it is not anticipated. For example, a hospitalized patient is expected to feel happy, not depressed, when told that he or she is to be discharged. Similarly, one might expect a patient in certain circumstances (e.g., one who is recuperating at home after successful treatment of breast cancer) to be happy. Of course, the opposite often is the case. Upon discharge from the hospital, the patient, physically and/or emotionally altered by an illness, must face up to the changes that have taken place. The breast cancer patient who has been rushed through a brief period of diagnosis and a short hospitalization in which she was kept both medicated and very busy will experience a delayed reaction to the enormity of the threat to her body and her life.

Gold (1987a:75) indicates that reactive depression usually eases with the patient's recovery and readjustment. We agree, but readjustment is a complicated process, necessitating grieving for the losses resulting from the illness and then making the adjustments necessary to continue with one's life. It is often imperative to deal with the depression first in order for these changes to occur.

It has long been known that dementia (the deterioration of intellectual capacity, generally but not always associated with aging) can produce depressive responses in conditions such as Huntington's disease, cerebrovascular insufficiency, and others. The prognoses for depressions accompanying these degenerative diseases are not favorable. (We discuss dementia further in chapter 18.)

3. *Physical and psychiatric illnesses may coexist without relationship to one another.* Many patients in psychiatric hospitals are also physically ill because, according to Gold, they do not receive good medical care. However, if the physical and psychiatric illnesses are not directly related, treating the physical disease "may have little or no bearing on the psychiatric symptoms" (1987a:75).

4. *Physical illness may be the direct result of emotional problems.* The vague, often overused term *psychosomatic* has long been a part of our clinical vocabulary. Currently, a great deal of research focuses on the mind/body connection. This research verifies a multitude of interactions.[3]

5. *Certain physical conditions may cause emotional disorders.* Some physical ailments first present as depression. The depression may be the first indication that there is something physically wrong with the patient. These "physical conditions are sometimes called 'somatopsychic disorders' " (Hall 1980).

Physical illnesses, of which depression may be an early symptom, may appear in any of the body's systems. Depression may be a consequence of infectious diseases such as influenza, of endocrine disorders, of tumors and cancers, collagen diseases (particularly systemic lupus erythematosus), neurological disorders (including multiple sclerosis), cerebral tumors, sleep disturbances, some dementias, and Parkinson's disease (Lobel and Hirschfeld 1984:35–36; Kathol 1985:748; Lentz 1990). It may be associated with nutritional problems, such as anemia, and may result from some drugs, such as steroid contraceptives, reserpine, amphetamine (in withdrawal) and, most certainly, alcohol and the other drugs of abuse (Whybrow, Akiskal, and McKinney 1984:176).

Gold states that at least seventy-five physical illnesses (or conditions) can cause symptoms of emotional disorders (1987a:xv). He calls these the "great mimickers" and points out that the physical illnesses must be treated for these emotional symptoms to disappear.

Other frequently encountered classes of mimickers are the conditions that are responses to drugs and alcohol, such as sleep disturbances, extremes of moods, neurological symptoms, lack of appetite, and others (Royce 1989). Patients with these symptoms are often put into a psychiatric hospital instead of being treated medically.

A number of legitimate drugs may also touch off depressive symptoms. Among these are drugs for treating hypertension (such as Serpasil and Aldomet), drugs to treat Parkinson's disease, certain hormones (estrogen and progesterone), antituberculosis agents, and anticancer drugs (Lobel and Hirschfeld 1984:36.)

Gold makes the astonishing and very disturbing statement that, "Study after study reveals that *up to 40 percent of all diagnoses of depression are misdiagnoses of common and uncommon physical illnesses*" (1987a:xv, emphasis in the original). Two other very prominent advocates and spokesmen for the biopsychiatric orientation to depression disagree, stating that "most patients with depression do not have another underlying medical condition" (Klein and Wender 1988:64).

There is also a lack of agreement on which physical illnesses cause depression. For example, two leading biopsychiatrists hold that two conditions that are thought to cause depression

> *rarely,* if ever do. . . . [One] is hypoglycemia, . . . a drop in the amount of sugar in the blood to an abnormal level. . . . The [other] . . . is an allergic reaction to food or to *common* environmental chemicals. [They state that] there is no evidence that serious depressive illness is ever produced by such allergies. Considerable time and money are sometimes wasted pursuing these medical "will-o'-the wisps." (Klein and Wender 1988:61–62, emphasis in the original)

Part of this controversy may be a problem of definition rather than of diagnosis. Kaplan and Sadock (1990:149) point out that people with hypoglycemia often display signs of "depression with fatigue."

Hall (1980) has cautioned that when a patient shows symptoms of depression, the availability of antidepressant medications may lead many physicians into mistakenly prescribing them, which—if done without careful physical *and* psychiatric evaluations—may lessen the severity of the depressive symptoms. The patient may seem to get better but the underlying physical disease not only may go undetected but may even worsen through unintended neglect and oversight.

It is imperative that therapists *always* have a patient's physical condition evaluated to be sure the patient is not suffering from a physical illness that may be causing or contributing to the symptoms. We cannot overemphasize the importance of a complete and relevant physical examination. In chapter 16 we discuss how to make this examination as relevant as possible for treating the depression.

Organic Mood Syndrome: A Mood Disorder Caused by Physical Illness

■■ Organic mood syndrome is an example of a physical condi-
■■ tion "caused" by an emotional disorder. This is a major depression or marked mood upswing caused by a "specific organic factor" (D.S.M.-III-R 1987:111). These organic factors may include en- docrine disorders, diseases, injuries and other insults to the brain, and other disorders and diseases. Depression may be secondary to the traumatic effects, both psychological and physical, of the particular medical illness.

We discuss this syndrome further in chapter 3, where we elaborate upon the specific criteria for diagnosis, for it is ruled out if there are other conditions, such as delirium and/or attention disorder (D.S.M.-III-R 1987:112). We also mention it again in chapter 18, on "Depression and Aging," for this condition is often confused with the dementias.

Masked, or Hidden, Depression

■■ *Masked depression* is one of the most controversial terms en-
■■ countered in the psychiatric literature. Lesse (1974) was one of the first to use this term. He noticed, as had many others before him, that although many of his patients on both psychiatric and medical services exhibited a wide variety of complaints, further examination often revealed an underlayer of unrecognized and undiagnosed depres- sion. The depressions were "masked" by the complaints. The cause of the patient's problem is really a depression, even though the symptoms

do not appear initially as depression (Wender and Klein 1981:63). The symptoms may occur in many forms in any of the body's systems. They seem to appear most often as pain, anorexia (loss of appetite), self-destructive behavior, and panic disorders.

The term *masked depression* is also used to characterize drug abuse, alcoholism, criminal and delinquent behavior, spouse abuse, and behavior and habit disorders where the observable behavior is felt to cover an underlying depression. The term has been applied to so many conditions that many investigators feel it is useless (Cytryn, McKnew, and Bunney 1980; Bower 1989). It is nonspecific, and it offers little help in indicating a treatment approach (Wender and Klein 1981:64). However, the term *is* used in the literature, especially when dealing with the interplay of psychological and medical factors (e.g., psychosomatic medicine) (Fisch 1987; Makanjuola and Olaifa 1987) and with addictions and antisocial behaviors. Other terms used to describe this condition are *depressive equivalent, affective equivalent,* and *smiling depression,* which is still used widely throughout the psychotherapy literature. (Antisocial behavior and masked depression are discussed further in chapter 19.)

2

The Symptoms of Depression

A wide variety of symptoms may indicate depression, and a therapist must be sensitive to them. These symptoms are not of equal seriousness or toxicity, and they may or may not reach the criterion level to merit a formal diagnosis of depression in this country.[1]

The Most Common Indicators of Depression

Klerman (1988:310–311) has compiled a very useful list of the symptoms of depression. The reader should bear in mind that these symptoms may also be present in disorders other than depression.

1. *Depressed mood.* More than 90 percent of depressed clients *appear* to be depressed (Klerman 1988:311, emphasis added). They look sad. Their mouths are often turned down at the corners, their eyes may appear red and swollen from crying, and they may lack a sense of humor. They often speak of feeling "low," "blue," and/or "down."

Initially, however, some do not appear depressed. These are the so-called masked or smiling depressives, exhibiting what can be described as the "Pagliacci syndrome"; they laugh though their hearts may be breaking. However, one senses, while talking with them, that sadness and often despair are just beneath the surface; that their defenses will crumble if the right, or wrong, word is said. Denial is involved here, and these smiling depressives must also be considered at risk for suicide.

2. *Anhedonia.* Many depressed people experience anhedonia, or lack of pleasure. Nothing they do makes them happy—eating, going out, seeing friends, engaging in sports. In short, they derive little pleasure from anything.

3. *Feelings of fatigue.* Depressed people are often very tired. They complain of a lack of energy, weakness, exhaustion, aches, and pains. They feel "washed out," even when they are inactive. They have trou-

ble beginning tasks and often cannot finish them. (This fatigue may also result from sleep problems, another common symptom of depression.)

4. *Retardation of speech, thought, and movement.* Depressed patients often speak very slowly. They can be difficult to interview because it may take them a long time to answer a question, and if they do respond it may only be in a monosyllable. Therapists often report feeling exhausted after a session with such a client.

5. *Appetite changes.* Many depressives eat very little. They report that, "Even the thought of food makes me ill." They may refuse food or just nibble, even when favorite dishes are presented to them. Shopping for food, preparing it, or even eating it takes energy they do not have.

In 70–80 percent of cases, depressives suffer a loss of appetite and lose weight (Klerman 1978:255). Other depressed people may gain weight, often because of increased eating during the evening hours, which an authority on eating disorders called the *night eating syndrome* (Stunkard, Grace, and Wolff 1955). Food provides them with a ready source of comfort. (Craving carbohydrates and being comforted by foods high in carbohydrates may be symptoms of a form of seasonal affective disorder, which we shall discuss in chapter 9.)

6. *Sleep disorders.* Seventy to 80 percent of all depressives have some form of insomnia (Klerman 1988:312). The most frequent type is one in which the individual, who is usually exhausted and has no trouble falling asleep, wakes up after several hours and is unable to get back to sleep. This is called *early morning insomnia, middle waking,* or *terminal insomnia.* Another kind of sleep disorder is inability to fall asleep, which is associated more often, but not always, with anxiety rather than with depression.

Some depressed individuals have hypersomnia: They sleep excessively. This is avoidance of the pain they experience when they are awake. It may also be a symptom of seasonal affective disorder (SAD).

7. *Physical (somatic) ailments.* Depressives commonly have physical complaints. Prior to seeing a psychotherapist, they may have extensive tests and treatments to attempt to alleviate their pain. They often visit ambulatory care clinics and emergency rooms and may inappropriately overutilize such facilities. Klerman (1988:312) lists the following commonly presented symptoms: headache, neck ache, back pain, muscle cramps, nausea, vomiting, lump in the throat, sour taste in the mouth, dry mouth, constipation, heartburn, indigestion, flatulence, blurred vision, and pain on urination, among others.

8. *Agitation.* Depressives sometimes show extreme restlessness or tension, constantly moving about, pacing the floor, wringing their hands, exhibiting jerky movements, and so forth. Anyone who has worked in a psychiatric ward can recall patients with sad expressions who moved

about constantly. These activities are "ego alien" and do not provide any comfort; consequently, they do not ease tension (Klerman 1988:312).

9. *A drop in libido.* A lack of interest in sex often parallels the drop in energy and the general anhedonia so typical of the depressive. Sexual problems may also be side effects of medications or may be caused by other physical and/or psychogenic problems. However, depression is often involved and frequently overlooked, even by marital therapists and particularly by narrowly trained sex therapists.

10. *A drop in interest in the usual activities of work and play.* Depressives often state that even routine activities are very difficult for them and that they perform below their own expectations and those of others, such as their employers or spouses. These perceptions of their low level of achievement are not always realistic. The individual with these symptoms receives no pleasure or comfort from the usual activities of work or play. In behavioral terms, these activities are "nonreinforcing"; consequently, the person may give them up. (The behavior is "extinguished.")

11. *A diminished ability to think and concentrate.* The thought processes of depressed people often slow down, and this is sometimes accompanied by memory lapses. Depressives may also dwell on some thoughts until they become obsessional, and they may find everyday decisions difficult.

12. *Feelings of worthlessness, self-reproach, guilt, and shame.* These symptoms are often a central feature of depression. In depressions that used to be diagnosed as *neurotic depression* the feelings were thought to cause pain. They were "ego-alien"; consequently, the client wanted to get rid of them. In what used to be diagnosed as *psychotic depression*, it was believed that the clients often felt the feelings were proper punishment for real or imagined transgressions and shortcomings and therefore *should* be punished. One way to administer this punishment was through suicide, where the depressed people themselves delivered the punishment for their transgressions.

13. *Anxiety.* From 60 to 70 percent of depressed patients report feelings of anxiety and sometimes extreme worrying (Klerman 1988). This symptom can present many problems. For example, a nonpsychiatric physician who hears a patient complain of anxiety often prescribes a tranquilizer such as Valium, which may be ineffective and counterindicated for depression.

14. *Lowered self-esteem.* This includes a sense of inadequacy and feelings of despondency that accompany the client's belief that he or she is a failure and will continue to be a failure and a disappointment.

Authorities on depression disagree on whether low self-esteem is a cause or a result of depression. It is often very difficult to tell the difference, especially when the depression is long-standing.

15. *Feelings of helplessness, pessimism, and hopelessness.* These often go together. The world, as seen by depressed people, is overwhelming, especially if their often unrealistically high standards for themselves are not achieved. Because they feel overwhelmed, they are helpless to change things and thus become both hopeless and helpless, thereby increasing their extreme feelings of pessimism and gloom.

Unfortunately, one action that can be taken to relieve the feelings of helplessness and hopelessness is suicide. When the depressive is able to take this active step, the feelings of helplessness may disappear. Suicide then becomes a logical, even appealing way out of pain for some depressed patients. (Suicide as a "way out" partially explains the euphoric mood seen in some depressed patients after a decision to attempt suicide.)

16. *Thoughts of death and suicide.* Many depressives think about death. They typically state, "I'd like to get away from it all"; "I have nothing to live for"; "I wish I had never been born," and many think about suicide as the means to death. Only a portion of depressed people attempt suicide, but the risk of suicide in *all* depressives cannot be overstressed. The therapist must be especially sensitive to a client who mentions suicide. The old canard that "they won't do it if they talk about it" is absolutely wrong. Many, if not most, of those who attempt suicide speak of their intentions before they do it. Later in this book we discuss the detection and treatment of suicidal tendencies and acts.[2]

Other Symptoms of Depression

■■ We discuss other symptoms of depression in the sections on
■■ formal diagnosis and treatment. These include constipation, amenorrhea, and dry mouth (which can also result from antidepression medication). Some depressives suffer from *worsened early morning mood* (i.e., they are most depressed in the morning and feel better as the day progresses).

Ways of Categorizing the Symptoms of Depression

■■ The symptoms of depression have been categorized in a
■■ number of ways. For example:

Affective symptoms, including feelings of sadness, anxiety, guilt, anger, hostility, and irritability.
Behavioral symptoms, such as agitation, depressed facial appearance,

psychomotor retardation, slowness of speech and thought, crying, and suicide attempts.

Attitudes toward self and the environment, including self-reproach; low self-esteem; feelings of helplessness, pessimism, and hopelessness; thoughts of death and suicide.

Cognitive impairment, including decreased ability to think or concentrate.

Physiological changes and bodily complaints (sometimes called *vegetative symptoms*), such as inability to experience pleasure, loss of appetite, sleep disturbance, loss of energy, decrease in sexual interest, and bodily complaints (Klerman et al. 1984:31).

3

The Formal Diagnosis of Depression

The diagnostic systems for clinical diagnosis of the depressions are not universally accepted. Although many investigators use the "Research Diagnostic Criteria" (Spitzer, Endicott, and Robins 1978), we shall utilize the system advanced by the American Psychiatric Association, because it is the most widely used. These formal diagnostic criteria appear in the current *Diagnostic and Statistical Manual of Mental Disorders* (D.S.M-III-R).[1]

The D.S.M.-III-R sets forth a system for providing professionals (e.g., clinicians, researchers, and teachers) with precise, standardized criteria for diagnosing mental disorders. The manual gives specific information for each disorder, such as a description of the symptoms (usually based on the amount of distress or pain the person experiences, and the related impairment in functioning) and a specification of the number of symptoms that must be present to meet the criteria for diagnosis.

Diagnosis is multidimensional (necessitating a variety of information) and consists of five divisions, or *axes*. Axis I contains the *clinical syndromes* (including the depressions) and the *V codes*, which are conditions not attributable to a mental disorder, such as marital problems, parent/child problems, malingering, and others. Axis II consists of the developmental disorders and the personality disorders; axis III provides for inclusion of physical disorders and conditions; axis IV is a rating of severity of psychosocial stressors; and axis V is global assessment of functioning.

Just as some praise or criticize the manual as a whole, others accept or question the sections on mood disorders. Its proponents have praised the manual for defining disorders precisely, for basing criteria on empirical evidence, for drawing away from a psychoanalytic orientation and coming closer to a *medical model* (one of the goals was to make the manual atheoretical), and for heightening communication among therapists. Its detractors say that it did not go far enough toward the medical model, that it heightened reliability at the cost of validity (not really portraying the disorders vividly enough), and, particularly applicable to the depressions, that the diagnoses do not help the clinician

Table 3.1. Depression-related Diagnoses Recognized in the D.S.M.-III-R

Major Category/Diagnostic Subtype	Page Numbers in D.S.M.-III-R
Organic mood syndrome (293.83)—A prominent and persistent depressed mood resembling a major depressive episode that is due to a specific organic factor (e.g., hormone- or drug-induced depression).	111–112
Schizoaffective disorder (295.70)—At some time in the disturbance there is either a major depressive or manic syndrome concurrent with symptoms that meet certain criteria of schizophrenia.	208–210
Mood disorders	213–214
Bipolar disorders[a]—The essential feature is the presence of one or more manic or hypomanic episodes (usually with a history of major depressive episodes).	214–218
Bipolar disorder (296.XX)—One or more manic episodes.	225–226
Cyclothymia (301.13)—Numerous hypomanic episodes and numerous periods with depressive symptoms.	226–228
Bipolar disorder NOS—Residual category that includes disorders with hypomanic and full major depressive episodes, sometimes referred to as bipolar, II.	
Depressive disorders[b]—The essential feature is the presence of one or more periods of depression (syndrome) *without* a history of either manic or hypomanic episodes.	218–224
Major depression[c] (296.XX)—One or more major depressive episodes; can be specified as recurrent.	228–230

Note. D.S.M.-III-R = *Diagnostic and Statistical Manual of Mental Disorders (Third Edition-Revised)* (American Psychiatric Association, 1987); NOS = not otherwise specified. Numbers in parentheses are code numbers.
[a] For bipolar and bipolar NOS, a further specification is "seasonal pattern."
[b] For a current bipolar disorder or major depression, the episode can be subclassed as psychotic features. For recurrent major depression and depressive disorder NOS, a further specification is "seasonal pattern."
[c] A current major depressive episode can be specified as "melancholic" or "chronic" type.

differentiate between which client will respond to medication, which will respond to psychotherapy, and which will be helped by a combination of the two.

Much of the criticism of the D.S.M. is directed toward statements such as the following: A diagnosis of depression must include "at least five of the following nine" symptoms. Critics point out that all nine classes of symptoms are not equally severe. For example, *fatigue* is hardly as serious as *recurrent suicidal ideation* or *suicide attempt*. Nonetheless, the criteria have a good heuristic use, for they encourage more careful use of the diagnostic label *depression*.

Major Category/Diagnostic Subtype	Page Numbers in D.S.M.-III-R
Dysthymia (300.40)—A history of depressed mood more days than not for at least two years, which did not begin with a major depressive episode.	230–233
Depressive disorder NOS (311.00)	223
Adjustment disorders—A maladaptive reaction to an identifiable psychosocial stressor.	329–330
Adjustment disorder with depressed mood (309.00)—An "incomplete depressive syndrome" that develops in response to a psychosocial stressor; predominant symptoms include depressed mood, tearfulness, and feelings of hopelessness.	331
Personality disorders	
Dependent personality disorder (301.60)—Frequently complicated by depressive disorders.	354
Codes for conditions not attributable to a mental disorder	359–362
Uncomplicated bereavement (V62.82)—Normal reaction to the loss of a loved one. Can include a "full depressive syndrome."	361–362
Late luteal phase dysphoric disorder—A proposed diagnostic category needing further study, coded as "300.90 unspecified mental disorder (late luteal phase dysphoric disorder)."	367–369
Decision tree for differential diagnosis of mood disturbances	380–381

The Mood Disorders

■■ In the latest manual, the section covering the depressions is
■■ entitled "Mood Disorders." (This section was called "Affective Disorders" in previous editions.) *Mood* is defined as a "prolonged emotion that colors the whole psychic life; it generally involves either depression or elation" (D.S.M.-III-R 1987:213). Information relating to mood disorders also occurs at several points in the D.S.M.-III-R. (Table 3.1 lists the depression-related categories, gives their main features, and indicates their location in the D.S.M.-III-R.)

The D.S.M.-III-R states explicitly that the diagnosis of a mood disorder is to be made only if the condition is not due to any physical disorder, such as a brain tumor, or to any other mental disorder. The manual emphasizes objectively verifiable constellations of observable symptoms and their persistence over time as prerequisites for a diagnosis of depression.

The manual uses the terms *mood syndromes, mood episodes,* and *mood disorders* (D.S.M.-III-R 1987:213–214). A mood syndrome is a combination of mood symptoms that occur at the same time, such as depressed mood, loss of interest (e.g., in work and sex), lack of appetite, and so on. Although mood syndromes may be part of a mood disorder (defined later), they may also be seen in physical disorders and other mental disorders that are not primarily mood disorders, such as schizophrenia, or in some organic disorders, such as organic mood syndrome, that result from specific organic factors.

When a mood syndrome (referring to the cluster of symptoms) is not attributable to any organic disorder or to any other "nonmood psychotic disorder," it is called a *mood episode*. Mood episodes are groups of mood symptoms that appear for a specified minimum period of time. Mood syndromes (the combinations of symptoms) can be chronic, or they can appear from time to time—thus the name *mood episode*. However, as we previously stated, the term *mood episode* is reserved for the mood disorders (e.g., major depression) in which organic and nonmood psychotic disorders have been ruled out.[2]

Mood disorders are "determined by the *pattern* of Mood Episodes" (D.S.M.-III-R 1987:214, emphasis added). For example, if there have been one or more major depressive episodes, but no manic or hypomanic episodes, then the diagnosis would be a depressive disorder (e.g., major depression). If there have been episodes of both mania and depression, then the diagnosis would be bipolar disorder (e.g., bipolar disorder, mixed) (D.S.M.-III-R 1987:214, emphasis added).

In our discussion of the mood disorders, we shall follow the axis I classifications of major clinical syndromes (D.S.M.-III-R 1987:7). The mood disorders are divided into two main categories: bipolar disorders and depressive disorders.

The Bipolar Disorders

As previously described, bipolar disorders are conditions in which there is marked fluctuation in mood, with periods of highs (manic episodes) usually, but not always, alternating with lows, which may or may not include a depressive episode (Goodwin and Guze 1989:7). Other bipolar disorders are cyclothymia and bipolar disorder NOS (not otherwise specified).

The criteria for a manic episode consist, briefly, of (1) a "distinct period of abnormality and persistently elevated, expansive or irritable mood"; (2) at least three of the following seven symptoms: "inflated self-esteem, decreased need for sleep, [extreme talkativeness], flight of ideas, distractibility, [an] increase in goal-directed activity, [agitation, and] excessive involvement in pleasurable activities . . . [with] high potential for painful consequences . . . e.g., . . . buying sprees, sexual indiscretions, or foolish business investments" (D.S.M.-III-R 1987:217–218); (3) a severe impairment in social and other relationships. There should be no delusions when there are no mood symptoms, and no schizophrenia or organic factors.

A hypomanic episode meets numbers 1 and 2 but not number 3 of the preceding criteria; it is not severe enough to cause "marked impairment." (Hypomania is "mild . . . excitement with moderate change in behavior" [Thomas 1989:876].)

Bipolar disorders may be classified, on the fourth digit of the code, as *mixed, manic,* or *depressed,* depending upon the current clinical picture or upon the latest episode, if the client is in remission (D.S.M.-III-R 1987:225). *Manic* indicates that the latest episode is mania, and *depressed* means the latest episode is one of depression. A *mixed* episode is one in which both manic and major depressive symptoms characterize the latest episode. The major depressive symptoms in this case do not last for two weeks without mixing, or rapidly alternating with mania (sometimes called *rapidly cycling,* a very serious and disturbing situation).

On the fifth digit, if the client fulfills the criteria for a manic, depressed, or mixed specification, the episode is classified as mild, moderate, severe with or severe without psychotic features (D.S.M.-III-R 1987:217–218). If the episode does not fulfill the criteria for either of the preceding, it is rated as *partial* or *full remission* (D.S.M.-III-R 1987:217–218).

The second major classification, cyclothymia, is a "chronic mood disturbance, [of] at least two years duration (one year for children and adolescents) involving numerous Hypomanic Episodes and numerous periods of depressed mood, or loss of interest or pleasure, of insufficient severity or duration to meet the criteria for Major Depressive or Manic Episode. [It] . . . must [last for] . . . a two-year period . . . in which the person is never without hypomanic or depressive symptoms for more than two months . . . [with] no Manic Episode or Major Depressive Episode during [the] first two years." The condition is not a psychosis, nor is it due to organic factors (D.S.M.-III-R 1987:228).

The diagnosis of cyclothymia is controversial. Some say it is a condition in its own right; others consider it a less severe kind of bipolar disorder (D.S.M.-III-R 1987:226).

The third category, bipolar disorder, NOS (not otherwise specified), is a residual category for "disorders with manic or hypomanic features that do not meet the criteria for any specific bipolar disorder" (D.S.M.-III-R 1987:228). One example is "bipolar II," where there is at least one major depressive episode, possibly a hypomanic episode, but never a true manic episode or cyclothymia. (The Research Diagnostic Criteria refer to bipolar with mania as bipolar I and bipolar with hypomania as bipolar II [Spitzer, Endicott, and Robins 1978:775].)

Goodwin and Jamison (1990:14) think that hypomania is underdiagnosed, which they believe accounts for the underdiagnosis of bipolar disorder. They suggest that untreated bipolar II disorders can develop into full-blown mania.

Both bipolar disorders and major depression may also be classified as "seasonal pattern," either bipolar disorder or recurrent major depression (of several varieties) (D.S.M.-III-R 1987:224). (We discuss seasonal affective disorder in chapter 9.)

The Depressive Disorders

There are two categories of depressive disorders in the D.S.M.-III-R: major depression—in which there is at least one and often more depressive episodes—and dysthymia, a condition in which "there is a history of a depressed mood more days than not for at least two years and in which, during the first two years of the disturbance, the condition did not meet the criteria for a Major Depressive Disorder" (D.S.M.-III-R 1987:214). There is also a residual category: depressive disorder, NOS.

For the diagnosis of major depression, a person must have had at least five of the specified group of symptoms for a two-week period, and at least one must be either "depressed mood or loss of interest or pleasure." Excluded are symptoms due to physical conditions, delusions, drugs, and so on. The specified symptoms are "depressed mood; . . . diminished interest or pleasure in all, or almost all activities, most of the day, nearly every day; . . . significant weight loss or gain when not dieting (more than 5 percent of weight in a month) or decrease or increase in appetite; . . . insomnia or hypersomnia nearly every day; . . . psychomotor agitation or retardation nearly every day; . . . fatigue . . . [and/or] loss of energy; . . . feelings of worthlessness or excessive or inappropriate guilt; . . . diminished ability to think or concentrate; . . . recurrent thoughts of death [not just fear of dying], recurrent suicidal ideation without a specific plan, or a suicide attempt or a specific plan for committing suicide" (D.S.M.-III-R 1987:222–224).

The depression should not be the consequence of organic factors, nor should it be a "normal" grief reaction to the death of someone close (uncomplicated bereavement). There should be no hallucinations or schizophrenia or complications of drugs (D.S.M.-III-R 1987:222–223).

Major depression may also be subcategorized as *melancholic type* (D.S.M.-III-R 1987:224) or as *seasonal pattern (seasonal affective disorder)*.

Melancholic type is viewed as a very serious, or deep, depression, particularly responsive to either medication or electroconvulsive therapy (ECT) (Goodwin and Guze 1989). The major depressive episode(s) must have the

> presence of at least five of the following to be further specified as Melancholic:
> 1. loss of interest or pleasure in all, or almost all, activities
> 2. lack of reactivity to usually pleasurable stimuli (does not feel much better, even temporarily, when something good happens)
> 3. depression regularly worse in the morning
> 4. early morning awakening (at least two hours before usual time of awakening)
> 5. psychomotor retardation or agitation (not merely subjective complaints)
> 6. significant anorexia or weight loss (e.g., more than 5 percent of body weight in a month)
> 7. no significant personality disturbance before first Major Depressive Episode
> 8. one or more previous Major Depressive Episodes followed by complete, or nearly complete, recovery
> 9. previous good response to specific and adequate somatic antidepressant therapy (e.g., tricyclics, ECT, MAOIs, lithium). (D.S.M.-III-R 1987:224)

Dysthymia, which used to be called depressive neurosis, is a chronic disorder, for the person must have had a depressed mood for "most of the day more days than not, for at least two years (one year . . . for children and adolescents)" (D.S.M. III-R 1987:230). Dysthymia might also be a "consequence of a preexisting, chronic nonmood . . . disorder . . . e.g., anorexia, somatization disorder, . . . arthritis . . . etc." (D.S.M.-III-R 1987:230).

A diagnosis of dysthymia is given when there is a depressed mood, if the individual has had the symptoms without interruption for more than a two-month period and if at least two of the following symptoms are present: "poor appetite or overeating; insomnia or hypersomnia; low energy or fatigue; low self-esteem; poor concentration, difficulty making decisions; feelings of hopelessness" (D.S.M.-III-R 1987:232). A major depression or a manic episode or any sign of psychosis will rule out this diagnosis.

Dysthymia may be primary, where there is no preexisting condition, or it may be secondary to a preexisting chronic, nonmood, mental or physical disorder (D.S.M.-III-R 1987:233).

The residual category, *depressive disorder, NOS,* covers those conditions that do not fit the other depressive diagnoses, such as adjustment reaction with depressed mood, and depressions associated with any of the other mood disorders, such as a major depression superimposed on residual schizophrenia (D.S.M.-III-R 1987:233).

Atypical Depression

The diagnosis of *atypical depression,* which is classified in the D.S.M.-III-R under the heading *depressive disorder not otherwise specified,* is controversial (1987:233).

Some depressed clients appear with a number of symptoms, some different from—even opposite to—those of major depression. These "atypical" symptoms include a mood that is intermittently sad but that can be raised with sympathy and praise; oversleeping; worsened evening, rather than morning mood; a large number of psychosomatic symptoms; heavy feelings in the arms and legs; excessive eating; phobias; panic attacks; and premenstrual symptoms. The person often has an extreme need for attention and is hypersensitive to perceived rejection (Frances 1989).

Acute symptoms, such as tearfulness, can often be traced to a recent specific incident, such as the breakup of a relationship. The client exhibiting these symptoms often has low self-esteem and frequently uses drugs, particularly alcohol. Most important clinically, the client's depressive symptoms are improved by taking a monoamine oxidase inhibitor (MAOI) rather than a tricyclic drug. The different symptom picture and the consistent response to the MAOIs have led some observers to conclude that this is a specific subcategory of depression (Liebowitz et al. 1988; Parsons et al. 1989). (The antidepressant medications will be discussed in chapter 6.)

The reliability and validity of this diagnosis are controversial. Convincing evidence on genetic transmission is lacking, and it is not known if the symptoms or the positive reaction to MAO inhibitors might be linked to family transmission. Above all, the constellation of symptoms and the diagnosis of atypical depression do not tell us much about the future path of the condition. Because of these and other inconsistencies in psychological and biological (vegetative) symptoms, it has been suggested that there needs to be even further specification and elaboration of all the categories of mood disorders.

Some think that atypical depression is closer to the personality disorders, such as histrionic personality or borderline personality. (Many borderline personality disorder patients are also seriously depressed.) There may be a "chicken-and-egg" problem here, in that some depressed people may appear, after time, to resemble borderline personalities.

It is also hard to differentiate between atypical depression and bipolar disorders or cyclothymia, particularly with "rapid-cycling" bipolars. The change from the high to the low mood, or vice versa, may be very rapid and/or very subtle.

It is suggested that a combination of psychotherapy and drugs might help these patients, but a number of researchers feel that this symptom picture is not distinctive enough to merit still another diagnostic category and that the clients are better served by the existing diagnostic categories (Davidson et al. 1982).

Double Depression

■■ Patients who have had a long-term chronic depression (dys-
■■ thymia) may experience one or more major depressive episodes, and in some instances, manic episodes, on top of the existing dysthymia. This condition is called a *double depression* (not a formal D.S.M.-III-R label). There are still many unanswered questions as to the genesis and course of "double depression." Although long observed clinically, the condition was first described in the literature by Keller and Shapiro (1982) and confirmed by later observers. In lay terms, the depression "seems to be a part of these people"; it seems almost characterological.

The diagnosis of double depression is difficult and can only be made after careful history taking. The manual specifically states that the diagnoses of both dysthymia and major depression should be made, for dysthymia usually persists after the major depressive episode ends (D.S.M.-III-R 1987:232).

Researchers have observed that clients who have experienced double depression often suffer from guilt because they feel they have been malingering. This unrealistic guilt is frequently relieved when they are reassured that the periodic lows are beyond their control and part of the depressive disorder. Intervention depends upon the subtype, history, and so on, but clients often respond to medication as a first step, easing the major depressive episode and making psychotherapy possible, particularly focusing on the consequences or the effects of the long-lasting dysthymia (Akiskal and Simmons 1985).

Schizoaffective Disorder

■■
■■   The classification of schizoaffective disorder, which even the manual calls confusing and very ill defined, is sometimes considered a mood disorder but is actually a psychotic disorder. The classification is used when the client experiences psychosis, sometimes with mood symptoms and at other times without. The category is only used when the client does not meet conditions for schizophrenia or mood disorder. Differential diagnosis can be very difficult, for clients with bipolar disorders, at the height of manic excitement, may appear with delusions and sometimes hallucinations.

The criteria state that schizoaffective disorder is a "disturbance . . . [in which] at some time, there is either a major depressive or [a] manic syndrome concurrent with symptoms that meet the A group [a D.S.M.-III-R category] of criteria of Schizophrenia . . . [with no] delusions or hallucinations for at least two weeks, but [with] no prominent mood symptoms." The diagnosis is made only after possible organic factors have been ruled out (D.S.M.-III-R 1987:210). This disorder may be specified as a bipolar type or as a depressive type.

Organic Mood Syndrome

■■
■■   The diagnosis of organic mood syndrome, which we mentioned briefly in chapter 1 and discuss again in chapter 18, is listed under "Organic Mental Syndromes and Disorders" (D.S.M.-III-R 1987:112). It refers to a brain dysfunction, temporary or permanent, caused by insults to the brain, such as stroke, Alzheimer's disease, and reactions to medications (such as reserpine, used to treat high blood pressure) and toxins (poisons) and by certain physical illnesses, such as cancer of the pancreas, viral illness, endocrine disorders, and other conditions. These illnesses may cause lasting brain damage or a transient disturbance of brain functioning, either of which may mimic depression (Billig 1987:61–62).[3]

There are specific criteria for the diagnosis of organic mood disorder: "[A] Prominent and persistent depressed, elevated, or expansive mood. . . . [and] evidence from the history, physical examination, or laboratory tests of a specific organic factor (or factors) judged to be etiologically related to the disturbance . . . [and] not occurring exclusively during the course of Delirium" (D.S.M.-III-R 1987:112).

The crucial element for making this diagnosis is that there must be a specific organic factor that is etiologically related to the mood disturbance (depression or mania). These are the illnesses and other conditions listed earlier.[4]

An absence of mood disorder in the person, or family, also "suggests an organic mood syndrome" (D.S.M.-III-R 1987:112).

When changes in mood, either elevated or depressed, are due to definite organic factors, differential diagnosis depends upon specific indicators and obviously should be made, or confirmed, by a physician or a medical team. (A person with this syndrome is most likely already in the care of a physician, perhaps even hospitalized.) For example, differential diagnosis sometimes has to be made in elderly patients where dementia is suspected. However, this is a rare condition (Billig, 1987). The differential diagnosis becomes difficult, for the vegetative symptoms of depression may be confused with the symptoms of the medical illness. (For a case example see Frances and Popkin 1988.)

Adjustment Disorder with Depressed Mood

■■ Adjustment disorders are reactions to psychosocial stressors
■■ that must be specific enough to be identifiable. For this classification, the reactions should take place not more than three months after the appearance of the stressor and should not last longer than six months. During this time the person's functioning (e.g., at work or school or at home) is impaired. To justify the diagnosis of adjustment disorder, the degree of response should be more than just overreaction; it is a genuine impairment of a person's functions, which will improve either when the stressor disappears or when the person adapts to the new stressful condition(s). Divorce, business failure, and marital problems are all examples, cited in the manual, of stressors that can trigger these severe adjustment reactions.

Adjustment disorder with depressed mood is an incomplete depressive syndrome (D.S.M.-III-R 1987:329). The main symptoms are "depressed mood, tearfulness, and feelings of hopelessness" (D.S.M.-III-R 1987:331).

Uncomplicated Bereavement

■■ Uncomplicated bereavement is "distinguished from a Major
■■ Depressive Episode and is not considered a mental disorder

even when associated with the full depressive syndrome. However, morbid preoccupation with worthlessness, suicidal ideation, marked functional impairment or psychomotor retardation, or prolonged duration, suggests that bereavement is complicated by a Major Depressive Episode'' (D.S.M.-III-R 1987:222).

Biological Theories and Treatments of Depression

The "modern" view that depression is primarily a medical or a biological condition can be traced back to the time of the early Greeks, when Galen, within the framework of the four humors, believed that melancholia resulted from an excess of black bile (Thase, Frank, and Kupfer 1985:817). Kraepelin's studies, in the early 1920s, began to provide evidence of biological irregularities. Other researchers followed, continuing this line of investigation. By the middle of the twentieth century a number of somatic treatments for depression, including lithium, antidepressant medications (e.g., imipramine), and electroconvulsive therapy (ECT) were in use.

During the next three to four decades new technologies led to enormous advances in knowledge of the body and the brain's physiology and chemistry, which have facilitated the study of the biology of depression. In addition, a new discipline, *neuroscience* (a combination of anatomy, pathology, pharmacology, chemistry, and psychology), has emerged that focuses on the physical relationship of the brain and brain structure to "thoughts, feelings, and behaviors" (Andreasen 1984:27).

New data continually reveal information about these biological factors and their relationship to depression, and some suggestive findings and intriguing working hypotheses have resulted. For example, Thase, Frank, and Kupfer (1985:816) believe that the appearance of "abnormalities in several biological systems discriminate depression from normal states or other psychopathological conditions." There have also been some clearly delineated associations between the *hypothesized* biological factors and some categories of clinical depression, primarily in the endogenous, or "vital"; the bipolar; and the delusional (psychotic) subtypes. The associations between biological abnormalities and the nonendogenous, nonbipolar (unipolar), and nonpsychotic depressions—the majority of the cases seen by most psychotherapists—have been weaker or, so far, have not been proved (Thase, Frank, and Kupfer 1985:879).

We emphasize the word *hypotheses*, as many of the findings are still in a formulative stage. Leading authorities, including some prominent researchers in the field, have cautioned against a premature closure on the evidence, noting that a "complete synthesis, or accurate model, of the biochemistry of these disorders [including depression] has not yet been developed" (Green, Mooney, and Schildkraut 1988:129).

The biological orientation to treating depression is currently dominant; it is seen as being more "scientific," and thus is held by many practitioners to be more valuable, despite the tentative nature of much of today's evidence and theorizing in depression research. The biological hypotheses and findings are nevertheless very important, and there are valuable treatments based on these hypotheses, such as the various antidepressant medications.

Clinicians must have a basic knowledge of how certain body systems function if they are to understand the biological theories on the nature of depression and the treatment approaches based on these theories. Yet many therapists are not familiar with this material. These will be explained in part 2.

In part 2 we first discuss the genetic process, then include a brief review of the biological systems involved in depression. These are followed by individual chapters on the neurochemical, the neuroendocrine, and the circulatory systems. We discuss the chronobiology of depression, including sleep and seasonal disorders. Then a number of other biological factors are addressed: pharmacotherapy, lithium and electroconvulsive therapy, substance abuse, and the eating disorders. Finally, we illustrate the clinical approach of biologically oriented psychiatrists.

In the following chapters, we discuss the pioneering biogenic amine hypothesis of depression as well as other current theories related to each biological system. Throughout, there are brief overviews of the main relevant investigations, including those avenues of research that have produced laboratory tests for biological markers such as the dexamethasone suppression test (the DST). The somatic treatments, including the antidepressant medications, are also covered.

4

Heredity and the Genetic Basis of Depression

Some families seem to have higher rates of depression than others. This raises the question of a hereditary component in mood disorders. Researchers first have attempted to verify that the rates in these families *are* higher than expected in the general population and then have asked, "Is depression, or a tendency to develop it, genetically based? Or is the apparent clustering in families socially determined (e.g., by children imitating and identifying with depressed parents and thereby learning a depressed coping style)?" The question, then, is one of nature versus nurture (Bertelsen 1988).

To follow the discussion on the possibility of genetic determination of affective disorders, the reader will need to understand some basic principles of biology and chemistry as they relate to genetics. For those who have not studied these subjects or who no longer remember some details, we shall present a very brief and vastly oversimplified review of this topic.

The first time we define a term, it will be printed in italic type to assist the reader who may need to refer back to it. The reader may wonder why we bother to define "simple" terms like *protein* and *tissue*, and in later chapters *brain, gland,* and *nerve*. It is because we may use these words frequently, and correctly, without recalling all their particular connections and functions in the body—the specific information that will be needed to understand the genetic and biological aspects of the depressions.

The Biology and Chemistry of Genetics: A Very Brief Review

■■ A human body is made up of billions of cells. The *cell* is the
■■ physical basis of life and of all life processes. Each individual human cell contains *protoplasm*, which includes a nucleus that is surrounded by *cytoplasm* (a thick, jellylike substance made mostly of proteins and water); and each cell is enclosed within a thin, selectively

permeable *membrane* ("A thin, soft, pliable layer of tissue that lines a tube or cavity, covers an organ or structure, or separates one part from another" (Thomas 1989:1100). This membrane controls the materials that enter and exit the cell.

Cells organize into structures with different functions and different locations (e.g., muscle, nerve, and skin) and connective *tissue* (groups of specialized cells). Cells grow by enlarging or dividing (multiplying), obtaining their fuel by burning *molecules* ("the smallest quantity into which a substance may be divided without loss of its characteristics" [Thomas 1989:1140]) composed of *carbohydrates* (sugars and starches), proteins, and fat. These three molecules, along with vitamins and nucleic acids, are the "five major organic molecules of life" (Sherman and Sherman 1983:55). The process of energy transformation is assisted by catalysts called *enzymes*, which are a class of protein. (A *catalyst* is a general term for a "substance that speeds up the rate of a chemical reaction without . . . being permanently altered" [Thomas 1989:303]. Enzymes are catalysts with specific functions [Thomas 1989:602].)

Many thousands of different chemicals help to form cells. The primary structural material consists of *proteins,* which are long molecules that often assume a twisted structure called an *alpha helix.* Proteins are composed of *amino acids* ("the building blocks of protein and basic constituents of living organisms" [Sherman and Sherman 1983:12]) linked in one or more *polypeptide chains.* (Polypeptides are a "union of two or more amino acids" [Thomas 1989:1447].) The sequence of amino acids is considered the backbone (or *main chain*). Each amino acid also has an additional cluster of atoms (a *side chain*) that is different for each one. Since there are about twenty different amino acids, billions of combinations are possible. In addition to the complexities of the molecules themselves, the way the molecules are folded and their level of organization vary according to their function. For example, they can be fibrous (e.g., *fibrin,* a blood protein involved in clotting) or globular (e.g., *hemoglobin,* the pigment of red blood cells). Proteins can change their shape and structure (e.g., when heated), thus changing their function or causing them to become inactive. They continually wear out and need to be renewed or replaced. This replacement process involves nucleic acid, another important substance found in cells.

Nucleic acids are large, complex molecules that direct the synthesis of proteins in the cells. (*Synthesis* is the combining of simple elements to produce a more complex substance.) Like proteins, nucleic acids are long-chain molecules, but their building blocks are nucleotides rather than amino acids. (A *nucleotide* is a "compound . . . [that] constitute[s] the structural unit of nucleic acid" [Thomas 1989:1227].) There are two distinct types of nucleic acids: *deoxyribonucleic acid (DNA)* and *ribonucleic acid (RNA)*; these have different kinds of base sugars. Each cell contains two noninterchangeable sets of nucleic acids (nucleotides) that are the building blocks for DNA and for RNA. Each molecule of DNA has two twisted strands (a *double helix* configuration) that are not identical but are complementary, in the sense that one supplies what the other lacks. (Together they are "complete.") They fit together (*bond*) only when properly paired (i.e., when one strand has a specific sequence of nucleotides that are the correct partners for the other strand). The sequence of the nucleotides (*bases*) on one strand is determined by the sequence of the nucleotides on the other strand. RNA strands are generally single.

DNA, being the substance of which genes are made, is the basis of heredity. It reproduces exact copies of itself through the process of *mitosis* (division of the cell in which the nucleus is duplicated). Each new strand of DNA contains the blueprint (*genetic code* or *genome*) of the new cells. Although each cell contains the total genome, only certain genes may be activated in a particular cell or tissue. The timing of activation and deactivation (*suppression*) of genes is also under genetic control. DNA molecules can be altered (*mutated*)—for example, by exposure to radiation or, in rare instances, spontaneously.

For the body to use the information contained in the DNA it must first be moved from the *inside* of the cell nucleus to the cytoplasm *outside* of the nucleus. Then its coded blueprint must be deciphered (Sherman and Sherman 1983:110). This is accomplished via RNA. RNA is formed from a DNA template ("a molecule, as of DNA, that serves as a pattern for the generation of another macromolecule, [e.g.] . . . messenger RNA" [*Webster's* 1989:1214]). There are different types of RNA molecules, with different functions. *Messenger RNA (mRNA)* copies the DNA codes (a process called *transcription*) and transfers the information that is stored in the DNA by moving it to the cytoplasm, activating the protein-building process according to the particular instructions in each cell. In a process called *translation, transfer RNA (tRNA)* lines up the amino acids in the cytoplasm in specific sequences. These amino acids are then bonded into the polypeptide chains that comprise proteins. There are different kinds of transfer RNA, each associated with a particular amino acid.

In summary, DNA is a template for mRNA that moves out of the cell nucleus; tRNA interprets (decodes) the mRNA information into arrangements of amino acids, forming proteins that then build cell structures or form enzymes that assist in the building process.

Each cell contains thousands of *genes* (a gene is the "basic unit of heredity. . . . [They are] self-producing ultramicroscopic particles" [Thomas 1989:726]), which are composed of DNA. Genes are particular arrangements of nucleic acids that form the strands of DNA. These DNA strands combine with certain proteins to form *chromosomes*. Each chromosome has numerous genes, which are located in specific areas of the chromosome. Human cells have forty-six chromosomes. They are arranged into two sets (referred to as the *diploid number*) of twenty-three pairs (called a *karyotype*). Twenty-two pairs (called *autosomes*) are similar in all humans, but one pair (referred to as the sex chromosomes) is different: A female has two X chromosomes and a male has one X and one Y chromosome. Although all cells have an entire set of genes, the genetic codes instruct each cell to use only specific parts of the code, depending on the cell's purpose.

In the reproductive process, each chromosome pair splits, in a process called *meiosis*. Each separate strand, or *gamete* (egg or sperm), contains one entire set of genes (twenty-three chromosomes), which joins with the gamete from the opposite sex parent. Variations can occur because during the early stage of meiosis, both strands of DNA coil and exchange materials. (This process is called *crossover*.) Thus the new strands contain different combinations of genes that each parent received from his or her parents, so that every child inherits characteristics, or *traits*, from both parental lines. Genes located close to each other on a particular chromosome are referred to as *linked* and are often transmitted together, so that a child may inherit certain groups of characteristics from one parent and other groups from the other parent.

Two basic principles govern the transmission of genes from parent to child. These are referred to as *Mendel's laws*, because they were identified by Gregor Mendel, an Austrian monk. The first principle, called the *law of segregation*, points out that genes function independently, as units. They pair but do not blend; they are passed on intact to the next generation. When *gametes* (egg or sperm) are produced by the next generation, the genes segregate (separate) and recombine, forming any of a number of possible combinations. This is known as Mendel's *law of independent assortment* or *principle of recombination* (Sherman and Sherman 1983:448).

The genetic makeup of an individual is called the *genotype*. This refers to the individual's DNA, which contains all the factors the individual inherits; that is, all of his or her potential. Some of these characteristics will be revealed (*expressed*) in the individual. Other characteristics will not be expressed but will still be carried in the genes and may be passed on to future generations. The way the DNA expresses itself—that is, the factors that are actually revealed, such as the individual's physical makeup, including outward appearance—is his or her *phenotype*. These factors are said to be *expressed phenotypically*. In recent literature, some authors distinguish between the identification of processes inside the cell, which they call the *endophenotype,* and the external expression of the gene, called the *exophenotype* (McGuffin and Sargeant 1991:22–24).

Individuals inherit two of each gene. The two genes in this pair may or may not be identical. Some genes exert a stronger influence than others and are said to be *dominant;* they inhibit (or mask) the expression of the paired gene, which is said to be *recessive.* A single dominant gene can exert a very strong effect and be expressed phenotypically, whereas recessive genes usually have to be present in pairs to have this effect.

Various genetic errors or mutations can cause disorders. Rauch (1988:389–390) describes four types of associations: "(1) single gene inheritance. . . . a condition associated with a specific abnormal [dominant] gene" (e.g., Huntington's disease); "(2) multifactorial inheritance. . . . which involves the [additional] effect of . . . the environment" (e.g., diabetes and asthma); "(3) chromosome aberrations—chromosomes that are broken or have missing or extra pieces"; and "(4) exposure to harmful environmental agents." This last type can occur prenatally (e.g., as with fetal alcohol syndrome), or it can occur at any time after birth.

Genetic Research

■■ The field of genetics is usually divided into a number of
■■ broad areas, such as *biochemical genetics,* the study of the mechanisms of inheritance, including genetic influence; *molecular genetics,* the study of the makeup and workings of genes; *clinical genetics,* the study of the significance of genetics to health and illness; *cytogenetics,* the study of chromosomes; and *analytic genetics,* the study of modes of inheritance and linkage.

Until recently, genetic research on affective disorders was mainly in the first area: Researchers studied the distribution of phenotypes in families (e.g., mood disorders), and they reached conclusions based on inferences made after the fact. Recent technological developments have led to *genetic engineering,* the construction of techniques that enable researchers to work directly with genetic material. For example, using *gene splicing,* DNA can be cut from one organism and transplanted into the DNA of another organism. When the genetic material of the host organism reproduces, the resulting *recombinant DNA* contains the genetic material of both organisms (Thomas 1989:1568). This technology has reversed the research process, as scientists can now focus on genotypes—for example, by examining the structure of genes, such as sequences of base pairs that comprise particular genes. Scientists are charting mutations and variations that are not visible to the naked eye and that may have biological consequences. Studies of particular conditions and diseases and *genetic markers* ("a usually dominant gene or trait that serves especially to identify genes or traits linked with it" [*Webster's* 1989:511]) are enabling researchers to pinpoint the specific chromosomes on which these genes are located.

Human genetic mapping is the systematic construction of maps of the structure of the twenty-two autosomes and the two sex chromosomes. Scientists are exploring this area in great detail. (One report referred to this procedure as "looking for an address for every gene" [*Consumer Reports* 1990:484]).[1] Researchers are also examining genetic function (or expression) by identifying internal phenotypes (endophenotypes). This involves analyzing mRNA in the cells and is helping to pinpoint *state markers* (markers indicating the condition or form of the organism). Various other techniques are also in use.[2]

The Evidence for a Genetic Component in Depression

■■ McGuffin and Sargeant (1991) have described the strategies
■■ being used in the investigation of the genetic components of depression in two groups: (1) genetic influence; and (2) mode of inheritance. These provide a good framework for surveying the research.

Genetic Influence

McGuffin and Sargeant (1991:165) describe research done with families, twins in the same family, and twins who were separated by adoption, in an attempt to ascertain the "lifetime expectancy (. . . lifetime incidence) of developing a disorder." As they point out, the symptoms of affective disorders are so common that genetic researchers cannot simply count cases; they generally focus on those involving hospital referral, which tend to be the most severe. This approach is not without problems, for these referrals to hospitals tend to represent disproportionately people who live close to the hospital and, in the case of urban hospitals, to oversample women and poor people (McGuffin and Sargeant 1991:166).

FAMILY STUDIES

A review of a large number of studies of first-degree relatives (siblings and parents) of bipolar patients reveals higher proportions of affected relatives, beyond normal probability expectations. These rates are about 14 percent, with a range, in different studies of 4–24 percent (Bertelsen 1988). These proportions are high, considering that about 1 percent of the general population is conservatively estimated to suffer from bipolar disorders (Mendlewicz 1985:797–799).

Over a lifetime the risk of having unipolar or bipolar depression is about three and a half times higher for first-degree relatives of identified cases of affective disorders than it is for the general population (Smeraldi 1988:56).

The evidence for familial clustering is the strongest in bipolar disorders—from 10 to 20 percent higher than would be expected by chance. In fact, a child whose parents are both diagnosed with bipolar disorder has been estimated to have a 75 percent risk of developing a mood disorder (Grinspoon and Bakalar 1990:3). Children and other first-degree relatives of those with bipolar disorders seem generally vulnerable to mood disorders. On the other hand, relatives of those with unipolar depression do not show higher than expected rates of mood disorders (Bertelsen 1988). The evidence is stronger for a genetic basis of bipolar mood disorders than it is for a genetic cause of unipolar disorders.

TWIN STUDIES

Identical twins originate from the same fertilized egg and are called *monozygotic (MZ)*. Fraternal twins, called *dizygotic (DZ)*, originate from separate egg and sperm products and are no more similar genetically than any other siblings. Studies of both kinds of twins have provided a good deal of evidence, some of it controversial, in the nature-versus-nurture debates.

With bipolar disorders the evidence is consistent and well beyond chance that hereditary factors play a role in this condition: If one identical twin has a bipolar disorder, the probability that the other twin will have some sort of mood disorder is nearly 100 percent, and the probability that it will be bipolar is 80 percent. If one fraternal twin has a bipolar disorder, the chance of the other twin having *any* mood disorder is no higher than that of any other sibling (Grinspoon and Bakalar 1990:4). Gold (1987a:199) states that "depending upon the criteria . . . both identical twins become depressed in forty to approximately seventy-eight percent of the cases; . . . [in] bipolar it is even higher . . . [while] in nonidentical twins . . . [the] rate is the same . . . [as for] non-twin siblings, zero to thirteen percent."

Bertelsen (1988:51) states that identical twins show a high *concordance* (agreement) rate compared with fraternal twins, by a factor of from 2 to 6.[3] He emphasizes that any concordance rate of less than 100 percent (which would show complete genetic control) provides evidence of the influence of environmental factors. In other words, if the depression is entirely genetic, when one MZ twin develops an affective disorder, the other twin should always develop this disorder.

Another literature review indicates that in seven studies identical twins showed a concordance rate for mood disorders of 76 percent, compared to a rate for fraternal twins of only 19 percent. The authors suggest that these data uphold the argument for a genetic component in affective disorders but that they still fail to sort out the differential effects of heredity and environment (Papolos and Papolos 1987). These research projects investigated identical and fraternal twins reared in the same households and, thus, an apparently equal environment. However, we know that two siblings—even twins—rarely experience the same environment or are treated the same by parents, even when parents attempt to be consistent.

ADOPTION STUDIES

Another way to sort out the nature-versus-nurture question has been to study identical and fraternal twins who were separated at birth and reared apart. This is called the *adoption strategy*. Only a few studies have dealt with MZ twins with affective disorders who were reared apart. In eight of twelve pairs of separated twins with bipolar illness, the concordance rate for the bipolar disease was the same as that for those pairs of twins who were reared together, suggesting very strong evidence for a genetic factor (Bertelsen 1988:52). Papolos and Papolos (1987:45) point out that there may be a genetic component, but it is not wholly genetic, as some 33 percent were not in concordance. Obviously, social and environmental factors played a role.

SUMMARY

In short, the findings from the family, twin, and adoption studies indicate that genetic factors contribute to affective disorders, although the precise nature of this contribution has yet to be explained. The mechanisms of inheritance for so heterogeneous a diagnosis as depression are more complicated than those for such straightforward conditions as Huntington's disease (McGuffin and Sargeant 1991). (We discuss this further later.)

Mode of Inheritance

The search for mode of inheritance has been a search for *genetic markers*. According to McGuffin and Sargeant this term "in the stricter sense . . . [means] an inherited characteristic . . . [with] a simple mode of transmission . . . [with] two or more *alleles*" (1991:171). (An allele is a "pair of genes situated on the same site on paired chromosomes, containing specific inheritable characteristics" [Thomas 1989:65]). Genetic markers "must be capable of being reliably detected and are stable over time," as compared with *state-dependent markers,* which mark the similarities or differences in genetic makeup that reveal how a particular characteristic (e.g., an inherited disease) is transmitted. Finding a trait marker for a particular disease identifies those who are at risk for it. Some confusion occurs because the term *genetic marker* is sometimes used (or misused) to describe "virtually any biological finding that may be inherited and can be potentially related to psychiatric illness" (McGuffin and Sargeant 1991:171).

The search for genetic markers generally focuses either on trying to find association markers or on locating linkage markers. *Association markers* "provide evidence of an association between a particular marker phenotype and the disease" (McGuffin and Sargeant 1991:171). Association studies compare how often a specific marker gene appears in ill people in the population with how often it appears in an ethnically comparable group that does not show this illness. *Linkage studies* look for evidence in families that the marker gene and the illness are being transmitted together. *Linkage* provides evidence that two genes are physically located near each other on a chromosome.

ASSOCIATION STUDIES

Association studies include the analysis of such classical markers as those that determine blood types and certain antigens. (An *antigen* is a "substance which induces the formation of antibodies" [Thomas 1989:113].) Although some associations with affective disorders have been reported, after reviewing the available research, McGuffin and Sargeant (1991:171–173) stated that the results currently seem puzzling and are not consistent enough to conclude that there are significant associations between association markers and affective illness. Research in this area is appealing but fraught with many complications, including the difficulty in finding research subjects and appropriate control groups.

LINKAGE ANALYSIS

Linkage analysis is an important method of identifying the presence of genes in the determination of a phenotype. This is an expanding field, as new potential markers are now being identified throughout the genome with the advent of DNA technology. For example, some evidence has indicated a link between affective disorders and color blindness, among other factors. However, the affective disorders constitute a very heterogeneous group of conditions, and some linkages may apply to specific subgroups of families with mood disorders.

Several types of linkage markers have been studied in relation to affective disorders. These include the following:

1. *Classical markers.* Studies have investigated the possibility of linkage involving classical markers, particularly of the *HLA system* (the human leukocyte antigen system, which is involved with the immune system). McGuffin and Sargeant (1991:174) reviewed a small number of studies of this type of linkage and reported that they yielded only mildly positive linkage scores. However, they feel that this area is probably worthy of follow-up.

2. *X-linked studies.* McGuffin and Sargeant (1991:174–175) reviewed research based on the thesis that affective disorders were transmitted via an X-linked gene (i.e., they are transmitted along with the chromosomes that determine gender). Although this thesis received some support, the results were considered questionable.

3. *DNA markers.* The best-known linkage analysis of affective disorders is a family study on the Old Order Amish. Using recombinant DNA gene-mapping techniques, a specific gene was found in a number of families with a higher than expected incidence of manic depression. The bipolar disorder was allegedly linked to genetic markers "in or near two genes on chromosome 11" (Kolata 1987). As reported in the media this "genetic marker . . . [is] a piece of DNA so near the Manic-Depression gene that it is inherited along with the disease-causing gene" (Schmeck 1987; Kolata 1987:1139). Kolata's article reported that two other studies of manic depression in other populations could not find the marker.[4] Yet a researcher at M.I.T. reported that "now that the manic-depression genetic marker has been found, mental illness research has taken a new turn. For the first time molecular genetics has entered the arena of psychiatric disorders" (Kolata 1987:1140).

Very recently, serious doubt has been cast on the Old Order Amish studies (Schmeck 1989). There now seems to be agreement that no gene for affective disorder exists on this part of chromosome 11 (McGuffin and Sargeant 1991:177).

This controversy surrounding the findings on chromosome 11 provides some insight into the research process of such a complex problem as that of genetic inheritance. The hypothesis of genetic linkage and control of depression is certainly tenable but is obviously unproven. It was unfortunate that when the previous claims about chromosome 11 were so widely publicized, the cautions, such as the one by Kolata (1987) that this linkage was found in only one of the three groups studied, were largely ignored, certainly by the popular press.

SUMMARY

McGuffin and Sargeant (1991:170–171) report that "Affective illness, particularly of the BP [bipolar] type, has a large genetic component, but the main justification for searching for major genes is there is no compelling evidence against their existence at least in some families." After a careful review of the literature on studies of genetic markers, they conclude that the "yield so far . . . has been confusing and disappointing" (Kolata 1987:178).

Problems of Conducting Investigations into the Genetic Basis of Depression

■■ The fact that we are not dealing with a single condition or
■■ illness complicates the investigation of the evidence for genetic influences on depression. We are dealing with a complex disorder, actually with a group of disorders. There *are* differences, clinically and phenomenologically, between bipolar and unipolar disorders, and further differences in the subclassifications of each of these disorders. Smeraldi (1988:56) states, "There are no clinical, biological, or pharmacological data to indicate whether or not the affective disorders are . . . etiopathogenetically homogeneous [the cause of the disease is genetically uniform in composition, structure and nature], and *the relevant genetic system whose segregation pattern we want to know may also not be unitary, even for a single clinical phenotype*" (emphasis added). Whatley and Owen (1991:24) point out that even a simply expressed disorder may have a genetic base that is quite complex (e.g., involving several regulator genes at various locations).

Smeraldi (1988:56) further states, "That genetic factors are involved has been demonstrated, but neither their nature nor their mode of action, nor their pattern of transmission has been defined." Papolos and Papolos (1987:44) think that the "next few years should yield some heady things about the genetics of mood disorders, but right now . . . current research indicates only that the vulnerability to these disorders is 'passed down' in families. . . . But how does a scientist disentangle the subtle strands of heredity from those of environment?"

Not only is it difficult to investigate direct genetic control of the affective disorders, but the problems are enormous in studying the mode of their transmission. One major problem is the need to study very large families, particularly families without other complicating illness, which can be very hard to locate.

Some problems relate to the organism itself. For example, Whatley and Owen (1991:24) indicate that in the study of state markers, the mRNA can only give a picture of the existing pattern at the time of extraction, and this pattern may be changed by drugs and other factors.

Defining and using terms also entail difficulties. *Genetic predisposition* may have different implications for different diseases. For example, Huntington's disease is inherited through a dominant single gene. A person who has inherited a single copy of the HD gene will develop the disorder, but the time required for the disease to develop and its progression vary. The correspondence between the presence of a gene (or genes) and the variety of conditions known as mood disorders may be less direct.

McGuffin and Sargeant (1991:177–178) call research on genetic markers a hazardous pursuit. Since we do not clearly understand how affective illnesses are transmitted, geneticists must make assumptions that may not be true. The major research strategy that has been used—a random search through available markers—has not yet yielded significant results in the affective disorders, although it has been more successful in single-gene disorders such as Huntington's disease. Focusing on genes having a putative relationship is another possible research strategy, as is making a systematic search of *all* the pairs of chromosomes for such candidate genes.

Although the study of DNA has always been known to involve an awesome number of factors, it has become very obvious that DNA is even more complex than previously thought. Furthermore, it is increasingly apparent that DNA—in fact, inheritance and genetics—does not operate as directly, mechanically, and predictably as originally thought. DNA contains the directions for the synthesis of proteins, and proteins need to be replaced continuously. In this process, the genes are constantly being "turned on" to access the building instructions contained in the DNA and then "turned off." Earlier, it was thought that these instructions were established at conception and remained constant, except for changes that might result from damage or deterioration. However, evidence now suggests that neurotransmitters and antidepressant drugs, among other substances, can actually *alter* expression of the DNA. This hypothesis, which is explained in chapter 6, has reshaped the biological theories on the causes of depression. We emphasize the use of the term *theories,* because much is not yet understood, and much of this theorizing is at the cutting edge of current molecular biological research. We do not yet have an answer to exactly what is happening in the chain of change, but it is now clear that genetic endowment is not final at birth. "Rather, the environment is regulating gene expression on a minute to minute basis" (Hyman 1991a).

With the growing emphasis on the environmental factors that affect nurture, we now realize that we must expand our definition of *environmental*. In addition to "upbringing, personal relations, and social stress," we must look at physical illness (including viral infections, which may alter DNA,) accidents and random events, and nutritional status, among other factors (Plomin 1990:5).

Despite the current problems and limitations, molecular biologists are hopeful, even "confident that if major genes exist [in affective disorders] . . . they will be detected" (McGuffin and Sargeant 1991:178). At a recent conference on affective disorders, a member of the NIMH team studying genetic disorders stated that this discovery is only a matter of time. These researchers are studying the twenty-two pairs of autosomes, one at a time, and they are certain that they will turn up evidence of genes controlling these phenotypes (Barrington 1991). McGuffin and Sargeant (1991:178) believe that this ambitious project will require collaborative studies, carried out in many different research facilities, which are currently being set up. This is moving psychiatry into the era of "big science."

The Implications of Genetic Research and Genetic Engineering

■■ Genetic information is already leading to greater understand-
■■ ing of affective and other disorders. The possible benefits are clear: new, perhaps better treatments, and predictive tests that might result in early preventive measures. There are also serious risks. Tests will probably not always be able to predict accurately if an at-risk individual will develop a disease or when it might occur and how severe it might be if the disease does develop. Nonetheless, test results could lead to discrimination: At-risk individuals may be defined as unemployable, untrainable, and uninsurable. Mental health professionals will have to keep abreast of this process, which is already under way. The knowledge that, based on genetic inheritance, one might develop an illness such as an affective disorder may also have very negative, stressful effects on the individual and his or her family and close friends.

Nature or Nurture?

■■ We know, statistically, that there is a greater prevalence of
■■ depression in identical (MZ) twins than in fraternal (DZ) twins. Yet even in identical twins and for bipolar disorders, for which

the genetic evidence seems stronger, the concordance rate is not 100 percent. The most biologically oriented of the researchers acknowledge, if only in the most general terms, the relevance of the environment, of life history, of interpersonal relations, and of stresses and trauma to the development of depression.

Further complicating the issue is a distortion of what is meant by *genetic transmission*. It has been argued that genetic endowment may increase one's susceptibility to such disorders as depression. However, environmental factors may exert a great deal of influence. It may very well be that one identical twin may receive (or even perceive) more support from a parent or a loved one, or there may be another significant factor that is different. From this they may obtain strength or resistance that deters the tendency to depression, and so this twin will not develop the disorder. Heightened susceptibility, therefore, does not mean absolute determinism.

Gold, who has stated that depression is an inherited disease, adds, "Our genes are *not* our destiny. . . . Inborn errors can be corrected. Vulnerabilities can be avoided. We can change . . . counter or correct many of the genetic as well as experiential factors that trigger depression." He says that these changes may be brought about by "biopsychiatric treatment for depression. . . . [including] psychotherapies . . . to counter interpersonal, cognitive and behavioral triggers [and]. . . . provide strength to cope with life events and psychological stressors that can touch off a depression in a vulnerable individual" (1987a:202–203).

Hyman (1991a) points out that "depression is not a genetic disease in the same sense as Huntington's disease because Huntington's disease has 100 percent *penetrance*," meaning that "if you live long enough you will get it." In contrast, based on what we know from twin studies, not everyone with a genetic vulnerability to depression will develop the disease. (It has reduced penetrance.) Moreover, since identical twins, who share 100 percent of the DNA, have less than 100 percent concordance for either bipolar or unipolar disorder, some environmental factors, currently unknown, must be involved.

Behavioral geneticists are examining *genotype-environment (GE)* interactions—the mutual effect and influence that genetic and environmental factors have on each other. Plomin states that better definitions are needed, both of environmental factors (e.g., how to describe selection and construction of one's experience) and of genetic markers, that will help to index individual genotypes (1990:5). These geneticists hope to be able to measure the proportion of the contribution of nature and of nurture, and eventually, of the "developmental interface between the two" (Plomin 1990:6).

Plomin (1990:4) points out that whereas environmentalism was once the predominant theory in psychiatric research, and genetic factors were downplayed or overlooked, genetic or biological determinism is now being emphasized. He cautions that neither aspect should be ignored.

5

The Biology of Depression

The Biological Systems Associated with Depression: A Brief Review

■■ The body is a marvel of complex chemical controls and bal-
■■ ances. A single action may trigger a chain of events: A gland
is stimulated and then produces a hormone that inhibits, or stimulates,
the secretion of another hormone in another gland. A series of actions
may occur in a fraction of a second and produce a single, specific result.
These internal actions produce both chemical and behavioral changes.
The chemical changes may also be produced by external factors: Psychological and social stresses are known to affect an individual's biochemical systems profoundly. External events—light and darkness, heat
and cold, seasonal variations in temperature, length of day—also affect
internal biochemistry.

Conversely, individuals can exercise control over their environment,
which can affect the chemical balances in their bodies. For example,
they can ingest foods or medications that have beneficial or harmful
results; they can schedule work and sleep to fit with the environmental
cycles of light and dark (Whybrow, Akiskal, and McKinney 1984:113–
114).

Although much is not understood about these biological processes,
the information that is available has helped us understand the course of
depression and the chemical changes associated with it. This knowledge has resulted in a number of theories based on assumptions of
various malfunctions in the biological systems, and these theories have
in turn led to new treatments. Although these biological systems are
intricately interconnected, we describe them separately to facilitate the
reader's understanding of this material.

First, we consider two of the major body systems, the nervous (including the brain and the brain's limbic system) and the endocrine
systems, which are involved with communication and control—"the
decisive mediators between the internal and external environment"
(Whybrow, Akiskal, and McKinney 1984:113). We then describe the

circulatory system, particularly the role of blood and blood plasma. Later, we focus on particular subsystems, including the functions of several neurotransmitters and hormones and of particular organs, such as the hypothalamus, the thyroid, and the pineal gland.

The Nervous System

■■ The *nervous system* has been compared with an electric mes-
■■ senger service that very rapidly sends messages that control movement and feeling throughout the body (Bruun and Bruun 1982:68). It gathers information from outside the body and processes it in a number of ways. It may use it to move muscles or control the heart's rate; it may store it in memory; it may recall stored memories to understand and process information further; and so on.

This system is made up of delicate *nerve cells* or *neurons* (bundles or groups of fibers that connect the various parts of the system). The system includes the brain and the spinal cord, nerves, *ganglia* (masses of nerve cell bodies outside of and along the side of the brain and spinal cord) and parts of *receptor organs* (groups of cells that receive stimuli).

The nervous system receives and interprets stimuli and rapidly transmits impulses to the effector organs. (*Organs* are differentiated structures, made up of cells, that perform specific functions in an organism. For example, *effector organs,* such as glands or muscles, respond to motor stimulation. *Glands* are cells and groups of cells that respond by selectively removing substances from the blood, concentrating or altering them, and secreting them for further use or elimination. *Muscles* contract, when stimulated, to produce or check movement.)

The nervous system functions primarily through electrical impulses (stimuli) that travel down individual cells, stimulating the release of chemicals called *neurotransmitters,* which carry the stimuli from one cell to another, triggering the next electrical impulse. This process, called *neurotransmission,* is repeated over and over again, sending impulses throughout the body. (We shall discuss this process in greater detail later.)

A number of the body's chemicals have dual roles. For example, *hormones* (chemicals secreted by the endocrine glands, whose primary purpose is to stimulate particular activities, such as the secretion of other hormones) may also function in the nervous system as neurotransmitters.

Nerves are classified functionally, depending on the direction of conducted impulses. For example, *sensory nerves* conduct sensory impulses from receptors to the central nervous system; *motor nerves* conduct motor impulses to a muscle or gland.

The *nervous system* can be divided into two general parts: the *central nervous system (CNS)* and the *peripheral nervous system (PNS)*. (See figure 5.1.)

The *central nervous system,* which includes the brain and spinal cord, controls the body's relationship to its outside environment. The *spinal cord* is a longitudinal cord of nerve tissue that extends from the brain, along the back, and is contained within the spinal column. It carries messages to and from the brain and other parts of the body.

The *peripheral nervous system* coordinates and integrates nervous functions. It includes the very great network of nerves and ganglia found mainly along the spinal column. This system "carries messages connecting sensory receptors with the central nervous system and the central nervous system with muscles and glands" (Bootzin, Loftus, and Zajonc 1983:49).

The peripheral nervous system has two branches: the *somatic nervous system,* which controls muscles that act voluntarily in relationship to the outside world (e.g., the muscles that can move finger bones to grasp items), and the *autonomic nervous system,* which supplies nerves to smooth (involuntary) and cardiac muscles and glandular tissue, and regulates many of the inner organs and body processes. These processes, such as digestion, blood pressure, body temperature, and breathing, were once thought to be entirely involuntary or autonomous, thus the origin of the name. Recently, however, procedures such as biofeedback have shown that, to some degree, these processes can be controlled voluntarily. Now the autonomic nervous system is usually defined as the system governing the body's internal environment.

The controlling centers of the autonomic nervous system are in the brain and are considered part of the central nervous system. The nerve

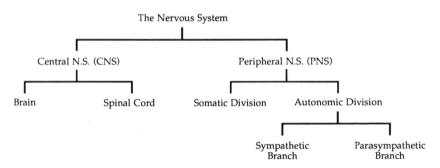

Figure 5.1. The Divisions of the Nervous System

portions are subdivided by function into two parts: the *sympathetic* and the *parasympathetic* divisions. The *sympathetic* branch expends energy; it prepares the body for action by stimulating the flow of adrenalin, which increases heartbeat and narrows certain blood vessels. This is the part of the nervous system that deals with stress. The *parasympathetic* branch functions in many ways opposite to the sympathetic: It slows the body's actions by reducing the heart rate, increasing the tone and contractability of the smooth muscles, and causes blood vessels to dilate. This system supplies nerves to the glands, eyes, heart, lungs, genitals, and more. The vegetative symptoms of depression are associated with this parasympathetic branch of the nervous system.

The Brain's Structure and Functional Organization

The *brain* is a soft mass of nerve tissue. Enclosed within the hard bones of the skull, it is a part of the central nervous system. It regulates and coordinates all the body's activities, primarily by (1) receiving messages from outside and inside the brain (called *input*), (2) processing these messages, and (3) sending messages (stimuli) to *effector* organs, such as glands and muscles, which results in the body responding to internal or external changes in the environment (called *output*) (Mesulam 1988:91).

Andreasen (1984:89—91) describes the brain as an extremely complex structure consisting of multiple structures and "three dimensional [systems] stretching from the front of the brain to the back and from one side to the other, as well as being nested inside each other." It is difficult both to portray and even to imagine. While all the levels are interconnected, and these connections are its essence, the brain must be arbitrarily divided into segments to achieve even a vastly oversimplified understanding of its functions.[1] These divisions are the *cerebrum* (the *cerebral hemispheres*), the *diencephalon*, the *basal ganglia*, the *brainstem* (composed of the *midbrain*; the *pons*, or *bridge*; and the *medulla*, or *middle part*), and the *cerebellum*.[2] There are also four cavities (*ventricles*). (Figure 5.2 illustrates some of the structures of the brain.)

The *cerebral hemispheres*, derived from the *telencephalon* (*tele*, "distant"/ "end"; *enkephalos*, "brain") are the largest structures, located at the top of the brain, one on each side, and interconnected by a band of nerve fibers called the *corpus callosum*. Each cerebral hemisphere has four divisions: the *frontal lobe, parietal lobe, occipital lobe,* and *temporal lobe.* (The temporal lobe contains a small structure called the *amygdala*, which we shall refer to later in our discussion of the diencephalon-limbic system.) The varied functions of the lobes include the processing of memories, feelings, body sensations, visual and auditory information,

and much more. The covering of the cerebrum (the *cerebral cortex*) consists of heavily folded layers of tightly packed cells and is called *gray
matter*, because it appears to be gray. Beneath the cortex are concentrated nerve fibers, the so-called *white matter*. The nerve fibers of the
white matter are the "wiring that connects various regions of the cortex
to other brain centers" (Andreasen 1984:92).

Important processing centers are located deep inside the middle part
of the brain. Among other structures, these include the *thalamus*, which
processes both sensory and motor information, and the *hypothalamus*,
which controls metabolism. The *basal ganglia*, also found in the central
part of the brain, are involved in the governing of movement. The
brainstem, located between the brain and the spinal cord, modulates the
functioning of the heart and of vital functions, such as breathing. Located in this general region is a small cluster of cells called the *locus
ceruleus*. Another important structure in the brainstem is made up of
the *raphe nuclei*. The *cerebellum*, which is connected to the brainstem, is
also involved in regulating movement. The interconnecting *ventricles*,—
which are located in the cerebral hemispheres, the diencephalon, and
the medulla—contain cerebrospinal fluid. Also of interest to us is the
pineal gland, attached to the rear of the third ventricle, which regulates
the sleep/wake cycle via the secretion of melatonin. (We discuss this in
chapter 9.)

Mesulam (1988:91) explains that the intermediary function of central
nervous system neurons—the procedure in between input into the
brain and output—is the one that involves "thought, language, memory, self-awareness and even many aspects of mood and affect. . . ."
From this behavioral perspective, there are four primary parts in the
cerebral hemispheres: "primary sensory cortex, primary motor cortex,
association cortex, and [part of] the limbic system." The limbic system
is the one we are currently most interested in.

The Limbic-Diencephalon System

Many scientists who are currently conducting research on the
depressions, among other disorders, are focusing on the *limbic-dience-
phalon system*. This name refers to a mixed group of structures, including
parts of the diencephalon and the bodies they connect with, such as the
thalamus (mediator of sensory and motor signals), the *hypothalamus*, and
the attached pituitary gland that it controls, the amygdala, locus ceruleus, raphe nuclei, and more. (The limbic system is illustrated in figure
5.2.)

The limbic system is the regulator of emotions, sexual feelings, and
"other appetitive and consummatory behaviors and the self-protective

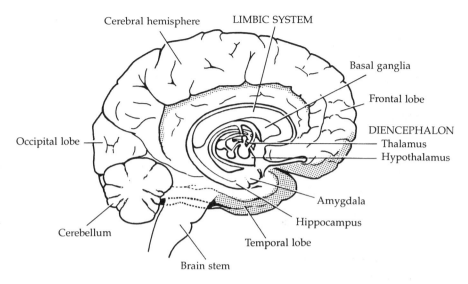

Figure 5.2. Some Structures of the Brain, Including the Limbic System

mechanism of flight or fight" (Papolos and Papolos 1987:57–58). In other words, most of what is popularly called "individual personality, cognitive style, and patterns of behavior" (Andreasen 1984:103). It is involved with memory, including memory distortion and partial and full memory failure (amnesia); with some forms of epilepsy; and with certain patterns of autonomic responses, such as those associated with stress (activation of high blood pressure, ulcer formation, irregular heartbeat, and so on). The limbic system is now thought to be so important that Andreasen feels that the "limbic system and its connections. . . . may be the part of the brain that has somehow 'broken' in at least some of those patients suffering from the schizophrenias or the affective disorders" (1984:103).

The Endocrine System

■■
■■ The *endocrine system* is a chemical messenger service. It is second in importance to the brain in its critical functions of regulating control and communication in the body. A relatively slower-functioning system, it is involved in the coordination of long-term, continuing processes, such as growth, metabolism, the development and functions of the reproductive organs and personality (characteristic ways of responding), the body's ability to respond and adapt to stress, and more. It is a system of glands located in different areas in the body

whose chemical secretions, or *hormones*, have far-reaching effects on cells and organs. The actions of many hormones are interrelated: a change in the amount of one hormone in a particular subsystem will produce a change in the amount of another hormone in that system. Levels of hormones secreted by one subsystem may also affect levels in another subsystem.

Endocrine glands, which secrete their products into the bloodstream, are also called *ductless glands*. Another system of glands produces liquids that are secreted via ducts to surrounding tissues; these are called *exocrine glands*. Some of these liquids (e.g., saliva and sweat) pass to the outside of the body; others (e.g., digestive juices) work inside the body.

The endocrine system includes the thyroid gland and parathyroid glands, the adrenal glands, the pituitary gland, the thymus, the pineal gland, and the testes and ovaries. The testes and ovaries are the *reproductive glands*, or *gonads*, and are a separate system in themselves. The islets of Langerhans, groups of cells that produce insulin, are also part of the endocrine system, although they are not distinct organs; they are located in the pancreas.

The Circulatory System

■■ The circulatory system (sometimes called the *cardiovascular,*
■■ or *transport, system*) consists of the *heart,* a large, muscular organ that functions as a pump; *blood* (actually a tissue in liquid form), composed of plasma (fluid) and various solid particles, such as cells, platelets, and chemicals; and a complicated system of *blood vessels* (capillaries, veins, and arteries). *Veins* carry blood to the heart, and *arteries* carry it from the heart. The heart pumps blood to every cell in the human body, bringing oxygen, digested food, and other necessary substances and removing waste materials.

Blood, particularly blood plasma, is intricately involved in the biochemistry of depression.

In the following chapters we discuss all these biological systems and substances as they relate to depression.

6

The Neurochemical System and Depression

The Biogenic Amine Hypothesis of Depression

■■ The theory that initially focused the attention of investigators
■■ on the neurobiology of depression is called the *biogenic amine hypothesis of depression*. (*Biogenic* means "produced by living organisms"; *amine* refers to a particular biochemical group of compounds.) It is also known as the *monoamine hypothesis of depression*. This theory is based on the role of the brain as a communication circuit, consisting of neurotransmitter networks that control cognition, sleep, sex and appetite, and other processes in which many of the symptoms of depression appear. Many of these networks are separate "systems" that maintain their chemical balance via an intricate process of transmission of particular neurochemicals (neurotransmitters). The biogenic amine theory holds that depression results from chemical imbalances in one or more of these systems in which biogenic amines function as neurotransmitters.

The chemical structures of neurotransmitters vary. The biogenic amines, which we shall discuss in their roles as neurotransmitters, are *monoamines* ("amine[s] that . . . [have] one organic substituent attached to the nitrogen, especially one . . . that is functionally important in neurotransmission" [*Webster's* 1989:767]). A substituent is an "atom or group that replaces another atom or group in a molecule" (*Webster's* 1989:1176). In contrast, some neurotransmitters (e.g., *peptides*) are made up of short chains of amino acids joined together. Some monoamines are also classified as *catecholamines* or *indoleamines*, based on their particular chemical makeup (Edelson 1988; Strand 1983).

There are many different kinds of neurotransmitters, which exist in various neurons throughout the central nervous system. We are particularly interested in the biogenic amines. Included in this group of neurotransmitters are the catecholamines norepinephrine (NE), epinephrine (EP), and dopamine (DA). In the *periphery* ("the outer part . . . of a body; part away from the center" [Thomas 1989:1366]), norepinephrine and epinephrine constrict many arteries and veins, speed the heart, increase the flow of blood to the muscles, dilate *bronchi* (branches from the lungs through which air passes), and slow the activity of the gastrointestinal system. Also in the periphery, dopamine can both dilate arteries and increase blood pressure. In the brain, dopamine neurons seem to be related to schizophrenia and Parkinson's disease; current thinking is that a deficiency in dopamine is not directly involved in the depressions (Thase, Frank, and Kupfer 1985:828; Cohen 1988:16–25).

Serotonin (5-HT) is another biogenic amine of interest to us. It is not a catecholamine but an *indoleamine* (a derivative of an *indole*—a compound produced by the decomposition of proteins such as tryptophan [Thomas 1989:90]).[1] This amine is a very strong vasoconstrictor. It is also believed to play a role in the mechanisms of sleep.

The Classical Model of Neurotransmission

To understand the biogenic amine theory, one must try to visualize the billions of nerve cells (called *neurons*) in the brain. Neurons function in the manner of electric wires. Each is a separate entity, composed of the cell *body*, an *axon* (a thin, tubelike projection that may vary from less than an inch to several feet long), and *dendrites*, which are short, branching fibers that project outward toward other cells but do not touch them. The physical gap between two communicating cells is called a *synaptic cleft*. (See figures 6.1 and 6.2.)

The brain's complex signaling system has both chemical and electrical elements. When a nerve cell (neuron) is stimulated, the cell *fires*: An impulse, or surge of electrical energy, moves down the axon until it reaches the end of the cell, where it stops. In most cases it cannot travel across the synaptic cleft. At that point chemical neurotransmitters that have been stored in small *vesicles* ("small sac[s] or bladder[s] containing fluid" [Thomas 1989:1989]) are released into the synaptic cleft. These chemical messengers are needed to carry the information signal across the synapse to the next cell.

Some of the chemicals diffuse (extend or spread) across the gap (the synaptic cleft) from the *firing cell* (or *presynaptic neuron*) to another cell, the *receptor cell* (or *postsynaptic neuron*). Depending on a number of factors, such as the receptor cell's sensitivity, they may bind to the cell's dendrites. Andrews (1990) provided a very good explanation of this process: "[The] neurotransmitters bind to proteins on the surfaces of cells called receptors; receptors act like molecular switches and turn [stimulate] production of chemicals and proteins on and off. . . . Each type of switch on a receptor has a distinctly shaped crevice, and the neurotransmitter fits into the crevice the way a key fits into an automobile ignition." (The functioning of receptor cells is currently the focus of

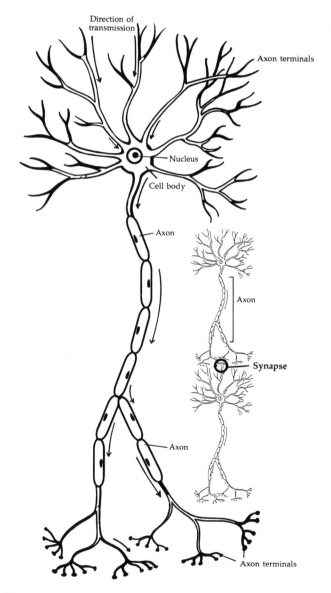

Figure 6.1.
Neurotransmission: A Typical Neuron, Showing Location of Synapse

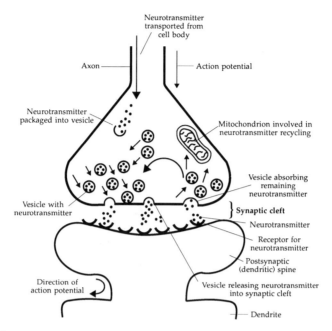

Figure 6.2.
Detail of a Synapse, Showing Action of Neurotransmission

much research on the neurobiology of depression, as we shall discuss later in this chapter.)

After activating the receptor molecules, the neurotransmitters are released back into the synaptic cleft. They must be rapidly cleared out to avoid excess stimulation (Whybrow, Akiskal, and McKinney 1984:109). This clearance is regulated by several mechanisms. Some of the neurotransmitter may be inactivated by the enzyme *monoamine oxidase (MAO)*. Some neurotransmitter (only of catecholamines) is metabolized just outside of the cell: While in the synaptic cleft, this catecholamine neurotransmitter comes in contact with the enzyme *catechol-O-methyl transferase (COMT)*, which immediately inactivates some of it. In many cases, much of the neurotransmitter may be "inactivated [by being broken down] into smaller molecules . . . or [may be] . . . 'reuptaken' [that is,] sponged up into the presynaptic nerve terminal. . . . processes [which] clear the site for the arrival of the next chemical messenger" (Papolos and Papolos 1987:59–60). The extent to which the firing cell reabsorbs (reuptakes) the neurotransmitters also seems very important. As Wender and Klein (1981:198) point out, "In this way, the cell continues to use its supply of neurotransmitters over and over again in an economical manner."

If it is stimulated, the receptor cell becomes a firing cell itself, thus repeating the process millions of times from cell to cell in minute fractions of seconds and producing widespread effects. This process in which signals are transmitted via neurotransmitters to receptors to which they bind, activating a series of additional signals, is called *signal transduction*—signals are transduced, that is, they are "converted from one form of energy to another" (Thomas 1989:1891). (See figure 6.3).

The configuration of the three contact points—(1) where one neuron ends, (2) the space between the end of this neuron and the next one (the synaptic cleft), and (3) the receptor (binding) site at the next neuron—is called a *synapse*. (See figure 6.2.) (This explanation is greatly simplified. As Andreasen [1984:132] points out, the "synapse [is not] a one-to-one connection between neurons . . . each neuron cell body or dendrite receives input from hundreds of nerve terminals. The receptor neuron will 'decide' to fire only if it receives strong excitatory input.")

There are different patterns and rates of firing. Transmitters may be *excitatory* (resulting in a higher firing rate and releasing a larger amount of transmitter chemicals) or *inhibitory* (decreasing the firing rate and releasing a smaller amount of transmitter chemicals). A postsynaptic (receptor) cell will receive thousands of electrical signals. Some instruct it to fire and some instruct it not to fire. These contradictory signals are quickly processed; the decision depends on the balance of the signals (The Diagram Group 1987:40–41). Later in this chapter we explain in greater detail the electrical processes that control the neurons' firing rate.

Imbalances may occur that result in extremes of behavior. Too much of a particular neurotransmitter may produce great excitement/elation, anxiety, excessive aggressiveness, great anger, agitation, and hyperactivity. Too little may produce the opposite: very passive, even lethargic behavior—the retarded behavioral symptoms of depression. An exact balance results in no change at all.

The process of neurotransmission can be affected by a number of factors: A firing cell may not be able to release its neurotransmitters, or it may be unable to synthesize them. If the receptor cell's sensitivity diminishes, it would be less stimulated to fire, and the entire chain of transmission would be impaired. If the firing cell is unable to reuptake the neurotransmitter, the neurotransmitter would accumulate in the synaptic cleft and this high concentration would interfere with the usual functioning of the receiving cell (Wender and Klein 1981:198).

This greatly simplified description of the process of neurotransmission is known as the *classical model.* It has recently been revised, as we shall see later in this chapter.

THE RELATIONSHIP OF NEUROTRANSMITTERS
TO DEPRESSION

Associations have been found between depression and the balance of certain chemicals in cells, as well as the quantity and quality of chemicals conducted from cell to cell. The biogenic amine theory stipulates that depression results from a deficiency of norepinephrine (NE) at a number of synapses in the brain. In other words, when nerve cells of depressed individuals are stimulated, the amount of NE that successfully crosses the synaptic cleft and binds to the receptor cells is less than the amount that crosses and binds in people who are not depressed. Either too little crosses, reuptake by the firing cell is too rapid, or the receptor cell is insensitive. (It was originally thought that mania was due to an excess of NE crossing the synaptic cleft, but this theory was quickly discarded.)

A number of authorities believe that depression in some people is related to disorders in serotonin (Green, Mooney, and Schildkraut 1988:133). This suggests the possibility of two different kinds of depression—one related to a lack of serotonin and the other to a lack of norepinephrine and has resulted in a serotonin hypothesis, in addition to the catecholamine hypothesis (Andreasen 1984:234). The evidence for the two separate hypotheses is derived from the actions of antidepressant medications: Some work on one neurotransmitter, and some on others. Some (the tricyclics, which we discuss later) prevent the reuptake of both norepinephrine and serotonin during neurotransmission (Andreasen 1984:234).

Andrews (1990) reports that researchers who have been studying serotonin receptors now believe that a number of distinct types exist, each with a few subtypes, and that they have different effects. The blocking of the serotonin receptors, located chiefly in the brain and some blood vessels, seems to alleviate anxiety and depression. The object of research is to locate the "switches" in this process and to find drugs to block their action that do not have significant side effects. Although the hypotheses are promising, the report ends with the usual warning that the knowledge of serotonin's action in the brain is still uncertain.

Recent research has examined the roles of other chemicals involved in neurotransmission, such as acetylcholine (ACh). Acetylcholine is an ester of choline, an amine found in animal tissues and considered essential for metabolism of fat and carbohydrates. (An *ester* is a "compound formed by the combination of an organic acid with an alcohol" [Thomas 1989:624]). Acetylcholine is involved in transmitting nerve impulses at certain cell synapses. At the synapse between neurons and muscle cells, surpluses or deficits of acetylcholine block neuromuscular activity (Thomas 1989:20). It is impossible to obtain "accurate non-invasive measurements of ACh" (Thase, Frank, and Kupfer 1985:833). Its role in depression is controversial.[2] (We discuss acetylcholine further in chapter 8.)

Later research emphasized deficiencies in receptor functions in the receiving cells. Depression came to be viewed more as the result of insufficient norepinephrine being bound by these receptors and less as the result of an insufficient amount crossing the synaptic cleft. Hyman (1991b:27) reviewed a number of the studies investigating the theory that individuals with major depressive disorders have abnormalities in monoamine receptors that disrupt neurotransmission. He concluded that although evidence existed for disrupted regulation, it was not robust and that the theory was unconvincing. Nevertheless, the hypotheses were very important, for they redirected the research on depression and on the development of antidepressant drugs.

CONTRIBUTIONS OF THE BIOGENIC AMINE HYPOTHESIS

The biogenic amine hypothesis has always had some serious limitations. Some of the theory's authors acknowledged its limitations themselves when it was first introduced in 1965 (Koslow and Gaist 1987:110). In a thoughtful review, Thase, Frank, and Kupfer (1985:828) noted that "twenty years of research activity have failed to support the original monoamine hypothesis of depression." Nevertheless, "this milestone hypothesis has been the guiding impetus for depression research for the last two decades. . . . [setting] the stage for what has been one of the most intensive and extensive research endeavors of modern psychiatry" (Koslow and Gaist 1987:110). This theory and related research have led to a greater understanding of the neurobiology of the affective disorders. Hyman (1991a) pointed out that "it focussed psychiatry on the important actors." Other authorities have noted that the research has provided some useful and potentially useful evidence, such as indicators of biological subgroups among unipolar depressed patients (Green, Mooney, and Schildkraut 1988:131–132). It also stimulated the development of a number of antidepressant medications.

Pharmacological Treatments Based on the Biogenic Amine Hypothesis

The antidepressant drugs are generally divided into the tricyclic antidepressants, the MAO inhibitors, the atypical drugs (in which we shall, for convenience sake, include stimulant drugs), and some newer second-generation antidepressants.

The initial drugs were called the tricyclics, directly referring to their chemical structure. Some of the more recent drugs are not tricyclic; some authors have used the terms *tetracyclics* and *heterocyclic* antidepressants (Schoonover 1983b:28). However, one expert has stated that the "general, trivial term 'tricyclic antidepressants' can be retained. Alternatives, [e.g.] 'tetracyclic' . . . or . . . 'cyclic' or 'heterocyclic' are chemically imprecise" (Baldessarini 1985:134–135). We shall generally follow the suggestion of Baldessarini (a leading authority) and use the term *tricyclic*.[3]

THE TRICYCLIC ANTIDEPRESSANTS

The tricyclic drugs, introduced in the late 1950s, are still the ones most often used for depression. They primarily block the reuptake (reabsorption) of the neurotransmitter norepinephrine and also effect receptor sensitivity to NE. Currently, nine tricyclic-type drugs, which work particularly on norepinephrine, are in use: imipramine (trade name Tofranil), amitriptyline (Elavil), doxepin (Sinequan), trimipramine (Surmontil), desipramine (Norpramin), nortriptyline (Pamelor), and protriptyline (Vivactil). Two additional drugs (usually called tetracyclics) are amoxapine (Asendin) and maprotiline (Ludiomil).

Some antidepressant drugs (most are technically not tricyclics but act as if they were) also block the reuptake of serotonin at the synaptic cleft, thus increasing the amount of serotonin available to cross the synapse (Andreasen 1984:234). These currently include fluoxetine (Prozac),[4] trazodone (Desyrel), an atypical tricyclic antidepressant clomipramine (Anafranil), and the experimental drugs fluvoxamine and citalopram. Of these, fluoxetine (Prozac) seems to be the most popular; its effects are long-lived, though the recommended dosages are still being established. An adequate explanation to account for the antidepressant effects of these drugs is still lacking.

The symptoms of approximately 70 percent of depressed clients who take tricyclics ease considerably in four to six weeks. (However, 20–40 percent respond to placebos [Baldessarini 1990:5].) It has been speculated that it may take this long for the medication to affect the levels of norepinephrine and serotonin. Then the nerve cells, confronted with increased levels of norepinephrine and serotonin, alter the number of receptors on their surface, which changes mood (DePaulo and Ablow 1989). (This theory about receptor sensitivity is discussed later in this chapter.)

THE MAO INHIBITORS

The drugs categorized as MAO inhibitors work by blocking (inhibiting) the action of the MAO enzyme, so that less NE is metabolized and more is available to cross the synaptic cleft.

At present the most frequently used MAO inhibitors are isocarboxazid (trade name Marplan), phenelzine (Nardil), and tranylcypromine (Parnate). Some recent MAO inhibitors (still considered experimental), such as clorgyline and brofaromine, inhibit only one type of MAO (Baldessarini 1990).

The MAO inhibitors came into use earlier than the tricyclics, but they fell out of favor for a while because of their potential for toxicity. Because of their many negative side effects, the MAO inhibitors are sometimes used as a second or third choice in treating major depressions or for dysthymia, when the tricyclics do not work in clinical application. In these situations the tricyclic first has to be discontinued, and the patient must wait seven to ten days while it clears from the body before using the MAO inhibitor, to prevent a potentially problematic interaction. Used inappropriately in combination with the tricyclics, these drugs sometimes cause seizures and even death (Baldessarini and Cole 1988:520). In fact, Baldessarini and Cole (1988:518) recommend electroconvulsive therapy (ECT) with hospitalization as the treatment of choice for severe depression rather than the MAO inhibitors.

Increased information about the utility of MAO inhibitors, and when they are effective, has led to a growth in their use in this country. For example, the MAOIs seem particularly effective with atypical depressions. In the United Kingdom, where they are sometimes used in combination with the tricyclics (Nies and Robinson 1982:259), they have generally been held in more favor than in the United States.[5] However, this practice of combining MAO inhibitors and tricyclics generally "cannot be recommended as a safe practice and has not been demonstrated to offer consistent additional benefits over single-drug treatments" (Baldessarini and Cole 1988:519).

ATYPICAL DRUGS

A recent, also atypical drug is bupropion (Wellbutrin), which inhibits the reuptake of both dopamine and norepinephrine. Pharmacologically, it is similar to such stimulants as the amphetamines (e.g., Ritalin).

Other drugs are in use, including lithium, which we discuss in chapter 10. By the time this book is in print, additional drugs may be on the market.

THE SIDE EFFECTS OF ANTIDEPRESSANT MEDICATIONS

Antidepressant drugs have a number of side effects, which are often intensifications of their pharmacological actions. These include such anticholinergic effects (the inhibition of parasympathetic responses) as tachycardia (rapid heartbeat), dry mouth, blurred vision, constipation, and urinary retention (Noll, Davis, and DeLeon-Jones 1985:240); autonomic symptoms, such as acute salivation, gastrointestinal, and bladder problems; reduced libido; confusion; delirium; sensitivity to heat; weight gain; and cardiac problems. The central nervous system is also affected, generating dizziness, light-headedness, and skin reactions. These drugs are powerful and can be used to commit suicide. A drug overdose may produce comas, seizures, cardiac toxicity, and death. Because of this they represent a real management problem, which, as stated previously, is primarily the responsibility of the physician who prescribes the drugs but must also be taken seriously by all therapists (Baldessarini and Cole 1988:516).

Tricyclics may interact negatively with other substances, including alcohol, barbiturates, and other medications, and can cause a wide variety of side effects, including seizures, deepening depression, agitation, and other problems. They may cause an increased sensitivity to sunshine (photosensitivity), resulting in reactions ranging from painful sunburn to various skin irritations, such as eczema and hives. Even when the medication is stopped, this sensitivity can continue for a few days (Schatzberg and Cole 1991:40). Depressed patients who are also on antihypertension medication may become overly sedated. When antidepressants are being taken, less antihypertension medication may be indicated (Baldessarini and Cole 1988:517). Hypertensive patients need close medical supervision and may require help with maintaining compliance. The safety of these drugs during pregnancy and lactation has not been sufficiently established, but so far there seems to be no evidence of danger of deformed fetuses.

One side effect of the tricyclics that we feel has not been given enough prominence is tinnitus, a constant buzzing or ringing in the ears, often loud enough to cause acute discomfort and, in some clients, distress severe enough to lead to thoughts of, and even attempts at, suicide. Withdrawal of the drug may relieve the tinnitus in some patients. However, in others there may be permanent damage to the middle ear, leading to lasting hearing loss, particularly in the extreme high and low registers. Although it is estimated that tinnitus is a side effect for approximately only 1 percent of people taking the tricyclics, this is a significant number, considering how many people are taking these drugs (Laird and Lydiard 1989).

The numerous side effects of the MAO inhibitors include hypotension (abnormally low blood pressure), dry mouth, bladder and bowel problems, sexual dysfunctions, sleep disturbances, fainting, and hypertensive crisis. Furthermore, these drugs do not interact well with a number of substances, including nose drops, cold remedies, barbiturates, opiates (e.g., Demerol), and a large number of foods. The patient taking them must follow a very strict diet, eliminating certain common foods. The food avoidance list, at one time exceedingly prohibitive, has been shortened and now includes overripe, fermented, and aged foods, especially those high in proteins, including red wine (and other foods containing the amine tyramine); certain kinds of beans; and pickled meats and aged cheeses. Coffee, chocolate, and cola are among the foods that were previously on the list and are now considered safe (McCabe and Tsuang 1982:178–181).

Research in many different areas is providing additional information on the effects and side effects of antidepressant medications. For example, in a study of patients with major depressions who also exhibited increased appetite and carbohydrate-craving symptoms, it was found that these symptoms were actually induced by antidepressant drugs (Yeragani et al. 1988). By the time this book is published, additional factors may have been found explaining these linkages.

INDICATIONS FOR USING THE TRICYCLICS AND MAO INHIBITORS

The tricyclic drugs and the MAO inhibitors seem most effective when used for the acute and major depressions, especially where the endogenous or melancholic features predominate. Some authorities maintain that they are not effective with reactive depressions, although the diagnostic line can be hard to draw. When the reactive depression is severe and/or the patient has been depressed for a while, the drugs may relieve some symptoms, particularly the vegetative symptoms of depression.

There is little evidence that these drugs are effective for the more moderate (less severe) depressions. Two leading experts, Baldessarini and Cole (1988:521) have stated that "their effects are not much better than those of antianxiety agents, a placebo, or other nonspecific treatments, nor are they impressively better than psychotherapy." Furthermore, the drugs usually do not take effect for at least one week, often longer, and the relapse rate is high, especially several months after a patient has discontinued taking the drug (Baldessarini and Cole 1988:521). It is also imperative that dosage(s) be closely monitored by the prescribing physician, because some patients develop a tolerance to the drugs, resulting in a drop in their effectiveness.

Antidepressant drugs are useful when they are chosen after careful examination of their efficacy for a particular depressed individual. However, in our opinion, they are currently being used too widely, are not chosen carefully enough, and often are not properly supervised. In addition, new drugs are needed. These important issues are discussed further in chapter 10, in the section on "Pharmacotherapy and Depression."

The MHPG Test: A Test Based on the Biogenic Amine Hypothesis

Much current research has been devoted to 3–methoxy-4–hydroxyphenyl glycol (MHPG), a metabolite of norepinephrine that can be measured in the urine. (A *metabolite* is the product of metabolism, which is the sum of all the physical and chemical changes that occur in cells, involving both the building up and tearing down of cell materials found in body fluids.) The focus on MHPG is based on the evidence that about half of the MHPG in the urine originates from the central nervous system, whereas only a very small part of the "other indole amine and catecholamine metabolites" comes from this system (Whybrow, Akiskal, and McKinney 1984:109).

According to the biogenic amine hypothesis, the levels of norepinephrine (NE) that reach the brain should be lower in depressed individuals than in the nondepressed, and the level of MHPG should be higher than expected (above normal) during manic episodes. Therefore, by assessing the levels of MHPG in a patient's urine, a clinician could predict the type of medication to which the patient would respond. For example, if low MHPG actually proved to be evidence of a lack of NE, that would indicate using a drug that acted to block the reuptake of NE. It was also hypothesized that the MHPG test could be used both as a diagnostic tool and as a means of measuring the progress of the illness (Fawcett and Kravitz 1985:449).

Careful evaluation of the results of the research on the MHPG test has led many experts to conclude that the promise of MHPG theory has not yet been fulfilled. Test results show that levels of urinary MHPG vary widely in patients with unipolar depression, which may reflect NE metabolism but also may result from other physiological processes. In addition, it was found that less urinary MHPG is derived from brain NE than was originally hypothesized (Thase, Frank, and Kupfer 1985:827). Diet, activity levels, withdrawal of drugs, and anxiety levels, among other factors, all affect MHPG, which confuses the issue in depression research. In fact, "time of day seems . . . [more closely] related to MHPG levels than a diagnosis of depression" (Thase, Frank, and Kupfer 1985:827). Contrary to the theory, treatment with antidepressant drugs does not always raise the level of urinary MHPG. Finally, the correlations between urinary MHPG and the response to antidepressant drugs are much less clear than expected (Thase, Frank, and Kupfer 1985:827; Green, Mooney, and Schildkraut 1988:131).

Nevertheless, opinions differ widely on the usefulness of the MHPG test. For example, Andreasen (1984:184) states that the MHPG is useful in helping doctors match medication to particular patients. But Lieber (1987:6–7), who reported using the MHPG test in a clinical rather than in a research setting, stated that the procedure was discontinued because it was "cumbersome, expensive. . . . fraught with possibilities for errors in collection and processing . . . [and] it yielded little clinical information."

The Current Status of the Biogenic Amine Hypothesis

After more than a quarter of a century of research, recently aided by sophisticated technology, serious questions have emerged about the validity of the biogenic amine hypothesis of depression. Hyman (1991b:26) expressed the view of many current authorities when he stated that "this simple hypothesis has not been borne out."

We referred previously to the gaps and limitations in the biogenic amine hypothesis of depression. One problem area has been the evaluation of the actions of neurotransmitters in the brain and of the effects of antidepressant drugs upon these actions. A major difficulty is that much of the human research on the action of the antidepressant drugs on neurotransmitters does not measure the amines directly.[6] In research on animals, the measurement technology is primarily invasive; the body is actually entered, which may interrupt functioning. In human research, measurements are made by using the metabolites in body fluids, and the accuracy of these noninvasive procedures is uncertain (Lieber 1987).[7] For obvious reasons it is difficult to observe and experiment with the live human brain, and postmortem studies yield less data than expected. Not only do the last few hours of life have a great effect on the physical status and appearance of the brain, but there is often a delay between death and the availability of the brain for examination, which results in additional changes (Hyman 1991a).

Finding increased quantities of the metabolites of norepinephrine and serotonin in urine and other body fluids of depressed people would have lent support to the biogenic amine hypothesis. However, studies that measured these metabolites (using the MHPG test we have just reviewed, and neuroendocrine tests we discuss in chapter 7) did not fully support the hypothesis; the evidence they provided was not conclusive. For example, investigators were unsuccessful in identifying any systematic configurations in patients who had been diagnosed as having endogenous depression. Furthermore, the hypothesis that there were two types of depression, one based on norepinephrine reuptake and one based on serotonin uptake (in response to different antidepressant medications), was ultimately not upheld by the research testing this theory. Patients did not divide so neatly into two separate groups (Hyman 1991a).

Many authorities came to believe that, although neurotransmitters appear to be important regulators of mood, it seemed unlikely they could account for all the behavioral changes that are symptomatic of depression (Papolos and Papolos 1987:66). Also, although there is some evidence, based on clinical observations, that biogenic amines change during depression, the meaning of this is unclear. Moreover, it is difficult to differentiate cause from effect. For example, when NE deficits are observed, it is hard to determine if the lowered levels of NE cause depression or result from it, a secondary effect of low levels of behavior. (Later in this chapter, we describe an experiment showing that similar changes in receptor cells were brought about by both chemical and behavioral interventions.)

Another observation that led to a revision of the view that depression was caused just by norepinephrine (NE) or serotonin (5-HT) deficits and that it could be treated by increasing the transmission of these substances across the synaptic cleft, was related to the actions of the antidepressant medications. Antidepressants *are* successful in changing transmission of NE and 5-HT in approximately 70–80 percent of those who take these drugs. But these changes occur fairly rapidly, sometimes in hours, while it takes from one to four weeks and longer for the depression to ease. This "lag time" (Koslow and Gaist 1987:119), and other questions, led to further searches for evidence of other mechanisms to explain the *pathophysiological processes* (how disease alters normal physiological courses) in the affective disorders. New theories have been developed, which we describe later.

With the development of advanced research technology, scientists began to accumulate evidence that the nervous system was much more complex than previously thought. Among other findings, it became apparent that neurons often contained multiple transmitters, that many different kinds of neurotransmitters might be involved with depression, that there are many different kinds of receptor sites and theoretically a very large number of possible interactions, and that many of the signaling chemicals do not act according to the classic theory of synaptic transmission. They also made new discoveries about the significance of the reuptake mechanisms in neurotransmission (Hyman 1988a:161–162).

This led to important changes in the theories of neurotransmission and the neurobiology of the depressive disorders.

The Effects of Antidepressants on Receptor Sensitivity

Researchers began to look more closely at the receptors to which neurotransmitters bind by studying brain tissue of rats. They investigated both pre- and postsynaptic receptor sites to determine where they are located and how they are regulated.

One area of investigation focused on *receptor sensitivity,* particularly in relation to the changes caused by antidepressant medications. When receptors are sensitive, they are more open to accepting a neurotransmitter and seem to be more numerous. When they lose sensitivity the quantity or density lessens: Some "seem to sink back into the cell membrane and become temporarily inaccessible to the neurotransmitters" (Papolos and Papolos 1987:64).

Studies revealed changes in the sensitivity of receptors in rats that had been given antidepressant medications: after a few days to several weeks, norepinephrine receptors seemed to lose some sensitivity, resulting in fewer sites where the NE could bind. This is known as *downregulation;* increased sensitivity is known as *upregulation.* These conditions can be measured directly in animals or inferred in humans by decreased or increased effects of *drug challenges* ("the process of provoking or testing physiological activity by exposure to a specific substance" [*Webster's* 1989:224]). Since the downregulation seemed to result from the antidepressant medication, the researchers theorized that to compensate for this loss, there must be a balancing release of NE within its particular system (Papolos and Papolos 1987:64). Hyman (1991b:32) has stated that the downregulation of particular receptors after the administration of antidepressant medications might be due to these *homeostatic mechanisms* (referring to a state of dynamic equilibrium), although the mechanisms are not understood. Hyman cautions that these changes have been demonstrated in experiments with normal rats. We do not know if the effects are the same in depressed humans.

Further investigations identified specific areas of the brain where changes take place. Henn, Edwards, and Anderson, (1986), in a study testing Seligman's learned helplessness theory (which we discuss in chapter 14), administered electric shocks to rats. At first the rats could escape the shocks; then the escape mechanism was removed, and when they tried to escape they were helpless—an aspect of depression. When the escape mechanism was reinstituted, the rats' helplessness continued—they no longer attempted to escape. Receptors in the hypothalamus of these rats were then examined and found to be downregulated;

receptors in the hippocampus were upregulated. After antidepressant medications were administered, the helpless behavior was reversed, and the receptor cells reverted to their previous state. In a very interesting follow-up study, the experimenters omitted the antidepressants in the last part of the experiment and taught the rats to go through the behaviors needed to avoid the escapable shocks. As in the previous experiments, the "depression" seemed to lift and the receptor sites returned to normal. The experimenters concluded that "just as neurochemistry affects behavior, behavior affects neurochemistry" (Papolos and Papolos 1987:65–66.)

Hyman (1991b:34) believes that receptor regulation is *not* the "mechanism of therapeutic action of antidepressants"; if it were, "receptor regulation would occur in drug responders but not nonresponders." He reminds us that this statement refers to the studies done with rats; we do not yet know whether this is the case in humans. According to Koslow and Gaist (1987:119), researchers also disagree on important aspects of the hypotheses on neurotransmitter receptors, which are still being investigated. They also indicate that many of the studies of the effects of medication on receptors were demonstrated with semichronic or chronic drug administration and that we still have much to learn about how antidepressants work. However, because the studies consistently show that all antidepressant agents (including electroconvulsive therapy) seem to produce downregulation of particular receptors, they feel this suggests that "specific receptor abnormalities may be a key factor in the underlying biochemistry of depression" (Koslow and Gaist 1987:120). They emphasize the complexity of the processes of neurotransmission and of antidepressant drug action and believe that although drugs may act via multiple molecular mechanisms, there may prove to be a final common pathway (Koslow and Gaist 1987:124). However, they stress that the research findings on receptor sensitivity have not always been consistent and that additional research is needed.

Although receptor regulation did not explain the delay in the effectiveness of antidepressant medications, the evidence of downregulation, showing that there are actual modifications in the cells—changes that may at least correlate with the therapeutic effect (Hyman 1991a)—did support the view that the slow onset of the medications' effectiveness points to "chronic adaptations in brain function rather than simple increases in synaptic norepinephrine and serotonin [underlying] their therapeutic effect" (Hyman 1991b:32). Hyman believes that these neurotransmitters are "major players" in depression and that, assuming the body is made up of widely projecting systems, they may be responsible for the varied and pervasive symptoms of the depressions. It is not at all clear, however, what goes wrong in norepinephrine (NE) and serotonin (5-HT) neurons—or their brainstem, hypothalamic, limbic, and cortical targets—and how this is reversed by antidepressants (Hyman 1991a).

The immediate effects of antidepressants (reuptake blocking, or MAO inhibition) *are* important, but these are *triggers* for the slow-onset therapeutic mechanism. Since NE and 5-HT are always involved, actions probably involve both neurotransmitter systems (Hyman 1991a). Since NE and 5-HT do not have an immediate clinical impact, it has been hypothesized that there must be some adaptive changes occurring inside the cell, and this unknown process is probably the "cause" of the therapeutic change. The current thinking is that it may be due to the impact of a "second messenger system" that brings about internal changes and adaptations. This is the focus of new theorizing.

A Revised Theory of Neurotransmission and Depression: Long-Term Adaptations in Brain Function

The studies of the effects of antidepressants on receptor regulation provided additional information about the actions of these drugs. The consistency of findings that the antidepressants resulted in downregulating certain receptor cells—markers of actual changes in cells—was another important step in the attempt to understand how these medications work. But there was not yet an explanation clarifying the entire therapeutic process, particularly the lag time between the administration and the effectiveness of these drugs.

Neurobiologists such as Hyman (1991a) were still asking, "What is taking so long?" They considered it possible that events occurring after neurotransmission played a more important part in implementing the drugs' effects than was previously thought to be the case. This led researchers to examine more closely the details of what happens after neurotransmitters cross the synapse and then bind to the receptor sites— a process called *signal transduction* (Hyman 1988d:373).

Signal transduction is extremely complex. These are the essential steps as described by Koslow and Gaist (1987:117): After a neurotransmitter (or *first messenger*) is released and crosses the synaptic cleft, its molecules bind to a receptor (binding) site in the receiving cell's membrane, which causes the cell to be *activated*—an enzyme is released, which then acts as a catalyst, triggering the release of other chemicals, which eventually activate a *second messenger system*—an *intracellular mechanism*. (One second messenger is cyclic adenosine monophosphate, or cAMP.) This second messenger system then activates the release of *protein kinases*. A kinase ("an organic substance which activates an enzyme" [Thomas 1977:K-9]) can modify proteins that bind to DNA, thus altering the functions of cells and producing a physiological response.[8] (See figure 6.3.)

Each step in this procedure depends upon activating a chemical, which triggers another chemical, which in turn causes another to become active, and so on. In other words, each successive transmitter is changed from its resting state to its active state. This is accomplished through a forced change in the lineup of proteins making up the substance. As Hyman (1988d:373) points out, "When the conformations of proteins are changed, their functions are changed, thus enzymes are activated or deactivated and ion channels are opened or closed." These changes develop slowly, which may explain the lag time between taking antidepressant medication and the lessening of the depression (Hyman 1988d:377).

This process has been clarified recently. Electrical signals transmitted via pathways along the cell membrane are thought to be the activating agents. Nerve cells have a *resting potential* to fire at higher or lower rates. How they actually perform depends upon a number of different electrical and chemical elements. In common with all cells (as described in chapter 4), neurons contain protoplasm, which is divided into a nucleus (center) surrounded by cytoplasm. Each of these parts is enveloped by a thin, semipermeable regulatory membrane. Neurons contain particles with electrical charges called *ions,* which are *polarized* (those inside the cell nucleus tend to be negatively charged; the ones in the cytoplasm are usually positively charged). Each cell membrane has various ion *channels* (or *gates*) through which the ions pass when these channels are open. Channels open and close according to the various signals they receive, which also control how long they remain open and

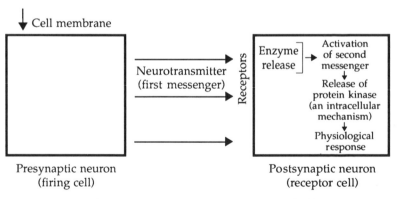

Figure 6.3. Signal Transduction Process (Simplified), Showing Actions of "Second Messenger" System

the power with which their signals are transmitted. Some channels open when a neurotransmitter binds to a receptor; these are called *ligand-gated channels*. (A *ligand* is a molecule of any kind that attaches to a receptor.) *Voltage-gated* channels open or close in response to changes in the polarization of the membranes. The gates of these channels, which control the important function of transmitting electrical signals, are carefully regulated by the body (Hyman 1988a:157–159).

When negatively charged channels open, they admit ions with negative charges (*anions*), usually chlorine (Cl⁻). Positively charged channels open to admit *cations* (positively charged ions) of sodium (NA^+), potassium (K^+), and chlorine (Cl^+). Chlorine is a powerful ion, as it is composed of two atoms; it "has a major role in the control of crucial cell functions, [e.g.] activation of certain enzymes" (Hyman 1988a:158).

Some neurotransmitters open ligand-gated channels that allow negatively charged ions to enter. These are *inhibitory*—the neuron is hyperpolarized, which reduces its potential to fire (its *synaptic potential*). Some open ligand-gated channels that allow entry to positively charged ions, depolarizing the neuron, and increasing its synaptic potential; these are *excitatory*. If the sum of this localized activity (the total of both potentials) exceeds a particular amount, it causes a voltage channel to open, and an *action potential* is triggered, releasing the neurotransmitter. This results in a sequence of similar openings of these channels along the cell's axon (Hyman 1988a:157–159).

The verification of this theory—that ion channels exist on the surface of cells and that they control the passage of electrically charged ions through these cells—was so important that the scientists who made this discovery, Erwin Neber and Bert Sakmann, were awarded a Nobel Prize in October 1991. They used a ground-breaking research technique, which they had developed a number of years earlier called *patch clamping*. In this procedure, a "recording electrode fastens to a microscopic patch of the cell's membrane . . . [enabling the identification] of very specific details of cell physiology. . . . [and the detection of] incredibly small electric currents that pass through a single ion channel" on the surface of a cell (Altman 1991b). Patch clamping was used to record how a single channel molecule alters its shape, and in that way controls the flow of current. . . . [It] conclusively established that ion channels do exist" (Altman 1991b).

Changes in DNA Instructions; Changes in Cell Function

A very recent hypothesis stipulates that the adaptations that take place via the second messenger system and that lead to changes in the function of proteins of nerve cells may be controlled by instructions coming from the individual's genes. In addition, these instructions, which were thought to be fixed in the DNA, are actually *altered* by chemical neurotransmitters and antidepressant medications (Hyman 1991b:34). As Hyman stated, "A profound way to change the way a cell functions is to change the rate of DNA transcription." He believes that these hypothesized alterations would account for the fact that the perceptions of depressed individuals often differ from those of people who are not depressed (Hyman 1991a).

Currently, this theory has not yet been published. We look forward to its publication and to the research that will follow. We hope that it will add to our understanding of the pathophysiology of the depressions and their treatment.

Summary

■■ Following the classical model of neurotransmission, much
■■ previous theorizing and experimentation on the neurobiology of depression was based on the view of the brain as a "hard-wired [communication] network" that utilized some chemical procedures but these were secondary to electrical conduction (Hyman 1988a:161). Neurotransmission was seen as a simple process of communication between cells. But the "brain cannot be viewed like a computer . . . unless it is one in which the hardware itself is undergoing constant modification" (Hyman 1988a:165). Neurotransmission is now thought to be a complex process of adaptation in which the function of the cell is changed. The hypothesis that the changes involve altering the cell's genetic instructions may necessitate a dynamic reinterpretation of the theories on the genetic aspects of depression, which we have discussed in chapter 4.

This work is of great theoretical importance not only for understanding depression but for understanding all psychiatric disorders, as well as for expanding our knowledge of how the brain works. However, "much more work is needed before clinical observations can be understood in terms of basic neurobiological mechanisms" (Hyman 1988d:377).

Many of the explanations of what causes depression and how antidepressants work are speculative. At present, we do not even have satisfactory animal models of all the major psychiatric conditions, including depression. Humans, to state the obvious, are more complicated—if only in the cognitive sphere. Furthermore, even diseases and abnormalities that have been studied at length have not provided much insight into the mechanics of pathophysiology because of the multitude of interacting control systems. Changes in one system often produce unpredictable changes in other systems. What we see may be effects that are far removed from etiology. We need to learn much more about the brain before we can understand the pharmacological and endocrine abnormalities in depression and other psychiatric conditions (Hyman 1988c:331).

7

The Neuroendocrine System
and Depression

The neuroendocrine system involves the workings and relationships of the hormones that are released and controlled by the nervous system. These *neurohormones* (hormones produced by or acting on the nervous system) include norepinephrine (NE), discussed earlier in its role as a neurotransmitter.

Neurohormones carry messages (*stimuli*) from the brain, via the hypothalamus (defined, below), to the pituitary gland. The pituitary gland, which is stimulated by these neurohormones, sends other messages, through hormones such as ACTH (explained later) to other glands, including both endocrine and exocrine glands. These glands, in turn, are stimulated to produce other hormones, which complete the system by sending messages back to the brain. Although each hormone has its own particular route, the hormones are also interrelated. They all communicate via an elaborate system of feedback to maintain the body's chemical balance. One of these complicated sets of interactions is illustrated in figure 7.1.

The Hypothalamus

■■ The hypothalamus, a small structure in the brain, is impor-
■■ tant in both the nervous and endocrine systems. In fact, its cells have characteristics of both endocrine and nerve cells (Whybrow, Akiskal, and McKinney 1984:111). Andreasen (1984:121) calls the hypothalamus the "command center of the neuroendocrine system," for it regulates the pituitary gland, to which it is linked, as well as the endocrine system, acting as a "mediator between the brain and body." Some of the important functions regulated by the hypothalamus are sleep and wakefulness, body temperature, appetite and thirst, and sex drive.

The Hypothalamic-Pituitary-Adrenal (HPA) Axis: Cortisol, Dexamethasone Suppression, and Depression

■■ One of the central topics of inquiry in research on depression
■■ is the hypothalamic-pituitary-adrenal (HPA) axis. This system regulates such functions as appetite and sleep and adaptation to stress (Andreasen 1984:121–122). Since malfunctions in these areas are symptomatic of depression, a connection between depression and an imbalance in this HPA axis is possible. (See figure 7.1.)

Andreasen (1984:180–182) provides an excellent explanation, which we have adapted, of how the hypothalamic-pituitary-adrenal axis functions. When we experience major stress, psychological or physical, we need additional energy and readiness to deal with it. In chemical terms, the body needs more cortisol, the main hormone that deals with stress. The brain, which recognizes this need, signals the hypothalamus, which releases a messenger—*corticotrophin-releasing factor (CRF)*, a peptide hormone. The CRF travels to the pituitary gland, stimulating it to release *adrenocorticotropic hormone (ACTH)*, which travels to the adrenal glands

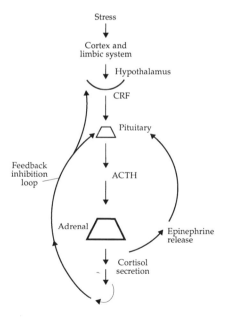

Figure 7.1. The Hypothalamic-Pituitary-Adrenal (HPA) Axis, Showing Feedback Inhibition Loop

and stimulates them to release cortisol. The hypothalamus constantly monitors the amount of cortisol in the blood. If there is not enough, it starts the process again by releasing more CRF; if there is enough or too much, it stops the process, inhibiting further production (Grinspoon and Bakalar 1990:4–5).

In normal individuals cortisol and ACTH seem to be released periodically throughout the day, synchronized with the sleep/wake cycle (see chapter 9). The peak release is between 5:00 A.M. and 9:00 A.M.; very little is released during the late evening and early morning. Depressed individuals show a different pattern: It is less distinct, the peak release occurs earlier, and higher levels of cortisol and ACTH seem to be released (Whybrow, Akiskal, and McKinney 1984:140). Studies have verified that many individuals with major unipolar depression have elevated levels of cortisol and ACTH (Lobel and Hirschfeld 1984:2). The oversecretion of these hormones suggests that the processes that normally control the release of cortisol are not working properly.

Other neurotransmitters may be involved in this process. For example, deficiencies of norepinephrine or serotonin may cause an excess of ACTH, thereby resulting in too much cortisol-releasing hormone, which stimulates the adrenal glands to produce excessive amounts of cortisol.

The Dexamethasone Suppression Test

The dexamethasone suppression test (DST) is used to diagnose depression. Based on the functioning of the HPA sequence (which was just described), it seeks to uncover defects, or interruptions, in the interactions (the communication system) between the brain and the adrenal glands (Andreasen 1984:182).

The laboratory test is fairly direct. Dexamethasone (synthetic cortisol) is given orally, usually prior to bedtime, and is monitored by drawing and analyzing blood samples several times after administration. In nondepressed individuals the dexamethasone mimics the action of cortisol: The brain, perceiving the drug to be cortisol, signals the hypothalamus to stop releasing CRF, which tells the pituitary gland to stop sending ACTH to the adrenal glands, which cues them to stop releasing cortisol. Thus *normal suppression* occurs.

In many, but not all, depressed patients the dexamethasone fails to suppress the releasing of CRF and the cortisol levels remain high. However, as Whybrow, Akiskal, and McKinney (1984:141) point out, as the patient recovers from depression there is a predictable pattern of change toward normal when the dexamethasone is administered.

The DST was thought to have good prospects as a biological marker.

After an initial wide acceptance, continued research began to reveal some shortcomings, and its usefulness became very controversial (Grinspoon and Bakalar 1990:6; Rodin, Craven, and Littlefield 1991:90–96). Reading the varying reports in the literature is an interesting exercise in how research data can be interpreted in different, even opposite, ways.[1]

Pohl, who questions the usefulness of the DST, points out that the test lacks adequate *specificity* (the ability to differentiate one diagnosis from others or from normal), as "nonsuppression occurs in approximately 40 percent of patients with a major depressive disorder . . . [while] approximately 8 percent of normal controls have a false positive (nonsuppression) DST" (1987:16).[2] He points out that many other conditions produce nonsuppression and high rates of false positives and that states such as stress also reduce the accuracy of the test. He also feels that *sensitivity* (being able to detect the presence of a condition) is a major issue (Pohl 1987:12). Fifty-five percent of a depressed population does not manifest abnormal DSTs (will not show as depressed on the DST). He states that this can be dangerously misleading; a clinician who relies on the DST results may overlook a depression in a client whose test results are negative and thus fail to provide proper treatment. Furthermore, according to Pohl, the DST does not predict how depressed individuals will respond to drug treatment. He concludes that it is not useful in routine diagnosis and that it can even be harmful—for example, if used in situations where diagnosis is a "close call" or when it is used to rule out a diagnosis of depression.

Lieber, a proponent of the DST who has been using the test since 1980, feels that it is worthwhile and has several important functions. One is that it can validate a diagnosis of major depression, discriminating between major and minor, in about 50 percent of those identified as suffering from a mood disorder. Furthermore, it can discriminate major depression from schizophrenia and endogenous from nonendogenous depression. He acknowledges the shortcomings of the test but feels that when the "dust settles, the DST will take its rightful place in clinical practice" (Lieber 1987:6–8).

A conference on the DST sponsored by the National Institute of Mental Health (NIMH) concluded that even though there are questions about the DST and depression, the test is helpful for research, although there are no "clear indications for its routine use in the diagnosis or clinical management of depression. . . . [and the] search should continue for possible specificity of treatment modality on [the] basis of [the] DST" (Hirschfeld, Koslow, and Kupfer 1985).

We believe that the DST has not yet lived up to its promise of providing a true biological marker. Even this brief review of the literature shows that a great deal of investigation and clarification is still needed to resolve some important questions about the test. For example, although nonsuppression shows dysfunctions of the HPA axis, its relationship to depression is unclear. The "chicken-or-egg" question is also unresolved. It is not known whether the lack of suppression is a biological cause of depression or a result of depression.

We think that many who advocate the DST are operating within a predominantly biological definition of depression, a condition with vast sociological and psychological (i.e., nonbiological) consequences or contributing factors. The "jury is still out," while the research and the debate continue.

The Hypothalamic-Pituitary-Thyroid (HPT) Axis

■■ The interactions between the thyroid glands and the brain as
■■ they relate to the affective disorders have also come under greater scrutiny lately.

Hormones produced by the thyroid glands control the rate of metabolism of every cell in the body (Gold 1987a:144–145). The thyroid glands help control important functions, including growth, body temperature, and pulse rate. This control results from regulating the production of a hormone, *thyroxine*, that has several different forms, including L-*triiodothyronine* (*T-3*), and L-*thyroxine* (*T-4*).

The hypothalamic-pituitary-thyroid (HPT) axis functions similarly to the processes described for the hypothalamic-pituitary-adrenal axis (HPA), although different hormones are involved. An event (e.g., a cold temperature) is perceived by the brain, which then signals the hypothalamus to release a substance called *thyrotropin-releasing factor* (*TRF*). The TRF travels to the pituitary glands, stimulating them to release *thyrotropin* (known as *TSH—thyroid stimulating hormone*). The thyrotropin is carried via the blood to the thyroid glands, stimulating the release of *thyroid hormone*. The production of a certain amount of thyroid hormone inhibits the further production of TSH and stops the cycle (Andreasen 1984:121; Grinspoon and Bakalar 1990:5).

Outside factors can influence this feedback system, including psychosocial and physical events, which can result in the release of another hormone, *thyrotropin-releasing hormone* (*TRH*), a small peptide messenger that may also stimulate the pituitary to release TSH (Whybrow, Akiskal, and McKinney 1984:99–100). (Some of the literature refers to TRH as *hypothalamic TRH* and to TSH as *pituitary TSH*.)

Malfunctions of the thyroid glands are fairly common, especially in women, and when the thyroid and the adrenal glands do not operate as they should, people may experience such symptoms as fatigue, changes in appetite, or insomnia, which mimic the symptoms of depression (Andreasen 1984:180). For example, the presence of excessive thyroxine (known as *hyperthyroid* condition) is characterized by elevated rates of pulse, body temperature, and metabolism, which produce symptoms that can be confused with panic attacks or other anxiety reactions. Insufficient thyroxine (or *hypothyroid* condition) is characterized by lowered rates of pulse, body temperature, and metabolism. A deficiency of thyroxine is associated with the distorted cognition and "down" feelings of depression.

Other connections have been noted between the thyroid hormones and depression. Whybrow, Akiskal, and McKinney (1984:12) point out that administering thyroid hormones sometimes produces episodes of hypomania. They note, however, that adding small doses of thyroid hormone to antidepressant medication can hasten recovery from depression, particularly in women (1984:39). The thyroid hormone, which is initially helpful in relieving depression, may sometimes precipitate a manic attack in bipolar patients (Whybrow, Akiskal, and McKinney 1984:167–168). This evidence confirms the hypothesis that thyroid hormones influence the actions of the biogenic amines.

These findings have contributed to the understanding of the biochemical aspects of depression and to biochemical treatments. For example, responses to particular antidepression medications seem to vary, depending on the amounts of such substances as thyroxine and cortisol circulating in the blood. They have also been the basis of such tests as the DST (dexamethasone suppression test), already described, and the thyrotropin-releasing hormone suppression test (TRHST), which we describe later.

The Thyrotropin-releasing Hormone Suppression Test

The thyrotropin-releasing hormone suppression test (TRHST) has been developed to determine if the hypothalamus-pituitary-thyroid axis is functioning normally. This is done by measuring the levels of thyroid stimulating hormone (TSH) in the blood.

Since TSH levels vary during a normal daily cycle, the first step is to take some precautions that will maximize the accuracy of the test. The individual must fast overnight and be rested. A baseline measure of TSH is then taken. Synthetic thyroid releasing hormone (TRH) is then injected intravenously and the individual's blood is tested at several intervals following the injection. In normal individuals the injected TRH will produce an increase in the level of TSH in the blood. In depressed individuals (including those with normal thyroid function) this response is lower, or *blunted*. Reported percentages seem to vary from 25 percent to 70 percent, with women showing higher rates. Blunted responses are more prevalent in individuals with major depressive disorders than in those with minor disorders and are more prevalent in those with unipolar depressions than in those with bipolar ones. The test also helps to distinguish mania (which shows a blunted response) from schizophrenia (Whybrow, Akiskal, and McKinney 1984:210; Fawcett and Kravitz 1985:465).

The TRHST also reveals thyroid dysfunction. Thyroid abnormality, especially in the early stages, is one of the most common medical *mimickers* of depression. (A mimicker is a condition with presenting symptoms that are the same as, or similar to, another condition.) Thyroid problems are too often improperly treated as depression (Gold 1987a:140). Gold strongly urges administration of the TRHST, claiming that 10–15 percent of patients diagnosed as depressed have some form of thyroid illness and that diagnosis of this condition without the TRHST is impossible. Gold is adamant in stating that overlooking thyroid problems is the "single most important area of misdiagnosis" in the depressions (1987a:145).

Gold's enthusiasm for the TRHST is not matched by many other authors, whose reports tend to be mixed (Grinspoon and Bakalar 1990:5). The major criticism of the test is that the criteria for measuring the TSH levels have not been standardized. For example, a blunted response can be a *false positive*, caused by such factors as age, maleness, anorexia, and alcoholism. It can also result from the presence of thyroid hormone or from dexamethasone from DST and TRHST tests given within the past few days (Fawcett and Kravitz 1985:465–466). This lack of standardization undoubtedly accounts for the wide variations in percentages of blunted responses reported by different researchers.

The functional significance of a blunted TSH level is still not completely understood. It may or may not be related to the cause of the depression (which is unknown), and although about 30 percent of depressed individuals show abnormal results on both the TRHST and the DST, the significance of this is unclear (Fawcett and Kravitz 1985:466). Fawcett and Kravitz conclude that, although the test is safe and easy to administer, its data are questionable and the test should be used only as part of an overall careful clinical assessment.

Thyroid disease is found in about one woman in fifteen, with an estimated total of ten million cases in the United States. The high prevalence in women may contribute to, and confound, the persistent data indicating that depression—especially "neurotic" depression—is diagnosed much more among women than among men (Gold 1987a:149; 1987b).

8

The Circulatory System and Depression

The Role of Blood Plasma

■■ Blood plasma contains proteins, glucose, sodium, and potas-
■■ sium, among other substances; some of these circulating
substances are needed in neurotransmission—for example, in building
new neurotransmitters and eliminating worn-out ones. Certain proteins
are essential for transporting substances to the brain and for manufac-
turing neurotransmitters. Sodium and potassium ions, which are
positively charged, are important in the electrical signaling process
and in neurotransmission and hormone release. However, these
substances must first reach the brain, which involves overcoming some
obstacles.

Blood plasma also contains substances that could harm the brain,
which must maintain a relatively constant environment. The brain must
be protected from these harmful substances and from abrupt changes.To
provide this environment and protect the brain against potentially harmful
elements, there is a protective mechanism—the blood-brain barrier—
that effectively separates the brain and the spinal cord from the remain-
der of the body and allows only specific substances to enter.

The Blood-Brain Barrier

■■ The blood-brain barrier (sometimes described as a "gate-
■■ house") is an intricate mechanism composed of tightly interconnected cells that line blood capillaries in the brain. (*Capillaries* are
"minute blood vessels . . . [that] connect the ends of the smallest arteries . . . with the beginnings of the smallest veins" [Thomas 1989:279].)
These are both endothelial cells (a particular type that lines the various
body cavities) and "curious . . . astrocytes . . . [which are] cells form[ing]
flattened 'end feet' which line up side by side to contribute an additional layer around the capillary wall" (The Diagram Group 1987:158).
This cellular barrier protects the extremely sensitive tissues in the brain

from potentially harmful substances (e.g., certain chemical compounds and bacteria) that circulate in the blood. It is a "waterproof protein shield . . . linking the cells lining [the] tiny blood vessels" and has been compared to a "moat around the mind. Impassable to all but a few types of molecules" (Thompson 1989).

Most water-soluble substances cannot cross this waterproof barrier, but fat-soluble substances (e.g., alcohol, heroin, cocaine, and L-dopa) apparently have little difficulty. However, some mechanisms in the brain (sometimes referred to as "revolving doors") allow the entry of molecules of certain nutrients the brain requires, such as glucose and amino acids. These molecules, which seem to be selected for entry according to their size and shape, are called *transport systems*. Researchers have now identified at least ten of these doors, or systems. Most drugs currently available to treat depression and other diseases believed to be brain related, are water-soluble. Because they cannot cross the blood-brain barrier, they are not as effective as they might be in treating these disorders.

Another protective system regulates and filters the fluids in the brain, periodically (in approximately eight-hour cycles) washing out any chemicals that find their way in. This process (much more complex than we have described) is an additional deterrent to medicating directly to the brain.

Facilitating Neurotransmission Through Nutrition: The Precursor Theory

■■ The role of nutrients, both in neurotransmission and as po-
■■ tential antidepressant medications, has been highlighted by orthomolecular psychiatrists for a number of years. This approach, associated primarily with Dr. Linus Pauling and his followers, states that "mental illness is due to biochemical abnormalities" that can be treated with vitamins and minerals (Thomas 1989:1271). It focuses on providing the body with the "optimum concentration of substances" in the brain (Linus Pauling, quoted in Ross 1975:70). In fact, Ross (1975:214) stated that vitamin therapy (often involving megavitamins) frequently is the most neglected medical treatment for depression. Many authorities strongly disagree with this hypothesis.

Over the years, there had been widespread agreement that severe, long-term nutritional deficiencies have behavioral and cognitive consequences, including depression. But because of the protective mechanism of the blood-brain barrier, the belief that there could be short-term consequences (e.g., from the nutrients in a single snack or a meal) had been considered "in the territory of nutritional gurus and quacks" (Freedman 1987:5). This territory included orthomolecular psychiatry.

Increasing knowledge of the biochemistry of the brain, including the functions of the blood-brain barrier, has recently led reputable investigators to reexamine the relationship of nutritional intake to cognition and behavior. They believe they are finding evidence of just such short-term effects (Freedman 1987:225). They have developed a number of hypotheses, which are presently *very controversial*, on the relationship of nutrition to neurotransmission and hope that verifying them will provide more understanding of the biochemistry of the depressions. They also hope that clarifying which nutrients do what, and how, will lead to treatments for the depressions that use ordinary foods and substances derived from them.

Richard J. Wurtman, who is currently with the Massachusetts Institute of Technology Department of Brain and Cognitive Sciences, has examined in detail what happens in the brain after certain foods or nutrients are consumed, particularly those involved in the process of neurotransmission. He analyzed blood plasma and hypothesized that certain nutrients found there affect the amount of related neurotransmitters in the brain. Wurtman called his hypothesis the *precursor theory*, based on the role these nutrients play when they get to the brain, where they function as precursors, "signaling the brain to make more of certain brain chemicals" (Goleman 1988b). (*Precursors* are "substances that precede and indicate the approach of another . . . [or] from which others are formed" [*Webster's* 1989:926].) This signaling (precursor) function affects the quantity of related neurotransmitters that are synthesized in the brain, causing a series of chemical changes that eventually produce changes in behavior and mood. Wurtman hypothesizes that this process works both ways (is bidirectional): Certain changes in the brain (e.g., a lowered rate of serotonin) stimulate a craving for the substance (e.g., carbohydrate, if serotonin is low) that theoretically will make up the deficiency.

We described specific transport mechanisms that allow nutrients into the brain. The nutrients, which are carried in the blood plasma, travel along the transport pathways, across the blood-brain barrier, and into the brain via carrier molecules. These carrier molecules tend to be unsaturated ("capable of absorbing or dissolving more of something" [*Webster's* 1989:1293]). Because these transport molecules can reach the brain, an increase or decrease in the amount of carrier molecules in the blood plasma can quickly change the quantity of these substances that go to the brain or come out of it (Wurtman 1987:228). Nutritional pathways provide very limited access to the brain. The single amino acids tryptophan and tyrosine have the "unique property, once they are digested and enter the blood plasma, of readily crossing" the blood-brain barrier (Goleman 1988b). However, seven other of these *large neutral amino acids* (*LNAAs*) may cross the barrier, and they all compete for entry.

Wurtman believes that certain foods are "behaviorally active," which means that they can alter the release of neurotransmitters associated with behavior. Eating these foods produces changes in the composition of the blood plasma, increasing the amounts of some nutrients and decreasing the amounts of others. These levels consequently influence the quantity of each of these nutrients that reaches the brain (Wurtman 1987:226). When the nutrients from these behaviorally active foods are precursors for neurotransmitters such as serotonin, there is a resulting change in mood and behavior.

According to Wurtman's theory, the nutrients in some foods apparently reach the brain quickly and thus are said to have direct effects on mood, because the results may be visible several hours after the foods are eaten. However, most nutrients must be ingested in pure, concentrated form to get into the brain and gain entrance in high enough quantities to have the desired effects on mood. Wurtman (1987:228–229) believes that there are probably "buffering mechanisms" in the brain to prevent transmissions that are out of the physiological range in the event that excessive amounts of precursor nutrients are eaten.

Wurtman's research has focused on three substances affected by behaviorally active foods: the amino acids tryptophan and tyrosine, and another widely distributed amine, choline. These are all chemicals that can cross the blood-brain barrier, and they are all precursors for neurotransmitters.

1. *Tryptophan*, a precursor of serotonin, is found in foods high in protein. It seems to lessen both the psychological and physiological effects of stress, and it regulates sleep. It was the first substance to be studied by Wurtman and his colleagues, as a number of previous studies, first with animals, then with humans, showed that the "administration of tryptophan, in pharmacologic doses does elevate brain serotonin levels" (Wurtman 1987:227). However, as studies of the effects of high-protein meals progressed, a paradox emerged: Measurements confirmed that eating foods high in protein raised the levels of plasma tryptophan but lowered the levels of brain tryptophan, whereas eating high-carbohydrate meals with no protein (therefore no tryptophan) raised the levels of brain tryptophan. It was later determined that this was due both to the competition for transportation across the blood-brain barrier and to a unique property of tryptophan: When protein is ingested, the tryptophan competes with other amino acids in the blood plasma for transportation to the brain, and only small quantities make this journey.

When carbohydrates are ingested, they trigger the release of insulin, which causes the plasma amino acids to be absorbed by muscle. Tryptophan, however, is not affected by insulin; it remains in the plasma and may be transported to the brain.

Although the therapeutic effects of most foods are smaller than the effects of taking concentrated ("pure") extracts of particular nutrients, foods rich in carbohydrates are the exception as long as they are not taken with foods containing protein, for the reasons described earlier. Some other differences became apparent in a study measuring the effects of eating a meal consisting of pasta, which is high in carbohydrates: It caused women to feel sleepy and men to feel calm; and those over 40 showed increased errors on performance tests (Wurtman 1987:229).

Wurtman and his colleagues feel that if depression, or a form of depression, results from inadequate serotonin in the brain, then tryptophan could be useful in treatment. Tryptophan converts into a pure form in the brain—5–HTP, which is currently used as an adjunct in treating depression in a number of countries, but not in the United States. The pure form of tryptophan seems to be most effective when taken with a food high in carbohydrates, such as fruit, rather than with one that is high in protein. 5-HTP is also used in combination with other antidepressant medications. Wurtman (1987:229) lists a number of studies showing antidepressant effects from tryptophan, particularly when taken in combination with MAO inhibitors.

2. *Tyrosine*, a precursor of dopamine and norepinephrine, helps to regulate mood, including depression. The tyrosine in blood plasma comes from two sources: protein and phenylalanine, another amino acid found in certain foods. When tyrosine levels are low or absent and levels of phenylalanine are simultaneously low, this amino acid seems to act as a partial substitute for tyrosine and promotes the release of dopamine. When plasma levels of tyrosine are normal and, at the same time, concentrations of phenylalanine are high, the phenylalanine seems to restrain the tyrosine and suppresses the release of dopamine. According to Wurtman (1987:234), "This inhibition might become clinically significant in people who consume very large quantities of the dipeptide sweetener aspartame" (a protein that is unique in that it has no competitors for entry into the brain). Ingesting large amounts of aspartame, especially when combined with carbohydrates that cause the release of insulin (and thus remove potentially competitive amino acids), results in very high levels of phenylalanine in the brain. These high levels are typical of lower synthesis (production) of neurotransmitters.

In a recent review of studies examining the possibility of toxic effects from aspartame, the data seemed to indicate that ingesting normal levels of aspartame was not harmful (Kanarek and Marks-Kaufman 1991:196). However, the authors cautioned that foods and beverages sweetened with aspartame are often consumed with foods high in phenylalanine, which increases the risk of neurological and behavioral symptoms, such as alterations in mood.

Research on tyrosine had not been as extensive as research on tryptophan, because it had been thought that the "catecholamine neurotransmitters were not under precursor control" (Wurtman 1987:232). This has proven incorrect, and research is increasing. Tyrosine, used alone or as a supplement to tryptophan, has been shown to be useful in treating depression (van Praag and Lemus 1986). If depression results from insufficient norepinephrine in the brain, tyrosine could have great potential in its treatment.

3. *Choline,* a precursor of the neurotransmitter acetylcholine, is also thought to be involved with depression, especially mania, and with Alzheimer's disease. It is part of the fatty substance lecithin, which is found in such foods as soybeans, egg yolk, and the fatty tissues of meat, including liver.[1] Some research with manic depressives has shown that choline increases the effectiveness of antipsychotic medications and shortens the periods of mania (Goleman 1988b).

In summary, Wurtman points out that tryptophan is currently an approved prescription drug in Canada, for use as an *adjunct* in the drug treatment of depression. He cautions that present data are insufficient to justify the use of tryptophan or tyrosine or any other nutrient alone for the treatment of depression: "much more is needed in the way of well-designed positive studies" (Wurtman, personal communication, October 29, 1991).

Evaluations of the Precursor Theory

Wurtman's precursor theory on the role of nutrients in facilitating neurotransmission is highly controversial, having been both praised and criticized by authorities in the field. For example, Carlsson (1987:238) finds it "stimulating and provocative. . . . [but] difficult to prove. . . . [with an] absence of direct evidence." Pirke (1987:240) finds the theory easily conceivable and states that studies on weight-reducing diets confirm Wurtman's results. However, he questions some of the findings regarding the eating disorders. Loffelholz (1987:242) considers these theories lawful and plausible but oversimplistic, believing that there are some discrepancies and that important supportive data are missing. Van Praag (1987:246–247) applauds this work as having seminal significance, particularly with regard to monoamines, but finds the conclusions about tryptophan ambiguous. He feels that it is at best a marginal antidepressant unless it is combined with tyrosine. Pardridge (1987:248) says that the precursor theory is a practical paradigm that grows stronger with each additional year of supportive data." Moller and Kirk (1987:249–253) find the evidence suggestive but feel that "determination of the precursor plasma amino acids alone does not accurately reflect brain metabolism." Menolascino (1987:254–255) states that Wurtman has clarified the "scientific basis for the role of dietary nutrients in modifying the neurotransmission basis of behaviors" but cautions that some of Wurtman's information "is not firmly validated by data from other investigators." Kaye (1987:255–256) feels that Wurtman's work has "exciting theoretical implications for understanding the pathophysiology of the eating disorders," warning that although some of the hypotheses are plausible, they are supported by limited data." Garattini (1989:235) also finds these hypotheses very attractive but says that several aspects are still to be proved."

Some of those who question Wurtman's theories feel he has not taken into account important mechanisms that regulate the body's basic biological functioning. For example, Carlsson (1987:238–239) points out that in neurotransmission there are "powerful feedback mechanisms, which are brought into play when the balance is upset by interventions of various kinds . . . a homeostatic mechanism, whose efficiency is well established." Loffelholz (1987:242) also refers to the body's dynamic equilibrium—its self-regulatory mechanisms, specifically the "general belief in the constancy of transmitter storage and release . . . [that] contributes to . . . the constancy of the internal environment." He outlines a number of mysteries that need to be resolved—for example, what he feels is a discrepancy between the "timing of brain biochemical events and the timing of behaviors they are thought to explain." Wurtman's research has also been criticized for producing meager data from small samples attained with poorly controlled experimental conditions (Garattini 1989:237).

This brief summary of evaluations of the precursor theory gives some indication of the complexities of research on the immensely intricate workings of the human body. Although critics have offered alternative explanations for different aspects of the hypothesis, Freedman (1987:225), among others, emphasizes that Wurtman's pioneering work has generated a large amount of research. This research may well have enormous implications for health care, including the treatment of depression and that of the related eating disorders.

Diet-induced Depression: Sugar (Carbohydrates) and Caffeine

■■ Low blood sugar (hypoglycemia) causes the release of insu-
■■ lin, which can result in severe changes in mood, including depression, anxiety, and anger. High blood sugar (diabetes), which also involves periods of low blood sugar, has similar consequences.

In most people, caffeine, a central nervous system stimulant, has the opposite effect on mood: Regular consumption seems to have an antidepressant effect. As explained by Christensen and Burrows (1990), the adrenal glands are stimulated by caffeine, causing the release of adrenalin, which can change body and brain chemistry and reduce depression. However, caffeine often affects sleep patterns, resulting in symptoms associated with depression, including a delay in falling asleep, a shorter period of sleep, lighter sleep, and "worsening [of] the subjective quality of sleep" (Kanarek and Marks-Kaufman 1991:156).

Caffeine and carbohydrates, such as refined sucrose (e.g., granulated sugar), seem to induce depression rather than diminish it in certain individuals who are sensitive to these substances (Christensen and Burrows 1990). In one study of dietary-induced depression, when all "sensitive" foods were removed from the diet of the test group, depression decreased significantly (Christensen and Burrows 1990:184–185). The researchers concluded that refined sucrose seems to heighten depression but cautioned that further verification is needed because "elimination of refined sucrose serves the purpose of reducing overall carbohydrate intake and increasing protein intake . . . [thus] the beneficial effect observed . . . may be from this dietary alteration" (Christensen and Burrows 1990:192). Christensen also suggested that there is a need to study what happens when caffeine is eliminated from the diets of patients who are clinically depressed.

The relationship of blood sugar levels and depression is highly controversial. As we stated earlier, some prominent biopsychiatrists hold that hypoglycemia, which is a low level of sugar in the blood, is "hardly ever the cause of depressive illness" (Klein and Wender 1988:62).

Vitamins, Minerals, and Depression

■■ The body's thirteen *vitamins* ("a group of organic substances
■■ . . . essential for normal metabolism, growth and development" [Thomas 1989:2000]) and a number of *minerals* (organic com-

pounds, usually solid) have profound effects on the central nervous system. Deficiencies of these substances may cause depression or symptoms of depression.

Vitamin and mineral deficiencies can develop from genetic conditions, disease, and drug and alcohol intake, among other factors. Their major cause, however, is that they are not consumed in sufficient quantities, either because insufficient food is eaten or because the foods that are eaten do not contain all the vitamins and minerals required for good health (Kanarek and Marks-Kaufman 1991:35).

Each vitamin has a different role. Generally, vitamins act as catalysts, helping to metabolize nutrients and to maintain various physiological functions, especially in the central nervous system (Kanarek and Marks-Kaufman 1991:35). *Thiamine* (vitamin B-1), acting as an enzyme, is important in the synthesis and release of neurotransmitters; it also helps to conduct electrical signals throughout the nervous system. Thiamine deficiency seems to cause degeneration of neurons as well as changes in neurotransmitters, results in injury to many parts of the brain (e.g., the thalamus, hypothalamus, cerebellum, and brain stem), and affects the activity of a number of neurotransmitter systems, including reducing the metabolism of norepinephrine and serotonin (Kanarek and Marks-Kaufman 1991:39–42). *Niacin* (vitamin B-3), which is needed by all cells, is essential to the metabolism of fat, carbohydrate, and amino acids and other substances. A severe shortage of this vitamin can lead to biochemical and physiological changes throughout the nervous system, including symptoms of emotional instability. *Pyridoxine* (vitamin B-6), which is essential in metabolizing proteins and amino acids, is involved in synthesizing a number of neurotransmitters, including norepinephrine and serotonin. A deficiency of this vitamin may have serious consequences, such as decreased levels of these neurotransmitters in the brain—an indicator of depression. (As we shall discuss in chapter 17, oral contraceptives can cause a deficiency of this vitamin.) An inadequate supply of another B vitamin—*cobalamin*, or vitamin B-12—can cause anxiety, which has symptoms of fatigue and anorexia—an eating disorder often closely related to depression. (We discuss anorexia in chapter 10.) Severe deficiency of this vitamin may lead to central nervous system impairment and accompanying symptoms, including depression. One of the most commonly occurring vitamin deficiencies is that of *folic acid*, which is characterized by a number of psychiatric symptoms, including depression and psychotic behavior. Kanarek and Marks-Kaufman (1991:53–54) indicate that these symptoms, which are often more severe in patients who are physically ill, may be caused by anticonvulsant drugs. They also caution that, although taking this vitamin may improve neuropsychological functioning, excessive amounts may be toxic, resulting in sleep disturbance, excitability, irritability, and other symptoms.

Sodium, potassium, and *calcium* are some of the essential *trace minerals* (i.e., those in very small quantities) reviewed by Kanarek and Marks-Kaufman (1991:57–75). As we discussed in chapter 6, these minerals are important in conducting nerve impulses; changes in quantity in and around cells can affect the process of neurotransmission. Since only small amounts of these three minerals are needed, deficiencies tend to occur in abnormal situations. For example, sodium deficiencies may be found with some chronic illnesses, such as cancer, colitis, and liver disease. Potassium deficiency may occur after surgery or may result from conditions associated with malnutrition, such as alcoholism, anorexia, and diets with insufficient amounts of carbohydrate. Shortages of *iron*—which is crucial for such biochemical processes as the transport of oxygen and the "synthesis of the neurotransmitters dopamine, norepinephrine and serotonin"—may affect the manufacture of these substances. Inadequate amounts of *zinc,* also needed for metabolism, result in irritability and emotional instability. A deficiency of *iodine,* which is essential in producing the thyroid hormones, causes many symptoms of depression, including slowed reflexes, fatigue, and apathy (Kanarek and Marks-Kaufman 1991:73).

Kanarek and Marks-Kaufman (1991:54) conclude that vitamins and minerals are "important in the synthesis of neurotransmitters, maintenance of neuronal integrity, myelination of neurons [the process of acquiring the soft sheath of somewhat fatty tissue that surrounds some nerve fibers (*Webster's* 1989:784)] and conduction of electrical potential." Vitamin and mineral deficiencies may have serious consequences. However, Kanarek and Marks-Kaufman (1991:79) state that treating these deficiencies with megavitamin therapy ("the use of massive doses of vitamins . . . and large amounts of minerals in the treatment of disease") is not only controversial, because the evidence for it is inconclusive, but potentially harmful. They suggest that the problems resulting from vitamin and mineral deficiencies often can be reversed simply by a nutritionally sound diet.

The increasing evidence of associations between deficiencies in vitamins and minerals, and depression—or sometimes symptoms mimicking depression—emphasizes the importance of physical examinations of depressed clients to identify, or rule out, any dietary causes. We shall discuss this further in chapter 16.

The Chronobiology of Depression: Our Biological Clocks

Circadian Cycles and Depression

■■ Various cycles shape our lives. Daily or *circadian cycles* (*circa*,
■■ "approximately"; *dies*, "day"), such as periods of light and
dark, largely determine when we go to sleep and wake up. Internal
daily cycles include variations in body temperature and the release of
certain chemicals, such as the hormone cortisol. There are many such
cycles, and recent research focuses on their identification and interrelationships. The study of these "timing characteristics of the life processes" is known as *chronobiology* (*chronos*, "time"; *bios*, "life"; *logos*,
"study") (Thomas 1989:357).

Through evolution, these basic rhythms have become an internalized
part of our *biological template* (the molecules, such as RNA, that carry
genetic codes). We generally refer to this biological template as our
biological clock (Whybrow, Akiskal, and McKinney 1984:157).

All living beings must maintain states of biological and psychological
stability in a constantly changing environment. They must be stable, to
maintain balance, yet be flexible enough to adapt to changing conditions (Whybrow, Akiskal, and McKinney 1984:156–157). Our biological
clocks are vital in maintaining this stability—for example, through the
flexibility in the system of daily stimulation, which allows us to adjust
to such variations as the changing amounts of daily light. This is accomplished via *melatonin*, a light-sensitive hormone controlled by the pineal
gland, which is located in the brain but is not part of it. High levels of
melatonin are released at night. In the morning, when the body perceives sunrise, this daylight causes the melatonin to be suppressed;
blood levels drop rapidly; and the body is signaled to awake. This
process is known as the *sleep/wake cycle*.

Disturbances in the sleep/wake cycle are commonly associated with
depression. Connections have also been found between depression and
seasonal variations in light. For example, during the months when
daylight is shorter, some individuals suffer from a type of depression
called seasonal affective disorder (SAD).

Sleep Disturbances and Depression

■■ Sleep disorders have been the focus of a great deal of atten-
■■ tion and research in recent years. This extensive research has
evolved into a specialization known as *sleep disorders medicine*.

Sleep has been studied subjectively, by interviewing individuals about
their sleep patterns (questions commonly asked by therapists when
taking case histories), and it has been studied objectively in sleep laboratories using both observers and instruments that measure electrical
brain waves, eye movement, rates of heartbeat and breathing, body
movement, and so on. This process is called *polysomnography*.

Through polysomnography three relevant states have been identified: (1) the state of being awake, (2) *non-rapid-eye-movement sleep* (NREM—
also called *synchronized, orthodox, simple,* or *quiet* sleep, or *nondreaming*
sleep), and (3) *rapid-eye-movement sleep* (REM—also called *desynchronized,
paradoxical, active,* or *dreaming* sleep) (Hartmann 1988:152). In NREM
sleep, brain waves are slow and uniform, but the body moves frequently. In REM sleep the brain waves are irregular, the eyes move or
blink rapidly, but the body is very still (Lamberg 1988:24). REM sleep is
a qualitatively different kind of sleep (Hartmann 1988:155).

Studies of electrical brain patterns during sleep have identified four
distinct *stages of NREM sleep,* ranging from stage 1, the lightest, to stage
4, the heaviest sleep. Stages 3 and 4 (in recent literature these stages are
combined) are sometimes referred to as *slow-wave sleep (s.w.s.),* or *delta
sleep.*

The studies have also shown that sleep occurs in predictable *cycles*. A
normal individual usually progresses from NREM stage 1 to stage 4
(from lightest to deepest NREM sleep) in about one to one-and-a-half
hours, followed by a period of REM sleep. This cycle is repeated several
times, depending on the length of the total period of sleep. As sleep
progresses, the periods of REM and of NREM light sleep, get longer,
and the amount of heavy sleep decreases. In one sleep period, the
normal individual may go from NREM stage 1 to stage 4, followed by
REM, one or two times. He or she will then go from NREM stage 1 to
stage 3, followed by REM, then from NREM stage 1 to stage 2, followed
by REM. The cycling back and forth between NREM and REM sleep is
sometimes referred to as the *sleep/dream cycle.*

A normal period of sleep usually lasts from about six to nine hours.
The REM sleep usually takes up about one and one-half hours, or from
20 to 25 percent of the entire sleeping period (Hartmann 1988:154).
Young adults average about seven and one-half hours, with surprisingly few geographic or cultural variations (Hartmann 1988:159). Some

adults show wide variations (e.g., Thomas Edison apparently slept for only four hours each night, but Albert Einstein normally slept for twelve hours).

Individuals need sufficient amounts of both NREM sleep (especially the deep or delta sleep of stages 3 and 4) and REM sleep. Metabolism occurs during delta sleep: Proteins and ribonucleic acid (RNA) are synthesized; afterward the person feels physically restored. The person who does not get enough NREM sleep will wake up feeling exhausted, headachy, and generally washed out. During REM sleep dreams occur and information is stored in the brain. A person who does not get enough REM sleep will not feel alert and may find it difficult to concentrate and remember things.

In most normal individuals the sleep/wake cycle follows a predictable twenty-four-hour pattern, though it is interesting to note that in laboratory tests, when external cues to day and night are removed, the sleep/wake pattern usually readjusts to a twenty-five- or twenty-six-hour cycle that has been named *long days*. However, body temperature follows a constant twenty-four-hour cycle. When an individual does not sleep for a number of days, these two cycles grow more and more apart. Eventually, the individual falls asleep, generally in response to a drop in body temperature, thus reestablishing a normal cycle.

These patterns of long days may be similar to those found in people with bipolar illness who display "quickly shifting cycles," moving rapidly from manic excitement to depression. As summarized by Whybrow, Akiskal, and McKinney (1984:159), these shifts, although assumed to be internal, are also influenced by external *zeitgebers* ("time-givers" in German). Zeitgebers are periodic events, such as the appearance of light and the sound of an alarm clock, that help to set our biological clocks. Researchers report that these zeitgebers influence sleep and are a factor in the depressions.

The *sleep disorders*, as classified in the *Diagnostic and Statistical Manual of Mental Disorders* (D.S.M.-III-R 1987), are separated into two major subgroups—the dyssomnias and the parasomnias. Briefly, the *dyssomnias* are disturbances in "the amount, quality, or timing of sleep." They include *insomnia* (characterized by trouble falling asleep, staying asleep, or not feeling rested after sleep), *hypersomnia* (feeling excessively sleepy in the daytime, or having difficulty making the transition from the state of sleep to feeling awake), and *sleep-wake schedule disorder* (a mismatch between a person's environmental pattern and circadian pattern, resulting in either insomnia or hypersomnia). In *parasomnia* disorders the primary complaints are about such events as frightening dreams and "sleep terrors," rather than loss of sleep.

Three kinds of *sleep/wake schedule disorders* are listed in the D.S.M.-III-R (1987:307): *frequently changing*, which is characterized by numerous changes in the times of awaking and going to sleep, common to travelers to different time zones, or to frequent changes in work shifts; *advanced* or *delayed*, where the biological clock is often at odds with the demands imposed by conventional society, such as the need to be at work during particular hours; and *disorganized*, in which sleep patterns are random, with no regular daily major period of sleep.

Changes in the sleep/wake cycle seem to upset internal rhythms, which generally results in malaise and lack of energy. Individuals suffering from the *frequently changing* disorders may exhibit rapid mood switches and deficiencies in mental abilities. Long periods of sleep deprivation may lead to ego disorganization, hallucinations, and delusions. Some researchers feel that extended sleep deprivation would eventually develop into psychosis, but this has not been tested (Hartmann 1988:158).

A high percentage of depressives report sleep disturbances, usually some form of insomnia. These disturbances may take several forms, the most common of which is *terminal* (also known as *early-morning* or *middle-waking*) insomnia, where people wake up anywhere from two to four hours after falling asleep and often cannot get back to sleep. Many depressed people have trouble falling asleep, especially the 60–70 percent who also report symptoms of anxiety. Some unfortunate individuals experience both kinds of insomnia—difficulty falling asleep and then early awakening. Insomniacs also tend to present many general complaints, including "disturbances in mood, memory and concentration" (DSM-III-R 1987:298).[1]

Bipolar and unipolar depressives seem to have different patterns of sleep (Whybrow, Akiskal, and McKinney 1984:10). Bipolar depressives sleep more while in the depressed phase. During manic episodes they seem to need less sleep. In fact, they may have periods of heightened activity, often lasting twenty-four to thirty-six hours, during which they may not sleep or even appear tired. Unipolar depression is frequently characterized by disrupted sleep (e.g., early-morning awakening); the depressed person sleeps less and often awakes feeling very tired.

Some depressed individuals suffer from hypersomnia; they sleep excessively and may become demoralized. Sleep is an obvious, although usually not consciously determined, way of escape from the pain they feel while awake.

Laboratory tests show different sleep patterns for normal and depressed individuals. A depressed person often attains REM sleep in about forty-five minutes as compared with ninety minutes for a normal person. (In some of the literature this is referred to as a *shortened REM latency period* or *shortened REML*.) In depressives, periods of REM sleep tend to be longer; conversely, periods of NREM sleep are shorter and have less depth (i.e., sleep stages 3 and 4 may be shorter or even absent). Depressed people experience more cycling or shifting of sleep stages. Again, the total period of sleep is often shorter.

The evidence that depressed individuals experience more light sleep and insufficient heavy sleep may explain their heightened sensitivity to noise and tendency to awaken easily. They also seem to have trouble falling back to sleep, thus increasing their sleep deprivation.

Changes in sleep patterns may be useful in predicting depression. When some individuals are becoming depressed, they wake more during the night, awaken earlier in the morning, cannot return to sleep, and feel more and more exhausted in the morning (Hartmann 1988:161). One of the early symptoms of a manic episode is that the individual begins to sleep for shorter periods of time, simultaneously feeling that he or she needs less sleep.

Changes in sleep patterns may also be of value in confirming diagnoses of depression and in monitoring the progress of treatment. Some experiments have identified characteristic shapes of periods of REM sleep. Depressed individuals showed significant differences in terms of the number of REM sleep periods and levels of intensity. These might be used as a baseline to predict clinical response and to measure long-term response to antidepressant medication. Further research is needed, especially long-term studies, to determine if, among other things, these patterns of REM sleep change during remission.

Rapid changes in patterns of dreams may be significant in diagnosing depression. Persons who are becoming clinically depressed may report that they have suddenly stopped dreaming or that they have begun having nightmares. The laboratory analysis of sleep patterns may also be used to make differential diagnoses, although there is a question about the cost effectiveness of these tests and the difficulties of arranging the necessary "ideal conditions" (Hartmann 1988:162). Whybrow, Akiskal, and McKinney (1984:210) state that exhibiting *REM latency* (achieving REM sleep in a shorter than normal time) for two consecutive nights on the sleep *EEG* ("*electro-encephalogram,* a record of the electrical activity of the brain [Thomas 1989:568]) differentiates primary depression from secondary, barring confounding factors such as drug withdrawal.

Changes in sleep patterns are also symptomatic of many other disorders. All health and mental health professionals must be cautious about basing a diagnosis of depression primarily on a client's reports of sleep problems. Among these other conditions are any painful or uncomfortable condition, such as muscle spasms; psychiatric disorders other than depression; the use of, or withdrawal from, various drugs and addictive substances; sleep dysfunctions, such as narcolepsy (recurring periods of uncontrollable drowsiness or deep sleep) or sleep apnea (temporary "cessation of breathing during sleep" [Thomas 1989:1693]); medical illnesses (e.g., metabolic diseases and brain lesions), toxic, and environmental conditions; menstrual associated syndrome; dietary factors; and so on (Hartmann 1988:163–164). Hartmann gives an example of a patient who, after ten years of unsuccessful treatment for "mild depression," was properly diagnosed as having sleep apnea (1988:163–164).

Two commonly used substances, alcohol and nicotine, can also disrupt normal sleep. Ironically, they are both frequently used as sleep aids, and although they may initially cause drowsiness, which helps the person fall asleep, they cause restless sleep and often result in the person waking during the night.[2]

The Treatment of Sleep Disorders

THE CHANGING OF SLEEP PATTERNS

A growing number of researchers believe that some of the mood disorders may really be disorders of circadian rhythm (Wehr et al. 1979; Wehr and Wirz-Justice 1982). This theory is based on evidence that the sleep patterns of depressed individuals differ from those of nondepressed people. In addition, medications used for unipolar depressions may lessen REM sleep, and drugs that raise the amount of NREM sleep may retard behavior and reaction times (Lamberg 1984:253).

In some depressed individuals there may be discrepancies between the time of going to sleep and the activity of their biological clocks, particularly of the functions that help to regulate the REM stage of sleep and the release of cortisol. Excessive amounts of chemicals may be released, or their release may be badly timed—for example, coming much earlier than the usual bedtimes of these individuals (Lamberg 1984:255–256).

This hypothesis has resulted in some interesting experiments in treating depression by intervening in sleep rhythms. The experiments, carried out in sleep laboratories, involved depriving depressed persons of all sleep; depriving them of sleep for part of the night; and advancing the time of sleep, in some cases by as much as six hours (introducing a "kind of therapeutic jet lag") (Lamberg 1984:254). Experiments also have combined full or partial sleep deprivation with such medications as lithium and clomipramine (Doghramji 1989:36). These linked approaches were developed for clients who could not carry out regularly scheduled programs of sleep manipulation. Many of the subjects in these experiments were helped; their depressions lifted. However, all the subjects eventually fell asleep, and when they did, they relapsed. Subjects with endogenous symptom patterns benefited the most from these treatments (Noll, David, and DeLeon-Jones 1985:279). Interestingly, those who did not improve after being deprived of REM sleep also did not respond to the standard antidepressant medications. Interrupting the sleep cycle may also worsen depression in some individuals, and it can trigger a manic attack in bipolar depressives.

Another interesting theory is that a neural oscillator moves back and forth between generating REM sleep and inhibiting it. Some depressives may have a damaged or weakened oscillator, which either plays some part in producing depression or accompanies it. Sleep deprivation may stimulate the oscillator, thus lessening the depression to the extent that the oscillator is stimulated. The mechanisms of circadian oscillators are now being studied to determine both their composition and their controlling process (Raju et al. 1991:673).

These studies are clarifying some of the mysteries of depression. Additional knowledge of REM sleep changes in depression may eventually increase understanding of the pathophysiology of depression (Kupfer, Targ, and Stack 1982).

CONDUCTING LABORATORY SLEEP TESTS AND RESEARCH: PROBLEMS AND QUESTIONS

Conducting tests and research on sleep can be very expensive, time-consuming, and inconvenient for subjects. It is hard to deprive someone of sleep for a long time or to keep him or her awake when it is dark. To do so, a very bright, interesting environment must be provided. The tests must be done in well-equipped laboratories under the supervision of highly trained technicians. A subject must be free of drugs for two weeks and spend a minimum of two nights in the laboratory.[3] Furthermore, we currently lack standardized criterion values and measurements (Fawcett and Kravitz 1985:483).

One authority on sleep says that overnight tests in a sleep laboratory are necessary (and cost-effective) only in certain cases, such as an elderly patient, especially one who has cardiac problems and/or is reluctant to try ECT, or has not responded to several trials of antidepressant medication. He believes that it is less complicated to attempt antidepressant medications on an outpatient basis than to go to the trouble and expense of using the sleep laboratory, unless the sleep problems complicate the case and/or the diagnosis is difficult. If diagnosis is a problem, then the sleep lab might be used in conjunction with such tests as the dexamethasone suppression test (Hartmann 1988:162).

Another drawback to the sleep laboratory is that the research findings thus far have been shown to be most applicable to the major mood disorders. The findings also seem to hold for schizoaffective disorders, but not for schizophrenia, the dysthymic disorders, or the neurotic depressions (Hartmann 1988:162). They are least relevant to the depressives who form the majority of the outpatients seen by mental health personnel: the unipolar, exogenous, nonpsychotic depressive.

A number of questions about sleep research remain, many of which are being asked by the experimenters themselves. For example, is a shortened REM latency enough to diagnose depression? Since it is found in other conditions, such as borderline personality disorders, tests may produce false-positive results. However, these conditions *do* overlap with mood disorders (Thase, Frank, and Kupfer 1985:840). Findings about the suppression or nonsuppression of REM sleep resulting from treatment with antidepressant medications and by electroconvulsive therapy have also raised questions. The interested reader is referred to Vogel (1983).

THE USE OF SLEEPING PILLS (HYPNOTICS)

Hypnotics (literally, "sleep-causing") work by blocking various pathways in the nervous system. They may lessen or slow down breathing, vision, and reflexes of various kinds, and they cause some of the bodily changes that occur during sleep. Hypnotics are considered effective sleep aids for a short time and for people without previous sleep disturbances who are reacting to identifiable stressors. They are not effective for chronic insomnia or depression (Gillin 1990:5).

These widely used pills have serious, often dangerous consequences. Yet many who use them often know surprisingly little about their effects and side effects. It is not unusual for a person having difficulty sleeping to ask a doctor to prescribe one of these medications or to take one or more of the readily available over-the-counter drugs without inquiring about the possible consequences.

All hypnotics present a number of possible problems. Although they generally can be effective in inducing sleep, that sleep is not normal— either REM sleep or NREM sleep is insufficient. Consequently, a person who takes a sleeping medication may awake feeling tired, washed out, and somewhat disoriented or confused, depending on the particular medication.

Sleeping pills have other drawbacks. They can be very strong and very toxic, and often they do not combine well with other substances. For example, a small overdose of a barbiturate can be lethal, as can the combination of a barbiturate with alcohol. A hypnotic may negate the effects of other medications, and because the body may adjust quickly to a hypnotic, larger and larger amounts may be required to achieve an effect. Because hypnotics depress the functions of the nervous system, they can be dangerous, especially for those who suffer from respiratory and related problems.

Additional negative effects include excessive sleep, or excessive deep sleep, from which an individual may be unable to awake, even in an emergency. Hypnotics may also lead to *rebound daytime anxiety*—grogginess and confusion that last for a time after waking. (This may cause automobile accidents and injuries due to falls, especially in the elderly.) These symptoms may result from the long "half-life" of some of these drugs. They do not clear the body until several hours after waking. Many of the drugs can be addictive, with severe withdrawal symptoms, which Hartmann (1988:160) thinks is a danger that is still not sufficiently appreciated. Someone may take medication for a transient problem and then stop taking it. If the person does not know of the predictable withdrawal effects, these disturbing symptoms may cause him to think that he probably needs more medications, which could result in taking the medication on a long-term basis (Hartmann 1988:160).[4]

The benzodiazepines (e.g., Dalmane, Halcion, Restoril, Librium, and Valium), which are prescribed primarily for anxiety, are also used widely to help people fall asleep. They are generally considered safer than the barbiturates and just as effective as hypnotics. Moreover, tolerance does not build up as rapidly. The benzodiazepines are currently the most widely prescribed drugs to help people sleep, to lessen anxiety, or to provide sedation for other purposes (Schatzberg and Cole 1991:231). However, as seen by the recent difficulties with Halcion (see Dyer 1991), these drugs are also problematic.

Both prescription and over-the-counter sleeping medications are often taken by those who are depressed but not yet diagnosed and who think that they merely have a "sleep problem." Although we lack definitive data, clinical experience has shown that many depressed people, desperate for sleep, use these medications.

Despite the accumulated knowledge about hypnotics and the questions about benefits versus risks, "sleeping pills remain among the most widely used of all drugs" (Lamberg 1984:135). Questions about the use of hypnotics have led to an increased interest in nonbiological approaches to treating sleep disorders.

THE USE OF FOODS AND NUTRITIONAL SUPPLEMENTS

We have described Wurtman's controversial theory that mood can be directly influenced by foods, including those believed to contribute to the levels of serotonin in the brain. These "behaviorally active" foods increase the levels of serotonin, producing calming effects on the body and inducing drowsiness. If this theory proves correct, then certain foods or nutritional supplements derived from them could be used instead of drugs to treat sleep disorders.

An important benefit of using foods and other natural substances is that they do not have the negative side effects of hypnotics and other drugs. However, besides the mixed evidence of the effectiveness of these substances, they are not presently regulated by the F.D.A. or any other regulatory body, and their safety is not assured (Burros 1991). Recently, a contaminated product (a batch of L-tryptophan extract) was found to cause serious and sometimes fatal illness.[5] One report cited this as a "reminder that so-called natural remedies are really quite artificial. There is nothing natural about consuming half a dozen grams a day of a pure amino acid . . . [produced in manufacturing] processes that are subject to failure or contamination" (Bennett 1990:2).

PROCEDURES THAT ENCOURAGE SLEEP

A variety of nonmedical procedures may encourage sleep: The sufferer should try to reduce stimulation in the evening. Exercise, smoking, alcoholic beverages, certain medications (e.g., those with stimulants, such as decongestants and pain medications containing caffeine), and caffeine should all be avoided. Instead, foods that are believed to enhance relaxation, such as warm milk, should be taken. Deep breathing and other relaxation procedures can be helpful. Another effective technique is to establish *stimulus control* by using the bedroom only for sleep, arranging the bedroom to encourage sleep (e.g., keeping the room cool and quiet and maintaining adequate humidity; using enough blankets to stay warm; lessening distractions; and so on), and following a regular bedtime routine. This includes going to bed at the same time each night and getting up at the same time each morning. Avoiding daytime naps can also be helpful, as can regular exercise, as long as it is not done in the late afternoon or evening (Schwartz and Aaron 1979).

Comments on Sleep and Depression

The report from a recent meeting of the Association of Professional Sleep Societies (APSS) states that even though a lot of information has been obtained about physiological changes during sleep, we still know little about the *function* of sleep or why it is needed (Palca 1989:351, emphasis added). A professor of psychiatry asked, "Is sleep, or a certain amount of sleep or type of sleep, somehow bad for people who are depressed? Or is it the timing of sleep that has gone awry in depression?" (C. Gillian, quoted in Lamberg 1984:254). These and many other questions remain unanswered, including the familiar and difficult question of which came first, the sleep disorder or the depression.

Clearly, much of the theorizing on the relationship between sleep disturbances and depression remains just that—theorizing. However, some findings *are* consistent: Sleep disturbances as vegetative symptoms respond to some of the antidepressant medications. Manipulations of the sleep cycle (e.g., partial or total deprivation of sleep, deprivation of REM sleep, or advancement of the phases of sleep) have also proven effective, individually or when supplemented with medications (Doghramji 1989:36). Although it is unclear why sleep manipulation is effective, Doghramji holds that it can ease even severe depressions in a few days.

Helping depressed individuals regain adequate sleep, using one or more of the approaches we have reviewed, is crucial for their health and functioning. It is also extremely difficult to conduct psychotherapy with a sleep-deprived person.

Seasonal Affective Disorder

■■ We have been aware of "spring fever" and "winter dol-
■■ drums" for over two thousand years. Hippocrates, Aristotle, Pinel, and many other physicians and philosophers believed that certain illnesses were connected to changes in the seasons, and they even observed that some people seemed best suited to winter weather but others did best during the summer.

Recent research has verified that these seasonally changing moods are symptomatic of certain disorders, now specified as *seasonal pattern* in the D.S.M.-III-R (1987:224). The first seasonal pattern studied was an increase in depression in the fall and winter, with remission in the spring; now called *winter SAD* (seasonal affective disorder). It was later determined that a sizable number of people become depressed during the warm, summer weather—the pattern now called *summer SAD*. Some experience both winter and summer depression and feel fine in the spring and fall. Seasonal variations are also present, in varying degrees, in all people, as well as in those suffering from various affective disorders (Lacoste and Wirz-Justice 1989). Both children and adults display them.

Seasonal changes in mood seem to be associated with variations in the daily cycles of light and dark, which are believed to be connected to the role of melatonin in the sleep/wake cycle, described earlier. The hypothesis is that as winter approaches and sunlight (the body's wake-up signal) arrives later and later, the suppression of melatonin (the body's signal for darkness/sleep) also comes later and later. If a person's biological clock does not adapt properly to these changes, the cycles become "out of synch," resulting in feelings of depression. This hypothesis has not yet been completely confirmed.

The causes of summer SAD are less clear, and it is not known why some individuals experience both variations. Recent research has identified two other disorders, also characterized by disturbances in mood, associated with seasonal variations in light and dark. One is carbohydrate craving obesity (CCO), which we discuss later in this chapter. The other is a subtype of late luteal phase dysphoric disorder (commonly called premenstrual syndrome, or PMS) which will be discussed in chapter 17, Gender and Depression.

About 25 percent of the entire population is estimated to suffer from a mild form of seasonal depression (Blehar and Rosenthal 1989:4). This disorder, called S-SAD or *winter blues* (*W.B.*), does not seem to interfere with the ability to cope with the responsibilities of daily living, such as employment and family care (Whybrow, Akiskal, and McKinney 1984:162).

About 5 percent of the population experiences the more severe (clinical) form of the disorder, which was identified in a study conducted at the National Institute of Mental Health (NIMH) in the early 1980s (Blehar and Rosenthal 1989:4). SAD patients are thought to comprise only a small part of the total percentage of depressed people (Whybrow, Akiskal, and McKinney 1984:162).

In general, the degree of severity of SAD is less than that of major depression: Sufferers seldom need to be hospitalized, nor do they become psychotic; and although suicidal ideation is certainly present, and always a danger, the rates are reported to be low (Blehar and Rosenthal 1989:3). Rosenthal (1989b) pointed out that women are especially susceptible to SAD in their reproductive years. The ratio of women SAD patients to men is 4:1, compared with 2:1 in general surveys of depression (Blehar and Rosenthal 1989:3). More than half the patients seen at four centers reported a first-degree relative as having an affective disorder, a higher than expected figure; from 15 to 28 percent reported relatives with SAD; and from 17 to 42 percent reported alcoholism (Hellekson 1989:39). Almost one-half of SAD patients told of periodic, seasonal swings in mood in adolescence or childhood, much earlier than other depressives or the general population (Thase 1989:70).

Estimates keep increasing as research continues. For example, in a recent sizable study by Wehr and Kasper, 27 percent of the respondents had S-SAD, and between 4 and 10 percent suffered from a full-fledged SAD (Rovner 1989).

Winter SAD

Winter SAD usually begins in the fall and worsens as the winter progresses and the days grow shorter; it eases as the days begin to lengthen; and then disappears with the bright, longer summer days. A very high proportion (89 percent) of winter SAD patients repeatedly experience mild hypomanic episodes in spring or the beginning of summer (Thase 1989:68). As described by Wurtman and Wurtman (1989:68), "Once spring arrives SAD patients are full of energy and creativity, they are almost manic in their zest for life." It is difficult to determine if this is true mania or just extreme activity based on feelings of relief after the winter's gloominess. The unreliability of client self-report heightens the difficulty of determining the extent of the "mania."

People with winter SAD present an atypical symptom picture of the depressed client. Their symptoms include irritability, sadness, some slowing of movement, carbohydrate craving and weight gain, social withdrawal, diminished sexual desire, retardation (slowing down) of behavior, daytime drowsiness and excessive sleeping (hypersomnia), after which they wake up tired rather than rested. They have difficulties at work and with people (Thase, Frank, and Kupfer 1985:877; Hellekson 1989). Anxiety and arthritis-like pains may also be present (Pekkanen 1983:61).

Because of the question of mania and hypomania (often troublesome to diagnose) and the unreliability of client self-reports, authorities disagree on whether bipolar disorder or unipolar disorder occurs more frequently (Blehar and Rosenthal 1989:2). The DSM-III-R allows both.

Summer SAD

In their continuing studies of seasonal depressions NIMH scientists have been uncovering a growing number of individuals who suffer from the "flip side" of winter SAD—summer SAD. Those who suffer from this disorder experience depression, ranging from mild to severe, in the summertime (Wehr, Sack, and Rosenthal 1987). The symptoms, which usually begin in the late spring, include loss of appetite and a resulting weight loss, agitation, and insomnia, particularly early-morning insomnia. The symptoms are much closer to those of endogenous depression. These clients have also reported more suicidal thoughts and more depression in first-degree relatives than winter-SAD clients, but the differences were not statistically significant (Wehr et al. 1989:58).

Summertime depression has been verified in a number of countries—for example, in a British sample (Thompson and Isaacs 1988:9) and with patients in the Southern Hemisphere (Boyce and Parker 1988). Some of the individuals in the latter study seemed to have a mild form of summer SAD. They reported not feeling depressed but "in a holding action . . . not running on all cylinders"; and they tended to withdraw (Thomas Wehr, quoted in Rovner 1989:9).

SAD and other seasonal mood variations may play a role in the seasonal variations in successful suicides. Rosenthal (quoted in Krucoff 1989:13) hypothesizes that a minority of individuals do not seem able to make a "high-energy shift" in the springtime, which results in an "agitated, depressed state [that] is more dangerous in terms of suicide than is the depression of SAD." In his words, "It's like the horse pulling ahead, but the cart doesn't follow. The reins snap." If, as experts now believe, there may be more people suffering from summer SAD than winter SAD, this could explain the large number of suicides in May and June.

Although there is a consensus that winter SAD seems to be related to light, agreement is not as strong on the causes of summer SAD. Many clients believe the major factor to be the way the body responds to hot weather (Wehr et al. 1989:61). Some clients have reported relief from summer SAD by staying in airconditioned rooms, and one reported the beneficial, if sometimes impractical, effects of cold showers.

Confounding the question on etiology is that some individuals with summer SAD state their depression seems to lift when they spend time in the dark. Wehr (1989) has experimented with a number of therapeutic procedures that either block out light or lower room or body temperature, including wearing dark glasses and taking cold baths. Patients reported a lessening of symptoms in four to five days. In another systematic experiment, involving only six subjects, light and cold were tested in a crossover design (one in which the order of presentation of the stimuli is alternated). Clients responded positively to both dark and cold. These results were questioned, because the experimental variables might well have been confounded during the study (Wehr et al. 1989:60).

The Influence of Other Environmental Factors

It is obvious that in both winter and summer SAD, we are dealing with at least two manifestations of the effects of climate and other environmental variables. The two types of depression may be "exaggerated expressions of normal behavioral and physiological adaptations to environmental conditions that prevail in summer and winter, respectively" (Wehr et al. 1989:59). Another interesting speculation is that, although there are definite changes in individuals according to the length of the day and seasonal temperature, there may also be subtle, persistent shifts—that is, a "conditioned behavioral response [e.g., to] 'winter blahs and spring irritability' " that overlie these changes, especially in wintertime in the north (Lacoste and Wirz-Justice 1989:219). Seasonality may well turn out to be primarily a factor in adjustment and coping. Further research is needed, and is under way, to clarify the meaning of these effects, their etiology, their treatment, and eventually methods of prevention.

The relationship between environmental factors and depression is receiving increasing attention. Evidence is mounting that atmospheric conditions, including heat, humidity, and air pollution, worsen nonseasonal depressions, as well as other psychiatric disorders. Visits to emergency rooms for treatment of depression reportedly increase during days of low barometric pressure, and associations have been made between hot, dry winds and increased mental hospital admissions, heightened irritability, and diminished problem-solving ability. Heat may not be the cause of these difficulties, but it can be the final straw in making existing problems worse (Folkenberg and Spritzer 1989). Wehr (1989:11) advises that it is important to understand these environmental factors because evidence suggests they may trigger an episode of depression and may sometimes terminate one.

A controversial study evaluating patients reporting environmental illnesses found that almost all were suffering from, or had suffered from, such psychiatric problems as depression (Black, Rathe, and Goldstein, 1990). These problems, not environmental factors, were deemed to be the cause of their illness. Proponents of the existence of environmental illness criticized the methodology used in this study, adding that illness may result in feeling depressed. Other experts have pointed out that the depression may have been triggered by toxic chemicals in the environment (Angier 1990b).

The Diagnosis of SAD

The latest edition of the D.S.M.-III-R does not have a category for SAD. However, both bipolar and major depression can be subclassified as "seasonal pattern" (D.S.M.-III-R 1987:224).[6]

Hellekson (1989:43) has recommended modifying the manual's concept of seasonal pattern by including *seasonal psychosocial stressors* (e.g., being regularly unemployed every winter) and by adding hyperthymia to full remissions. The modified criteria for SAD would be the following:

> A. There has been a regular temporal relationship between the onset of an episode of bipolar disorder (including bipolar disorder NOS) or recurrent major depression (including depressive disorder NOS) and a particular 60–day period of the year (e.g., regular appearance of depression between the beginning of October and the end of November).

B. Full remissions . . . (or a change from depression to mania or hypomania) . . . within a particular 60–day period of the year (e.g., depression disappears from mid-February to mid-April).

C. . . . at least three episodes of mood disturbance in three separate years that demonstrated the temporal seasonal relationship defined in A and B; at least two of the years were consecutive.

D. Seasonal episodes of mood disturbance, as described above, outnumbered any nonseasonal episodes of such disturbance that may have occurred by more than three to one [Hellekson 1989:43].

The original criteria for SAD required two episodes (Rosenthal et al. 1984). This was increased to three to minimize the possibility of a diagnosis based on chance occurrence of two episodes. Two of the three must be consecutive (Spitzer and Williams 1989:83). Investigators have noticed that after the onset of SAD, it "tends to recur annually unless the patient moves to a place where day length does not decrease significantly in fall and winter" (Wurtman and Wurtman 1989:68).

Based on the available information, we recommend that formal diagnosis of SAD follow the D.S.M.-III-R. For intervention purposes, other sources should be consulted (Rosenthal and Blehar 1989, among others).

SAD in Children and Adolescents

Seasonal affective disorders have been identified in children and labeled *SAD-CA* (with *CA* signifying "children and adolescents"). The number of young people that suffer from these conditions is unknown, but the incidence is thought to be comparatively rare. (Almost 50 percent of adult SAD patients's seasonal mood swings began, however, when they were children or adolescents [Thase 1989:70].)

Still less is known about the biology of SAD-CA, in which lessened sleep and heightened irritability are exhibited, but there is less evidence of reduced activity, sadness, anxiety, and increased appetite (Sonis 1989:52). Like adults, children and adolescents apparently respond to phototherapy.

Phototherapy for SAD

Winter SAD seems to lift with a change in environment (e.g., if the patient leaves a cold, northern city in the wintertime and goes south, to a place with longer days). If that is impossible, *phototherapy*— exposure to very bright, daylight-imitating (therapeutic) light—is currently the primary treatment.

PHOTOTHERAPY BASED ON THE MELATONIN HYPOTHESIS

Currently, two hypotheses attempt to explain how light corrects the "out-of-synch" circadian cycles. The first (and older) one, associated primarily with Rosenthal and his followers, holds that light therapy suppresses melatonin, artificially lengthening the day. This is known as the *melatonin hypothesis* (Lewy et al. 1989:295–296). The phase shift hypothesis (to be discussed later) focuses on advancing the release of melatonin.

Phototherapy was first developed and evaluated on the basis of the melatonin hypothesis. Initially, it was thought that phototherapy was most effective when administered in the morning, or before dawn. Subsequent research has suggested that it can also be effective when administered in the afternoon and in the evening, after dusk. As research in this area progresses, experimenters have been evaluating different patterns, varying the time and length of exposure and the brightness of the light and alternating treatment days. Although some researchers have concluded that morning treatments are more effective (Lewy et al. 1987:353), the consensus is that time of treatment is less important than brightness of the light (Wehr et al. 1986:870). A complicating factor is that much of the research has defined effectiveness according to the melatonin hypothesis. Research based on the phase-shift hypothesis could account for some of the differences in opinion. Differences in individual responses may provide evidence of which factors are effective (Zucker 1989:157–159).

Effective phototherapy has the following characteristics: intensity of at least 2,500 lux (10,000 lux is the amount of light reaching your eyes if you look up at the sky within thirty minutes after sunrise; 500 lux is the amount in a room with average lighting) (Rosenthal 1989a; Rosenthal et al. 1989). Although some people respond better to intensities of less than 2,500 lux, experimental work indicates that some depressives may need intensities of as much as 10,000 lux. Preliminary findings show that using these intensities of light (about four times as bright as usual) may enable treatment time to be shortened without lowering effectiveness (Terman 1989:365). Light must be absorbed by the eyes, with the light spectrum visible. The type of light used is usually full-spectrum fluorescent light (Rosenthal et al. 1989:287–288). Rosenthal cautions that it is important to deal with patients' schedules and preferences in planning treatment.

Side effects of phototherapy treatment include irritability (hypomania), eyestrain, headaches, insomnia (especially if the treatment is late at night), and, very rarely, mania.

The length of treatment (exposure) is considered important but varies greatly from person to person, by time of year, amount of light, and intensity and source of light. The number of studies is still insufficient to specify more definitive criteria (Rosenthal et al. 1989:287). Treatment generally seems to be effective after approximately two to four days, and relapse occurs from two to four days after treatments are stopped (Rosenthal et al. 1989:276). In other words, to be effective, these treatments must continuously manipulate the existing body clock.[7] In the initial NIMH experiments some subjects who had improved were then given melatonin, and the depression returned immediately. When the melatonin was withdrawn, the depression lifted.

A special light box, containing fluorescent tubes, can be purchased and used in the home. The patient can engage in other activities while sitting in front of the light and occasionally must look directly at it. This has proven to be very effective for those who suffer from SAD. Researchers are in the process of developing a light box in the form of a "visor," which allows the wearer greater mobility.[8]

Current evidence suggests that individuals with other forms of depression do not seem to benefit from phototherapy (Thase, Frank, and Kupfer 1985:877). However, there is enough evidence of benefit to "justify further testing" (Kripke et al. 1989:353).

Light treatment has been called an "exciting new therapeutic modality. . . . [that] closely aligns the biology of the disorder with its treatment" (Blehar and Rosenthal 1989:2). Rosenthal (1989b) has emphasized that light is a powerful drug, with many uses. For example, it helps to mediate withdrawal from alcohol; it has been shown to raise the level of norepinephrine, which is low in depressed patients, and to normalize serotonin receptors, the dopamine system, and metabolism rates. Conversely, sensitivity to light may set off some psychiatric problems, touch off migraines, and even trigger mania (Hellekson 1989:40). Rosenthal (1989a) suggests that the use of phototherapy be considered "one tool in the treatment armamentarium."

PHOTOTHERAPY BASED ON THE PHASE-SHIFT HYPOTHESIS

Both the causes of seasonal disorders and the most effective treatment method are controversial. Wehr, one of the pioneer researchers in this area, and his followers believed that what has been called SAD "relates more to circadian rhythms than to seasonal rhythms" (Wehr et al. 1979). They agree that phototherapy is an effective treatment but believe the critical factor is not that it extends daylight but that it corrects abnormal circadian rhythms by changing the time that melatonin is released.

This theory, known as the *phase-shift hypothesis,* is based on an assumption of two phases of circadian response (the phase response curve, or PRC); one occurring in the early part of the night and one in the later part, with a defined middle point. In experiments with animals, then with humans, it was shown that exposure to a short pulse of light during the first phase produced a *phase advance*—that is, it advanced the timing of the release of melatonin, or artificially advanced dawn. Conversely, exposure to light during the latter part of the night delayed the release of melatonin, or artificially delayed dawn. Thus, "contrary to what was previously thought, human circadian rhythms can be shifted by the light–dark cycle independent of the sleep–wake rhythms" (Lewy et al. 1989:296).

These researchers also hypothesize that there are phase types of mood disorders: a *phase-advance type* and a *phase-delay type*. Winter depression is phase-delayed and is therefore treated most effectively with morning light (Lewy et al. 1989:297–298; 304).

The phase-shift hypothesis has been called highly controversial and is the subject of much ongoing evaluation (Blehar and Rosenthal 1989:6).

Additional Research Findings on SAD

Research on seasonal disorders has covered many areas, including the neurobiological, neurochemical, physiological, and behavioral aspects. The following are a few findings that are interesting and relevant: Some body functions do not vary with seasons (e.g., blood pressure, body temperature, and glucose); others are bimodal (e.g., melatonin, fatigue, depressivity [sic], and circadian phase). Some studies show different courses in males and in females (Lacoste and Wirz-Justice 1989:209). An analysis of patients beginning antidepressant drug treatment also revealed differences for males and females; men showed peak usage in June and December, whereas women showed a spring peak and a lesser winter peak (Harris, 1984, cited in Lacoste and Wirz-Justice 1989:218). Some evidence suggests that responses of SAD patients on TRH tests are higher in the winter than in the summer. Similarly, depressed patients show greater response to the DST in winter and in the higher latitudes (Lacoste and Wirz-Justice 1989:209;216). Studies on the possible role of serotonin suggest that there may well be a relationship between serotonin regulation and SAD (Jacobsen, Murphy, and Rosenthal 1989:339).

After reviewing numerous studies on the neurobiology of SAD (including catecholamines, the HPA axis, thyroid, metabolism, immune function, and so forth), Skwerer concludes that the light sensitivity seen in SAD patients may eventually prove to be a useful biological marker (Skwerer et al. 1989:327). A number of other researchers point out that genetic inheritance may play a role. They note that when a disorder such as depression occurs periodically, it may be the result of physiological susceptibility (Lacoste and Wirz-Justice 1989:167). Findings that the mood of some normal individuals is enhanced by increasing environmental light, while others do not respond positively, have led to speculation that responsive individuals might have a genetic vulnerability to SAD, especially in view of a study showing that children whose parents had bipolar disorders showed greater suppression of melatonin after exposure to light than subjects in the control group (Kasper et al. 1989:268; see also Rosenthal and Blehar 1989).

Carbohydrate Craving Obesity (CCO)

Carbohydrate craving has been identified as a common symptom of SAD. As researchers have learned more about the complexities of this condition, it has been defined as a distinct disorder and labeled *carbohydrate craving obesity (CCO)*.

Individuals suffering from CCO tend to eat normally at mealtimes, and usually select an assortment of foods, including proteins. However, they experience a craving for carbohydrates, typically in the late afternoon or early evening of every day, and then snack on very large amounts of foods high in carbohydrates. Researchers found that these snacks were generally overlooked and not reported to them.

Studies of carbohydrate cravers revealed clinical depression, as measured by the Hamilton Rating Scale for Depression and the Beck Depression Inventory (both standard tests for depression). These individuals ate not to satisfy hunger but to cope with tension, anxiety, or mental fatigue (Wurtman and Wurtman 1989:71). Eating carbohydrates made them feel calmer, and mood tests showed them to be markedly less depressed—so much so that it was speculated that consumption of excessive carbohydrates might even be a kind of self-medication or "substance abuse." The antidepressant effects are so great that individuals overindulge even though they may become obese and otherwise affect their health and physical appearance negatively. Wurtman and Wurtman (1989:71) state that perhaps two-thirds of all obese people are carbohydrate cravers.

Some carbohydrate cravers are not obese; they watch their calorie intake by eating the lower-calorie carbohydrates (e.g., unbuttered popcorn, pretzels, and unsweetened dry cereal), and they exercise to control their weight (Wurtman and Wurtman 1989). Similarly, some bulimics (bulimia is a disorder characterized by "bouts of overeating followed by voluntary vomiting" [Thomas 1989:258]) binge on carbohydrate-rich foods, but there is hardly any weight gain, even without vomiting. This type of bulimia may be, like CCO, a seasonal affective disorder (Wurtman and Wurtman 1989).

Many aspects of CCO have been investigated, including the role of the neurotransmitter serotonin, which regulates the desire for foods rich in carbohydrates. Evidence links seasonal changes to variations in the functions of serotonin (Jacobsen, Murphy, and Rosenthal 1989:334). Changes in serotonin, mood, and carbohydrate consumption may produce symptoms of depression, lethargy, inability to concentrate, and in some individuals, weight gain classified as "moderately obese (from 20 to 39 percent above ideal body weight)" to "obese (from 40 to 80 percent above ideal body weight)" (Wurtman and Wurtman 1989:69). When SAD patients with carbohydrate-craving symptoms were given phototherapy treatments, over half of the patients showed complete relief from both symptoms of depression and cravings for carbohydrates after a few days. The others showed some improvement (Terman 1988).

Speculations about the causes of CCO include a number of interesting hypotheses—for example, that the feedback mechanism that tells the brain that carbohydrates have been consumed is not operating properly and that this malfunction is greatest in the late afternoon or early evening (Wurtman and Wurtman 1989:71).[9] Wurtman (1987:230) cautions that patients with impaired serotonin functioning might seek treatment for obesity or depression or both. Sometimes one will be diagnosed as *primary* and the other as *secondary,* and vice versa. He also points out that serotonin is involved in both weight reduction and antidepressant drugs, providing a further connection between CCO and the mood disorders.

In a review of a number of studies of CCO, Kanarek and Marks-Kaufman (1991:234–235) point out that these studies did not state objective criteria for carbohydrate craving; the subjects were all self-designated. Moreover, *high-carbohydrate foods* was not well defined. Many of the foods were actually high in fat, which is highly palatable. Therefore the food craving might actually be a "desire for a pleasurable sensory experience rather than for a particular nutrient" (Kanarek and Marks-Kaufman 1991:235).

Summary of SAD

The points of agreement on SAD are the following: The condition appears frequently, the symptoms do not reflect the typical depression pattern, and phototherapy treatment is effective (Blehar and Rosenthal 1989:7). Areas of disagreement include such basic questions as the causes of SAD and how phototherapy works. The present body of knowledge is fragmented and needs to be refined into an all-inclusive theory of seasonal physiology (Lacoste and Wirz-Justice 1989:218–219). More data are needed in such important areas as clarification of the intensity and duration of phototherapy used for easing depressive symptoms and the need for further definition of the subtypes of SAD.

A great deal of research is currently being done in this area, and important findings are regularly being published, which not only have implications for economical, efficient, and effective treatment of seasonal depression but also increase our general understanding of human chronobiology.

10

Other Biological Factors and Treatments

Pharmacotherapy and Depression

Treatment with Antidepressant Medications

As the use of medication to treat depression increases, and as the type and number of drugs increase, treatment of depression requires collaboration with a psychopharmacologist or a physician with a good, current knowledge of these drugs.[1] Michael Basch, a Chicago psychoanalyst, said:

> As a psychiatrist who almost exclusively practices psychotherapy and psychoanalysis, I have found that psychopharmacology has become so complex as to constitute a sub-specialty beyond my ken. With patients like Dr. Osgood [note: a pseudonym], for whom both psychotherapy and medication are indicated, I still prescribe simple antidepressant medication to accompany my psychotherapeutic efforts. If, however, satisfactory results are not forthcoming, I refer that person, after discussing the situation with him or her, to a colleague skilled in such matters while I continue to conduct the psychotherapy [Basch 1988:118].

In a collaborative treatment approach, psychotherapists and other mental health professionals must be well informed about the antidepressant drugs, to ensure that their clients are treated properly by whoever is prescribing the medication. Drug treatment is *not* a precise science, and often it is not carefully controlled. Confounding the issue of drug effectiveness is that of patient compliance (Blackwell 1979). However, practitioners who follow the established guidelines should be able to provide their clients with the most effective, least harmful, and most economical treatment available for each individual.

We believe that currently, there is a great deal of inappropriate medicating of depressed patients, often through insufficient knowledge and experience but also through inadequate monitoring and control. Baldessarini (1990:5) points out that antidepressants should be used more often and in higher dosages. He feels that despite the risks, proper medication would actually decrease the mortality rate for those who are depressed.

Guidelines for Using Antidepressant Medications

We are summarizing the broad clinical guidelines developed to help the medical practitioner use drugs to treat depression (Bassuk, Schoonover, and Gelenberg 1983:9–18). These are the following:

1. The patient should be interviewed and a complete history taken; if this is not possible, the significant others should be interviewed.
2. Use drugs only when no nonbiological treatments are as effective, but do not withhold them if they can help the patient.
3. Select the drug that provides the greatest benefit with the lowest risk.
4. Learn the pharmacokinetics (explained later) of each drug, as well as the differences between the types of preparations.
5. Prescribe the smallest effective dose for the shortest amount of time, and use the least complicated regimen in order to enhance compliance.[2]
6. When there is a choice, use the least expensive drug (e.g., a generic drug) and try to avoid combining medications.[3]
7. Take additional precautions with patients who are medically ill.
8. Form a therapeutic relationship with the patient, encouraging him to participate in his care.
9. Complete a clinical drug trial by administering the drug until it is effective, has immediate adverse effects, or proves ineffective.

The *pharmacokinetic* characteristics of drugs include the rate at which they are absorbed by the body, distributed, metabolized, and eliminated. These factors, which determine how soon a drug will take effect and how long the effect will last, are considered when determining the amount and timing of the drug regimen. Pharmacotherapists usually consider a drug's *half-life*—that is, the time it takes for half of a dosage of a drug to be eliminated from the body. If patients take a new dose of medication before the previous dose has been eliminated, the drug accumulates in their body tissues. This affects how individuals tolerate this drug and may increase the potential for side effects and addiction.

All patients are not the same. A particular medication can well have different effects on different patients.[4] It may also affect the same patient differently at different times, because the internal environment of the body changes constantly. For example, psychotropic drugs seem to affect women differently at various stages of the menstrual cycle. Men too may react differently to a drug at different times (Kahn 1991). Patients also vary in their compliance in taking medications, and not all patients comply to the same extent at all times. These important variables should be taken into consideration in the prescription and monitoring process.

The Availability of Drugs

Another important factor in determining treatment is the choice of drugs. Many drugs are currently being marketed. Experts agree that a good number of them are inadequate and need to be improved. These problems were discussed at a recent conference sponsored by the National Foundation for Depressive Illnesses and the Center for the Study of Drug Development. The conference report stated that, of the millions of patients receiving drug treatment, about one-third do not benefit, and many others discontinue taking medications because of negative side effects (Thompson 1989).

Developing new drugs presents many problems, including identifying or designing potentially effective substances and testing them sufficiently to receive FDA approval—an expensive, often time-consuming process with legal risks. Because of these factors, members of the conference committee agreed the government should take some action and recommended the following: setting up a panel to review drugs currently used in other countries, thus bypassing the lengthy F.D.A. review process; searching for ways to test new drugs in women of childbearing age (currently prohibited by the F.D.A.); and doing more research on the body's blood-brain barrier, which prevents many potentially effective substances from entering the brain (as we shall discuss later).[5] Calling for a major government initiative, a prominent member of the conference group, Louis Lasagna, suggested that "patient advocacy groups have the best shot at getting Congress's attention . . . [as] advocates for mental patients are the most credible and the least criticizable" (Thompson 1989).

A serious impediment to the development and use of drugs to treat depression is found in the brain itself. This is the blood-brain barrier, which we discussed in chapter 8. Researchers are concentrating on ways to breach the barrier safely—that is, without affecting its ability to protect the brain from bacteria and other harmful substances. One way is to develop new medications such as peptides (made from protein), which might fit into existing receptors in the brain. Monoclonal antibodies ("clones of immune system proteins that bind only to specific receptors" [Fisher 1991]) are also being developed as carriers. Another possible way of safely crossing the barrier might be to flood its cells with a rich solution of glucose. The theory is that this should temporarily shrink the tightly packed barrier cells and result in some gaps that would allow medications to pass through. Another possibility would be to try to link a medication to a fatty molecule, thus facilitating its entry. Researchers are also attempting to develop molecules that will open the nutrient "doors" so that existing medications can be pushed in.

A leading authority on depression, Ross J. Baldessarini, is concerned that, because antidepressant medications are felt to be so effective, there has been a decrease in rigorously controlled experiments, with less emphasis on the use of placebos, and an inappropriate inclusion of less seriously depressed persons or atypical patients who do not improve with other treatments. He emphasizes that since "our understanding of [the] mood disturbances remains incomplete . . . [and] there are . . . biologically dissimilar types of depression, . . . we should not expect all antidepressants to . . . have a common action. A more coherent theory of antidepressant activity (and of depression itself) is needed to guide the development of better drugs. Meanwhile, . . . [we need] . . . broader clinical experimentation even at the risk of side effects" (Baldessarini 1990:6).

We recommend that mental health professionals who work with depressed patients follow the developments and debates in this important area and actively advocate changes—such as more rapid and more open communication on research and the effects of drugs—that will improve treatment for depressed individuals. They should also encourage and support patient advocacy groups in these efforts.[6]

Lithium

■■ Lithium (actually, lithium salt, a naturally occurring mineral)
■■ is widely used in the treatment of the mood disorders, primarily the bipolar disorders. Its utility in treating mania was discovered by an Australian physician in 1949. It began to be widely used in Europe a decade later but was not used in the United States until about 1970. The delay was due to lack of commercial interest in developing this inexpensive, unpatentable mineral (Baldessarini and Cole 1988:500) and to early reports that it was unsafe. These studies were later shown to have been poorly controlled.

Lithium is now considered a very beneficial drug, both for the acute states of mania and for maintenance. Rates of symptom relief range from 70 to 80 percent, within ten to fourteen days of initial administration. Good evidence exists for its effectiveness in preventing recurring mania, and both manic and (to a lesser degree) depressive episodes in bipolar disorders (Baldessarini and Cole 1988:502). Long-term lithium management (one to five years) also seems to reduce symptoms in recurrent unipolar depression (Lepkifker, Horesh, and Floru 1988). Increasingly, lithium is being combined with the tricyclic antidepressants for difficult and recalcitrant cases (Murray 1990; Kim, Delva, and Lawson 1990). With very disruptive patients, sedative and antipsychotic drugs are often given first.

Only fifty thousand patients currently receive this drug, but an estimated one million or more persons could benefit from it (Baldessarini and Cole 1988:501). Some observers speculate that doctors are reluctant to use it because they lack knowledge of its properties and because of the persistence of early controversies surrounding its use.

Lithium is generally prescribed for patients who clearly have a bipolar disorder. However, not all bipolar patients respond to it, and others cannot tolerate its side effects. It is usually given during acute episodes of mania or hypomania, most often while a patient is hospitalized (Baldessarini and Cole 1988:502). If lithium is properly prescribed and monitored, it may be given for a long time; it is considered a safe and effective drug.

Before taking lithium, the patient must have a complete medical evaluation, including tests of cardiovascular, thyroid, and kidney function. In addition, a family history should be taken. Those with a family history of bipolar disorders seem to be good candidates for long-term treatment with this drug (Mendlewicz 1985:808).

It is very important that patients receiving lithium comply with stringent therapeutic instructions. Lithium is a powerful medication with a narrow *therapeutic index:* The therapeutic dosage is close to the lethal dosage. Since the patient must take the medication two or three times a day to lessen the risk of toxicity, the difficulties of proper compliance are increased. The patient must also carefully observe a number of dietary restrictions, particularly limiting the intake of substances that raise or lower the blood levels of lithium. For example, tea and coffee are diuretics that cause such decreases.

Prescribing the right amount of lithium is crucial. The dosage must be sufficient to be therapeutic but must not reach a toxic level. With many psychotropic drugs, this is accomplished by trial and error. Obviously, this is inappropriate with lithium (Noll, David, and DeLeon-Jones 1985:258). There is a simple test that predicts proper dosage on the basis of the amount of lithium in a patient's blood sample (Cooper, Bergnor, and Simpson 1973; Cooper and Simpson 1976). Since this amount can vary greatly between individuals, as well as within individuals at different times of day, routine blood monitoring is extremely important. Periodic monitoring of thyroid and kidney function is also indicated (Gelenberg, Bassuk, and Schoonover 1991).

After lithium is administered, the dosage is increased very slowly until the drug reaches the desired level. The response to lithium seems to be "all or none"; the patient *must* reach the proper blood level to benefit from the drug. In fact, underprescribing the drug seems to be the most frequent reason for treatment failure in patients who might otherwise benefit from lithium (Alda 1988).

The patient must be advised of the many common substances that may interact negatively with the lithium and produce toxicity. These include such common drugs as ibuprofen and aspirin (Schvehla et al. 1987). Anything that increases or decreases the amount of fluid in the blood will affect the concentration and absorption of lithium and must be taken into account. This includes heavy perspiration or urination (e.g., due to such diuretics as tea and coffee), retention of excessive amounts of fluid, loss of blood, vomiting, diarrhea, and so on. This is a complicated situation, as some of these conditions may be side effects of taking the lithium. Or they may be related to side effects. For example, the patient may exercise more to offset weight gain—a side effect—which may produce excessive perspiration, especially in the summertime.

Lithium has a number of potentially negative side effects. In most patients who can tolerate the drug these are transient mild gastrointestinal symptoms (e.g., stomach pain, nausea, vomiting, and occasional diarrhea) and decrease in appetite. More severe symptoms, especially those associated with central nervous system functioning, may indicate lithium poisoning. Some early signs are heightened tremor, with shaky handwriting; general weakness and drowsiness; ataxia (lack of coordination, especially of voluntary movements); giddiness; slurred speech; blurred vision; and tinnitus (Baldessarini and Cole 1988:504–505). Other symptoms include changes in electroencephalogram (EEG), electrocardiogram (EKG), and number of white blood cells; weight gain; diabetes insipidus; and hypothyroidism. Troublesome skin rashes, cardiovascular problems, and kidney malfunctioning may also occur.

One side effect, not spoken of enough, is that even though the extreme ups and downs of bipolar illness or mania are curbed by lithium, psychological and social problems may remain. Paradoxically, because of lithium's effectiveness in regulating mood, many therapists overlook the social and psychological problems that may remain and that need to be treated with psychotherapy. Not addressing them can lead to noncompliance and relapse, worsening the situation of the patient, particularly the bipolar patient (Van Gent, Vida, and Zwart 1988).

Patients who tolerate lithium seem to be able to take it for a long time. A study of life satisfaction and adjustment of fifty patients with unipolar and fifty with bipolar disorders being treated with lithium found that neither lithium nor the mood disorder lessened satisfaction or interfered with functioning during remission (Lepkifker, Horesh, and Floru 1988).

From 20 to 40 percent of patients with bipolar disorders do not seem to improve or cannot stand the side effects of lithium (Wise 1989). For those who cannot tolerate lithium, some alternate drugs are often effective—for example, carbamazepine (Tegretol), an anticonvulsant. In one study, 80 percent of twenty-four patients treated with carbamazepine improved, with infrequent side effects (Stuppaeck et al. 1990). The drug has some adverse effects, primarily skin reactions and blood and kidney disorders, most of which seem to appear in the first two months of therapy (Askmark and Wiholm 1990). Carbamazepine is being given in combination with lithium, with very promising results for serious affective disorders (Kramlinger and Post 1990).[7] It is also used for "rapid-cyclers, [these are] bipolar patients with four or more affective episodes per year" (Bauer and Whybrow 1991:191).

Patients who cannot be relied upon to comply with medication regimes are considered poor risks for lithium treatment, as are those who are impulsive or suicidal, unless the substance is given in a controlled environment such as a hospital (Baldessarini and Cole 1988:502). Pregnant women who must take lithium have to be supervised very closely in the first trimester. Additional precautions must also be observed with elderly patents. Since lithium is eliminated through the kidneys—a process that usually slows with aging—the half-life of lithium increases. Therefore the dosages for elderly patients must be decreased, sometimes by as much as 50 percent. Elderly patients are also more prone to the serious side effects of lithium (Stoudemire and Blazer 1985:560–561).

Lithium has been used successfully for over four decades. However, despite much research and theoretical speculation, how it works is still not understood (Noll, Davis, and DeLeon-Jones 1985:263), but there is great interest in discovering how this simple substance relieves symptoms so effectively. Researchers hope that this understanding would shed light on the causes of depression.

Conversely, one expert stated that "[perhaps] if we understood better the chemical and electrical abnormalities at the root of depression and mania, we might see more clearly how a simple metal lends a very welcome hand" (DePaulo 1989:147). Research on the postsynaptic phase of neurotransmission (discussed in chapter 6) has led to a theory that the remedial action of lithium is located in one of the second messenger systems (Hyman 1988d:374). Another recent theory is that lithium heightens serotonin operations by offsetting as yet unspecified abnormalities of serotonin. This is taken as additional evidence for a serotonin hypothesis of depression (Price et al. 1990).

Lithium has been called a miracle drug. Many anecdotal records and recent autobiographies by celebrities have attested to its power and have described lives that were torturous before the diagnosis of bipolar disorder and the administration of lithium. (See, for example, the autobiography of the film star Patty Duke [Duke and Turan 1987].)

Another famous sufferer from manic depression was the late Broadway director Joshua Logan. He spoke very frankly and eloquently of his life-long struggle with the extreme ups and downs of manic depression and the relief he experienced from lithium. In his own words:

Free! For the first time in my life. Free from the fear I have waked up with since I was a youth: the fear of my illness, manic depression. It's not just an illness; it is like a ride on the giant swing at Coney Island. It swoops its victims from low to high without warning—from ink black depression where life is all hopelessness and despair to a wild state past happiness and joy of life to the upper regions of irresponsibility. . . . Free and unfettered willfulness takes over until the patient must be incarcerated to protect those around him. (Logan 1978:342)

Describing how he felt after he began taking lithium in 1969, he stated:

Although I no longer ever reach an elated state where I make no sense, I am still as volatile as I have always been. I yell and jump around when enthusiastic. I can write or direct and cast plays or pictures with the same zeal. . . . I talk passionately to actors. I am still recognizable as myself. I go far in my moods, but not beyond reality into fantasy. (Logan 1978:343)

Logan's writings indicate that taking lithium did not interfere with his creativity. Recent studies on the association between manic depression and creative abilities have shown that this may occur among a minority of artists, especially when patients are taking higher doses of lithium and their moods are not carefully monitored (Raymond 1989).

Electroconvulsive Therapy (ECT)

■■ No psychiatric treatment is more controversial than electro-
■■ convulsive therapy (ECT)—a direct but highly technical procedure that artificially induces a therapeutic brain seizure by passing an electric current through the recipient's brain (Fink 1990b:77).

ECT was developed in 1934 by a Hungarian psychiatrist, Laszlo Meduna, who had observed that individuals suffering from epilepsy (which is characterized by brain seizures) did not suffer from schizophrenia. He hypothesized that artificially producing seizures or convulsions in schizophrenics might relieve their psychotic symptoms. His initial observation was wrong. Epilepsy and schizophrenia can exist in the same individual. His hypothesis about the therapeutic effects of the convulsions proved to be correct (Wender and Klein 1981:144). He succeeded in producing seizures by using camphor, which had a number of undesirable effects. Several years later, two Italian doctors, Ugo Cerletti and Lucino Bini, used electric current, which was equally effective but had fewer negative consequences.

ECT was first used in the United States in the 1940s with a number of conditions, particularly schizophrenia, although later evidence showed it was not the most effective treatment for this disorder. It was also used excessively. The senior author of this book, who worked as a mental hospital attendant in the late 1940s, often encountered patients who had received fifty, seventy-five, and even a hundred or more treatments, which, to make matters worse, were often given on several consecutive days!

The immoderate (in retrospect) use of electric current—often as much as 150 volts—(O'Connor 1985) produced violent contractions. Broken bones were common side effects. The mortality rate was high—0.1 percent (one death per one thousand patients) (NIH/NIMH Consensus Statement 1985). Nevertheless, it was considered a humanitarian treatment, compared to existing treatments for schizophrenics and other "unruly" patients, which included coma induced with insulin, heavy sedation, psychosurgery (particularly lobotomies) and restraints by wet-sheet packs and even straitjackets (Squire 1987). Unfortunately, it was also used as a punitive disciplinary procedure, particularly when there were staff shortages (e.g., during World War II) (O'Connor 1985). This was vividly portrayed in the popular movie "One Flew Over the Cuckoo's Nest."

In the mid-1950s, methodology began to change significantly. ECT treatment now has been modified and greatly improved since its early days. The average number of treatments has been reduced to between six and twelve, which are generally given two to three times per week over a three- to four-week period (Frankel 1988:581; American Psychiatric Association 1990:108). The equipment has been refined, and two new types of machines are in use: One provides a constant and slow electric current, and one provides constant voltage consisting of a series of very small pulses. Both use considerably less electrical current than earlier machines, and both seem equally effective (Railton et al. 1987; Fox, Rosen, and Campbell 1989). The Task Force Report (American Psychiatric Association 1990:101) states that a "constant-current brief pulse stimulus is recommended for routine use . . . [although] higher energy waveforms . . . may be effective in otherwise refractory cases, though present evidence for such an effect is not convincing." Other technicalities of application have also been refined, including the placement of the electrodes. Until recently it was felt that placing both electrodes on one side of the temple (unilateral placement) was more effective than the earlier method of placement on opposing sides (bilateral). The evidence is now less clear-cut and both approaches have their advocates (Frankel 1990:80). Other changes include the type of current used (described earlier), the amount of current (between 80 and 170 volts) and the length of time it is administered (currently ranging from 0.5 to 1.0 second) (Frankel 1988:580). The latest report avoided specifying a stimulus intensity, citing that "seizure threshold varies among patients over a 40–fold range" (American Psychiatric Association 1990:104).

More attention is paid to preparing the patient for treatment by administering such drugs as muscle relaxants, to lessen the possibility of bone breakage from spasms; tranquilizers and anesthetics that allow the patient to sleep during the treatment; and atropine, which prevents irregular cardiac rhythms (Frankel 1988:580; American Psychiatric Association 1990:97–99.)

The improvements in ECT methodology virtually eliminated bone fractures as a side effect of treatment and reduced the mortality from one per thousand in the early years of treatment, to 2.9 per ten thousand (or about one in over thirty-four hundred). This is the "risk . . . associated with the use of short-acting barbiturate anesthetics" (NIH/NIMH Consensus Statement 1985:3). Another source reported 4.5 deaths per 100,000 treatments (about one in over twenty-two thousand) (NIH/NIMH Consensus Statement 1985:3).

ECT treatment can result in a number of adverse and potentially dangerous reactions, including rapid and/or irregular heartbeat, hypotension, and high blood pressure. If these changes occur, they usually do not last long. For a short time the patient may also feel confused, have sore muscles and a headache, and experience a loss of memory, which may persist for a time after treatment. Some experts claim that these losses are short-lived and that memory returns to normal within several weeks. In follow-up studies some patients report much longer periods.

There are obviously great individual differences in both objective and subjective perception of memory loss. The Consensus Report cited studies showing that self-reports by patients, as long as three years after treatment, indicated a subjective perception of memory loss. However, it states that a contributing factor might be that elderly patients treated with ECT may be more conscious of some of the "normal" memory loss that occurs with age and attribute this loss to the treatment (NIH/NIMH Consensus Statement 1985:3). These varying and disputed degrees of memory loss (and alleged brain damage) have created so much conflict among professionals and lay persons that much of the debate is based on ideology and belief rather than on data.

Accurate diagnosis and assessment are essential to maximize the benefits of ECT and minimize the risk. Potential candidates should be carefully screened, with an extensive history-taking, physical examination, and laboratory tests. Selection should be on the basis of type and severity of the depression, degree of the patient's suffering, risk of suicide, treatment options, personal factors, and medical status (American Psychiatric Association 1990:90–92, 98–101).[8] *Informed consent*—a legal procedure that implies the patient is competent and understands the risks of a treatment—is required. This means a prospective patient may refuse treatment. This is a complex and disputed process. When consent *is* obtained, treatments should be administered by trained, qualified professionals who closely monitor the patient before, during, and after the treatments. These issues, particularly informed consent, are spelled out in the Task Force Report (American Psychiatric Association 1990).

The customary treatment procedure is to use ECT when a patient is extremely depressed and to stop using it when symptoms ease. *Continuation therapy* used to be standard treatment after ECT but was discontinued, giving rise to recent speculations that clients were being undertreated and may need either continuation or maintenance ECT, possibly in combination with antidepressant medication and/or lithium to lessen the chance of relapse (Fink 1990a:8).

The increased use of antidepressant medications in the 1970s was paralleled by a decrease in the use of ECT. As it became clear that some patients were not helped by these medications, the use of ECT began to increase. For those 20–30 percent of depressed patients who do not respond to medication, ECT is said to have an improvement rate of from 80 to 90 percent (O'Connor 1985).

ECT with Children and Adolescents

Although ECT has been used with children as young as four years old, the literature is contradictory and its use with children and adolescents has not been included in the various consensus statements and task force reports. A number of case and clinical reports exist, but there seems to have been no systematic and controlled study of ECT in children and adolescents (Guttmacher and Cretella 1988). Guttmacher and Cretella, in reviewing this anecdotal literature, report contradictory opinions (1988). They surveyed physicians who had seen over one thousand patients and gleaned case reports of four patients, only one of which showed a positive response to treatment, even though three of the four did exhibit seizures that were predictive of successful response in adults (Guttmacher and Cretella 1988). McGough, McCall, and Shelp (1989) pointed out, in response to Guttmacher and Cretella, that ECT is most effective in major depression and that only one of the children received that diagnosis. They concluded that "ECT [is] a safe and effective treatment in selected childhood disorders . . . [especially] since depressive disorders in children and adolescents are often refractory to treatment" (McGough, McCall, and Shelp 1989:106). In their response, Guttmacher, Cretella, and Houghtalen (1989:106–107) present a fifth case and defend their assertion of the unproven efficacy of ECT in children and adults. They do agree on the need for extended research.

The Consensus Conference and the Task Force Report on ECT

Because of recurring questions about the efficacy, safety, and ethical use of ECT, the NIH and NIMH convened a special "Consensus Development Conference on Electroconvulsive Therapy" on June 2, 1985. Discussants included physicians, various other health and mental health professionals, epidemiologists, lawyers, and interested lay people. They evaluated all the current evidence, and their findings were published as a "Consensus Development Conference Statement" (vol. 5, no. 11). It is this Consensus Statement to which we have referred in these pages, as well as the more recent Task Force Report of the American Psychiatric Association (APA), which also was interdisciplinary, although it consisted primarily of psychiatrists (American Psychiatric Association 1990).[9]

The Consensus Statement indicated that in 1980 an estimated 33,384 patients were treated with ECT—2.4 percent of all admissions to psychiatric facilities. This percentage has certainly risen. Other yearly estimates state that ECT is given to about 100,000 patients (Squires 1987), eighty-eight thousand (The American Psychiatric Association), and between thirty-five thousand and 100,000 (The National Institute of Mental Health 1985) (Frankel 1988:586). The preliminary report of the APA Task Force (1990) did not give these data.

The Task Force Report (American Psychiatric Association 1990:87—88) stated that ECT is an effective treatment for all subtypes of unipolar major depression, the bipolar disorders, all subtypes of mania, and several types of schizophrenia as well as other disorders. Its primary use is where there is a "need for rapid, definitive response . . . [and where the] risks of other treatments outweigh the risks of ECT, . . . [if the patient has had a] history of poor drug response and/or good ECT . . . [and if the] patient [states a] preference [for ECT]" (American Psychiatric Association 1990:86). ECT can be used as a second choice of treatment when primary-choice therapies fail or have an adverse effect such as marked patient deterioration (American Psychiatric Association 1990:87–88).

ECT was evaluated as particularly effective for delusional and severe endogenous depressions—an important minority of depressive disorders. A review of pertinent studies showed ECT to be at least as effective as the tricyclics and more effective than the MAO inhibitors. It was about as effective as lithium for acute mania, and both were superior to hospitalization without somatic therapy. The Consensus Review Committee stated, "Not a single controlled study has shown another form of treatment to be superior to ECT in the short-term management of severe depressions." The Consensus Statement cautions that these studies concentrated on the short term, which restricts interpretation of the results (NIMH Consensus Report 1985).

In the past, ECT had not been recommended for reactive depressions, especially when the external stressor was recent and the person had not been depressed long. It was not used when a number of medical conditions coexisted with the depression, although quite elderly patients frequently received it. Since the term *reactive depression* is not used in the D.S.M.-III-R, the Task Force Report did not specifically refer to it. However, it specified all subtypes of major depression, in essence, endorsing its use for this type of mood disorder. Although ECT was used extensively in the past for schizophrenia, neuroleptic drugs are now recommended as first choice.

ECT allegedly works faster than medication, with one source stating that most patients showed "significant improvement" in one week and some complete recovery after a "single treatment" (Noll, Davis, and DeLeon-Jones 1985:272). These authors cite a growing body of evidence of the effectiveness of ECT with severely depressed individuals who do not respond to medications and/or to psychotherapy and who show vegetative symptoms such as sleep disturbance, weight loss, and diminished sex drive. Patients with delusions are also thought to be responsive to the treatment. A high risk of suicide is another indicator cited for using ECT, especially because of its immediate short-term effectiveness.

The rate of relapse after treatment is significantly lower for patients receiving periodic continuation ECT after remission (Fink 1990a:8), and the Consensus Report recommends it. The timing will vary. For example, some elderly patients require treatments every one to four weeks, followed by decreasing amounts until treatments can be terminated in approximately six to twelve months. Some may require additional treatments (Frances, Weiner, and Coffey 1989:242).

Current Controversies Over ECT

There are many detailed descriptions of the effects of ECT but not much convincing evidence of how it works. As one observer said, "the knowledge of how ECT works is primitive, [but] the technology is state-of-the-art" (O'Connor 1985). Fink (1990b:77) feels that, although the exact mode of operation is unknown, knowledge of ECT "is broad; we seem to know as much (or more) about the central effects of ECT as we know about other psychiatric therapies. . . . [We] no longer need [to] apologize to recommend its use. . . . [T]he efficacy of ECT . . . [is as great for depression] as that of psychotherapy or pharmacotherapy."

There have been a number of useful findings and some interesting speculations on the workings of ECT. For example, a 1984 NIMH study measured "before" and "after" levels of "three neurotransmitter systems—serotonin, norepinephrine and dopamine—that have been associated with major depression." The researchers, who had hypothesized that the actions of ECT would parallel those of antidepressant medications, were surprised to find that "ECT has almost no effect on the first two systems and a striking influence on the third" (Squires 1987). In studies investigating the effects of ECT on the sleep/wake cycle, measurements of results showed improvement. A number of studies compared the effects of ECT and tricyclic antidepressants in treating depression. However, a review of nine of these controlled studies concluded that all were methodologically deficient and did not provide conclusive evidence one way or the other (Rifkin 1988).

Matthew Rudorfer (who currently directs ECT research at NIMH) stated that he believes ECT "does more than simply raise or lower critical substances in the brain. . . . It's something about the balance" (quoted in Squires 1987). Max Fink, a psychiatrist at the State University of New York at Buffalo, feels that in "major depressive disorders . . . something's missing in the brain . . . [and] the seizure stimulates the brain to produce what's missing (quoted in Bor 1989).

Research findings fueled the burgeoning conflict over the use of ECT and provided justification both for those in favor of its use and for those against it. This controversy currently focuses primarily on its negative side effects and on the issue of informed consent to treatment.

The main argument advanced by many proponents of ECT treatment is that in many case situations "nothing works as well as ECT" (Robert Temple, quoted in Bor 1989). The advocates, including many psychiatrists and other medically trained therapists, deny or minimize the claims of serious negative effects, such as severe or permanent memory loss and possible brain damage. They do not deny the importance of informed consent but believe that the side effects are often overstated, which tends to frighten patients who could benefit from ECT treatment, and they consider this unethical (Squires 1987). They also emphasize that the treatment is economical. Studies have shown that patients receiving ECT spent an average of thirteen fewer days in the hospital than patients on antidepressant medication, with average savings of $6,400 (Markowitz et al. 1987).

Among the most enthusiastic advocates of ECT are some of the patients who have received it and their family members. A moving account was given by a psychiatrist whose fifty-two-year-old father became severely depressed. Over a two-year period he was treated, in succession, in three well-known and highly regarded psychiatric hospitals. He received contradictory diagnoses and various combinations of medications and psychotherapies, with no positive results. Finally, he entered a small suburban hospital, where he received ECT and in six weeks he was "cured." He returned to work, and saw a psychiatrist only one more time. There was "no insight, no awareness, no motivation to get well. There remains no evidence of depression or any other illness" (D'Agostino 1975). There have been many similar reports, although in most cases, one of the psychotherapies was combined with the ECT.

Proponents of ECT are not without their criticism of it. Rudorfer, a physician who has used it extensively, has called it a "dirty drug . . . [using it is] taking a giant paint brush to touch up a tiny crack—you get the job done, but in the process you do some unnecessary painting." He hopes that ECT will eventually be replaced (Matthew Rudorfer, quoted in Squires 1987). The director of a support group for ECT patients and their significant others, stated, "A lot of us view ECT as the one thing we can rely on if all else fails. . . . It scares me. But I like knowing it is there" (Nancy Scheff, quoted in Squires 1987).

Opponents of ECT also include both physicians and patients. In 1978 the American Psychiatric Association polled psychiatrists and found that "one-third . . . were generally opposed or 'more opposed than favorable' to its use" (O'Connor 1985). (It was not clear, in the O'Connor report, whether this opposition stemmed from a negative view of the treatment or a reluctance to use a controversial procedure.) A prominent psychiatrist feels that evidence of long-term benefits of ECT is lacking (John Pinel, quoted in O'Connor 1985). One widely cited author has asserted that ECT is really a form of legalized brain damage (Breggin 1991).

Former patients are also among the most outspoken critics of ECT. There have been moving testimonies, mostly about how the resulting loss of memory rendered them unable to continue their former work, ruining their careers and their lives. Many reports are mixed: A patient whose depression caused her to be "almost catatonic" was vastly improved by ECT treatment. However, six months later she stated, "I guess you can't put me down as totally against ECT, because I am functioning and talking to you as a well individual. But I wish I wouldn't have had to pay the price for it of having such memory loss and not being able to use my brain in the intellectual fashion that I was used to" (O'Connor 1985).

Critics of ECT believe that it is very important that individuals considering treatment be made aware of all of the negative side effects. This can be difficult as patients who are being considered for ECT are usually too depressed or disturbed to understand the many aspects of the treatment. As discussed earlier, many opponents of ECT believe that the side effects are much more severe than most doctors who offer the treatments believe.

The Consensus Report (NIH/NIMH Consensus Report 1985) and the Task Force of the American Psychiatric Association (American Psychiatric Association 1990:90–93) emphasize the importance of the consent process and suggest that consent be reexamined periodically, with the patient's family involved if the patient agrees to this. Some hospitals have developed videotapes showing interviews with patients who have received ECT and presenting the procedure and explaining its risks and benefits. These videotapes have been found to be an effective means of educating the prospective patient and/or his family (Squires 1987). A New York State task force on "Life and the Law" recommended that every patient appoint a "health care proxy," who could act on his behalf, in the event that he or she was unable to do so (Squires 1987).

Some former ECT recipients have become politically active, monitoring what goes on in regard to this treatment.[10] In fact, a long-time recipient was responsible for instituting a successful campaign to ban ECT in Berkeley, California, in 1982. In 1991 the San Francisco Board of Supervisors passed a resolution "repudiating ECT and urging that its use be restricted" (Cody 1991). Over thirty-five states currently have laws limiting its use. The irony is that the depressed patient who is now admitted to an expensive private hospital or treatment facility is more likely to receive ECT, as these facilities do not seem to be as restricted as the larger, public state hospitals, which are subject to direct political control.

ECT treatments can be given on an outpatient basis; a typical series costs about $5,000 (Boodman 1990b). Ablow (1990b) points out that since ECT is inexpensive and is not profitable to industry, psychiatrists are not flooded with the usual hard-sell literature on it. This affects the acceptability of the treatment, and contributes to psychiatrists' unwillingness to use it.

Summary of ECT

It may very well be that future developments in medications and other therapies will make ECT obsolete. However, in view of the current lack of effective treatment for some of the very severe depressions, ECT remains a tenable treatment, to be used only after careful study and diagnosis.

We agree that much additional research is needed not only on how ECT works but on specifying the conditions under which it is successful and unsuccessful, and spelling out more precisely the groups of patients for whom the treatment is either helpful or harmful. We also agree with the final recommendation in the Consensus Task Force Statement that, "A national survey should be conducted on the manner and extent of ECT use in the United States" (Consensus Statement 1985:6).

Substance Abuse and Depression

The Use of Drugs of Abuse

Stimulant and sedative drugs, as well as a variety of other substances, are used widely by people who are trying to ward off or cope with depression. The stimulants may provide an immediate but short-lived "high"; and opiates may provide a temporary numbing of physical and emotional pain as well as a transient euphoria. These short-lived effects are followed by a "crash" that can be devastating, sometimes more devastating than the depression. Furthermore, these substances can have some severe consequences, such as triggering paranoid reactions. Needless to say, these drugs are not recommended for treating depression, and the practitioner must be aware that patients might use them as a form of self-medication.

Depression is obviously not the only reason that people use these chemicals. Among other reasons, they are also used for avoidance and escape, to conform to peer group influences, to feel good, and to attempt to deal with frustration and feelings of powerlessness (Boodman 1989:12). However, a bout of depression is often what brings a drug abuser into a treatment program, where he or she then receives a dual diagnosis. For example, opiate abusers suffer from "chronic low level of depressive symptoms punctuated by exacerbations when stressed" (Lehman 1985:679). This sequence, of the interplay of depression and substance abuse, also occurs with a number of other drugs. In addition, depression frequently accompanies withdrawal from a variety of drugs of abuse.

The issues around the causes and treatment of substance abuse are complex, and most are beyond the scope of this book. Here we shall briefly review some aspects that are relevant to depression. Because there are many commonalities, we shall discuss the drugs of abuse as a group, except for alcohol. Alcohol is of particular interest to us because of the many individuals who are dually diagnosed as depressed and alcoholic and because depressed alcoholics tend to abuse other drugs as well as alcohol (Schuckit:1983a).

The Drugs of Abuse

Many substances are currently being abused. Some, such as alcohol and nicotine, can be obtained lawfully; others are illegal. The patterns of use vary, as do the substances, with new ones being marketed periodically. These drugs may be classified in different ways—for example, by "chemical similarities, the tendency to cause similar behavioral outcomes, activity at identical sites in the brain, or classification in the same schedule under federal and state law" (Roffman 1987:478). We have grouped them by behavioral outcome, as follows: the *sedatives* (sometimes referred to as sedative-hypnotics) and the *central nervous system depressants*, which calm and tranquilize. These include the barbiturates such as phenobarbital (trade name Amytal; called "blues") and others (e.g., Nembutal, or "yellow jackets," and Seconal, or "reds"—"red jackets"). Benzodiazepines—Valium, Dalmane, and Librium, among others—are also in this class. *Alcohol,* although in a separate category, is also categorized as a sedative.

The opposite effect is produced by the *stimulants* (central nervous system stimulants), which produce a brief but powerful and energizing rush (period of euphoria). These are the amphetamines and amphetamine derivatives, including Dexedrine, Ritalin, and Benzedrine; and *cocaine* (in a separate category), including "crack" and "ice," which are smokable forms of cocaine and methamphetamine and are currently widely used. Nicotine and caffeine are also classified as stimulant drugs. *Opiates* (*narcotics*; sometimes called narcotic-analgesics) include some that are found naturally—such as opium, morphine, and codeine—and some that are semi- or completely synthetic, including heroin, and drugs with the trade names Percodan, Dilaudid, Demerol, Darvon, and Talwin. The opiates also produce a euphoric rush, followed by a profound sense of tranquility (Mirin and Weiss 1983:223). *Psychedelic drugs* (*hallucinogens*) such as LSD (D-lysergic acid diethylamide) and PCP (phencyclidine; also called "angel dust," "crystal," and "hog") produce disorientation and distortions in perception. *Marijuana,* a complex drug that is in a separate category, has both sedative and stimulant (euphoriant) properties. A group of *inhalants* (*volatile substances*), such as glue, rubber cement, and cleaning and lighter fluids, also have various effects on the nervous system (Mirin and Weiss 1983:273–275).

Defining Drug Abuse

Drugs may have different effects on different people. They may also have different effects on the same person, depending on a number of factors, such as the quantity ingested and when, how, and conditions under which the drug is taken.

The drugs of abuse may sometimes be used with no ill effects; the line between use and abuse is not always clear. When use becomes "excessive . . . [at] . . . a level inconsistent with acceptable medical practice," it is *drug abuse* (Vaillant 1988:799). Additional characteristics of drug abuse are that it involves "deviation from societal norms [and is] harmful to physical and mental health" (Mirin and Weiss 1983:221). The term *drug abuse* has legal as well as medical implications.

Drug dependence involves a "compulsion to take the drug on either a continuous or periodic basis," either for its effects or to escape the distress of its absence (Vaillant 1988:700). *Physical dependence* is an "altered physiological state . . . [caused] by frequent use of a drug and resulting in physiological symptoms on withdrawal" (Vaillant 1988:700). When the compulsion to use drugs is mainly psychological and the withdrawal produces psychological symptoms but no physiological symptoms, it is called *psychic dependence* (Vaillant 1988:700). *Tolerance* occurs when more of the drug is required to produce the same effect, or the person shows decreased responses to the same dosage (Thomas 1989:1873). *Cross tolerance* occurs when this decreased sensitivity generalizes to different drugs, usually in the same class (Mirin and Weiss 1983:222.)

Drug dependence has also been viewed by behavioral scientists as maladaptive habitual behavior. The various drugs of abuse we have mentioned have different mechanisms of action, but they all provide pleasure (or they reverse feelings of pain and depression).[11] They stimulate an area in the brain known as the *pleasure pathways*, which results in intense feelings of pleasure; the drug abuser wants to keep experiencing this pleasure (Gawin 1991:1583). The effects of the drugs are a powerful reinforcer for drug taking behavior (Bohm 1984:443). In other words, taking drugs is a learned behavior. This implies that education about drugs may be useful in both lessening and treating drug addiction.

As previously discussed, depression is believed to be associated with a lower than normal amount of certain neurotransmitters in the brain—

for example, norepinephrine, dopamine, and serotonin. Stimulant drugs, such as cocaine, inhibit neuronal reuptake of serotonin, norepinephrine, and dopamine. However, cocaine's action on the dopaminergic pathways is believed to be the important one for drug abuse.[12] For example, in normal dopamine transmission there is an impulse, which results in the release of a certain amount of dopamine (the cell fires). Some of the dopamine is metabolized by MAO before it enters the synaptic cleft; some is metabolized by another enzyme (COMT) *in* the synaptic cleft, then, depending on factors regulating receptivity, the remaining dopamine bonds to the receptor cell, passing along the electrical impulse; it is then released back into the synaptic cleft and quickly cleared. (We describe this process in chapter 6.) When cocaine is used, there is a significantly stronger impulse, and the dopamine accumulates because cocaine inhibits its reuptake, thus sustaining the stimulation of the recipient cell. This action has been called "revving up the pleasure centers," because dopamine triggers feelings of euphoria (Boodman 1989).

Regarding the apparent effects of the drugs of abuse, it is interesting to note that recent evidence shows that they *all* increase the levels of dopamine in the brain but that those levels are much higher after taking cocaine or amphetamines (Kuhar, Ritz, and Boja 1991:300).

Vulnerability to Addiction

Recent research is beginning to provide some information on how and why addiction occurs, as well as how drug addiction relates to depression. A number of prominent researchers believe that those who become addicted to a particular type of drug or substance have an imbalance in brain chemistry that makes them susceptible (or vulnerable) to this chemical group because it acts like a medication. It immediately stabilizes the imbalance. They cite examples of individuals who typically recalled that the first time they took this substance they felt "normal for the first time." This very controversial theory has been called the *self-medication theory of drug abuse* (Khantzian 1986:1989).

Some authorities think that a susceptibility to addiction is inherited, although the exact biological mechanisms are uncertain. Various studies have been cited as substantiating this hypothesis. A significant one was reported in April of 1990. Scientists at the University of California, Los Angeles, found a particular gene in 77 percent of a research sample of alcoholics. This gene was linked to the receptors for dopamine (Blum et al. 1990). They also reported that alcoholic subjects who had alcoholic fathers had lower levels of the neurotransmitter *GABA* (gamma-aminobutyric acid)—levels that were equalized when vodka was ingested (Moss et al. 1990). One of the researchers feels that "there are specific neurotransmitter irregularities for each addiction" (Kenneth Blum, University of Texas, San Antonio, quoted in Goleman 1990). Another estimates that as many as 33–50 percent of those who abuse a particular drug may have a genetic irregularity (Frederick Goodman, Federal Alcohol, Drug Abuse and Mental Health Administration, also quoted in Goleman 1990). They believe that individuals with specific irregularities also display certain typical and identifiable behavior patterns (Goleman 1990).

Researchers in Sweden recently reported higher rates of addiction for individuals whose mothers received narcotics (barbiturates, opiates, or nitrous oxide) as painkillers ten hours or less prior to birth, as compared with siblings who were not exposed. These researchers also speculated that this early exposure to these drugs of abuse resulted in increased vulnerability later in life (Jacobson et al. 1990).

Two types of individuals are thought to become rapidly addicted to cocaine—the depressed and the extroverted. The former, who presumably have lower than normal levels of dopamine, experience a lift in their mood when their brain levels of dopamine increase after taking cocaine. When they stop taking the drug, they become deeply depressed—"the heavier the cocaine habit the deeper the depression" (Goleman 1990). People in the latter group, who are normally energetic and outgoing, presumably have higher-than-average levels of dopamine to begin with. These users experience a very intense response that "seems to intensify the biology" (one user described it as "like an orgasm" [Goleman 1990]). Their response is even greater when using crack cocaine, because it reaches the brain faster and in higher concentrations, since it is smoked. These individuals become addicted to the feeling of very great pleasure. This response is not unique to cocaine; dependency on many drugs is clearly sustained by their effects, especially those that are felt almost immediately. There is evidence that cocaine and other fat-soluble drugs, such as alcohol and heroin, quickly cross the blood-brain barrier. This would account for the rapid euphoria felt by users of these drugs (Goleman 1990).

Addiction to sedatives (e.g., alcohol and opiate drugs) seems to be associated with lower levels of serotonin and monoamine oxidase (MAO). These deficiencies are thought to produce feelings of tension and anxiety. The prototype of the alcohol abuser is of a "chronic, aggressive troublemaker"; a brooding individual, full of rage and resentment, who has difficulty controlling impulsive behavior. The sedative drugs calm them and produce feelings of euphoria. Lower levels of MAO are also seen in those who exhibit antisocial behavior. It is believed that they are "at greater risk for drug abuse of all kinds, in addition to alcohol" (Goleman 1990).

Lower levels of certain opiatelike substances found in the brain have been linked with anger and agitation (Trachtenberg and Blum 1987; Blum and Trachtenberg 1988). Opioid drugs such as heroin lessen these feelings, possibly by substituting for the natural analgesics (painkillers), the endorphins and enkephalins (Blum and Trachtenberg 1988). It is also thought that certain hallucinogenic drugs may be taken up by some nerve terminals in lieu of the neurotransmitter serotonin (Grinspoon 1990b).

Social scientists have criticized these biological theories of chemical imbalances, including the self-medication hypothesis, as having too narrow a focus. They feel that more attention should be paid to social circumstances, such as urban poverty and rates of addiction in children "from impoverished, single-parent families in drug-ridden neighborhoods, with no strong counterbalance from church and school" (Jessor, quoted in Goleman 1990). Members of the legal profession have objected to these theories on legal and ethical grounds. They are particularly concerned about issues of consent to treatment, such as the legal right of individuals to refuse to agree to be tested and/or treated. Another concern is that those who are identified as vulnerable to substance abuse might be discriminated against when applying for jobs, insurance, and so on.

This approach has also been challenged by researchers such as Zinberg (1990) who have studied "chippers," people who use drugs periodically—for example, on weekends ("weekend warriors")—and who do *not* become addicted. Zinberg feels that although these drugs are very potent and there *might* be a genetic vulnerability, other factors are potent enough to offset the effects of the drugs. These other factors include satisfying work, intimate relationships, and reachable goals. Some seem to be able to avoid addiction because the frequent use of drugs is not in keeping with their standards and life-style (Zinberg 1990). However, there is a difference between comparatively healthy people, whose drug use is seen as problem-solving behavior, and those who use drugs to alleviate mental or physical health problems (Ray 1972:5).

People who suffer from depression (including manic depression) and from anxiety, as well as those who are antisocial and borderline, are at higher risk for using and abusing drugs. This is sometimes referred to in the literature as *comorbidity*. For example, a major study on dual diagnosis investigated a group of five thousand eighteen- to thirty-year-olds in five settings. Twenty-two percent abused various drugs, alcohol, or both, and four-fifths started using these substances of abuse prior to age twenty. In this group, major depression was found at rates that were 2.7 times higher than average, and anxiety disorders were 1.7 times above average. A distinct pattern emerged: The anxiety started at about fifteen years of age; substance abuse started at about nineteen; the average age for alcohol abuse was twenty-one; depression was seen at age twenty-four. Three-fourths of the time, the mood or anxiety disorders came before the abuse. The previous existence of either a mood disorder or anxiety did not increase the probability of alcoholism. However, when depression was a preexisting condition, the probability of substance abuse was doubled (Christie et al. 1988).

Besides the need for symptom relief, other identified risk factors for substance abuse include cultural, hereditary, environmental, and personality factors; the availability of the substances; and certain of their characteristics, including type of action and timing (Vaillant 1988:702–704). It is hard to predict susceptibility and risk on the basis of such broad and diverse factors.

Certain risk factors, such as "psychodynamic, environmental, and physiological stressors [may] combine to make the drug abuser particularly vulnerable to depression" (Lehmann 1985:679). Depression may also result from the drug abuse, as we stated previously. Such drugs as amphetamines and cocaine (but not "crack") seem to be taken in cycles: Users often take them heavily for a time (called a "run"), then stop using them (withdraw or "crash") for a time. When the user's brain is deprived of the cocaine or other substance, it must adjust to the changes. This produces effects opposite to those of the drugs. Depression occurs frequently during the period of withdrawal; its degree varies, depending on the substance used. For example, amphetamine withdrawal is characterized by depressions and lethargy, which may reach suicidal intensity and last for a few weeks (Grinspoon and Bakalar 1988:419).

Opiates induce a continuing low level of depression. Those who abuse them have been described as "trapped between the depression associated with sedative drug effects and that associated with the chronic withdrawal most of them suffer" (Woody, O'Brien, and Rickels 1975). The hallucinogens also produce depression, especially when there is a bad "trip" (Grinspoon and Bakalar 1988:431). Cocaine abstinence (there is some disagreement about cocaine *withdrawal*) produces agitation, then depression. Nicotine withdrawal also produces symptoms similar to those of mood disorders. Marijuana can produce serious depression, especially in beginning users who may already have an underlying depression (Grinspoon and Bakalar 1988:425).

Multiple substance abuse is common. Different classes of substances may be taken for their apparently opposite effects. Stimulant abusers may feel extremely jittery after a while and take sedatives to calm themselves, and some sedative abusers may take stimulants to feel better. Since very powerful drugs cannot be ingested continuously, many users periodically switch substances. This also occurs after developing tolerance to a particular substance.

Treating Substance Abuse

Treatment for substance abuse is difficult. Individuals become substance abusers for many different reasons, and their causes can be difficult to isolate. There is a great deal of multiple drug abuse, and most experts agree that multiple drug users are very hard to treat. The symptoms experienced by individual abusers also vary greatly.

Quite a few special treatment programs are available for substance abusers. Unfortunately, care often begins with emergency treatment for an overdose or for a particularly bad "trip." This detoxification may involve administering oxygen and drugs to counteract the effects of the substances that have been ingested. Tricyclic antidepressants and lithium may also be given, as well as various painkillers. Detoxification stabilizes the abuser's physical condition; it is not treatment for the substance abuse.

After abstinence is achieved, the next step is usually some form of psychological therapy, or a combination of treatments. Because substance abusers have tried to solve their problems by using drugs, they may not be ready for psychotherapy at this time (Grinspoon and Bakalar 1988). Supportive therapy in self-help groups such as Narcotics Anonymous (N.A.), Rational Recovery (R.R.), and Alcoholics Anonymous (A.A.) is usually recommended. Later on, supportive psychotherapy, often in combination with N.A., is recommended to help the patient abstain from drug use and learn ways to cope with whatever problems or conditions initiated the use (Grinspoon and Bakalar 1988:421).

The literature also mentions various behavior therapy approaches as specific treatments for substance abuse. These include cognitive-behavior therapy and several behavior modification techniques. Social skills training is particularly recommended, especially for long-term abusers, for the comparatively simple behaviors of looking for drugs—for a "score"—are the overwhelming occupation of the addicted; abstinence and withdrawal often leave large behavioral voids in their lives. (These treatment approaches are described in chapters 14 and 15.)

Pharmacological treatments are also used. The most significant one for treating opioid addictions (e.g., heroin) has been methadone, a synthetic opioid that exhibits cross tolerance with other drugs in this class. It is a very controversial drug because users also become addicted to it. However, it has a number of advantages over heroin: It is taken only once a day, by mouth, in pure (unadulterated) form, in a therapeutic environment. Some reports have suggested that the antidepressants desipramine and imipramine have been successful in controlling the craving for cocaine (Isikoff:1990). Carbamazepine (which we have mentioned in reference to treating manic depressives) is also being used to treat cocaine addiction, because it seems both to minimize dangerous side effects and to lessen desire for the drug ("Two Treatments for Cocaine Addiction" 1990). Other experiments have focused on magnesium (a neurobiologically significant nutrient) that, in laboratory experiments with rodents, seems to produce behavior changes and reactions similar to those of cocaine but also blocks the "behavioral disruptions and neurological changes" of cocaine (Kantak et al. 1991). These experiments are currently being repeated with primates and are expected to be conducted on humans.

There is an ongoing search for other drugs able to counteract the effects of the various abused substances. The difficulties of finding suitable drugs are intensified by the prominence of multiple drug use. Proponents of the self-medication theory of drug abuse, who are seeking to identify those they consider are biologically vulnerable to specific addictions, are also looking for specific drugs to counteract the various theoretical underlying imbalances.[13]

Acupuncture is now being considered as a promising treatment for cocaine abuse. When it is combined with some form of psychotherapy (including attending Narcotics Anonymous groups), it seems to relax addicts and lessen their craving for cocaine. At the time of the writing of this book, several studies were in progress, but the results were not yet available. Preliminary reports suggested that the success rate was as good as that achieved with other approaches. There is great interest in this treatment approach. It is very easy to administer, and very economical, currently costing approximately $21 per outpatient office visit (Boodman 1989:14).

The costs of drug treatment programs can be enormous! Certain programs that combine detoxification and counseling (individual and group) in a thirty-day stay at a nonprofit clinic can easily cost about $5,400 at the present time, and a comparable program at a profit-making hospital can cost $1,000 a day (Boodman 1989:13–14). These programs are obviously designed for people who work and have good insurance coverage. The typical substance abuser usually does not have a job, insurance, or a supportive spouse, relatives, or friends. The ability of significant others to be supportive usually deteriorates along with almost everything else in the substance abuser's life.

The abstinence achieved by these treatments does not always continue when they end. When the client leaves the controlled environment and reenters the world, where the "real work of recovery begins," relapse often follows (Washton, quoted in Boodman 1990a).

Outpatient treatment is considerably cheaper, and it can be very effective. For example, in a study of 164 alcoholics in need of detoxification (but without severe symptoms such as delirium tremens) treatment approaches were compared by randomly assigning about half of the group ($n = 87$) to outpatient treatment and the balance ($n = 77$) to inpatient treatment. Both groups were given antianxiety drugs to ease the symptoms of withdrawal, and both received some form of counseling. The results were similar, although the dropout rate was higher for the outpatient group (25 percent compared with 5 percent). Six months later, the remission rate was the same for both groups—about 25 percent. The most significant difference was in the cost of treatment which was "$175 to $400 for outpatient detoxification and $3300 to $3700 for hospitalization" (Hayashida et al. 1989).

The Combination of Alcoholism and Depression

Alcohol, a central nervous system depressant, may deaden the sensibilities and is often used to escape the aversive conditions of life. Many who use, and abuse, alcohol seem to be self-medicating for depression. They appear to be trying to deaden the pain of living: the pain in their minds and sometimes the pain in their bodies as well. Bipolar depressives, for example, often drink heavily while in a manic episode. However, other factors must be significant, because heavy consumption of alcohol usually continues after their mood improves (Pary and Lippmann 1989:8).

Kanarek and Marks-Kaufman (1991:205–209) point out that because alcohol is one of the drugs of abuse, we tend to overlook its role as a nutrient. Most alcoholic beverages add calories and little else of value to the diet, and they have a number of negative effects on the consumer. The chronic alcoholic, who tends to substitute drink for food, is often undernourished, lacking vitamins and minerals important to his or her well-being. Even when normal quantities of vitamins are ingested, alcohol consumption lessens their value. For example, the absorption of thiamine and B-12 are impaired because of damage to digestive organs. (Deficiencies of these vitamins are connected to a number of psychological disorders, including depression, as we explained in chapter 8.) Liver damage interferes with the body's ability to use nutrients as well as with the functioning of the immune system. Weight loss is not uncommon, resulting in higher levels of alcohol in the blood when alcohol is consumed. Among other effects, alcohol decreases REM sleep and impairs vision and intellectual and motor skills, including memory. It may cause brain damage in the adult and disrupt the manufacture and functioning of many neurotransmitters and neuromodulators, including those associated with depression—norepinephrine, dopamine, and serotonin (Royce 1989:67). Alcohol may also lead to physical and mental damage to children whose mothers abused it while they were pregnant; this is known as *fetal alcohol syndrome* (Kanarek and Marks-Kaufman 1991:209). Some experts think exposure of the fetus to alcohol in utero may be a factor leading to alcohol abuse later in life (Hodgkinson, Mullan, and Murray 1991:188).

Depression is the condition most often linked with alcoholism. We have discussed evidence of a possible genetic susceptibility to alcohol abuse. There may also be a genetic vulnerability to both conditions (Lehmann 1985:677). For example, in those diagnosed as having depressive spectrum disorder, the depressive symptoms in this low-grade, chronic disorder are usually less severe than in the major depressions. However, more patients with the spectrum disorder have a higher number of alcohol abusers in their first-degree relatives than do those with any other mood disorders. They do not show the same absence of suppression on the dexamethasone suppression test (DST) as do endogenous depressives; and their condition improves when treated with ECT or serotinergic (influencing or affecting serotonin) antidepressants (Lehmann 1985:677).

Others reject this genetic theory. Although biological markers are thought to be linked to heavy drinking, only a minority of this group reveals these markers; most do not become alcoholics (Fingarette 1990). Evidence from studies of twins so far has not confirmed genetic causes. The risk of an identical twin of an alcoholic developing alcoholism is 60 percent, and the risk in a fraternal twin is only 20–30 percent, which is higher than expected in the population but does not show complete concordance (Schuckit 1986:8).

A recent report on the possibility of a genetic predisposition failed to confirm this hypothesis, and the investigators, stating that "more work will be needed to identify any gene or genes that may be at fault," voiced their doubts that "alcoholism could be explained so simply" (Kolata 1990).

Primary mood disorder and alcoholism are the two disorders that seem most associated with suicide (Goodwin and Guze 1989:23). Part of the reason for the higher rates of suicide attempts, and successful suicides, in depressed alcoholics (as compared to nondepressed alcoholics) is that alcohol and alcohol intoxication can temporarily lift the mood of the alcoholic and energize him or her enough to attempt suicide. Resistance to suicide seems to be disinhibited and the rise in mood is often accompanied by impaired judgment. Alcohol itself can be a way to commit suicide, either by drinking large amounts or by mixing it with other substances. Suicides almost always take place when the alcoholic is intoxicated (Avery 1987:2). For these reasons, and others, alcoholism can be seen as a form of chronic suicide, a term used many years ago by Menninger (1938).

Alcoholism has also been called a form of masked depression because it is often difficult, in the clinical situation, to differentiate the two conditions (Arieti and Bemporad 1978:67). The most commonly utilized screening tests for depression are very poor in detecting clinical depression in alcohol abusers (Grant et al. 1989).

Individuals may appear with the symptoms of either depression or alcoholism and may fulfill the criteria for diagnosis of a mood disorder as well as those for alcohol abuse. Many of the symptoms of depression—sadness, disruptions of sleep and appetite, lessening of libido, a drop both in energy and interest in events, guilt, verbalizations and feelings of hopelessness, and even suicidal thoughts—are symptoms that may also be seen in someone who abuses alcohol or another substance. Additional indicators of primary depression include the markers for medication, such as a family history of mood disorders, and other positive biological markers, as determined by responses to certain tests for depressive disorders. An outstanding feature of true alcohol dependence and abuse is chronicity; usually, the client has been addicted for a long time.

According to one source, 42 percent of alcoholics are diagnosed at intake as clinically depressed, whereas only 6 percent remain so after four weeks of treatment and abstinence (Brown and Schuckit 1988). This has led some observers to label the depression in alcoholics as transitory (Schmeck 1988). However, there are disparities in the statistical estimates of the coexistence (morbidity) of the two conditions. The estimated rates of primary depression coexisting with alcoholism run from 28 to 51 percent in a minority (15 percent) of female alcoholics and in a smaller number (5 percent) of male alcoholics. In these depressions (which preceded the alcohol abuse), the course of the disorder, including reaction to treatment, is closer to the mood disorders than to alcoholism (Lehmann 1985:676).

Some studies have shown that, in clients diagnosed as having primary depression, the diagnosis of secondary alcoholism runs from 8 to 32 percent (Avery 1987:2). The estimates of primary alcoholism with secondary depression vary from 6 to 98 percent. This range is so large that it obviously reflects problems in the accuracy of the statistics, such as a failure to use standardized criteria in diagnosis. When standard psychiatric diagnostic criteria are used, about 25 percent of primary depressives are also found to have secondary alcoholism; however, when rating scales are used, about 50 percent of those diagnosed with alcohol abuse are classified as having secondary depression (Avery 1987:2).

Some authorities feel the proportion of alcoholism among depressed people has been exaggerated; it appears to be high because the depression, or another mental disorder, brings the alcoholic into treatment, not the alcoholism.

One study of a sample of alcohol abusers revealed that 3 percent of the men but approximately 25 percent of the women had primary depression. A follow-up study conducted three years later showed that the women with a dual diagnosis of primary depression with secondary alcoholism did markedly better than women who had been diagnosed as having primary alcoholism (Avery 1987:2). Alcoholism may present a much more difficult problem for women than depression. We can only speculate whether it is because of the efficacy of the treatments for depressions and/or the great stigma attached to female alcoholism in this country; we do know that more women hide alcoholism than men (Royce 1989:172–174). As a group, women become problem drinkers at an older age than men; therefore there is a longer time in which an existing depression can be diagnosed. This may account for the higher rates of primary depression in women (Goodwin and Guze 1989:23). Colleagues of the authors have reported observing, in their clinical practices, that the depression progresses faster in females than in males, and they seem to have greater psychological after-effects (or sequelae) than males.

Because of the depressiogenic effects of alcohol abuse, the beginning of detoxification treatment is a critical time (Schuckit 1983b, cited in Lehmann 1985:676). In the first weeks of treatment, as many as 95 percent of patients undergoing detoxification may be depressed enough to be diagnosed as having a mood disorder under the D.S.M.-III criteria. This may reflect a number of genuine tensions and losses, including loss of home, because the patient is residing in a treatment center. In many cases, as the patient becomes sober, these depressive symptoms may ease and even go away. However, it is a dangerous period, for as the depression lifts, the patient may voice, and act upon, suicidal impulses (Schuckit 1983b).

Alcoholics who have relied on alcohol to ease social relations experience an additional loss during detoxification. The depression understandably worsens as they withdraw from alcohol and lose social support. Support groups such as Alcoholics Anonymous or Rational Recovery can be very helpful for these individuals (Nakamura et al. 1983).

Since the period of withdrawal from alcohol is usually a time of great mood instability, depression may be hard to diagnose and may be confused with *alcoholic sadness*, a down mood caused by the depressive effects of alcohol on the central nervous system. It lifts with sobriety. Relief from depression, with sobriety, is rare. A period of abstinence must occur before this diagnosis can be made. Such a lapse of time is becoming more and more difficult, however, because of the increasing emphasis on curtailing stays in hospitals and the consequently rapid evaluations that must be made (Pary and Lippmann 1989:8).

Alcoholics who have been abstinent, including those in the first three weeks of detoxification, show a lowered REM latency. As we discussed previously, this is considered a distinct biological marker for depression (Lehmann 1985:678). Response to the DST may show false positive during alcohol withdrawal, but this should disappear after three to four weeks of nondrinking (Majumdar, Shaw, and Bridges 1988). Some consider the DST to be capable of detecting depression in alcoholics, holding that alcoholism alone will not produce a false positive (Lehmann 1985:678). Others feel that until there is more agreement on the validity of the DST, it is not useful for diagnosis (Pary and Lippmann 1989:8). (We have discussed the pros and cons of the DST in chapter 7.)

Alcohol abusers who have relapsed seem to have a greater rate of depression than those who have not relapsed, although it is difficult to tell if the depression is a consequence or a cause of the relapse (Lehmann 1985:677).

What causes depression in alcohol abusers? The physiological properties of alcohol were once thought to be the cause. However, this thesis has been renounced, because the multiplicity of depressive criteria met by these patients goes beyond a purely physiological interpretation (Lehmann 1985:677). In reality, it can be very hard to determine which is cause and which is effect—if the drinking followed the depression, or the depression followed the alcohol abuse (Khantzian 1987; Pary and Lippmann 1989).

When the drinking is long term, many clients may be unable to remember which came first. The chances of memory lapse are, of course, even greater if there is brain damage, which may result from long-term drinking. When direct questioning of the client does not produce the required information, it is common that collateral sources, such as relatives, also fail to do so.

TREATMENT OF THE DUAL DIAGNOSIS

In the treatment of depression, alcoholism is considered such a serious complication that it is a contraindication for brief psychodynamically oriented psychotherapy (Rosenberg 1985:101).

Intervention should certainly vary according to the individual situation. Usually, this depends on a determination of the primary diagnosis—a differentiation that may be very difficult to make. If the mood disturbance came before the alcoholism, then it is more likely that antidepressant medications and/or lithium might be used. When the patient's biological markers are more pronounced, a positive response to medication is more likely. However, this response does not eliminate the utility of some form of psychotherapy. This is supported in the literature (Pary, Lippmann, and Tobias 1988).

Depressives who suffer from alcoholism generally do not stop drinking when their mood improves (Pary and Lippmann 1989). The alcohol abuse itself requires therapeutic attention. If the alcoholism preceded the depression, it is generally suggested that the addiction be treated first. The recommended treatment is usually a multidisciplinary approach that includes supportive group treatment, such as that provided by Alcoholics Anonymous or Rational Recovery. The focus of treatment should be on practical resolution of problems rather than on the development of insight. Because of low mood, pessimism, and passivity, cognitive-behavior therapy rather than insight therapy is highly recommended (Lehmann 1985:677–678).

Care should be exercised in using antidepressant medication when the primary diagnosis is alcohol abuse. However, when a client has been alcohol-free for a few weeks and still shows symptoms of depression, treatment with antidepressant medication can be considered (Avery 1987:3).

We do not have many long-term controlled studies on the effectiveness of antidepressant medications with depressed alcohol abusers. One major study of depressed and nondepressed alcoholics, covering a fifty-two-week period, showed that lithium had no effect on the alcohol abuse of either group. There was also no difference in the modification of the depth of depression between lithium and placebo, nor did lithium have an effect on the length of abstinence or the degree of alcoholism (Dorus et al. 1989). Still, it is currently thought that antidepressant medications may be used with depressed alcohol abusers up to the higher levels of therapeutic dosages (Pary and Lippmann 1989).

There are a number of problems in studying treatment outcome. One is that alcoholism is a very complicated disease with many periods of relapse and remission that do not follow any regular pattern. Another is that when patients start treatment they are usually at their lowest state and nearly always improve somewhat. Prognosis is best for those who are married, have a steady work history, have no criminal record, are on their first admission, are in a stable social situation, and do not suffer from any other psychiatric illness (Vaillant 1988:712).

Confounding the treatment of depression and alcoholism, and similar to the treatment of alcoholism alone, is the fact that alcoholics as a group often do not comply with their treatment regimens, particularly when it comes to taking medication. The antidepressant medications can also be deadly. If alcoholics are depressed, or have worked themselves up to self-destruction, the available antidepressant medications are an all-too-efficient means of suicide. Another frequent complication, as previously noted, is that depressed alcoholics use other addictive substances much more frequently than alcoholics who do not suffer from a mood disorder (Schuckit 1983).

Alcoholics who stop drinking have been described as going through a period during which they are like prisoners of war returning home. The world of being sober is strange, because their previous world was formed by alcohol (Styron 1990:40–43). Recuperation is a period of rehabilitation and is usually very stressful. It is a time of anxiety, tension, and depression, in which the former alcoholics must assume responsibility for their lives. They must learn many new behaviors and do a lot of reconstructing. Often they do not anticipate this, expecting that the multiplicity of problems they (and their significant others) have been dealing with—problems they have been blaming on alcohol—will disappear when the drinking stops. Because of these unrealistic expectations, patients and their significant others can become greatly disillusioned. The rehabilitation process may take two or three years and is marked by instability, which leads to difficulties in keeping employment and maintaining relationships. Many relationships that have endured through the "hard times" end *after* the drinking is terminated.

Summary: Treating Drug and Alcohol Addiction

There is obviously a tremendous need for treatment of alcoholism and the other addictions. Between the years 1978 and 1984, private facilities for treating alcoholism increased fourfold; and hospitalization of adolescents in private centers—many of them for abuse of drugs and alcohol—increased 450 percent (Peele 1991:5). The average cost for a hospital stay was $18,000 (Peele 1991:5).

Recently, the effectiveness of treating the addictions in institutions has been questioned. There is very little evidence to show that expensive residential treatment is better than cheaper outpatient treatment (Peele 1991:5). A theory has been advanced that "natural remission" is as effective as planned inpatient care (Peele 1991:5), for both alcoholism and other drug abuse. Vaillant (quoted in Peele 1991:5) states that the "most important single prognostic variable associated with remission among alcoholics who attend alcohol clinics is having something to lose if they continue to abuse alcohol."

Peele (1991:6) states that the "best way to discourage addictive behavior is to show people how to meet the demands of life without drinking or drug use." In other words, people should be taught job and interpersonal skills as well as self-control and stress management. This orientation, more social and behavioral than medical, has been increasingly adopted, even in private facilities, with promising results. Although the research for this approach also is inadequate, Peele (1991:6) stresses that little of a medical nature is done in alcoholism and drug treatment programs. Similarly, there is no evidence for the efficacy of genetically oriented treatment approaches. In summary, among other suggestions, Peele (1991:6) recommends rejecting the total dominance of the disease concept and reconsidering both AA-based and inpatient treatment. There should also be more emphasis on cost effectiveness; research on what actually goes on in treatment programs, accompanied by an emphasis on skill training; more study of people who remit on their own; more matching of patients to treatment; a reduction in the output of accredited alcoholism counselors; and—very important—minimal treatment in the beginning. In short, a pluralistic system of alcoholism and drug treatment should be created (Peele 1991:7).

The Eating Disorders and Depression

Anorexia Nervosa and Bulimia

Anorexia nervosa and bulimia are the two eating disorders associated most closely with depression. They have many features in common. Problems with self-image are universal among patients with eating disorders, but they may or may not have common origins (Treasure and Holland 1991:199).

Anorexia nervosa (*an*, "absent"; *orexia*, "appetite") is a conscious and deliberate refusal to eat, frequently accompanied by the person feeling that he or she is unattractive and obese. This feeling persists even after the person loses a great deal of weight—an obvious disturbance of body image. There may be forced vomiting, voluntary fasting, and use of laxatives to purge the body and stay thin.

There are definite criteria for a D.S.M.-III-R diagnosis of anorexia nervosa. These include a "refusal" (the term used in the D.S.M.) to sustain weight above a minimum appropriate for age and height, or "body weight 15 percent below that expected," or—if still growing—a failure to gain weight, resulting in "body weight 15 percent below that expected." There may be an intense dread of gaining weight or growing fat, even if the person is underweight. There is usually a disturbance in the way weight, size, or shape is perceived. In women, there is "absence of at least three consecutive menstrual cycles . . . (primary or secondary amenorrhea). . . . (A woman is considered to have amenorrhea if her periods occur only following hormone, e.g., estrogen, administration)" (D.S.M.-III-R 1987:67). Anorectics often do not feel distress over their condition, deny there is a problem, and resist help.

Bulimia (*bul*, "cattle head"; *limos*, "hunger"), called bulimia nervosa in the D.S.M.-III-R (1987:67), is a "neurotic disorder, especially of adolescent and young adult women, characterized by bouts of overeating followed by voluntary vomiting, fasting or induced diarrhea" (Thomas 1989:258). The criteria for diagnosis include recurring bouts of *binge eating* ("rapid consumption of a large amount of food in a discrete period of time" [D.S.M.-III-R 1987:67]) often accompanied by a feeling that eating is out of control. There may be "self-induced vomiting, [frequent] use of laxatives or diuretics, strict dieting or fasting, or vigorous exercises" to keep from gaining weight. There must be a "minimum of two binge eating episodes a week for at least three months" often accompanied by "overconcern with body shape and weight" (D.S.M.-III-R 1987:68–69).

A frequent pattern is to binge, particularly on carbohydrates, and then feel shame after eating, further lowering self-esteem (Herzog 1988:435).[14] Unlike the anorectic, bulimics may feel distressed and will often accept help (Herzog 1988:435). Much of the binge eating is a result of both dietary restraint and depression. The presence of both dietary restriction and a bipolar mood disorder is a good predictor of the severity of binge eating (Greenberg and Harvey 1987).

Goodwin and Guze (1989:288) caution against confusing the weight loss often seen in major depression with the more extreme weight loss in the eating disorders. The weight loss in depression is involuntary; the loss of appetite is a by-product of lowered energy and other aspects of depression. The loss of weight in the eating disorders is more deliberate; it is a goal—the result of thoughtful choices not to eat and of deliberate actions, such as vomiting and purging, taken to achieve this goal.

Proponents of the precursor theory (described in chapter 8), such as Pirke and Ploog (1987:241), point out that anorectic patients not only starve themselves by reducing their intake of calories, but eat a nutritionally unbalanced diet. Studies of bulimic patients also reveal signs of starvation even among those who do not lose weight. (In this context, *starvation* is defined as "a condition in which the supply of . . . specific food[s] is below minimum bodily requirements" [Thomas 1989:1743]. There are numerous related complications.) The body responds to this intermittent or permanent starvation by reducing the flow of norepinephrine, which may result in depression, among other changes. Lowered amounts of tyrosine (the precursor for norepinephrine and dopamine) seem to play a part in this process. However, studies have shown that as the carbohydrate content in diets is lowered, producing lower levels of brain tryptophan (as previously explained), the moods of the subjects were lowered (Pirke and Ploog 1987:241). Pirke and Ploog (1987:241) hypothesize that the reduced tryptophan availability may cause reduced serotonin turnover in anorexia and bulimia.

Other researchers have evaluated the binging and vomiting behavior of bulimics as the body's way to suppress appetite and to ease dysphoria (Kaye et al. 1988). (*"Dysphoria* is general dissatisfaction . . . discomfort, unhappiness" [Thomas 1989:547].) This theory is based on studies showing that an increase of carbohydrates in the diet heightens the amount of tryptophan (the precursor for serotonin) that enters the brain. These behaviors (binging/vomiting) may change the balance of amino acids, which increases brain serotonin and thereby improves mood. Studies have shown that plasma levels of tryptophan increase after bouts of binging and vomiting, resulting in lower rates of these behaviors. (Again, we must stress that these theories are controversial.)

Young women increasingly are consuming crack and cocaine in the mistaken belief that they are rapid, inexpensive ways to lose weight. Crack, in particular, deceives the senses, producing feelings of being well fed, so that the user may not eat for several days. One hospital unit specializing in the treatment of eating disorders estimated that 40 percent of its patients had abused cocaine and that 25 percent of entering patients were severely addicted (Newman 1990). Clients with anorexia nervosa also frequently abuse alcohol.

Anorexia nervosa and bulimia overwhelmingly affect adolescent or young women; 90–95 percent of all cases are women (Herzog 1988:435). Anorexia nervosa usually occurs at an earlier age than bulimia. The onset is from twelve years of age to the middle thirties, with peaks at thirteen to fourteen and seventeen to eighteen. Onset for bulimia is usually between seventeen and twenty-five years of age (Herzog 1988:435).

The same person may suffer from both anorexia nervosa and bulimia. (This is sometimes called *bulimarexia* [McGrath et al. 1990:92].) Both disorders involve severe disturbances in self-esteem, including perceptions of the body and body image. In both, the individuals feel their weight is completely out of control; they feel unattractive, fat, and gross. This feeling may persist, even when they become underweight or emaciated. This distortion of body image often has little or no relationship to reality.

The suicide rate ranges from 2 to 5 percent in chronic anorectics, and a follow-up study of 435 sufferers showed that over one-half "suffer[ed] [from] recurrent affective disorder, . . . [and] a quarter did not regain their menses or attain 75 percent of [their] ideal weight" (Herzog 1988:435).

Although the real extent of these eating disorders might never be known, a survey in northern California of 646 tenth-grade females showed that 10.3 percent were diagnosable as bulimic and another 10.4 percent admitted vomiting to control their weight. The bulimics and purgers reported higher rates of drunkenness, marijuana use, cigarette use and greater levels of depressive symptoms (Killern et al. 1987). Similarly, a study of bulimic female outpatients showed that over their lifetimes there was a high rate of major affective disorder, anxiety disorders, substance abuse, and atypical depression. This study supported previous work implying a relationship between bulimia and major affective disorder (Hudson et al. 1987).

From 25 to 50 percent of clients with eating disorders can also be diagnosed as suffering from major depressive disorder. It is often difficult to determine which came first, for the depression may be a cause or an effect (Herzog 1988:438). Certainly, the extreme eating patterns associated with both anorexia nervosa and bulimia have biological consequences that will also have psychological repercussions (Laessle, Schweiger, and Pirke 1988). A study of the symptoms of depression in bulimic, depressed, and control groups of women showed that it was impossible to differentiate the bulimic from the depressed women on the items on the Hamilton Rating Scale for depression and that both groups were markedly different from control subjects (Pope, Hudson, and Yurgelun-Todd 1989).

Theories on the Causes of Eating Disorders

There are a number of theories on the causes of eating disorders. Some hypothesize a biological origin and some a psychological origin, although most agree that the disorders have both components.

Some researchers have been investigating the possibility that the eating disorders involve a genetic predisposition. In a review of a number of studies of twins, Treasure and Holland (1991:202–208) state that there is consistent evidence that if one identical (MZ) twin develops anorexia nervosa, there is a higher than normal probability that the other will develop it. For example, in one study of thirty pairs of female MZ twins, 55 percent of the siblings became anorectic. Treasure and Holland (1991:204), the authors of this study, acknowledge that their sample was small but feel that their evidence is supported by a "larger study of eating attitudes in normal twins." These studies of identical twins have revealed insignificant evidence of a genetic predisposition to bulimia.

Kanarek and Marks-Kaufman (1991:277) concur with Treasure and Holland that the evidence supports a theory of genetic vulnerability to anorexia nervosa. They hypothesize that this vulnerability may be due to a "defect in the homeostatic mechanisms that normally ensure weight gain after a period of weight loss." However, they also point out that more than one factor must predispose an individual to such a disorder.

One area of investigation has focused on the family. Published and unpublished reports indicate that families of anorectics are so protective and intrusive that their children have difficulty progressing through the normal stages of separating from the family and developing self-identity. This may be one of the factors predisposing these children to self-destructive behaviors such as those displayed in anorexia nervosa. These families also seem to be excessively worried about "external standards for determining self-worth and success," valuing slimness and fitness (Kanarek and Marks-Kaufman 1991:277–278). Furthermore, studies have shown that first- and second-degree relatives of eating-disorder patients have a higher than expected incidence of depression and alcoholism. Agreement on familial factors, though, is not universal. A study of relatives of eating-disorder patients, depressed patients, and normal controls did reveal a relationship between eating disorders and major depression, but it did not show a relationship between these disorders and either alcoholism or drug abuse (Logue, Crowe, and Bean 1989).

In addition to having difficulty establishing autonomy, anorectics have been described as "obsessional . . . hysterical . . . compliant, perfectionist, obedient, eager to please, oversubmissive, lacking in responsiveness to inner needs. . . . [with] extremely high expectations and need to please others in order to maintain their sense of self-worth" (Kanarek and Marks-Kaufman 1991:276–277).

Women suffering from bulimia scored significantly higher on several scales of depression, including the Beck Depression Inventory, than those who did not have eating disorders. Particularly noticeable was the finding that these bulimic women displayed dysfunctional attitudes and depressive attributional styles, although these attitudes and styles were not associated with the depth of the affective disorder (Goebel et al. 1989). A review of eleven studies of anorectic patients showed that a majority of the female subjects exhibited marked obsessive-compulsive traits, leading to speculation that anorexia nervosa and depression may both be linked to an obsessive-compulsive syndrome (Rothenberg 1988). Another study showed that bulimic women displayed distorted patterns of thinking, similar to those of depressives, but it was felt that although there is a high frequency of depression among bulimics, the maladaptive cognitions of bulimic women were more specific to the eating disorder (Schlesier-Carter et al. 1989). A follow-up of women with affective and anxiety disorders, who were diagnosed as anorectic five to fourteen years earlier, established that in one-half of the depression cases and in three-quarters of the anxiety cases these conditions were manifested before the onset of the eating disorder (Toner, Garfinkel, and Garner 1988).

Some have expressed reservations about the relationship of bulimia to depression. Early studies showed a high occurrence of depression in bulimics and in their families. More recent research hypothesizes that bulimia and major depression are distinct syndromes, based on studies of the clinical data, family studies, pharmacotherapy, and neurobiology of both depression and bulimia (Levy, Dixon, and Stern 1989).

Other factors contribute to anorexia nervosa and bulimia—for example, sociocultural factors that emphasize or overstress thinness (Kanarek and Marks-Kaufman 1991:278–279). It is obvious that the eating disorders are complicated and are probably caused by many different factors.

Treatment of Anorexia Nervosa and Bulimia

Treatment of the eating disorders can be very complex because it is difficult to ascertain etiology, which may raise questions of where to begin treatment. A multisystems approach is usually followed. The priority is to stabilize the patient's medical condition and then to treat the psychological problems.

Treatment generally consists of two phases. The first phase is often carried out in a hospital, because of weight loss and the accompanying nutritional deprivation, which can be life-threatening. During hospitalization, the emphasis is on medical stabilization, including restoring nutritional balance and blocking the symptoms, to halt the eating-disorder behavior. In this process, the weight loss may be reversed. However, gaining weight, per se, often is not the main issue. As the late expert Hilde Bruch (1988) stated, the eating disorder may be just a smoke screen, for the real problem is what the person feels about herself. This is usually addressed in the second phase of treatment, which may also be carried out within the controlled environment of a hospital, using behavioral treatment approaches such as cognitive-behavioral therapy and cognitive restructuring for bulimia and using reinforcement procedures and generalization training for anorexia nervosa (O'Leary and Wilson 1987:281–291). (These procedures are explained in chapters 14 and 15.) Family therapy may also be initiated, first emphasizing the alteration of patterns of eating, then addressing specific problems within the family unit (Kanarek and Marks-Kaufman 1991:285).

Upon discharge from the hospital or controlled environment and reentry into the natural environment, the therapy (including nutritional, medical, and dental care) must continue and must focus on more central and dynamic issues, such as self-esteem, the primary and early relationship of the patient with her mother, and so forth (Stunkard and Mahoney 1976:48; O'Leary and Wilson 1987:289). At this point it is appropriate to use a combination of more traditional therapies, such as group therapies, intensive individual and family psychotherapies, and perhaps cognitive-behavioral and even psychoeducational family therapies (Herzog 1988:439–445).

Studies have indicated that serotonin is involved with anorexia nervosa (Neill and Cooper 1989). Others have determined that norepinephrine, corticotropic releasing factors, and beta-endorphin (Giannini 1988); melatonin levels (Kennedy et al. 1989); and cortico-releasing hormone (CRH) are all common to a number of disorders with features of depression, including anorexia nervosa and bulimia (Smith et al. 1989). Thus antidepressant medications have been used in the treatment of the eating disorders, and have, for example, been useful in reducing the frequency of binging and vomiting in bulimia (Blouin et al. 1989). However, in long-term studies it has been found that recovery from bulimia has little effect upon depression and vice versa (Herzog 1988:438).

Furthermore, many neurotransmitters that have an effect on appetite may also impact on other behaviors, increasing the probability of side effects from the medication (Morley 1989). It does stand to reason that antidepressant medication, which also modulates these neurotransmitters, may have unexpected and often unwanted side effects. The use of the antidepressant medications increases the need for medical consultation and supervision in the therapies of these sometimes life-threatening disorders.

Summary: The Eating Disorders and Depression

After reviewing the current evidence on the relationship of anorexia nervosa, bulimia and the depressions, McGrath and colleagues (1990) conclude that there is clearly a relationship among these disorders. However, current evidence does not indicate "whether it is a correlate, a cause, or a consequence." They emphasize the need to carry out additional studies in these important areas.

11

The Biopsychiatric Approach to Treating Depression

The view that depression is primarily a medical or a biological condition, like diabetes, heart disease, or cancer, caused essentially by biological factors located primarily in the brain is expressed by Gold and Andreasen, among others. Andreasen (1984:30) states that the goal of psychiatry (psychiatry based on neuroscience) should be to find these biological factors—what is "broken" in the brain—and repair them using somatic therapies. Wender and Klein (1981:20) have suggested that these orientations might be encompassed ideally in a third view, a *biopsychiatric approach.*

As examples, we shall discuss the work of Gold, Andreasen, and Papolos, three biopsychiatrists who have described this approach in their writings, and we shall describe it in a clinic with which we are familiar.

Gold's Approach to Treatment

Mark Gold has given an informative description of the therapeutic approach of a biopsychiatrist. Gold (1987a:245–252) begins by taking an extensive history and may also use some standard questionnaires. He tries to speak with members of the patient's family. If the patient's condition permits, he allows a period during which the patient receives no drugs of any kind. In this period, laboratory and psychological tests are given, both to rule out illnesses that resemble depression (the *mimickers*) and to determine if other mental illnesses or conditions exist.

Some laboratory tests are administered to identify neuroendocrine markers of biological depression—for example, the dexamethasone suppression test (DST) plus one other neuroendocrine test, usually the TRH-TSH test (Gold 1987a:246). (This is the same test we discussed in chapter 7 as the TRHST, or thyrotropin-releasing hormone suppression test.) Gold emphasizes that there may be normal suppression but that a patient may still have a hypothalamic-pituitary-thyroid abnormality. If the tests are negative but he still suspects a biological factor, Gold uses other tests (which he did not specify.) He then makes an assessment based on all the preceding factors and refers clients to other specialists as needed. For example, in the case of a coexisting addiction, he sends the patient to a drug or alcohol treatment program.

Treatment usually begins with a combination of medication and psychotherapy, especially if one of the tests reveals what he believes to be a biological factor. If there is uncertainty, he administers a test to gauge *response prediction*. For example, if the patient's mood improves after a single dose of an amphetamine, this is an indication that the patient will respond positively to antidepressant medication (Gold 1987a: 246).

Gold is adamant against prescribing antidepressants for everyone "just in case they might work." He states that "drugs are not the answer to everything, in medicine or in life" (1987a:246). He recommends psychotherapy, without medication, "when neuroendocrine testing is consistently negative" (1987a:246).

When Gold prescribes an antidepressant, he begins with a tricyclic, relying upon specific tests to indicate which one should be tried first (1987a:247). A test dose is administered. After twenty-four hours he assesses how much of the medication remains in the blood plasma, and then sets a dosage, lessening the need to change the dosage and, it is hoped, keeping side effects to a minimum.

The choice of drug depends, among other factors, on the extent and the nature of the side effects. In the example Gold gives of a busy executive, he states that prescribing a drug with a heavy sedative effect is "asking for failure." He emphasizes the potentially aversive nature of side effects, for if they are too great, or too incapacitating, they might be too much for a depressed person and might even heighten the possibility of suicide.

Gold states that 85 percent of his patients improve within three weeks after taking medication at the therapeutic level. By this time the patient will have been in his care for about four weeks. For the 15 percent who do not respond to a single medication, he may supplement the medication, sometimes with thyroid hormone, tyrosine or tryptophan (the amino acids we discussed in chapter 8), or lithium.

If, after a week or two, the patient still has not improved, Gold reevaluates the problem and tries another approach, depending not only upon the details of what has already been tried but also upon the seriousness of the patient's condition. If the danger of suicide is low, he may try another tricyclic or switch to an MAO inhibitor—a procedure that may take three or more weeks to institute. He feels that the dangers of the MAO inhibitors have been exaggerated and that they are safer than reputed (Gold 1987a:249). However, there is one limitation, or risk, to these drugs, and that is the requirement that the patient observe some fairly strict diet restrictions. (This was discussed in chapter 6.)

Gold may consider electroconvulsive therapy (ECT) for patients who remain depressed, especially if the patient is not responding to medication and if there is a high probability of suicide, or when other conditions, such as physical health or certain management problems, indicate that a quicker relief from the depression is essential for the well-being of the patient. He views ECT as a therapy of "last resort for all but a limited number of patients" and states that "we know too little still about why it works or how the treatment changes the brain for better and for worse" (Gold 1987a:251).

If the patient shows clinical improvement after any therapy and the symptoms of depression lessen, Gold repeats the DST and other biological tests to confirm that the "biological state markers of depression" have disappeared. He regards absence of these markers as the true indication that the treatment has worked. In his view, if there is clinical improvement but the markers are still there, the patient will relapse (Gold 1987a:251). Adequate treatment is described as the elimination of the "underlying condition" (Gold 1987a:252). If these tests still show abnormalities, then treatment should continue and the patient should be observed closely. An abnormal response on the DST, according to Gold, indicates a potential suicide. Many of the patients who later kill themselves seem to have improved symptomatically but retain these biological underpinnings of depression (Gold 1987a:252). If the vegetative symptoms are relieved and test results are normal, then psychotherapy is definitely indicated. With bipolar patients, the medication (usually lithium) is continued.

Gold believes psychotherapy can help prevent relapse by increasing, even teaching, coping abilities and by helping the patient learn a way of living other than the learned life-style of the chronic depressive. Although it is unclear in this description whether Gold does the psychotherapy himself, the implication is that he refers patients to others for this phase of combined therapy. This is inferred from his comments that although only a biopsychiatrist can make a diagnosis and prescribe the best kind of treatment, one need not be a biopsychiatrist or even a psychiatrist to practice psychotherapy. He states that psychologists, social workers, and nurses "may be equally competent, sometimes even better trained in certain psychotherapeutic techniques" (Gold 1987a:270).

Andreasen's Approach to Treatment

■■ Nancy Andreasen (1984:27–31) also presents a biological or
■■ medical model, which she attributes first to the works of Kraepelin and his followers and more recently to the developments in

neuroscience. She states with assurance her view that psychiatric conditions are diseases, mostly in the brain, with biological etiologies. Her approach emphasizes that this biological model is more appropriate for the graver mental conditions, including depression, and the treatment is basically somatic, including medication and ECT—both of which are aimed at correcting biological aberrations.

As with Gold, diagnosis includes careful history taking (family and personal medical), including detailed descriptions of symptoms, physical examination, and laboratory tests. Making an accurate diagnosis also includes watching the symptoms over time.

After the initial interview, Andreasen states that the patient usually is told what the physician thinks is wrong. A medication is then prescribed and careful instructions are given about its effects and side effects. The patient usually returns within a week or two, but follow-up visits tend to run from fifteen to thirty minutes rather than the customary psychiatric visit of from forty-five minutes to an hour. The purpose of the return visits is to determine if the client is improving and if his symptoms have had an impact on other parts of his life, for Andreasen holds that a biopsychiatrist treats the whole person. Treatment is very focused and very brief. Andreasen feels that the psychiatrist does not have to invest a lot of time in conversation because the patients who understand that their illnesses have biological roots do not suffer from guilt feelings, nor do their significant others.

Andreasen believes that this biological model of psychiatry not only is beneficial to patients but leads to better health care. She says that the antidepressant medications are "almost miraculously effective" but that since "not all biological treatments are miraculous cures, . . . [expectations should not be] excessively high" (Andreasen 1984:32).

Treatment in Psychiatric Outpatient Clinics

■■ For both technical and financial reasons, clients with mood
■■ disorders are being seen increasingly in outpatient clinics of psychiatric and medical hospitals. These clinics usually use a team approach to treatment. Because hospitals tend to have staffs comprised of individuals from many disciplines, the treatment team may include psychiatrists, social workers, psychologists, psychiatric nurses, and often occupational therapists, recreational therapists, and chaplains. Team members may also consult with various medical specialists as needed.

In some of these clinics the roles of each individual are clearcut; in others they may overlap. However, in a hospital setting the team leader is usually a physician (in this case, a psychiatrist), who has overall responsibility for all team staff members and clinic patients. The role of the team leader may vary and include supervision of staff, direct care of patients, leadership of diagnostic and treatment seminars, and responsibility for and supervision of medication.

The initial intake, which includes evaluating an applicant's eligibility for the program, is usually done by a social worker, psychologist, or psychiatric nurse. A potentially acceptable patient is then usually evaluated by a psychiatrist. Sometimes standardized scales are used to help diagnose and evaluate the patient and sometimes to gather data for research. The patient may be examined physically and given some medical tests. The criteria for acceptance may vary considerably, depending on the setting or the goals of a particular clinic's program. For example, a hospital may have been chosen to test a particular medication and may therefore be interested primarily in patients with a particular diagnosis or history.

Various combinations of medications and psychotherapies may be prescribed. Usually a nonphysician provides the psychotherapy—most often a social worker, although some clinics utilize other trained mental health professionals, particularly nurses. A physician, often a psychiatrist who may also be an expert in pharmacotherapy, prescribes and monitors medication. Usually, team members have regular meetings or consultations to discuss each patient's progress and evaluate the need for continuing treatment.

Treatment centers such as the Anxiety/Depression Clinic at the University of Chicago, which we describe later, tend to treat severely depressed patients. Many, if not most, of these patients have at least two diagnoses, such as depression and anxiety, depression and borderline personality disorder, or depression and substance abuse (particularly alcohol abuse, especially in bipolar patients).[1]

The Anxiety/Depression Clinic in the Department of Psychiatry of the University of Chicago Hospitals is an example of an outpatient clinic that follows a biopsychiatric team approach to patient treatment.[2]

Clients are referred to the Anxiety/Depression Clinic from a number of sources. All go through a diagnostic evaluation that includes a clinical interview, during which *face sheet information* (pertinent personal data) is gathered. Then the Structured Clinical Interview for Diagnosis (S.C.I.D.) is given by the interviewer. There are three self-administered scales: a Symptom Check List (SCL-90) (Derogatis and Cleary 1977), a scale devised by Ganellen to evaluate cognitive factors, and a standardized sleep questionnaire, designed to evaluate patterns of sleep. A Life Style–Life Events Interview designed to identify potentially precipitating events is administered. They also carefully assess current use of all types of drugs. Very complete medical and family histories are taken of the patient and his family, the latter in an attempt to identify genetic and familial factors; medical records are also requested. All patients are given thyroid function tests. Since the clinic maintains close contact with referring physicians, physical examinations are not required of clients who were referred by doctors, but they are given if the information is lacking or if there is some indication that a physical exam is needed. If medication is to be prescribed, then an electrocardiograph (EKG) is also given.

Three types of treatment are provided: One is medication alone, which is received by approximately one-third of those who attend the clinic. The usual procedure is to begin with a tricyclic (e.g., imipramine [Tofranil] or Prozac) and, if there is no response, to move to another tricyclic or to a MAOI (usually Nardil), then to other medications or combinations of medications. Another treatment is verbal therapy alone, received by about one-sixth of clinic patients. The third is combined verbal therapy and medication, which is received by about one-half of the patients. Usually, the most severely depressed receive combined therapy.

The verbal therapy, given by staff members of all disciplines, may be one of a range of therapies, including behavioral therapy, cognitive-behavioral therapy, and brief insight therapy. Interpersonal psychotherapy (IPT) will soon be added as a treatment approach. (These therapies will be explained in part 3.) If the therapist who provides the verbal therapy is not a physician, then there is periodic consultation on medication with a staff physician. In a number of these cross-disciplinary settings, all therapists—physicians and nonphysicians—soon become very sensitive to differing patient reactions to medications and are adept at alerting and requesting physician adjustment of the medication.

The Ideal Clinic of Papolos and Papolos

■■ Demitri and Janice Papolos (one is a psychiatrist and the
■■ other a journalist) discuss the changes in the treatment of depression that came about with the growth of recent information from the neurosciences. They feel that the replacement of psychotherapy by medications "was short-sighted . . . a serious clinical oversight and a gross scientific presumption" (Papolos and Papolos 1987:139). They propose an integrated treatment approach combining psychopharmacological management and psychotherapeutic dialogue in three areas (Papolos and Papolos 1987:143–144).

Under *medical* they visualize the physician prescribing the appropriate medication and establishing a recording system for past and future cycle frequency (rather than episodes, indicating that they deal with more bipolar disorders than the milder or even more severe unipolar disorders). The physician, in discussion with the patient, spells out maintenance medications and monitors the medications periodically. For example, there are monthly observations of patients taking lithium (if prescribed) and thyroid and kidney examinations every six months to a year.

Under *educational* is the provision of information about depression, including course, symptoms and signs, cycles, and the medications used to treat depression. One aspect of this phase that we feel is particularly useful is that the "patient learns to differentiate normal mood variations from episodes of illness" (Papolos and Papolos 1987:144).

The third part of the approach, *psychological*, includes the formation of a collaborative, trusting relationship with the therapist. Papolos and Papolos decry what they see as an artificial division between medicine and psychology; they approve of nonmedical psychotherapy as long as the therapist, physician, or otherwise, has a "solid understanding of the disorder, its course and medical treatment" (1987:159). Although they do not advocate any one approach, they specifically mention marital therapy, cognitive therapy, and interpersonal psychotherapy (IPT) (Papolos and Papolos 1987:149–155). During the therapy, the focus is first on the psychological meaning of taking the medications, then on discussion of self-esteem, life goals and relationships, defenses and coping strategies, and stigma. (These elements are common to many of the approaches we discuss in part 3.) They state, as part of the psychological approach, that the patient must accept the disorder (1987:144).

Papolos and Papolos (1987:161–162) acknowledge that there are some shortcomings in the organization of health care, and they propose a clinic that offers a program for clients and their families that "would serve as a diagnostic, medical treatment and education center. . . . assess[ing] the psychological impact of the illness on both patients and families and offering supportive service for long-term management of the disorder."

During intake, a client would be interviewed for several sessions, in the course of which an individual and a family history would be taken, focusing on the number and length of past and present periods of depression. Previous treatments and their consequences, including side effects, would be reviewed. There would be a complete evaluation by physicians, including a physical examination and the ruling out of any other condition that might account for or complicate the depression. As described earlier, treatment would begin with the prescription of medication and would include careful testing and monitoring. Education and psychotherapy are also considered part of the treatment.

After the diagnosis, the patient and family would be given "psycho-education" through a workshop where the "nature, course, possible causes and treatments of the disorder are reviewed." The family would have the option of "several sessions of family counseling" (1987:161).

Follow-up treatment would be provided. A psychiatrist would stay with each client for individual long-term medical treatment, although some clients might also opt for individual psychotherapy, and their families might keep going to treatment groups focusing on family issues. The clinic would have support groups, run by patients and their families, both for manic-depressives and for patients with other kinds of depression.

The clinics could also serve as a source for information on the hypothesized genetic causes and genetic markers for depression, thereby heightening understanding.

As Papolos and Papolos say, "Unfortunately, such a comprehensive program is not commonly available. . . . If patients and family members come together and work with the leaders of such clinics, they can sensitize them to the services they need and want, and thus forge a better system. A group of people bound by ideas, commitment and strong resolve could have their say and effect change" (1987:162).

Some Comments on the Biopsychiatric Approach to Treatment

■■ As the name indicates, the biopsychiatric approach to treat-
■■ ment is a combined approach that emphasizes biological treatment yet includes the talking therapies. Biological treatment may be any of the approaches we have reviewed, including antidepressant medication, lithium, electroconvulsive therapy, phototherapy, the somatic treatments for substance abuse disorders, sleep disorders, eating disorders, and so on. It also embraces the tests we have discussed (e.g., for biological markers). Although much of the theory is still unproven, some of the tests are useful diagnostic tools, and many of the somatic treatments are clearly effective in relieving a great deal of the distress of the depressions (Coyne 1987:393).

Since psychological treatments—the talking therapies—also have much to offer in the treatment of the depressions, as we shall explain in the next sections of this book, the biopsychiatric approach would seem to be an effective, logical process if it truly combines the best of both orientations. For example, Gold's practice, as reflected in his writings, stresses pharmacotherapy, or pharmacotherapy combined with psychotherapy for the more seriously depressed, and recognizes the importance of the psychotherapies, especially for the milder and more moderate depressions. We believe that Gold's recognition of the importance of each approach is an ideal to be strived toward rather than the reality of most current biopsychiatric practice.

Current biopsychiatric treatment by an individual practitioner is probably much closer to Andreasen's description. Although she recognizes the need for treating the whole person, most psychotherapists would object to what she describes as psychiatric treatment. On the other hand, we know of many instances where depressed patients are seen by biologically oriented psychiatrists who merely prescribe antidepressant medications and do not use *any* form of psychotherapy.

We are also concerned about some of the practices of prescribing antidepressant medications. Unlike Gold, who emphasizes that he does not prescribe medication for every depressed patient, many psychiatrists who do not know enough about the pharmacology of these drugs prescribe them easily and frequently. They often err on the side of undermedication, and this is most often responsible for patient nonresponse (Baldessarini 1986).

A psychiatric resident recently wrote an article that reflects our thinking on the biological approaches to the treatment of depression. Keith Ablow (1990a) stated that when he was a medical student he found the medical model of mental illness, which he described as "accidents of biology . . . [resulting from] . . . abnormal brain chemistry," to be appealing and understandable. He could picture in his mind the faulty neurotransmission being corrected by medication and the faulty "chemical wiring between neurons" being fixed by ECT. He states that all that is true and that "many patients . . . thankfully, get better on the right combination of medicines." On the other hand, he describes interactions with anguished patients who were "sick and defeated and alone. . . . [and] . . . . whose needs for affection and security and understanding . . . [were] unmet. . . . [who used] desperate survival strategies . . . to provide some insulation against the chaos of their lives." One depressed psychotic patient, technically able to be cured by medications, did not want to take them, because he felt desperately lonely without the "voices. . . . [especially] the good voices . . . that talked to each other." Although Ablow found this to be not very scientific, he started developing a third ear and began to listen to the patient as well as to himself. He concluded that the "art of psychiatry is in marrying empathy and science in service to the patient."

The multidisciplinary clinics, preferably following the combined approach proposed by the Papolos, among others, will probably become the most commonly utilized sources of treatment for mood disorders. Because they are staffed by people from various disciplines, there can be a fusion of knowledge of all aspects of the depressions: the social, economic, and familial factors as well as the psychological and the biological. As the knowledge of biological factors increase, so will the knowledge about the psychotherapies and the psychosocial and psychoeducational means of interventions. If present trends persist, they will continue to focus on comparatively short-term therapies, more and more specifically designed for treatment of the mood disorders—therapies such as cognitive, cognitive-behavioral, and interpersonal psychotherapy (IPT). (We describe these therapies in part 3.) In addition to the scientific developments, the rising costs of health care and the dictates of third-party reimbursement sources have led to changes in the distribution of health care. As health maintenance organizations and managed-care facilities continue to grow, mental health care will become increasingly focused on the short-term team approaches. We view this as a positive, not only for the potentially higher level of care but for more careful diagnostic assessment, particularly the weeding out of mimickers and the increase in the treatment of coexisting conditions.

Summary of Part II

We have reviewed a number of theories proposing that the depressions, as well as various associated problems—such as sleep disorders, eating disorders, and substance abuse—have a genetic basis or component and/or are caused by malfunctions in brain chemistry. We have also discussed the somatic treatments based on these theories, which were developed to correct the hypothesized biochemical imbalances and malfunctions.

Although most of these theories are controversial, evidence increasingly suggests that many of the *processes* described are correct. As our technology improves, this evidence may become clearer, as we are able actually to see the neurochemical and other body systems at work. Even at the present time, sophisticated machinery such as positron emission tomography (PET) has made it possible to see receptor binding inside the living brain (Hyman 1988b:255).

Improvements in technology should facilitate the development of even more effective antidepressant medications and somatic treatments. The emphasis has already evolved from concentrating on neurotransmitter accessibility to emphasizing the sensitivity of cell receptors (Andreasen 1984:137) to focusing on postreceptor events (Hyman 1991a). Other aspects are similarly being explored, such as neuroendocrine functioning, the pathway of amino acids across the blood-brain barrier, and other biological systems.

What the research has not provided is firm evidence of causation—the chicken-or-egg question we have been interjecting from time to time. Whybrow, Akiskal, and McKinney (1984:121) warn us about interpreting this evidence: "Biological complexity appears easily confused with etiology. That changes in the metabolites of biogenic amines may be defined in the affective disorders does not necessarily imply that biogenic amine change is a *more* likely explanation of the *origin* of affective disorder than is perceived loss of self-esteem" (emphasis in the original).

In these chapters, we have cited the cautions that many of the most responsible investigators in this field have placed on their research reports, as well as their evaluations of work by colleagues. Although many therapists also are convinced that in the depressions, we are dealing with a biological, or perhaps biopsychosocial phenomenon, they warn us to be cautious about what is actually proven and to be careful to differentiate fact from hypothesis. For example, Matussek (1988:97) has stated that "for many years a great number of research groups worldwide have made many efforts to elucidate the neurobiological functions in affective disorders. So far no unequivocal, generally accepted, and reproducible results have been obtained. We do not yet know the neurobiological changes of brain functions during an endogenous, neurotic or reactive depression responsible for the symptomatology."

Beckham (1990) has stated that more naturalistic (nonexperimental) longitudinal research must be done to identify the elements involved in treating the depressions. We could cite additional statements by other researchers and therapists, but we feel we have made the point. It is obvious that the depressions are complicated phenomena that cannot be explained satisfactorily by any single biological or biochemical factor (Baldessarini 1985b). Of course, they also cannot be explained by any single social or psychological factor.

While the debate continues, millions of depressed individuals need treatment, and choices must be made. Perhaps it is not so important for therapists who treat these depressed patients to be entirely constrained by the question of what *causes* the depressions. Even if many theories have not yet *proven* to be correct, they have provided some useful indicators for treatment that could be attempted, cautiously, as long as they will not harm the patient. For example, although the theories that a patient may be self-medicating for depression by eating carbohydrates or using one of the substances of abuse have not been proven, the knowledge of these possibilities could certainly be taken into consideration. If an obese patient is a carbohydrate craver, the possibility of depression should be explored prior to treatment. If the patient attempts to diet, he or she should be carefully monitored.

From the viewpoint of direct treatment, the focus should be on the client and his or her needs—symptoms, functioning, what the patient says, and so on. There is ample evidence (e.g., as stated by Ablow and seen by many therapists) that, based on biological tests, patients may be "cured" of depression but still may not feel good and may not function at a normal level.

We feel that pharmacotherapy and psychotherapy are both relevant to different aspects of the many kinds of depression. We agree with Wender and Klein (1981) that the biological and psychological orientation to treating depression may ideally be encompassed in a third orientation. However, rather than a biopsychological approach, we envision one that is psychobiological, which we shall present in part 3.

Psychological Theories and Treatments of Depression

The clinical descriptions of depression have remained fairly constant for many centuries, but the theoretical explanations of depression and treatments for it have changed many times. Different approaches appear periodically, are popular for a while, and then fade away or survive, usually in an altered form. Some of these new theories and therapies are genuine advances; some are not.

When we examine the psychotherapies, we often confront a surplus of theory and a paucity of evidence. Fortunately, we have recently seen some increase in research and systematic investigation of psychotherapeutic treatment alternatives to depression. The National Institute of Mental Health (NIMH) has also sponsored a major study, which has compared two of the major psychotherapies for depression—cognitive-behavioral and interpersonal psychotherapy (IPT)—with drug treatments. Although all the results of this long-term study are not yet in, we shall refer to this study and its importance for treating depression.

In the following chapters we present a brief overview of the current major psychotherapies for depression. "These psychotherapies are basically divided according to their emphasis on one or more of the various ways of describing human beings: what they are feeling—their *affects/emotions*; what they are doing—their *behaviors*; and what they are thinking—their *cognitions*" (Schwartz 1982:2). In chapter 12 we begin with the oldest and most central, the psychodynamic. In chapter 13 we discuss interpersonal psychotherapy (IPT), a comparatively new development. Chapter 14 explores the behavioral approaches, and chapter 15 covers the cognitive-behavioral psychotherapies.

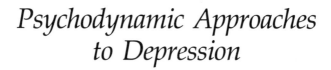

12

Psychodynamic Approaches to Depression

Freud's View of Depression

■■ The roots of our present psychological approaches to depres-
■■ sion can be found in the works of Karl Abraham and Sigmund Freud, particularly Freud's masterful essay "Mourning and Melancholia" (1917), a paper that was said to have "changed the course of
psychoanalysis" (Arieti and Bemporad 1978:21).

In 1911, Abraham presented his view that depression is related to
the abandonment of libidinal strivings ("psychic energy . . . which
drives the individual towards the gratification of desires" [Walrond-
Skinner 1986:205]), a thesis later elaborated by Freud, who said,
"Depression is hostility turned inward," or what Rado called retro-
flexed rage (1928).

This view of depression as hostility turned inward refers to a situation in which a person has invested love and libidinal (emotional or
psychic) energy in another individual and then finds the relationship
terminated. When the relationship is ended through death, we go through
a mourning process. Freud stated that in "normal mourning" or grieving we remember the dead one, both positively and not so positively,
and gradually withdraw (reclaim) the energy invested in the other as
we let him go. As described by Arieti (1982), the survivor comes to grips
with the reality that the person is dead. "By being unpleasant, sadness
seems to have a function—its own elimination" (Arieti 1982:298). The
survivor is then free to redirect this energy (libido) elsewhere. After a
period of slowed behavior, activity returns and the mourner resumes a
more usual, or "normal," round of activity.

In mourning the loss is real, and feeling it is conscious and socially
sanctioned (ego-syntonic). Every major religion has provisions for
mourning, or "grief work," which is recognized as normal and necessary to enable the bereaved person to go on with life. However, the
person who becomes depressed cannot spring back; he cannot do what
Arieti calls sorrow-work (1982:298).

Whether a relationship is ended by death or by rejection, grieving over its loss may persist and become melancholia. In melancholia—now categorized as a type of major depressive episode—a person has suffered a loss, real or imaginary, that may not even be consciously identified. He is enraged and hurt by the loss and directs these feelings against the most accessible target, the part of the other person now inside himself (the "introjected other"). This anger is experienced primarily as self-reproach: guilt due to perceived inadequacies in the relationship with the deceased or absent person. The feelings and the symptoms, which are perceived as depression, are really the unconscious manifestations of these feelings about the lost person. As frequently quoted, "in grief the world becomes poor and empty; in melancholia it is the ego itself" (Freud 1917:167). A survivor whose feelings for the deceased person (the former love object) were ambivalent often experiences additional confused emotions, which are worsened by the suffering and the sense of loss.

When relationships, especially love relationships, end for reasons other than death, termination is often perceived as desertion or rejection. The rage that the person feels about the relationship being broken, especially about being rejected, becomes focused on the part of the other that has been internalized. In other words, it is actually directed inward against the person himself. Under extreme conditions the depressed person may commit suicide in an attempt to punish the "other," now internalized in himself.

Psychodynamic thought has changed and advanced in many ways from the early drive-theory hypothesis, yet one still hears the early theory propounded. Although the idea that dammed-up sexual energy can be transformed into another emotion (e.g., anxiety) has not survived, the notion that aggression turned inward somehow becomes transformed into depression has endured. A number of authors have stated that the whole vague area of "hostility" varies so markedly from patient to patient that it does not seem valuable in explaining depression, despite the fact that the theory of aggression turned inward persists (Whybrow, Akiskal, and McKinney 1984:34).

The tenacity of this difficult-to-prove thesis poses a problem: Some therapists encourage depressed patients to express hostility outwardly toward others, allegedly to relieve this self-punishment. Although some patients *do* feel an immediate relief when they express anger, it is often short-lived and is frequently followed by feelings of guilt. Since some depressed patients do not express self-reproach and some have not experienced loss, either in the present or in the past, the "therapeutic" hostility may be expressed against the wrong person. Of course, for some patients, rage itself, which is an active feeling, may serve as a defense—an attempt to ward off depression.

Recent writings in self psychology (a contemporary development in psychoanalytic theory stressing the importance of narcissistic development and the self system) state another view that takes issue with the view that depression is hostility turned against oneself. Although there may be depressive responses when the individual experiences conflict about unconscious rage, the "two are not inevitably linked. It is a therapeutic and technical mistake to assume, as is still often done, that where there is depression there is hidden aggression; and that if such feelings do not appear in the clinical material, the patient is of necessity concealing them from the therapist" (Basch 1988:114).

Old concepts sometimes die hard, and we feel the survival of this oversimplified, difficult-to-research theory has impeded the investigation of psychodynamic treatments of depression.

Later Developments in the Psychodynamic Views of Depression

■■ Later psychodynamic theories of depression moved away
■■ from the "hostility-turned-inward" hypothesis based on drive theory, toward viewing depression in terms of ego functioning, especially that of adaptation. Ego psychology viewed losses as injuries more to the individual's view of himself (his ego) than to displaced libido. Bibring (1953) in particular stated that when a person falls short in achieving what he expected, he suffers a loss of self-esteem that is experienced as depression; there is a gap between the ideal self and the actual self. These reformulations of diminished self-esteem by Bibring and others made it easier to include social and external (environmental) variables in conceptualizing depression.

Basch (1980) has commented that the central characteristic of depression is the feeling that life is meaningless; that one's perception of oneself is "no longer a unifying focus for ambitions and ideals . . . [for] the goals that ordinarily organize behavior seem to have been lost." This observation reflects the contributions of the later self psychologists, who thought that the many symptoms of depression serve to protect a self-system that can no longer function and meet its goals. The symptoms are a way of communicating that this particular self-system is in despair and hopeless and thus needs help from others to restore some sort of meaning to life (Basch 1988:114). Basch also states that symptom removal is not the primary goal of therapy; he emphasizes that the end of symptoms and discomfort does not mean the end of the disorder but that the person is once again able to engage in behaviors (carry out procedures) that will enable him to reach constructive (therapeutic) goals (1980:136–137).

The concept of a *dominant other* was another important development. According to this theory, depressives often feel subjected to extraordinary demands by significant others in their environments. Their perceptions, which usually begin in childhood, may be correct or incorrect, but the difference is often moot. The person perceived to be making these demands, called the dominant other, is usually a parent or spouse, although it could be any other person (Arieti and Bemporad 1978). The demands of this dominant other are soon perceived to be so great that they become overwhelming, and a good portion of the individual's energies must be devoted to fulfilling them. Individuals may come to feel that they live mainly (frequently only) to satisfy the dominant other. If they cannot change their goals and achieve the perceived demands, they feel helpless and hopeless and may become depressed.

This history of unfulfilled demands and low self-esteem provides an orientation toward life for the depressed person, especially for the chronically depressed—or as some call it, the *depressive personality*. Many depressed persons see themselves and the rest of the world through a particular filter, which Arieti calls an *ideology* (1982:298). This ideology of pessimism and low self-esteem forms the foundation for depression that is often long-lasting and chronic.

Bemporad, in discussing the depressive personality, states that depressed individuals display pathological dependency and self-inhibition (1985:88). These personality traits contrast markedly with the surface appearance, for depressives often seem mature, high-achieving, and psychologically healthy. Although outwardly hard-working and productive, the depressive gets little pleasure from his work, for his efforts are not motivated by desire for achievement or altruism but by desire for praise from dominant others and as a means of easing guilt and ultimately avoiding perceived abandonment.

Despite the vast amount of work attempting to associate specific personality types with depression, no agreement has been achieved on the characteristics of depressive personalities, nor has evidence been discovered linking specific personality types to etiology (Millon and Kotik 1985:700).[1]

The preceding review is only a very small sampling of the sizable psychodynamic literature on depression. Although much has been written on this subject, Karasu (1990a:135) points out that the applications of psychodynamic *techniques* to the treatment of depression actually "have been relatively sparse," since the psychodynamic procedures were initially intended for "general application to neurotic personality structure" rather than designed specifically for the treatment of depression, as were cognitive therapy and interpersonal psychotherapy (IPT). He also points out that psychoanalytic thought has developed into many different approaches, both long and short term, and emphasizes many different aspects of theory and therapy.

Long-Term Psychodynamic Psychotherapy for Depression

■■ Long-lasting, chronic depressions are sometimes called *char-*
■■ *acterological.* They often have origins deep in childhood and are consistently reinforced by others. Usually, they do not respond to the shorter forms of therapy, which seem to provide relief only for individual depressive episodes, leaving the person at high risk for recurrence of severe depression. Bemporad (1985) proposes analytic therapy, which we understand to mean long-term analytic therapy, in these cases where depression is very much a part of the patient's personality structure.

We shall describe the general principles and the process of long-term psychodynamic therapy for depression, rather than presenting a case history, since the length and nature of the treatment make generalization difficult.[2]

In the course of analytic therapy, patients review their lives, analyzing those forces from the past that govern and determine their current pathological behavior. Bemporad particularly stresses the importance of assessing the patient's perception of demands made by dominant others and the often self-defeating and ineffectual modes of responding that the patient has adopted. Patients examine their views of themselves that have been based on the impossibilities of pleasing dominant others. They learn the origins of their faulty thoughts and responses and, through treatment, learn to give up these self-defeating patterns and learn new ways of coping, obtaining gratification, and maintaining self-esteem. They restructure their lives and abandon the old imperatives (the old "shoulds"). Part of the therapy is to use knowledge of the impact of these old patterns on the present and thus prevent recurrence of depression (Bemporad 1985).

Medication may be used to alleviate the patients's vegetative symptoms, thereby lessening the patient's focus on them and using them to resist in-depth exploration and insight. According to Arieti and Bemporad, drugs help in some cases, but not the most serious ones, which may require electroshock therapy or hospitalization. They stress that there is also a need for psychotherapy in *all* cases of depression (Arieti and Bemporad 1978:212–214).

In the beginning of therapy, the therapist assumes the role of a significant other but not of a dominant other (Arieti and Bemporad 1978:215). The therapist is flexible, dependable, and central to the patient's life and aims to be perceived by the patient as a helping and nondemanding person. It is also important that the therapy be perceived from the beginning as a joint venture. The therapist lets the client know that the therapist does not have total responsibility for the "cure"; the client must also be responsible and must do a lot of the work. It is felt that if the therapist assumes the main responsibility, sooner or later the depressed client, living out the patterns determined by the past, will manipulate the situation so that it works eventually to his (or her) disadvantage. In a typical sequence of events, the patient begins by making the therapist the center of his life and trying to please the therapist by increasing his performance. After a while the patient starts to understand that he is not acting on his own initiative, but in response to perceived (in this case, clearly imagined) demands of the therapist, who has now become a new dominant other. The patient eventually concludes that, like so many others in the past, the therapist is disappointed in him and that their relationship, like the others, will end in disaster and depression. This often becomes a self-fulfilling prophecy. However, the experienced therapist always remains acutely aware of this possible scenario.

During the middle part of therapy, one of the important tasks is for the patient to expand his (or her) horizons by looking for pleasurable activities in the outside world so that the reliance on a depressed mode of adaptation can be relinquished. Many depressed people fight this expansion of activities, which requires giving up old patterns of behavior. They may become angry with the therapist, who is seen as making familiar, impossible demands. The patient may also resist treatment or there may be relapses during treatment.

A crucial part of the middle and last phases of therapy is achieving an understanding of the conditions that produced the depression. Helping the client reach this understanding is a central focus of this approach.

Another goal is a change in personality. As we interpret it, this goal is to make changes in processes—the individual's ways of adapting and interacting with the environment. The client's depressive ideology must be replaced by a more optimistic way of looking at the world. The depressive must also master more adaptive personal and social skills. In this process the poor self-image and low self-esteem should be replaced by a greater sense of personal worth and a more optimistic outlook. Ghosts from the past must be dealt with. The dominant others who have made exorbitant demands must be understood as fallible and often vulnerable human beings, not as "evil people." As stated by Arieti and Bemporad (1978:311), "Before termination of therapy, the past must be accepted without excessive rancor."

Arieti and Bemporad's work is basic and essential for a complete understanding of depression. They call their psychodynamic approach cognitive, stating the relevance of the depressive ideology we mentioned earlier. This ideology, which may be partly conscious and partly unconscious, is not only an organizing principle for the depressed person but also a way of coping—a defense that enables the patient to function. In their view, the main function of therapy is to examine and replace the depressive ideology with a more adaptive, less self-punishing, and more optimistic way of looking at the world. Although Arieti and Bemporad emphasize the cognitive nature of depression, they do not diminish the importance of the pain felt by the patient, on both a conscious and an unconscious level.

In chapter 15 we shall discuss the approach of Aaron Beck, who feels that cognitive distortions and dysfunctional information processing cause depressions. Arieti and Bemporad differ from Beck, holding that the distortions and the dysfunctional processes are not the causes but the *results* of a person's history and experiences, including the development of the largely unconscious depressive ideology. In their view, cognition is only a part of the total picture of depression (Arieti and Bemporad 1978:80).

The Effectiveness of Long-Term Psychodynamic Therapy

No controlled or comparative studies and only a very few long-term follow-up reports exist on long-term psychodynamic treatment of depression (Bemporad 1985:97). Much of the theory is based on clinical case studies. Bemporad (1985) quotes Jacobson (1971:319–324), who reports on some depressed people "doing well" twenty years after the termination of analysis. Arieti (1977) reported on a three-year follow-up of twelve patients showing seven with full recovery (no relapse), four with marked improvement, and one failure.

The lack of controlled long-term research on the results of psychoanalytic treatment is not restricted to depression. Because of the nature of this highly individualized, highly idiosyncratic long-term treatment, it would be extremely difficult to do the kind of systematic research that seems to be increasingly demanded of therapy. According to Rosenberg (1985:116–117), there are three major methodological problems in researching psychoanalytically oriented psychotherapy: the lack of specification of the techniques used; the irrelevance of diagnostic systems, such as the DSM-III-R, for psychodynamic therapy; and the difficulty of translating the concepts that are most useful to psychodynamic therapists into researchable terms.

Karasu (1990a:135) has stated that because psychoanalytic thought has developed into a number of different orientations with alterations in theory and technique, the dynamic approaches have lagged behind others (such as behavioral and cognitive) in being translated into standardized treatment manuals, which would make it easier to evaluate the effectiveness of psychodynamic therapies.

There are certainly enough clinical accounts of successful psychoanalytic and dynamically oriented therapy to confirm that whatever the nature of the process, some patients benefit from it. We believe that the difficulty of researching these therapies (unlike the methodologically stringent trials available for testing drug effects) and the current emphasis on a cost/benefit approach to treatment have reduced the use of psychotherapy in favor of more economical (but not always more appropriate or successful) drug therapy.

Short-Term Psychodynamic Psychotherapy for Depression

■■ The psychodynamically based interventions for depression
■■ have become shorter and more focused. There are few conceptual differences between the long-term and short-term psychodynamic therapies for depression. Strupp and colleagues (1982) state that time limitation is the main factor that distinguishes the shorter- from the longer-term, more classic treatments.

Short-term psychodynamic therapy for depression has much in common with other short-term approaches. Many of the differences might well be entirely semantic. However, one real difference is in the use and interpretation of the transference relationship. Transference occurs in *all* forms of therapy.[3] In short-term psychodynamic therapy it is actively used, unlike most other therapies, with the possible exception of interpersonal psychotherapy (IPT), as we discuss in the next chapter.

The classification of short-term therapy is arbitrary (Rosenberg 1985:107). No one agrees on how many sessions differentiate short-term from long-term therapy. The number may vary from a minimum of perhaps six to a maximum of from twelve to twenty-five or even as many as forty—a rather wide range.

Brief (time-limited) therapy is obviously not open-ended. The limitations on time provide an organizing framework. The theory holds that this limitation on the number of sessions provides not only greater motivation for help but more movement (Reid and Shyne 1969).

Both long- and short-term treatments involve an intense interpersonal relationship with the therapist and assume that during treatment the patient will exhibit the same coping strategies used both outside the therapy and in the past. These strategies then become the focus of treatment. However, just a few topics can be chosen for discussion because of the time limitations of the approach. These time limitations also make it necessary that the therapist have the skill and that the client be able and ready to connect current conflicts with core conflicts (Rush 1986).

According to psychodynamic theory, core (inner) conflicts are the causes of depression. Strupp and colleagues (1982) state that these conflicts stem from past and present interpersonal relations, from early childhood experiences of being disappointed by others, from inadequate nurturing, and from other factors. Depression also results from an inability to adapt to the gap between aspirations and achievements and from a reduction in self-esteem, especially due to disappointment and loss—experiences that predispose the individual to helplessness and worsen the initial inner conflicts. These initial and subsequent conflicts retrigger rage that cannot be expressed and is therefore turned inward.

Long-term therapy may examine any number of topics: unresolved grief, disappointments, poor self-esteem, guilt, problems with aggression, and so on. In short-term therapy only one or two issues may be discussed. These are usually past and present relationships, including the therapeutic relationship. There is greater focusing, the therapist is more active, and interpretations are more direct than in long-term therapy (Strupp et al. 1982).

There is early and assertive exploration and clarification of the transference—what is occurring in the relationship. The therapist and client examine the client's defenses and ways of coping with anxiety and impulses, and the therapist illuminates how these factors are interrelated and are a manifestation of the old maladaptive patterns of coping (Rush 1986).

Since one of the main assumptions of the psychodynamic orientation is that depression is a symptom of an underlying conflict, brief psychodynamic therapy, although time-limited, aims not only at the presenting problem (or symptom) but at the underlying problem. This assumption is contrary to the theories of the other brief therapies, which focus more upon the symptoms of depression.

The proper focus of short-term therapy is controversial. Some authorities (e.g., Strupp et al. 1982) consciously focus on the transference as the main medium of change. Others center on *chronically endured pain*—the "long term feelings of failure and victimization" (Mann 1973, cited in Rosenberg 1985:103) or on the relationship of childhood experiences to current problems and symptoms (Malan 1976, cited in Rosenberg 1985:104).

Patients selected for short-term dynamic therapy must be able to deal with the fast pace of this therapy. Rush (1986) states that suitable patients are motivated for change; able to develop mutual, mature relationships; have ego strength; are psychologically minded (which we interpret to mean open to the therapist's interpretations and connections); and have a focal (central or dominating) conflict. Rosenberg (1985) excludes psychotics, manic depressives, and those who are impulsive, are narcissistic, and have problems with alcohol (1985). He feels that suicidal patients should also be excluded, but the criteria for exclusion is active suicidal behavior rather than suicidal ideation. Clients whose defenses are rigid and who need the extreme dependency of a longer-term therapy are also poor candidates.

A Case of Depression Treated with Short-Term Psychodynamic Therapy

Lester Ashkenazi (a pseudonym) appeared for treatment at a student mental health clinic, referred by one of his professors. He was a twenty-two-year-old first-year medical student at a midwestern state university.

Lester had completed an undergraduate degree in a small, highly regarded, midwestern liberal arts college. He attended this school against the wishes of his parents, who wanted him to attend an Ivy League school such as Harvard, Yale, or Princeton. (He had been accepted at all three.) He stated that he chose the smaller school because of its size, thinking it would give him more opportunities for close friendships and the attention of professors. As it developed in the first interview, he actually chose it for two other reasons: It was one of his few acts of defying his parents, and although he did not initially admit this to himself, he was afraid of what he felt would be intense competition at the large Ivy League schools. His father constantly stated that if he had taken his advice, he would be in medical school at a prestigious university instead of this large state medical school.

Lester was the youngest of five children and the only son. His father, a physician, was also a professor of biochemistry at an Ivy League school and an internationally known authority in his field. His mother was a successful author of children's books. His sisters were each considered successful. Except for the sister who was immediately older than Lester, all were married. Each had either earned or was in the process of earning a graduate degree. The two oldest sisters had also produced grandchildren, on whom Lester's parents doted.

Lester said he wanted desperately to succeed in medical school, but he was having difficulties. Although he worked hard, he felt he was in over his head. He felt he had difficulty understanding some of the material in courses such as anatomy and biochemistry, although his work was more than adequate. He began to have trouble falling asleep and described his sleep as restless; he seldom woke feeling rested. He also began to skip meals and lose weight. Physical examination and tests by the campus health service showed nothing.

Lester had had previous counseling when he was twelve years old and having difficulty preparing for his Bar Mitzvah (confirmation). The ceremony was to be followed by a lavish party. His parents had been involved in every step of the preparations. His father constantly quizzed him on his speech and other parts of the ritual, continually criticizing and correcting his pronunciation, singing, speaking, and so forth, to the point where Lester was unable to proceed with his preparation. The principal of the religious school finally intervened, and the family eased its pressure. Lester performed well at the ceremony.

The pressure that his family put on Lester over the Bar Mitzvah was typical of what occurred during his entire schooling. This family put considerable emphasis on performance and achievement, particularly academic achievement. In an early session, Lester stated that he could remember his father grunting and nodding at his straight A's, for this was expected; anything less than that provoked arguments, scoldings, and groundings, often for months at a time. He could not remember his father ever hugging or kissing him.

Lester's mother also emphasized achievement. When he did not clean his room, or finish what he had been served at meals, or did poorly in school, she told him he did not love her. Lester told the therapist he loved his mother but that she favored his sisters and gave them a lot of attention. He could recall no instance in which his mother praised him and described his parents as giving openly and freely to their grandchildren, spending a lot of time with them, and showering them with affection and attention.

He was dating several women but none with whom he had a commitment. He preferred to remain unattached.

INITIAL PHASE OF THERAPY

Since the student mental health clinic was a short-term treatment facility, the limited and focused nature of the available help was explained to Lester. He was assessed as an appropriate candidate for short-term help, for he was highly motivated for change (he was petrified of doing poorly in medical school), he had ego strength and was psychologically minded, and he seemed to have a capacity for relationships, as evidenced by his dating and by his wide circle of friends in college and medical school.

In the early phases of the therapy Lester seemed an ideal client. He was on time or early for every appointment. He was verbal and spoke animatedly and at length about his early family relationships. When asked about his dreams, he immediately began to bring in notes and discuss vivid, interesting dreams with the therapist. He eagerly answered the therapist's questions, and he free-associated to the dreams with enthusiasm. He seemed to place the therapist on a pedestal, clinging to his every word.

After he entered therapy, Lester's anxiety seemed to ease, and his sleep problems ended almost immediately. He was much more cheerful and was able to concentrate upon his studies. His work improved.

The beginning phase of therapy lasted three sessions.

MIDDLE PHASE

The therapist introduced the idea of the dominant other, pointing out to Lester that much of his life had been spent in trying to please others through his accomplishments. He was aware, intellectually, that his parents' approval of him depended on his achievements. He said this somewhat blandly, denying hostility toward them and his sisters. He dismissed the problems over his Bar Mitzvah as adolescent conflict over religion rather than as ambivalence at being shown off by his parents as another achievement. He resisted exploring what the therapist felt was considerable underlying anger. The therapist attempted to focus on the link between his feelings of depression and his feelings of frustration in not being able to fulfill his parents'—particularly his father's—expectations of him.

To this point, Lester had related well to the therapist, trying hard to please him by praising the therapist's sometimes routine comments. He had tried, unsuccessfully, to increase the frequency of the sessions. He had asked to see the therapist on weekends and had begun to telephone between sessions. On one occasion, Lester made an unscheduled visit to the therapist (a university professor who was also affiliated with the student mental health clinic) in his office in another school on the campus, a highly inappropriate behavior.

During this middle phase the therapist began to interpret the transference relationship: Lester was trying to please the therapist by performing for him, bringing in dreams, free-associating, and praising him excessively. Actually, Lester was attempting to convert the therapist into a dominant other from whom he could receive praise and encouragement.

When the therapist connected Lester's current behavior with his old, deeply ingrained patterns of interacting with his family, Lester was at first incredulous. He rejected the idea and was acutely angry with the therapist for rejecting him. Lester then attacked the therapist, stating that the therapist, much like his father, did not care for him as a person but only as an object. The therapist only wanted another success story that he could write up for a book. He questioned his credentials, asking "Why aren't you a psychiatrist?," and in one session he attempted to discuss the catecholamine hypotheses of depression, "which you, as a nonmedical person, couldn't possibly understand!"

The anger that Lester felt when presented with the observations on his relationship with the therapist was connected to the long-denied feelings of rejection by his parents and to the helplessness he felt at being able to satisfy them only through academic accomplishments. He began to express anger at his parents for this lack of acceptance. Several dreams featured hostile themes, one of which was the death of his father. In another dream Lester presented a paper at a scientific conference where he received much praise. The topic of the paper was in biochemistry!

When the therapist did not act defensively in response to Lester's attacks and did not withdraw attention, Lester came to realize that this relationship with the therapist was really quite unlike the one he had with his father, for the therapist did not make his acceptance conditional upon Lester's performance as a client.

During this middle phase, Lester did not go home for one of the school holidays but spent the time at a friend's home. He was admittedly much too angry at his parents and was not yet able to handle his new insights on his compulsion to dedicate his life to pleasing the dominant other.

This middle phase ran from session 4 to session 22.

END PHASE

The termination phase covered three sessions. Lester became morose when the therapist mentioned termination. Initially he perceived this as a rejection, although he knew that the therapy was time-limited and focused on clearing up this central conflict.

By not allowing the therapy to be drawn into other areas, the therapist resisted becoming the new dominant other. The therapist continued to insist that their contacts be limited to meetings in the student mental health office and emphasized that with the clearing up of this central issue their joint work would be finished. However, this resolution involved Lester's coming to "peace" with his family, particularly his father, and attempting to understand that his parents acted not out of malice but because of their own limitations and needs.

Therapy was terminated at the end of the twenty-fifth session. Six years later, Lester and the therapist met by chance at a conference. Lester had finished medical school and was in a residency in internal medicine. He had married a woman from his college who was an instructor at a local university. He was considering taking a public health degree, much against the wishes of his father, who wanted him to go into biochemistry and research. Lester reported that he and his father were friendly but distant, that they could not get any closer. He said that from time to time when things got a little overwhelming, he did suffer down moods, but nothing like those in medical school. He did not feel the need for additional therapy.

DISCUSSION OF THE CASE

Lester's case represents a good application of short-term psychodynamically oriented therapy. The work focused on the relationship of inner conflicts to the current problem situation. The conflicts were core conflicts, and both Lester and the therapist addressed them directly. The intense transference relationship was used to interpret the way Lester continued to use very maladaptive and unsatisfactory ways to obtain approval (repeating with the therapist the approval-seeking behavior he had learned from his parents).

A great deal was done in a short time to alter central coping responses. Of course, Lester was an ideal candidate for this and perhaps any other kind of therapy: He was young, bright, and highly motivated, albeit the motivation (the fear of failing in medical school) was a negative one. He was certainly psychologically minded, and the conflict was focal and serious. He worked hard and cooperated with the therapy; his resistances (which we touched upon briefly) were not central to his functioning, and he was quick to surrender them.

The gains seemed to be long-lasting, as evidenced by the accidental meeting of Lester and the therapist some years later.

The Effectiveness of Short-Term Psychodynamic Therapy

In a recent review of the literature, Jarrett and Rush (1991) stated that there are few published results of short-term dynamic therapy with depressives. Existing studies have not defined the presenting problems as clearly as the other short-term therapies, nor have they specified the techniques used. In fact, the psychodynamic approaches downplay techniques, making comparisons even more difficult. Finally, the dependent (or outcome) variables in these studies have been vague, since easing of depression is often regarded as *only* symptomatic improvement.

It is also felt that in many of these studies of short-term treatment, the patients are chosen more on the basis of the criteria for brief dynamic psychotherapy than on diagnostic grounds (Rosenberg 1985:115). In other words, the patients are chosen to fit the format rather than the format being adapted to the needs of the individual patients.

In five studies of short-term dynamic, or insight-oriented, therapy of depressed patients reviewed by Jarrett and Rush (1991), in no case was insight-oriented therapy superior to other therapies, such as behavioral or cognitive-behavioral, and in at least one case it was less effective than comparison treatments and controls.

Because of the theoretical and methodological shortcomings mentioned earlier, we agree with Jarrett and Rush (1991), who say there is insufficient evidence either to advocate for short-term dynamic therapy or to say, convincingly, that it has no effect. Until definitive research is conducted, the jury is out. Suggestions for further research have stressed the importance of spelling out in greater detail the process of therapy between client and therapist (using more operationalized measures), the techniques used by the therapist (perhaps with the use of treatment manuals), and "dispositional characteristics" (Rosenberg 1985:120).

Some psychodynamic therapists have lamented that "no *specific* psychoanalytic treatment for depression has emerged" (Strupp et al. 1982:217, emphasis in the original). One reason advanced for this lack of specific approaches is that within psychoanalytic theory, depression is seen as associated with many neurotic disorders rather than as a disorder in its own right (Strupp et al. 1982:242). However, as we shall see in the following chapters, which discuss other theoretical approaches to depression, the insights of the psychoanalytic orientations have enhanced these differing schools of therapy.

13

The Interpersonal Psychotherapy (IPT) Approach

Interpersonal therapy (IPT) was developed at Yale University by an interdisciplinary team of psychiatrists, social workers, psychologists, and nurses as a short-term, focused therapy for depressed patients. (Much of this account draws heavily from Klerman et al. 1984.) IPT emphasizes that depression takes place in the context of a person's relationships with others and that it affects these relationships. The treatment of the depression must involve discussing and changing these relationships. This approach also takes into account the importance of biological factors in both causation and treatment.

IPT evolved from the writings of Adolph Meyer, professor of psychiatry at Johns Hopkins University Hospital in Baltimore. He was one of the first psychiatrists to emphasize the influence of social and interpersonal (environmental), as well as biological, factors in mental disorders. Meyer stressed that psychiatric symptoms reflect the patient's efforts to adapt to often stressful environments. Adaptive capacities are formed in early family relations and are influenced, both while growing up and in adulthood, by relationships with various social groups. Meyer used such concepts as role adaptation in clarifying the nature of psychiatric disturbances (Rounsaville et al. 1985:127).

IPT also incorporates the views of Harry Stack Sullivan (an influential psychoanalyst who stressed interpersonal relations) that much of what is called psychiatric illness is related to, if not caused by, faulty interpersonal relationships.

The interpersonal school of psychiatry stresses concepts adapted from the social sciences, particularly the importance of primary groups, such as the family, and relationships with immediate significant others. It recognizes the importance of the different roles people play, the different statuses they occupy, and the rewards (consequences) of successful or unsuccessful fulfillment of these role requirements. This approach is also heavily influenced by G. H. Mead, of the Chicago School of Sociology, and his writings on the self (Mead 1934). Mead viewed the self as arising from people's interactions with others, originating in the initial interactions of children with parents and continuing with a positive or a negative impact throughout life.

The interpersonal approach also focuses on the effects of specific environmental (social) stresses in producing depression, such as losing a job, divorce, lack of or deterioration of social support systems, lack of intimacy, and the presence of marital conflict. Also significant is loss of a parent, the presence of one or more depressed adults in the immediate environment, and a history of depression in the family.

Even though IPT was created by therapists who are highly social in their orientation, the Yale Group considers depression a clinical disorder within a medical model (Klerman et al. 1984:37). They believe that classifying clients as patients is justified by the reassurance that depressed individuals feel when they are given a label for what they have been experiencing. Identifying it as a medical condition also offers hope that the client can be helped. We believe that this reasoning is valid, for many depressed people are unaware that they are depressed; many think that they are malingering or not living up to their responsibilities. This is especially true if people close to them are telling them to "snap out of it," "pull yourself out of it," "stop giving in to yourself"— attitudes that may be reinforced by certain simplistic, misleading popular books on how to cope with depression.

The IPT group holds a pluralistic view of causation, stating that no single cause can explain depression. It can be produced by environmental stress, early childhood experiences, genetic and other biological factors, and many other factors, either by themselves or in combination. They stress the multifaceted nature of depression, maintaining that it is more correct to speak of the *depressions*. In their view, depression may be an exaggeration of a normal mood, a symptom of a physical or psychiatric state, or a syndrome in its own right (Klerman et al. 1984:38).

Treatment is aimed at the type of depression classified as a clinical syndrome. The group stresses that one function of the diagnostic process is to differentiate the clinical syndrome from "feeling down," which is in the normal range of experience. They specifically define depression within the guidelines of the D.S.M.-III-R and the Research Diagnostic Criteria and stress that three processes are involved in clinical depression:

1. *Symptom formation,* which refers to the signs, symptoms, and so on, which may have biological and/or psychological bases.
2. *Social and interpersonal relations,* related to social roles, reflecting past learning, current patterns of interactions with others, and a possible inadequacy in these areas.
3. *Personality and character problems,* which refers to personality traits, deficits in communication, and lack of self-esteem. These are personality patterns that are thought to predispose individuals to

depression (Klerman et al. 1984:6–7). (The idea that personality patterns predispose individuals to or cause depression is not universally accepted.)

Intervention in IPT is focused on the first two processes: symptoms and social and interpersonal relations. IPT is aimed at easing the symptoms of the depression and working with the depressed person to develop new, more effective ways (strategies) of handling the current interpersonal relations that are linked with the beginning of depressive symptoms (Klerman et al. 1984:7). The authors state, and we agree, that not enough attention has been paid, in treating depressives, to specific techniques that can reduce the pain of depression and improve their interpersonal relations (Klerman et al. 1984:7).

According to its founders, the briefness of IPT therapy tends to rule out changes or lasting effects on personality structure. They do emphasize, though, that personality function is assessed (Klerman et al. 1984:7).

The Process of Interpersonal Therapy

██ The IPT approach tends to be structured, although it is
██ adaptable to individual needs. The originators have stated that although IPT may be similar to other therapies in techniques and orientation, it differs on the level of strategies, emphasizing strategies oriented to specific problem areas or tasks (Klerman et al. 1984:73). The structure, techniques, and stance of IPT are spelled out in a detailed outline (Klerman et al. 1984:73–76), which we shall summarize and quote from in describing the process of intervention. They view intervention as occurring in three stages of treatment: initial phase, intermediate phase, and termination.

Initial Phase

The first task is to deal with the depression. The depression is diagnosed and the need for medication is assessed.

Next, the depression is defined, or redefined, within the interpersonal context. In other words, the depression is interpreted to the client as being related to difficulties, in the present and the past, that the individual is having in interactions with significant others. Information is elicited about the mutual expectations the client and these others have had, whether they were achieved, and whether there was disappointment (Klerman et al. 1984:74).

The major problem areas are then specified and related to the current depression. Pinpointing which relationships or factors in a relationship are connected to the depression leads to a consideration of changes that might be made in these relationships.

The IPT approach is interpreted to the client: The emphasis is on the present, on open discussion, and on interpersonal relations. As early as the first interview, the therapist gives his or her perception of the problem, discusses the treatment goals, and emphasizes the need to agree on those goals (to set a "contract"). The mechanics of the therapy are discussed, such as frequency of visits, length of therapy, fees, and other policy matters (Klerman et al. 1984:74).

This initial phase, usually completed in two to four interviews, is common to all the problem areas.

Intermediate Phase: Dealing with the Problem Areas

The intermediate phase focuses on the "major, current, interpersonal problem areas" mutually defined by the client and the therapist. IPT emphasizes relieving depression by focusing upon communication and other problems with significant others in any one or more of the selected problem areas. Those problem areas considered most important are abnormal grief, interpersonal role disputes, role transitions, and interpersonal deficits. Since specific strategies have been developed for each of these problem areas, we shall later discuss them separately, giving the individual therapeutic strategies followed by case illustrations.

The structured tasks include homework assignments that direct the client in trying out, in actual life situations, the skills and self-confidence that he or she has been acquiring in the therapy sessions. Discussion of the client's experiences in practicing these new skills provides the opportunity for feedback from the therapist. It is important for the therapist to reinforce each accomplishment of the client by praising attempts at new ways of coping, buttressing the hope that change is possible and achievable.

Termination of Treatment

The third phase, termination, is considered particularly important. Because the therapy is short term, the client must form a relationship, examine his or her problems, work on them, acquire skills to deal with future stresses, and then relinquish the relationship, all within a comparatively brief time. This is often difficult for a depressed client, especially since he or she may perceive termination as rejection by the therapist and may respond with additional symptoms of depression, particularly hopelessness.

The IPT manual calls for the therapist and client to begin talking of termination from two to four sessions before the end of treatment. The therapist and client should review the client's progress and expressly discuss the termination of treatment and the naturalness of a feeling of loss and possibly of mourning that revives past deprivations and losses. In addition, the client should acknowledge his or her new skills and competencies (Klerman et al. 1984:138).

Included in the termination process are discussions of possible future difficulties to attune the client to the symptoms that may indicate a return of the depression. As with all therapies, this includes the ability to differentiate between the so-called normal depressive reactions and the reactions that indicate that something more serious is happening and that additional professional help may be needed. Of course the therapist (and the agency or clinic) should be available if the need arises in the future.

Treatment is brief. All but one case presented by Klerman and colleagues was terminated after twelve sessions; one was terminated after the thirteenth session. If the treatment must end because the time limit has been reached and the client wants to continue, at least four to eight weeks should elapse before additional treatment is offered, unless the client is still severely symptomatic and/or has not shown sufficient progress in therapy. In these cases, other therapies and/or medications should be considered. Klerman and colleagues (1984:140–141) state that long-term treatment may be needed for some clients, especially those with chronic personality problems with severe interpersonal deficits not responsive to IPT, those who require maintenance treatment, and those who remain depressed for various other reasons and who have not responded to IPT (Klerman et al. 1984:140–141).

The Therapist/Client Relationship

In IPT the relationship between the client and the therapist is explicitly not the primary focus of treatment; unlike some of the more traditional therapies, it is not the main modality of change (Klerman et al. 1984:149–150). Although IPT stresses the here and now, it recognizes the reality that certain of the client's feelings (called transference in other approaches) can interfere with progress and, if unaddressed, produce resistance to the therapeutic work or even unplanned termination. The client's feelings and behaviors toward the therapist must be addressed if and when they interfere with therapy.

The therapist/client relationship is viewed as a model for relationships outside of the therapeutic work. Acting as a model, the therapist provides immediate feedback to the client in a corrective way, so that behavior change can be facilitated. To do this, the client is encouraged to report both positive and negative feelings to the therapist.

These instructions, among others, are explicitly stated by the creators of IPT, who provide "specific guidelines for using the therapeutic relationship" (Klerman et al. 1984:150). They also detail the difficulties in the process of IPT, many of which involve the relationship between client and therapist. The role of the therapist using IPT is also spelled out in considerable and helpful detail (Klerman et al. 1984:201–212).

The Main Problem Areas Treated with IPT: Descriptions, Strategies, and Cases

IPT Treatment of Abnormal Grief

Depression associated with abnormal grief is one of the problems targeted for IPT treatment.

Freud (1917) theorized that the reaction of the mourner greatly resembled the symptoms of depression. In both there is crying, sadness, disturbance of usual sleep patterns, and because of the preoccupation with the loss of a loved one, a reduced ability to carry on with the activities of daily living. Although it is sometimes difficult to tell the difference between normal and pathological mourning, normal grief is generally considered to lessen within two to four months. Then everyday activities are resumed and preoccupation with the memories of the person who has died lessens (Klerman et al. 1984:96). Evidence of abnormal grief might be multiple losses (other losses, not necessarily deaths) occurring at the time of the death; more than one death; insufficient expression of grief (e.g., the person may have engaged in avoidance behavior about the death, such as not going to the funeral); symptoms centering around a significant date (e.g., the anniversary of a death); an obsessive fear of the illness that killed the significant other; preservation of things exactly the way they were when the loved one died (e.g., making a shrine out of the home); and a lack of social support in the period after the death (Klerman et al. 1984:98).

One of the assumptions of IPT is that inadequate grieving leads to delayed or distorted grief reactions. In delayed grief, the person does not show grief immediately after the death but may react strongly some time later, often in response to another event: the death of a pet, the loss of a favorite possession, and so on. In distorted grief reactions, which may come immediately or may be postponed, the grief is not expressed in the usual manner, but there may be physical symptoms and/or other problems.

Distorted and delayed grief reactions sometimes coexist, producing an excessive reaction—for example, constant crying or elevation of the one who has died into near sainthood. This is shown in the case that follows.

The goals for this problem area are to help the person mourn and, through mourning, to get back into his work and life to compensate for his loss (Klerman et al. 1984:74). The strategies utilized are to "review the depressive symptoms . . . [and to] relate . . . [their] onset to [the] death of the significant other; reconstruct the patient's relations with the deceased [and] . . . the events just prior to, during and after the death; . . . explore . . . [the associated] feelings . . . [and] consider . . . ways of becoming involved with others" (Klerman et al. 1984:74).

A Case of IPT Focusing on Grief

INITIAL PHASE (SESSIONS 1–3).

Inga Mueller (a pseudonym) was referred to the clinic by her internist. Although she had no outstanding health problems, she was having difficulty sleeping. She woke early every morning and could not return to sleep. She was unable to work or continue her studies and found herself increasingly isolated and subject to worry, with very pessimistic thoughts about the future.

Inga, who was forty-six years old, was born in Germany during the last days of World War II, and was one of six children. Her mother, to whom she was close, later spoke of the continual bombardments and air raids. Her father, who had been in the military service for several years, rejoined the family about eighteen months after the end of the war, having been released from a prisoner-of-war camp. Inga describes her childhood as one of intense material deprivation. She remembers her father drinking excessively, fighting with her mother, and eventually abandoning the family.

Inga was very bright and talented. As a young woman, she managed to win scholarships first to a private school in Germany and then to an art school in Italy. During her studies in Italy she met Sam, an American who was studying literature in Rome under the GI Bill of Rights (a postwar act that enabled American veterans to attend college by paying for their tuition, supplies, and living expenses). Handsome, witty, and very taken with Inga, he did not pay much attention to his studies, spending most of his time in cafes with a large circle of friends. After a short courtship in this romantic atmosphere, they married and returned to Sam's home town, Detroit.

Inga worked and attempted to go to school at night while Sam tried his hand at a number of jobs, including teaching, truck driving, and bartending. He worked most often as a bartender, where he was well liked and had a good following. He also began to drink heavily, much more than in Rome. Warned that his drinking was excessive, at several points he "went on the wagon" but always relapsed. During this time Inga neglected her painting and did not finish her degree. This pattern persisted for several years until Sam, suffering the effects of severe cirrhosis of the liver, died of pneumonia.

Initially, Inga was devastated but she seemed to recuperate rapidly and was observed by friends to be cheerful and taking it well. However, she left Sam's clothes in his part of the closet they had shared. In addition, she mounted several paintings she had done of Sam in happier days and even periodically shined his shoes, which she still kept under the bed. (A friend commented that Inga had made a shrine out of the apartment.)

It took three sessions to obtain this information. During the first two sessions Inga denied any negative feelings about Sam or his death and described their relationship in almost idyllic terms. She was critical of herself for being unable to keep Sam from drinking and for failing to keep him sober.

Inga interpreted her sleeplessness and feelings of agitation and hopelessness as a shortcoming on her part, a weakness, rather than depression, and considered herself as inept in controlling herself as she had been in helping Sam.

The first phase of treatment ended with the formulation of a contract to help Inga resolve her feelings about Sam—actually, to help her go through the mourning process and to plan for the future (establish new ties and, if possible, reestablish old ones).

MIDDLE PHASE (SESSIONS 4–9).

With the help of the therapist, Inga first reviewed her relationship with Sam, starting with some of the positive aspects, the almost idyllic situation of being carefree students in a very romantic setting abroad. Then she spoke of some of the negative aspects, such as returning to live in Detroit—for her a dismal, foreign place. She gradually related the harsh realities of having to earn a living while adapting to life in a new country, with a language that she was only beginning to master and a husband whose "lighthearted" drinking became excessive as he grew financially more dependent upon her.

As Inga began to analyze the relationship, her previously denied anger at Sam emerged. Rather than being carefree and loving, she began to describe him as irresponsible. Furthermore, she expressed her anger at their diminished sexual activity, which was exacerbated by Sam's drinking and health-related problems. During one session she lamented that they had never had a child, which she really had wanted but had never been able to discuss with Sam.

Initially, her expressions of anger were accompanied by crying and then were followed by guilt. Both these emotions decreased, although they did not stop during this middle phase.

The therapist encouraged Inga to contact a local art school, where she began to take courses in painting. She also applied to a local branch of the city university system, where her academic credits from Germany and Italy were evaluated. She received two years of credits and began to take courses part time toward completing a degree in art education.

Inga was then encouraged to contact some of the friends she had made when she first came to Detroit and to pursue relationships with some of the acquaintances she had made in the art institute and at the university. She joined a church near her house and began to take part in some of the activities. She also started to plan and save for a trip back to Germany.

TERMINATION PHASE (SESSIONS 10–12).

Inga continued with her studies and part-time job. Her sleep patterns became more regular, especially after she started a regime of exercise and moderate diet. She redecorated her house, replacing the pictures of Sam with some of her landscapes. She donated his clothing to a charitable organization and made a contribution in his name to the local church. She was able to speak with nostalgia of the student days in Rome and some of the more pleasant times in Detroit, genuinely lamenting that things had not gone better but being more realistic about Sam's alcoholism and her youthful inability to understand, let alone control, his drinking.

Therapy terminated. Inga agreed to contact the clinic if she felt herself becoming depressed. Follow-up several years later showed she was teaching in a local school while continuing to take part-time art lessons. She had a wide circle of friends, mostly women, and was busily involved in church activities.

IPT Treatment of Interpersonal Disputes

A second problem area is that of interpersonal role disputes, circumstances in which two people have differing definitions or expectations of their relationship. These differences can often be central to the development and the continuance of depression. If the disputes continue and the likelihood of resolving them seems small, some people may consider the difficulty to be all their own fault and evidence of their worthlessness. This is further proof of the client's inability to function, to control his or her life, or to communicate effectively (Klerman et al. 1984:104–119).

To make this diagnosis, there must be overt or covert evidence of a conflict between the client and a significant person. Identifying this conflict may be difficult, for many depressed people blame themselves and accept all responsibility for any problem in a relationship. These conflicts are most often found in marital, parent/child, and employer/employee relationships.

The goals of the middle phase of treatment are to identify the disputes and spell out their nature in interpersonal terms and to help the client decide how to resolve them.

In IPT the therapist assesses a role dispute as being at one of three stages: (1) *renegotiation,* where the client and the other person know that there are disagreements and they may even be attempting to resolve the differences; (2) *impasse,* where there is no dialogue between the two, although the emotions may persist; and (3) *dissolution,* where the client feels the relationship cannot be healed or reestablished (Klerman et al. 1984:106).

It is important to identify and differentiate among the three phases, for each phase necessitates a different strategy. If the stage is renegotiation, part of the therapist's task may be to calm both individuals so that they can talk with each other. In an impasse, one strategy is to increase the conflict temporarily, to start a dialogue. With dissolution, which is similar to grief, the therapist works with the client to understand what happened in the relationship, helping him or her to realize that the relationship is dead and facilitating mourning so the client can form new relationships (Klerman et al. 1984:106).

The strategies for dealing with interpersonal disputes include reviewing symptoms, relating symptom onset to disputes, establishing the stage of the disputes, examining role expectations in relation to disputes (issues, differences, options, alternatives, available resources), exploring equivalent behavior in other relationships (the "gain" assumption underlying behavior), exploring how the disagreement is perpetuated (Klerman et al. 1984:75).

A Case of IPT Focusing on Interpersonal Disputes

INITIAL PHASE (SESSIONS 1 AND 2).

Mary McCarthy (a pseudonym), just turning twenty-three, had been tearful and sleepless, was having "dark thoughts," and saw the future as hopeless. A neighbor who had been treated successfully for depression referred her to the mental health clinic.

Mary, who was employed as a data processor and computer technician at an insurance company, was very bright. She had started to take night courses at college. She liked these courses and the people she met but discontinued night school when her boyfriend David complained that he wanted more of her company.

Mary had been dating David for over four years and had known him since they were both in grade school. At one time she had been eager to marry him, but recently she had begun to feel increasingly uncomfortable in the relationship. In the first interview, she stated that she could no longer talk to David. Communication between the two had dwindled, and now, more often than not, consisted of arguments or extended silences. They went out infrequently, either to a local movie or to the neighborhood pub, where they drank (often to excess) with David's friends. The sexual relationship between the two, which Mary initially found pleasurable, had become perfunctory and unsatisfying.

Recently, their arguing had become ugly, with verbal but no physical abuse from David. Arguing centered around Mary's wishing to return to school, which David vehemently opposed. After these arguments she felt that life had no meaning. She felt "like a worm," slept a lot, but was tired and listless at work. In the evenings when she was not seeing David, she watched a lot of television. She had recently thought of suicide. She felt that the future was bleak and did not know what she was going to do, but she avoided pressure from David to set a marriage date.

Mary responded positively to the therapist's diagnosis of depression. She quickly grasped the connection between the depressed moods and the unresolved relationship with David. Part of the depression was related to their decreasing ability to communicate and Mary's growing, but not consciously acknowledged, doubts about marrying David. She also quickly understood the relationship of the arguments and David's assaults to her feelings of depression and lowered self-esteem.

Both the therapist and Mary felt that medication was not indicated at the time because of the primarily reactive nature of the symptomatology.

In setting the contract for the therapy, Mary and the therapist agreed that in the initial phase they would closely examine the couple's current and past relationship. They would assess the positive and negative factors as well as the behaviors (and attitudes) that might be contributing to the currently poor relationship. The ultimate goal was to determine Mary's true feelings for David before she made a decision about marriage. They would also assess the possibilities of improving the relationship.

Mary was also to examine her options in the situation: staying with David and working on the relationship, temporarily interrupting the relationship (not seeing David), or breaking off with him. She rejected the last two options. David had refused to attend the sessions, calling the therapy nonsense and stating that all Mary had to do to get better was to "snap out of it" and to marry him.

A portion of the discussion was to focus on Mary's occupational status and her desire for more education, what this meant to her, and what it implied for the relationship. Also to be examined were her other relationships, an assessment of her social networks and what could be done to widen them (Klerman et al. 1984:115). Central to these discussions was an examination of the relationship of the depressive reactions to these interpersonal disputes.

MIDDLE PHASE (SESSIONS 3–11).

Mary and the therapist agreed that the discussions about marriage seemed to be at the impasse stage. Since David chose not to be involved in the therapy, Mary and the therapist explored Mary's perception of the points of agreement and disagreement between them as well as both of their hopes for the relationship. Central to the dispute, and to her increasing resistance to the marriage, was Mary's thwarted desire for more education. She received high praise for her work as a computer technician but had risen as far as she could go within the company without further technical training or, preferably, a college degree. In the course of the sessions, Mary came to realize how badly she wanted this advanced training and how unwilling she was to settle for the traditional role of wife. David had firmly stated his expectation that *his* wife would not have a career; she would stay at home, take care of their house, and raise their children.

Mary attempted to convey these feelings to David, who responded with either verbal abuse or silence, often not calling Mary for several days and not returning her phone calls. When Mary told David how hurt she was by his behavior and by his lack of even trying to understand how she felt, he responded with, "Then let's break up."

Mary and the therapist examined the alternatives, with the therapist steadfastly refusing to make Mary's decisions for her. They discussed the future of the relationship and the possibility of working out an alternative that would allow Mary both the relationship and the future job training. Mary decided against marriage in the near future.

With the therapist's encouragement Mary explored her options for education. She found that her company would pay for her college courses if she earned certain minimum grades and would make a commitment to remain with the firm for a specified time. The company would even allow her a few hours of paid time off each week so that she could attend classes. With this information, she enrolled in school. When David presented her with another ultimatum, she ended the relationship.

TERMINATION PHASE (SESSIONS 12–13).

In the termination phase Mary discussed her now ended relationship with David, her previous denial of her own needs and wants, and her lack of assertive behavior with David. Initially devastated by the breakup, Mary nevertheless responded enthusiastically to school. As she began to verbalize her hostility to David and her long-suppressed discontent with the relationship, her depressive moods lifted. She also began to shop for new clothing, in preparation for expanding her social life.

An avid reader, Mary began to read self-help books on depression and on male/female relationships, recommended by the therapist. Increasingly, she could connect her feelings of depression and her interactions with others, particularly men, in her environment. She was symptom-free for the last three sessions and, upon follow-up, was busily attending school and dating several young men.

IPT Treatment of Role Transitions

We all experience changes in our lives. Some are positive and some are negative; some are planned (e.g., a move to another location to take a new job), and some are unplanned (e.g., an undesired transfer). Role transitions are commonly associated with the aging process, such as the midlife crises of both men and women, which may be accompanied by a feeling (often reflecting reality) of lack of success in career, marriage, or parenting. The alleged golden years may well be anything but that with decline in health and income, death of friends, and so forth. These changes may lead to alterations in one or more of our roles.

Our various roles both determine and are determined by our interactions with others. They are closely linked to how we view ourselves— our self-esteem. Sometimes role transitions bring anticipated changes, such as those that accompany human developmental phases. Other transitions have unanticipated elements, such as the reality of the lifestyle changes brought about by having a child or of obligations incurred with marriage—where the problems are often not anticipated as clearly as the advantages.

Role transitions (e.g., those involving a move to a new city) may mean the loss of friends and family—a person's support systems. These transitions are sometimes associated with troubling emotions: feelings of rage, fright, fear, failure, and more. This is especially true if a new role is seen as too demanding. The new roles may require social skills and behaviors that are not in the person's repertoire, and they may result in such drastic changes in an individual's patterns of behavior (including the way he or she copes with these changes) that they produce both depression and an accompanying drop in self-esteem (Klerman et al. 1984:121). In fact, depression may be a way of coping with these changes, albeit at great cost. The cost and difficulty in coping are especially great when these new roles require immediate and drastic changes in behavior.

An individual may feel reluctant to give up old roles. New behaviors cause anxiety; old roles and statuses may have at least provided security, and deprivation of this security may be experienced as a loss. Loss is central to many views of depression.

Inability to function in new roles may worsen a depressive reaction, which may be related to the individual's lack of awareness of what is involved in the new roles—often a focus in IPT treatment.

The assessment of role transition as a problem area requires that the depression be in reaction to, related to, or following life changes related to role transitions (Klerman et al. 1984:122). Work in therapy may focus on "(1) giving up the old role; (2) expressing guilt, anger, loss; (3) acquiring new skills; and (4) developing new attachments and support groups" (Klerman et al. 1984:122). The strategies are as follows: "Review depressive symptoms [and] relate . . . [them] to . . . coping [difficulties around] . . . recent life changes; review . . . old and new roles . . . [and] feelings about . . . [loss and] change; explore opportunities in new role[s] . . . [and] evaluate what is lost; . . . [encourage] appropriate release of affect . . . [and development of] support system and . . . new skills . . . [needed for a] new role" (Klerman et al. 1984:75).

A Case of IPT Focusing on Role Transitions

INITIAL PHASE (SESSIONS 1–3).

William (Bill) Rodgers (a pseudonym), fifty-nine years old, was referred by his minister. At his wife's urging, Bill had consulted the minister for spiritual help. He felt "down" and thought that his life had no purpose. He had difficulty sleeping and reported a lack of interest in most things, including sex with his wife. He also reported a drop in his appetite and was losing weight. A recent physical examination revealed no problems, and his physician recommended a vacation.

Bill was a professional accountant employed by one of the nation's leading accounting and business management firms. He was the father of four grown children, who were all married, pursuing careers, and seemingly happy. He had recently become a grandfather to twin girls. His wife, who was supportive, realized that something was bothering him and was troubled by the lack of sex, although she knew that he was not involved with another woman.

Bill accepted the referral for therapy, although he maintained that there was nothing wrong. In the initial interview the therapist learned that Bill's company had an inflexible policy of retiring people at age sixty. Although he was financially successful and a "key player" in his business, his involuntary retirement was less than a year away. Money was not a problem; Bill was well paid, had made many good investments, and the company's pension plan was generous.

His father, also an accountant, was one of the founders of the firm and the author of a series of tax guides that had become a standard reference work in the field. Bill had always assisted his father in the annual revisions of these tax guides, and as his father aged, Bill took over more and more of the work. When his father died two years earlier, Bill assumed editorship and sole ownership of these publications.

Bill felt that he was a failure; that he had never lived up to his potential. He viewed retirement as a "death sentence" and the end of any opportunity to demonstrate that he could match his father's achievements. He saw the future as desolate, questioned the purpose of living, and was disturbed that he was not as excited as his wife about their first grandchildren. He viewed his current lack of interest in sex as evidence that he was "over the hill." He denied any thought of suicide, although he said, "I would be relieved if I were hit by a car." His drinking was limited to an occasional glass of wine or brandy and was not a problem; he took no medications.

The therapist and Bill decided to focus, during the first three sessions, on what would be lost when the retirement—which was beyond Bill's control—occurred. The client and the therapist would jointly examine Bill's relationship with his father, focusing particularly upon his competition with his father and the future potential for gainful work on the tax guides. They also agreed to work on the marital relationship, with the possibility of involving his wife in the therapy at some point in the future.

MIDDLE PHASE (SESSIONS 4–10).

During the middle phase, Bill began to examine his relationship with his father. He said that his first love was history and that he had originally planned on advanced studies in history and teaching in a small college. When his father resisted this plan, Bill abandoned it and took degrees in accounting and law. He was at or near the top of his class in all of his studies.

When he graduated, Bill had his choice of many jobs, but, again in response to parental pressure, he entered his father's firm, where he rapidly became a partner. Although some of his peers implied that this advancement was because of his father's influence, Bill's ability and talents obviously merited these promotions. However, Bill took some of these criticisms very much to heart, and he felt that continuing his father's work on the tax guides was also "riding on his father's name." However, during the therapy sessions, Bill explained that he had not only taken over the editorship but had redirected the focus and emphasis of the guides. Under his leadership, the guides improved so much that accountants came to consider them indispensable. Sales increased enormously. He related all this in a self-deprecating way.

Bill did express some hostility at his father's directing him away from a career in teaching, but he also liked the things money could buy and realized that he would not have earned as much if he had been a college teacher. For the first time in his life, he admitted to himself that the switch was not entirely his father's wish, that his father had really only objected mildly to a teaching career.

In reviewing future options, it was apparent that editing the tax guides could either be done at home or in a rented office; Bill really did not need the firm to continue this work. In fact, being relieved of the obligations of partnership meant that Bill could have time to do some things he had always wanted to do, such as travel. Over the years his wife had often suggested travel but Bill had resisted, because of the pressure of work.

As part of the therapy Bill and the therapist discussed plans for him to continue work on the tax guides. Bill was encouraged to begin cutting down on his hours at the firm, to sign up for an exercise course, and to keep more regular hours.

Bill's acceptance of the responsibility for choosing his career and of the credit for improving and expanding the tax guides led him to acknowledge that his work in this area was an important contribution to the field and that it would be facilitated when he retired. As his enthusiasms grew, his spirits rose. One evening, after spending a long time planning a trip to Scandinavia, he and his wife had a frank talk about sex and shortly afterward resumed sexual relations.

TERMINATION PHASE (SESSIONS 11–12).

Bill's symptoms of depression eased and then disappeared as the realities of the involuntary retirement were clarified and as he began to see that retirement had more positive aspects than negative ones. By this time he had made a number of plans, including the trip to Scandinavia and the rental of an office to continue his work on the tax guides. At his own instigation he looked into an organization of retired business-men who volunteered their time helping inexperienced younger people establish small businesses. He decided that he would join this group when he retired.

Bill continued his exercise program and his travel plans. He seemed to resolve his ambivalence toward his father and his profession as he came to see that life would not be over with retirement and that he would actually be entering a stimulating new phase.

The depressive symptoms disappeared. Upon follow-up, Bill reported only mild, occasional "down" periods, which he handled by working and exercising.

IPT Treatment of Interpersonal Deficits

A fourth important problem area in IPT is that of interpersonal deficits. Clients often appear with a history of severe interpersonal loneliness because of a lack of social relations, which frequently dates back to childhood, even early childhood. They often seem to lack social skills and in many ways show inadequacies in relating to other people.

Deficits in social skills can be temporary or chronic. For example, if the person is alone or does not work, he or she may have little opportunity for intimate relationships. This lack of contact with others may be a crucial factor in their depressions and may become a focus of treatment. Such clients may be more seriously disturbed than others who are depressed (Klerman et al. 1984:129).

The treatment goals for these clients are to lessen or eliminate their social isolation and to learn how to form new relationships. This may well include the client learning new social skills.

The strategies used are to review depressive symptoms and relate them to "social isolation or unfulfillment; review past relationships . . . [and] repetitive patterns in relationships [and] discuss . . . positive and negative feelings about therapist and seek parallels in other relationships" (Klerman et al. 1984:76).

A Case of a Client with Interpersonal Deficits

INITIAL PHASE (SESSIONS 1 AND 2).

Jane Smith (a pseudonym), aged thirty-four, was self-referred to a university mental health clinic after reading about it in the university newspaper. She reported herself to be very anxious and very depressed. She had a graduate degree in library science and worked in a university library, where she was considered very competent. Her training equipped her for a supervisory position; however, because of her shyness and lack of confidence she chose to do comparatively dull, lower-level work cataloging books. The chief librarian had given up trying to persuade her to take a higher-level job in the Circulation Department, where she would be in charge of a large number of student and other part-time workers and be in contact with many people.

In her initial interview Jane said that she was born in a small town in Nebraska, the only child of parents who were in their mid-forties at the time of her birth. She commented that they seemed more like grandparents. They emphasized achievement, neatness, and cleanliness, and the high opinion of the neighbors. While living at home and commuting by bus, Jane attended a small church-related college on a scholarship and did extremely well. Upon graduation, she worked in a library in her home town and kept busy with church work and a circle of women friends. She did not date. She reported that at this time she had intervals of "feeling blue," although she managed to work and to function reasonably well.

Jane's parents died within six months of each other, leaving her a small inheritance. Feeling alone and hemmed in, she went to Chicago, where she completed her graduate degree. During the time in graduate school, she lived in a dormitory. After graduation she took a job at another university in Chicago.

Jane currently lived alone in a small apartment with two cats, on whom she doted. When she was not at work she was at home. She had discontinued attending church and had no interests outside of work. Her health was good, except that she had periods of great lassitude and lack of energy. She reported sleep problems, nervousness, and occasional lack of appetite that caused her to skip meals and sometimes feel faint.

In the past six months Jane had cried a lot, the result of thinking of her isolation and loneliness. She felt very pessimistic about the future, although she denied any thoughts of suicide. She very much wanted to change her life but had no idea of how to proceed. She vehemently rejected the therapist's suggestion of a psychiatric consultation for medication, stating that she did not smoke, drink, or use drugs of any kind. The use of antidepressants was put off, with the agreement that they were to be considered if therapy did not result in symptomatic improvement.

The therapeutic contract was set: to focus on reducing the client's social isolation and to work with her to form relationships.

INTERMEDIATE PHASE (SESSIONS 3–10).

The client, who was very verbal, was aware that she grew up essentially an isolated child. She did not feel close to either parent, stating that she always felt that she was unwanted, an "accident" late in her parents' marriage. Furthermore, she felt that there was always too much attention given to achievement and appearances and not enough to her as a person. Even as a child she had difficulty relating to other children. During all the time she attended school, from elementary to graduate school, she felt isolated from the other students. She could talk of only a few close relationships she had with women and none with men during her lifetime. Jane also became aware, while talking with the therapist, that she had probably been depressed to some degree for most of her life: Much of her quiet and good behavior in the past was either accompanied by or heightened by depressed feelings.

Jane then recounted the loneliness of her current life and her dim view of the future. In conversations with the therapist, after tearful sessions, she began to talk of what she would like to happen: to make new friends and increase her social activities. She decided that she would become active in the professional librarian's organization (overwhelmingly women) and that she would begin by attending their meetings. This not only would give her some social contacts but would help her professionally.

Since Jane was hesitant about the most basic elements of making social contacts with people, with the therapist's help she began a program of extensive reading on this topic, coupled with in-session training to heighten her social skills. Jane loved to read, and she began to read self-help books, such as those written by Dale Carnegie, as well as several books on depression.

Helped by structured homework assignments, Jane began to join her co-workers for lunch at the library cafeteria and then volunteered to assist in a local political organization. Here she met a number of people, some her own age, but mostly older married couples who were friendly and outgoing. Several meetings of this political organization were in people's homes. Jane particularly enjoyed these meetings, because she had some contact with their young children and young baby-sitters. She began to fantasize about a future marriage and family.

During this part of the therapy, Jane began to dress in a more stylish and becoming manner, with more youthful (and less severe) colors and styles. She became attentive to the therapist, arriving early for sessions, attempting to lengthen the sessions, and trying to schedule meetings more often than once a week. She also began to ask more personal questions of the therapist (a male, married, approximately twenty years older than Jane). When the therapist discussed this behavior with her, Jane shyly stated, "I am in love with you because you are trying to help me." When this response was discussed further, Jane said that she loved him because he was the first person that she could remember who was concerned about her and liked her for herself.

Jane's desires for increased contact were explored as being natural but inappropriate in this situation. She had to search for deeper relationships in other settings and with other people. The therapist pointed out Jane's efforts to make conversation with him, her reaching out and showing interest—actions that revealed growing skills and capabilities that could be focused on other people. The relationship with the therapist began to serve as a model for other relationships in other settings.

Jane's depressive episodes became less frequent and shorter as she became involved in activities and relationships outside of her work. The request for additional sessions stopped at the tenth session.

TERMINATION PHASE (SESSIONS 11–13).

The client seemed free of depression (more than passing and short periods of feeling low) for the last three weeks of the treatment. Her social life had become busy, and although she had not yet begun to date (a goal), she had met several interesting men at the library, an older graduate student and an assistant professor, and had spoken with them during long coffee breaks.

She was feeling increasingly comfortable in her new activities and new interests. Although she felt sad about the coming termination of treatment, she stated, correctly, that she knew that she and the therapist would see each other from time to time, because the therapist, a university faculty member, had a study in the library where she worked. Her laughing comment at the last session was, "I know where to find you!"

She did not have to "find" the therapist, although in the next few months they occasionally passed and greeted each other in the library.

Comment on the Cases

The preceding vignettes have been edited to illustrate the main areas of IPT focus. In practice, most cases are not so clear-cut. Although the strategy of IPT calls for focusing on one area (or sometimes two), the problem areas might be handled serially. It is also common for progress in one area to result in progress in another.

The Effectiveness of IPT

IPT was one of the two psychotherapies for depression tested in a significant National Institute of Mental Health (NIMH) study; the other was cognitive-behavioral therapy (CBT). The purpose of the research was to compare the two psychotherapies. Both psychotherapies were also compared with a drug, imipramine, and a control condition—clinical management (management of medication combined with support and encouragement [Elkin et al. 1989:973]). The inclusion of IPT was based on the observation that a "number of studies have provided support for the effectiveness of . . . IPT in treating depressed patients" (Elkin et al. 1985:307).

The preliminary results from the NIMH data show that patients in all four conditions improved. In the analysis of the entire sample "there was no evidence that either of the psychotherapies was significantly less (or more) effective than [a control condition] imipramine [and] clinical management." When compared to placebo-clinical management, "there was limited evidence of the specific effectiveness of IPT and no evidence of the specific effectiveness of CBT . . . in the major outcome analysis. Patients treated with IPT had the lowest drop-out rate of any of the groups, 23 percent as compared to 32 percent for CBT and 32 percent for the entire sample" (Elkin et al. 1989:974).

For the most depressed and impaired, IPT seemed more effective than CBT but less effective than imipramine plus clinical management. For the less severely depressed, the differences among the four conditions were insignificant (Elkin et al. 1989:971).

The minor differences among the treatment conditions, as well as the fact that patients improved under *all* conditions, prompted the observation that for the moderately depressed, one intervention may be "watchful waiting, support, sympathetic curiosity and encouraging support" (Freedman 1989:983). Another interpretation may be that for the moderately disturbed the use of drugs, in the beginning of the therapy and especially in the absence of severe symptoms, may be counterindicated.

Critics have pointed out that it is almost impossible to judge the effectiveness of IPT versus CBT without carefully analyzing the procedures of the *therapists*, which would require finer examination of the data. We hope this question will be answered in future analyses, for it may well prove to be a serious shortcoming of the study.

Despite the extent, time, and expense of the NIMH study, the editor of the prestigious *Archives of General Psychiatry* has called it a "truly unique and complex *pilot* study" (Freedman 1989:983, emphasis added). In other words, the findings are suggestive rather than definitive, and many of our questions on the efficacy of the psychotherapies and of drug treatment remain unanswered.

Prior to the NIMH studies, Jarrett and Rush (1991) concluded that IPT, used by itself, could reduce the symptoms of depression and better the social relations of some depressed patients. IPT combined with drugs not only lessened resistance to treatment but seemed to work against premature termination. At least one study pointed out that a combination of drugs and IPT is the therapy most likely to be effective with endogenous depressions. IPT has been shown to be effective in reducing depressive symptoms when compared to an antidepressant medication, and some data indicate that combining it with medication may enhance long-term remission of depressive symptoms (O'Leary and Wilson 1987).

Additional research has been done on IPT. A summary of studies by one of the developers of IPT showed it to be effective compared to both controls and amitriptyline, and when used in conjunction with amitriptyline, more effective than either alone (Klerman 1989; Klerman 1990).

Much of the recent ongoing research on IPT is aimed at specifying exactly *which* aspects of the IPT process are responsible for effecting change. Not surprising for a therapy oriented toward interpersonal relations, it was found that the severity of the patient's presenting problem was less relevant to positive outcome than the patient's ability to become involved in a productive relationship with the therapist (Foley et al., 1987). In other words, the capacity for relationship was a key factor in successful outcome. A further specification of "ability" showed that patients with negative expectations of therapy proved to be more difficult to treat and that, consequently, therapists were less successful with these patients. This research seems to buttress the importance of relationship in the treatment of depression, especially in the interpersonal treatment (IPT) of depression. Positive expectations are particularly important and often create a self-fulfilling prophecy.

Another attribute of IPT is that there is growing evidence that experienced therapists, especially those with psychodynamic training, can use IPT manuals to become competent in the approach after a short period of training (Rounsaville et al., 1988). The fact that IPT is outlined and described in a usable treatment manual also renders it easier to examine methodologically, including making comparisons from one therapist to another and from one client to another.

IPT as a focused, short-term therapy for depression appears to show promise as an economical, effective approach for some depressives. Results of treatment combining IPT and antidepressant medication are also promising. The emphasis upon the interpersonal aspects of the depressive disorders is a marked contribution of this approach. Elements of this approach will most likely become part of even more effective models in the future.

14

Behavioral Approaches to Depression

The behavior therapies originally stemmed from the experimental psychology laboratories. Psychologists attempted to apply their observations of animal behavior to procedures that would help humans. They stressed measurement, research, and accountability in the treatment of *observable* conditions. In short, they attempted to develop a scientific approach to intervention. Their early focus was on overt and observable disorders, such as overeating, smoking, stuttering, alcoholism, and other behaviors. However, therapists utilizing structured behavioral procedures produced impressive evidence of positive results in treating depression, an affective disorder. Furthermore, the behavioral techniques have been combined successfully with other therapeutic approaches in treating the depressions (Schwartz 1982).

Classical (Stimulus-Response) Conditioning Models

Pavlov's Conditioning Experiments with Dogs

The earliest behavioral models were based on the experiments of Ivan Pavlov (1849–1936), a Russian physiologist. In his famous experiments, Pavlov placed meat powder—an *unconditioned stimulus* (one that occurs without training or history)—in front of a hungry dog, and the dog salivated—an *unconditioned response* (a response that occurs without previous history or training). Pavlov then rang a bell—a *neutral stimulus* (one that does not elicit a given response [Reese, Howard, and Reese 1978:13]) at the same time he presented the powder to the dog; he rang the bell again but omitted the powder, and the dog salivated. This is a *conditioned response*—the animal was now trained (conditioned) to respond to the bell in the way he had responded to the food. The bell and the food are both *antecedent stimuli*, as they were both presented prior to the behavior (the unconditioned response.) This model is also referred to as the *classical*, or *stimulus-response*, or *Pavlovian* approach.

Harlow's Conditioning Experiments with Monkeys

Another early animal experimentalist was Harry Harlow, who, with his associates, isolated infant monkeys from their mothers (McKinney, Suomi, and Harlow 1971; Suomi and Harlow 1977). The pitiful infants responded with apathy and with lowered behavior and mood: a condition that seemed to these observers close to human depression. They later "cured" these young monkeys by pairing them with older female "therapist monkeys." Although there is a debate in the literature as to whether the condition suffered by these animals is really the equivalent of human depression, there is general agreement that the despair, failure to thrive, and other signs displayed by these baby monkeys is the equivalent of anaclitic depression in human babies, very similar to the pathetic infants studied by Spitz (1965).[1] (Anaclitic depression results when an infant is separated from his or her mother and not reunited or given adequate nurturing by a substitute or surrogate mother.)

Harlow's work led to further formulations of theories of human depression based on observation of animals, such as the work of Seligman.

Seligman's Theory of Learned Helplessness and Its Reformulation

In other experiments with animals, Martin E. P. Seligman put a naive dog (one not previously exposed to the experimental condition) into a cage divided by a barrier. Electricity was sent through the part of the cage where the dog stood. The dog could avoid the shock by jumping over the barrier into the other part of the cage, where there was no current. If the dog did not jump the first time, he was shown that he could. When the experiment was repeated, he jumped over the barrier. Seligman then put that dog into a harness, from which the dog could not escape, since he was immobilized, and subjected him to a series of electric shocks. He later put the same dog back into the cage without the harness and readministered shock. In contrast to his earlier behavior, the dog did not try to jump over the barrier and escape the shock but ran around, barking and yelping pitifully until the shock was turned off.

In the first part of the experiment the dog learned that he could avoid the shock by jumping over the barrier—he was able to affect (control) his environment. In the second part, when he could not escape the shock, he learned he could not have an effect on the punitive environment and felt powerless—he experienced *learned helplessness*. In the third part, he clearly had given up trying to change his environment, even when it became possible to do so (Seligman 1975).

Seligman's theory is useful as a hypothesis to help us understand the alleged predisposition of some people to depression and to identify the numbing effects of early trauma, poverty, discrimination, and political and social oppression.

Some people who have been subjected, particularly in their early lives, to severe and often prolonged trauma and deprivation appear to be depressed, but others do not. Following Seligman's theory, one of the crucial differentiating factors is the extent to which the person subjected to the trauma felt that he or she could have an impact upon the punitive environment. Those who had some success in easing or avoiding the pain and/or had the support of significant others seem to keep on trying and do not become depressed.[2] The others develop learned helplessness; they lack hope and feel helpless. They often display lowered self-esteem and vegetative symptoms. In other words, they become depressed.

Critics considered the original model of learned helplessness inadequate to explain human behavior because it did not account for the far greater complexity of depression in humans than what was produced in laboratory animals. A reformulation of the theory included the individual's views of why these uncontrollable things were happening to him.[3]

This revised theory postulates four major elements in the development of learned helplessness.

1. Depressed individuals anticipate that whatever happens to them will be very bad (aversive) and that, conversely, good things are not likely to happen to them.
2. They feel that they can do nothing to prevent these bad things from happening.
3. Their misfortunes are their own fault. They are due to things inside them that are unchanging and, therefore, these misfortunes will happen again and again. Good things that happen result from specific external factors or circumstances over which they have no control; they do not last and probably will not happen again (a *maladaptive attributional style* that is often seen in depressed people).
4. The more people are sure that bad (aversive) events will happen to them and the more they think they cannot control them, the lower will be their motivation and ability to deal with these matters. In other words, the motivational and cognitive deficits will be greater. Similarly, the more important an uncontrollable circumstance is to them, the more extensive will be the loss in self-esteem and the greater the depressive reaction.

Although the reformulated theory states that all four factors are involved in depression, most of the professional interest has been on the third factor, maladaptive attributional style. Some critics of the model state that it does not account for genetic and biological factors; others question its validity. At this point we agree with Williams's understated comment that the "attributional model is 'not proven' "(1984:16). Nevertheless, there are some positive aspects to the theory and its reformulation. It has generated a great deal of empirical research and has enlivened the theoretical and therapeutic debate about depression. The theory has enriched clinical work with depressives.

Wolpe's Behavioral Theories of Depression

Another application of conditioning principles to work with humans is exemplified by the work of the psychiatrist Joseph Wolpe, a pioneering behavior therapist who has had a great impact upon not only the behavior therapies but the psychotherapies in general. Wolpe's therapeutic techniques, which are expansions of the respondent (stimulus-response) approaches, were developed first to treat phobias and then broadened to encompass other conditions, including the depressions.

Wolpe has described three kinds of depressions. The first are what he calls *situational depressions.* These are the depressions suffered by all of us; the normal drops in spirits, particularly in reaction to a failure, loss, or deprivation (Wolpe 1982:271). A second category is *biological depressions,* which have a variety of causes and vary in seriousness from the extremes of bipolar illness to the side effects of drugs, physical disorders, and so on. Wolpe feels that these depressions may or may not be triggered by external events, but since they are related to biological processes, they are best treated with biological treatments (Wolpe 1982:271). The third category is *neurotic depressions,* often called *reactive depressions,* although Wolpe feels this latter term should be abandoned, as situational depressions are often reactive, and endogenous (biological) depressions may be triggered by stress. He states that many neurotic depressions are the result of a conditioning process. People develop conditioned responses of anxiety to various stimuli in their environments. For some people this anxiety is an antecedent (stimulus) for neurotic (reactive) depression. Although many depressed people also experience anxiety, depression frequently becomes their dominant mood state.

Wolpe believes that the neurotic depressions are appropriate for behavioral treatments. Viewing reactive (neurotic) depression as a conditioned response resulting from anxiety means that the various counterconditioning therapies devised by Wolpe can be used to treat these types of depressions.

Despite the differences in language and terminology, Wolpe's views of neurotic depressions as conditioned phenomena have much in common with psychodynamic and other views of depression. For example, in an analysis of a number of his own cases, Wolpe differentiated four types of neurotic depression, which illustrate these commonalities. Type 1 views depression as a "consequence of severe, directly conditioned anxiety." In this type, behavior is inhibited to the extent that it approaches helplessness. Wolpe states that this type of depressive responds well to systematic desensitization or other methods intended to reduce the anxiety, which will then reduce the depression.

Type 2 is neurotic depression that follows anxiety based on "erroneous self-devaluative cognitions" (Wolpe 1990:277). Wolpe, who is generally opposed to many of the newer cognitive and cognitive-behavioral developments, states that this type is comparatively rare.

Type 3 is illustrated by people who are dominated by other people because they cannot satisfactorily control interpersonal situations. They usually find themselves in a submissive role because they are overwhelmed by anxiety that makes them incapable of action. This incapacity develops into depression, which further increases the lack of activity and thus heightens the depression. Part of the treatment, according to Wolpe, would involve some sort of assertive training, either by itself or preferably as part of a larger treatment package.

Wolpe's view of a neurotic depressive being overwhelmed by other people has elements that are similar to Arieti's and Bemporad's psychodynamic concept of the dominant other.

Type 4 depression is an "exaggeration of the normal response to loss." This excessive response to loss has long been familiar to us as one of the central themes in Freud's classic essay "Mourning and Melancholia" (Freud 1917).

WOLPE'S BEHAVIOR THERAPY: RECIPROCAL INHIBITION THROUGH SYSTEMATIC DESENSITIZATION

Wolpe developed a set of specific procedures called reciprocal inhibition through systematic desensitization—usually referred to as *systematic desensitization*, based on the fact that the body's nervous system cannot simultaneously process conflicting states such as tension and relaxation. Wolpe hypothesized that if an individual could learn to relax in tension-producing situations, the tension would be eliminated. In systematic desensitization an individual is first taught to relax, using standard relaxation procedures, and while relaxed is slowly and systematically exposed to the tension-producing situations. This is usually done "in imagination" in the therapist's office, but it may also be done in vivo (in real life), where the therapist accompanies the patient to the actual place in which the "threat" occurs.

Systematic desensitization is, theoretically, individualized for each client. There is an assessment in which a complete history is taken. Wolpe then administers standardized tests, including the "Willoughby Personality Schedule, a Fear Survey Schedule, and a Bernreuter (an instrument to determine 'self-sufficiency' " (Schwartz 1982:26). An examination by a physician may be required if physical complications are suspected. If the client is taking any type of tranquilizer, including antianxiety medications, these are suspended, as they may interfere with the therapy; they may mask the anxiety. In addition, learning that occurs while taking medications may be lost when the client stops taking them (Schwartz 1982:27).

There are four steps in systematic desensitization. The first is to teach the client a deep muscle relaxation procedure—a useful tool to ease anxiety in general (Jacobson 1938). Although some of Wolpe's followers feel this must be done in the therapy session, Wolpe and others (these authors included) go through the procedures in the therapy session, and when they feel the client is ready, they provide him or her with a tape recording of the procedures, so that they can be practiced at home.

In the second step the therapist and client develop a scale of "subjective anxiety." The client is asked to visualize various anxiety-producing situations and rate them on Wolpe's scale of subjective units of disturbance (*sud*); a scale of 0–100 (from no anxiety to extreme anxiety).

Next, a hierarchy of subjective discomfort is developed, based on the client's anxiety-producing scenes. The hierarchy starts with the scene that causes the least amount of anxiety and ends with the one that produces the most. A hierarchy may focus on time or distance from the scene, or it may combine both elements.

In the last step, called relearning, the client must first become relaxed. Then he or she systematically reviews the anxiety-producing scenes, starting with the one lowest on the hierarchy, and "erases" them one at a time. The therapist presents a scene and the client states the unit of discomfort he feels according to the sud scale; that is, the degree of anxiety felt when visualizing the scene. If there is no anxiety or a low amount (usually under 25), the therapist proceeds to the next scene. If the client states that he is anxious (feels anxiety above 25 on the sud scale), he is instructed to practice the muscle relaxation procedures until he feels relaxed. When he can do this, the scene is considered no longer capable of causing anxiety and the next one on the hierarchy is presented. In other words, he is learning, by practicing in his imagination, to be relaxed in a situation in which he usually feels anxious.

Treatment of Depression with Wolpean Behavior Therapy: A Case

Barry Pratt, a thirty-nine-year-old unmarried man, was referred by his family doctor for treatment of depression. He appeared very early for the appointment, dressed in fashionable but conservative clothing, all of which hung loosely on him. He was well shaven and extremely neat. His face reflected despair. He had been losing weight and complained of sleeplessness and feelings of being "down." His physician had ruled out organic reasons for these conditions, including hypoglycemia, allergies, and so forth; all tests, including thyroid function, were within the normal range. He did not smoke, drink, or use any of the drugs of abuse. He does not take medication; he stated, "Thoughts of medication fill me with panic; I won't take drugs."

Barry worked as a computer programmer and a systems analyst with a prestigious insurance firm. He received bachelor and master's degrees in computer science from a large state university. He had been urged to take an MBA (Master of Business Administration) degree so that he could go into management, combining his technical background with sales. If he were to do so, his duties would change from working primarily with machines to working primarily with people, and his salary would be greatly increased. He declined to study for the MBA, for one of his problems was extreme shyness and anxiety when near people.

Barry is the youngest of five children and is presently the only one who is unmarried, despite the urging of his parents. He has had no relationships with women and describes himself as interested in several women but sure that these feelings are not reciprocated. In fact, he has not even dated the women he described. He says he is clumsy and uncomfortable near women. There have been a few contacts with prostitutes, which he found very unsatisfactory. He says he has had no homosexual experiences or desires.

Barry has no personal friends, although he sometimes discusses sports with a few men at work. He used to go to a baseball or hockey game from time to time but has not done so for several years. He describes himself as very bored and says he would like to get out of the rut he feels he is in. He remembers himself as having been tense all his life. Many things trigger tension, especially contact with women and with his superiors, with whom he cannot assert himself.

Barry lives alone and keeps his apartment very clean. He often skips meals, not being hungry and not liking to eat alone. When he is not working, he either watches TV or sleeps. Sometimes he has trouble falling asleep, but once he drops off, he sleeps soundly. He frequently awakens feeling tired, even if he has slept eight or nine hours.

Barry describes himself as a spectator rather than a participant.

Assessment. Wolpe viewed neurotic depression as the result of an exaggerated and extended reaction to loss, commonly associated with severe anxiety and/or failure to control interpersonal situations (1982:278–279).

Barry Pratt's depression does not seem a magnified response to loss. He does exhibit severe anxiety and feels unable to control interpersonal situations. He also seems to have poor self-esteem, poor self-image, and a lack of confidence. However, a Wolpean behavior therapist would hypothesize that easing the anxiety should eliminate the conditioned linkage between low self-image (and lack of confidence) and the anxiety that is triggered when the individual finds himself in threatening situations. Moreover, it should ease the depression that often follows this linkage. The therapeutic task is to identify those stimulus conditions that trigger anxiety.

Both the client and the therapist set the priorities. They decided to treat the shyness around women first. Barry felt that if this shyness were alleviated, much of his depression would lift. However, both he and the therapist realized that this was only one aspect of Barry's depression. They would then begin a course of assertiveness training. This sequential application of procedures is a common practice in Wolpean behavior therapy (Wolpe 1976:279).

The shyness was to be treated by systematic desensitization to the anxiety-producing situations. We shall limit our case to the first part of the therapy, the desensitization of anxiety produced by the presence of women.

Preparing for the therapy. During the first two sessions, Barry learned the relaxation procedures (the first step) by practicing during the session and listening to a tape at home. Then he and the therapist reviewed a variety of anxiety-causing situations. These scenes were rated from zero on the sud scale (no disturbance) to 100 suds (extreme disturbance). This was the second step. The third step was constructing the anxiety hierarchy by rearranging these situations according to the amount of anxiety they produced. The hierarchy we shall use for illustration combined physical distance from, and social interaction with, women. The following is a condensed depiction of this first hierarchy:

1. Stand at a distance of 30 feet from Jane (an older married woman who is a file clerk).
2. Stand 25 feet from Jane.
3. Stand 20 feet from Jane.
4. Stand 10 feet from Jane.
5. Stand 5 feet from Jane.
6. Stand 1 foot from Jane.
7. Ask Jane to find a particular file.
8. Take the file from Jane.
9. Approach Mary (a younger computer programmer who is married and also a subordinate) and ask her to check a program.
10. Ask Mary to bring the work into your office to discuss it.
11. Approach Sarah (another programmer, young and unmarried) and ask her to check a program.
12. Ask Sarah to check another program.
13. Ask Sarah to bring the program into your office to discuss it.
14. Ask Sarah to revise part of the program.
15. Ask Sarah to bring the revision into your office to discuss it.
16. In the cafeteria in the building, sit at a table with an older, married female coworker.
17. Sit at the table with a younger female coworker and several men.
18. Sit at a table with a younger female coworker and one other man.
19. Sit alone at the table with this female coworker.
20. Speak with the young woman about work.
21. Ask her how she likes the food that is served.
22. Ask her her name.
23. Etc.

Relearning (step 4) summarized. In step 4, the relearning phase of treatment, Barry practiced gradually increasing his approach behavior to women, in his imagination. He began each of the sessions in the relearning process by going through the series of relaxation procedures until he was relaxed. The therapist then presented a scene from the hierarchy they had agreed upon, starting with the one lowest on the scale of subjective discomfort. Barry was asked to raise a finger to indicate when the scene was in his mind. He was asked to keep it there for a short time. After a few seconds (usually five to seven) had passed, the therapist instructed him to erase the scene and then rate it on the sud scale. As this process was repeated, the sud rating for the scene became lower and lower. When it reached zero, they moved up the scale to the next item.

Barry became more comfortable, (was *desensitized*) in imagination, with the anxiety-producing situations in the hierarchy he was working on. After he had finished going through the hierarchy, in imagination, the plan was to carry out a series of similar steps in vivo, first approaching and then talking with various women in his office. At this point the therapist suggested that he simultaneously begin a program of assertiveness training. Considering Barry's isolation, the therapist suggested that this be done in a group and referred him to an appropriate resource.

Barry participated in an assertiveness training group where the leader and the group members modeled assertive behaviors and coached him. Barry had the opportunity to practice assertive behavior. The group was invaluable in providing feedback and reactions to the homework assignments he was carrying out as part of his therapy. Group procedures, as we shall see later in this chapter, have been quite successful with depressed patients (Lewinsohn et al. 1984).

As he became free of the anxiety that had preceded his depression and learned new approach behaviors aided by the assertiveness training, Barry's depression began to lift. He reopened discussion with his company about enrolling for the MBA in the next class, about ten months away. He also started to attend a social club, joining the members for coffee after the meetings. He began to date one of the members of the group and, at six-month follow-up, they were discussing marriage.

COMMENTS ON WOLPEAN BEHAVIOR THERAPY FOR DEPRESSION

In his text on behavior therapy, Wolpe (1982) presented a summary of twenty-five cases of reactive depression, all but one of which used some form of desensitization and/or relaxation techniques, a few combined with *cognitive correction*. Of these twenty-five cases, twenty-two were either recovered or "much improved." The mean number of sessions was 30.2, more than Wolpe usually reports for treating the phobias, attesting to the more complicated nature of the depressions.

The deconditioning approaches are generally held to be more effective than traditional psychotherapy, although less effective than imipramine or behavioral skills training in the treatment of depression (Hollon 1981:48). However, the research substantiating these techniques has been criticized as being based on "methodologically inadequate case studies or nonequivalent group designs" (Hollon 1981:48). For example, in a review of the treatment of depression with systematic desensitization, Turner, DiTomasso, and Deluty (1985:30) state that although Wolpe's case studies do lend some support for his position, "in the absence of controlled studies, the efficacy of desensitization in this area remains as yet undemonstrated."

In our view, Wolpe's techniques, particularly the relaxation procedures, are useful, especially when combined with other forms of therapy. Lehrer and Woolfolk (1985:102–103) reported that, "All systematic relaxation techniques produced reliable decreases in self-reported anxiety, anger, and depression." However, although they are frequently correct, Wolpe's views of depression as primarily a conditioned phenomenon seem limited, for, in our opinion, they are based on a narrow view of the emotional disorders in general and of depression in particular. Many depressed people *do* have high levels of anxiety, and this anxiety is often accidentally conditioned. However, cognitive, biological, and other factors are also central to understanding depression. Furthermore, from a behavioral point of view, the Wolpean approach does not sufficiently stress the *consequences* of depression, the positive reinforcements from significant others in the depressed person's environment, and the reinforcing elements of the depression itself. (In this context, a positive reinforcer refers to any event or action that maintains or increases the frequency of a behavior. We shall expand on this later in this chapter.)

Wolpe was a pioneer in offering a behavioral alternative to psychodynamically oriented theories. The Wolpean behavior therapy approach has been slowly supplanted, or supplemented (for the two often overlap) by the operant conditioning views associated with B. F. Skinner, currently the predominant orientation in behavioral psychology (Schwartz 1982).

Operant Conditioning Approaches

The Language of the Operant Conditioning Approaches

The operant conditioning approaches use specific terms to explain the operant procedures. This terminology may sometimes be confusing, because we use some of these terms (e.g., *positive, negative, punishment,* and *reinforcement*) every day. However, when they are used in the context of operant conditioning, they have specific meanings that may differ from their common usage.

We shall list these terms in italic type when they are used for the first time and shall give the technical definitions as well as examples. Since these terms are used throughout the balance of the chapter, the reader who is new to operant conditioning terminology is cautioned to keep these definitions in mind or refer back to them as needed.

Skinner's Operant Conditioning Theory

Operant conditioning is associated with the eminent psychologist B. F. Skinner. This approach is based on the observation that behavior has an effect (operates) on the environment—in contrast to the respondent view that it occurs automatically in response to environmental stimuli (S–R). (Much of this discussion on operant conditioning draws from Schwartz [1982, 1983].)

Behavior is viewed within an *A-B-C* (*antecedent-behavior-consequence*) framework. Every behavior has an *antecedent* (*A*), which can be a particular event (e.g., a light turning green or red)—something that precedes the *behavior* (*B*), setting the conditions under which the behavior is likely to occur. For example, a green light indicates that the appropriate behavior is to continue going through the intersection; a red light indicates that the appropriate behavior is to stop. Each behavior has a *consequence* (*C*). Going through the green light has the consequence of continuing on one's trip without being delayed; stopping when the light is red avoids (takes away the threat of) getting a ticket, or avoids being hit by another car. An antecedent condition can be a person as well as an event. A teacher coming into a class (A) indicates to the pupils that they should stop talking and face the front of the class (B). When the students stop talking and face the teacher, she smiles at them and begins teaching (C). In summary:

(A) Light turns green, indicates (B) continuing, which results in (C) continuing on trip.

(A) Light turns red, indicates (B) stopping, which results in (C) not getting a ticket.

(A) Teacher enters classroom, the cue for (B) pupils to stop talking and face teacher, resulting in (C) teacher smiles and starts teaching.

Consequences also determine the rate or frequency of behavior. Some consequences cause the rate of a behavior to be maintained or to increase, in which case the behavior is said to be *reinforced*. Other consequences cause the rate of a behavior to diminish or stop, in which case the behavior is said to be *punished*. For example, when an individual reaches out and starts a conversation with a person at work and that person shows interest, the speaker usually continues to talk and will engage in future conversations. His or her behavior is *reinforced* (maintained or increased) by the consequences (the response of the other). If he starts a conversation and the other person "snaps" at him, his "starting-a-conversation" behavior tends to drop; it is *punished* (decreased) by the consequences. A child may act out in class (behavior considered undesirable by the teacher) because he wants the attention of the teacher (consequence desired by the child). If, in response, the teacher scolds and disciplines him (thus giving him attention) and if his acting-out behavior continues, it is being reinforced (usually inadvertently) despite his having been disciplined ("punished," in the common use of the word) by being sent to the principal's office. If the teacher makes him do an unpleasant chore or takes away his free time (consequences the child does *not* desire) and the acting-out behavior lessens, we call this procedure *punishment*. If the teacher is able to ignore him (an alternate consequence), it is likely that this response will ultimately result in his acting-out behavior diminishing, and eventually stopping, thereby being *extinguished*. In summary:

1. (A) Coworker's presence leads to (B) starting a conversation, resulting in (C) interest shown. If (B) continues or increases—(B) is said to be *reinforced*.

   (A) Coworker's presence leads to (B) starting a conversation, resulting in (C) a brusque response. If (B) decreases—(B) is said to be *punished*.

2. (A) Teacher's presence, leads to (B) acting out, which results in (C) teacher scolding/disciplining (giving attention). If (B) continues or increases—(B) is said to be *reinforced*.

   (A) Teacher's presence, leads to (B) acting out, which results in (C) teacher scolding. If (B) diminishes—(B) is said to be *punished*.

   If (C) the teacher ignores the (B) acting-out behavior and the behavior drops, it is said to be *extinguished*.

Whether behavior occurs, and keeps on occurring, as the result of a consequence in which something is presented (e.g., response to conversation) or a consequence of something removed (e.g., the removal of the threat of getting a traffic ticket), as long as the consequences maintain or strengthen the behavior the process is called *reinforcement*. In the case of the consequence being presented, it is *positive reinforcement*; when the consequence is removed, it is *negative reinforcement*. For example, if the children stop talking, the teacher smiles, and the silence is maintained or increases, then the reaction of the teacher is positive reinforcement, for something is presented (a smile) that maintains or increases the rate of the behavior (remaining silent). If the teacher threatens to make the children do extra work if they continue to talk and they then remain silent, the procedure is negative reinforcement— the behavior (keeping silent) is maintained because something (the threat of extra work) is taken away. (Negative reinforcement is an aversive procedure because it is obviously unpleasant to the children.) Similarly, when behavior drops (is punished) as a result of a consequence being presented (e.g., a child is slapped), this is *positive punishment*. If it drops because the consequence is removed (e.g., a child is grounded), this is *negative punishment*. Operant therapists usually use the word *punishment* to stand for both positive punishment and negative punishment; both are aversive procedures. In summary, in operant behavior language:

Positive—always indicates that consequences are presented (e.g., the teacher's smile, the teacher's scolding, the coworker's interested response to conversation).

Negative—always indicates that consequences are removed (e.g., the threat of a traffic ticket; the threat of extra schoolwork).

Reinforcement—always indicates that the consequences of a behavior result in that behavior being maintained or increased. (The teacher's smile maintained the class's silence; the coworker's interest maintained continuing conversation.)

Punishment—always indicates that the consequences of a behavior result in that behavior decreasing. (The teacher's scolding of acting out lessened this behavior; the coworker's brusque response lessened initiating conversations.)

Positive reinforcement—always indicates that behavior is maintained or increased via a *positive* consequence (something presented—e.g., the teacher's smile and the response to conversation).

Negative reinforcement—always indicates that behavior is maintained or increased via a *negative* consequence (something aversive being removed—e.g., the threat of a traffic ticket or of extra schoolwork).

Positive punishment—always indicates that behavior is diminished via a *positive* consequence (e.g., a slap—which is presented).

Negative punishment—always indicates that behavior is diminished via a *negative* consequence (e.g., grounding—which removes a privilege).

The antecedent event (A), which may be the cue for a behavior to take place, as we just described, is also the *rule* that indicates what will be the consequence for which behavior. In other words, certain behaviors tend to occur only when specific antecedents are present and will not occur when others are present. For example, a child who wants to stay up later than his bedtime (a desired consequence) may have a temper tantrum when his baby-sitter is present, because he knows from past experience that this will result in (have the consequence of) her allowing him to stay up late and watch television. He will not have a temper tantrum when his mother is present, because he knows that the consequence of this same behavior (a temper tantrum) will be a spanking and being put to bed. This is called *stimulus discrimination*: The child has learned that his behavior (a temper tantrum) produces different consequences in the presence of the two different antecedents—the presence of the baby-sitter and the presence of his mother. When he alters his behavior accordingly, he is discriminating between the two on the basis of the consequences; he has learned stimulus discrimination. The baby-sitter has become the *discriminative stimulus* for the tantrum behavior; the mother is the discriminative stimulus for going to bed on time. In summary:

(A) Baby-sitter present, leads to (B) a temper tantrum, to get (C) to stay up later (a desired consequence—from the viewpoint of the child).

(A) Mother present, leads to (B) going to bed on time, to avoid (C) a spanking (an undesired consequence—from the viewpoint of the child).

In the preceding situations, the child's behavior (even the temper tantrum when the baby-sitter is present) actually fits the situation. When individuals behave in ways that do not fit the situation (their behavior is *maladaptive*)—for example, reading comic books during study period, then doing math homework in music class, or doing work in the cafeteria during lunch hour and trying to engage coworkers in conversation during working hours—they are said to be "under inappropriate stimulus control. . . . [and people must learn] to engage in the appropriate behavior in the appropriate situation" (Schwartz 1982:66). In other words, they are not paying attention to or are ignoring or misinterpreting the antecedent cues (in the preceding examples, the study hall or the lunch room).

In the operant model we speak of the *probabilities of behavior*. The probability that a particular behavior will occur and the rate of its occurrence are determined sometimes by the antecedents, but largely by the consequences of the behavior. The driver will probably stop at a red light when others (e.g., a policeman) are present, to avoid getting a traffic ticket; the probability that he will stop lessens when no one is around to observe him and give him a ticket. The students will probably stop talking and face the teacher when she comes in and looks at them approvingly; they may not stop talking if she comes into the room, sits right down at her desk, and starts to read her record book. In summary:

(A) A red light, will probably lead to (B) stopping, to avoid (C) getting a ticket—when there is a high probability that this consequence might occur (e.g., in the daytime, when the behavior may be seen by a policeman).

(A) A red light will less often lead to (B) stopping, to avoid (C) getting a ticket—when there is a low probability that this consequence will occur (e.g., late at night, when the behavior may not be seen by a policeman).

A consequence may be self-programmed and self-administered. For example, one may give a reward to oneself for performing a desired behavior that is difficult or unpleasant (e.g., dieting, exercising, homework, and so on). This procedure is called *self-reinforcement*. Self-created consequences such as self-rewards are usually used for a period of time to get a behavior started. After a while, the natural consequences of the desired behavior (e.g., weight loss, feeling good, better grades) become reinforcers in their own right; they are now "intrinsically reinforcers" (Reese, Howard, and Reese 1978:55).

Unlike the respondent model, where there is a response after each eliciting stimulus, in the operant model behavior may occur according to various *schedules of reinforcement*. When a response occurs after every behavior, this is a *continuous schedule of reinforcement*; if it does not occurs each time the behavior occurs, it is an *intermittent schedule of reinforcement*. Reinforcement may occur after either a fixed or a variable number of responses, or a fixed or a variable period of time. Schedules of reinforcement may be simple (one type) or complex (a combination of different schedules). An individual's schedules of reinforcement provides important information about how certain undesirable or maladaptive behaviors are maintained (reinforced), giving indicators for intervention. Reinforcement schedules are closely examined in depressed clients, as we shall explain.

The interrelations of the antecedent, the behavior, the consequences, and the individual are called *contingency relationships*—meaning that behavior is contingent upon, or likely to occur as the result of, these other factors. The person in the situation may or may not be consciously aware of the interconnections of these contingency relationships. "The analysis of behavior within the Skinnerian or operant approach is an analysis of the individual within the whole set of his contingency relationships. . . . [which is] equivalent to the social work principle of 'the individual in the situation' " (Schwartz 1983:209).

These concepts are fundamental to operant behavioral treatment approaches.

TREATMENT PRINCIPLES

In treatment based on operant principles, the therapeutic task is to examine and change the contingencies (the conditions) that govern maladaptive behaviors, not just to change these behaviors. The treatment approach is very explicit and straightforward. It begins with diagnostic interviews to identify the problem behaviors, the contingencies controlling these behaviors (within the A-B-C framework), and the goals of treatment. Problems are pinpointed by asking specific questions, such as, "How long has this been a problem? . . . Is this a problem all the time? Are there some times when this is not a problem? . . . What happens when [it] occurs? What are the reactions of others? Has this always been a problem?" (Schwartz 1982:67–69).

Very specific goals are determined based on the client's view of what life would be like when the goals are achieved and how that would differ from the current situation. The client's strengths are examined. Client and therapist together develop a program that uses the client's strengths to achieve the treatment goals. The procedures are spelled out, and the first step of the program is mutually determined. The goals of the therapy and the program procedures are usually formalized in either a verbal or a written contract. At the end of the diagnostic session or sessions the therapist gives the client the opportunity to ask questions about any aspect of the treatment and gives feedback on his or her view of the client's problem(s) and whether they can be treated with behavioral intervention.

The therapy emphasizes analyzing the contingency relationships in the client's behavior. The client is frequently asked to keep *logs*, which are charts with recordings of behaviors with their antecedents and consequences, including mood. Programing procedures are used to help the client make necessary changes in these contingency relationships. This is usually done by helping the client to learn new behaviors, increase the performance of desired behaviors already in the client's repertoire, reduce the frequency of undesired behaviors, eliminate certain undesirable behaviors, and learn to discriminate what situations are appropriate for which behaviors. Common techniques include *shaping* (working in very small steps to change the nature of a behavior already known, often ending in a new behavior—sometimes called the method of *successive approximations*); *chaining* (linking one behavior to another, in small steps, to end in a new behavior); and *prompting and fading* (inserting cues to redirect behavior, then gradually withdrawing them).[4] Although operant methods are used both to increase desired behaviors and to decrease undesired behaviors, most operant procedures emphasize positive reinforcement, encouraging desired behaviors, especially desired behaviors that are incompatible with the undesired behaviors, rather than eliminating undesired behaviors by using aversive procedures.

An important goal of treatment is for the client to learn skills that will enable him to maintain the gains he has made. This is done through processes of *generalization,* where the skills that the client learns in the treatment situation are transferred to outside situations, and by the client learning to analyze his contingency relationships and deal with them in the ways learned in treatment (monitoring antecedents and consequences of behavior, arranging or rearranging these consequences as needed, and so on).

THE OPERANT CONDITIONING VIEWS OF DEPRESSION

Skinner originally considered depression to be the result of an extended process of extinction in which behavior that had previously been reinforced was no longer reinforced. For example, a woman whose husband has died may no longer feel like cooking dinner, since her efforts are not "consequented" (i.e., reinforced by her husband's response—his eating the food) (Skinner 1953). Sometimes the cue (discriminative stimulus) for behavior (e.g., her husband coming home at a particular time for dinner) is lost along with the reinforcers.

Extinction may also occur when the schedule of reinforcement is weakened: a slow decrease of reinforcement that leads to less behavior, leading to less reinforcement, then extinction. The nonreinforcement (extinction) of previously reinforced behavior is often accompanied by certain feelings—a conditioned emotional response experienced by the individual as "depression" (Ferster 1973).

The concept of previously reinforced behavior that is in extinction is a central theme in behavioral formulations of depression. It has been pointed out that extinction is a "thesis similar to loss" and that psychoanalytic theory hypothesizes that loss is central to the etiology of depression (Agras 1978:45–46; Schwartz 1982:180–185).

Potential reinforcements may be available, but the individual may not be behaving in ways that will elicit these reinforcements. Such a case would be that of a socially isolated college student who is not dating. This individual may benefit enormously from social skills training, discussed later in this chapter .

Sometimes the behavior exhibited by a person meets with very aversive responses from the environment, and thus the rate of this behavior is lowered (punished). An individual may be engaging in behavior that elicits these responses. For example, a student may act awkwardly toward women, who then consistently reject him. This causes him to shy away from women. The response of the women is a "punishment," because it lowers his approach behavior. He might also experience this lowered behavior, with its consequent effect on his self-esteem, as depression.

Determining the sequence of events is part of the behavioral assessment of depression. There are other aspects to an operant analysis of depression, such as examining the effects of different schedules of reinforcement, the loss of *stimulus props* (constant factors during the learning of behavior, such as a particular classroom), the loss of *reinforcer effectiveness* (responses that no longer maintain rates of behavior— e.g., food is no longer reinforcing when a person is no longer hungry) (Costello 1972), *ratio strain* (where too much behavior is demanded for too little reinforcement), and others.[5]

One aspect of the behavior-consequence (reinforcement) view of depression that is sometimes overlooked is that the depression itself is often reinforced. That is, the depressed person may be ignored when he or she is nondepressed. However, when the individual is depressed, people in the immediate environment may show concern, ask questions, and be solicitous. In this situation, the person would have low motivation for not being depressed; depression may become an operant to receive attention (Falloon et al., 1988:117–118). (An *operant* is a "behavior [that] operates, or has an effect, on its environment" [Schwartz, 1982:53].) In psychodynamic terms, this reinforcing effect of attention may be labeled as a secondary gain of the depression. It may be hard to eliminate, for this secondary gain may be one of the maintaining variables, reducing the depressed person's motivation to give up the depression. A psychoanalytic interpretation is that for some persons, depression is a an active, interpersonal manipulative maneuver, usually on an unconscious level, not only to obtain attention but to control others (Bonime 1966).

TREATMENT OF DEPRESSION WITH OPERANT CONDITIONING THERAPY: A CASE RECONSIDERED

Earlier in this chapter we presented a case illustrating how Barry Pratt was treated by a Wolpean behavior therapist. We now present the same case from an operant conditioning point of view.

In operant conditioning terms, Barry's depression is seen as more than just an accompaniment of the anxiety set off by certain stimuli. More emphasis is placed on the role of the *consequences* of the depression as well as the antecedent stimuli that trigger the anxiety and depression. An operant therapist would try to ascertain if the depression is being reinforced (maintained) by the attention it draws from significant others, if there was a sudden cessation of reinforcement by these people in his environment, or if the depression was being negatively reinforced (i.e., it is a way of coping by *escaping* or *avoiding* unpleasant things in the depressed person's life). The depression might be a result of *punishment* (e.g., caused by harsh comments delivered by significant others who find the depressive's behavior very aversive or undesirable).[6]

In a behaviorally oriented initial interview, the information would be gathered for an analysis of the factors that affect the behavior-depression linkage. The client is often asked to keep logs, a record of the events of each day, with one entry an hour (if feasible) and a rating of mood. Some therapists use Wolpe's hundred-point rating system (0 is the lowest rating; 100, the highest). We have had success with a ten-point scale, with 10 = high, 0 = very low, and 5 = "in between." The important differences are between the large intervals (e.g., 7 and 2); the small intervals (e.g., between 6 and 7) are not meaningful in practice.

Since Barry reported that he worked long hours and did little else, there were few differences in his workday logs (Monday to Friday). For illustration we present a workday (Tuesday) and a weekend day (Saturday). (See logs 14.1 and 14.2.) This kind of record is better than attempts to recall past events, providing both the therapist and client with a good picture of the details of a client's day.

Barry's logs for the two days showed very little behavior that provided pleasure, which is typical of many depressives. It also revealed low mood and no reinforcements from others, because he did not act

Log 14.1. Daily Log: Tuesday, July 11

Time	Where	Who Was There	What I Wanted	What I Got	Mood	Comments
7:00 A.M.	bed	alone	get up	got up	2	not looking forward to work
8–8:30	car	alone	get to work	got to work	4	felt a little better
9–12	desk	alone	work; talk	work with people	5–6	felt better working, but no conversations
12–1	Cafeteria	alone	lunch; talk with people	lunch	2	did not approach anyone; bolted food, took a walk
1–5	desk	alone	work, talk with people	work	4	did a good job; did not talk with anyone
5–6	car	alone	get home	got home	7	no rush to get home; took new route, interesting
6–11	house	alone	eat, TV	ate, TV	3	TV dinner; nothing on TV: tried to read, but distracted by my lousy life situation
11	bed	alone	sleep	tossing	2	felt very down

Log 14.2. Weekend Log: Saturday, July 15

Time	Where	Who Was There	What I Wanted	What I Got	Mood	Comments
10 A.M.	bed	alone	get up	stayed in bed till 11:15	2	felt down, lonely, hopeless
11:30	kitchen	alone	eat	only coffee	2	did not feel like preparing food
12–2	liv. rm.	alone	distraction	watched TV	3	feel lousy
2–4	bed	alone	escape	nap	4	felt dragged when I woke up
4–5	market	people	shop, talk	groceries, no talk	2	felt alone (couples, kids, families, all shopping)
5–6	kitchen	alone	eat	ate cheese sandwich	3	I hate cheese sandwiches
6–10	liv. rm.	alone	kill time	watched videos	5	felt somewhat better, but still lousy
10–11	liv. rm.	alone	watch TV news	TV news	3	down again, another lonely weekend .. to parents tomorrow
11:15	bed	alone	sleep	eventually, fell asleep	2	took over an hour to fall asleep

(behave) to elicit reinforcement. There was little interaction with people. His appetite was poor and he had trouble falling asleep.

The highest rating, 7 (one of the few above the mean of 5) was given when he *on his own* examined a new route home, which gave him a lot of pleasure and even a sense of control. This venture was a good prognostic sign, for it showed that he had the potential to adapt to new activities.

The chief feature of Barry's records is that they show he *is* "in a rut." He is acutely aware of this, and very unhappy with his life situation. His logs show little that would earn him reinforcements from others, if there *were* others to reinforce him. The first therapeutic task is to break the extinction cycle or, in other words, for Barry to begin to engage in new behaviors, including meeting new people who could provide reinforcements. (This same approach, utilizing a different theory and a different therapy, is proposed by Arieti and Bemporad 1978:306.)

The opening and middle phases of treatment focused on Barry's behavior and factors controlling his behavior (the contingencies). The therapist and the client planned some behavioral steps Barry could take to break the extinction cycle. The first priority, chosen by Barry and the therapist, was eating: Barry was to try to eat at least two meals a day, planning the meals at least one day ahead of time. (Barry, who was a computer programmer, liked this suggestion so much that he actually planned a whole week's menus.) A second behavioral requirement was to engage in at least one activity each day that would take him out of his home and include at least one interaction with another person. It was decided that another homework assignment for this week would be to go to a grocery store and speak with one clerk. The purpose here was to begin to engage him in safe (nonthreatening), somewhat impersonal interactions with one or two people and then gradually shape his behavior, in slow steps, by associating with people in relationships increasingly more personal and thus more meaningful.

Another goal was to interact more with people at work. The therapist and Barry role-played how to approach and talk with young women at work, as preparation for actually carrying this out at his office. In addition, he responded enthusiastically to a suggestion that he explore joining a group at church. This was a group of accomplished people, like Barry, but slightly older and more established, who met weekly for intensive discussion of the Bible. The group was ecumenical as well as multiaged, although, unfortunately, it consisted only of men. Several of these men responded positively to Barry and to his increasingly cogent contributions. Invitations to dinners followed, where there were other guests, including young women. These invitations and dinners were both material for discussion and places where Barry could try out new behaviors.

As expected, increasing the levels of Barry's behavior led to obtaining more reinforcements from the environment and caused changes in his affects. The increased rates of behavior slowed down the extended extinction process—the retarded behavior that characterizes many reactive depressions.

If Barry had been engaging in behavior that was aversive to other people, which caused them to "punish" him, then this behavior would have been analyzed and other courses of behavior would have been discussed to increase his ability to elicit positive responses and positive reinforcements.

Barry slowly began to move out of his rut. He began to attend meetings of several social clubs and gradually made overtures to several young women at these clubs. He started to rethink the company's offer of MBA training and was seriously considering attending school for this advanced degree. He also began to socialize more with the people at work.

In the last phase of treatment, as Barry's treatment goals were being accomplished, both the therapist and Barry focused on the specific contingency relationships that had previously resulted in episodes of depression. They reviewed the procedures for analyzing these relationships and for engaging in the patterns of desirable behavior that tended to prevent depression. In other words, a final goal was for Barry to learn to be his own behavior therapist by the time treatment ended.

Comments on Operant Conditioning Therapy for Depression

Barry and the therapist were aware of internal events, such as feelings of low self-esteem; however, the focus of treatment was on increasing some external behaviors that could elicit reinforcement, thus lessening the depression (breaking the extinction process).

Barry was a responsive client who was increasingly able to engage in actions that brought him into contact with other people. He began to feel less gloomy when he behaved in ways that obtained the reinforcements so lacking in his life. However, if asked, "How do you feel?" Barry continued to reply, "I still feel hollow; empty inside."

What happened with Barry sometimes happens with clients treated with behavior therapy: As the rate of behavior goes up, the client does feel better, but he may still have feelings of worthlessness. He may be "behaving" more, and this does elicit reinforcements, but the feelings of pessimism and sadness may persist. In fact, more traditionally oriented therapists may insist that he is, in effect, still depressed, and they may be correct.

We believe the behavioral approaches have enormous utility, especially in the beginning phases of treatment, in providing both an analysis of the actual circumstances and the nature of the depression as well as succinct methods for breaking the downward spiral of the depression cycle. These specific procedures may, of course, hasten the client's natural tendency to "come out of it." However, if the internal factors, such as lack of self-esteem, are not worked out, the depressive episodes may very well recur. In addition to changing his behavior, Barry must change the way he sees himself and the way he sees the world. In short, although it has much to recommend it, a purely operant behavioral therapy approach has its limitations, and these have probably provided the main impetus for development into the cognitive areas. We believe this evolution is a positive one in the treatment of the depressions.

Lazarus's Time Projection and Affective Expression Procedures

Lazarus introduced two innovative and useful interventions. One was a *time projection* procedure that motivates the client to picture himself at some point in the future—for example, by making plans for some future event, like celebrating a birthday or attending a nephew's confirmation. This is a sensitive and effective therapeutic procedure, especially useful for treating those depressed clients with suicidal ideation (Lazarus 1968). The rationale behind the procedure is that if depression is seen as resulting from inadequate reinforcers, this technique will enable the client to imagine himself freed of his oppressive inertia to enjoy some potential reinforcers in the future that will lessen his depression (Lazarus 1971:228).

Lazarus also recommended *affective expression,* where the therapist encourages or provokes the client to express a great deal of feeling, which halts the downward spiral of the depression (1968). This behavioral maneuver is similar to the psychodynamic technique of catharsis. Affective expression (like catharsis) may lead to temporary relief of the feelings of depression. However, unless there is an analysis of and intervention into the total behavior-contingency relationships, the positive effects of this procedure will be short-lived (Schwartz 1982).

The Social-Learning Approach of Lewinsohn

Much of the contemporary work in the behavioral orientations is a combination of behavioral, cognitive, and sometimes even affective (including psychodynamic) procedures. A major theory that spans these divisions but that seems most appropriately classified with operant behavioral reinforcement theories is the social-learning model of Peter M. Lewinsohn. This model draws from Bandura's views that there is *reciprocal determinism:* the environment, the person (including cognitive and other internal factors), and the behavior all interact and influence each other (Bandura 1986).

Lewinsohn and his colleagues at the University of Oregon agreed with the operant behavioral view that depressed individuals often do not behave in ways that elicit reinforcements from others, and sometimes their behaviors elicit a high rate of punishment. Lewinsohn believed that part of the reason for the low rates of behavior (and thus low rates of reinforcement) typical of these depressed individuals was that they lacked social skills. Lewinsohn and his colleagues developed a social skills training therapy for these individuals, an approach that focused on increasing positive interactions and decreasing punishing interactions with people.

Although this approach has been used with individuals, in our opinion the most important aspect of Lewinsohn's work is the therapy done within groups. Most treatments for depression, especially behavioral and cognitive-behavioral treatments, are not offered in groups. Group therapy theory tends to advise against forming groups solely of depressed individuals. Lewinsohn's results indicate that some depressives work well within the group structure. The therapy groups may resemble groups in the natural environment, and they also provide a good support system (Lewinsohn and Hoberman 1985:198–199).

Lewinsohn has incorporated some cognitive features into his treatment supplementing what is primarily an operant behavioral approach. He recognized that cognitions, especially a client's expectations of failure, negatively affect his interaction with the environment and limit his ability to cope with depression. Thus the program includes a number of procedures, such as assertion training and time management techniques.

LEWINSOHN'S COPING WITH DEPRESSION COURSE

Lewinsohn's theory and strategies for intervention can be found primarily in three books: *Control Your Depression* (Lewinsohn et al. 1986), *The Coping with Depression Course* (Lewinsohn et al. 1984), and *Participant Workbook for the Coping with Depression Course* (Brown and Lewinsohn 1984). The first is a popular book; the second is a detailed treatment manual for professionals who lead the depression reduction course; and the third is a concise handbook for workshop participants.

The *Coping with Depression Course* runs for twelve sessions. Learning occurs within the group and through reading assigned chapters in *Control Your Depression*. Other homework assignments are given periodically—for example, keeping logs of activities and mood; making activity schedules; completing tasks including social activities; creating plans to deal with stress; and so on. In addition to leading the group meetings and teaching the course, the instructor plays a very active role monitoring and reinforcing the progress of each student and models social skills, such as assertiveness.

Goals, primarily learning to become "undepressed," are determined (Brown and Lewinsohn 1984:4). After reviewing a 320–item Pleasant Events Schedule, which provides a baseline of their current activities as well as for potentially reinforcing events, the participants are asked to keep logs monitoring daily moods. Next, they begin to plan for self-change, to overcome depression by learning new behaviors through a seven-step process: pinpointing, baselining (keeping statistical information), discovering antecedents, discovering consequences, setting goals, contracting, and choosing reinforcers. They plan pleasant events as rewards (reinforcers) for progress (changed behavior). They also learn relaxation procedures, cognitive change procedures (similar to the ones that will be discussed in chapter 15), and assertiveness training.

The final emphasis is on "using social skills," which is the heart of the Lewinsohn approach. This involves evaluation of current social skills, pleasant activities (both engaged in now and to be engaged in in the future), and homework assignments that are increasingly in the real world (i.e., outside the group). Maintaining gains and developing strategies to anticipate and ward off the return of depression are emphasized.

A number of outcome studies, mostly by Lewinsohn and his associates, show great reduction in symptomatology and maintenance of gains at follow-up intervals of one and six months. They claim that 80 percent of the students were not depressed after taking the course (Lewinsohn et al. 1984:vii). The therapy seems to be less effective with more seriously depressed clients, especially those who are suicidal. However, for many depressed clients who might not otherwise receive therapy and for those who are responsive to group approaches (and this does include some of the seriously depressed, socially isolated individuals) this approach is direct, effective, and economical.

Becker's Social Skills Training

Becker and his colleagues have also treated depression with social skills training (Becker et al. 1987). They assume that depression occurs when a person receives too little positive reinforcement and receives it infrequently. In addition, there is usually a deficit of other kinds of rewards, such as recognition, inclusion in social events, promotions, and so on, because the person's behavior is deficient: He is not acting in a way that would elicit these rewards. Social skills training is designed to help the person act in ways that will result in receiving these attentions from others. More reinforcements (a denser schedule of reinforcement) will lessen the depression.

Becker and his colleagues (1987:4–5) stress the importance of *key developmental periods* in the life of the depressive. An individual may have insufficient social skills because he or she was not taught certain behaviors or did not have the opportunity to observe or perform these behaviors at key times in life. Furthermore, the individual may have learned unsuitable or problematic behaviors at these times. These behavioral deficits may persist into adulthood and may result when adaptive behaviors, such as dating, are not used for a long time. They are not easily regained when needed again (e.g., if a married person becomes divorced or widowed or a long-term relationship ends). Furthermore, deficits in behavior often result when a person feels he will be unable to perform a behavior well enough, regardless of what he does. This is related to Seligman's concept of learned helplessness; it is also related to the impotence of the depressive when faced with demands from dominant others, a restatement of a psychodynamic concept from Arieti and Bemporad (1978).

These conceptualizations of depression as primarily a result of behavioral deficits are the justification for a behavior training approach to the treatment of depression. Similar to operant conditioning approaches, Becker's behavior training involves more than just learning and relearning specific behaviors. The individual must learn when and where certain behaviors are appropriate and when and where they are not. This inability to discriminate, especially in social situations, may result in a person's not engaging in desirable behaviors, or engaging in ill-timed or inappropriate behaviors. The client with this problem needs help with self-evaluation and self-reinforcement training.

BECKER'S PROGRAM OF SOCIAL SKILLS TRAINING

Treatment usually consists of eighteen individual, weekly, one-hour sessions. Scheduling is flexible to allow for client and therapist vacations, illnesses, and so on. As we shall see, the therapy involves much homework, and the eighteen-session limitation requires client cooperation.

Clinical assessment includes interviews and the completion of a number of rating scales both for evaluation of progress and for research: the Beck Depression Inventory (BDI), the Depression Adjective Checklist (DACL), the Hopkins Symptom Checklist (HSCL), the Zung Self-rating Depression Scales, the Raskin Global Severity of Depression Scale, and the Hamilton Rating Scale for Depression (Becker et al. 1987: 17–22).

The therapist uses interviews, role-playing, and self-assessments to evaluate social skills and deficits, social judgments, self-monitoring skills and deficits, and degrees of assertiveness (Becker et al. 1987:32–40). The rationale of the approach is made clear: The assessment procedure is, in effect, a rehearsal of the therapy to come.

Family members are included in the treatment by being given information about depression and the treatment process; any questions they may have are answered (Becker et al. 1987:89).

The initial focus is on *direct behavior training*. The goal is to teach *expressive communication skills,* including assertive behavior, and how to begin and sustain conversations. It is the "hows of effective social behavior" (Becker et al. 1987:9).

Role-playing begins with "as-if" situations and continues with real-life ones, followed by *flexibility training,* where the client is taught to assess social situations and adapt his behavior appropriately.

As stated by Becker and colleagues (1987:50–51), a typical session begins with a ten-minute review of homework, followed by approximately forty minutes of role-playing of specific client situations. In role-playing, the therapist analyzes the new behavior that is to be learned and then demonstrates it in a reverse role-play, where the therapist is the client and the client plays a person involved in the situation. The therapist judges the client's awareness of what is involved and then the client role-plays (imitates) the therapist's actions. The therapist gives feedback, including praise and constructive criticism. The role-play is repeated (the behavior is rehearsed) until the therapist and the client are satisfied with the client's accomplishments. The last ten minutes are devoted to deciding upon the next homework assignment. In the following session, the homework assignment is brought back to the therapist for review, feedback, and discussion of the things that went well and of the problems; the client is then praised for his or her efforts. Client logs are sometimes used.

Direct behavioral training is followed by *practice and generalization,* where the focus is on trying out new skills outside of the office but under the tutelage of the therapist (Becker et al. 1987:52).

The next segment concentrates on *social perception training,* called by the authors the "dynamics of social behaviors." This focuses on the more involved aspects of social interactions, including the client's perceptions (and often, misperceptions) of how others react to him and how he affects others. Attention is paid to the more subtle aspects of interactions, such as recognizing cues, assessing and demonstrating responses to them; understanding both verbal and nonverbal communication from the other person; and finding out how the other person feels. This is often difficult for depressed people, who tend to be preoccupied with their own emotions.

There is practice, feedback, role-play, homework, and more practice.

The next section of the therapy, focusing on self-evaluation and methods of self-reinforcement, attempts to help the client reduce the excessively stringent demands he often makes of himself. He is encouraged to set more realistic and achievable criteria for his behavior and for judging himself. The client also learns ways to reinforce himself, verbally and otherwise. This work on self-evaluation involves helping the depressed person to change the kinds of messages he is giving himself, thus expanding this very behavioral therapy into the areas of cognitions and cognitive processes.

A pattern of response to therapy emerged from Becker's investigation of eighty cases. In the first three or four weeks, there is a slight lessening of the depression. At the fifth or sixth week there is a drop that may last for several sessions. About the eleventh session, the depression again diminishes markedly and continues to lessen, often so much that scores on the scales used to measure it no longer indicate depression. They may rise again, but still remain low. At the end of treatment, depression scale ratings are in the nondepression ranges (Becker et al. 1987:88–89).

COMMENT ON SOCIAL SKILLS TRAINING TREATMENT FOR DEPRESSION

As stated by the authors, the "heart of this approach is a learning-oriented model" (Becker et al. 1987:83). It focuses on learning new skills and unlearning old, maladaptive behavior patterns. It is a structured therapy in the process of being developed, and although there is some ongoing research, there are currently insufficient data to indicate which type of depressed client would benefit from this treatment. The approach is obviously not for everyone. The authors feel that their therapy would not be applicable for clients who do not grasp the relation between interpersonal behavior and depression, who do not comply with therapy, who resist doing homework, and who display rigid and inflexible patterns of cognitions. Clients who are likely to benefit are those having problems with assertion, who agree that they must behave differently, and who have the support of family and friends (Becker et al. 1987:82).

Social skills training seems to be beneficial for the moderately depressed rather than the most severely depressed. In its current form it seems aimed primarily at outpatient treatment, although some aspects of the therapy could be incorporated into inpatient treatment, especially for the previously severely depressed patient prior to being discharged from the hospital.

We think that the elements of social skills training would be a positive addition to any therapy for depression. As currently conceived by Becker and his colleagues, social skills training is a therapy in its own right, with a heavy research and evaluation aspect. However, as we stated earlier, some elements of the approach, such as assertion training, social perception, evaluation of self-standards, and so on, are already being used with a number of therapies for depression, regardless of what label or name the therapy bears.

The Self-Control Model of Rehm

Lynn P. Rehm (1977), a psychologist, has developed a *self-control* model for treating depression. Rehm acknowledges the contributions of the Skinnerians, who stated that behavior was largely in response to environmental control, but stresses that the individual may take a more active role in influencing the nature of these behavior-consequence sequences. Although it includes direct cognitive change procedures, this approach stresses changing the nature of individual/environmental interactions. For this reason we include it in this chapter rather than in the chapter on cognitive or cognitive-behavioral approaches, as perhaps the most comprehensive of the behavioral approaches to depression.

In the self-control model it is believed that individuals may change their behaviors: They may discontinue dysfunctional behavior or begin to engage in behavior to elicit reinforcement, or they may behave in ways to avoid eliciting punishing responses. Therapy is aimed at helping individuals be more active in controlling their contingency relationships themselves, hence the title of *self-control.*

Rehm's model utilizes many of the self-control ideas of Kanfer and Gaelick (1986:288–289), who formulated a three-step process that individuals engage in when changing behavior. The first is *self-monitoring,* where people examine their behavior, what preceded it, and what followed it (the antecedents and the consequences). The second is *self-evaluation,* where they estimate whether their behavior has met a particular standard. This standard may be external, but more frequently it is internal and is usually very stringent. In the last step, based on whether their behaviors met the standard, they *self-reinforce* or *self-punish.*

There may be problems (*self-deficits*) at any phase of this three-step process. Depressed people often pay more attention to negatives than to positives. They judge themselves too harshly, and they seldom, if ever, engage in self-reinforcement, self-praise, or even positive self-evaluations. Because of their histories they expect failure rather than success, and they often act as if they have failed, thus setting up a self-fulfilling prophecy.

Rehm's short-term, structured therapy aims to correct deficiencies in all three phases of this process of self-control. The intervention was originally planned to last for six sessions, with sessions 1 and 2 focusing on the principles of the approach and self-monitoring. Sessions 3 and 4 emphasized self-evaluation. Individuals determined positive activities, set goals, and learned ways to attain their goals and how to evaluate whether they had succeeded in reaching them. Typical of behavioral interventions, the goals were specific, observable, and achievable. The fifth and sixth sessions focused on self-reinforcement. Self-rewards were given for achievement; the rewards were to be given immediately (often not an easy task for depressives), and time was spent on the development of skills and techniques to maintain these gains.

Because of the complicated nature of the depressions (they are more than just extinction trials or a lack of reinforcement), Rehm's intervention has been expanded to twelve sessions. Increased time is spent on self-monitoring, and there is increased emphasis on the activities for immediate reinforcement as well as upon learning the principles behind the activities. More therapist reinforcement and repetition have been added, including trying out additional activities and writing more logs.

A number of research projects have validated Rehm's approach, demonstrating remission of symptoms on the Beck Depression Inventory and on self-reports. Data also indicate that remission of symptoms lasts over a year after termination of therapy (O'Leary and Wilson 1987:222). Beach, Sandeen, and O'Leary (1990:37) state that altering self-monitoring, self-evaluation, and self-reinforcement can lessen depression; however, they say, "it remains unclear that these variables play an etiological role in nosological depression." Put another way, as we shall see in the next chapter on cognitive methods, data show that changing these factors does lessen depression but, at this stage in our knowledge, we are not sure which factors, or actions, cause which changes. (The reader may find detailed cases in Rehm [1981].)

Evaluating the Behavioral Approaches

■■
■■ Research on the behavioral approaches seems to provide varying amounts of evidence for the efficacy of each method in easing the symptoms of unipolar, reactive depression. Summaries of these researches can be found in Hoberman and Lewinsohn (1985) and Emmelkamp (1986:405–413).

The evidence strongly supports Rehm's concepts of the self-control theory of depression (Lewinsohn and Hoberman 1985:184–187). Limited experimental data support Seligman's original theory of learned helplessness, and much ongoing research generally confirms his reformulated attributional theory (Peterson and Seligman 1985). Lewinsohn and Hoberman (1985:188–194) list a large, and increasing, number of instruments and scales that can be used in research to assess these various aspects of depression.

A number of studies show that the behavioral procedures by themselves, as described in the research reports, do not seem to account for all the changes in the research subjects.

Some of these studies, as we shall discuss later, have been criticized for methodological shortcomings. The report of Blaney (1981:19) is typical. In discussing the use of pleasant events, Blaney states that although one study does support the use of the pleasant events, the "burden of proof must rest heavily with advocates of the pleasant-events model." This comment is fairly characteristic of the literature, where there seems to be some, but not conclusive or even substantial, evidence of the fit between the theory and the results of the interventions. Something obviously happens in behavioral treatments. What is needed now is to spell out in greater detail the techniques and, above all, to pinpoint what happens as a result of which specific techniques, used with which clients. In relation to methods, Marshall and Segal (1990:273) state that the "absence of a single approach or a common core element . . . [makes] outcome evaluations . . . not readily compatible." In other words, treatment elements have been increasingly mixed, so that what is actually being administered, in most of these behavioral therapies, is not a single behavioral technique but a "treatment package." Similarly, Freeman and Davis (1990:346) have pointed out that a large number of behavioral techniques have been absorbed into the cognitive and cognitive-behavioral approaches. Their partial list includes activity scheduling, mastery and pleasure ratings, social skills training, assertiveness training, bibliotherapy, graded task assignments, behavioral rehearsal and role-playing, homework assignments, and relaxation training.

Part of the difficulty of research with the depressions, regardless of the methods used, is that the complicated nature of the depressions makes straightforward, comparative controlled research, such as that done with drugs, very difficult.

Marshall and Segal (1990:276) state that the research studies evaluating patient outcomes "often obscure patient characteristics." For example, patient response differs based on the seriousness of the disorder. Although combined drug and behavior therapy (or cognitive behavior therapy) seems the most effective approach for seriously depressed patients, for the mildly depressed either behavior therapy or cognitive behavior therapy is sufficient; there is no need for medication. Furthermore, studies have shown differences between endogenous and exogenous patients, with the former more receptive to drugs and the latter doing better with social skills teaching. However, these dichotomies are not mutually exclusive; they overlap to a considerable extent.

Wolpe (1982:281–282), in commenting on the lack of outcome research on the depressions, also says that it is inappropriate to compare therapeutic techniques on depressions that are allegedly different (e.g., biological versus cognitive versus those depressions that are classically conditioned [1982:281–282]). He also criticizes researchers for not differentiating among the depressions. For example, the NIMH collaborative research program (Elkin et al. 1985; 1989) was criticized for experimental and control groups consisting of undifferentiated depression (Wolpe 1982:282). Furthermore, Wolpe feels that much of the success of cognitively oriented therapies, particularly those of Beck (to be discussed in chapter 15), is due to "nonspecific emotional deconditioning" (1982:282). Other therapists have called this a placebo effect. It is unfortunate that these criticisms of Wolpe's have not been sufficiently answered, for his comments on the complexities of research on depression are valid.

Another problem encountered in research on the behavioral approaches is the difficulty in attributing the effects to the techniques. Lewinsohn and colleagues (1985:340) commented perceptively that the "functional systems (i.e., cognitive, behavioral and somatic) that are affected by depression, tend to change together; that is, they move en masse."

Although there have been problems in evaluation, we feel confident that the behavior theories and therapies have had a positive effect upon the understanding and treatment of depression. The early behavioral emphasis on observable factors added to clinical understanding of depression by lessening the emphasis upon abstract and nonempirical theories. However, although the early respondent and operant therapies proved to be limited, albeit useful, it was necessary to go back "inside the organism" and once again to deal with such abstractions as patterns of thoughts—in other words, cognitions. With the increasing awareness within the behavioral orientations of the complexity of the depressions and the need for multifaceted models, the behavior therapies evolved into the "cognitive-behavioral" therapies—now the leading behavioral therapies for the depressions (Craighead 1990).

15

Cognitive and Cognitive-Behavioral Approaches to Depression

The early operant behavioral theories advocated treatments that focused on a narrow view of depression, which was considered an extinction phenomenon (a conditioned emotional response accompanying an absence or weakening of reinforcement). The goal of treatment was to interrupt and break the downward extinction cycle. There were interventions to raise the level of behavior and elicit reinforcement from significant others in the environment, interventions with these significant others to increase the level of reinforcement, and procedures to decrease aversive behaviors that elicited punishment from the environment (Liberman and Raskin 1971). We have described these various procedures in detail in chapter 14.

Therapists using these procedures seemed successful in helping depressed clients go rapidly from low rates to high rates of behavior: These clients got out of bed in the morning, dressed themselves, went to work, and so on. However, when asked, "How do you feel?" they often responded, "I feel terrible. There is no pleasure in my life." The behavioral treatments for depression were obviously effective in stopping the downward part of the depression cycle. However, if success was measured by how the client felt, then treatment needed to be directed to other aspects of the depressions, including low self-esteem, self-blame, and feelings of worthlessness, failure, helplessness, a pessimistic view of the future, and other negative thoughts. It became evident that it was necessary to help a client examine his thoughts and to change his self-statements; in other words, to focus on cognitions (Schwartz 1982:188).

Cognitive processes such as pessimistic thinking, gloomy thoughts, and a negative view of the future have long been observed as a part of depression. Aaron Beck has emphasized that these cognitive processes are not a by-product of depression but are integrally involved in the development and the continuance of depression.[1] Beck initially developed a treatment approach that he labeled *cognitive therapy*. Through practice, his work evolved into a cognitive-behavioral approach, for "clients are trained to use the outcomes of their behaviors to test the accuracy of their beliefs" (Hollon and Beck 1986:448.)

The Cognitive-Behavioral Approach of Aaron Beck

■■ Aaron Beck, a medically trained psychoanalyst working in
■■ Philadelphia, tested Freud's central thesis that depression
was hostility turned inward. He examined the dreams of depressed
patients and found no evidence for this thesis. He did find that many
depressed patients, unlike the nondepressed, experienced dreams in
which they were losers: They would put money into a soda machine
and receive no soda; they would call their therapist and get an automatic answering machine. Beck called these *masochistic dreams* (1972).

In studying these depressed patients and their activities when they
were awake, Beck found that fear of loss was a stronger emotion than
anger. He theorized that depression was not so much inverted hostility
(hostility turned inward) as fear of loss. The patients thought that if
they expressed anger at their significant others, they would lose their
love and support. The difference is subtle, but extremely meaningful
(Schwartz 1982:189). This sense of loss is central to the etiology of
depression. Loss is a theme that seems to run through all theories of
depression, from Freud to Skinner to Beck.[2]

Although anger, sadness, and sense of loss characterize many depressed people, Beck has theorized that depressions are more closely
linked to the way a person thinks; to his cognitions or patterns of
thought. Beck sees depression as resulting primarily from the negative
cognitions of the patient (1979). In other words, depression is the result
(the consequence) of these negative cognitions being triggered or reac-
tivated. Based on these negative cognitions, the depressed person (and
the depression-prone person) begins to interpret his past and present
experiences as failures and anticipates that his future experiences will
also be failures. He comes to view himself as inadequate or flawed. The
lowered self-esteem of the depressive is the result of these negative
cognitions and negative cognitive sets.

The Cognitive Triad

Beck called a typical disturbance of thought patterns common to
many depressives the *cognitive triad* (Beck et al. 1979:11). First, the
patient's life experience has so far been negative. He sees the world as
a hostile, nongiving, aversive place. These perceptions may be based
on reality, but they are generalized into a more widespread pattern of
pessimism and defeat. Next, the patient has a very negative view of
himself, thinking of himself as somehow faulty. This perception is
partly, sometimes totally, based on his dismal life experiences. His

defects and shortcomings, real or imagined, contribute to feelings of helplessness and hopelessness. If the past has been horrible, and the client thinks he is presently worthless, then things are certainly not going to change. The person has a very negative, almost nihilistic, view of the future. The presence of this last part of the triad may indicate future suicidal potential.[3]

Schema

A concept used by Beck that is helpful in explaining the persistence of negative and pessimistic thoughts is the notion of *schema*. Beck says that each person responds to and interprets stimuli from the environment in a unique, personal way. These responses, based on his previous life experiences, form a pattern of summarizing and interpreting (making sense of) whatever is happening. These patterns, which Beck states are "relatively stable," provide a framework—the schema—for interpreting and reacting to situations (Beck et al. 1979:12). The schema both screen out and include elements of the reality the person is facing and help him to formulate and categorize his experiences (Beck et al. 1979:13). Sometimes this is functional and sometimes, especially with the depressive, dysfunctional. The negative and pessimistic schema of the depressive often facilitate self-fulfilling dismal prophecies. They have been called *depressiogenic schemata* (Williams 1984:17).

Automatic Thoughts

Another contribution made by Beck in his explorations of the role of cognitions in depressions is the existence and influence of what he calls *automatic thoughts* (1976:29–38). In his practice of psychoanalytic therapy, Beck found that when patients were free-associating, often a stream of thoughts occurred at the same time. The patient usually reported one thought to the therapist and either was not fully conscious of the others or was reluctant to report them. These are often negative automatic thoughts (Williams 1984:16). For example, a woman who was discussing some of her conflicts about sex was also showing signs of anxiety. When questioned by Beck, she reported these thoughts, which kept intruding upon her free association: "I am not expressing myself clearly. . . . He is bored with me." In analyzing these automatic thoughts, Beck came to the conclusion that her central conflict was not about sex but about self-esteem (1976:31–32). Automatic thoughts may well play a role in the formation and maintenance of the three elements of the cognitive triad.

Examining automatic thoughts often gives information for understanding emotional conditions such as depression. This examination, which occurs during the course of the therapy, has several phases (Young and Beck 1982:193). The first is to elicit the thoughts, to make the client aware of the parallel stream of thoughts. The second is to test the automatic thoughts: The thoughts are not treated as the truth but as a hypothesis. The client and therapist examine whether these thoughts are valid (Young and Beck 1982:197–198). The third phase is to identify any underlying assumptions that may be maladaptive and then to examine the truth of these assumptions. Identifying and analyzing these dysfunctional assumptions can be helpful in changing cognitions, which eventually changes the behavior that follows the cognitions. According to Beck's theory, this will ease and eventually overcome the depression.

Beck's writings and his cognitive-behavioral therapy have had a great impact on the theories and treatments of depression. His writings are essential reading for any mental health professional who works with depressed people.[4]

The Views of Albert Ellis: Rational Emotive Therapy

■■ Albert Ellis, a psychologist, has stated that there are ele-
■■ ments in the environment, *activating events* (A), that have *consequences* (C) for the individual and that the nature of these consequences is shaped by the *intervening belief system* (B), or *cognitive map* (1962). In other words, when something happens (A), we do not necessarily respond on a factual or rational basis, but we act according to what we believe about it (B), and this belief may be irrational.

The following example shows how irrational beliefs lead to undesirable emotional and behavioral consequences:

> *Activating event* (A). I asked Mary to go to a party with me and she turned me down because
> *Irrational belief* (B). I am unattractive, unappealing, and dull.
> *Emotional consequences* (C). I feel very bad and worthless and depressed.
> *Behavioral consequences* (C). I won't ask Mary again; in fact, I won't ask anyone else for a date.

An individual acting according to more rational beliefs might have said to himself, "I don't like being rejected but there may be reasons; Mary might already have a date or she may be involved with someone." The desirable emotional and behavioral consequences might be, "I shall ask someone else—Joan might be available. Perhaps Mary doesn't like large parties. I'll ask her to dinner next time."[5]

Ellis has developed a therapy called *rational emotive therapy (RET)* that is based on this A-B-C model and adds D and E. The therapist has the client examine and modify irrational ideas, such as those in the preceding example. This is done through a process of (D) *disputing* the irrational beliefs and substituting more appropriate ideas and thoughts, which would lead to (E) *more appropriate emotional and desirable behaviors.* In the preceding example, disputing might include asking, "What is so terrible about being turned down? Why does this make me a terrible person? Why do I think I'll never get another date?" More appropriate feelings and behaviors (E) might be, "I don't like being turned down, but it's not so terrible; it doesn't mean I'm a terrible person." "I don't like being rejected, but I can tolerate it. It may be hard to get a date for this party, but not impossible. If I can't get one, I can go alone." As a result of these new, rational ideas, the client's behaviors and affects are also modified (Ellis and Geiger 1977).[6] In the process of disputing irrational beliefs, the client is encouraged to express negative or bad feelings (anger, annoyance, frustration, disappointment) appropriate to the situation. These feelings are then put into perspective as bearable, and the client moves on to try to attain what he wanted through alternate behaviors—asking another person for a date, applying for another job, deciding to achieve additional job training to merit a promotion, and so on.

A Comparison of Beck's and Ellis's Views

■■ Beck's views parallel Ellis's formulations, adding that faulty
■■ ways of processing information perpetuate depression. These include arbitrary inference (drawing a conclusion either in the absence of evidence or against the evidence), selective abstraction (taking details out of context), overgeneralization (coming to a conclusion on the basis of a small detail or incident), magnification and minimization of the significance of an event, personalization (relating events to oneself when there is no reason to do this), and dichotomous, polarized thinking (everything is black or white; all good or all bad) (Beck et al. 1979:14).

A concept that both Beck and Ellis have incorporated into cognitive therapy is the *tyranny of the shoulds,* an idea initially set forth by Karen Horney (1950). Horney spoke of the neurotic who, in his drive for perfection, tries to hold himself to completely unrealistic standards. These internalized standards, which were learned within the family, often in childhood, are usually unattainable. An example given by

Horney is, "You should be able to endure everything, to understand everything, to like everybody, to be always productive" (1950:64–65).

These shoulds are usually coercive, that is, they are experienced as pressure on the person to achieve these unattainable standards (Horney 1950:73). They drive the person continually on, and the failure to attain them further reinforces the individual's idea of his own inadequacy. The shoulds are often related to the demands (real or imagined, or both) of the dominant other, as theorized by Arieti and Bemporad (1978).

Beck's Cognitive-Behavioral Course of Therapy

■■   Beck and his associates have developed a time-limited ap-
■■   proach to the treatment of depression that incorporates a number of behavioral procedures (Beck et al. 1979). The therapy is structured but conducted flexibly. The approach is based on what Beck calls *collaborative empiricism* as the therapist is active and constantly engaging with the client (Beck et al. 1979:6–7).

There is a comprehensive initial interview designed to elicit information on diagnostic, biographical, and background factors, including an assessment of the degree of depression and the possible existence of complicating medical and psychopathological factors. Some psychological tests, including the Beck Depression Inventory, are administered. The client is then started on a course of cognitive-behavioral therapy.

Initially, the therapist structures the intervention, individualizing the therapy to enlist the client as an active participant (a collaborator) in the work. Since the client may be depressed and confused at the beginning of the treatment, one of the the therapist's tasks is to encourage the client to become actively engaged as quickly and as fully as possible (Beck et al. 1979:7). This mutual activity is designed to prevent the client from sinking further into the passivity of depression or, as stated by Beck, the "morass of his negative preoccupations" (Beck et al. 1979:7).

The focus of the therapy is on present problems. Past events are explored only to the extent necessary to understand the present. The emphasis is on the client's present thoughts and feelings. There is no interpretation of the unconscious (Beck et al. 1979:7). The therapist and the client work together (collaborate) to examine the client's thoughts and to formulate activities and assignments (homework) to be done outside of the sessions.

One such task is completing activity schedules. The activity schedule used by Beck is similar to other behavioral logs that detail the client's day. Sometimes clients are asked to rate their moods on these schedules. For example, depression might be rated, with 0 being a very low mood and 10 being complete absence of depression (Schwartz 1982:205). Beck asks his patients to rate activities from 0 to 5 on two factors: One is the degree of mastery (M) felt by the client and one is the extent of pleasure (P) related to each activity (Beck et al. 1979:124).

In addition to providing the therapist with a picture of the client's day, the activity record is used to verify or dispute the notion that the client "didn't do anything." It is also a way of identifying any activities the client has mastered to any degree and those that give him *some* pleasure—in other words, those that ease the feeling of depression (Beck et al. 1979:125). These client evaluations are extremely useful and provide a very personal and individualized baseline as a standard of comparison for each client.

Beck's work is comparatively direct and seems simple, but it is conceptually quite elegant. The utility of the approach can be illustrated best by a case.

A Case of Depression Treated with Beck's Cognitive-Behavioral Approach

Marian Johnson (a pseudonym), a thirty-two-year-old woman born in Brooklyn, New York, worked as a laboratory technician in a small hospital within walking distance of her home. The youngest of five children, there was a seven-year gap between Marian and the sibling just above her; she stated that she felt like an only child in a second family.

After graduating high school she commuted to Brooklyn College, where she completed a B.S. degree in biology. She described herself as a loner during her college days. She did not date and had only a few women friends. Although an attractive woman, she thought of herself as homely and obese. (She was about ten pounds overweight—certainly not obese.)

Marian had considered going to medical school, but she did not share these thoughts with anyone, including her family. After graduation she took a job as a technician in a Brooklyn hospital and continued to live at home. While working in the hospital, she became friendly with a resident, William, whom she met in the cafeteria. They began to date and married about one year later when William finished his residency. Her family opposed the marriage, as William practiced a different religion. Relations with her family are still strained.

Marian and William moved to Philadelphia after he accepted a job in a local hospital. Marian obtained a part-time job as a lab technician and began to decorate a small townhouse they bought near the hospital. The marriage was not going smoothly: William worked long hours and was tired and uncommunicative when he was at home; Marian was socially isolated. However, she described this period as the happiest time of her life.

After living in Philadelphia three years, Marian was shocked when William came home one day and announced that he was going to leave her; he had been having an affair with a nurse on the night shift, who was pregnant with his child. Too stunned to respond, Marian was passive during the divorce proceedings. After the sale of the house and the division of community property, she was left with very little money.

Marian took a full-time job working nights in a hospital laboratory and spent her days sleeping and eating. Her weight ballooned to more than two hundred pounds. Finally, after attempting suicide by taking pills, she was committed to a psychiatric hospital, where she spent seven months as an inpatient. Since her discharge she has been on maintenance dosages of antidepressant medication. She dieted and took off most of the weight she had gained while she worked in the hospital. She received both individual and group outpatient psychotherapy for several years, but attended these sessions without enthusiasm and felt she got nothing out of them.

Marian still felt isolated from her family, although she now stated that they were "right about Bill from the start." There had been some sporadic communication with her family, but she had not visited them in Brooklyn since her marriage, for she felt ashamed, worthless, and ugly. She felt her work was boring and routine, yet she was reluctant to change jobs.

Marian continued on the medication, which she said helped her sleep and gave her energy. Every three months she faithfully checked in with the physician monitoring her medication, who finally strongly suggested that she see a psychotherapist who had recently completed training with Dr. Beck in Philadelphia.

Assessment

There was no question of the diagnosis of depression. In addition to the obvious presenting symptoms, Marian's score on the Beck Depression Inventory (BDI) was 39, indicating severe depression.

The plan for session 1, as proposed by Beck, has an agenda of specific items: The first is to discuss depression, including its symptoms, with the client (Beck et al. 1979:106). The risk of suicide was assessed—both suicidal behavior and suicidal thinking—including an evaluation of the client's feelings of hopelessness. In this first session, Marian stated that, although she felt hopeless, she would not try suicide again, even though she felt that things were not going to change.

When the therapist began to point out the relationship between her very negative thinking and her self-criticisms, Marian agreed but felt it could not be helped, that her "personality" made her depressed. The therapist stated that the negative thoughts were part of her depression rather than her personality.

The therapist pointed out the benefits that she was receiving from the medication, which helped sustain her behavior, but added that she needed to work on the other aspects of her depression, such as her negative expectations and view of the future, her low feeling state, and so forth. He also pointed out that the depression was involuntary and that the two of them could work on alleviating her pain. He explained the rationale of the approach and gave her several assignments. The first was to keep an activity schedule that could give them both a clearer, more objective view of her behavior and activities.[7]

When Marian returned for session 2, she tested 38 on the BDI, almost unchanged from her initial interview. She and the therapist again discussed her symptoms of depression, particularly the relationship of thoughts to depression. She was still feeling down, stating that "after looking at my activity records, I realized how empty my life is." She had filled out the activities chart and found that her life outside her job consisted of sleeping and eating—in essence, doing very little, yet she always felt tired.

Marian had been asked to keep such records for an entire week. Since many of her days were similar to each other, we shall reproduce a workday and a Sunday. These are preintervention baseline logs. (See logs 15.1 and 15.2.) These logs reveal very few activities that gave Marian any pleasure, although there were a few where she felt some mastery. She felt both mastery and pleasure at walking to work (a specific destination), and she felt competent at work, although she considered the work boring. She also felt able to do housework and shopping, although neither was exactly pleasurable. She obviously was removed from people and seemed not to get enough sleep. Late-night television was an escape for her, although ratings for both mastery and pleasure were low.

The log for the weekend even more vividly reflected Marian's depression and the bareness of her daily routine. Here she showed little mastery. She had no contact with people and spent her Sundays either napping or "killing time while watching television." (See log 15.2.)

After discussing these activity records, Marian and the therapist

Log 15.1. Daily Log: Monday

		M	P
9:00 A.M.	woke late	0	0
9:10–10:00	breakfast, newspaper	0	1
10–11	cleaned house	3	2
11–12	shopped, errands	3	2
12–2	napped	0	1
2–2:30	prepared for work	2	0
2:30–3:00	walked to work	4	4
3:00–4:30	ran tests in lab	4	0
4:30–5:00	conference with doctors	2	0
5:00–6:00	paper work	4	0
6–6:30	ate, alone in cafeteria	1	0
6:30–11:00	ran tests, paper work (very busy)	4	0
11:00–11:10	cab home	2	0
11:15–2:00 A.M.	ate, watched TV	2	1
2:00 A.M.–8:00	slept	2	0

worked on an Assigned Activity Schedule for the coming week. As envisioned by Beck, this consisted of a form, similar to the log, where the therapist and client agreed on activities for specific times, and when the client did them she also rated them for mastery and for pleasure (Beck et al. 1979:122–123).

One of the first goals was to increase Marian's contact with people. Part of the plan involved her reaching out to people, and she and the therapist discussed some assertive procedures. Marian and the therapist agreed that since she was capable of working on a number of behaviors simultaneously, they would try, very quickly and deliberately, to stop the escape behavior on the weekend. She was to wake up after only one extra hour of sleep; she was to schedule activities; she was to eliminate naps; and she was to minimize watching television during the day.

For this first week, Marian and the therapist agreed on four activities, which were listed on an activity schedule. The first was to set the alarm clock for 7:00 A.M. on workdays and 8:00 A.M. on weekends and to get out of bed when it rang. The second was a period of exercise, which could take place at different times on workdays and on the weekend. The third, which involved reaching out to people, was also varied and a little more complex: On weekdays Marian was to sit at a table with another person when she had dinner at her workplace and speak to that person. On Sunday she was to talk with at least one person at church. In addition, Marian elected to attend a foreign film festival and stay for the discussion that followed. A more difficult step—participating in the discussion—was added as an option. The fourth activity was to go to bed at midnight.

Two such schedules follow that were agreed upon by Marian and the therapist and that she carried out. (See log 15.3 and log 15.4.) Since Marian was going to bed earlier, she woke with less difficulty. Getting up earlier in the morning represented a real step forward for her. Again, work and physical exercise provided her with the greatest sense of mastery. She did speak to someone in the dining hall; she was intensely nervous, but this gave her a moderate degree of pleasure. Her activity schedule for Sunday showed an even more dramatic change. (See log 15.4.)

As the activity schedule shows, Marian was successful in increasing her activities, and she actually attended the film festival. She felt extremely ill at ease in the strange group but enjoyed the movie and was pleased that she had taken the step to attend. At this first time, she spoke only with an usher; she chose not to pressure herself by participating in the discussion on the film.

Marian and the therapist reviewed the activity schedule, checking for possible omissions and distortions. When they examined the experiences she had recorded, they looked for connections between thinking, behavior, and affect. For example, Marian was interested in the discussion following the Japanese film she saw on Sunday, but she did not participate because she felt inadequate and inept. She was sure that she would say something stupid and that she would be ridiculed. This resulted in the rating of 0 in the mastery column, although the pleasure

Log 15.2. Weekend Log: Sunday

		M	P
9:00 A.M.	woke up	0	0
9:00–2	ate, papers, TV	3	2
2–4	nap	2	0
4–6	TV	2	2
6–7	ate, TV	2	1
7–8	nap	0	0
8–2:00 A.M.	TV	1	1
2:00 A.M.	sleep	2	0

Log 15.3. Daily Log: Monday

		M	P
7:00 A.M.	woke up when alarm rang	4	3
7–8	breakfast	0	0
8–11	housework, shopping, errands	3	3
11:30–12:30 P.M.	exercised	4	4
12:30–1	walked to library	4	4
1–1:30	library	2	4
1:30–2	walked home	4	4
2:00–3:00	prepared for and went to work	0	0
3–6	worked	4	1
6–6:30	dinner, sat at table with Gloria, spoke with her	1	3
6:30–11	worked	4	1
11:10	home by taxi	3	3
11:10–12	drank cocoa; TV news	3	2
12:00	WENT TO BED!	3	0

rating was 3. The fact that she was able to feel this moderate amount of pleasure despite her negative thoughts about herself was a good prognostic sign.

The homework assignment for the next session was to carry on with her activity schedule. Marian was to attempt one or more mastery and/or pleasure activities. She was also to pay close attention to the times when she felt depressed in order to try to discover what factors might be setting off or adding to her depression.

In the third session (BDI score 33) Marian and the therapist continued to examine the mastery and pleasure activities and to monitor the cognitions associated with feelings of depression. For example, although she liked food and liked to eat, eating alone was always very unpleasant for her, for it reminded her of how alone and unloved she felt. She would also think of her failed marriage. She usually tried to finish eating as quickly as possible, bolting her food. She rarely bothered to cook ("Who wants to cook for just one person?") and often ate fast food and take-out food, which were, of course, high in calories and often tasteless. This further emphasized both a lack of mastery and a lack of pleasure.

Marian's homework assignment was to continue keeping the activity schedules; writing down her cognitions during periods of sadness, anxiety, anger, and lethargy; and searching for connections between these emotions and her thoughts and behaviors.

In the fourth session (BDI 29), there was further examination of which cognitions led to which emotions, especially feelings of depression and discouragement. The homework assignment was for Marian to continue recording her cognitions when she felt certain emotions and to search for other explanations than negative, self-destructive ones. Marian was urged to change the messages she was sending to herself —that is, to avoid labels such as "incompetent" and "selfish," negative terms, which are not helpful in understanding problems. There was a homework assignment to shop for and cook at least one meal a day, not counting breakfast.

At this point Marian was also asked to rate on a scale of 0–10 the degree to which *she* wanted to complete the activities, as opposed to meeting the therapist's expectations or doing what she felt she should be doing. They discussed the "tyranny of the shoulds," identifying the role of these shoulds in producing negative self-statements and deepening depression.

Session 5 (BDI 31) focused on analyzing Marian's cognitions; frequent patterns were pinpointed. The homework was to continue to record thoughts, in a continuing attempt to illustrate the connection between her conscious and automatic thoughts and the feelings of depression.

Log 15.4. Weekend Log: Sunday

		M	*P*
8:00	woke up when alarm rang	4	0
8:00–8:30	breakfast, read paper	0	1
8:30–9:30	jogged	4	4
9:30–10:30	home, showered, dressed	1	1
11–12	church; spoke with one person	1	2
12–1	lunch, TV	0	2
2–4	worked in garden	4	4
4–5	cleaned up, ate	0	0
5–7	film festival, Japanese film; stayed for discussion, spoke with an usher	0	3
7–8	home	0	0
8–12	laundry, read; tv news at 11	2	3
12	WENT TO BED!	3	0

In sessions 6 (BDI 28), 7 (BDI 20), and 8 (BDI 20) (nearing the middle phase) Marian continued to monitor cognitions, particularly her expectations of herself and her shoulds rather than her wants. She continued to discuss her thoughts and feelings about her work responsibilities and her acute loneliness. This enabled her to talk about dating, specifically her fear of repeating the traumatic relationship with William and her feelings that no man would want her. The homework was to keep on identifying cognitive mistakes and search for alternative reasons for her negative automatic thoughts.

In sessions 9 (BDI 18), 10 (BDI 32), and 11 (BDI 20) the work centered on trying to replace Marian's almost constant and automatic self-criticisms with a careful analysis of problem situations. Marian gave an example of something that happened at work: She had delivered the results of some tests to a resident physician, who mixed them up with those of another patient. A subsequent confusion about medication resulted. Fortunately, it was corrected by the attending physician before any harm was done. The resident physician, in front of the attending physician, blamed Marian for the error. She was extremely upset at the accusation but did not defend herself, remaining mute during his tirade. She then went to the ladies room, where she cried for a long time. (This incident accounts for the BDI of 32 at the beginning of the tenth session.)

Marian obviously had not coped well with this episode. The therapist and Marian discussed its meaning. Even though she knew the doctor had been wrong in his accusation, Marian blamed herself, not the doctor, for the error, stating that she should have been clearer in her presentation of the results. She interpreted the doctor's criticism as further evidence of her inadequacy. As the therapist and Marian reviewed all aspects of the incident, Marian finally acknowledged that it was not her fault. She actually expressed some anger during this session!

Following Beck's emphasis on the improvement of realistic coping responses, Marian and the therapist discussed how to avoid such encounters in the future and ways that Marian could defend herself if they occurred. This included things that she might have said as well as enlisting the aid of her supervisor. She reluctantly agreed, at least verbally, that the young doctor should be held accountable for his errors.

In sessions 12 (BDI 18), 13 (BDI 18), 14 (BDI 16), and 15 (BDI 15) the work continued to focus on self-criticism, with increased attention to awareness of the incorrect assumptions that governed Marian's behavior and thoughts. The therapist and Marian continued analyzing wants, linking these wants to future goals. The next homework assignment was to list wants, particularly future goals, and to differentiate them from shoulds.

In sessions 16–19 (BDI 15, 15, 12, 10) Marian and the therapist worked on furthering the client's understanding of her patterns of thought and behavior and the emotions resulting from these patterns. Marian was instructed to rehearse and then actually try out more adaptive thinking and behavioral actions to offset these dysfunctional cognitions. The homework was to look for ways of increasing interactions with people, both outside of work and on the job. She practiced opening conversations with the therapist as part of an effort to be more assertive. These actions were aimed at diminishing her feelings of loneliness and unworthiness, in turn lessening her feelings of depression.

Sessions 20 (BDI 10), 21 (BDI 8), and 22 (BDI 6) focused on solidifying the achievements Marian had made and arranging for follow-up contacts in preparation for termination of treatment. She had applied to switch to the day shift at the hospital and was promised the next assignment. She preferred to wait rather than change jobs. In addition, she took a course in computers offered by the hospital and was considering other classes and possibly an advanced degree in the use of computers in biological laboratories.

Following Beck's procedures, the therapist had follow-up contacts with Marian at one- (BDI 6), two- (BDI 5), and six-month intervals (BDI 2). Marian succeeded in continuing to monitor her automatic thoughts and the interconnections with cognitions, moods, and behaviors. She had transferred to the day shift, had signed up for two courses at the University of Pennsylvania, and was active in several social groups: one at work and one at church. Although she talked of dating, she had not done it yet. Her depressions were mild; she continued on maintenance doses of antidepressant medication, which were to be discontinued within a few months.

The Effectiveness of the Cognitive and Cognitive-Behavioral Therapies

■■ The treatment of depression with cognitive and cognitive-
■■ behavioral therapy has been one of the most investigated areas in the entire literature of psychotherapy research (Hollon and Najavits 1988:646). This research has focused mainly on patients with primary depressions who are nonpsychotic, nonbipolar, and treated on an outpatient basis. The research on patients with secondary depressions who are psychotic or bipolar and inpatients has been on a case study basis, not as part of controlled experimentation.[8]

Some studies have compared short-term cognitive therapy with tricyclic antidepressants. Tricyclics are seen as effective interventions for depressed people and have been extensively researched, thus providing a recognized standard for comparison (Hollon and Najavits 1988:648). In comparison to medication alone, in the acute phase there is good evidence that cognitive therapy alone is as effective as tricyclic medication in lessening acute symptoms (Hollon and Najavits 1988:649). A "small but potentially clinically meaningful advantage for the combination of the two" has been identified; however, the data are relatively sparse (Hollon 1990:255).[9] Recent criticism has also pointed out that in these studies comparing cognitive therapy with medication, medication was prematurely withdrawn (Hollon 1990:255).

Hollon (1990:258) states that "cognitive therapy *does* appear to provide some protection against relapse following treatment termination, perhaps approaching that provided by continuing pharmacotherapy. . . . Combined treatment [cognitive therapy plus antidepressant medication], while not clearly superior to either . . . *does* appear to provide as much protection against subsequent relapse as cognitive therapy alone" (emphasis added). Hollon emphasizes, though, that the "existing literature is too sparse . . . [and there are too many] methodological problems . . . to warrant real confidence" (1990:258).

In a comprehensive summary of research from six centers, Beck (1986) cited three studies indicating that cognitive therapy by itself was superior to medication and three studies showing it to be as effective as medication. He noted that adding cognitive therapy to drug therapy made drug treatment more effective, but the reverse was not seen; the addition of drugs did not improve the efficacy of cognitive therapy alone. He further noted four studies indicating that cognitive therapy was superior to drugs in sustaining improved functioning as well as lessening depressive symptoms. Three of the studies covered a two-year period, and one was a follow-up at one year (Beck 1986:3).

A few of the studies comparing cognitive therapies with other kinds of therapy hint that cognitive therapy might be more effective than psychodynamic therapies, but the comparison loses meaning because therapy in these psychodynamic interventions may not have been adequately conducted, as we previously discussed (Hollon and Najavits 1988:647).

Cognitive-behavior therapy (CBT) was compared with interpersonal therapy (IPT), with antidepressant drugs, and with "clinical management" in the NIMH comparative study on the treatment of depression. In the first preliminary account the reports of the efficacy of CBT were somewhat mixed (Elkin et al. 1989). Patients treated with CBT showed significant reduction in symptoms and increase in functioning while being treated. However, it was about equal to IPT, less effective than imipramine with clinical management, and more effective than placebo and clinical management. In terms of the total sample, CBT was judged to be as effective as IPT. However, in comparison with "placebo plus clinical management" there was limited evidence for IPT and none for CBT. In a secondary analysis, with those patients who were the most depressed, there was some evidence that IPT was effective, and the evidence was strong for the effectiveness of imipramine plus clinical management. Among the less severely depressed, however, there seemed to be no differences between IPT, CBT, and the other conditions, including placebo and clinical management.

Elkin and colleagues specified that there "is no evidence of greater effectiveness of one of the psychotherapies compared with the other and no evidence that either of . . . [them] . . . was significantly less effective than the standard reference treatment, which was imipramine plus clinical management" (1985:311). The results did state that IPT and imipramine plus clinical management were consistently superior to placebo-clinical management, but CBT was not (Elkin et al. 1985:311). The authors emphasize that these are short-term results, and there will have to be follow-up at six, twelve, and eighteen months (Elkin et al. 1989:980).

Frankly, these findings are difficult to interpret. At the time of the writing of this chapter, only the first of a projected series of reports has been issued (Elkin et al. 1989). As we mentioned in discussing IPT, at this stage of the analysis of the NIMH project it is almost impossible to avoid concluding that part of the reason for the lack of definitive results is that the study itself was flawed. In addition to the shortcomings mentioned earlier, Hollon (1990:251) points out that the NIMH study may not have provided a proper test for cognitive therapy, since most of the therapists, although experienced, had little background in cognitive therapy and only one supervisory session per month.

In other studies, when straight cognitive therapy (without behavioral techniques) is compared with straight behavior therapy (no cognitive change techniques), they yield about the same results in treating depression. However, in comparing cognitive-behavioral with straight behavioral therapy, the cognitive-behavioral is more effective. These studies indicate that cognitive-behavioral therapy is also more effective than insight or relational/insight therapies, as it was shown to be superior to nondirective therapy. Early comparisons with IPT show mixed results: The two were found to be equivalent in one study, and cognitive-behavioral was found to be less effective in one but equivalent on follow-up (Sacco and Beck 1985:26). Most of these studies seem to have been done by partisans of each approach, and more objective testing is needed.

Dobson (1989) did a "meta-analysis" of all the studies from January 1976 to December 1987 that reported using Aaron Beck's cognitive approach and treatment manual as well as the Beck Depression Inventory (BDI) as an outcome measure.[10] Dobson located twenty-eight studies that indicated a greater improvement for cognitive therapy over waiting list (no treatment control), pharmacotherapy, behavior therapy, and a scattering of other psychotherapies. Outcome was not related to length of therapy or percentage of women in sample. (Most studies had a ratio of three females to one male.) Although there was not really a representative sample by age in these studies, in most the average age was between thirty-two and thirty-nine and a half years, and the younger clients seemed to do better (Dobson 1989:417). Although the methodology of meta-analysis has been severely criticized, Dobson's study can be viewed as support for the efficacy of cognitive therapy.

Cognitive therapy is considered to be effective with depression, although how or why it works is unknown. The outstanding hypothesis is that by changing beliefs or correcting faulty information processing, mood and behavior will be improved. Whether these same processes occur in pharmacotherapy or, for that matter, in the other psychotherapies has not been sufficiently investigated. It may well be that changes in cognitions are not the cause of an easing of depression but the results of a lessening of depression achieved through other means, which at this point are viewed as nonexplicit factors. In other words, cognitive distortions may be symptoms rather than causes of depression (Bellack 1985:207). This is also the view of Arieti and Bemporad (1978:46).

In an earlier review of the research literature, Lewinsohn and Hoberman (1985) also voiced a contrary opinion. They found little support for Beck's hypotheses that failure makes depressed people become more negative in their self-esteem, in their expectations of themselves and the future, and in their evaluations of their own performances. They did not support Beck's hypothesis that depressed individuals express less positive feelings after being successful than nondepressed persons. Moreover, laboratory studies have not substantiated the idea that depressed people show distorted perceptions of feedback from others, overemphasizing the negative.

Research has upheld Beck's hypothesis that depressed people tend to forget pleasant events but remember unpleasant ones and negative information. Similarly, the idea that they have negative expectancies has been strongly supported, as has their tendency to show more irrational beliefs, as Ellis calls them.

Beck, in his numerous publications, has held that changes in cognitions are present or may be the essential element of change in *all* forms of psychotherapy. Both evidence and clinical wisdom suggest that cognition may well play a central role.

Another factor related to effectiveness might be the format of treatment. If highly structured and organized therapy, especially short-term therapies such as Beck's, have such an impact on a client, it may well be that the *form* of the therapy is more *efficient*, that is, it works better in less time.

A feature of the cognitive-behavioral models is the use of well-prepared and complete therapeutic manuals that spell out the procedures and provide a clear idea of what is actually done in therapy. This facilitates the replication and evaluation of the interventions as well as the development of new treatment procedures and techniques.[11]

A growing body of comparative research contrasts one approach with another, but more research is needed that matches patient deficiencies to the type of therapy. For example, if a patient has adequate social skills, it is redundant to treat him with therapy aimed at building skills. Similarly, if the depressed patient has no cognitive deficiencies, it might be inappropriate to treat him with Beck's approach or another of the cognitive therapies. This theme is developed in Hollon and Beck (1986:412–413).

As we have stated under the discussion of IPT, it is highly likely that Beck's procedures in cognitive therapy, especially as enriched by its evolution into a cognitive-behavioral therapy, will be eventually absorbed into an integrative, more comprehensive therapy for depression. Meanwhile, Beck's procedures can, and should, be used when appropriate, as we shall discuss in our integrative orientation to treatment in chapter 16.

A Commentary on Behavioral and Cognitive-Behavioral Approaches

O'Leary and Wilson (1987), in referring to the models of Beck, Lewinsohn, Rehm, and Weissman (IPT), observed that each was supported by some research evidence and each has been adopted in a number of therapy programs. They commented, however, that these approaches should be seen as complementary, rather than as competing (O'Leary and Wilson 1987:226). Each view stresses that depressed people see themselves, their worlds, and their existences as negative; experience comparatively fewer positive reinforcements; and are alienated from most people. They refer to the NIMH study, where preliminary evidence shows good results with the psychotherapies as compared to drugs and controls. Considering the high rates of dropouts, noncompliance with and lack of response to drug treatments, and the frequent return of symptoms if medication is withdrawn, these short-term, focused therapies are "highly effective . . . with comparatively few dropouts and essentially no adverse side effects" (O'Leary and Wilson 1987:226–227).

Summary of Part III

In part 3 we reviewed a number of theoretical approaches to understanding psychotherapy of the depressions. There is clearly a steady trend toward short-term, more focused approaches in all psychotherapies. There also seems to be much less emphasis on the historical antecedents of depression and more on therapies aimed at alleviating the "symptoms" of depression. Of course, one might argue that the symptoms of depression and depression itself may be considered one and the same; research linking depression to specific personality variables has been slow and, in general, not convincing.

Ironically, this trend toward briefer, more focused psychotherapies is related to the developments of the antidepressant medications. Although part of the impetus for the development of the shorter-term therapies was to alleviate patient suffering, part was certainly the competition, obviously still ongoing, with the comparatively rapid effectiveness of antidepressant medications. Even though many of these medications may take three weeks or longer to have an effect, the time is still short compared with many of the older, more long-term therapies.

Other factors hastening the growth of these briefer interventions are the rising costs of mental health care and the increasing resistance of insurance companies and government-subsidized programs to reimburse for therapies that are considered excessively long (and therefore expensive) or are not validated with sufficient empirical research. We believe that this situation will continue, if not increase, in the future.

This recent emphasis on the more structured techniques, which we view as a positive development, should not be interpreted as precluding, or invalidating, the insights of the more traditional approaches, in particular the psychodynamic theories of depression. In fact, much of the theory that underlies these newer approaches is a reinterpretation, and perhaps a different application, if not a rediscovery, of some of these older theories. The psychodynamic literature is extremely useful in helping the therapist to understand the depressed client. We particularly have in mind the psychodynamic insights of Arieti and Bemporad (1978), whom we have quoted throughout this book. For example, knowledge of the concept of the *dominant other*, which is in the background of many depressed clients, will help the therapist understand something of what is behind the pain of many clients and will facilitate the application of techniques, both short term and structured. These theories ought certainly to be part of a clinician's whole general orientation toward a depressed person—what might be called his "tacit knowing." Schoen (1983:49–52) calls this "tacit knowing" knowledge that we use but cannot identify and that forms part of our "view" (our term) of the client and his situation. The training of a professional, of course, is aimed at making this tacit knowledge as overt and as subject to verification as possible.

We have discussed the pros and cons of antidepressant medications, emphasizing throughout this book our view that psychotherapy ("talking therapy") should be part of every intervention for depression, whether or not these medications are used. Jerome Frank (1974) has stated that the question might well be one of "symptom comfort versus social effectiveness"; drugs may very well be appropriate and effective for the first, even in cases where there are mild symptoms. However, the psychotherapies are necessary for social effectiveness—which means, in effect, some form of talking therapy for *all* depressives.

There are still many things we don't know about drug therapy, including the many uncertainties about their effects, especially their long-term effects. There are also unknowns about psychotherapy; just as we are beginning to identify certain indicators for the use of certain drugs, so are we now beginning to identify the indicators for the use of certain psychotherapies with depressed clients. Klerman (1989:245) has said that "it would be an error to conclude that all forms of medication are useful for all types of depression, ... [and] it would be an error to conclude that all forms of psychotherapy are efficacious for all forms of depression."

There is increasing research on the many types of psychotherapy for the depressions. We agree with Emmelkamp (1986) that the growing body of research indicates the successful psychotherapies for depression have a number of things in common. First, they all have specific and identifiable theories and principles, which present the client with a "new vocabulary" that enables the client to look at himself and his depression from a new point of view. Second, the newer therapies tend to be "highly structured" (also shorter and focused). Third, the therapies (through the therapist, of course) provide "feedback and support," often immediate, that is vital for the client. In other words, as shown by many research studies, the therapist is still an important factor.

There are many treatments for the depressions. As well put by Noll, Davis, and DeLeon-Jones (1985:282–283) there are "standard treatments . . . unusual treatments . . . [and] combinations of treatments." We too feel that there are grounds for great optimism. Not only are the depressions currently treatable, but an enormous amount of research is going on, examining both the psychotherapies and the antidepressant medications. Month by month, we are learning more about the nature and treatment of depressions, and the future looks even brighter.

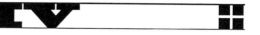

A Unified Approach to Treating the Depressions

In this section we offer guiding principles for interviewing depressed clients and assessing and treating their depressions. We draw from a number of theories and viewpoints described in parts 2 and 3 of this book that have been shown to be effective. The standard diagnostic criteria have been described in chapter 3; in this chapter we focus on the specific factors, problems, and behaviors that are indicators for selecting particular treatments and/or treatment techniques. We also offer guidelines for determining when referral to other resources is needed.

The Assessment Guide was developed within the framework of Western culture, using the criteria of mood assessment in the D.S.M.-III-R; treatments were also evaluated on this basis. However, the guide is flexible enough to be used with various ethnic groups and minority populations, with some adaptations. These are discussed in chapter 21, where we examine sociocultural variations in the diagnosis and treatment of depression.

We wish to emphasize that the content of this section should not be taken as a blueprint but should be used as a frame of reference for making clinical decisions. These decisions should direct the practitioner to utilize the interventions that will best help each client at every step in the treatment process. Sometimes the best intervention will be an entire treatment approach (e.g., an IPT strategy for abnormal grief); more often it will be individual techniques and procedures taken from different therapeutic orientations and integrated into whichever treatment approach a therapist normally uses.

We urge the reader not to settle on a single philosophy of therapy but to consider the approaches or techniques that might best help the client at various phases of therapy.

16

Assessing and Treating the Depressions: A Unified Approach

Interviewing a Depressed Person

■■ Interviewing a depressed person may present situations dif-
■■ ferent from those of other clients. Among these situations
are the following:

Be prepared for interviews that are difficult. Interviewing a depressed
person can be difficult and trying. Some clients exhibit symptoms of
psychomotor retardation and their affect is often very flat. They may
lack facial expression and can be very slow to respond, with very long
periods of silence between answers. They may speak in a monotonous
voice. Others, such as agitated depressives, can be hard to pin down;
they are tense, fidgety, and very restless. Some clients will appear very
sad and in great pain; they may cry continuously, especially in the
initial interview; others may have masked symptoms, but the therapist
will usually sense the depression underneath the smiling affect.

Assess suicide risk. In addition to the preceding factors, all of which
may make the therapist uncomfortable, there is the added responsibility
of the therapist to attempt to gauge the danger and extent of the
possibility of suicide. Needless to say, all therapists are very concerned
about the consequences of a wrong judgment.

Use short sentences. While speaking with a depressed person, it is
important to use short sentences. The interviewer should also pause
after a question to allow the client to answer, but the pause should not
last long, for many depressed people have impaired concentration;
if a pause is too long, they may forget the question. Since clients
who are very depressed often cannot tolerate a long interview, it may
take more than one session to obtain the information needed for assessment.

Terms should be clarified. For example, the word *depressed* has different
meanings to different people. It is important to find out exactly what
clients mean when they say they are depressed. The therapist must also
treat with caution the client's interpretation of *what* has happened and

why. The client's description of the cause of the depression may not be an accurate picture of the etiology of the depressive symptoms.

Ascertain the time frame. It is important to be sure that both the therapist and the client are using the same time frame, so that when the therapist asks a specific question (e.g., about mood or suicidal feelings), the client's answers refer to the same time periods as the interviewer's questions. Depressed clients often have a distorted sense of time and may honestly speak of yesterday's events as having occurred long ago, or vice versa.

Obtain precise information. It is especially important when interviewing a depressed client not to rely solely upon clinical impressions but to obtain information that is as precise as possible. To obtain accurate information about a client it is sometimes helpful to speak with significant others, such as relatives of the client. If necessary, this should be done with the client's consent early in the treatment process, both to corroborate information and to assess their roles, considering how and when to involve them in the therapeutic process. It may also be done later in treatment, as needed.[1]

Keep the interviews short. The interviewer must always bear in mind that the client is depressed and may not have the attention span to tolerate a long interview. He or she should not be pressed or overtaxed to obtain information. The interviewer should be flexible and sensitive to the client's ability to cooperate. It may be necessary to focus on obtaining only the minimum amount of information needed to begin treatment and fill in the rest of the data sometime in the future.

Making an Assessment

■■ Some information *must* be obtained in the process of making
■■ a differential diagnosis and assessment. This information may be obtained in a formal mental status examination, such as the one presented by Nicholi (1988:35–42), or it may be interwoven in an intake or initial interview.

Standard questionnaires are often used for evaluating depression, such as the Schedule for Affective Disorders and Schizophrenia (SADS) (Endicott and Spitzer 1978) and the Mood Syndromes section of the Structured Clinical Interview for the D.S.M.-III-R (the SCID) (Spitzer et al. 1990).[2] However, the process of assessing a depressed client is complicated by the reality that "there are not universally accepted interview questions to elicit information regarding depressive symptoms" (Leber, Beckham, and Danker-Brown 1985:364).

Whether one uses standardized questionnaires, interview guides, a

Mental Status Examination, and/or a personalized interview, we feel it is essential that the information be obtained by the therapist rather than by a questionnaire that the client completes himself, for depressed people may not understand all the questions and therefore may give incorrect answers. In addition, therapists should not miss the valuable opportunity to pick up cues from the patient's answers and from their observations of the patient's affect as they answer the questions.

Guide for an Initial Interview

■■ The following outline covers the categories of information
■■ usually needed to begin intervention with a depressed client. These categories should be considered as guidelines—perhaps even as a checklist—for the initial interview. Practitioners need not cover all these areas in the first interview or interviews; priorities may have to be set, depending upon the condition of the client.

The therapist may guide the client, encourage him to talk, and elicit further information by asking questions. We suggest some questions that might be asked; the exact wording of most of the questions is not as important as the therapist's comfort with the questions and the effectiveness of the questions in eliciting the desired information.

I. Inquiring about the nature of the problem

The client should be encouraged to state his problem in his own words. This may not be possible when a client is very depressed and mute.

1. Statement of the problem

Can you tell me why you are here?
What is the problem?

Questions must be asked selectively, and very carefully. For example, sometimes, when the depression is very obvious, an inquiry such as, "What is the problem?" not only may be unnecessary but may offend the client, and it may get the interview off to a bad start.

2. What brought the client to therapy at this time?

What brought you in to see me at this time?
[Or] What is depressing you at this time?

This is an attempt to *pinpoint,* to determine if there is a specific, identifiable stressor or, possibly, if the client's reactions to stress are out of proportion.

3. How has the client been coping with the specified problem?

How have you been coping with (or dealing with) these feelings (the depression)?

What (if any) other ways of dealing with these feelings have you tried? [Or] What alternative solutions have you tried?

4. Further specification of the presenting problem

Have you experienced these feelings in the past? When did they begin? How did you handle them at that time?

When/under what circumstances (conditions) is it (the presenting problem) not a problem? How do you handle it when it is not a problem?

The purpose of these questions is (1) to differentiate the conditions that will produce depression from those that will not; and (2) to identify strengths—for example, the strategies used by the client in those circumstances where the client can cope with the situation. These questions also tap into the history of the problem.

5. Probing for other problems

Is there anything else that is troubling you at this time?

[Or] Is there anything else that is a problem (that concerns you) at this time?

II. Assessing the depression: Is it *really* clinical depression?

The next task facing the therapist is to determine if the client is clinically depressed or if he is experiencing normal sadness—for example, a reaction to a loss (is in a state of mourning)—a state that is usually time-limited and ordinarily does not require clinical intervention. This differentiation is central to selecting the most appropriate treatment.

We have discussed one widely held view that sadness is a normal emotion, a response to a loss or disappointment or setback, whereas depression is an illness (Burns 1980:207). "Normal sadness is the emotional effect on a human being when he apprehends a situation that he would have preferred not to occur, and which he considers adverse to his well-being" (Arieti and Bemporad 1978:110). However, making an assessment on this basis can be difficult, for mild depression *can* have "biological" aspects, such as vegetative symptoms, whereas severe depression can be "psychological" or reactive to real setbacks in life, such as failures, losses, grief, and so forth. The differences between depressive illness and sadness may most often be revealed through such symptoms as loss of pleasure and energy, low self-esteem, guilt, and changes in appetite and sleep (Klein and Wender 1988:80). (For a more detailed discussion on the differentiation between normal sadness and clinical depression, we refer the reader back to chapter 1.)

In clinical depression, unlike sadness, some central complaints occur over and over again. These complaints, which may also be symptoms, must be pinpointed to determine if the client meets the criteria for a diagnosis of clinical depression and to determine the formal category of the depression. (The symptoms of depression were detailed in chapter 2, and the criteria for a formal diagnosis of clinical depression were discussed in chapter 3.)

If the client's symptomatology is comparatively uncomplicated, diagnosis can be relatively easy; otherwise it is usually more difficult. The therapist must also be aware that at the time of the interview the client may not exhibit the symptoms that meet the criteria for a particular diagnosis, but if he has had these symptoms within the past month or so he might still fit the criteria (Leber, Beckham, and Danker-Brown 1985:363).

A. Evaluating the presence or absence of clinical symptoms

Sometimes it is very difficult to tell the difference between the milder vital or biological depressions and symptoms that stem from the everyday problems of living that are understandable (normal) reactions to stressful situations such as physical illness. This differentiation can be made while assessing the client's symptoms. Leber, Beckham, and Danker-Brown present two useful guidelines for judging the absence or presence of symptoms (1985:363): "(1) Is it different from their normal self? (2) Does it seem to be a problem for them? . . . Are they bothered by the symptoms? . . . If the answer to both of these questions is 'yes,' then it is probably best to count it as a clinical symptom."

B. Evaluating the quality of the symptoms

As symptoms are disclosed, the therapist should remember that to make a formal diagnosis of depression, information will be needed on symptoms associated with the diagnostic categories. This includes the amount of distress the individual experiences with each symptom, the related impairment in functioning, and sometimes the length of time the individual has been experiencing these symptoms. This information on the *quality* of the symptoms is often more important than the quantity of symptoms.

If the therapist judges the client to be moderately depressed (if the client is not seriously depressed), the client might be asked to judge the severity of the symptoms. A guideline that might prove useful to the therapist, both in shaping the way the questions are asked and in assessing the response of the client, is the D.S.M.-III-R categorization system for coding the fifth digit of the diagnosis (D.S.M.-III-R 1987:223): 1 = mild, 2 = moderate, 3 = severe without psychotic features, 4 = severe with psychotic features, 5 = in partial remission, 6 = in full remission, and 0 = unspecified. The manual spells out, although sometimes vaguely, parameters for the classification of the fifth digit. Of course, the therapist sometimes must make this classification anyhow, as part of the formal diagnosis.

Probes for this information might include the following:

On a scale of 1–10, with 10 being the largest amount: How much distress does this (symptom) cause (you)?

[Or] How much does this (symptom) interfere with your (functioning?) (ability to work/carry out your daily responsibilities?)

Would you try to give me some idea of how long you have experienced this particular feeling (symptom)? How long does it last when it appears?

C. Differentiating clinical from normal depression by symptoms.

For convenience in interviewing, we have grouped the most common symptoms of depression according to type of symptom, cautioning that these categories are not mutually exclusive and, in fact, often overlap.

1. Affective symptoms

Does the patient have depressed mood—speaks of feeling low, down, and so on? Does he feel anxious, guilty, angry, hostile, irritable? Is anhedonia reflected in the tone and content of his speech? Does he seem to lack a sense of humor?

Have you been feeling low, down, blue? [If yes] Please tell me about this. (Please tell me more about this.)

Has there been a change in the number of times you go out? in the amount of time you spend with your friends?

Have you been feeling more [anxious] lately? More [irritable] than usual? *

How does this differ from how you normally feel? *

How much are you bothered by these feelings? *

Do you feel this way at certain times/in certain situations? *

[If yes] Does it always happen in these situations? Does it happen every day? nearly every day? * *[Attempt to differentiate from those times when it doesn't elicit depression.]*

---

* Note: These questions (probes) can be repeated after any of the questions that follow. Bracketed words in the third question may be replaced by the specific symptoms in each category.

2. Behavioral symptoms

Is there agitation (e.g., does the client seem tense/restless, exhibit jerky movements)? Is there depressed appearance? (Does the client look sad, e.g., mouth turned down?) Has the client been crying (e.g., red, swollen eyes)? Do you sense a masked or hidden depression (e.g., is the client "putting on a happy face" but seems depressed underneath it)? Is there psychomotor retardation (e.g., slowness of speech, thought; slowness in responding to questions, responding in monosyllables, and so on)? Is there diminished ability to concentrate? Are there memory lapses?

> *Have you been feeling very agitated/tense/restless lately? What, specifically, makes you feel that way? Is it different from how you normally feel? Please tell me more (please explain).*
>
> *Have you been crying? Have you been crying more than usual? What makes you cry? How do you feel after you cry?*
>
> *Have you been finding it difficult to concentrate?*
>
> *[Probe] To make decisions about everyday things?*
>
> *[Probe] Any memory lapses?*

3. Attitude toward self or the environment

Does the client express or exhibit self-reproach, low self-esteem, helplessness, pessimism, hopelessness? Are there thoughts of death or suicide? Have there been suicide attempts or self-destructive behavior? Are there any symptoms of extreme anxiety, or even panic disorder?

> *Tell me how you feel about yourself.*
>
> *[Or] Can you tell me how you feel about yourself?*
>
> *[Or] What do you feel about yourself?*
>
> *What do you think of the future?*
>
> *[Alternate] Do you ever think of the future?*
>
> *[Probe] What do you think of when you think about the future?*
>
> *Have you ever thought of hurting yourself?*
>
> *[If so] Have you thought about how you were going to do it?*
>
> *Do you think of being punished?*
>
> *[Alternative] Do you think you deserve to be punished?*
>
> *[Probe:] Why? Can you tell me about it?*
>
> *Have you thought of death?*
>
> *[Probe]*

Because assessing the risk of suicide is so important, these questions can be repeated and expanded upon later in the interview. (See section II.E.2.)

4. Physiological changes and bodily complaints

Are there vegetative symptoms? Is there an inability to experience pleasure; a loss of appetite; any sleep disturbances; any loss of energy; any decrease in sexual interest? Does the client experience any bodily complaints, fatigue or exhaustion, aches/pains?

> *What gives you pleasure?*
>
> *What are the demands upon your time/energy? Do you often feel tired/ lack energy/feel washed out? Do you ever feel this way when you are not very (not at all) busy?*
>
> *Are there any times when you are more tired than usual? Any time of day?*
>
> *[Probe for early morning, atypical, or seasonal affective disorder] Do you feel worse in the morning? in the evening? in the winter or summertime?*
>
> *Have there been any changes in your appetite? Any increase or de- crease? Any loss of interest in eating? Has your weight changed in the last month or two?*
>
> *[Probe: gain or loss, and* specify *within which time interval. If eating more, probe for night eating syndrome and carbohydrate craving:] Does this tend to happen at a particular time of day/night? Do you crave any particular kind of food?*
>
> *Any change in your interest in sex? Any change in your sexual activities?*
>
> *[Alternate, less desirable question] Any changes in your sex life?*
>
> *Tell me about your sleeping.*
>
> *[Or] How would you describe your sleep now?*
>
> *[Probe: especially regarding either sleep deprivation or hypersomnia.]*
>
> *Have you been experiencing any physical problems/symptoms? [Probe for: aches in head, neck, back, muscle (pain or cramps); pain on urination; other pain; blurred vision; nausea; vomiting, anorexia, lump in throat, sour taste in mouth, dry mouth; flatulence, consti- pation; menstrual difficulties; and so on.]*

D. Differentiating mourning from clinical depression

1. Assessing losses

Among the stressors that we must be alert to are changes, espe- cially losses such as the death of a significant person and those that are typical of certain stages of life. Changes that result from role transitions (e.g., retirement, parenthood, departure of chil- dren from home, and grandparenthood) are expected and normal in the life span. However, a client's reactions to these changes may be greater than one would normally expect, resulting in clini- cal depression. (Problems associated with role transitions were discussed in chapter 13.)

Have you recently experienced the serious illness or death of someone
close to you? (someone significant in your life?) (someone important
to you?)
Have there been any other significant losses such as divorce, separa-
tion, termination of a meaningful relationship? Have you recently
changed your job? moved? lost family/friends through any change
in your (or their) life situation?

Obviously, if there has been a death of someone important to the
client, he or she may be evidencing a reaction to the loss and is
mourning. This is not clinical depression, unless the depression
becomes extended and magnified. What we mean by "extended
and magnified," of course, is the central issue. (This was discussed at greater length in chapters 12 and 13.)

2. Assessment of other life stresses
This area may be explored by using open-ended questions, such
as the following:

Have you been experiencing other kinds of stresses at home? at work?
in other areas of your life?

3. Assessment of physical/sexual abuse and/or exploitation, past
or present
Certain issues related to role and status in society are thought to
contribute directly to the development of depression or to increase
vulnerability to it. This is especially true for women, although it
may also be true for men. These issues include being exploited,
abused, or victimized, physically, mentally, or sexually, in the
present or in the past. If these issues do not emerge from the
open-ended questions (see question 2), they should be explored
directly:

How have things been going in your relationship/marriage? Any ar-
guing or fighting? Has there been any physical abuse? (If positive
response, or indicators, continue to probe.)
Have you ever been involved in a relationship in which you were
abused, exploited, or felt victimized physically, mentally, or sex-
ually? in your personal life? in an employment situation? other?

E. Determining the degree/seriousness of the depression
The *quality* of the depression is central to the diagnosis and the
planning of the treatment; basing the diagnosis on the client showing
a minimum number of symptoms is often faulty. A person can be
seriously depressed and not fulfill the criteria for a formal diagnosis
of depression. One reason is that the symptoms are not equal in

seriousness: For example, suicidal attempts, or ideation, cannot be equated with sleep disorders.

The extent of the depression must be determined. The immediate purpose of this assessment is to evaluate current functioning or, to be more precise, the symptoms during the most severe period of the current episode, rather than to determine etiology. The therapist must also assess the potential for suicide.

1. Assessment of functioning and symptoms

During the last time that you were depressed, how would you describe the lowest point that you felt during the most severe period (of the current episode)?

2. Assessment of suicide risk

In assessing the risk of suicide, the therapist should try to differentiate between (1) the client who thinks about suicide but would never carry it out and (2) the client who might go through with it. In the first category, the therapist must probe for reasons the client would not do so (e.g., presence of young children in the home, religious convictions, and so on) and try to evaluate the sincerity of this motivation. In the second category, it is important to explore how far the client's thoughts, or plans, have taken him. For example, has he thought of how he would accomplish this act, or taken specific steps, such as purchasing a gun or stockpiling pills? Has he thought of, or actually written a note or a will? Has he planned on giving away specific possessions or actually done so?

It has been stated that raising the possibility of suicide might put it into the client's mind. Most therapists who are experienced in working with depressed clients downplay the risk of iatrogenic suicide. They feel that the suicidal thoughts are often there and that it is better to bring them out into the open.

During this time, have you ever thought of hurting yourself?
[If yes] How did you plan to do this? What have you done to do this? (to make it work?)
Have you told anybody about your plans? Have you written anything (to anyone) about your plans? Do you have a will? (Have you made out a will lately?) Have you given away (have you thought of giving away) any of your possessions?

As we have stressed throughout this book, even though depressions—regardless of their nature or classification—are often time-limited, there is always the danger of suicide. Although present at all points of a depressive episode, the danger of suicide is highest when the person is on an upward swing. In reactive, or what used to be called neurotic depression, the highest point of danger may well be nine months, or more, after the lowest point of a depressive episode.

F. Is the depression seasonal (seasonal affective disorder)?

Rosenthal (1989a) developed some guidelines to identify seasonal patterns of depression and to distinguish mild "winter blues" from the more severe and serious conditions of winter and summer seasonal affective disorders. The main distinguishing characteristic of seasonal affective disorder (SAD) is the degree to which an individual experiences impaired physical and mental functioning, including a significant amount of depression. The questions that follow were adapted from "How Seasonal Are You?" in Rosenthal's *Seasons of the Mind* (1989a:33–43).

> *Have you noticed that you feel depressed at a particular time of year (e.g., in the winter or summer months—or both)? (Do you feel that you would like to hibernate like a bear? Is your energy very low?)*
>
> *Do you find that you weigh more/have more of an appetite during the winter/summer months? Do you feel sleepier? tend to be less active? socialize less?*
>
> *How severe are these changes? Do they present problems? [Probe for additional information on changes from "no change [to] slight change, moderate change, marked change [and] extremely marked change" (Rosenthal 1989a:35) and the severity of problems ranging from "mild, moderate, marked, severe or disabling" (Rosenthal 1989a:40).]*

G. Is the depression primary or secondary?

If the client is judged to be clinically depressed the next task is to determine if the depression is primary or if it is secondary either to a physical disturbance or to another psychological disturbance. In making a formal diagnosis of depression, the therapist must first rule out the presence of these potentially complicating factors, which must be identified and treated, either prior to or simultaneously with the treatment of the depression.

1. Indicators of physical illness

We cannot overstress that depression may be one of the first indications that there is something physically wrong with the client. A number of illnesses first appear as depression—the "mimickers" of depression. We have discussed these in chapter 1. A complete discussion of physical illnesses masquerading as depression can also be found in Gold (1987a).

Among the questions designed to elicit this kind of information are the following:

How would you describe your current state of health? [Additional probes as indicated.]

Are you being treated or monitored by a doctor for any physical problems now or in the recent past?

When was your last complete physical? [Include ob/gyn exam for women.] What were the findings? (What did the doctor say at that time?)

Do you have any physical problems that are not being treated, or are not being treated by a physician? [If yes to last question] Who is treating this/these problems?

Are you taking any drugs/medications? [This includes everything from over-the-counter and prescription medications to tobacco, alcohol, and other substances of abuse. Probe for specific drugs: aspirin, Tylenol, Advil, antacids, decongestants or antihistamines, vitamin pills, sleep or diet pills.]

2. Indicators of other psychiatric disorders

In the more traditional psychiatric status examination the questioner is advised to start with open-ended questions and then to focus on leads given by the client. It is assumed that the questioning, by this time, will have proceeded to the point where the therapist can focus on more specific items.[3] These open-ended questions might include the following:

Have there been other things that have been bothering you? Do you feel that you have been having any other problems?

Have you had any additional problems getting along with people?

Have you had any trouble remembering things lately?

III. Making a formal diagnosis

After reviewing the client's symptoms, the next step is usually to make a formal diagnosis. Ideally, a formal diagnosis is useful in determining treatment; according to Goodwin and Guze (1989:xi) "diagnosis is prognosis." Although the utility of the formal diagnosis is often debated, such a diagnosis may provide information that can help determine the possible use of medication. It may also be necessary for other purposes, such as insurance claims.

The formal diagnosis is determined according to the criteria in either the D.S.M.-III-R (1987) or the International Classification of Disease (I.C.D.-9 1978).[4]

IV. Taking a short personal history

This information should be filled in at this time, if it was not given earlier. In each category, observe the client's affect and probe for problems related to the information that is given.

1. Occupation

What kind of work do you do? [Ask for specific details such as hours.]
How do you feel about your work? [Probe for satisfaction level.]
How stressful is your job? [Probe for specific problems/problem areas.]

2. Education

Please tell me about your education. [Ask for details—e.g., kind of education, level reached, any specific training, and so on.]

3. Marital/family status

Are you single/married/involved?
[If appropriate] Is this your first marriage? Any divorces? [Probe for factors that might be affecting current mental status, including contacts with ex-spouses, alimony, and so on.]
[If involved in a relationship] Current picture? satisfactions? problems?
What is your spouse's/partner's/significant other's evaluation of and response to your depression (to your depressive symptoms)?
[If appropriate] Any children?
[If yes] What are their ages? Where are they living? What are their occupations? How are they doing? [Probe for other relevant information.]

4. Family of origin

Where were you born? Are your parents alive? Do you have any siblings?
[If yes] Where do they live; what do they do? How close are you? [Probe: nature and closeness of relationship with client.]
Any family history of depressive illness/of symptoms you have?

5. Exploration of family roles

What did you feel your parents expected of you when you were a child? What do they expect of you now?
When you were a child, what did you expect of your parents? What do you expect of them now?
How were your grandparents involved in your upbringing? Were there many conflicts between the different generations? [If yes] How were these handled?

6. Significant others

Tell me about your friends/the people who are important (to you) (in your life) other than family members. [Probe to identify the client's significant others, particularly those who do, or may, provide emotional support and help.]

7. Religious background

What is your religious orientation?

[If the answer is "none"] What was the religious orientation in your house when you were a child?

Have you had any religious training?

What are your current religious practices? [Probe for any problems in this area.]

8. Economic status

What is your approximate salary/income? Any financial worries? [Probe, carefully, for problems/concerns, or anything producing stress in this area.]

At this point, if it seems appropriate, or toward the end of the interview it may be necessary to ask some questions about the client's health coverage.

V. Discussing psychological treatment

1. Present/past treatment

Are you receiving any kind of therapy now? Have you had any therapy in the past?

[If yes to either question, ask as appropriate] When and where? What happened to bring you into therapy? (What were the presenting problems?) What happened during the therapy? What were the results of the therapy (outcome[s])? [Probe for feelings toward previous therapy/therapist(s).]

2. Expectations of current therapy

These are *crucial questions*; they are the beginning of the identification of treatment goals. If a very depressed person is unable to answer at this time, the questions should be repeated later in the process, especially when the depression begins to lift.

Assuming that we work together and that the therapy is successful (everything comes out all right), what would things (life) be like for you? (Note: It is important to get specific information here; help the client to specify in as observable terms as possible, i.e., recognizable changes.)

What would not change?

VI. Probing for additional information

Is there anything we have left out?

[Or] Is there anything we haven't covered adequately (or to your satisfaction)? Is there anything you'd like to talk about more? Is there anything else you would like to add?

What do you think is going on?

[Or] What do you think is causing you to feel the way you do now?

Asking these open-ended questions toward the end of the interview gives prospective or beginning clients the opportunity to add information they feel is important—information not covered previously or not covered to their satisfaction. It reinforces the democratic nature of the therapy, which means, essentially, that the therapist and client *share* the responsibility rather than the therapist assuming total responsibility for a "cure" (Arieti and Bemporad 1978:293). This series of questions also heightens a feeling of trust for the therapist and may elicit important information that the client was reluctant to reveal earlier in the interview. However, since many depressed clients lack the energy to ask questions, these questions can be repeated at a later time during the therapy.

VII. Providing information about the therapist

At the end of the initial interview, we like to provide clients with an opportunity to voice any questions they may have about the therapist, the methodologies to be used, or any other matter. The client needs this information to make an informed decision about treatment. However, many individuals are afraid to ask questions, fearing that they may be inappropriate or that they may offend "the doctor."

The following open-ended questions not only encourage prospective clients to ask for information but also provide permission for them to do so. We have found that clients generally respond well to this opportunity, although some depressed clients do not ask any questions; they may be too worn out this late in the interview, or they may be disinterested or too self-absorbed or pessimistic to care. Nevertheless, it is good to provide an opportunity for this turnabout. If clients are too depressed to ask questions, these open-ended questions can be asked, or repeated, later in the process.

> *I've asked you a lot of questions. Is there any question you would like to ask me?*
>
> *Is there anything you'd like to know about me? [Encouragement] My background? My training?*

VIII. Exchanging reactions about assessment/treatment

A. Feedback from the therapist to the client

Sometimes the client may be too depressed either to ask for or to utilize any feedback. However, if the therapist thinks that enough information has been obtained so that feedback is possible and that it will be useful to the client, then the therapist might want to give feedback in the form of a tentative evaluation and possibly a prognosis.

1. Assessment of the client's problem(s)

A brief, preliminary assessment of the prospective client's problems, including if and how the therapist feels he or she can help this person, and a short description of the treatment methodology.

If the term has not been used or if the client is still unaware of the nature of the problem, this might be a good place to introduce the word *depression* and to discuss this diagnosis.

2. Assessment of length of treatment

If possible and/or advisable a tentative time limit may be set for the initial evaluation and/or trial of treatment.

B. Opportunity for client response to feedback

1. Reaction to therapy session.

At the end of an interview, it is appropriate for the therapist to elicit the client's reaction to what took place during the interview. The therapist may obtain this feedback with questions such as

> *How do you feel (feel now)?*
> *[Or] What are your thoughts at the end of this interview?*

2. Decision about continuing therapy

At this time, if the client has not already indicated his/her wishes, the therapist should ask if the client wants to make another appointment (wants to continue with treatment). The decision may depend on a number of factors: whether the client is there voluntarily and, in a fee-for-service setting, whether it is financially possible for the client to continue.

> *How do you feel about continuing?*
> *[Or] Shall we set the next appointment now?*

A depressed client may be unable to make a decision or to verbalize an answer at this time. The therapist might have to state the alternatives and try to help the client to decide, or perhaps make only a tentative decision.

IX. Closing the interview

A. When the client has decided to continue in treatment

1. Discussion of the mechanics of treatment

In closing an interview with a voluntary outpatient, there is usually a discussion of the mechanics of therapy, such as fees, how the client will pay for treatment (e.g., the client's insurance coverage, if appropriate), the therapist's policies about contacts such as phone calls and canceling or postponing sessions, and so forth. The extent to which these details are discussed depends on the degree to which the client is depressed. When it is possible, these matters should be discussed as fully as possible to heighten the client's participation in therapy and to emphasize the mutual responsibility for the course of therapy.

2. Homework assignments

There may also be homework assignments, especially if the therapist will be using a behavioral or cognitive-behavioral approach. Since the client is usually tired at this point and may feel flooded with a lot of information, it may be very helpful to have written instructions prepared in advance for homework assignments. For example, if the client will be asked to keep a log of activities or of certain behaviors, it is useful if the therapist provides a copy of a form (see, for example, the form used in chapter 14) with instructions on how the log should be kept. Providing a notebook, an audio tape, or a pad also expedites fulfilling assignments.

3. Assessment of client's mood

The initial interview should be ended with a general question, such as "How do you feel?"

This has the obvious purpose of assessing the impact of the interview on the client and possibly gauging his/her ability to respond to reinforcements. When a client seems very depressed at the start of an interview, a markedly elevated mood at the end of the interview can be a very positive sign that he or she will respond to external stimulation and reinforcement. However, therapists are cautioned against excessive immediate reinforcement, such as telling the client how well he is doing in the interview, praising his seemingly higher spirits, or even telling him he has "much to be grateful for" or "a lot going" for him. When a client feels so much better, perhaps even praising the therapist when leaving the session, this excessive reinforcement may cause him to think that the therapist did not take him seriously and does not realize how bad he feels. This client may not return for a second interview.

B. When the client has decided against continuing treatment

If the client decides against having *any* treatment and the therapist feels that further treatment is needed, this should be discussed with the client. If the client understands that treatment is needed but feels that this is not the right setting for any of a number of reasons, he or she may be referred to another therapist or to another resource, if appropriate. Another reason for referral, of course, is that the therapist may consider another therapist or setting is in the client's best interest; this should be discussed with the client.

Making Referrals

■■ It is often necessary to refer a client for evaluation or for
■■ specialized treatment. Sometimes it is also in a client's best interest to be referred to another therapist. This is particularly true if there is a medical complication, a coexisting psychiatric condition, or an addiction that may require specialized care, such as hospitalization or a particular team treatment approach.

Referral is a serious matter involving ethical responsibilities; it should not be seen as a chance to get rid of a difficult or nonresponsive client. The referring therapist should help the client locate the needed service or individual and should facilitate the connection. The therapist should act as the client's advocate in these situations, preparing the client by giving him information and instructions (e.g., about asking certain questions). With the client's permission the therapist should also contact this new resource and give information about the client to facilitate entry.

Referral for a Physical Examination

A thorough physical examination is usually necessary to diagnose primary or secondary depression and to rule out the possibility of complicating physical factors. If the client has not had a complete physical examination recently, one should be arranged and carried out as soon as possible. We hesitate to specify a time period, for changes in a client's condition, even within days or weeks, may negate the usefulness of even a recent physical.

To derive the greatest benefit from a physical examination and make it as relevant as possible to the diagnosis and treatment of the depression, the client should be instructed to bring to the examination a written list of symptoms and questions. Each symptom should be described as clearly as possible: The client should try to indicate how long it has been present, what problem it presents, when the symptoms appear (e.g., at a particular time of day or year), and any other connections that can be made—for example, if they are increased by stressful events.

All the medications the patient is taking should also be listed, including prescription and over-the-counter medications (aspirin, sleeping pills, cold medications, antihistamines, and so on), vitamins, mineral supplements, and any other substances being ingested, regardless of how innocent they may appear. A list of the quantities of alcohol, nicotine, and any other addictive substance that the client uses should be compiled that is as accurate as possible. It is useful to list the actual quantities or doses as well as the specific times they are taken.

Since it can be difficult for a depressed patient to concentrate and the patient may have a distorted sense of time, the therapist should be prepared to help the patient compile this list and write it down. The client should be encouraged to have someone accompany him to the examination to help convey this information and, if needed, to take down the physician's instructions. The therapist should obtain the patient's consent to talk with this physician and to request a written report.

It is also helpful if the therapist speaks with the patient's physician prior to this examination, alerting the doctor to the symptoms of depression and asking that the patient be screened for the kinds of diseases that mimic depression. Gold covers an index of suspicion that includes "drug . . . and alcohol reactions . . . endocrine disorders (e.g., hypothyroidism, diabetes). . . . diseases of the central nervous system (including Alzheimer's disease and multiple sclerosis), infectious diseases, cancers, metabolic conditions, nutritional and toxic disorders, plus a large miscellaneous category. . . . [including] vitamin deficiency, heavy metals, toxins [and] drug abuse or withdrawal" (1987a:78–84).[5] In addition to routine blood and urine tests, Gold suggests that the patient be screened for illicit drugs and be given neuroendocrine tests (1987a:78–79).

A female patient may report premenstrual symptoms ranging from troublesome to severe. She may be suffering from premenstrual syndrome (P.M.S.), which is actually not one condition but a group of conditions. (See chapter 17 for a fuller discussion of this topic.) Therapists should have on their referral roster the names of specialists in gynecology who are knowledgeable and up-to-date about P.M.S. It is important that this condition be treated initially as a physical, rather than as a psychological, problem; it is destructive to the self-esteem of female patients to have their symptoms dismissed as "merely psychological" when there is an increasing literature on the physical basis of the symptoms as well as the development of some effective methods for treating these problems.

Referring the Client for Evaluation for Antidepressant Medication

Following the guidelines that we discuss later, a therapist sometimes needs to consider referring a client for an evaluation for possible treatment with an antidepressant medication.

We have stressed that both the nonmedically trained therapist and the psychiatrist who is not an expert in the pharmacotherapy of depression should refer clients to a specialist in this area. Therapists should decide upon one or two specialists to whom they can comfortably refer their clients; it is helpful to interview these specialists in advance about their credentials and treatment philosophy and the procedures they follow when prescribing and monitoring medications. These should conform to the guidelines suggested in chapter 10.

The therapist should help arrange the appointment and prepare the patient for the visit to the pharmacotherapist. Before the visit, the therapist should discuss any expectations and fears the client may have about antidepressant medications. The client should be encouraged to tell the pharmacotherapist about these fears and expectations.

If medication is prescribed, the client should have a list of questions to ask about the medication and its effects. For example:

1. Why do you feel I need medication? Are there any other effective treatments that don't require the use of medication?
2. What is the name of the medication you are prescribing? (generic name? trade name?)
3. Why do you recommend this particular medication? What would happen if I do not take it?
4. When and how should I take this medication?
   How many times per day?
   Before, during, or after meals?
   Shall I take it with water or milk? With something else?
   Are there any foods/liquids that I should avoid when taking this drug?
5. What are the positive effects that I should expect? How long should it take for these to occur? What should I do if I do not experience these effects?
6. What are the negative side effects?
   How long might it take for these to occur?
   Will these effects last as long as I am taking the medication? If not, when can I expect them to stop?
7. What should I do if I experience these negative effects? Should I stop taking the medication?

Should I call you?

Where can you be reached?

When is the best time to call you?

If I cannot reach you at the number you have given me, what should I do?

8. Is there anything else I should know about this drug and its effects?

9. How long do you expect that I will be taking this drug?

10. Would it be helpful if I keep a record of when I take the medication and how it makes me feel? [If yes] What is the best way to record this information?

11. Is there anything I forgot to ask about?

12. May I read back the instructions you gave me so that I am sure they are correct?

13. Will you send a report on this to my therapist?

14. When will I need to see you again?

The therapist should help the client write this list, leaving adequate room for answers. If possible, the client should bring someone with him to the pharmacotherapist to assist in providing information and taking notes. Some doctors will permit a small tape recorder, but permission should be obtained in advance.

Later, the client should be encouraged to call the pharmacotherapist with any additional questions. The pharmacist who fills the prescription is also an excellent—and largely overlooked—source of information about medications. The client should be advised of the benefits of filling *all* prescriptions at a pharmacy with a computerized system that will alert the pharmacist to any negative interactions among the drugs.

In most situations, the referring therapist will continue to do the psychotherapy, and the specialist will prescribe and monitor the medication. In these instances, the referring therapist should be aware of the expected effects of the medication and of any side effects. The therapist should monitor these effects by observing and talking with the patient as well as asking for periodic reports from the specialist.

The therapist should also understand that a common problem with antidepressant medications is that if they are to be effective, they often must be given in dosages strong enough to produce side effects (Baldessarini 1990:5). Some doctors seem to be reluctant to prescribe such strong dosages and underprescribe. This causes the medications to be ineffective, or less effective than they could be. If the medication does not have the desired effects, the therapist might want to check on the dosage and discuss this with the prescribing physician.

Another problem may be patient compliance. Instructions for taking medications are often misunderstood, or a client may decide to alter the prescribed regime. If the client seems not to respond to the medication, the therapist might well verify that the correct dosage is being taken at the prescribed time intervals.

From time to time a patient taking an antidepressant will feel that the medication has been so beneficial that psychotherapy is no longer needed. The therapist may or may not agree. However, if the patient does not wish to continue in therapy, the therapist should offer to be available if the patient wants to talk with someone other than the pharmacotherapist. The availability of this support is important, and helpful, even if the patient never calls.

Referral for Other Types of Treatment

It is sometimes necessary to hospitalize a seriously depressed client, especially one who is suicidal and needs to be monitored closely. In most states this requires consultation with a psychiatrist, although some states give privileges to psychologists, social workers, and sometimes psychiatric nurses. Obviously, hospitalization is a serious matter. However, *not* using a hospital is very bad practice if the client is in danger. The judgment of whether to hospitalize is best made in consultation with another mental health professional and should be made with no other thought than the best interests of the patient.

Other facilities or programs may be needed: an addiction treatment program, an eating or sleep disorders clinic, phototherapy treatment for SAD, and so forth. These facilities may be used in conjunction with psychotherapy, although they may sometimes be used either instead of or as a preliminary to psychotherapy. Referral to some facilities, such as a sleep disorders clinic, may be primarily for diagnosis and evaluation.

There may be a number of reasons for wanting to refer a client to another psychotherapist. It may be the client's decision: The client might prefer a therapist of a different gender or theoretical orientation. The therapist might feel that he or she would not work well with a particular client. It may become clear quickly that a client is not a good candidate for the type of treatment a therapist offers. Or a client may not be making progress and he or she might do better with a different person. Sometimes a client's health insurance policy may stipulate a particular treatment group or program or may rule out a therapist's approach (e.g., long-term therapy). Or the client may be unable to pay the therapist, even at the lowest end of his fee scale. Sometimes it is simply a matter of convenience: A depressed client may feel the therapist's office is too hard to get to, or the treatment hours may be inconvenient.

When a referral is needed, the therapist should carefully select several appropriate therapists and give the patient a choice. The therapist should tell the patient that a new therapist will usually want to contact the referring therapist to make sure that the client has terminated treatment and perhaps to exchange some basic information. The therapist should assure the patient that he or she will talk with the new therapist when permission is granted.

Deciding on Treatment: Psychotherapy, Medication, and Other Alternatives

■■ When a client enters treatment, the therapist must decide
■■ whether to use psychotherapy alone, psychotherapy and medication, or another alternative, such as institutionalization or ECT. The real question is not the use of one or the other, but under *which* conditions *each* should be used. Differential diagnosis of which depressions will respond to psychotherapy alone and which will respond to medication is difficult. A general indicator is that with the milder depressions that are "psychological" in nature, psychotherapy is the usual method of intervention. Depressions that can be more easily classified as "illnesses," are more likely to respond to medication. However, as we stated earlier, these categories are not mutually exclusive.

Other important indicators are the level of functioning and the presence or absence of vegetative symptoms. Focusing on the numbers of symptoms (e.g., as listed in the D.S.M.-III-R [1987]) can be misleading in deciding treatment. As we have pointed out, symptoms are not equally serious: One individual may have all the symptoms listed as criteria for a formal diagnosis of depression yet not be seriously depressed; another may have fewer symptoms, but in such depth or severity that they may equal clinical depression. The *quality* of the symptoms is central to the diagnosis and planning of treatment. First, it must be determined if symptoms exist; then the severity of the symptoms must be judged.

There are some rough indicators that can help the therapist decide if psychotherapy should be tried without medication or if medication should be initiated immediately along with the psychotherapy. Indicators for hospitalization or ECT are also included. These have been gathered from a number of sources, including Wender and Klein (1981), Rush (1982), Burns (1980), Arieti and Bemporad (1978), and Karasu (1990b:274). Most of these indicators should not be used alone to determine treatment; the clinician must consider the entire picture, the total situation of this particular client at this time in his or her life.

Because of the difficulty, in the clinical situation, of differentiating "biological" from "psychological" symptoms, some overlap and repetition in the following discussion are inevitable. Sometimes the same symptom or symptoms may be viewed from either the biological or psychological perspective. For example, vegetative symptoms are more often, but not always, related to a physiological depression (depression as an "illness,") for which medications are often indicated. Treatment indicators may also overlap. For example, if depression has lasted for some time, even if it is basically "psychological," vegetative symptoms may develop and the person might well respond to antidepressant medication along with psychotherapy.

Indicators for Psychotherapy

The following conditions are indicators for psychotherapy:

Mild depression with mild vegetative symptoms. If the depression is mild according to the D.S.M. criteria that state, "Few, if any, symptoms in excess of those required to make the diagnosis, *and* symptoms result in only minor impairment in occupational functioning or in usual social activities or relationships with others" (D.S.M.-III-R 1987:223, emphasis in the original) or if it is judged to be mild by the clinician, *and if there is little apparent threat of suicide.*[6] The potential utility of medication should be reevaluated if after three months of psychotherapy the depression is not noticeably relieved.

   The severity of the vegetative, or physiological, symptoms is a very important indicator. If they are comparatively mild (e.g., there is little loss of appetite and little or only moderate weight loss or gain), then psychotherapy alone is indicated. Other vegetative symptoms that, if absent or mild, may indicate psychotherapy are no dryness of mouth, minimal or no constipation, and skin that is not excessively dry. In women there should be no hypomenorrhea (regular menstrual period with subnormal flow) or amenorrhea (absence of menstrual period).

Reactive mood. If the mood is basically reactive and this reactive mood is not so intense that it "pervades all aspects of the person and his or her functioning" (Whybrow, Akiskal, and McKinney 1984:15), then the client may well respond to psychotherapy alone.

Nonendogenous, nonpsychotic depression. Particularly relevant is the following: "In patients with nonendogenous or nonmelancholic depression without psychosis (i.e., the *majority of depressed patients*) psychotherapeutic treatments may well have the most powerful effect" (Rush 1982:14–15, emphasis added). Similarly, an indicator for psychotherapy is the absence of hallucinations or delusions (in other words, the patient is not psychotic). Although it is less used today than it once was, the neurotic/psychotic division is still a good, although crude, guideline for differentiating between psychotherapy alone and psychotherapy with medication.

Insignificant or no psychomotor changes. If psychomotor changes are nonexistent or insignificant, the person may respond to psychotherapy alone. (More serious psychomotor changes may require medication.)

Sleep-onset problems. If the sleep problems tend to be sleep-onset problems rather than terminal insomnia, the client may well respond to psychotherapy without medication. Terminal insomnia, also called middle waking or early-morning awakening, usually responds to medication.

Lack of worsened early-morning mood. If the client's mood is not worse in the morning, with progressive improvement during the day, this is another indication for psychotherapy alone.

Mood rises with comfort/positive events. If the depressed mood rises when the client is comforted and/or he does acknowledge and respond to pleasant (positive) events and people in his environment, this is an indicator for psychotherapy without medication.

Gradual onset of symptoms. Psychotherapy without medication is indicated if there is a gradual onset of the symptoms and the patient has not recognized the symptoms and the onset of the depressive episode.

Negative cognitions. Another indicator for psychotherapy alone is a flow of negative cognitions set off by external events, especially discernible, specific external events, such as the death of someone close, a loss of a job, a real or perceived failure in school or in a job, and so on.

Absence of pathological guilt. Some depressives, particularly psychotic or severely disturbed depressives, show pathological guilt; they may dwell upon the past or engage in excessive self-blame for either minor or imagined errors in the past. Absence of this persistent rumination and self-blame is an indicator for psychotherapy by itself.

Absence of suicidal thoughts; presence of nonoverwhelming suicidal thoughts. The presence or absence of suicidal thoughts and actions is crucial to diagnosis and treatment. The indicators for psychotherapy without medication are the following: when a person evidences no thought of suicide and there is no history of suicidal attempts;

when suicidal thoughts are not an overwhelming factor; when suicidal emotions are present but are related to feelings of failure or frustration rather than to a view of suicide as a way to ease deep internal psychic pain. (The neurotic and usually milder depressive wants to get rid of the undesirable depression and pain but usually does not consider suicide as the way to ease the depression and the pain; the more seriously depressed person may see killing himself as the most likely way to eliminate the pain.)

A therapist must always be aware of the possibility of being deceived by a potentially suicidal client or of failing to detect suicidal tendencies. It should always be remembered that alternative treatments such as medications or even hospitalization might be needed for suicidal patients.

Close interpersonal relationships in the past. The depressed person who has had close interpersonal relationships before becoming depressed can usually utilize psychotherapy by itself more than the person who has *not* had these previous close interpersonal relationships, although medication may sometimes be indicated, depending upon the total symptom picture.

Strong social support system(s). Another indicator for psychotherapy alone is the presence of a strong social support system, or of some significant others who can support the person during and after the depressive episode (Brown and Harris 1978).

Personality disorders. According to Karasu (1990b:274), psychotherapy without medication is indicated for some personality disorders, such as dependent, inadequate, and masochistic personality disorders but not for others (see later under "medications").

An absence of depression in first-degree relatives. This has frequently been listed as an indicator for psychotherapy alone, but it has recently been questioned. In our opinion, depression in near relatives has not yet been established as proof of a genetic factor. This indicator must be treated with caution, especially when dealing with children, where often much depressive-like behavior is acquired through learning (e.g., by imitation and identification).

Unwillingness to take drugs. Some clients will refuse to take drugs. For example, some have suffered severe side effects from medications in the past; some have an extreme sensitivity to medications; some are hypochondriacs; others simply do not want to take drugs. Psychotherapy alone would seem to be a logical first step with these individuals; however, if it proves ineffective, medications should not be ruled out. The problem should be addressed, and if the patient will consent, consultation should be sought. Perhaps what is indicated in many of these cases is not eliminating medication but changing previous medication and/or dosage.

Indicators for Medication

The depressions that can be more easily classified as "illnesses," regardless of their degree, seem to be the conditions that are most likely to respond to medication. These generally include the endogenous or vital depressions, where the individuals will usually show marked vegetative or physiological symptoms, particularly early-morning awakening, drops in appetite for food and sex, constipation, dryness of skin, earlier REM sleep, and so on.

The following conditions are indicators for medication:

Functional impairment/marked psychomotor changes. Medication is indicated when the patient is functionally impaired, the depression interferes with the activities of daily living, and the depression is severe (Burns 1980:394–395). Marked psychomotor changes also indicate the need for medication.

Bipolar disorder/manic attacks. Bipolar disorders, including both the episodes of depression and the manic attacks, generally require medication along with psychotherapy. The accompanying psychotherapy is important, especially in more serious and severe cases, to enhance compliance with treatment and to clarify issues once the extremes of mood swings have lessened.

Clear-cut onset of depression; feeling substantially different from normal. Burns states that if the depression "had a reasonably clear-cut beginning and if . . . symptoms are substantially different from the way . . . [the client] normally feel[s]," then this makes a case for medication (1980).

Terminal insomnia. Many depressed patients report that they have no trouble falling asleep, but they wake two or three hours later and have trouble falling asleep again. This terminal insomnia (or middle waking or early-morning insomnia), which is usually part of a larger symptom picture, responds to medications.

Worsened morning mood. Depressives who feel worst in the morning and better as the day goes on tend to respond to antidepressant medication.

Lack of response to comfort/pleasant events. When a rise in mood does not occur after the individual is comforted and he or she cannot respond to pleasant events in the environment, these are indicators that the depressive disorder should also be treated with drugs.

Deep psychic pain/suicidal thoughts/suicidal attempts. If there are marked somatic symptoms, the patient does not enjoy consummatory behavior, and the risk of suicide is severe, these are indicators for drugs. ECT and hospitalization may also be necessary. For example, when a depressed individual has deep internal (*psychic*) pain, the more seriously depressed person, especially the psychotically depressed, may feel that he deserves the pain; that the depression is punishment for his sins; and that he *should* be punished (Arieti and Bemporad 1978:148). Suicide is sometimes the punishment he selects; of course, if a voice—internal or external—is telling him to commit suicide, he may respond to it. Here we are obviously dealing with a severely, possibly psychotically depressed person; immediate hospitalization must be considered.

Abnormalities on biological tests. About 80 percent of individuals with endogenous depression show biological abnormalities on such tests as sleep polysomnographs, EEG, and/or the DST. These are strong indicators for medication (Rush 1982:13).

Personality disorders. Karasu (1990b:274) has stated that pharmacotherapy is indicated in borderline, histrionic, and obsessive-compulsive personality disorders.

Lack of response to psychotherapy. When a depression that is seen as primarily psychological in origin, such as one following a loss or a setback, does not respond to psychotherapy after about three months (assuming no suicidal ideation or attempts, or other consequences), the therapist should seek a consultation for possible use of medication to stabilize symptomatology and facilitate the psychotherapy.

If a depression has lasted for some time, even if basically psychological in nature, vegetative symptoms may develop and the person might well respond to antidepressant medication along with psychotherapy.

Retrial of medication after unfavorable reaction. Klein and Wender (1988:94–95) hold that about 80 percent of depressives will react favorably to at least one of three drugs if they are given in strong enough doses for at least six weeks, but 20 percent will not respond. In the latter case, if the therapist is a biopsychiatrist they recommend a second opinion if there have been three trials of medicine, each six weeks long, with no improvement. If the therapist is not a biopsychiatrist, then they recommend an opinion after only two trials of six weeks.

Treatment with Psychotherapy and Medication Combined

As we have consistently stated throughout this book, we believe that some form of talking therapy is necessary for *all* depressive conditions, even those treated with medication or other approaches. This view is upheld by many psychotherapists and psychiatrists, including a small but influential number of biopsychiatrists, such as Klein and Wender (1988:82), who state that problems and symptoms arising from the depression, as well as environmental, family, and individual pressures, may necessitate medication *and* counseling, and possibly social skills training and adopting a different way of life. Klein and Wender are also most explicit in stating that psychological problems caused by depression, even "biological depression," may last longer than the actual depressive episode. These problems are not neurotic but realistic consequences of the patient's former inabilities (1988:82–83).

However, even the biopsychiatrists disagree. For example, Wender and Klein (1988:67) state that since "mild depression is self-limiting and goes away without treatment . . . medication for mild depression is not always wise." Other biopsychiatrists, along with many psychiatrists argue against this view and state, "Antidepressant medications are the cornerstone of treatment for major depression and also have an important role to play in the treatment of moderate and even mild depression" (Greist and Jefferson 1984:84).

The clinician faced with deciding when it is appropriate to use psychotherapy with and when it is best to use it without medication is hindered by such contradictory opinions. Further complicating the choice is the observation by the dissenting biopsychiatrists who state that "failure to respond to all known biological treatments does not necessarily mean the patient's problems are strictly psychological. It may simply mean that useful biological treatments have not yet been developed for his particular illness" (Klein and Wender 1988:67). This latter comment is of small consolation to the therapist and even less to the client.

Nor does nonresponse to psychotherapy always indicate that the depression should be treated with medication. The client may be unable to "change entrenched ways"; or there may be a "mismatch between patient and treatment (or patient and therapist)" (Klein and Wender 1988:67).

Unfortunately, there is a trial-and-error quality to much of the prescription of antidepressant medications, especially with the current lack of reliable and valid tests of biological markers. "Although the major classes of antidepressant drugs have been available for over 30 years, clinicians are still unable to predict accurately the response of their depressed patients to medication" (Joyce and Paykel 1989:89).

The preceding indications and observations are meant to serve as guidelines, and *general guidelines*, at that. No one factor should determine whether to use psychotherapy with or without medication. The entire picture should be considered in the assessment process. When in doubt, *consult* with other therapists, and do not limit the assessment to one session, unless, of course, there is a serious suicide and/or health threat. (The recommendation for consultation is not meant to be limited to the use or nonuse of medication. Consultation is a good method of coping with difficult issues in treatment, with dealing with resistant or nonresponsive clients, and is often a good way to gauge a patient's progress—or the lack of it.)

The Next Decision: What Kind of Psychotherapy?

■■ The next decision facing a therapist is what kind of talking
■■ therapy to use. Ideally, all therapists would be versed in multiple methods and would be able to conduct the most appropriate psychotherapy for *each* client. In reality, however, proficiency in more than one model is rare. The treatment approach a therapist selects is usually the model or orientation in which the therapist has been trained, even if it is not the most appropriate available for the particular problems of a particular client. As Abraham Maslow has commented, "I suppose it is tempting, if the only tool you have is a hammer, to treat everything as if it were a nail" (1969:15–16).

In part 3 we described the major approaches to the psychotherapies of the depressions and the specific techniques in each approach applicable to the treatment of the various symptoms of depression. We believe that therapists of differing treatment orientations can adapt these interventions to fit the needs of each client. They can change the emphasis of their work with the client and can selectively use the interventions that the current research findings suggest are the most appropriate. We shall list the major indicators later.

The therapist must first determine priorities—the problems of greatest saliency and greatest threat to the well-being of the client and to those involved with him. This initial assessment of the client's presenting problems, particularly the identification of the most pressing problem areas, should direct the selection of intervention(s) for the initial phases of treatment. This process of selection and treatment should continue throughout therapy.[7]

Some Indicators for Using Behavioral Methods

The following are some indicators for using behavioral methods:

Low rate of behavior/retarded behavior. If you have depressed clients who are showing a very low rate or a retarded rate of behavior, the behavioral techniques (as we described in chapter 14) are particularly well suited to halt the downward spiral of low behavior, low reinforcement, even lower behavior, even lower reinforcement—the extended extinction trial. We are not suggesting that therapists ignore the lowered mood and the distorted cognitions that often accompany depression, but they should consider these behavioral procedures as a *first* phase of therapy, to stop the downward phase of the depressive cycle as quickly as possible.

Medication sometimes stops the downward spiral and often alleviates some of the vegetative symptoms. However, as Frank (1961) observed, although medication will alleviate symptom discomfort, psychotherapy is needed to restore interpersonal and social competence.

Lack of behavior/lack of reinforcement. Similarly, if there is a *lack* of behavior resulting in a lack of reinforcement, there are useful behavioral procedures specifically designed to increase the client's repertoire of behaviors. New or increased behaviors might elicit reinforcements, especially social reinforcements, thus stopping the downward spiral. Especially relevant are the approaches to treating depression (e.g., those of Becker et al. 1989) that stress the acquisition of social skills.

Lack of social skills. If there is a lack of social skills, one of the more behavioral or cognitive-behavioral approaches should be used, at least in the initial phases of the therapy, to help the client develop social skills, such as making conversation, approaching other people, job hunting, and so on.

The fourth area of IPT, interpersonal deficits, also focuses on the lack of social skills.

Severe anxiety/phobias leading to depression. Another symptom picture that one often encounters with depressed people is the presence of severe anxiety that leads to depression. This anxiety often manifests itself as a phobia (e.g., being overwhelmed by situations and by people). In these situations, as a part of the beginning phase of therapy, some of Wolpe's procedures, such as systematic desensitization and, later, assertiveness training, may raise the level of the client's competence and thus help to combat the depression and enrich the client's repertoire of coping maneuvers.

Learned helplessness. Such behavioral procedures as self-programming, shaping, successive approximations, modeling, and positive self-talk are applicable for overcoming the kind of obstacles that have been described as learned helplessness. (These procedures were described in chapters 14 and 15.) Cognitive restructuring and perhaps some psychodynamically oriented treatment for raising self-esteem might be employed later in the therapy.

Negative views/overly stringent standards/negative self-evaluation. If depressives have a pessimistic outlook on life and engage in self-defeating patterns of behavior because their standards are impossible to reach, some of the behavioral and cognitive-behavioral methods are applicable, particularly the self-control model of Rehm, described in chapter 14.

Some Indicators for Using Cognitive Methods

The following are some indicators for cognitive treatment methods:

High rate of behavior; distorted cognitions; self-defeating/subvocal verbalizations/automatic thoughts. A therapist may be treating a depressed person who has a high rate of behavior or whose low rate of behavior has been remedied by antidepressant medications or by some other therapeutic intervention. At this point, the strictly behavioral methods would not be needed. If the depressed individual displayed distorted cognitions and engaged in self-defeating self-talk, and/or the automatic thoughts were self-defeating and negative, then one of the cognitive therapies, such as Aaron Beck's or Albert Ellis's, might be appropriate.

Pessimistic view of the future. The cognitive methods are particularly useful in the phase of therapy when clients discuss—usually with pessimistic outlooks—their views of the future. A nihilistic view of the future is part of the cognitive triad, amenable to Beck's cognitive therapy (discussed in chapter 15); the other parts of the triad are a negative history and a poor self-image.

Behavioral deficits/faulty information processing. If there is a combination of behavioral deficits and faulty information processing, then the cognitive-behavioral methods might well be indicated.

Some Indicators for Using Psychodynamic Methods

LONG-TERM PSYCHODYNAMIC TREATMENT

The following are some indicators for long-term psychodynamic treatment:

Depressive life-style/dominant other/problems with core characteristics. The psychodynamic approaches to therapy, both short-term and long-term, as we discussed in chapter 12, are usually conceptualized as aiming to achieve changes in *personality*. That is, changes in the ways of coping and adapting plus (and it is an important plus) the resolution of problems associated with *core characteristics*.

These core problems are maladaptive ways of coping that originated in childhood. We particularly have in mind those whose depression or whose depressive style of living has been learned, or nurtured, by contact with a dominant other. The usually life-long patterns of coping (which may be called personality) are often deeply ingrained and sometimes require long-term therapy if they tend to persist even after the more symptomatic aspects of depression—ways of behaving and even ways of thinking—have been changed.

One will also encounter clients who will respond—sometimes because of specific stimuli in the environment and sometimes as a general reaction, where there seems to be no particular stimulus—with reactions that may be called depressions. These individuals may have experienced many traumas when they were very young, including the deaths of parents. These early traumas seem to have resulted in the individual adopting unrewarding and pathological ways of coping and relating to people. These patterns may be accompanied by unconscious irrational beliefs. Within the psychodynamic frame of reference, these core or inner conflicts are thought to cause depression or, perhaps more accurately, heighten the use of depression as a coping mechanism or even as a way of life.

Gap between perceived aspirations and perceived achievements. These core conflicts (underlying neurotic problems, characterological defenses, and so on) may manifest themselves as, or be worsened by, a gap between the aspirations of the person and what he feels he has achieved. Depressed people may achieve a great deal, but it is usually less than what they feel they should have achieved. Depression is the consequence, and it is often highly colored with disappointment, particularly about the loss of what might have been.

Rigid defenses/extreme dependence. Long-term psychodynamically oriented therapy is often appropriate for those with rigid defenses and those who are extremely dependent and need to work through this dependency in a long-term relationship with a therapist.

Recurrence of depression in patient receiving antidepressants. Recurrence of the depressive episodes, especially if the client is receiving antidepressant medication and has successfully changed behaviors, ways of thinking, and so forth, may well indicate that long-term treatment is needed for core problems.

SHORT-TERM PSYCHODYNAMIC TREATMENT

As we emphasized in chapter 12, the psychodynamic treatments for depression are becoming increasingly shorter and more focused. Of course, the shorter time means that there are some differences in the emphasis of treatment: Some short-term approaches focus on transference, others on the origin of depression in childhood, and so forth. Adherents feel that the limitation on the number of sessions not only organizes the focus of the therapy but increases client motivation. The various short-term dynamic treatments are conceptually similar. In one way or another, all center on the core conflicts of the client.

According to psychodynamic theorists, the short-term interventions often only relieve the episodes of depression; deeper, more long-term treatment is needed to prevent their recurrence. However, in our experience, since many depressions are self-limiting, the short-term interventions are often surprisingly effective and the changes often long-lasting.

INTERPERSONAL THERAPY (IPT)

If the client's problems are mainly in the interpersonal area, such as interpersonal disputes or problems with role transitions (usually transitions connected with the life cycle), then IPT would be the intervention of choice.

Where problems are connected with the death of significant others, such as abnormal grief reaction or the lack of the opportunity to mourn these deaths, a course of therapy with IPT may facilitate the mourning and alleviate the depression. If the short-term intervention of IPT is insufficient, and/or the depressive state returns, then a reevaluation (perhaps including a second opinion) may indicate the need for longer-term, psychodynamically oriented therapy.

Problems to Be Addressed in All Forms of Therapy

■■ Karasu (1990b:275) has identified the following conditions,
■■ which should be examined and addressed, as needed, in all forms of therapy of depression: "hopelessness, helplessness, apathy, decreased enjoyment, diminished desire or gratification, too high ego ideals and expectations, . . . feelings of restlessness or being slowed down, lack of motivation, low self-esteem, inappropriate or excessive guilt and self-reproach, . . . [the] wish . . . to be dead, . . . fear of rejection or failure." His observations parallel ours: Certain themes,

such as "chronic sense of emptiness and underestimation of self-worth," are particularly amenable to psychodynamic therapies; malfunctioning of thought processes about self, world, and the future (the cognitive triad) are amenable to cognitive therapy; and disagreements with significant others, social problems, and grief reactions are appropriate for IPT. However, we think that he has understated the utility of behavioral methods as a first step in restoring the level of behavior and stopping the downward depressive spiral. We agree with Karasu's observation that the various therapies are probably not so distinct and identifiable in practice and that the common elements tend to override the theoretical uniqueness of each approach (Karasu 1990b:276).

The Course of Treatment

■■ Treatment is not a matter of short-term versus long-term
■■ therapy, or of the behavioral therapies versus the cognitive versus the psychodynamic, and so on. We believe that these various approaches address different aspects of the depressions. Therapy *can* be adapted to fit the needs of each client at each phase of the treatment process. Following Freud's principle, we also recommend that therapists not use a complicated therapy until they have tried a simpler approach.

We have provided a general outline of the treatment process, divided into three phases, listing the tasks that typically (but not always) need to be addressed in each phase. This outline is an illustration, not a prescription. The number and intensity of tasks and problem areas obviously will vary considerably from client to client, as will the order in which they need to be addressed. For those depressed individuals who can be seen on an outpatient basis, the following general comments are applicable.

Beginning Phase of Intervention

The beginning phase of intervention consists of the following:
The immediate decisions. When depressed clients are treated, immediate decisions must be made, the first of which is whether hospitalization or ECT is needed, and then whether medication will be necessary. Certain diagnostic classifications, such as mania (manic episodes) or bipolar disorder, also will require consultation regarding the use of medication.
Establishing priorities for treatment. After immediate dangers, such as suicide threats, have been brought under control, the remaining symp-

tom picture must be examined and the first interventions chosen. The therapist begins by constructing a hierarchy of importance, starting with the problems that cause the greatest immediate discomfort. For a positive treatment outcome, it is extremely important to try to begin treatment by working on a problem, or problems, that seem to have the potential for providing the client with a "success experience" in this first effort at recovery. When a depressed, usually pessimistic client (who may also have experienced learned helplessness), achieves success, he or she also learns by experience that personal efforts *can* make a difference. This helps to set a positive tone for continuing treatment and may increase the client's involvement and motivation to continue with the difficult work of treatment.

Stopping the downward spiral of depression. This problem area is often a logical place to begin the intervention process, especially when there is an extreme absence of behavior, or behavioral deficits (and hence a paucity of social reinforcements). The behavioral methods are suggested as an immediate first step to stop the downward spiral of the depression. This can often be accomplished fairly rapidly, thus also providing the client with the success experience mentioned earlier.

Increasing and maintaining rises in behavior. Cognitive, or cognitive-behavioral, methods may be used next to maintain the rise in behavior and to help the client find alternate sources of reinforcement (social reinforcement). If faulty thinking patterns are part of the presenting, or developing, picture, then the cognitive therapies are particularly recommended.

Resolving problems in the interpersonal area. If there are a number of problems in the interpersonal areas, especially role conflicts around life cycle changes, or the breakup of close relationships, then one of the focused IPT procedures is indicated. There may also be an advantage to using a cognitive-behavioral approach in combination with IPT.

Dealing with low self-esteem. Where self-esteem is low and patterns of attempting the impossible task of pleasing real or perceived dominant others are repeated, a psychodynamic approach may be appropriate after the downward spiral of the depression has been stabilized. These problems may also be worked on later, at the mutual discretion of therapist and client.

Intermediate/Middle Phase

In the intermediate, or middle, phase of treatment the following issues may be considered:

Maintaining gains in behavior/correcting distorted thinking. In this stage of treatment, cognitive and cognitive-behavioral methods may be used to maintain gains in behavior and to begin correcting distorted thinking patterns and faulty information processing. IPT techniques may be used for interpersonal problems, particularly where mourning has been incomplete or absent.

Dealing with low self-esteem/persisting influence of dominant others. IPT and other psychodynamic methods can be used throughout the treatment process for problems with low self-esteem and—along with behavioral methods such as assertiveness training and desensitization—for learning how to deal with dominant others, both present and past. (These problems may be addressed at different stages in the treatment process, or they may be worked on periodically or continuously, as needed.)

Refocusing treatment to external interests/broadening the client's frame of reference. Around the latter part of the middle phase of *all* therapies, short or long term, we feel it is necessary to help the depressed client begin to seek increased pleasure in his or her environment. This includes helping the client identify interesting and enjoyable activities, such as social/political groups, concerts, plays, and the like; hobbies; and so on—depending on what the client enjoys or may find pleasurable. This increased activity also helps to lessen the frequent self-absorption of the depressive. Increased pleasure may also ease punitive self-judgment.

Treatment of demoralization. Sometimes behavior has been increased, dysfunctional thinking has been corrected and/or eliminated, and symptoms of depression are mild or nonexistent, but the client still does not feel optimistic about the present or the future. He or she may say, "I still don't feel any pleasure," or may ask, "Is this *all* there is in life?" Such individuals can be described as demoralized. Unfortunately, demoralization often follows when depressive symptoms lift, especially when these symptoms have been alleviated by medication. (Of course, one of the positive aspects of medication is that it may ease depressive symptoms to the point where psychotherapy becomes possible.) This feeling that life is still bleak is often coupled with lingering deficits in self-esteem. These symptoms may necessitate continuing psychotherapy, especially to work on persistent problems such as the client's low self-esteem.

Coming to grips with rage. Some clients have been depressed for a long time, and their depression involves long-held feelings of rage. These feelings often linger and are not open to resolution in the earlier phases of treatment. The feelings of rage are particularly relevant when based on real events in the client's past life, such as child abuse, abandonment, parental alcoholism, and parental sexual abuse. These feelings of rage are often the focus of the middle and the end phases of treatment.

Arieti and Bemporad (1978:311) have stated, "Before termination of therapy, the past must be accepted without excessive rancor." It has been our experience, especially when working with the more structured and the shorter forms of therapy, that when the therapy seems to draw out, the cause is often this unresolved anger stemming from the past, which gets in the way of the client's full acceptance of his or her newly gained competence as a nondepressed person.

Using books and tapes as an adjunct to treatment. Books and tapes (both audio and video tapes) may sometimes be useful adjuncts to therapy. For clients who like to read, assignments may be made on such topics as relaxation training, assertiveness training, sleep, the breakup of relationships, and even mood disorders and pharmacotherapy.[8] Some excellent audio tapes are also available, particularly for relaxation training and dealing with sleep problems. Since many self-help books and tapes are on the market, and the covers and ads may be exaggerated and misleading, the therapist should carefully review all material before recommending it to a client.

A survey of psychologists has shown that about 70 percent consider self-help books helpful and prescribe them, and less than 10 percent say they have heard of clients being hurt by them (Kingsbury 1992).

The timing of the use of books (*bibliotherapy*) and tapes is vital. Relaxation training and sleep tapes may sometimes be used effectively even early in treatment, and books may be used early with mild or moderately depressed individuals, especially in short-term treatment. In fact, clients may bring up the topic and mention a book they have heard about or read. However, more seriously depressed individuals are usually not ready, or able, to utilize books and tapes until their mood stabilizes and they make other gains in therapy. Our experience has shown that using these resources in the late middle phase of long-term therapy often facilitates and shortens therapy. They may help the client assess his own situation and help him become more assertive in effecting change in himself—in other words, to become a cotherapist. These skills are extremely useful in teaching the client to maintain the gains made in therapy, as therapy terminates.

End Phase: Termination

Termination should be thought of as a *process*. We find it useful to phase out treatment gradually, in stages. For example, one might begin by extending the time between appointments from one week to two, then make appointments every three weeks, then once a month, then have a follow-up session every three or six months. Telephone contacts can be made available to the client, and they might also be scheduled farther and farther apart. Of course, clients always have the option of returning to therapy if they are in genuine distress.

There are a number of issues to deal with in the last phase of treatment. Some of these issues are related to the client, and some are related to his relationships with significant others.

Learning to differentiate between normal and clinical depression. Many clients are very fearful that their depressions will return. Although it is true that many depressions are self-limiting, it is also true that they often recur. All people experience periods of feeling down, usually for short periods of time, but sometimes these feelings are so intense that they are the equivalent of clinical depression. These episodes usually pass in time or ease in response to any number of things: support from a friend, a change of scenery, and so on. Most of us learn that we can ride out a depression and that eventually we will feel better. However, when the person who has been clinically depressed experiences these feelings, he will immediately think, "Oh, oh. Here I go again." He will confuse the feelings of normal depression with clinical depression. This is why *all* therapy with depressed people should include helping the patient to learn to discriminate, to tell the differences between normal depression and clinical depression. This essential task should be part of the process of separation and termination in both short- and long-term therapies.

Helping the client accept gains/changes/make role transitions. As the client improves, he becomes more able to analyze his environments and his reactions to them—skills he has learned during treatment. He becomes more optimistic and is more competent, with newer, healthier, better ways of coping—in other words, he no longer has a "depressive personality."

However, many clients who have been depressed often have had life-long coping patterns that are depressive in style. When such a person is faced with difficulties, these older and more well-established patterns may well emerge and be stronger than the newer, healthier patterns of coping. If the depressive patterns begin to reemerge, it may be a sign that these newer patterns may need more clinical trials; that is, the individual needs increased practice for these patterns to dominate the older ones. It may also be a sign that the depressed client needs additional reassurance and reinforcement of the new ways of coping.

As therapy nears an end, symptoms may reappear; this phenomenon is common to many kinds of intervention. The client may grow fearful and begin to distrust his newly gained coping skills. He may express extreme doubts and try to postpone the end of therapy, especially pleading that he is not yet ready. The return of symptoms and client uneasiness should not by themselves delay the end of the therapy (Klerman et al. 1984:140).

Acceptance by significant others. Another issue in termination, and one that can be a problem, deals with the significant others in the client's environments. Long used to dealing with a depressed spouse, friend, or colleague, they have usually achieved a balance, or homeostasis, adjusting their behaviors as well as their expectations of the client's ability to cope. The longer the patient was depressed, the more deeply ingrained their adjusted behavior tends to be. Such individuals sometimes have difficulties dealing with the changes in the client, who may now be a different person with different, healthier ways of coping. Family members, unused to these new behaviors, may react negatively, even possibly sabotaging therapy. In these situations, it may be advisable to involve the family and/or spouse in an educational manner in the ending phases of therapy.

Resolving irrational aspects of relationship with the therapist (transference issues). As therapy is phased out, any irrational aspects of the client's relationship with the therapist must be addressed and resolved. Within the psychodynamic framework, this is referred to as working through the transference relationship.

Referral

If the client does not seem to be progressing in therapy (e.g., if an impasse has been reached), the therapist might first consider a consultation with another therapist to discuss the case and possibly gain some insight on other ways of working with this client. This is also the time to consider if the client might benefit from changing therapists. If so, this should be discussed with the client.

Support and Self-Help Groups

Before ending treatment, the therapist might want to discuss the possibility of the client becoming involved with a support or self-help group; or the client may bring up this topic. Recently, these organizations have grown markedly. A number of different kinds are available. *Support groups* are usually led by a professional and *self-help groups* are led by a lay person, often a member of the group. They may be open-ended or they may have a limited time frame (Knight 1990). They are often connected with a hospital and sometimes are affiliated with a national organization. Some of these groups serve individuals with specific problems, such as bipolar disorders or major depression.[9]

Support groups can be extremely helpful, but they can also be harmful. For example, an inappropriate mix of clients (e.g., recent and acute depressives mixed with long-term, chronic, and burned-out depressives) could be dangerous. Prior to making a recommendation, a therapist should get some information about these resources, including the type of group, the quality of the leadership, the makeup of particular groups, and, if possible, their reputation. We generally recommend a time-limited group, to avoid the possibility of a client becoming too dependent upon the group. We have real questions about self-help groups because of the lack of professional leadership, and we hesitate to recommend them to all our clients. We do advocate the judicious use of support groups.

Summary

■■ In this chapter we have presented a model incorporating the
■■ theories and viewpoints on depression described in parts II and III of this book. Although each of these paradigms has set forth a particular view of depression and treatment, the model we have offered is based on the assumption that the various existing treatments and treatment techniques can, and should, be adapted selectively by therapists and used in the specific situations where they have been shown to be effective. We believe that this can be done by all therapists, regardless of the treatment model in which they were trained.

We have presented guidelines showing how the therapist can make an assessment enabling him or her to judge under which conditions each approach could be used. Within the framework of our belief that talking therapy is always needed for depressed clients, we gave general indicators for using psychotherapy alone or in conjunction with medication. These indicators focused on using the most appropriate therapy for each client, for his or her particular problems, at each step in the treatment process.

Assessment emphasizes eliciting a picture of the client within the context of family and friends, education, training and skills, work, economic status, religion, goals, and so forth. We also focus on the importance of the client's significant others—on pinpointing who they are and how they help (or could help) the client, and on their role of supporting (or potentially sabotaging) treatment, especially in the termination phase of treatment.

The model highlights a democratic, ethical approach to treatment in which therapist and client share responsibility. It emphasizes providing a client with information on the therapy and on the therapist as well as inviting or eliciting client response (feedback)—in other words, helping the client to be an informed consumer of health care. Treatment options are discussed. Whenever feasible, treatment decisions are made conjointly, and there is an ongoing process of review. When referral may be indicated, we stress giving the client his or her choice, and the importance of the therapist acting as the client's advocate by facilitating the referral.

Concern for the client's best interest includes preparing the client to cope with life after therapy by emphasizing the skills that will be needed to function in relationships and work, as well as the role of support and self-help groups for posttreatment.

Ways to improve the treatments for depression continue to be sought and the existing treatment approaches are continually being reevaluated. Because of the rapid changes in treatments in general and in the depressions in particular, it is important to keep up with the literature and to be assertive in utilizing promising new approaches.

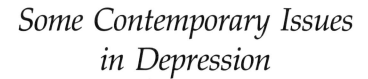

Some Contemporary Issues in Depression

In this last part, we deal with five topics: gender and depression, depression and aging, depression in children and adolescents, depression in couples and families, and sociocultural variations in the diagnosis and treatment of depression.

These chapters focus on factual information and related research. We have avoided extended discussion of theoretical controversies in favor of providing the reader with information useful in clinical practice.

17

Gender and Depression

Depression has been called a women's disease (Gold 1987b). Many have long believed that more women than men suffer from depression. Are these differences real?

The data from many sources and studies seem to indicate that in the bipolar disorders there is little, if any, difference between the genders (Whybrow, Akiskal, and McKinney 1984:182; Leber, Beckham, and Danker-Brown 1985:353). The risk of developing bipolar illness during a lifetime is practically equal for men and women, about 1 percent for each gender (Kaplan and Sadock 1990:88).

The situation is different for the unipolar disorders. The rates of *diagnosed* depression do differ between men and women who have unipolar disorders, including major depression and dysthymia. Weissman (1986) found that about 20–26 percent of women and 8–12 percent of men will probably suffer from major depression in their lifetimes. This finding was also reported in an important study by Weissman and Boyd (1983:31) and in one by Klerman (1988). Weissman (1986) further states that these higher rates of major depression diagnosed in women are true for almost all major industrialized countries, where twice as many women as men are diagnosed as suffering from major depression.

Others have stated that the rates of depression for men and women do not differ, that the apparent differences result from biases in reporting the data. One of these alleged biases is that the diagnoses are made by predominantly male psychiatrists, who are influenced by culturally accepted norms of passivity and obedience and tend to overlabel women as depressed (Chesler 1972).

Another view holds that the numbers of depressed men and women are similar but that men display symptoms of depression differently. Men use more alcohol and drugs in an attempt to self-medicate and deny; consequently, their depressive symptoms are masked. The studies of affective disorders among the Amish (a tightly knit group whose members do not drink alcohol) support this view. Here the rates of mood disorders among men and women are close to being even (Egeland and Hostetter 1983; Egeland, Hostetter, and Eshleman 1983; Thase, Frank, and Kupfer 1985:871). However, whether alcoholism in men is comparable to depression in women is debatable (Weissman and Klerman 1985:417).

In addition, more women than men seek medical help; therefore more women are likely to be diagnosed as depressed. This situation may reflect the apparent (some observers say real) willingness of women to report symptoms and, correspondingly, to show less denial than men. Since men are generally expected to be more stolid about physical illness, "male pride" may stand in the way of their seeking medical help.

Some interesting questions have been raised. In a review of four major studies, from 1947 to 1976 (two in the United States, one in Canada, and one in Sweden), Murphy (1986) has held that when these studies began, women had a higher rate of depression across all four studies and in all three countries. However, two studies observed that there was a trend for the rates for both men and women to grow closer to each other. In Sweden the Lundy Study showed a rise in depression in men in their twenties and thirties (Murphy 1986:120). In the Midtown Manhattan study, the rates of depression among middle-aged men and women were fairly close, about 9 percent in each group (Srole et al. 1962). In the 1950 study, women easily predominated over men (Murphy 1986:121); and in Stirling County, higher rates for women prevailed over the course of the study, but there was a lessening gap between the genders.

Weissman is convinced that the differences are real, not a reflection of more women seeking help and therefore being diagnosed more frequently as depressed. She observes that in community studies of people who have *not* sought help (studies that avoid the bias of reporting only self-identified cases) there are still approximately twice as many depressed women as men (Weissman 1986:11). In the NIMH Epidemiologic Catchment Area Study, carried out in five sites, the rates for major depression, over a six-month period ranged from 1.3 to 2.2 percent for men and 2.5 to 4.8 percent for women (Weissman 1986:2). A study of over two thousand relatives of depressed clients (in the NIMH Collaborative Study of the Psychobiology of Depression) showed that although the difference in rates between men and women could not be explained by a disparity in the reported number of all symptoms, women displayed higher rates of depressive symptoms, suggesting a genuinely higher rate of depression for women and not just better recall or greater willingness to report depression (Young et al. 1990).

The problems in comparing the rates for treated cases with those for untreated cases are obvious. Furthermore, it is sometimes difficult to compare data from one study to another because of the unreliability of, and the variance in, the diagnoses of affective disorders. Biopsychiatrist Mark Gold states that this labeling may be based on conclusions drawn from biased research. He concludes that although the rates for women may or may not be higher than those for men, "depression is less a male/female issue than it is a family affair" (Gold 1987b:11). There is truth in Gold's statement. Depression does have an effect on the entire family unit. Although such authorities as Weissman and Klerman (1985) find real differences between men and women, we feel that too many questions remain unanswered to decide one way or the other.

Women, Men, and the Biology of Depression

■■ One suggested cause of higher depression rates reported for
■■ women is the obvious difference in physiology, particularly hormones. However, there is very little to substantiate a link between these hormonal differences and symptoms of major depression (Thase, Frank, and Kupfer 1985:870). Weissman and Klerman find no consistent relationship between endocrine status and clinical status (1985:419). We lack studies using "modern endocrinological methods or sensitive quantitative hormonal assays" that connect clinical state with female endocrine status (Weissman and Klerman 1985:419). Although some part of the differences in the rates of depression in men and women "*may* be explained endocrinologically, . . . [particularly during the childbearing years], this factor does not seem sufficient to account for the large differences" (Weissman and Klerman 1985:419, emphasis added.)

Among the hormones that have been the focus of attention are those secreted by the anterior of the pituitary gland, including thyroid and adrenal cortical hormones and estrogen and progesterone. Dix (1985:23) points out that high levels of estrogen are associated with feelings of well-being, high levels of progesterone provide a sedative effect, and high thyroid levels "make us speedy and overanxious." When the levels of these hormones decrease (for example, after childbirth), the flow of norepinephrine, serotonin, and dopamine also decrease. Low levels of these neurohormones, which also act as neurotransmitters, are thought to be associated with depressed mood.

The physiological factors that might indirectly result in a higher rate of depression in women include a higher rate of hypothyroidism, particularly the asymptomatic forms, which may show not as thyroid symptoms but as depression (Gold and Pearsall 1983). Oral contraceptives may also play a role but probably only a small one (Weissman and

Klerman 1985:419). These contraceptives contain progesterone, a steroid hormone secreted during the later part of the menstrual cycle. The steroid hormones and a group of vitamins (B-6) compete for receptor sites, which results in a deficiency (more accurately, an increased need that is not met) of B-6 vitamins. This "deficiency" results in diminished levels of serotonin neurotransmitters, among others. As we have discussed, low serotonin levels are thought to be associated with depression. Administering supplemental B-6 seems to improve this type of depression (Kanarek and Marks-Kaufman 1991:49).

Other areas that need further investigation, which are seen to be the *cause* of depression by some observers and the *result* of depression by others, are the postnatal (postpartum) time and the changes associated with the menstrual cycle, particularly the premenstrual period and the climacterium (menopause). We shall discuss each of these later.

Parry (1989) holds that women *are* at a greater risk for depression during their reproductive years, that there is a connection between depression and the use of contraceptives, abortion, the premenstrual period, childbirth, and menopause. She thinks that hypothyroidism is associated with the end of pregnancy and the postpartum period, which may also trigger rapid-cycling affective disorders, and that a history of postpartum disturbances places the woman at higher risk for further occurrences of depression. Difficulties during pregnancy also make the woman vulnerable to other depressive reactions related to reproduction. Parry thinks that much additional research is needed to understand the links among hormones, the reproductive years, and depression. Whybrow, Akiskal, and McKinney (1984:182) believe the following biological factors raise the risk in women: "(1) Higher levels of brain monoamine oxidase. . . . (2) Precarious thyroid economy. . . . (3) Two x chromosomes (relevant if x-linkage is the mode of transmission of a genetic subtype of bipolar illness." However, Thase, Frank, and Kupfer (1985) and Weissman and Klerman (1985), among others, believe that, although these factors may cause *some* rise in depression, they cannot account for the difference in rates between the genders.

An interesting point has been made by Kovacs and colleagues (1988), who found that there was a higher ratio of conduct disorders among boys and a higher occurrence of depressive disorders among girls, *before* the onset of puberty, in other words, before the impact of hormonal differences (Thase, Frank, and Kupfer 1985:871). Social conditioning may be a factor here: Conduct disorders may be less socially acceptable for young girls, whereas the passivity of mood disorders may not be acceptable to young boys.

Female Menopause

Although previous editions of diagnostic manuals and earlier psychiatric textbooks used to talk of "involutional melancholia" (a term no longer used), no evidence seems to support an increased risk of depression in women during menopause (Weissman and Klerman 1977:106). In fact, the data show that the highest rate of depression for women occurs between the ages of thirty-five and forty-five, which is younger than the usual onset of menopause. (The average age of nonsurgical menopause in the United States is around fifty [Norris 1983:180; Dalton 1987:57].)

Weissman (1986) further points out that a number of studies in Great Britain, Scandinavia, and the United States show that the rates of major depression not only do not go up during the menopausal years but actually decline. However, some evidence suggests a small increase in the rate of depression may occur in women *over* the age of fifty-five (Weissman and Boyd 1983). This might well be due to the social effects of aging rather than to hormonal changes. Weissman and Boyd (1983) conclude that depression during the menopausal period is not a distinct entity in terms of the patterns of symptoms, their severity, or even precipitating factors.

Perhaps more relevant to the discussion of the alleged connection between menopause and depression is the work of Pauline Bart (1971; 1975), who, in a series of provocative publications, downplays the function of physiological factors in the depressions of middle-aged women. She holds that much of so-called middle-aged depression is due to role loss and other social and psychological changes that are the lot of the aging woman. (We shall discuss this issue later.)

Male Menopause: Is It Real?

The rate for depression in men certainly increases with age (Weissman and Boyd 1983:31).

"Male menopause" has received some attention recently, primarily in the popular literature and in television talk shows. A more appropriate term, however, would be *midlife crisis*. Although the aging male does experience biological changes, some of which are similar to those in the female, they are usually slower and less marked than the cessation of menstruation. The changes in men are more closely linked to social roles, individual expectations, and psychological changes. An apt description is found in the German word *Torschlusspanik* (literally, "panic at the closing of the gate"), used to refer to the "middle-aged person [who] seeks gratification while it is still possible . . . [especially] the frenzied anxiety-driven efforts of a man to make the most of his waning potency by pursuing young women" (Lidz 1968:468).

Comfort (1990:139) stated appropriately, "Men have no menopause, but between forty and fifty they are forced to reassess their success in attaining goals. The 'male menopause' is a gimmicky title for the second identity crisis in males. It has no basis in biology and merits decent burial as a phrase, for there is no male hormonal change as sharp as that which occurs in women."

Postpartum (Postnatal) Depression

■■ Most women experience some form of down mood after
■■ childbirth. These feelings have been given a number of names, including the "new-baby blues" (Weissman 1986). Typically, the woman feels "low" on the third or fourth day after giving birth, and these feelings last only a day or two. These blues happen so often that many women consider them an inevitable part of having a baby.

Most of the time the blues go away without treatment. However, sometimes they persist and may approach diagnosable clinical depression, which is called *postpartum depression*, or PPD. (The American Medical Association uses the term *postnatal depression* [Clayman and Kunz 1986:141].)[1]

In an early work, Dalton (1980) stated that about half of British women giving birth experience maternity blues, with about one in ten developing into postnatal depression. Gold (1987a:280) estimates that 70–80 percent of women experience the mildest form of postpartum depression, and 10–20 percent feel a full-blown clinical depression. This usually lasts from two to eight weeks, but it can last as long as a year. An estimated one in one thousand develop a postpartum depressive psychosis.

It is difficult to determine how widespread PPD is, for many women either deny the seriousness of the depressive reactions or feel so guilty at what they consider their own shortcomings (e.g., lack of maternal feelings) that they suffer in silence. Often contributing to their misery are the reactions of husbands and other relatives who insist they can "snap out of it." Unfortunately, not all obstetricians or pediatricians are sensitive and alert to the need to probe for these potentially serious depressive reactions.

Furthermore, the morbidity data for postpartum depression are often combined, and confused, with the broader categorization of postpartum psychosis, which may include serious mental disorders other then depression. The criteria vary, but in a summary of a number of studies,

Pitt (1982:362) stated that "severe (but not psychotic) depression occurs in about 3 percent of births . . . moderate, 'neurotic' or 'atypical depression' in from 7 to 11 percent and mild in 18 to 30 percent."

Another difficulty in determining the prevalence of postpartum depression is that the term *postpartum* is used in three different ways: One refers to the first ten days after childbirth, another to the first three months, and a third to the first six months (Scarf 1980:277). Regardless of the usage, professionals generally agree that in the first six months after childbirth, women are at greater risk than usual for major mental disturbances (Weissman 1986). One of these disorders is depression.[2]

The identified cases of PPD may well be just a small fraction that represents many unreported, potentially serious cases that go untreated. Another difficulty is that a number of the studies are retrospective rather than projected and use nonspecific instruments (Steiner 1990).

There is no relationship between social class or race and serious postpartum mental illness (Pitt 1982:370). Harris (1981), in a fascinating study in a clinic in Tanzania, found that despite a radically different culture, mothers there manifested depressive reactions similar to mothers in more developed countries. Seventy-six percent showed "overall blues"; fewer, but still a substantial number, showed serious reactions. Harris refers to studies in other cultures, such as Jamaica, which reported the same phenomenon. Dalton (1980:68–69) cites similar observations in studies in Britain, Guatemala, Sumatra, and Uganda, among other countries.

Controversies Over Postpartum Depression

The controversies over the cause of postpartum depression (PPD) and what it really is reflect the larger argument over the basic nature of depression: Is it primarily biological or is it in response to social pressures? Complicating the PPD debate is that this depression is apparently linked with, and attributed to, an identifiable stressor—childbirth. An interesting comment was made by Gold, who stated, "We may know little about PMS [postmenstrual syndrome—to be discussed later]; we know less about postpartum depression" (1987a:280).

There are conflicting perspectives on postpartum depression (PPD). There are currently four main points of view about PPD, and they overlap. One is that PPD is *not* caused by childbirth but reflects serious psychological problems of the woman that were brought to the surface by childbirth. Another view is the opposite, that the tensions of childbirth and of becoming a mother are the main, if not the only, cause of PPD. A third is that there are severe *social* stresses associated with childbirth that produce PPD. The fourth is that childbirth triggers neuroendocrinological changes not previously experienced (Dix 1985:42). A discussion of each follows:

1. *Childbirth is not the cause of PPD.* Some authorities believe that childbirth does not cause PPD, that the woman with PPD experienced psychological difficulties before becoming pregnant and giving birth. Pitt (1982:371), for example, states that the family history and the woman's individual history are the best predictors of psychiatric problems after childbirth and that other indicators have not been significant.

This view tends to dismiss the importance of childbirth as a stressor and denies the reality of PPD as a condition that by itself may need attention and that may be a syndrome. This position is indirectly substantiated by the D.S.M.-III-R, which has little in the section on mood disorders referring to PPD (1987). The term *postpartum depression* is not found in the index, in the table of contents, or in any lists of the diagnostic categories of the D.S.M.-III-R.

Although it may well be that some women who experience postpartum problems were vulnerable all along, this argument must be treated with a great deal of caution, for it has two possible negative effects. One is "blaming the victim"—that it was not the childbirth but the woman's vulnerabilities and predispositions that caused her disorder. It also lessens, or understates, the effect that childbirth has upon the adjustment, the coping abilities, and the biological and social status of women. Yalom and colleagues (1968) found that many situations that caused tears in women right after childbirth would not have produced them before childbirth. He found that in the first ten days after giving birth, women were approximately three times more likely to cry than they were in a similar time period during the eighth month of pregnancy.

2. *Childbirth is the cause of PPD.* In this view the stress of childbirth is seen as the *sole* cause of the woman's problems. This too is an oversimplification, for it overlooks the profound stresses that the new mother is experiencing, which, of course, are beyond her control.

In a sense, the first and second arguments are related. The first, by denying the importance of childbirth, holds the woman to be inadequate. The second also infers that the woman is somehow deficient in not being able to handle the "normal" stress of childbearing, which some feel is "part of being a woman."

Pitt (1982:369) characterized most of the psychogenic theories of PPD as picturing a woman who was unhappy that she was a woman, who would not accept the feminine role and thus did not experience pregnancy and childbirth as a joyous occasion but as reactivating old, unresolved psychological conflicts, particularly with her own mother. This caused the new mother to regard her child with anger and hostility.[3]

Certainly, complicated intrapsychic dynamics are connected with anything as involved and personal as the birth of a child. Without a doubt many women, especially with their first baby, worry about their adequacy as mothers and feel threatened in the presence of their baby, who is so demanding of time and energy. There may be feelings of competition, and comparisons with their own mothers, as well as identification with their infants.

3. *Social stress is the cause of PPD.* The mother experiences many stresses after childbirth, in addition to the physical strain on her body. We deliberately do not use the term *new mother,* which is often found in the literature, for a woman may not experience PPD with her first child or, at most, may experience only a fleeting period of the blues. However, with a second or third child she may experience serious depressive reactions. This may be related to a number of stressors: the reality of caring for an infant while simultaneously caring for a toddler (or two or three); there may be financial strains, or space problems (a house or apartment that is too small); the husband may have taken a second job to handle the extra bills and thus may be unable to provide support when it is needed, since he is not home very much.[4]

Although she does not overlook the biological aspects, Dix (1985:65) examines the social and psychological strains following childbirth, in essence trying to provide an answer to the provocative question asked by some women: "Why do I feel like this when I should be so happy?" Just a glance at the topic headings of sections in her book gives an overview of the many social stresses. The woman's sense of self is threatened, especially if she felt ambivalent about becoming a mother or about having another child. Many women feel trapped; feel a loss of identity; feel they do not have the time and energy to manage a household, a family, and a marital relationship that has to change with the addition of a child. They may also lose interest in sex.

These feelings are intensified by any difficulties, ranging from lack of sleep (because of the baby's sleeping and eating patterns) to colic to any of the normal demands an infant usually makes upon a parent, particularly the mother. For example, women who have difficulties breastfeeding often mistakenly feel it is because they are inadequate or not "feminine." If the child is premature or has any kind of problem and requires extra care, then the lack of time and the fatigue compound normal stress.

Another study showed that infants assessed (through observation, records, and testing) to be of a difficult temperament correlated highly with maternal depression (Cutrona and Troutman 1986). However, those mothers with strong social support seemed to fare better and they expressed greater self-efficacy (i.e., confidence in their own abilities to handle the child). As with other depressed individuals, strong social support was associated with greater coping ability. A single mother faced with raising a child alone often lacks support, which adds to her stress. Although some mothers "elect" to be single, the vast majority do not (Wortman 1981). It is interesting to note that many stepmothers also experience these depressive reactions, and it is not uncommon for mothers who adopt their children to have depressive reactions when they bring the baby home (Dix 1985:118).

The age of the mother is another variable. Childbearing may be delayed for many reasons: postponing a child until achieving some occupational success, not meeting the right man, being unable to conceive, and so on. Older mothers may bring a history of independence and achievement to a marriage, or they may be set in their ways and used to independence and freedom, which may make adapting to a child, or children, and the ensuing loss of independence more difficult than they are for a younger woman (Dix 1985:114–117). A carefully done study revealed that older women often had a greater sense of self, that their self-esteem was higher, and that they could cope better than young women with the feelings of isolation (Walter 1986). One of the most interesting findings of the study was that older mothers seemed to be much more at ease with their own dependency needs. They felt free to call upon others for help and did not view these requests as admissions of inadequacy. This contrasted with some younger mothers who did not have a history of work and achievement and regarded such requests as evidence of their lack of control over their own lives (Walter 1986:110–111).

Psychotherapists are seeing increasing numbers of women with conflicts over the need to return to work after childbirth. A woman may be eager to return, reluctant to return, or undecided about her feelings. She may see the child as exerting pressure, which may affect her attitude, inducing guilt if she takes time away from the child, which she may interpret as neglect. She often denies this guilt with the fiction that "quality time" is more important than "quantity time "(Dix 1985:148–151). These factors may be complicated, of course, by physical conditions, such as fatigue and poor health, pressures from her husband and from a job, and pressures from her family, often her own mother. Someone is usually critical of whatever decision she makes, and thus she may delay and be indecisive. A study of working-class women showed mothers working full-time were at high risk for depression, especially if they were under stress at work and/or with a partner or child. They interpreted job and interpersonal stress as evidence of their failure as a mother; this often paralleled a feeling of being trapped in negative work or interpersonal situations, or both (Brown and Bifulco 1990).

Arieti and Bemporad (1978:267–268) speak with a great deal of under-standing when they say that "male society does not know either the pain of labor or the status to which women are relegated. Pregnancy . . . keeps women in a secondary position, emphasizing their biological roles and depriving them of many opportunities. Pregnancy becomes a prison . . . [and may] lead to the death of existence as a total person."

4. *Biological stress, such as neuroendocrinological changes, is the cause of PPD.* Although social and psychological factors are considered impor-tant, there is also the view that the physiological changes of pregnancy, particularly the neuroendocrinological changes, trigger biological stresses that are sufficient to produce PPD. This prompts the question, "Are these changes, in and of themselves, adequate to set off PPD in a woman, or is it possible that the physiological stress and hormonal changes set off depression in a previously vulnerable woman"?

Hormone levels change rapidly after childbirth. Estrogen and proges-terone (produced by the ovaries and the placenta) are lower, and levels of prolactin (which stimulates the flow of milk) are higher. Dalton says that a "special sensitivity to hormonal changes *might* explain some of the symptoms" (1988).

Another change associated with depression is a marked drop in the level of thyroid hormone. The low level of this hormone could be partly due to the underactivity of the pituitary, which does not produce enough thyroid-stimulating hormone (TSH). TSH stimulates the thyroid to manufacture thyroxine. An abnormally low level of thyroxine slows down the pace of bodily functions. This produces such symptoms as feeling cold, dry skin, lanky hair, and slow pulse (Dalton 1980). Dalton makes the point, as does Gold (1987a), that a simple test will determine whether the thyroid gland is functioning properly.

Although it is true that low levels of thyroid hormone have not been firmly established as a cause of depression, experts such as Gold (1987a) consider it a strong element, possibly providing a susceptibility to depression. A low level of thyroid hormone is certainly associated with slowed thinking, physical exhaustion, and the lowered mood of depres-sion (Dalton 1980:18).

An insufficient supply of potassium can also cause exhaustion and may be due to poor diet during pregnancy or after birth or the overuse of diuretics (Dalton 1980:18). Anemia may be present, especially if there has been some pregnancy-related hemorrhaging, and this could cause fatigue as well as low rates of behavior, a feature of some depressions. This can also be detected with a simple medical test (Dalton 1980:19).

Dix (1985:48) states that after childbirth, there is actually a hypotha-lamic-pituitary collapse in which the pituitary becomes relatively inac-tive and sluggish. As we explained in chapter 7, the hypothalamic-pituitary-axis (HPA) regulates such functions as sleep and adaptation to stress, primarily through the release of ACTH, which signals the release of cortisol, among other hormones. An imbalance in the HPA axis is thought to be associated with depression.

A sluggish, inactive pituitary gland may fail to produce ACTH. Thus levels of cortisol in the blood would also be low after childbirth. At the same time, the new mother is under more emotional stress and is experiencing such emotions as joy. All these emotions are signals to the hypothalamus to release more cortisol. If more cortisol is not produced, the level of cortisol drops even lower and the hypothalamus sends out even more signals. Eventually, the hypothalamus overreacts, sending out nerve impulses to many other parts of the body and resulting in some symptoms of depression, such as sleep disturbance.

Weaning and Postpartum Depression

There has been comparatively little research, but much theoretical speculation, about the relationship of weaning to PPD. One review of the literature mentioned that there were no "endocrinologic or epidemiologic studies that dealt with a possible relationship between weaning and postpartum depression" (Susman and Katz 1988:498).

Dalton reported a higher ratio of depression among breast-feeding mothers than among non-breast-feeding mothers two weeks after birth, but the depression seemed short-lived (1971, cited in Susman and Katz 1988). Alder and Bancroft (1988) found that women who were breast-feeding, who theoretically had elevated prolactin and lowered estrogen and progesterone levels, tended to be slightly more depressed at three months after birth than non-breast-feeders, but the differences were gone by six months. The importance, the causes, and the interrelationships of breast-feeding, weaning, and depression after childbirth are not yet fully understood.

According to Dalton (1980:23), one sign that is positively diagnostic of postnatal depression is the appearance of breast milk two, and often more, months after weaning; it never appears in other kinds of depressions. The milk is called galactorrhea.

Hormones and Depression: A Real or Spurious Issue?

Weissman (1986), among others, has stated that the alleged link between hormonal changes and postpartum depression has not been substantiated by data. Furthermore, there is presently no understanding of the mechanism of any specific endocrine abnormality. As aptly put by Susman and Katz (1988:498), the relationship between these "endocrinologic changes and the coincident affective disturbances . . . have stimulated much theorizing and *some* study" (emphasis added). They make the further point that many of these studies of the relationship of mood and behavior changes to hormone changes in the puerperium (the "period of 42 days following childbirth and expulsion of the placenta" [Thomas 1989:1521]) usually focus on the first week after birth. They state that many changes in endocrine functioning, both premenstrually and postpartum, interact with each other and may play a part in these changes of mood and behavior. However, the "question of whether a correlation exists between maternity blues with its attendant hormonal profile and the development of postpartum depression *has not been carefully studied* (Susman and Katz 1988:499, emphasis added). They caution against simplistic explanations which suggest that the levels of one or more hormones could, by themselves, account for these changes and disturbance in mood. Nevertheless, they do find that the correlations between these hormonal changes and maternal blues have some support. Within the first few days of birth the levels of estrogen and progesterone drop and that of prolactin increases. However, the evidence they review is mixed. Some studies find no connection between these hormone levels; others report some evidence for the presence of high prolactin levels and low plasma estrogen.

Susman and Katz (1988:500) further speculate that PPD may be caused by hormonal patterns or changes in steady functioning that have not yet been identified and isolated. We agree with their caution against oversimplified thinking, especially the acceptance of a biological reductionism; the cases they discuss imply an interaction of biological and psychological components (Susman and Katz 1988:500). Campbell and Winokur (1985:34–35) also review the evidence for biological and biochemical factors. Although they find growing evidence for hormonal modulation of mood, it has not yet been proven; they also caution against premature closure.

Intervention in Postpartum Depression

Katherina Dalton, one of the pioneers in the treatment of PPD, states that "postnatal depression is not the same as typical depression, but a special type which needs special treatment" (1980:23).

Arieti and Bemporad (1978:80–81) contend that although PPD does not seem to differ substantially from other depressions, there is an added factor—the safety of the child. Many depressed women show disinterest or neglect of the child. Others show either phobic or obsessive fears that they will harm or possibly kill the child. Arieti and Bemporad hold that if a woman is obsessively fearful of hurting her child—is almost phobic about it—then the "danger is minimal or practically nonexistent." The mother will respond to reassurance that the problem is mainly fear of inadequacy as a mother rather than real fear of hurting the baby. However, they state that "if the patient has no obsessive-compulsive or phobic symptoms, is very depressed, and expresses or nourishes suicidal ideas, the risk is great not only for her but also for the baby." They point out that women with postpartum depressions may kill their children before they kill themselves, adding that the "greatest surveillance is necessary" (1978:80–81).

It should be assumed, until proven otherwise, that physiological factors are involved in postpartum depression. It is imperative that the woman's physical condition be medically evaluated. This evaluation must be done as soon as possible after symptoms are reported.

Dix (1985:49) proposes two treatments of PPD using medication. Following Dalton's procedure, progesterone is injected for several days after the delivery of a baby; then it is supplemented with progesterone pills for seven weeks. The theory is that progesterone injections help to avoid a drop in the progesterone level and prevent PPD. In one study testing this procedure, there was a low rate of recurrence (9 percent) among a group of seventy-seven women. Dalton uses natural progesterone synthesized from yams (Dix 1985:49). If, during this treatment, PPD does occur a week or two after birth, it indicates that the system has collapsed to the degree that progesterone alone cannot be used to revive it.

Antidepressant medications may sometimes be used for PPD, particularly the MAOIs (Dalton 1984:124; Dix 1985:52). The tricyclic antidepressants, which can take up to three weeks or more to be effective, do not always work. Lithium is usually not used for postpartum depression, although there is some mixed evidence for its effectiveness in PMS (Dalton 1984:124).

There is disagreement over the nature of postpartum, or postnatal, depression. There are still many unanswered questions about the relative roles of biological and sociocultural factors. However, from the viewpoint of the individual client, the most responsible intervention is a conservative approach. Postpartum depression should be treated as a genuine psychobiological or complex psychophysiological phenomenon. Even if there is marked physiological dysfunctioning, which may include noticeable fluctuations and changes in hormones and glands, social support and sometimes psychotherapeutic intervention are necessary.

PSYCHOTHERAPY FOR POSTPARTUM DEPRESSION

One of the first psychotherapeutic tasks is to reassure the woman suffering from PPD that she is not deficient or unfeminine; that what she is feeling, be it the three-day blues or a more serious depressive reaction, is not unusual and is fairly widespread. An explanation of what is happening inside her body, in terms the woman can understand, can be reassuring. Also helpful is the realistic reassurance that she is not "going crazy" and that effective interventions and procedures exist for relieving her symptoms.

Many new mothers need help. In addition to the stress of taking care of a new baby, they must take care of themselves and not become run down. These women must sleep enough, eat a proper diet, and find the time for regular exercise. The constant demands on the mother's time, which necessitate a realistic time-management plan, constitute another significant problem area, particularly for mothers who are single or without adequate support systems. A depressed mother might also need help formulating realistic expectations, for example, when there is great anxiety about failure to breast-feed or considerable difficulty in doing so.

Mothers with infants frequently complain of being isolated, and they often are, especially in comparison with their lives before the baby arrived. Lessening the feeling of isolation could be enormously helpful in coping both with these feelings and with the new infant. One ally may well be the woman's mother, who may have experienced these reactions herself and may be quite willing to assist. This could be a highly charged issue, but often the birth of a new grandchild may serve as the occasion for a woman and her own mother to improve their relationship.

Dix (1985:180) states that one of the best interventions is a sympathetic person just to listen and reassure. This could be a professional psychotherapist, a nurse, or a good friend (preferably someone who has been through the experience herself). The woman's physicians, usually including a pediatrician and a gynecologist, can also be helpful. If her present physician is not empathic, a woman's husband or friend can help find one who will be supportive. In addition, a number of support groups exist for women suffering depressive reactions.[5]

Pitt (1982:376) states that the prognosis for PPD is good but that there is a 20 percent risk of relapse with a subsequent child. According to his data, about 40 percent of women with PPD make "incomplete recoveries," which most likely means that although the presenting symptoms of the PPD may be eased, there is still considerable stress in the woman's life. This reinforces our view that in PPD, as with all depressions, the biochemical and physical changes are only part of the story.

Premenstrual Syndrome (PMS)

██ For many women the time in the menstrual cycle after ovu-
██ lation and before the onset of the menstrual flow is characterized by mood swings, including marked depressive reactions and
even clinical depression. These mood swings are known as premenstrual syndrome, or PMS; their description, causes, and even existence
are controversial.[6]

Johnson, McChesney, and Bean (1988), in a study of 996 nursing
school graduates (from 1963 to 1984) found that 87 percent of the 730
respondents stated that sometime in their lifetime they had experienced
premenstrual symptoms. Norris (1983) reported an earlier study of nurses
that showed such mood swings in about half of the women. Dalton
(1987), the physician credited with identifying the PMS syndrome, agrees
that these marked mood swings occur in 50 percent of women of men-
struating age.

Over two hundred symptoms have been associated with the premenstrual period (Woods 1987; Harrison 1985:11). One of the most common is depression: the blues, often severe enough to be classified as
clinical depression, characterized by crying jags, fatigue, a feeling of
losing control, and other problems. In a high percentage of women,
these feelings of being depressed stop with the onset of menstrual flow.
Yet one of the most commonly encountered psychological affects is
guilt—for somehow being responsible for these mood changes or perhaps not being "woman enough" or "adult enough" to overcome them.
This widespread guilt experience led Norris (1983:3) to begin his book
with the reassuring sentence, "Premenstrual syndrome, or PMS, is a
defect of physiology, not of character."

The disorders and the accompanying hormonal changes and guilt are
so serious that Norris (1983:45) states that about 30 percent of women
who have serious PMS will also develop clinical depression independent of the PMS. A depressive subscale of the Premenstrual Assessment Form (PAF) has greater ability to detect individuals with a high
probability of future major depressive disorder than either a family
history of depression or even a previous episode of depression (Graze,
Nee, and Endicott 1990). Often a therapist intent upon the depression
will overlook the physical and biological aspects of PMS. Sometimes the
gynecologist concentrating upon the PMS may minimize the symptoms
of a severe clinical depression, one that is often not a symptom of PMS
but a separate disorder.

According to Norris (1983:47), hormones play an obvious role in the
menstrual cycle and may be central to triggering PMS. For example,

Norris feels that birth control pills usually exacerbate the symptoms of PMS. About 60 percent of Norris's patients have taken birth control pills during their lifetime (1983:141). Halbreich, Holtz, and Paul (1988:185) state that women who used oral contraceptives report a decrease in premenstrual symptoms. They acknowledge that the pills contain high amounts of progesterone, which can themselves produce side effects, including PMS. Recent work has demonstrated that progesterone is not beneficial in the treatment of PMS ("PMS After Menstruation" 1992).

Norris (1983) holds that women who simultaneously experience both severe PMS and clinical depression must be treated for both disorders. The therapies most used for treating depression (psychotherapy, the antidepressant drugs, and other medications) will have no impact on the PMS. ECT is also ineffective for PMS (Harrison 1985:158). Norris has found that women suffering from both depression and PMS respond better to the MAO inhibitors and to lithium.

When the depression is a *product* of the PMS, the treatment for PMS will eliminate the depressive reaction (Norris 1983:47).

Treatments for PMS include change in diet, exercise, stress management and reduction exercises, hormonal treatments (e.g., progesterone), and vitamins (e.g., pyridoxine [vitamin B-6]). A British retrospective study of 630 PMS patients seen from 1976 to 1983 revealed that, depending upon dosage, from 40 to 60 percent showed good responses to vitamin B-6. If partial responses are included, the percentage rose from 68 percent with small dosage to 70–88 percent with much larger dosage. However, the investigators reported that with the partial responses there were still significant complaints. There were no side effects of peripheral neuropathy (diseases of the arteries or veins of the extremities [e.g., hands, leg, and so on]) (Brush, Bennett, and Hansen 1988).

A deficiency of vitamin B-6 produces inactivity, depression, and irritability, which is not, as originally thought, restricted to the premenstrual time but continues throughout the entire cycle. If a woman responds to this vitamin, it is a clue to examine her entire diet (Dalton 1984:125–126).

Some women with PMS also suffer from seasonal affective disorder (SAD), and they respond to the therapies for SAD, including phototherapy and sleep deprivation (Parry et al. 1990). Carbohydrate craving, a common symptom of SAD, has also been shown to be associated with PMS (Wurtman et al. 1989). (These topics were discussed in chapter 9.)

The PMS syndrome has recently received a great deal of attention. In fact, there has been increased awareness of the relation of PMS not only to depression but to emotional and behavioral disturbances, including crime and murder (Dalton 1987:113–116.) In a controversial action, the

American Psychiatric Association has proposed a diagnosis of *late luteal phase dysphoric disorder* to describe the premenstrual reactions as a psychiatric syndrome (D.S.M.-III-R 1987:367–369). It stated that the diagnosis should be limited to the late luteal phase and the few days after the onset of the follicular phase—usually a week before and a few days after the onset of the menses.[7] The proposal of this diagnostic category produced a massive reaction, not only from feminist groups but from conservative law authorities who felt that the adoption of this syndrome might, as with the defense of insanity, serve to justify or excuse crimes because the women who committed them were premenstrual.

PMS is a controversial and sensitive topic. All counselors and therapists who treat couples have seen the effect of the menstrual cycle, particularly during the period before the onset of menstrual flow, upon couples' relationships (Fitzgerald 1973). However, a good number of therapists continue to treat these symptoms as psychological. Popular mythology has long held that PMS is "just in a woman's mind." In fact, early psychological theorizing stated that PMS (also severe menstrual cramps) was due largely to women not accepting their roles as women (Harrison 1985:8). Surprisingly, some feminists similarly minimize PMS. For example, in the latest revision of the excellent book *The New Our Bodies Ourselves* (1984:214) there is only one short paragraph on PMS and five brief references in the index. Another expression of the view that everything is "in the mind" is the AMA handbook entitled *Women: How to Understand Your Symptoms,* which lists counseling as the first therapy for PMS (Clayman and Kunz 1986:119).

Women who experience the severe symptoms of PMS, including serious mood disorders, often submit to extreme measures and therapies to obtain some relief. One of the last resorts is hysterectomy, although in most cases PMS *worsens* after hysterectomy (Dalton 1987:147). In fact, severe depression following hysterectomy is a particular danger for women who experience PMS (Harrison 1985:158). Norris (1983:158) reports that depression is twice as common among women who have had hysterectomies as it is among those who have not. Ten percent of Norris's patients with severe PMS have had hysterectomies; many suffer from depression. He counsels against hysterectomy as a treatment for either PMS or depression. The rates of divorce and marital conflict are also higher among women who have had hysterectomies.

PMS is not a predictor of postpartum depression (PPD). Dalton (1980:68) states that only 26 percent of a large sample of women with PPD experienced PMS before developing the PPD. Since Dalton estimates that 26 percent is approximately the ratio of PMS among women who did not have children, this seems to indicate that PMS by itself was not predictive. However, a percentage of women whose PPD symptoms persist will develop PMS. In fact, with some women the depressive symptoms will develop with the onset of the first menstrual period after childbirth (Dalton 1980:92).

It is obvious that a careful differential diagnosis must be made in any case where a woman states that she suffers from severe depression premenstrually. If the depression is severe at *all* points of her cycle, then the diagnosis will probably be one of the mood disorders. However, if the depression eases with the onset of the menses, it is probably associated with some form of PMS.

In counseling women with PMS complaints, whether manifested as depression or as some other symptom(s), it is generally wise to assume that the problems are physical until they are proven otherwise. A consultation with a gynecologist, and possibly one with an endocrinologist, is indicated. Treatment includes proper diet, exercise, and possibly hormones. This does not rule out consequent or simultaneous psychotherapy to deal with interpersonal relations, self-esteem, and the like.

Marriage, Gender, and Depression

■■ Some authorities believe many social and psychosocial factors influence the comparative rates of depression between men and women. One of these factors is marriage, according to Weissman and Klerman (1977). The rate for married women is greater than that for married men or unmarried women, but the rate for single, divorced, and widowed women is less than that of single, divorced, and widowed men. Married women seem to be in one of the highest-risk groups for depression. However, the problem may be more complicated than it appears. The interrelation of marriage and depression is complex and will be discussed further in chapter 20.

Discussion and Conclusion

■■ After a careful review of the evidence, Weissman and Klerman (1977) have come to the conclusion that the differences in the rates of depression between men and women are genuine. They think that at the present time confirming evidence may be inadequate but that ultimately the explanation for higher female rates of depression will be found in the areas of psychosocial factors, genetic transmission and female endocrine physiology (Weissman and Klerman 1985:418).

This view may seem to contradict earlier statements that the evidence connecting genetics and hormones to depression is presently unconvincing. The relationship is quite complicated. With regard to hormones, Weissman and Klerman (1985:419) report that since newer diagnostic approaches have not yet been fully utilized in examining these issues, these connections might be found to be relevant in the future. In regard to genetic factors in the differences between the genders, Weissman and Klerman state that, "While the findings suggest that genetic factors cannot explain the preponderance of women in rates of depression, genetic factors are likely to be important in the transmission of some form of major depression for *both sexes* (1985:418, emphasis added).

These phenomena are very complex. Arriving at an understanding of differential rates of depression between men and women is more than just a matter of counting the number of cases in women and comparing them to the number of cases in men. Too many complicating factors are at work here, the effects of which we have yet to sort out—for example, greater urbanization, increased population, and longer life spans, especially for women. Although the percentage of male and female births has not changed, women live longer, so there is an increasing excess of women over men. This may affect the differences in rates of depression in subtle ways.

Among the social changes have been the substantial increase in the number of working women, later marriage for both genders, and lower birth rates, at least in the United States and many other developed countries. Rates of suicide and suicide attempts have also increased, as has the amount of abuse of alcohol and drugs.[8] Again, it is difficult to determine whether this is the result of or the cause of rises in rates of depression.

These trends imply that social or external forces are increasing the rates of depression, but much is still unknown. Understanding these trends is central to the issue of whether the sex differences in depression are real or illusory, stable or increasing (Weissman and Klerman 1985:418). What we do know is that depression for both women and men is a serious but very treatable problem.[9]

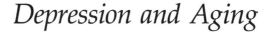

Depression and Aging

The essence of aging was encapsulated by Erik Erikson in his classic essay "The Eight Ages of Man" (1963). Erikson called the last stage of the life cycle "maturity" and viewed it as the culmination of the previous seven stages. He described a person who can accept his "one and only life cycle as something that had to be"—with its flaws, triumphs, and disappointments—as having *ego integrity.* Such a person could face death with no regrets ("death loses its sting" [Erikson 1963:268]). The person who cannot view his life with such equanimity is deeply fearful of death and full of despair. At this point there is no time to start over and try other pathways that might lead to ego integrity. Erikson calls the central conflict of this last age *ego integrity versus despair.*

Erikson's important formulation is relevant to any discussion of depression in the aged. Like people in other age groups, the older person is in a developmental phase, with tasks to complete. Too often older people are treated as if they no longer can develop or respond to treatment. (It is noteworthy that in many publications on depression reviewed for this book, the chapter on the aged was one of the shortest.)

How Many Older People Are Depressed?

We are an aging society. By the year 2000 at least 13 percent of us will be over sixty-five years old, and by the year 2030 this figure may reach 21.8 percent (Fowles 1988).

There is a widespread notion that depression, as well as other mental illness and emotional distress, is more common among the aged. No one really knows just how many of the elderly actually suffer from clinical depression, because in older people it frequently goes unseen and undiagnosed, sometimes worsening their health and even shortening their lives. Older people themselves may deny the symptoms, perhaps not wanting to appear frail. Since this often occurs unconsciously, symptoms may appear as other problems, resulting in considerable masked depression in this age group (Zisook 1989). Needless to say, unseen and undiagnosed depression is untreated. When clinical depression *is* diagnosed, it seems to be diagnosed more often for people under sixty than for those sixty and over.

Complicating any discussion of depression among the elderly is the frequent confusion of depression with dementia. Depressive symptoms may also be the consequence of, or secondary to, physical illness or overmedication, both of which *are* more frequent in the aged (Lobel and Hirschfeld 1984:45).

Recently, some experts have divided adulthood and old age into smaller categories. However, older people (usually meaning those sixty years old and more) are often lumped together in studies, which means considering a group with a span of thirty or more years as a single unit—an age range that is divided into several categories in younger people.[1] By considering older people as a homogeneous group, which they obviously are not, their distresses are not differentiated and examined to the extent of the ailments of younger people (Feinson 1985). In fact, few studies focus solely on "psychological distress" in older people (Feinson 1985).

Reviewing the results of twenty-eight measures of "psychological distress" in eighteen studies, Feinson (1985) found either no age differences in self-reports of distress or a greater incidence related by younger adults. She reports three studies where the results were mixed, with the youngest and oldest reporting the highest rates. Only three studies with three measures of distress show significantly more distress described by older adults. Three other studies reported a trend toward more distress in the older group. (Some technical statistical considerations beyond the scope of this chapter limit the usefulness of these three studies.) Utilizing two different, sophisticated problem checklists revealed that the only complaint positively associated with age was anxiety, not depression, and this was in the oldest group (over age eighty-five) (Feinson 1985:163).

In summarizing her work, Feinson states that she is not attempting to minimize the problems of older people but to challenge the belief that they have more mental health problems than younger people. She calls the idea that these problems are a part of the aging process a "scientific myth" (1985:167; 1987:710).

A Biopsychosocial View of Depression in the Elderly

■■ Stoudemire and Blazer (1985) state that depression, particu-
■■ larly in the elderly, should be seen within a biopsychosocial

model. They emphasize that there are aspects of biological, psychological, and social factors in depression. Their views provide a good framework for this discussion.

Biological Aspects of Aging

A number of conditions associated with aging may be involved in depression. One is that there may be an increase in monoamine oxidase (MAO), particularly in women. Estrogen is thought to be a natural inhibitor of MAO; hence less estrogen after menopause would disinhibit MAO. Since MAO is involved in metabolizing the neurotransmitter norepinephrine (NE), this would result in lower levels of NE being transmitted within the brain, a condition thought to be associated with depression. (The process of neurotransmission is described in chapter 6.)

Certain physical illnesses may first appear as depression or may manifest it as a secondary phenomenon. These conditions, which affect people of all ages but may be more common among the elderly, include diseases of the endocrine system (particularly diabetes); vitamin deficiencies leading to anemia (malnutrition is common among the aged); neurological conditions, such as Parkinson's disease; collagen vascular diseases (those affecting the connective tissues of the heart, blood vessels, and so on), such as rheumatoid arthritis; malignancies; cardiovascular problems, which often increase with age; metabolic illnesses; and infections, which the older person is less able to fight. Lists of these diseases may be seen in Stoudemire and Blazer (1985:565).

Several studies have shown that up to one in seven older medical patients may experience depression and that, among aged medical patients, depression occurs about seven times as often as it does among their healthy peers (Goleman 1988a.) Stereotyped thinking about the aged encourages considering sleep problems, lack of appetite, thoughts of death, and so on as normal rather than as treatable symptoms of depression. In one study, physicians did not detect any depressed aged patients, although reexamination by a psychiatric team diagnosed 15 percent as clinically depressed (Goleman 1988a). Again, dementia may be misdiagnosed as depression, or worse, depression may be mistaken for dementia.

Another serious danger for elderly people is falling. Many factors are associated with falls—for example, psychotropic medications, such as sleeping pills, antidepressants, and high-blood-pressure medication, all of which may produce lethargy and make an older person more likely to lose balance (Brozan 1988). Falls can have catastrophic effects on the health and independence—and thus the self-esteem—of older people.

A number of drugs may cause depressive symptoms, particularly antihypertensives, anti-Parkinsonian agents, and some hormonal medications (e.g., progesterone and estrogen) and psychiatric drugs. (A list can be found in Stoudemire and Blazer [1985:566].)

Older people may also be at risk for symptoms of depression if they take several medications simultaneously. These are frequently prescribed independently by different doctors, which is called *polypharmacy* ("excessive use of drugs or overdose of a drug; prescribing many drugs to be given at one time" [Thomas 1989:1447]). One study found an average of fourteen prescriptions for each hospitalized Medicare patient (Kasper 1982). These medications may interact negatively, creating problems that may not be attributed to them. As stated by one authority, the "sum total of the effects of these medications, especially in conjunction with moderate amounts of alcohol or over-the-counter preparations, can be a clinical picture indistinguishable from major depression" (Zisook 1989:3). (This happened to a personal friend of the authors, an energetic woman in her mid-seventies who suddenly appeared to be extremely confused, which more than one doctor labeled a sign of "normal aging." Her daughter, who questioned this diagnosis, admitted her mother to a well-known clinic for an evaluation. It was found that several of the medications she was taking were interacting negatively. With the change of a particular medication, all symptoms disappeared and the woman returned to her normal unconfused self.)

Alcoholism among older people has recently received more attention. Although it is difficult to determine the extent of abuse among the aged, more than a million of the twenty-eight million Americans over sixty-five are estimated to be problem drinkers. "Alcohol abuse or dependence [is] a problem for 1.4 to 3.8 percent of the men and from 0.1 to 0.7 percent of the women in an NIMH sample" (Collins 1985b). As the percentage of older people in the population increases, the absolute number of older people with drinking problems is also expected to rise.

Many elderly people may drink to self-medicate their depression and isolation (Collins 1985a). Alcohol is easy to obtain and comparatively cheap. Ultimately, excessive drinking worsens depression as alcohol acts as a depressant on the central nervous system (is depressiogenic).

Complicating both the diagnosis and the treatment of alcoholism, as well as general medical treatment in the elderly, is the association of alcohol abuse with a number of conditions, such as memory loss, paralysis, peripheral nerve problems, liver and kidney disorders and other physical problems (Collins 1985b).

Psychological Aspects of Aging

The last phase of life has its own adaptive problems. Negative cognitive changes can occur, with the elderly person accepting as fact some of the stereotypes of aging, leading to demoralization and depression.

Although earlier theorists, especially Freud, hypothesized much guilt and self-reproach in depression, later ego psychologists emphasized loss in self-esteem, which may be especially applicable to this age group. The losses of physical abilities and of support systems may readily diminish the older person's self-esteem and increase feelings of hopelessness and helplessness. Of course, these feelings are often based on reality.

Older people *do* experience loss and grief—for example, losses of jobs due to retirement and losses of relatives and friends because of death. Conway (1988) differentiates between external losses, such as the loss of a home because of fire, and internal losses, such as the loss of a personal belief system. She stresses that although external losses may be perceived and dealt with, internal losses may not be acknowledged and may be denied (1988:542). Loss and grief are inevitable, and Conway, among others, urges that they be seen as part of the normal developmental processes and not necessarily as pathological (our word). When they occur, they should be considered as problems to be solved, as they are with younger people.

All these psychological changes can result in a decreased ability to deal with the stresses of aging.

Social Aspects of Aging

The social aspects of aging related to depression include the ambiguous place of the aged in our society. Unlike societies that honor and revere the elderly (practices that are slowly fading), ours often pushes them out of mind, or into nursing homes. Our treatment of the aged makes them feel unwanted.

Complex social forces are at work here, such as increasing urbanization, increased mobility, and the breakup of larger family units. Another social factor is retirement, which can be positive if voluntary, planned for, and well financed; it can be difficult if involuntary, if money is insufficient, or if physical health deteriorates. Diminishing health alone would lessen social contacts, but far more often the death of significant others and the distance that members of the family live from one another account for the loss of social support networks. Symptoms of depression are inversely related to the existence of support systems and participation in organizations and religious activities. The less the participation, the higher the number of symptoms—and vice versa (Palinkas, Wingard, and Barrett-Connor 1990).

Diagnosis and Assessment of Depression in the Aged

■■ Differential assessment and diagnosis are important in work-
■■ ing with clients of all age groups, but they are especially
important with the aged. The basic criteria are those stated in the
D.S.M.-III-R. The major distinctions are among major depression, bipolar disorders, adjustment disorder, schizoaffective disorder, hypo-
chondriasis, uncomplicated bereavement, organic affective disorders,
and dementia (Stoudemire and Blazer 1985:566). If there are psychotic
signs, the mood disorder is very marked, and there are vegetative
symptoms, diagnosis can be subtyped "with melancholia." Major
depression should not be the diagnosis if schizophrenia, any organic
factor (physical illness, toxins, and medications), or uncomplicated bereavement is present. All the symptoms usually seen in major depression, such as the vegetative symptoms, can be triggered by disease or
medication (Stoudemire and Blazer 1985).

Zisook (1989:3) states that three forms of depression among the
elderly should be looked for: masked depression, pseudodementia, and delusional depression. He indicates that about 60 percent
of women and 50 percent of men whose first depressive episode
occurs after age sixty manifest delusions, especially paranoid thinking
(1989:10).

A careful history should be taken to the extent that the patient's
condition allows. Among other factors, special attention should be given
to previous bouts of depression, suicide attempts, number and kinds of
previous treatments (including any medication and/or electroconvulsive
therapy [ECT]), and family history of depression. Recent stressors, such
as deaths, money problems, and the like, should also be assessed. The
individual's medical history should be included, with a careful assessment of complaints about pain.

Another factor that complicates assessment of depression in the aged
is that most standard assessment scales were originally designed and
used ("normed") for much younger populations (Keane and Sells 1990).
Although some studies have stated that this factor has resulted in
overestimating depression among the aged, a more recent survey of
geriatric patients has held that a subgroup of older people may well
exist whose depressive disorders are not detected and who therefore
are not treated (Harper, Kotik-Harper, and Kirby 1990).

If the elderly depressed person has a caregiver, the assessment should
include this person, with questions asked about whether he or she has
someone with whom to talk, the elements of the relationship with the

depressed person that are disturbing, and, very important, whether the caregiver is also showing symptoms of depression (Gallo 1990). Organic factors in the aging person do not rule out psychotherapy and other social therapies. On the contrary, recent work, which we shall refer to later, increases our optimism for the utility of the psychotherapies for the elderly.

Dementia and Pseudodementia

■■ *Dementia* is characterized by the deterioration of cognitive
■■ functions, usually caused by physical changes in the brain (Billig 1987:63). There is a slow but steady disintegration of neurological and psychological functioning, including loss of memory, thinking, and concentration; these are often accompanied by disorientation. As the condition progresses, it may become impossible to carry out the activities of daily living, including dressing, toileting, and self-feeding (Billig 1987:63–64).

Since most dementias develop with age, they are found primarily in people sixty-five years of age or older, although they may appear in children as young as three or four. Kaplan and Sadock (1990:24) state that dementia is present in 5 percent of people over sixty-five and in 20 percent of those over eighty.

Many dementias are caused by physical illnesses such as Alzheimer's disease (which we shall discuss later), strokes (producing multi-infarct dementia, or MID), Parkinson's disease, Huntington's disease, and many other conditions, including acquired immune deficiency syndrome (AIDS). Some clients have mixed forms—for example, both Alzheimer's and multi-infarct dementia (Kaplan and Sadock, 1990:24–26). The symptoms of dementia (which are not always true dementia) may also result from some medications, irregularities of metabolism and endocrine malfunctioning, some neurological conditions, and depression (Billig 1987:67).

Patients with dementia may exhibit symptoms of major depression, particularly in the early phases of the dementia, making diagnosis and treatment difficult. These dementias show with generalized deterioration of intellectual skills, such as lessening of memory and abstract thinking, impairment in judgment, decline in motor performance, and diminished social skills, accompanied by a lack of motivation and a deterioration in personality (Stoudemire and Blazer 1985:568).

According to Kaplan and Sadock (1990:24), 25 percent of patients with dementia can be treated, and in 10 percent, where the dementia is caused by specific illnesses, it can be reversed. These illnesses include hypothyroidism, syphilis, subdural hematoma, vitamin B-12 deficiency, uremia, and hypoxia (Kaplan and Sadock 1990:26). They must be treated very rapidly or serious damage (e.g., to the brain) may result. The first step in the treatment process is laboratory testing to try to ascertain if one of the treatable illness is the cause. The next step is to treat any coexisting conditions that might aggravate the dementia. Eating a proper diet and keeping active are also emphasized. Supportive therapy and group therapy may be recommended for the patient, and caregivers may need support and sometimes even therapy themselves to deal with this difficult situation (Kaplan and Sadock 1990:24–27). Drugs may be used, but they must be prescribed and monitored by someone who is very knowledgeable about the drugs, the illness, and the elderly patient. Geriatric pharmacology is a specialty; older adults may differ from younger adults in dosages needed, the relative frequency or seriousness of different side effects, toxic levels, and even choice of drugs. However, at the present time, dementia by itself is not a sufficient indicator for drug treatment; this is an area that requires more and better studies (Schatzberg and Cole, 1991:329, 331).

Primary Degenerative Dementia of the Alzheimer's Type (DAT): Alzheimer's Disease

The most common and the best-known dementia is called Alzheimer's disease, categorized according to whether it begins prior to sixty-five years of age (called *presenile*) or after sixty-five (called *senile*) (Kaplan and Sadock 1990:27). There is some confusion in the literature about the correct terminology for this condition; as explained by Ornstein and Thompson (1984:145), it is now common to refer to all "senility that develops after sixty-five . . . as Alzheimer's disease," or technically, senile dementia of the Alzheimer's type (SDAT).

Similar to other dementias, Alzheimer's is a disease with an advancing decline in both intellectual and coping capacities. A journalist described it as the "theft of one's self" (Kobren 1989). The disease is progressive, with symptoms becoming more severe and more numerous, usually ending in death from five to fifteen years after onset. In fact, it is the fourth highest cause of death in the aged population of this country (Kaplan and Sadock 1990:208). Alzheimer's disease is a major health problem and often the chief cause of what is commonly referred to as senility.

The onset of Alzheimer's is usually slow and insidious. An early symptom is depression (never seen in the late stages), with crying, "sleep disturbance, suspiciousness, anxieties and agitation" (Kaplan and Sadock 1990:209). There are increasing, often hard-to-identify difficulties with thinking and memory (e.g., forgetting messages and appointments). Decreasing cognitive abilities increase passivity and lessen the person's participation in activities. In the early stages the client may show a mild *aphasia* ("absence or impairment of the ability to communicate through speech, writing or signs" [Thomas 1989:124]) and sometimes paranoid symptoms (e.g., mislaid objects may be thought to have been stolen). People in the first phases of Alzheimer's disease may be quite happy, not conscious of their increasing cognitive limitations and unaware of their prognosis. When there is some awareness of and concerns about these cognitive limitations, usually there are no feelings of guilt or suicidal thoughts (Rubin, Zorumski, and Burke 1988:1078).[2]

Age is a definite risk factor. Other potential high-risk factors, which are as yet unproven, include "maternal age at birth, exposure to aluminum, history of head trauma, deficiencies of brain choline, autoimmunity, and more" (Kaplan and Sadock 1990:28). Women are more likely to develop Alzheimer's disease than men, although this may be because they live longer (Kaplan and Sadock 1990:28). Heredity is thought to play a role. Risk, especially with particular types of DAT, is higher in individuals with a family history of the disease; twin studies show about a 40 percent concordance (indicating influence of something environmental); and a genetic defect has been identified in individuals with a family history of the illness (Kobren 1989).

Certain abnormalities characterize Alzheimer's disease, including clusters of abnormal cells, tangles of fibers inside nerve cells, deteriorated nerve cell dendrites, and loss of neurons (Ornstein and Thompson, 1984:145). (*Dendrites* are the branched part of a neuron that forms synaptic connections with other neurons [Thomas 1989:472].) The metabolism of acetylcholine in the brain also diminishes (Kaplan and Sadock 1990:28). Unfortunately, the only way to identify these abnormalities is through microscopic examination of the diseased brain tissue. At our present level of technology, a definitive diagnosis of Alzheimer's disease cannot be made without an autopsy ("Alzheimer's Disease" 1984).

We do not yet know what causes Alzheimer's disease, or the meaning of the relationship among the various characteristic abnormalities. There is currently some focus on the role of acetylcholine (ACh), the "neurotransmitter chemical at the neuromuscular junctions between all motor neurons and skeletal muscle fibers . . . causing muscles to contract" (Ornstein and Thompson 1984:146). ACh, which also functions as a neurotransmitter, is involved with memory. The brains of patients whose death was attributed to Alzheimer's disease showed very low levels of ACh. Since choline is found in many foods (e.g., in animal tissue and egg yolks), scientists are experimenting with various combinations of foods and drugs to try to increase the levels of ACh in the brain, thus enhancing cholinergic function (Ornstein and Thompson 1984:147.) Research is also focusing on the development of drugs to facilitate nerve growth.

By definition, Alzheimer's disease is a "progressive dementia in which all known reversible causes have been ruled out" (Kaplan and Sadock 1990:27). Although currently there is no cure for the disease, the symptoms may be alleviated with medication and psychotherapy. Both the patient and family can, and should be, counseled and supported (Billig 1987:64).[3]

In the last five or six years, there has been an explosion of research on the causes and possible treatments of Alzheimer's disease (Bulmahn 1990). A number of significant advances have recently been reported. Experiments have shown that certain brain hormones could block the kind of cell degeneration common to Alzheimer's disease (Maugh 1991). Next, a genetic flaw was found: a defect in a particular chromosome—a "modest bit of genetic material" inherited in triplicate, instead of duplicate (Angier 1991). Three defects were then found "at the same spot on the same gene that also causes Alzheimer's"; and these defects were shown to be passed on to several generations ("New Defects" 1991). It is still unknown if the disease is caused by this one defective gene or by others, or if there are other causes, such as viruses, toxins, or other, yet unidentified factors. However, these discoveries are accelerating the search for effective treatment and prevention of Alzheimer's disease. Wright (1991:270) cautions that this disease is a "highly complex, multi-factorial disorder in which simple solutions will be hard to find."

The term *pseudodementia* is used to describe patients who have the clinical signs and symptoms of dementia but who have a psychiatric disorder that includes perceived cognitive dysfunctioning (Stoudemire 1987). Although the term has been used with other diagnoses (including schizophrenia, Ganser's syndrome, mania, and hysteria), it usually refers to depression. The term is not universally accepted (we discuss this later), for these patients usually do not fulfill the criteria for an "organic mental disorder unless cognitive dysfunction was present prior to the onset of the affective illness" (Stoudemire 1987:2).

Some experts feel it is a mistake to think that affective illness can mimic dementia. Part of the problem is in diagnosis, because patients are not always able to cooperate and provide accurate information. Furthermore, the cognitive dysfunctions of mood disorders (e.g., of severe depression) rarely are serious enough to meet D.S.M.-III-R criteria for dementia. The term *pseudodementia* also confuses the reality that the two conditions *can*, and often do, occur simultaneously. When this happens, the depression heightens the deterioration of functioning, and the dementia usually worsens the symptoms of depression.

Differential Diagnosis Between Dementia and Depression

It can be difficult to differentiate between depressed patients with cognitive and memory symptoms resembling dementia (pseudodementia) and those suffering from true dementia.

Another confusion may be between these conditions and organic mood syndrome, which we discussed in chapters 1 and 3. Listed under the heading Organic Mental Syndromes and Disorders in the D.S.M.-III-R (1987:111–112), it is a brain dysfunction, temporary or permanent, caused by insults to the brain such as a stroke, Alzheimer's disease, reactions to medications and toxins, and certain physical illnesses. The disturbance of brain functioning, which may be transient or permanent, may mimic other kinds of depressions (Billig 1987:61–62). As we stated earlier, this condition is rare (Billig 1987:61–62).

Untreated depression in patients with dementia can have serious physical and psychological complications, including suicide and noncompliance, possibly resulting ultimately in the patient being "warehoused" in a caretaking facility. Treating depression in patients with dementia can improve their physical condition as well as their quality of life.

Clinicians disagree about ruling out dementia as a first step in making a differential diagnosis. The argument has been raised about the necessity of extensive work-ups using expensive procedures with negative side effects (e.g., CT scanning, EEG, and lumbar punctures) with patients who are relatively stable with no focal neurological findings. On the other hand, one of the treatable dementias could be missed if these thorough medical and neurological examinations and lab tests are not conducted (Stoudemire and Blazer 1985:570). When faced with this diagnostic dilemma, we agree that misdiagnosing a depressed patient who has cognitive deficits (pseudodementia) as being primarily demented is indeed a tragedy, especially when such patients are sent to nursing homes and not given the treatment that could reverse both their mood and cognitive disorders (Stoudemire and Blazer 1985:570).

Some general characteristics differentiate depression from dementia. Dementia is usually insidious: There is a lack of symptoms and the patient is unaware of the onset of the disease. Depression generally has a swifter onset: The depressed older person usually exhibits symptoms after several weeks or a few months, including a noticeable drop in mood, increased self-doubt, guilt and intrapunitiveness, suicidal ideation, diminished appetite, sleep disturbance, and decreased memory and concentration, and sometimes physical ailments.[4] Sometimes, depressive episodes have occurred earlier in the person's life, and there may be a family history of depression and/or suicide. In dementia, the symptoms are usually long-lasting; their duration in depression is shorter. Mood and behavior fluctuate in dementia, whereas in depression the mood is consistently down.

Both dementia and depression include cognitive motor and functional changes: agitation, passivity, diminishing interest in daily events, lessened concentration and energy; decreasing interactions with family, friends, and community; a reduced capacity for self-care; increased susceptibility to infection and a heightened death rate (Rubin, Zorumski, and Burke 1988:1078). In dementia, the cognitive impairment is relatively stable, whereas in depression it fluctuates greatly (Goodwin and Guze 1989:299–300).

The cognitive impairments of the depressed client are primarily related to attention, concentration, motivation, and memory. It is often difficult to assess if these symptoms are due to organic memory deficiencies or to other factors, such as reduced motivation and drive, which affect the client's ability to cooperate with the examination (e.g., by reducing responses to tests and questions) (Stoudemire 1987:2–3).

Generally (but not always), individuals with dementia give "near miss" answers to the assessment questions, but depressives are more likely to say, "I don't know." The patient with dementia may conceal, deny, or be unaware of his or her disabilities, but these are often highlighted by the depressive. In the more moderate and even severe depressions, where there is no underlying dementia, these cognitive deficits do not meet the criteria for primary dementia. Rather than use the confusing label pseudodementia, the diagnosis suggested is "depression with secondary cognitive impairment" (Stoudemire 1987:3).

Part of the difficulty in differentiating the symptoms of dementia from those of depression is that they are often confounded by physical illness. In addition, reactions to some medications produce dementia-like symptoms. Many patients with dementia will also show increased sensitivity and vulnerability to medication. A careful and detailed history and an itemization of current activities, medications, and illness are essential. Diagnosis and treatment must be done in cooperation with a physician or, even better, a medical team or clinic.

A differential diagnosis is still best determined by a clinical interview, including symptom profiles based on family history of depression, previous episodes, previous treatments, and the like. Stoudemire (1987:3) has stated that, "In their present stages of development, so-called 'biological' markers such as the dexamethasone suppression test, the thyrotropin stimulation hormone test, and sleep architecture studies do not have acceptable levels of diagnostic sensitivity and may be confounded by the presence of physical illnesses and medications." The electroencephalogram (the EEG) is not "sensitive or specific for dementia" and the DST gives positive results in over 50 percent of patients with dementia, who show no symptoms of depression. EEG sleep studies might be useful, but they are expensive and time-consuming; moreover, we lack normative information on their relevance (Stoudemire and Blazer 1985:569–570). (The preceding tests were discussed in chapters 7 and 9.)

More than one interview may be needed to make a differential diagnosis, and additional procedures outside of the therapist's province may be necessary. Differential diagnosis is made increasingly difficult when dementia and depression occur simultaneously. For example, about one-quarter to one-third of Alzheimer's patients exhibit symptoms of depression, although it is presently unknown whether depression is more common in Alzheimer's than in other long-term illnesses (Rubin, Zorumski, and Burke 1988:1078). It is obvious that a complete physical examination is necessary, possibly done by a specialist, such as a neurologist. When diagnosis is uncertain, a neurological psychologist and, if available, a geriatric psychiatrist might also be consulted. Neuropsychological testing may be required, because a number of neuropsychological abnormalities exist that are not seen in simple depression.

Unless there is a history of previous psychiatric illness, the diagnosis of an organic disorder obviously has the priority for treatment (Goodwin and Guze 1989:301). It has been stressed that if the "symptoms of one illness are the result of the other, then successful treatment of the primary illness should result in resolution of all symptoms" (Goodwin and Guze 1989:301).

In summary, the differential diagnosis of both dementia and depression is not easy, but it is essential to try to make this assessment and to determine how much each contributes to the patient's symptoms when they occur at the same time. It is important to remember that each condition deserves a complete work-up and diagnosis and that even when dementia is present, treating the depression can improve the older client's condition (Stoudemire 1987:3).[5]

Suicide Among Older Americans

■■ Suicide occurs more frequently in older people. In 1980, with
■■ 16 percent of the population in the United States over sixty,

23 percent of all suicides were in this age group. The highest rate occurs among those seventy-five to seventy-nine years old, a rate of forty-two per 100,000 (Morgan 1989:240). The rate for women peaks at sixty-five, whereas the rate for men continues to rise with age. The rate for whites is higher than that for blacks (Morgan 1989:240). Nearly thirty-five hundred white males over sixty-five killed themselves in 1982 (*Useful Information on Suicide*, 1986).

Suicide rates increased 25 percent from 1981 to 1986, elevating the rate among people sixty-five and older to 21.6 per 100,000 as compared to a total national rate of 12.8 per 100,000 (Tolchin 1989). A large part of this rise was in the white male group. The highest-risk person is a white fifty-five- to seventy-year-old male, living alone, retired or widowed, who is physically ill, addicted to alcohol, or both (Lobel and Hirschfeld 1984:46).

Suicide rates among elderly blacks are very low (Santos, Hubbard, and McIntosh 1983:57–58). However, there has been a sharp rise in the suicide rate among young black urban males (Gibbs 1984). Some have speculated that the survivor status of older blacks explains this difference (i.e., the weaker and more susceptible have already died), that they handle rage differently from younger blacks, and that they may expect less from "the system" than do younger blacks (Gibbs 1984:58–59).

The data on suicide rates among Hispanics are mixed and confusing; however, they show increasing rates of depression in Hispanics over forty-five years old. One study in New York City reported higher rates for Hispanic men than for white men (Monk and Warshauer 1974, cited by Santos, Hubbard, and McIntosh 1983:59).

Suicide rates among Native-Americans are high, but they appear at a younger age and peak from age twenty-nine to the early thirties (Santos, Hubbard, and McIntosh 1983:68). This may be a variation of the "survivor hypothesis"; the "suicide prone" probably kill themselves at a young age (Santos, Hubbard, and McIntosh 1983:68).

A frightening statistic is that the ratio of attempted suicide to successful suicide drops with age; from 20:1 (under forty years old) to 4:1 (over sixty) (Blazer 1987:4). Although the rate of suicides in older people is higher, the actual number of older people who kill themselves is small. Of course, other factors are involved here. The issues, which are complicated, involve loss of control in many areas: loss of independence, illness, feelings (often based on reality) of lessened capacity to deal with things, and deteriorating family situations. These all make the idea of suicide as a way out an active way of taking control and solving a problem—a step that may appear to the troubled person as a "rational" alternative. Hopelessness seems to be the emotion most frequently related to suicide among the elderly (Morgan 1989:242). The inability to control one's life or one's destiny seems reflected in hopelessness. Research in Seattle, Washington, showed a distinct relationship between suicide in people sixty and over and the anticipation of placement in a nursing home (Loebel et al., 1991).[6]

Lesnoff-Caravaglia (1988) states that older clients who attempt suicide have an overwhelming fear of being rescued from killing themselves and thus being denied their escape from further losses and increasing dependency. She stresses that suicide and suicide attempts among the elderly differ from those in other age groups and urges that mental health workers learn more about the interplay of physical and psychological factors in this group, particularly about loss (including the loss of identity) and elderly suicide. Those who work with older people need to be alert to the clues that they are considering suicide and must be aware of their own attitudes toward suicide. Knowledge about the client's financial resources is also very important, because it affects quality of life, which in turn affects mental health (Lesnoff-Caravaglia 1988:587).

Suicide as "Rational Behavior" for the Elderly

Many people believe that older people, especially if they are in pain, would elect to terminate their own lives, and this is sometimes true. A typical account is that of the suicide of Dr. Richard Schlatter, a seventy-five-year-old man with terminal cancer of the spine, who shot himself. Dr. Schlatter had had a brilliant career as a scholar and university administrator. After witnessing the prolonged sufferings of a close friend and colleague, he had previously told his family that he would kill himself if he ever suffered from a terminal disease, as several of his friends, in similar situations, had done. There were consequences to the suicide. Some friends were shocked and, perhaps, guilty. Others felt that "it makes . . . sense. He . . . lived a wonderful life . . . so this was his very rational way of seeing that his life ended well" (Erlanger 1987).[7]

There has been growing interest in the *living will*, a quasi-legal statement directing discontinuance of extraordinary life support measures that would keep a person alive under certain conditions (e.g., in an extended coma). The problem for the clinician, and for family members, is to decide whether, when a client indicates he does not want to live longer, such a statement is equivalent to those in a living will or shows a sense of hopelessness that reflects serious depression and a possibility of suicide. Sometimes the individual will make his decision about suicide, as did Dr. Schlatter. At other times, therapists and family members might have to make decisions about restricting the client, including his mobility, if the person seems clinically depressed.

One has to be careful in viewing suicide among older people as an acceptable, problem-solving "way out." Many older people who suffer losses and experience grief do not commit suicide. Suicidal thoughts may occur because of feelings of helplessness and despair, but they usually last only a short time (although they can recur). If the person receives some help during this period, the suicide can often be averted.

Suicide among the elderly presents a difficult situation and one that we believe will increase as the aged population grows larger. We call attention to it here because more and more people are discussing suicide as a "rational way out." Although there may be growing acceptance of suicide as a rational solution, we do not know how widespread this acceptance is. Perlin, of George Washington Medical School, theorized that rational suicides often involve the cooperation ("complicity") of adult children. The parent feels, "You would be better off without me," and the children concur (e.g., because the parent may be in pain). Perlin states that the "neutral stance in favor of rational suicide is actually collusion, as the parent is really reaching out to the child for affirmation of a desire to live" (S. Perlin, quoted in Tolchin 1989). This view was criticized as an "unsubstantiated, unjustified indictment of the families of older people. . . . [who] are the chief caregivers to the elderly. . . . [whose care] often delays or prevents nursing home placement" (Silverstone 1989).

Assessing the Risk of Suicide in the Elderly

Assessing the possibility of suicide should be a part of the treatment of the aged client. One way of doing this is to ask very directly if the patient has thought about suicide (Blazer 1987). (See the questions in the interview guide in chapter 16.) Another is to find out the extent to which the older depressive is demoralized. If he or she feels that there are no satisfactions in life and makes such statements as: "Things get worse when you get older," or "I am no longer of any use," then there is a definite risk of suicide (Blazer 1987:4).

Suicidal thoughts are usually transient, regardless of the age of the depressive. However (and this is true of all ages), there is a difference between thinking about suicide and actually taking a step toward killing oneself. There is obviously more risk with the action than with the thought. Some factors that increase the possibility of suicide are being widowed or divorced; bereavement; living alone; being retired or unemployed; being in poor physical health, particularly upon being diagnosed with a terminal illness; abusing drugs (alcohol, prescription drugs, or "hard" or polydrugs); and having a family history of suicide. Usually, the more of these factors that are present, the higher the potential for suicide. However, this assessment method is not infallible; there is an element of probability. For example, suicide is sometimes an impulsive act, done in an instant by a person who has not voiced suicidal thoughts (Blazer 1987:4).

A danger of suicide calls for immediate intervention (crisis intervention). The person may have to be placed under supervision, in a protective environment such as a hospital or, if at home, under constant surveillance. It is obvious that the means for committing suicide (weapons, pills, and so forth) should be removed. Necessary medications, such as antidepressants, should be very closely monitored to protect against an intentional overdose. Some experts recommend a "no-suicide contract" (usually only a few days long), but many older depressives will probably not be sufficiently alert for this technique to be effective. The problem must be discussed with the family. Part of the work with the family must involve some recognition that suicide is a danger in all depressions and sometimes occurs despite the best efforts and intentions of people involved with the depressed person.

Although technological advances have extended the lives of some sick people, they may well not have improved the quality of life. Tolchin (1989) believes many older people choose to commit suicide because they elect not to live a life of incapacity. There does seem to be evidence for this theory, especially since the numbers of suicides are probably underreported and probably do not include accidents and the incidents of older people who deliberately do not take medication or who starve themselves to death. Nevertheless, we must be careful before we accept this hypothesis as fact. This is an area that needs a great deal of investigation.

Treatment of the Older Depressed Person

■■ Whenever possible, intervention with the depressed older
■■ person should involve the family and even, in some cases, the extended family, friends and others—in short, whoever may comprise the support system of the depressed person.

As we have stressed earlier, a thorough process of assessment and diagnosis not only should precede work with the depressed older client but should continue during the intervention. Although diagnosis and assessment should be an ongoing process, continuing the process is particularly important in the case of the older depressed person, for a differential diagnosis is sometimes very difficult to make, especially at first. The overwhelming question here is that of possible complications of organicity.

The most common methods of intervention are some form of psychotherapy or social therapy ("talking"), antidepressant (and other) medications, and ECT (Billig 1987). These may be used separately or in various combinations. There is increasing evidence that, depending upon the nature and severity of the depression, a combination of therapies may be more effective than any single intervention, especially with clients whose depression is extended and marked by sleep and appetite disturbances (Tobias and Lippman 1988). However, as Billig (1987) points out, many of today's older adults have a greater prejudice against psychiatric help than younger people, and there may be resistance to undertaking nonsomatic, or talking therapy.

The Use of Antidepressant Drugs with Older People

The use of drugs presents particular problems with the older patient. Extra caution must be exercised because of the complications of age, such as cardiac problems and medication interactions. Although the psychotropic medications can be useful, the effectiveness and safety of these drugs is being increasingly questioned, particularly with older and weaker patients (Koenig and Breitner 1990). These concerns focus on several general areas: (1) With aging, changes in the central nervous system increase the risk of toxic reactions to these drugs; (2) the actions of these drugs (e.g., metabolism, distribution, and clearance) may be markedly different in the older person; (3) the problem of anxiety, which often accompanies depression, is also different in older patients (some of the antianxiety drugs also have toxic reactions in the elderly) (Salzman 1990).

The same medications are used with older patients and younger patients, but adjustments have to be made because of the often weaker physical condition of the older patient who may also be suffering from some illness or other organic condition. Dosage too must be considered carefully to get maximum results with minimum side effects (Billig 1987:80).

Increasingly, nortriptyline (Aventyl, or Pamelor) has been used; it has fewer sedative effects the day after administration and has fewer anticholinergic side effects (Billig 1987:80). The MAO inhibitors are used with the elderly, although precautions such as dietary restrictions must be very carefully observed (Kaplan and Sadock 1990:210). The newer heterocyclics, such as trazodone (Desyrel), fluoxetine (Prozac), and bupropion (Wellbutrin), are also used, especially in treating major depression (Schatzberg and Cole 1991:325).

Several authorities, including Billig (1987:83–85), assert that lithium can be used to prevent depressive episodes, even in the absence of manic episodes. He feels the side effects are minimal and that, with appropriate control, not only are complications few but lithium is safer than the tricyclics. Because of some aspects of aging, such as decrease in kidney functioning, the patient should be monitored closely, for the lithium blood levels may become toxic more quickly and less obviously than in younger patients (Schatzberg and Cole 1991:326–327). Lithium is also considered a useful supplement to the tricyclics and can be prescribed simultaneously with some tranquilizers if hallucinations or delusions are also seen along with mood swings. Billig feels that lithium is underused, considering its potential in treating and preventing serious disorders (Schatzberg and Cole 1991:85).[8]

Because of changes in the body's ability to process the drugs, it is recommended that beginning dosages be very small and be increased slowly and cautiously (Schatzberg and Cole 1991:325).

The sleep of many elderly patients is troubled, usually because of health problems, emotional upset, or even poor sleep practices, so physicians tend to prescribe that medications be taken once a day, in the evening. This is useful for those older patients who tend to be forgetful. As with younger patients, medication may take several weeks to take effect. In the interim, clients, or their caretakers, sometimes lose patience and abandon the medication.

Some physicians employ another, more empirical approach, which is probably more common. They begin by prescribing antidepressant medications or by using ECT. If there is no improvement in either mood or cognition, this indicates that further work-up is needed. If the client's memory improves as mood rises, this tends to verify a diagnosis of pseudodementia (Stoudemire and Blazer 1985:570). If the mood improves but cognition is still impaired, there is suspicion of a treatable dementia. If neither mood nor cognition improves, then more intensive medical examinations are indicated, to make sure that some underlying medical or neurological condition has not been missed. For example, a few patients with right cerebral hemispheric lesions appear to have deficiencies in showing affect and in understanding when others express affect. Although this condition has appeared in small numbers of patients, we cite it as an example of the necessity of a complete medical examination of the depressed older client (Stoudemire and Blazer 1985:570–571).

Medications must be closely monitored by a physician who knows about the pharmacokinetics of these prescribed drugs relevant to older patients (see chapter 10). The side effects can be serious, and sometimes the medications have unexpected effects, such as triggering mania. The elderly patient's psychotherapist has a lot to contribute in terms of observation of effectiveness and side effects and of unanticipated consequences of medications the patient is taking.

Compliance with the drug regimen can be a problem. If the older person is a resident of a nursing home or hospital, then there are trained personnel to supervise and make sure that the patient takes the medication. With outpatients, compliance must be stressed both with the patients and with their caretakers. A number of problems need to be considered, as succinctly stated by Charatan (1987), among others. One is the problem of deafness. (In patients who are depressed or suffering some degree of dementia, or both, the hearing impairment is often attributed to these deficits.) The therapist must make sure that the older person can hear the instructions and understand them. Some older patients may be timid and not speak up for themselves. Many suffer from anxiety, which also interferes with their perception of therapeutic instructions. Sometimes this anxiety takes the form of muteness; or the patient may become overly talkative, which may be annoying. A therapist must be direct, active, and willing to listen.

The therapist who prescribes drugs should be aware of their cost and how this may affect compliance. The older person may be unable to afford the drugs and therefore not buy them or may take inadequate dosages. A colleague conducting a drug study strongly suspected that one of the subjects was not taking her medication; the patient insisted that she was. The researcher later learned that this was true, but to save money she carefully cut each pill in half, and she did take the half-pills regularly.

The Use of ECT with Older Depressed People

A number of authorities are enthusiastic about the use of ECT with the aged. They believe the opposition to it is based on prejudice and hysteria rather than on data. (We have discussed some of these attitudes and controversies in chapter 10.)

Its advocates claim that ECT is more effective for the older depressed client than either the tricyclics or psychotherapy. They say that it works rapidly, often in less than a week, whereas medication takes several weeks, and psychotherapy may take even longer. ECT is thought to be particularly valuable if the client is withdrawn and has regressed, does not eat, is suicidal, or is suffering from delusions and hallucinations. It is also used when drug therapy is ineffective, although with some patients who have reappearing episodes its effectiveness stops, for unknown reasons, after the third to tenth course of treatment (Schatzberg and Cole 1991:326). ECT may be used in critical episodes and repeated depressions, often with quick results (Black 1987). However, up to 50 percent of responders to ECT may relapse within six months (Papolos and Papolos 1987:117). Thus for many clients, ECT may not prevent further episodes and may have to be combined with medication, such as the antidepressants or lithium, or both, or with booster administrations of ECT. Maintenance ECT is held to be useful in preventing relapse in older patients (Thienhaus, Margletta, and Bennett 1990). Cardiac complications may contraindicate ECT (Tobias and Lippman 1988:10).

Psychotherapy with the Older Depressed Person

The talking therapies seem to be underutilized with older clients. This may be partly due to the feeling, as we have stated, that they are "over the hill" and not treatable. However, substantial evidence indicates that many older patients respond to psychotherapy, and it should be used. Psychotherapy may be used alone, in combination with drugs, and with ECT.

The focused, short-term therapies for depression that work with younger patients also are effective with older patients (Steuer 1982; Gallagher and Thompson 1982; Thompson and Gallagher 1984; Thompson, Gallagher, and Breckenridge 1987). These are the psychotherapies described in part 3, particularly cognitive therapy (Riskind, Beck, and Steer 1985), the behavior therapies (Hussian and Davis 1985), IPT (Sholomskas et al. 1983), and group psychotherapy (Billig 1987:78).

Billig (1987:77) suggests that therapy be a combination of *dynamic* and *supportive* therapy, focusing on clients' feelings about themselves and their current and past relationships. The therapy would emphasize the coping procedures ("strengths and useful defenses") that the client has used in the past and that can be used to deal with current painful conditions or issues related to stage of life. Billig appropriately points out that there is little reason to dig up and rehash all the client's early life.

Despite the increasing evidence that psychotherapy with older adults is often effective, the literature on treating the older depressed patient is overwhelmingly oriented toward antidepressant medications and/or ECT. Yet a comprehensive approach involving psychotherapy combined with medication, if indicated, results in positive outcome "in weeks to months" for 75 percent of clients (Billig 1987:77).

Talking provides relief, and the older person often benefits from exposure to an optimistic mood. Reminiscence (specifically, a technique called *therapeutic reminiscence*) is particularly effective, especially when used within a group ("group reminiscence counseling") (Yousseff 1990).

The concept of *coordinated care* extends far beyond combining talking therapy with medication or ECT. The elderly patient is usually involved with a number of different kinds of health and mental health services. If the patient is covered by Medicare or another type of health insurance, he or she must usually deal with other personnel. The patient who is a candidate for therapy often cannot cope with a myriad of stresses. The therapist who assumes the role of patient advocate and helps his or her patient coordinate these various care segments (or helps a caregiver to assume this advocacy role) is providing a very useful service.

Hospitalization in the Treatment of the Older Depressed Person

Most elderly depressives can be treated on an outpatient basis, but sometimes a client must be hospitalized. There are several good reasons for considering hospitalization. For example, extensive diagnostic procedures might be needed to complete a diagnosis, such as ruling out organicity. In addition, a hospital provides a highly structured setting in which the patient can be closely supervised for diagnosis, for treatment of medical complications, or for interventions that need to be monitored (e.g., combinations of medicines, or ECT that cannot be done on an outpatient basis). Furthermore, some situations involve such a high risk of suicide that the person has to be hospitalized for self-protection, or, although comparatively rare, to prevent him from hurting someone else. Hospitalization must also be considered if the person is, or may be, psychotic. Psychiatric hospitalization is sometimes used (inappropriately, we feel) as an alternative to a nursing home.

Hospitalization is sometimes considered more for the caretaker's sake than for the patient's (Billig 1987; Cohen and Gans 1988). There are situations where the family members simply cannot handle the patient or have been so drained by caring for him or her that they desperately need respite (Billig 1987; Cohen and Gans 1988). A recent rise in respite-care programs for the elderly and their caretakers is lessening the need for this type of hospitalization and will, it is hoped, eventually eliminate this practice.

Discussion

■ ■ The biological, psychological, and social realities of aging
■ ■ often produce symptoms that resemble depression, but depression, demoralization, and despair, although often seen in older

clients, are not unavoidable aspects of aging. In working with older clients, one must be careful to differentiate the normal aging process from clinical depression and the dementias. Complicating this process is the number of physical ailments to which depression is a secondary phenomenon and the number of physical ailments that mimic depression.

Treatment of the conditions of the aged, including the dementias and the depressions, has improved considerably. The advanced age of a client need not be an impediment to successful treatment and management of depression. A careful physical examination and a differential diagnosis are essential for all aged clients, as is the involvement of family, significant others, and support groups.

Therapists who work with older clients must examine their own attitudes toward the process of aging, including their fears of aging and death. Often therapists fail to treat elderly clients properly because they have their own "irrational" resistances, rather than because of the realities of the client's situation. However, therapists who have previously avoided working with elderly clients often change their attitudes after being assigned such a person (Steuer 1982).

Many of the problems of depression in older clients ultimately relate to Erikson's formulation of the central developmental conflict of ego integrity versus despair. Part of the increasing work done in the treatment of the depressions, using drugs, ECT, and the psychotherapies, is based on evidence that older people (and the age limit keeps increasing) are responsive to therapeutic interventions. These treatments can help diminish despair and help achieve ego integrity in this last stage of life.

However, the elderly "use mental health services at less than half the rate of the general population" (Maldonado 1987:101). One reason for this may be the prejudice that these services should not be "wasted" on the elderly. Another issue may be the tendency to move older people from hospitals to nursing homes and from inpatient to outpatient status, where mental health services are usually inadequate (Maldonado 1987:101). Mental health professionals must advocate for the elderly, to ensure they receive adequate and appropriate care.

19

Depression in Children, Adolescents, and College Students

Depression in Children: Reality or Fiction?

■■ For a long time children were thought not to suffer from
■■ depression. The sadness and other symptoms they displayed were not considered true clinical depression. Some therapists
still believe this. Closely allied is the theory that depression in children
is not really depression but is only transitory (Hodges and Siegel 1985).
Others believe that children *do* show depressive signs but that these are
more likely to be depressive equivalents or masked depression. Some
clinicians hold that depression in children is very similar to depression
in adults; others state that childhood depression does exist but has
some characteristics unique to children (Pfeffer 1986:84).

Those who think that children do not experience clinical depression
generally hold two different views:

1. *Children cannot suffer from depression.* The basis of the view that
children do not experience true clinical depression is a misconception
that can be attributed to early psychoanalytic thinking. The original
Freud-Abraham-Rado theory is a complex set of ideas that postulated
the existence of a strong and punishing superego. A person had to
reach the stage of development of a superego to be mature enough to
exhibit "real" clinical depression. Since the development of the super-
ego occurs in late childhood and theoretically is not stable until late
adolescence, what was observed in children could not be depression.
According to this view, depression must also include an overwhelming
sense of guilt, which, it is hypothesized, cannot be found in very young
children. Furthermore, if depression is seen primarily as low self-esteem because of a gap between one's ideal self and one's real self, then
"there is great difficulty in applying this model to children" (Arieti and
Bemporad 1978:185).

The assumption that early childhood depression is not a diagnostic
entity was so firmly upheld that the authors of the leading paper given
at an important conference on childhood depression stated that they
focused their literature search on ages six and seven to adolescence

(Kovacs and Beck 1977:1–2). These investigators were also influenced by Piaget's statement that the child's use of language for conveying information does not become apparent until the age of seven (Kovacs and Beck 1977:2).

Part of the difficulty in determining whether depression existed in children lay in defining how the problem would appear in a child, a developing organism, as contrasted with a fully developed adult. Children certainly show depressive feelings. The question was whether these and other symptoms, such as sadness and physiological characteristics, were sufficient to be classified as a syndrome.

Furthermore, it was felt that some conditions that had been called depression, such as the pitiful infants studied by Spitz (1946) who were labeled as suffering from "anaclitic depression," were not really depression at all but a "deprivation reaction" (Malmquist 1977). Certain conditions, such as "failure to thrive," are considered by some to be developmental disruptions rather than true clinical depression.[1] The same might be said for the consequences of nutritional deficiencies and, of course, the reactions of abandoned or abused children.[2]

Another possible theoretical explanation of the depressive reaction in some children is that they have not completed the separation-individuation process but have instead merged with a depressed mother. They may very well show many of the signs of the depression of the mother. This is not the same as the "depressive position" that Melanie Klein hypothesized was part of the development of every infant (Segal 1979).

2. *Children experience transitory depressed moods that are not depression.* Another view is that sad feelings in children are often short-lived because the child cannot endure these painful feelings for any length of time. Children can shift their attention quickly, usually to more pleasurable matters, and they may fight depression by evasion and denial. Behaviors to ward off the pain of depression, such as hyperactivity, aggression, pretending to be happy, and so on, may not be depressive equivalents or masked depression but may be attempts to cope with the same kind of problems that produce depression in older people (Arieti and Bemporad 1978:91–92). The mixed nature of these behaviors contributes to the difficulty in diagnosing and selecting the appropriate treatment for the preadolescent child. As with adults, signs of depression, like periods of distress and sadness, are common but usually transitory in *all* children. Crying is certainly common in children, especially in younger children.

Many experts, however, believe that very young children do suffer from depression, although differential diagnosis is difficult in infants and children younger than five or six. Symptoms may very well be seen as developmental lags, failure to thrive, or "mere" sadness. Behavior problems may sometimes mask a depression, especially in older children (discussed later). Depression is usually detected through verbalizations, fantasies or reported dreams, play, and above all, outward expression of mood and observable behavior. If a child is not perceived as depressed, he or she obviously is not going to be treated for depression.

The views of those who believe that children do suffer from depression fall into two broad categories:

1. *Children show depressive equivalents and masked depression.* Whether the child in latency (or the juvenile era) shows true depression is controversial. Many children in this age group (about six or seven to approximately twelve years of age) *do* show depressive symptoms, such as feelings of inadequacy, worthlessness, low self-esteem, helplessness and hopelessness, withdrawal, apathy, retardation of behavior and thinking, sadness, supersensitivity, and appetite disturbances. However, much more common are behavior problems, school problems, phobias, and a myriad of other symptoms, including bed-wetting (enuresis). Some experts feel that many of these symptoms reflect an underlying depression, that these symptoms are really depressive equivalents. In other words, these children, especially those with behavior or school problems, are suffering from masked depression.

Depressive equivalents may include temper tantrums, disobedience, truancy, running away, delinquency, school phobia and avoidance, underachievement, accident proneness, masochism, self-destructive behavior, boredom, restlessness, sexual acting out, hyperactivity, aggressiveness, school failure, psychosomatic symptoms (e.g., vomiting, headaches, abdominal pains), irritability, temper outbursts, whining and whimpering, phobias, fire setting, and more (Kovacs and Beck 1977).

When reviewing such a list, one is tempted to ask, "If all of these are depressive equivalents, then what is left?" If the most common way of presenting depression in this age group is through masked depression, then all latency-aged children might seem depressed. What is the usefulness of the label, especially as an indicator of the need for treatment?

Confounding the issue is that some of these problem behaviors respond to antidepressants; for example, imipramine has been used to treat bed-wetting. (Although these medications are useful with some enuretics, alternative behavioral and psychological methods are preferred because they are more effective and usually have a lower rate of recurrence of the problem behavior [Schatzberg and Cole 1991:321].)

This questioning of the often confusing concept of masked depression, which confounds therapy by clouding the issue, is long overdue. Much more useful, in our opinion, is the notion that depression may be secondary to other presenting problems and thus needs treatment, in its own right, as much as the primary, or presenting, problems (Kovacs and Beck 1977:11; Pfeffer 1986:84).

2. *Children experience depression that is similar to adult depression.* Rutter (1988) emphasizes that, when assessing children, it is essential to distinguish between the normal down, or negative, moods of children and those that indicate clinical depression. He emphasizes that such cognitions as guilt and self-depreciation are a part of the diagnosis, and he further states that one cannot diagnose a child as depressed merely from a score on a questionnaire. Poznanski (1982:313), a leading authority, agrees, stating that to make a diagnosis of a depressive syndrome, as contrasted with a depressive affect, one needs a "clinical diagnosis, not a rating scale score."[3]

Poznanski (1982:312–313) differentiates between children with "depressive affect," regularly seen with other psychiatric conditions, and those with a "depressive syndrome," which fulfills the criteria for adult depressive disorders. She uses the criteria from the D.S.M.-III-R but judges the nonverbal behavior of the child to be equivalent to the adult's verbal portrayal of low feelings. To diagnose depression in the child, she thinks at least five of the following symptoms must be present: "anhedonia, low self-esteem, impairment of schoolwork, sleep difficulty, excessive fatigue, psychomotor retardation, social withdrawal and morbid or suicidal ideation" (Poznanski 1982:312).

According to Poznanski (1982:309) the down mood of the depressed child must last at least a month for a diagnosis of clinical depression. Estimates of the length of the time must come from a number of sources—for example, the child's teacher, in addition to the mother or father. Parents are often unreliable, because they are frequently not objective about their child and may minimize problems because of guilt, among other reasons. Furthermore, many parents are themselves depressed and may have either identified with their child or have withdrawn from close contact with their child. Children usually cannot evaluate their own affective state and, depressed or not, children have a distorted sense of time (Poznanski 1982:309).

Poznanski further states that in children six to twelve years old, depressed affect often coexists with other psychiatric illnesses, including schizophrenia and brain damage. Recent studies suggest strongly that children sometimes suffer from panic disorder simultaneously with depression (Moreau, Weissman, and Warner 1989). Severe psychiatric problems, including depression, often coexist with mental handicap (retardation), to a much larger degree than has been recognized (Matson, Barrett, and Helsel 1988).

Poznanski describes the affect of seriously depressed children vividly. It is not difficult to recognize these children as depressed: Smiles are fleeting and quickly replaced by a bland, frozen look of depression (Poznanski 1982:308). Children with milder depressions cannot be identified so easily, for many children are not spontaneous with strangers. Obtaining an accurate, realistic estimate of the child's affect is so important that if there is any doubt, an extended or second interview should be done.

Depressed children will appear down and unhappy, especially when talking about something sad (Poznanski 1982:309). They often cannot have fun and do not know how to play, which is their equivalent of anhedonia. Unlike most children, who openly show their pleasure in play, they may conceal, or mask, any pleasure they feel. When asked, "What do you do to have fun?" these children confused the seasons, saying they play baseball in the winter and they throw snowballs in the summer. Although all children complain of boredom from time to time, those who are depressed may do so from 50 to 90 percent of the time, showing little curiosity and inventiveness. They may sit for long periods of time in front of a television set, not paying much attention to the programs and responding very little, if at all, to what is being shown.

Relations with other children are poor, and often nonexistent. In fact, depressed children may act toward other children in ways that are bound to bring rejection. They may elicit belittling nicknames, which hurt them deeply, and then describe themselves as stupid and unpopular (Poznanski 1982). This is a circular process: The children act in ways that elicit negative responses; the negative responses lower their self-esteem, which often elicits further rejection. However, the negative attention may be better than no attention at all; it may be the only way these troubled children can relate to other children, and it may be the way they have learned to relate at home.

One study comparing the play of depressed and nondepressed fourth- and fifth-grade students showed that depressed children made more advances to other children and were approached more than nondepressed children. However, they also had higher rates of negative interchanges with other children, so they were alone more. They felt less socially adept, and deficient in a number of areas (Altmann and Gotlib 1988). Another study showed that isolation was particularly marked among boys in the fifth to ninth grades. The implication is that social isolation is a stronger indicator of depression among latency-aged boys than it is among girls of the same age (Larson et al. 1990).

It is difficult to assess the level of self-esteem in young children, especially since the concept of self is seen as developing between six and nine years of age. Depressed children with low self-esteem may try to deny or hide that they feel the rejection of other children very deeply. Guilt is also difficult to assess, but because the child does not talk about it does not mean that it is not there.

The schoolwork of depressed children is often unsatisfactory, even though they may have done very well before they became depressed. They may do well on some days but poorly on others, when their mood is low and they lack interest and cannot concentrate. In contrast to hyperactive children, who are easily distracted, severely depressed children may appear totally absorbed with themselves, shutting out the outside world.

Depressed children may show symptoms of fatigue, irritability, excessive or inappropriate crying, some somatic complaints, and retardation of both motor activities and speech. This inability to express themselves well makes it even more difficult for these children to discuss their feelings and fantasies.

Depressed children also exhibit problems in eating and sleeping. Sleep disturbances, including abnormalities that may be seen on polysomnographs (e.g., shortened REM latency), have been found in children (Emslie et al. 1990). They may describe their sleeping problems accurately but may minimize their eating problems, especially if they feel their parents may punish them for not eating.

Children may suffer from seasonal affective disorder. (We have discussed this in chapter 9.)

There is often a persistent morbid ideation about death, and some depressed children obsess on suicide. Many know what suicide is, particularly from viewing television. Suicidal thoughts are not uncommon and may be triggered by a death of someone or something they care about (e.g., a grandparent or even a pet). There are quantitative and qualitative differences to grief reactions in depressed children (Weller and Weller 1990b).

In summary, the literature agrees that children feel sadness and depression; they can even be said to become depressed. However, childhood depression is not a homogeneous clinical entity (Rutter 1988:8), and many experts have held that it is a complicated matter, as it is in adults.

The *nature* of children's feelings of sadness and depression and their extent, intensity, and duration are still uncertain. The implications of childhood depression are also uncertain. For example: Is it always a precursor of adult depression, especially if left untreated? Will it be possible someday to refine diagnostic categories, possibly by etiology, and especially with indicators for successful treatment? These and many other questions must be answered.

The Formal Diagnosis of Depression (*Mood Disorders*) in Children

Most experts agree that childhood depression *does* exist as a diagnostic entity in children. The acceptance of the validity of the diagnosis is reflected in the latest D.S.M.-III-R, where the criteria for the diagnosis are the same as those used to diagnose depression in adults. The section "Disorders Usually First Evident in Infancy, Childhood, or Adolescence" states, "Because the *essential* [emphasis in original] features of Mood Disorders and Schizophrenia are the same in children and adults, there are no special categories corresponding to these disorders in this section of the classification. Therefore if, for example, a child or adolescent has an illness that meets the criteria for Major Depression, Dysthymia, or Schizophrenia, these diagnoses should be given, regardless of the person's age" (D.S.M.-III-R 1987:27).

In preadolescents, the most frequent diagnoses are major depression, dysthymic disorder and adjustment disorder with depressive features. These children are often at high risk for suicide (Pfeffer 1986:107).

Bipolar disease is rarely seen in children under twelve (Carlson 1990:27). When it does occur in younger children, it is often confused with some of the schizophrenias (Kovacs 1989:210) or with attention deficit hyperactivity disorder (ADHD). Bipolar disorders are much more likely to appear in adolescence, and lithium may be used to treat them, although both the effectiveness and long-term effects have not been established (Koplan 1983). Children with parents who suffer from bipolar disorders are at higher risk for depressive disorders; the effects of imitation and modeling should not be overlooked here.

Depressive disorders are frequently seen in child psychiatric patients and patients with serious medical illnesses (Pfeffer 1986:107). In addition, children with dysthymic disorder are at high risk for developing a major depressive disorder; they often experience reappearing and chronic episodes and are frequently suicidal. Without treatment, the prognosis is not good (Harrington 1990).

Practitioners have been slow to use tests of biological markers for detecting depression in children. However, research is being conducted to validate the dexamethasone suppression test (DST) with children (Naylor, Greden, and Alessi 1990). When used as a screening device for depression, it is correct only about 12 percent of the time (Weller 1988), although nonsuppressors—about 50 percent of all depressed children—have a higher rate of relapse (Weller and Weller 1990a:7).

How Many Children Are Depressed?

Perhaps because of the lack of biological markers or because of the persistent idea that children cannot really be depressed, studies have shown that physicians tend to underestimate and underreport severe psychiatric problems in child patients. These same physicians exhibit very little agreement on prevalence with three other classes of informants: parents, child psychiatrists, and other children (Chang, Warner, and Weissman 1988).

Estimates on the number of depressed children vary. One study stated that using adult criteria, only one of a sample of 350 preschoolers was diagnosed as depressed—a prevalence rate of 0.3 percent—leading the authors to conclude that depression among preschoolers was uncommon. Depression was found twice as often in adolescents as in preschoolers, rising to 4.7 percent in a community sample of 150 fourteen- to sixteen-year-olds (Kashani and Sherman 1988:1). Other estimates state that community prevalence rates for major depression and dysthymia are about 2–5 percent; rates among hospitalized juveniles are much higher (Kovacs 1989:210).

In one study of hospitalized juvenile psychiatric patients, there was a high rate of rehospitalization of children diagnosed with major depression and/or dysthymia: 35 percent in the first year after hospitalization and 45 percent in the second year (Asarnow et al. 1988). Contributing to this high rate of rehospitalization is the problem of noncompliance with treatment, which in the younger children probably reflects family factors, including parental depression.

The estimate of how many children are depressed will obviously vary by the methods used to detect depression and, ultimately, by the definition of what constitutes depression in children (Kashani and Sherman 1988).

Depression as Learned Behavior in Young Children

When working with a child who is depressed, it is a good idea to find out if anyone in the immediate household is depressed. The presence of depression in a close family member may indicate some form of genetic transmission; however, it more likely reflects some imitation or modeling: Depression, and depressive reactions, might very well have been learned by the child from significant adults, particularly parents, as a way of coping. The child has a limited view of the world. What others might see as problematic or pathological, the child might consider to be the only, or best, way to behave, because it is the way presented (modeled) to him.

The family of the depressed child is an important factor in etiology, diagnosis, and treatment. We discuss family factors at greater length in chapter 20.

Early Parental Death and Depression in Children

Psychoanalytic theory has held that the death of a parent means the loss of a major source of psychological, emotional, and physical nurturing and predisposes a child to depression, or is sufficient cause for depression to develop.

Recently, the role that early parental loss plays in the etiology of depression in children and adolescents has been questioned. Some of the hypothesized changes in self-image that are due to these early losses are difficult to confirm. One theory states that if the child has positive memories, hopelessness will not develop (Tennant 1988). More recent theorists place greater emphasis on external events, including the influence of other family members, parent surrogates, and the like, in helping the infant or child cope with the loss.

In one study of the mourning process, following death, it was found that only one of forty aspects of the situation showed any relationship to depression: the degree of anxiety shown by siblings at the time of loss (Brown, Harris, and Bifulco 1986:272). In this study of working-class populations, the loss of a mother did increase the possibility of depression in adult life, but the authors pointed out that maternal deaths are actually low in Western society. In addition, factors of social class contaminate the connection between childhood maternal loss and depression. They concluded that the long-term effects of early parental loss are still undetermined (Brown, Harris, and Bifulco 1986:293).

In a comprehensive review of the literature, Tennant (1988) stated that the relation between parental loss and subsequent pathology was uncertain. He pointed out that only 5–8 percent of children experience a parental death, whereas from 30 to 40 percent experience divorce; these losses are obviously unequal. Wallerstein (1985) predicted that of children born in the early part of the 1980s, 45 percent will encounter parental divorce, 35 percent will see a parental remarriage, and 20 percent will experience a second parental divorce.

Divorce, by itself, or the early death of a parent is not considered predictive of pathology in adulthood, but the quality of the relationship with the remaining parent is an important predictive factor (Breier et al. 1988, emphasis added). The effect of the divorce seems more pronounced on older and teenaged children (Wallerstein and Blakeslee 1989).

Tennant specifies that his findings showing a lack of connection between parental death and subsequent depression have been substantiated by a number of other studies (Tennant 1988:1049). This is not to minimize the potentially traumatic effect of the loss of a parent but to emphasize that separation, by death or divorce, is only one factor, albeit an important one, in a constellation of factors. These studies by Tennant and others should make us wary of clinical overgeneralizations based on single factors or variables.

Suicide in the Young (Preadolescent) Child

Until recently, it was felt that suicide did not occur frequently enough in the preadolescent age group to be considered a problem or evidence of depression. Yet in a study in Toronto, seventy-five out of 505 children (approximately 15 percent) hospitalized for attempted suicide were between six and ten years old. The apparent high rate was attributed to a rise in one-parent families and to increased drug and/or alcohol abuse.

The definition of *suicidal behavior* for children parallels that for adults: "any self-destructive behavior that has an intent to seriously damage oneself or cause death" (Pfeffer 1986:14). *Mild suicide attempts* are those self-destructive actions that do not threaten life and do not require medical intervention, such as swallowing a few aspirin. *Serious suicide attempts* are those self-destructive actions that could lead to death and require intensive medical attention, such as jumping from a high structure.

Discussing suicide in preadolescent children presents a number of problems and issues. First, there are no government statistics on suicide in children younger than ten years of age. The data for 1981 show that suicide was the third highest cause of death in the age group fifteen to twenty-four; it was tenth for all age groups. For ages five to fourteen it was the seventh cause of death. This is eye-opening, for if there are no data before age ten, this means that the incidence for ages ten to fourteen are high enough to push suicide from the tenth cause of death to the seventh. These same data show "accidents" (many are undoubtedly suicide attempts) to be the primary cause of death in those fifteen to twenty-four, the fourth cause for all ages, and the first cause for children between five and fourteen years old.[4]

Suicides are probably underreported for a number of reasons: because of sensitivity to the feelings of the survivors, insurance, religion, and especially in the case of younger children, simple lack of recognition of the death as suicide!

Another difficulty in assessing suicidal behavior in children is that, from a developmental perspective, it is felt that children do not understand that death is final until they are at least ten years old. Many very young children engage in behavior that might be called self-destructive: "hair pulling, head banging, self-mutilation, anorexia, self-biting, wrist cutting, jumping from heights, . . . ingestion of toxic substances" and probably others (Pfeffer 1986:13).[5] Self-injurious behaviors may be found in about 15 percent of all normal toddlers nine to eighteen months old, but these behaviors decline with increasing age and vanish by the time the child is five years old (Shintoub and Soulairac 1961, cited in Pfeffer 1986:13).

Suicidal inclinations are felt to occur in children as young as two and a half to three years old. These children say that they want to kill themselves, and they have tried to jump from high places, take poison, and hang themselves. These observations are cited as evidence that "suicidal behavior can be expressed at any age or developmental level" (Rosenthal and Rosenthal 1984). Another study showed that children three to six years of age exhibited suicidal risk factors similar to those of older children: depression, preoccupation with death, parental psychopathology, and family instability, often with child abuse (Pfeffer and Trad 1988).

The idea that a child cannot be said to be suicidal because he does not understand the finality of death has been challenged. If a child expresses a wish to die, this wish makes us consider him suicidal: The child is feeling overwhelming distress, and his motivation is release from distress. Some children do think that death is reversible; a pleasant—and temporary—alternative to pain. The child may be unaware of the potential lethality of an action—for example, that jumping from a high place might result in death or serious injury.

Another problem in assessing suicide risk is that children who are thinking about suicide may talk less than adults do about intending to kill themselves. That is why it is extremely important to concentrate on observable behavior. When suicidal thoughts or intentions are suspected, the child should be interviewed, as should others involved with the child, such as the family and any caretakers, including regular daycare workers or baby-sitters. There may be little parental acknowledgment of these problems in preteen children, and sometimes little correspondence between the accounts of the child and those of the parent. The therapist must be very careful and observant.

Generally, it is agreed that the reported increase in juvenile suicide is not just the result of more accurate reporting but is a real rise in the number of preadolescent suicides. Suicide is a real and growing problem in all young people, from preschoolers to those of adolescent and college age. Many of these suicidal youngsters are depressed (Kovacs 1989:210). Teachers and others in frequent contact with children should be trained to recognize symptoms of depression, especially in young children, who often cannot verbalize their depression or suicidal thoughts (Brent and Kolko 1990:387).

Treatment of Depression in the School-aged (Preadolescent) Child

Although there is increasing awareness of the problem of depression among the school-aged pre-adolescent, unfortunately much of the literature on treatment is still based on case study and anecdotal material. A number of theories on the causes of childhood depression exist, and there are a number of treatments (Hodges and Siegel 1985:544–545). The drugs-versus-psychotherapy issues that dominate the treatment of adult depression also characterize the treatment of childhood depression.

THE SOMATIC TREATMENT OF CHILDHOOD DEPRESSION

One implication of the syndrome of childhood depression being accepted and considered equivalent to adult depression is an increasing emphasis (some would say an overemphasis) on somatic treatments, particularly the antidepressant medications.

The use of drugs with this age group is controversial. Teicher and Baldessarini (1987) hypothesize that children may well respond to antidepressants differently from adults. Hypotheses on the effects of medications on the developing brain are confounded by the reality that we have insufficient information on the long-term effects of some of these drugs on adults and our data on their effects on children are even more sparse. Based on more than twenty years of use with adults, one authority suggests that antidepressant drugs are not appropriate for children. "We may *infer* that the risks of unpredicted major developmental toxicity will probably be quite low . . . [but] careful observation of possible toxicological effects . . . will be needed" (Popper 1987:xvii, emphasis added).

Using antidepressant drugs with children also raises ethical questions, such as: What is informed consent? That is, who is capable of giving it? Can physicians ask parents for this consent when information on the long-term effects is insufficient (Popper 1987)?

One factor emphasized by a number of authorities on pediatric psychopharmacology is that the way symptoms and signs are expressed, particularly in depression, is obviously related to the child's age and stages of cognitive and affective development. Depression looks different at different developmental stages.

Furthermore, children often either cannot or will not verbalize their feelings, cognitions, and so on. Because their verbal ability is not fully developed, they may not talk about some of the undesirable side effects of the medications they take. Children may respond negatively even to low dosages of drugs because of their smaller body size, among many reasons (Koplan 1985:323). Overdosage, either through physician error, actions on the young client's part, or parental negligence, is an omnipresent problem. (The parents may be depressed themselves and incapable of administrating medication.)

The blood level necessary for antidepressant medications to be effective in children is uncertain. One clinician stated his own research showed that improvement often occurred within six weeks after the start of treatment with imipramine (Tofranil) when the blood levels varied from just below the cutoff point (150 nanograms per milliliter) to dosages about twice the amount of the usual prescription for children. He warns that the levels of medication in the blood must be carefully monitored because of the side effects (e.g., irregularities of the heart) that can be life threatening (Bower 1989:91). Schatzberg and Cole also emphasize this (1990:322).

The side effects of the antidepressants are considered to be the same for children as for adults: anticholinergic reactions, sleep problems, restlessness, and so on (Schatzberg and Cole 1991:322). For children the most serious side effects of the tricyclics are cardiac arrhythmia, convulsions, and coma—"the three C's" (Koplan 1983:324; Schatzberg and Cole 1991:321–322). Citing the possible cardiac complications of the tricyclics and the dietary restrictions of the MAOIs, Schatzberg and Cole recommend cautious trials of the newer drugs, such as fluoxetine (Prozac), bupropion (Wellbutrin), and trazodone (Desyrel) (1991:322).[6]

Papolos and Papolos (1987:124) stress that the administration of antidepression medication should be preceded by a complete physical examination, including blood tests, urinalysis, and an electrocardiogram (EKG). During treatment, blood pressure, pulse rate, and heart rhythm should be monitored. They recommend that imipramine be used with children, since it "is the most studied antidepressant for young children" (1987:124). Dosage must be adjusted to the weight of the child because of possible cardiac side effects. Medication should always be given by a parent or adult because of the danger of overdoses. Schatzberg and Cole (1991:322) in recommending the newer heterocyclics (see earlier) state, "All three are quite safe in overdose."

Not only is research on the use of antidepressants with children inadequate, but drug companies seem unwilling to develop drugs for this population. As stated by one authority, "The drug companies have already spent millions on tests proving these drugs are useful in adults.

. . . By the time we get around to asking about their effect in children, the companies' patents on the drugs are about to expire, so there is little incentive for them to spend millions more on new tests in children" (Poznanski, quoted in Van 1982).

A pediatric psychopharmacologist urges caution in using drugs: "for most depressed and unhappy children, psychotherapy, supportive measures and environmental manipulation are effective. . . . [If there are] symptoms of a major depressive syndrome, heterocyclic anti-depressants should be considered early in treatment . . . [for] melancholia responds to pharmacotherapy. . . . the final decision rests with the doctor and parents" (Koplan 1983:323). Another expert states, "I only use antidepressants for depressed children when other approaches fail. . . . Even then, I'm uncomfortable with larger doses" (Kashani, quoted in Bower 1989:91).

Kazdin (1990) thinks there has been evidence showing the effectiveness of some of the tricyclics, particularly imipramine and amitriptyline. He predicts that other medications will be developed that will be more effective but states that the treatment of depressed children should be "psychological interventions either alone or in combination with medication" (1990:148–149). Another leading authority on depression in children has said, "We're using medications more because we've learned more and we've learned that they can be beneficial when used carefully" (Dr. Cynthia Pfeffer, quoted in Shuchman 1991).

Once again, as with so many areas relating to the depressions, we encounter differences of opinion. It is obvious that there is insufficient evidence to render a definite statement. In light of these uncertainties, many authorities urge caution: "When a child is taking a medicine, you always have to ask, 'What is the alternative?' " (Dr. James Breiling, quoted in Shuchman 1991).

PSYCHOTHERAPY FOR CHILDHOOD DEPRESSION

The main therapeutic interventions with children are environmental manipulation and/or work with parents, teachers, and significant others to alleviate the child's stress. The various individual and group psychotherapies for children stem from the same theories as the therapies for adults, although most textbooks and handbooks have few references to direct treatment of depression in children. Still valuable is Arieti and Bemporad (1978); additional guidance on therapy with children may be found in Pfeffer (1986) and in Hodges and Siegel (1985) among others. Family and couple approaches are used when the child is the "bearer" of dysfunctioning in the "system" (Nichols 1988; Clarkin, Haas, and Glick 1988:118).

There are differences in therapy between adults and children. The first is that children cannot engage in abstract thinking to the degree that an adult does; the younger the child, the less the ability to verbalize, to understand interpretations, and to relate them to his or her life and problems. Clarifications and interpretations must be instantly understandable, and useful, but often a child cannot retain an interpretation from one session to be used in another. Second, therapeutic work with children should be a developmental experience in itself, aimed less at repair and more at enhancing the growth of the child (Arieti and Bemporad 1987:345–347).

Therapy is partly reliving earlier relations with the parent and partly a new occurrence that will change the way the child develops. The therapist should offer a relationship based on the here and now, with emphasis on the relationship itself. The therapist does not use verbal interpretations to the extent he does with an adult; instead he models behavior. He demonstrates to the child that he does not agree with the child's poor self-image, that he sees the child differently; and he holds this new view to the child as a possibility for the child to change his self-image and to grow differently (Arieti and Bemporad 1978:346).

Because the child is still developing, he or she is less likely to have absorbed and integrated certain ways of thinking of himself (schemas). Thus therapy may well be simpler and quicker than with adults. Trust in the therapist may bring rapid change and growth.

The controversies on whether children suffer from "true" depression or something else still continue. However, whether it is true depression, a reaction, or a combination of factors, most observers agree that many children are suffering from something. "[M]ental health professionals. . . . generally agree that about one in fifty school-age children . . . show signs of serious depression" (Bower 1989:90).

Most authorities agree that a conservative approach to treatment is indicated. Counseling, parent and family therapy, and other psychosocial interventions, including environmental manipulations, should be attempted before drugs are considered. We do not know enough about the effects of these medications upon children, and there is still too much disagreement among experts. For example, one authority found nortriptyline (a tricyclic) to be no more effective than an inactive placebo in treating depressed children, and she commented that "there's no good evidence showing these drugs work as well with children as they do with adults" (Barbara G. Geller, quoted in Bower 1989).

Adolescence and Depression

■■
■■ Although the existence of childhood depression is debatable, that of adolescent depression is not. For example, one study

showed a prevalence of 4.7 percent for major depression and 3.3 percent for dysthymic disorder (Kashani et al. 1987). (In this sample, all adolescents diagnosed with either depressive disorder also had other psychiatric diagnoses, particularly anxiety.) However, the *nature* of adolescent depression is controversial; many adolescents do display great mood swings, and often within very short periods of time. The following questions have been raised: Are the extreme down periods true depression? Are they comparable to depression in adults?

Adolescence is a time of heightened activity and frenetic movements (such as participating in loud rock music concerts) and declarations of independence and self-assertion. Adolescents frequently display uncertainty about roles, fluctuations in their views of themselves, impulsiveness, and sometimes immoderate and inappropriate responses. They are oriented very much to groups and are very sensitive to their environments and susceptible to the slights, real or imagined, or praises of their peers. They are caught in the turmoil of rapid physical and psychological changes. Part of this turbulence derives from the fact that as growing and developing individuals, they have not yet developed adequate skills to deal with loss, including coping with disappointments and rejections and loss of self-esteem. Their self-images may be very fragile. Classical Freudian theory holds that the ego does not achieve full development and steadiness until late adolescence, so that the marked moods of early adolescence mirror the "dominance of id or super-ego forces over a relatively weak ego" (Arieti and Bemporad 1978:100).

Because of their normal volatility in mood and frequent extreme and sudden mood swings, depression is often not as straightforward and easy to recognize in adolescents as it can be in adults. This confounds the problems of diagnosis of depression. It is often difficult to differentiate between the normal exuberance and striving toward independence and the frantic overactivity that is sometimes an adolescent's way of attempting to ward off a depression.

The question of mood swings and how pathological they are has been raised by Mihaly Csikszentmihalyi, a University of Chicago researcher, who stated, "If anything, it's the *lack* of both high euphoria and low despair that might be an indicator of pathology. . . . Many of the teen-agers' moods have a half-life of 15 minutes. This means that a high positive mood, or a low negative mood, is back to the midpoint in 15 minutes, whereas for adults it would take at least twice that long" (Csikszentmihalyi and Larson 1984).

Regarding the difference between the "truly depressed" and the adolescent who is displaying a passing depressive reaction, Anthony (1975) makes the perceptive comment that the usual variety is an "unstable interlude in an otherwise emotionally stable individual"; there is a reactive quality to the depressive reaction. McCoy (1982) also points out that most depressions suffered by adolescents seem reactive. For example, injuries (real or imagined) to the fragile self-esteem of adolescents may produce depressive reactions but not serious enough, or long-lasting enough, to be called true or clinical depression. Clinical depression, in the adolescent, is less reactive to the person's current life, although the depression can be an exaggerated response to very little external stimuli; the true depression seems more autonomous, with more of a life of its own, rather than an excessive response to current events in the person's life.

The concepts of masked depression or hidden depression, although controversial, may particularly apply to adolescents. Are these problems in their own right or are they the way that adolescents express depression?

Adolescents often express anger, rebelliousness, and acting out. These behaviors, which may also be exaggerations of normal adolescent behavior, include risk taking (sometimes a disguised suicide attempt), substance abuse (especially alcohol), accidents, sexual acting out, psychogenic illnesses, and talk of suicide or even suicide attempts. Other symptoms of depression, which some label masked depression or depressive equivalents, may include changes in patterns of sleeping and eating (including in its extreme forms, anorexia nervosa and bulimia); social isolation; sudden changes in behavior, including acting out or extreme isolation; hyperactivity (to be discussed later); intense self-criticism; various physical and medical complaints (including vague aches and pains); extreme passivity and, of course, a variety of problems connected with school, including school phobia, cutting classes, failing work, and so on (Kashani and Orvaschel 1988). Adolescent suicide, as we shall discuss later, is a major social concern.

Adolescent depression can be very intense and is often misread or minimized by parents, teachers, and family doctors. This can be especially problematic, for the consequences of the depression, and/or acting out, can be severe: dropping out of school, pregnancies, accidents that can be fatal or crippling, substance abuse that becomes an addiction (and may involve trouble with the law), and the ignored suicide threat that is sometimes successfully carried out.

Adolescent rebellion is often the norm for determining one's own identity; rebellious behavior is a way of separating from one's parents (McCoy 1982:41). Parents who have lived through the summer between a child's high school graduation and his or her leaving for college in the fall can empathize with the difficulties of this transition for both parents and child. Rebellion may also mask depression. Depressed adolescents who are rebellious may not elicit the sympathy given depressed adults who express depression overtly with sadness, slowness of behavior, and other known symptoms of depression. Instead, they may elicit from their parents and teachers the anger and rage of adults who misread their behavior, not recognizing the depression, masked or hidden, under the rebellion.

Another difficulty is determining whether such behavior as frequent and rapid mood swings, enthusiasms, restlessness, and extreme activity and energy so typical of adolescence falls within the normal range or is the high, up, or even manic phase of a bipolar disorder. Although the extent of mania and bipolar disturbance among teenagers is uncertain, some estimate that about 20 percent of depressed juveniles develop a bipolar disorder before adulthood. They are also susceptible to other psychiatric problems as a complication of depression (Kovacs 1989:210).

A confounding factor is that we do see adolescent flare-ups of behavior that appear maniclike. Part of the dynamic here is that many adolescents, like adults, may feel a depression coming on and will engage in a frantic burst of activity in an attempt to ward it off.

A discussion of the biology of depression in adolescents may be found in Puig-Antich (1986). He thinks that there is an effect of age and pubertal factors in the "psychobiological markers of depressive illness" but that the interrelationships are complicated and at this point in our knowledge suggestive rather than definitive. Shaffer (1986) adds that the biological markers are not specific to depression in adults. Furthermore, there may be great—and as of now, unknown—differences in these markers between children and adults that may negate their validity in assessing depression.

Adolescents may suffer from depressive carryovers from previous stages or may experience severe or clinical depression for the first time in adolescence. Depressions, and depressive reactions in adolescents, may parallel many of the causes and contributing factors characteristic of depression in adults. Yet the occurrence of these events during adolescence may be even more stressful to the growing adolescent than to the adult.

Such factors as the death of a parent or the divorce or separation of parents often deprive teenagers of consistency. This is especially true if there is a stressful custody fight and one parent takes the teenager to another town, where both the other parent and his or her peers are lost.

Becoming frustrated when seeking to lean on someone (fulfill dependency needs) may heighten a teenager's anxiety, and in an urgent need for a parental substitute, he or she might join a gang, use drugs, engage in promiscuous sexual behavior, and participate in group activities. Bemporad (1988:27) makes the sensitive point that although adolescents may well be preoccupied with sex, conflict over sex, especially in more recent years, has lessened as a source of shame and guilt. Instead, it has become an arena of competitiveness, acceptance, and exploration and of new desires for and demands for intimacy, which may worsen the adolescent's fears of rejection, inadequacy, or responsibility for which he or she is not ready.

We have referred to the adolescent's fragile self-esteem. Many adolescents, particularly those who are depressed, need great amounts of reassurance and support from others. They often cannot provide their own direction, nor can they function without this support (Bemporad 1988:266). The lack of inner resources is especially relevant to one of the chief developmental tasks of the adolescent, making the transition from home to society—be it school, army, or job. Adolescents, unlike older people, have not yet gained the achievements and the relationships that provide these psychic and social supports. When there are losses, and then new environments to adjust to, they may overrespond to real or perceived rebuffs, rejections, and testings, by the new people in their environments. In psychodynamic terms, there is a "marked narcissistic vulnerability" in adolescence (Bemporad 1988:27).

Sometimes adolescents who are, or feel, somehow different cope with their discontent with themselves, and their perceived lack of acceptance by others, by becoming depressed. Being short, overweight, or excessively ill or suffering physical symptoms (real or otherwise) may contribute to depression.

A common form of depression in teenagers is the letdown after achieving a goal (often the parents's goal and not the child's) and the feeling that it was not worth it. For example, the freshman who finally achieves entry into an Ivy League school may find out that not only is it difficult but that he does not want to be there. Failure to live up to the expectations of parents heightens a loss in self-esteem, which may result in depression or in depressive-equivalent behaviors, such as the acting out we described earlier.

Another factor that may cause depression is the loss of boundaries and guidelines for behavior. Some parents, often under the guise of love and permissiveness, do not discipline their child or apply limits. The child, allowed to do what he or she wants to do, interprets this lack of boundaries as lack of parental caring.

McCoy (1982) suggests that although such symptoms as rebellious behavior, doing nothing, and skipping school may be typical of adolescents, they may also be signs that something more is going on with the child. She suggests the following questions: "How frequent is this behavior and how intense is it?" (Implied, of course, is that the baseline, or comparison point, should be this particular child at previous points in his or her life.) "How long has it been going on?" and "Is this behavior change drastic for . . . [the] child?"

It is important to find out how long the adolescent has been depressed. Although the depression may first come to someone's notice during adolescence, the adolescent might have been depressed for a long time. Similarly, as related to our discussion earlier, the adolescent might have suffered some other problem during latency that was not recognized as depression but that, because of developmental factors, appeared for the first time in adolescence as depression. As with younger children, adolescents who are depressed may also have depressed parents.

Some Social Factors Related to Depression

Social factors are relevant to the development of depression. We shall list a few: The percentage of families headed by one parent, usually the mother, has increased. In 1980, over 82 percent of white children and over 42 percent of black children lived with both parents. By 1988 this had dropped to 79 percent of white and fewer than 40 percent of black children (Johnson 1989). Furthermore, in 1987 one in five school-age children and one in four preschoolers lived in poverty, and the rate of poor black and Hispanic children was estimated to be from two to three times that of white children.

The percentage of babies born to unmarried women increased sixfold from 1950 to 1986—from 142,000 to 878,000. Having a child without the psychological and financial support of a husband or a committed partner is an understandable cause of depression (Johnson 1989).

Violence, often closely interwoven with depression, has also increased for both blacks and whites. Between the ages of fifteen and nineteen, black males die by homicide, execution, or police action at the rate of 51.5 per 100,000 as compared to 8.6 per 100,000 for white males. Among black males twenty to twenty-four years of age, the rate jumps to 107.7 per 100,000.

Drugs and Adolescent Depression

The use of the drugs of abuse during the teenage years has increased enormously. The overuse of drugs among teenagers is related to a number of factors, such as adolescent feelings of loneliness and isolation, often part of a reality that adolescents find intolerable. Drugs are used not only as an escape from this reality but often in an attempt (as is hyperactivity) to deal with an oncoming or underlying depression. One unfortunate characteristic of both hyperactivity and drug use to deal with depression is that the person is unaware that depression underlies the discomfort or unhappiness, which means the depression goes treated.

Drugs are usually ineffective in warding off the depression and may themselves deepen the feelings of depression. This is certainly true of alcohol, the drug most abused by adolescents. Marijuana can also be depressiogenic, as is crack, a product of cocaine. Cessation or treatment of the drug abuse, as a first step, is only part of the therapy that must explore the coping styles of the individual (Nicholi 1988a). (Substance abuse was discussed at greater length in chapter 10.)

Adolescence and Suicide

Adolescent suicide and depression are national problems of epidemic proportions.[7] A combination of social forces puts the young under stress, alienates them, causes them to feel that they cannot live up to high expectations imposed by others, extends adolescence, triggers feelings of nonsupport from families, results in increased use of drugs and alcohol, and increases inability to cope with internal and external problems. These factors all make for an "impressively dangerous formula for self-destruction among our youth" (Curran 1987:11).

Suicide and suicide attempts are an increasingly common part of adolescence. The suicide rate for youths fifteen to twenty-four years old rose more than 230 percent between 1960 and 1980 (Gutstein and Rudd 1988). From another perspective, there has been a two- to threefold increase in suicide in youths aged fifteen to nineteen (Mack 1989:222).

Even though suicide is the second leading cause of death in the fifteen to twenty-four age group, second only to accidents, it is widely accepted that the number of suicides and suicide attempts is significantly underreported by doctors, family members, and clergy. Suicide is still considered sinful in some religions, and surviving family members who practice such religions often feel guilt and shame. This underreporting makes the official suicide statistics even more frightening. One source says that for every death that becomes an official statistic there may be as many as ten to sixty suicide attempts. Rates of attempted suicides for adolescents are, at a minimum, ten times higher than those of completed suicides in all groups. According to one estimate, from 250,000 to 500,000 nonfatal attempts per year occur in the fifteen- to twenty-four-year age group (Gutstein and Rudd 1988:5). A different estimate states that 220 attempts are made for every successful suicide (McIntire, Angle, and Schlicht 1980, cited in Curran 1987). Another source holds that about five thousand young people between the ages of fifteen and twenty-five kill themselves annually and that the rate of completed adolescent suicide has tripled in the last thirty years, exceeded only by accidents and homicides (Moore 1986:4).

A community prevalence study of youths twelve to sixteen years old in Ontario, Canada, showed that 5–10 percent of the males and 10–20 percent of the females reported suicidal behavior in a six-month period. This behavior was linked to psychiatric disorders, family disorganization, and parents' arrest (Joffee, Offord, and Boyle 1988). A study in Montreal showed that in a sample of youths ten to nineteen years old, the mean incidence of suicide was 5.92 per 100,000 (males, 9.52; females, 2.32). Suicide in ages fifteen to nineteen was ten times that in ages ten to fourteen, a constant difference across sex and time period. These observations hold in other studies (Cheifetz et al. 1987).

One fact is consistent: The number of adolescent females who *attempt* suicide is far greater than that for adolescent males. (The ratio is usually estimated at from 3:1 to 4:1, although some studies have it as high as 9:1 or 10:1.) However, more adolescent males *complete* suicide. This is largely a function of the method. Young women overwhelmingly choose self-ingestion of poison or sometimes one of the over-the-counter painkillers such as aspirin (which does not lessen the seriousness of the behavior). Males overwhelming choose firearms, hanging, automobiles, or jumping from heights. One-car accidents are particularly suspect, and of all suicide attempts, these are probably the most underreported. Unfortunately, the gap between attempted suicides and completed (successful) suicides is closing for adolescent girls. These generalizations apply to children of all social classes and social strata.

Adolescent suicide cannot be compared directly with adult suicide. The ratio of attempts to completions is much higher for adolescents than for adults. Many of the attempts by adolescents have been described as nonlethal, since the intent, on some level, is not to kill oneself. (Attempting suicide, however, is an extreme form of coping or problem solving.)

This is not meant to minimize the seriousness of this kind of behavior. In our opinion, one of the most destructive and least useful phrases in the whole psychiatric vocabulary is *suicide gesture*. The difference between an attempted suicide (a gesture) and a completed suicide sometimes depends on chance. An adolescent may take an overdose of pills in the afternoon, knowing that his or her parents will be home soon; however, this may be the night they stay out very late. The expression *suicide* (or *suicidal*) *gesture* should be banished from the professional vocabulary.

Bemporad (1988) states that suicide and such behaviors as substance abuse, membership in cults and gangs, obedience to a charismatic leader, promiscuity for the sake of acceptance, and criminal acts may be connected. They must all be considered grave, even those that are self-limited and reactive. One purpose of therapy in these situations is to prevent the adolescent from either performing an irrevocable act or becoming so committed to an "eventually harmful solution" that it acquires a momentum of its own and cannot be stopped. The therapist must help the patient keep his options open until the "dysphoria passes of its own accord" (Bemporad 1988:27).

Adolescents are knowledgeable about suicide, as vividly reported by Curran (1987) in a superb discussion of the phenomenon of adolescent suicide. In addition to what they learn from the media, most adolescents either personally know, or know of, someone who has attempted self-destruction or succeeded at it. Suicide, as a way of problem solving, has often been modeled: During interviews, many adolescents mention suicide as a possible way out of whatever personal difficulties they may be in. This consideration of suicide as a way to solve problems is by no means limited to adolescents who are "disturbed." Furthermore, there is an element of contagion. In the early part of the 1980s there were waves of suicides, almost epidemiclike, in such disparate places as Plano, Texas, and the exclusive North Shore suburbs of Chicago—the latter labeled a "suicide belt." [8]

Suicidal behavior may be the expression of very serious personal problems and may have been considered (perhaps not always consciously) for some time as a way of resolving problems and ending pain. This means that suicidal talk must always be taken seriously. Contrary to erroneous beliefs still found in professional circles, those who talk about it often *do* attempt it.

It is sometimes possible to identify a particular stress that may trigger suicide, but more often than not, this identifiable stressor may be the proverbial "straw that broke the camel's back." One study reported that the problems seen most frequently in those attempting suicide were school problems, problems with parents (often including faulty communication), strained relations with friends, and difficulties with the opposite sex (Spirito, Overholser, and Stark 1989).

Cohen classifies youth suicide according to three types: The first are primarily conduct disorders, often with drug abuse and mostly with males. Second are "pure" depressives, mostly female. The third are "hard-striving perfectionists," primarily male, who experience severe anxiety in any social or academic situation (Cohen, quoted by Holden 1986:839).

There are a number of warning signs: changes in interests, behavior, and mood; threat of suicide; lethargy; social withdrawal; substance abuse; sexual acting out; conflict with authorities; school problems, particularly falling grades; previous attempts at suicide; reckless behavior, often resulting in accidents; recent death in the family; repressed anger; depression or somatic symptoms; disruptions in close relationships; and the giving away of prized possessions, such as one's stereo system.

Referring to this last sign, Curran (1987:139) states that although giving away one's possessions is mentioned in all books on adolescent suicide, he has rarely seen it. He feels that it does not occur, at least not as often as is supposed, because most adolescent suicidal behavior is impulsive, without much planning, and because the adolescent may have a strong desire not to die. Curran acknowledges that when it does occur, the behavior should be taken very seriously; if it does not occur, however, one should not be lulled into thinking that suicide is unlikely.

Some have suggested that many adolescents attempt suicide in essentially nonlethal ways, for they do not conceive of death as permanent. Chronologically, adolescents should be able to think of death as permanent, but sometimes anxiety, denial, or both interfere with the adolescent grasping the significance of self-destructive behavior.

There are some myths about adolescence and suicide. Curran (1987:140–141) lists the following, along with rebuttals: (1) *If an adolescent has decided upon suicide, nothing can be done to stop him or her.* Actually, most desire to continue living but are disheartened and looking for encouragement. (2) *Those who fail once will inevitably succeed.* The data show that only 1–2 percent succeed in another attempt during the first year, and only 10 percent succeed within ten years. (3) *Talking about suicide will encourage it.* The contrary is true; talking often relieves these feelings. (4) *Adolescents who commit suicide come from certain types of backgrounds (e.g., poor families or families with mental illness) or have certain personality types.* The truth is that they come from many different backgrounds and from all social classes. This is related to the following myth: (5) *People seeing therapists will not commit suicide.* Being in therapy, unfortunately, is no guarantee against an eventually successful suicide. Linked to this false belief is another myth: (6) *Only professionals can detect a likely suicide.* Most individuals, especially adolescents, communicate their intentions to others, including their friends, family members, and teachers.

Suicide is seldom an individual act; it often reflects the pathology in a system (Arieti and Bemporad 1978:347). Yet in the current emphasis on family therapy and systems theory, the adolescent suicide attempt seems to be downplayed, being viewed as manipulative of the family system. Often the adolescent is seen as a messenger for the system and the suicide act is considered symbolic of, or symptomatic of, some dysfunctioning in the system. This may all be true, but adolescents can, and have, died from these "symbolic gestures." Regardless of whether their acts are symbolic of, or communications for, the family system, the act has sufficient potential for lethality that it should be viewed as a problem in its own right.

Many adolescents who attempt suicide are depressed, and their number is almost certainly underestimated. On the other hand, some authorities question the relationship of depression to this rising rate of suicide. Findings of a study of 160 youths in New York City showed that the majority of victims did not fulfill the D.S.M.-III criteria for depression but were heavily involved in antisocial behavior (frequently simultaneously using drugs) and that suicide was a response to these social difficulties rather than to a clinical depression. Only one-fifth of this sample fulfilled the criteria for diagnosis of depression. Furthermore, the preponderance of the sample did not show extended brooding behavior (David Shaffer, cited in Holden 1986). Part of the problem in reading these studies is that some, like Shaffer's, are based on community surveys that do not pay sufficient attention to the differences between individuals. Others, probably the majority cited in the psychiatric literature, are based on small, intensive case studies or control comparisons (Shaffi et al. 1988).

Treating the Depressed Adolescent

SUICIDE PREVENTION

The immediate emphasis in psychotherapy with adolescents is often suicide prevention. This reflects the reality that in the last thirty years suicide among adolescents has increased an estimated 300 percent (Sargent 1989). It is also a measure of the extent to which, understandably, suicide frightens parents, teachers, and others. When there has been a suicidal threat or attempt, the therapist must consider the lethality of the act: Has the client spoken of his plan to anyone? Is the method chosen very deadly (e.g., shooting)? How much secrecy was involved? (See the questions in the Interview Guide, chapter 16.)

As with all depressives, it might be necessary to consider hospitalization if the client is actively suicidal, the symptoms are severe, and there is a need for maximum control and security (Meeks 1980). Although hospitalization may temporarily alleviate the danger of suicide, risk may increase after discharge.

If therapy is to be on an outpatient basis, it may be necessary to involve the client and family in a cooperative effort to prevent suicide (Meeks 1980). It may be necessary to "sterilize the home," removing, to the extent possible, all potentially lethal materials, and to have someone there most of the time. If medication is used, it must be monitored carefully, and care must be exercised to control access to medications and to guard against the obvious potential of self-poisoning.

Meeks (1980) makes the very useful suggestion that it is helpful for a therapist to consult with an objective, noninvolved colleague regarding the management of a case involving a potential suicide. In addition, it will probably be necessary for a nonphysician therapist to consult with a psychiatrist knowledgeable about adolescents about the possible need for medication or hospitalization.

BEHAVIORAL AND COGNITIVE-BEHAVIORAL APPROACHES

Behavioral and cognitive-behavioral techniques, such as cognitive restructuring and skill building, are useful in intervention with the adolescent. These techniques should be used within a therapeutic understanding that the adolescent client is often undergoing a stressful phase of development. In other words, just as therapy with the younger depressed child is developmentally oriented, so is psychotherapy with the adolescent.

The therapeutic environment should be one of firmness, with set boundaries, which we feel are also compatible with acceptance and empathy. There must be flexibility, with an emphasis on enhancing the communication of the adolescent, for adolescents may use denial and intellectualization. Parents may have to be involved, with the aim of decreasing their resistance to the adolescent's growth and utilizing whatever positives that they may contribute to this process of growth (McCoy 1982:57).

Just about every therapeutic approach to adolescence speaks of increasing outside interests (i.e., outside of the family of origin), of heightening peer relations, improving the adolescent's sense of self and sense of achievement (which can be tricky, especially if the adolescent is striving for unrealistic goals). Medication may be useful for some clients (Schatzberg and Cole 1991:321–322). With a serious suicidal threat, short-term hospitalization may be necessary. Hospitalization can be very aversive, for many adolescents feel that their parents are "sloughing them off." Some well-meaning but frightened parents do send children to hospitals and residential treatment centers (often distant and usually very expensive) only to encounter the feeling on the part of their children that they were "dumped." This feeling may persist for a very long time.

Another emphasis is on the amount of family and environmental stress the client is experiencing. McCoy recommends that parents talk with teenagers about their worries if the parents see something that disturbs them. She urges parents to listen carefully to what the teens say, helping them to the limits of their ability but being ready to call upon others for help. Parents must deal with their own emotions and fears, and cope with guilt and anger. It usually helps parents of teenagers to talk with other parents of teenagers. The comparison of peer group behavior is often reassuring, although it can sometimes muddy the water, because parents can also frighten each other. Reading can often be helpful, and many good books are available such as McCoy's or the shorter pamphlet of Meeks (1988).

THE PSYCHODYNAMIC APPROACH

Bemporad (1988) thinks that depressed adolescents may be classified into one of two psychodynamic categories: anaclitic or introjective. Both types reflect difficulty in managing the developmental tasks of adolescence. *Anaclitic* alludes to adolescents who have not freed themselves from their families and may still be functioning in the latency stage of development (i.e., they cannot cope with the physiological changes in their bodies) and find their gratifications and their identifications within the family. In actuality, these families may have interfered with the development of these adolescents by infantilizing them or by forcing inappropriate roles on them, such as making parents out of the children (Bemporad 1988:29). The usual intense relations with peers or attachments to such adults as teachers is impeded. In these youngsters, depression is often triggered by loss, a move away from home, or another occurrence that may traumatically delay maturation. The adolescent feels overpowered and confused and has an overwhelming need to alleviate his or her anxiety and suffering.

Introjective adolescents may be more developed, more individualized, and able to move away from their families, but they have internalized excessively high expectations from their families. This type is often seen in students, especially college students. The failure to meet these standards (usually of academic achievement) often results in depression and a visit to the student mental health clinic. They display guilt and misgivings, often with submission to a life without much pleasure or perhaps a consideration (or action) of suicide as a way to resolve their problems.

Because both types—and they may overlap—often desperately seek approval and understanding, it is more important for the therapist to offer empathy than interpretation. The therapist may be perceived as a permissive adult who does not equate the value of the adolescent with such standards as high academic performance. Therapy for both types may involve a long period of support and reassurance, again with the therapist doing little interpretation but utilizing and emphasizing the strengths of the clients, assisting these adolescents to mature, and assisting them to handle the developmental tasks in the transitions of adolescence. The therapist helps these clients to relinquish unrealistic yearnings for childhood and to cope with the realities, and the different kinds of gratification, of adolescence and later adulthood (Bemporad 1988:30). The emphasis is on recognizing and encouraging the adolescents to assert their own standards and desires rather than those they have incorporated from their families. "The process of therapy aims at creating a more realistic and constructive sense of self built on true means of satisfaction rather than defensive denial of limitations or adherence to the standards of others" (Bemporad 1988:30).

Depression, Suicide, and the College Student

Much of what we have written about adolescents also applies to college students. Adolescence can no longer be defined solely by chronological age because it is conceived of as a transitional period from youth to adulthood, and part of adulthood is economic and psychological independence. Adolescents are dependent upon others, including parents. For those children whose education continues past high school, the period of economic dependence and psychological, if not chronological, adolescence has slowly been expanding into the college and, often graduate and postgraduate training years. It is not uncommon for some young people to stay in training (e.g., medical residencies and internships and graduate programs) into their late twenties or even thirties.

College can be stressful for many students. Students cope with these stresses with varying degrees of competence and success, often without the old supports, such as the familiar (and often smaller) high school faculty, the family, and old friends (Beck and Young 1978). Excessive pressure and ineffective coping may contribute to depressive reactions; the depressive reactions themselves may be a way of coping with these stresses.

College can be a great culture shock to young people. This is especially true for those colleges that have high entrance requirements and accept only the brightest students. Such students, always in the top part of their high school classes (sometimes without working hard at it), may suddenly be in a high-powered, highly competitive situation, very different from high school, where they may be in the middle or even the lower part of their freshman class. Those with high expectations of themselves, whose parents may also have similar expectations, may be very affected by what they (and their parents) perceive as substandard performance. They may feel that they are now working very hard but are producing very little, when actually they may be doing comparatively well.

In addition to academic pressures, both realistic and unrealistic, entering students may be pressured by feeling that they must choose a major and decide (irrevocably, from the viewpoints of many students) what their life work will be. Sometimes it is therapeutic to help students accept "permission" to delay this decision, exercising the option not to decide, at least until later in their college careers, when they have more information and have overcome some of the maturational hurdles.

Dormitory living can be very stressful because of lack of privacy, noise, and (a paradox, in view of today's allegedly relaxed standards) higher demands for social achievements and a tremendous emphasis on being socially successful (i.e., popular). Dormitories certainly are not conducive to study; they require that the student learn to live with others. The new coed dorms may not ease this transition, even making it worse.

College may turn out to be a lonely experience for some students. Their loneliness may result from difficulties in establishing relations with other people or may be a reaction to the changes in their lives and to a lack of intimacy (Beck and Young 1978).

In others, the loneliness may be due to a parent's death or to divorce by parents who had postponed separating until the youngsters were in college. Here the students inappropriately feel guilty that they are not home to keep parents together. Loneliness is also a common reaction in adjusting to a new place; it is usually short-lived and passes when the student makes friends with new classmates (Beck and Young 1978).

The data consistently show a rise in the number of suicides among college students. One source states that from 1981 to 1983, the rate was about 8.7 per 100,000 students, as compared with 6.9 per 100,000 in 1973. Among older adolescents (twenty to twenty-four), the rate rose 130 percent between 1960 and 1975 (Hawton 1986:19). In 1981 it was 26.8 per 100,000 for white males, compared to 184 per 100,000 for nonwhite males; for white females it was 5.9 per 100,000, compared to 3.8 per 100,000 for nonwhite females (National Center for Health Statistics, 1984, cited in Hawton 1986:22).

With college students, as with all adolescents, there are at least fifty attempts for every successful suicide. Women attempt suicide more frequently, but men succeed more, by a ratio of 4:1 or higher. More than twice as many women as men seek help, so the disturbed college man is often at high risk, and without treatment.

Data connecting education, IQ, and suicide are confounded, but one interesting observation, which holds across cultures, is that among college students, the more prestigious the college, the higher the rate of suicide. Suicide in Ivy League colleges is twice that of non-Ivy League schools and double the rate in the noncollege group (Curran 1987: 22–23).

The closeness of college life, especially dormitory living, has the potential for intimate contacts between faculty and students and between students and students. This has been utilized with some success in the identification and prevention of suicide. With proper training, college dormitory aides and dormitory heads watching for signs of depression and potential suicides can often prevent them. At the University of California at Los Angeles, all students receive a six-page pamphlet on suicide, urging them to be alert to certain early warning signs. The booklet lists hot-line phone numbers for students to call, including the campus counseling service and the campus police. UCLA was motivated to offer this service, because it has been having one to five suicides a year (Goleman 1986). It is reasonable to assume that this figure, like all data on all college suicides, is understated. It may well be that students commit suicide off campus and thus never make the official statistics.

Similar programs have been started at a number of schools. The investment of school time and energy is more than amply paid back by the successful track record of recognizing depression and preventing suicide. We believe that these programs should be mandatory in all colleges and that secondary schools, and even junior high schools, should consider instituting similar programs. (Similar hot-line services, unconnected with schools, also exist in many cities.)

As with younger depressed children and adolescents, much intervention consists first of crisis intervention, an easing of the immediate stresses and dangers, and then support and reassurance. Suicide threats and behavior should always be taken seriously.

20

Depression in Couples and Families

The first part of this chapter discusses the influence of couple relationships and relationships within the family upon the etiology and course of depression. We then briefly discuss treating depression within a couple and a family framework. Although there are differences in therapy for a couple and for a family, there are many similarities. Because of this overlapping, we have combined the two.

We shall present the evidence as it is reported in the literature. Most of the research in these areas has been done with married couples and in families headed by a heterosexual married couple. Therefore many of the findings will be on these pairs and groups. Nevertheless, much of this work is also applicable to couples in general and to families with different life-styles. There *are* some differences between married and unmarried couples: The chief one is that unmarried, cohabiting couples usually, but not always, are childless. There are also some differences in such central issues as commitment and the ability to terminate the relationship, allegedly with more ease and usually without the intervention of lawyers (Nichols 1988). However, these differences seem to be lessening as nontraditional relationships are becoming more common and are increasingly accepted. A great deal of research is needed in all these areas to bridge the gaps in our understanding of the functioning of the various kinds of couple and family patterns.

Depression: An Individual or a Family Matter?

■■ Most therapists view depression as an individual problem.
■■ Yet it can impact on others in contact with the depressed person.

Family therapists, on the other hand, see depression as a problem of a *system*, particularly the family system, where most, if not all, of the members of the system (the family) contribute to the problem(s). They state that an approach to treatment that focuses only on the individual tends to blame the victim (Haas and Clarkin 1988:3). This view is challenged by a leading authority, who states that the research does not support "an exclusive family systems view of depression, which sees the depressed patient's symptoms as a way of manipulating the family" (Weissman 1990:189).

This dichotomy between the individual and the family is artificial and somewhat forced. Depression often occurs within an interpersonal context; the couple relationship and that of the family are among the most relevant of these interpersonal environments. An awareness of these interpersonal factors is essential to the understanding and treatment of depression.

As we have discussed throughout this book, biological factors must be taken into account when depression is being considered. Yet, as Coyne (1987:404) points out, the literatures of both the biological and interpersonal aspects of depression seem to exist almost independently of each other. A well-rounded approach must also take social factors into account.

The Influence of the Family System on the Etiology of Depression

There is growing evidence of linkages (not necessarily causal linkages but connections and associations) between depression and marriage.

In a review of the literature, Coyne (1987:401) points out that the relationships between depressed persons and their spouses are frequently full of conflict and anger. When comparing depressed psychiatric patients, nondepressed medical patients, and nondepressed community controls, Gotlib and Whiffen (1989) found that in all couples the subjects were negative and critical of their partners. The depressed women were particularly so and continued in negative interactions longer than the women in the control groups. In an earlier study, Weissman and Paykel (1974) also found that depressives expressed a great deal of hostility toward their mates and even more toward their children. The depressed women functioned poorly as wives and mothers in marriages characterized by much interpersonal friction, low sexual satisfaction, bad communication, and a lack of affection between the spouses, albeit with much clinging and dependency upon these spouses.

These findings seem to contradict the early psychoanalytic belief that depressives do not show anger to other people because the depression is anger turned inward. As many experienced clinicians can verify, depressed people are often full of anger, and nowhere is this anger expressed more, both overtly and covertly, than within the couple relationship and within the family.

Coyne (1987:401) cited research showing that depressed people can make their spouses, partners, and families feel guilty. When this happens, these significant others may unknowingly trigger a "self-perpetuating system." When the depressed person provokes guilt, family members often feel angry and hostile, but they may not respond and may even deny the aversive behavior because they fear that any negative response might worsen the depression. The hostility, which may be inhibited for a short or a long time, is often expressed in other ways, and it almost always increases distance between the depressive and his or her partner or family.

In an interesting study in Great Britain, Hinchcliffe, Hooper, and Roberts (1978) approached depression from an interactional approach, as representing and perpetuating conflict within the marital dyad and within the family. They viewed depression as a disruption in communication between husband and wife. This communication was role-determined, reflecting conflict in the rules of the relationship. They found that there were, indeed, differences in communication between depressed men and depressed women. Depressed males showed elevated tension and hostility, and their wives were also tense and anxious. After an episode of depression, the males' attitudes and behaviors relaxed markedly; consequently, their wives were more relaxed and interaction between the two was less conflicted. Depressed women and their husbands were also tense and anxious during an episode. However, the tense interaction continued after the episode passed (Hinchcliffe, Hooper, and Roberts 1978:17). Analyzing this phenomenon within role theory, the authors theorized that the more instrumental role orientation of the male made it more difficult for him to be expressive and dependent when he became depressed.

Marriage, Sex Roles, Social Class, and Depression

Married women seem to be at the highest risk for depression, with higher rates than those for married men. Conversely, the rates for single, divorced, and widowed women are lower than those for single, divorced, and widowed men. However, the problem is certainly more complicated than it appears. It may not be marriage itself but the obligations and social roles that accompany it that may cause the higher rate. It may be that marriage results in a disadvantaged status for women.

Two hypotheses suggest that women experience a disadvantaged status that might account for a higher occurrence of depression. One is the "social status hypothesis," which contends that because of "real social discriminations . . . women cannot achieve mastery by direct action and self-assertion" (Weissman and Klerman 1985). For example, the credit ratings and charge accounts of many married women are in the names of their spouses, often regardless of income. The result of this and similar situations is "legal and economic helplessness, dependency on others, . . . low self-esteem, low aspirations and, ultimately, clinical depression" (Weissman and Klerman 1985:417).

A related hypothesis is *learned helplessness*, which maintains that women are reared, and conditioned, against expressing assertion and independence; being feminine is similar to the "learned helplessness characteristic of depression." However, Weissman and Klerman (1985:417) state that there is no evidence for personality differences between men and women related to learned helplessness.

A similar perception, from a psychodynamic point of view, is that of Notman (1989), who states that this greater incidence of depression results not only from the "normal feminine personality," with its emphasis on dependency, but from greater anxieties about loss of love and being abandoned. She feels this sensitivity to how one is valued by others accounts for much fluctuation in mood, including depressive reactions. Notman feels that society dictates basically passive roles for women, denying them outlets for aggression and "active mastery," by valuing "sacrifice and service." The situation is worsened both by the devaluation of the female body (with the emphasis upon perfection) and by the problem of identifying with one's own mother, who is often similarly devalued and frequently depressed. She states that these sex role stereotypes and life conditions support devaluation, subservience, and helplessness.

Hochschild (1989) has stated that the ambiguities and conflicts produced by the traditional female roles have not been eased by changes, whether real or perceived as real, in the last several decades. What has actually happened is that increasing demands for occupational achievement have been *added* to the traditional domestic and nurturing (maternal) role demands, all without further social support. The result has been a longer workweek and added stress on women.

Weissman and Klerman challenge this view, on the basis that recent epidemiological studies using D.S.M.-III criteria did not support these hypotheses; in fact, they state that "marriage is protective against major depression for both sexes" (1985:417). However, Weissman (1979) also states that the most commonly encountered depressed patient is most likely a woman who is married and having problems in a relationship. The reality is probably that "good" marriages often provide this protection but that discordant ones exacerbate personal adjustment and foster depression (Beach, Sandeen, and O'Leary 1990). Weissman and Paykel (1977) hold that marriage protects men (a consistent finding in community surveys) but often affects women negatively, for wives seem to need to make a bigger adjustment than husbands. In particular, the traditional feminine roles, which often are more expressive, integrative, and accommodating than male roles, make women more vulnerable to depression than men.

Coyne (1987:402) supports the broader view that study and treatment of the patient's marital, couple, and family relationships is vital in working with depressed clients. Coyne cites an earlier study by Brown and Harris (1978) in England, who found that the rate of depression was three times higher in women in unhappy relationships than in women in happy relationships. They found that those women who were in an intimate and confiding relationship with a man appeared to be protected from depression, because (in their sample) only 4 percent who described themselves in this kind of relationship became depressed, compared to 40 percent who were experiencing stress and did not have such a relationship. In several studies of depression and marital unhappiness, the marriages, even when stable, were unhappy and lacked intimacy. Women who had recently terminated this kind of relationship sometimes showed the most improvement in their depression.

Similarly, depressed unhappily married women were less likely to progress in individual psychotherapy, whereas all clients who had good relations with their spouses and partners improved. Response to antidepressant medication was poorer for those in conflicted relationships, but medication by itself did not impact upon the quality of the depressed person's engagement in the relationship (Rounsaville et al. 1979).

The reactions of the partner of the depressive, particularly angry criticism, were more highly correlated with relapse after hospitalization than was the degree of symptoms at the beginning of illness. Coyne thinks that these findings are important evidence for the centrality of marital or relationship factors in recovery from depression, regardless of whether the depression is biological or nonbiological (1987:403).

About 40 percent of the partners of these depressed persons were symptomatic enough to be referred for treatment. However, their disturbances involved more than just the consequences of living with a depressed partner; they resulted from a complicated set of factors. The women married to depressed men were themselves susceptible to depression, but the depressed women were often married to men who had a characterological disturbance or who abused alcohol or drugs (Coyne 1987:403).

In short, some stresses in marital and family relationships seem to trigger depression, especially in the (admittedly vague) case of the "biologically predisposed individual" (Haas, Clarkin, and Glick 1985:21). Similarly, the actions and the symptoms of the depressed family members may set off responses from other family members, such as anger and guilt, thus heightening conflict and aggravating the depression. All these interpersonal factors call for an evaluation of the family unit and its interactions, in addition to the evaluation of the depressed client; this is especially important if the identified patient is a child or an adolescent (Haas, Clarkin, and Glick 1985:21).

Much of the research on gender role and depression with women has focused on unipolar clients. However, one study comparing forty-two manic-depressive inpatients and thirty "normal" community couples revealed that the marriages of the inpatients were higher in conflict than the comparison couples. The couples in these marriages showed more complementarity than similarity. These findings emphasize the necessity of including spouses or other partners in the treatment of bipolar patients (Hoover and Fitzgerald 1981). It is clear that the relationship of social stress to traditional roles needs more research.

Boyd and Weissman (1982) contend that there is a social class difference in the rates of depression in women with children: women from the "working classes" (actually, lower income) are at higher risk than middle-class women with children. This is undoubtedly related not only to low income but to the accompanying cramped quarters, unemployment, and other factors that not only make the life of the working-class family more difficult but also emphasize the lack of control that lower-income families often feel (Boyd and Weissman 1982:118). In women without children, interestingly enough, there were no differences in the rates of depression between working-class women and women from the middle class (Boyd and Weissman 1982:118).

Keitner and colleagues (1990) and Coyne (1987:404) both state that the helping professionals are just beginning to identify the ways in which the depressed person, the spouse or the partner, and the children in a family are interconnected. There are actually very few substantiated conclusions in the current literature of family functioning and depression.

Depressed Parents and Children

Although it is difficult, if not impossible, to determine etiology and to separate genetics from environment issues, it is possible to observe the impact of depressed parents on children. The effects can be drastic: The literature overwhelmingly demonstrates that the children of depressed parents are at higher risk for psychiatric, behavior, and attention disorders, as well as accidents. (We discussed the genetic factors affecting depression in chapter 8.)

As a result of their experiences, children of depressed parents may well be more likely to be depressed when they are teenagers or adults. Because of their own pain, depressed parents may not be as sensitive to or have as much empathy with a child as a nondepressed parent. Furthermore, the evidence suggests that in addition to ignoring, or being insensitive to a child, depressed parents may be more critical and isolated and that this combination of aversive factors may interfere with the growth and development of their children.

A typical study showed that women diagnosed with unipolar depression showed comparatively fewer positive, and more negative and less task-focused actions toward their children than did nondepressed women. The depression of the women at the time of the study and the presence of persistent stress were better predictors of the way the mother would relate to the child than the extent and nature of her psychiatric history (Gordon et al. 1989).

Radke-Yarrow (cited in Goleman 1989a) found that depressed parents were less capable of handling resistant behavior of children, even if this behavior was nothing more than the expected and normal attempts at independence. Furthermore, they had difficulty with reasoning and modifying their own positions in arguments, and they were often bewildered by events. They spoke less with their children, and when they did speak, they were more negative.

Children of depressed mothers were found to have a higher proportion of clinically significant problems than children of nondepressed psychiatric patients, nondepressed medical patients, and nondepressed community mothers. However, there was sufficient overlap between the behaviors of children of depressed and nondepressed psychiatric patients to raise the question as to whether the children's adjustment problems were specific to parental depression or reflected maternal pathology in general (Lee and Gotlib 1989).

Depressed children of depressed parents exhibited their own depression at an earlier age, were depressed more frequently, and had more problems in school and with other children than did depressed children of nondepressed parents (Merikangas, Weissman, and Prusoff 1990).

In a comprehensive review of the literature, Gelfand and Teti (1990:331) concurred with the observation that "depressed people function poorly as parents." Although most of the research they examined focused on depressed mothers, they observed that depressed parents showed rumination and self-absorption and seemed less able than nondepressed parents to give their children "appropriate structure, guidance and rule enforcement" (1990:331). They also did not display "sensitive reciprocity, synchronicity and expressions of pleasure" toward their children (1990:331–332).

The literature suggests that depressed mothers seem unable to monitor what their children are doing and thus cannot guard them from such dangers as hazardous toys. The researchers cited several examples of these mothers not being sufficiently attentive when their children engaged in possibly dangerous activities; they cited the "gross inattention and obliviousness to potential danger . . . [as the reason for] abnormally high accident rates among children of depressed mothers" (Brown and Harris, 1978, quoted in Gelfand and Teti 1990:332). In conclusion, they stated that depressed mothers did not seem less happy with their children than nondepressed mothers, but they showed greater helplessness in trying to deal with them (Gelfand and Teti 1990:332). This helplessness was particularly evident in their inability to discipline their children (Gelfand and Teti 1990:333).

Although various studies reveal different statistics, up to 50 percent of the children with at least one depressed parent exhibited symptoms serious enough to be diagnosed. This risk is higher if the child is deprived of a parent and if there are marital problems; it is greatest when both parents are ill. However, if there is a supportive and constant adult accessible to the child, the risk may well be very greatly reduced. Studies have shown that the occurrence of divorce is responsible for a large part of the association between depression in the divorced mother and symptoms in the child.

The coexistence of substance abuse and depression complicates the family situation. Addicted parents are often depressed and usually have great difficulty taking care of their children. In one study, children of heroin-addicted parents suffered from a variety of disorders, primarily infectious and nutritional diseases, and the consequences of neglect and parental disinterest (Casado-Flores, Bano-Rodrigo, and Romero 1990). Disturbed parenting was observed in parents addicted to narcotics or alcohol (Bernardi, Jones, and Tennant 1989).

This situation is far from uncommon. Estimates are that at least one in every ten children born in the United States has one or two chemically dependent parents (Bays 1990). An addiction, whether of alcohol, another drug of abuse, or both, presents additional problems in working with parental, and often child, depression. The substance abuse must usually be given priority, often concurrent with or before the treatment of the depression. The coexistence of any addiction presents complications for drug therapy of depression. Above all, some talking therapy, and often a family approach, may be indicated in these situations.

Treating Depression Within a Couple and Family Framework

■■ We are just beginning to investigate the effects that de-
■■ pressed clients and their spouses and partners have on each
other. These interrelationships are certainly important enough that family therapy might well be one way of intervening in depression (Epstein
et al. 1988:157).

Family therapy and intervention in a family are not the same thing
(Lansky 1988:215). Therapists working with individual clients may
sometimes have to contact families—for example, when there is a risk
of suicide, when arrangements for hospitalization are necessary, or
some information on family history is required. We could expand this
list to include other interventions in the client's social fields, such as
talking with hospital personnel, other health care professionals, and so
forth. This might be called *family intervention,* and we assume that good
practice dictates the use of this approach when it is appropriate.

By *family therapy* we mean treatment in which one or both parents
are seen simultaneously with one or more children and sometimes
significant others. By *couple therapy* we mean therapy that is conducted
with the man and woman (or both single-sex partners) simultaneously,
which is also called *conjoint therapy.* Couple and family therapy may be
used by themselves or in combination with individual treatment and/or
antidepressant medication. These can be difficult treatment approaches.
For example, spouses, partners, children, and other family members
may resist cooperating with therapy, or will resist involvement, defining their function as helping the disturbed family member (or spouse or
partner) rather than as needing therapy for themselves.

There are a number of orientations to couple and family therapy, and
some authors (e.g., Nichols 1988) discuss the relevance and importance
of depression in both the couple and the family relationships. Good
discussions of the varying approaches may be found in Clarkin, Haas,
and Glick (1988). This volume focuses on couple and family therapy
with depressed clients and contains descriptions, with extensive docu-
mentation, on the following therapies of affective disorders within couple and family frameworks: cognitive therapy, behavioral therapy, strategic therapy, inpatient treatment, and combinations of pharmacological and family therapies.

Clarkin, Haas, and Glick (1988:47) hold that treating mood disorders
using conjoint or family treatment requires careful assessment of three
major areas: the symptoms of the individual, including an assessment
of the role the client plays in the family system; an evaluation of the

reactions (perceptions, cognitions, behaviors) of the spouse (or partner) and other people in the family; and a specification of the patterns of communication and the patterns of behavior of both the client and his or her family, particularly those patterns affected by the mood disturbance.

Families may respond to one of their members with a mood disorder in one of three patterns: There may be (1) a record of a fairly high level of functioning, including dealing positively with the depressed client; (2) a high level of functioning, except for dealing badly with the depressed client during depressive episodes; and (3) continual poor role performance and communication, and poor dealing with the client during the periods of upset (Haas, Clarkin, and Glick 1985).

Periods of stress within a couple, or a family, may precede an episode of depression or may heighten the susceptibility to depression in a vulnerable individual. Depression may also be a factor in worsening marital and family relationships, a factor that seems to work slowly and is not always recognized or that may work as an insidious process (Haas and Clarkin 1988:14). There seems to be an interplay (a continuous interaction or a feedback loop) between actions of a depressed individual and the spouse and/or family. We are only beginning to research and spell out the nature and the details of these circular processes.

We do know that there are very confused, mixed patterns of attribution, of blame and hostility, of hurt feelings and of disappointments, between depressed individuals and their family members. The identified patient is not always the most disturbed member of the system but is the one who has been labeled as such.

Coffman and Jacobson's Combined Treatment Approach

Coffman and Jacobson (1990) have developed a time-limited (twenty-session) model for family treatment combining cognitive-behavioral therapy for a depressed individual and conjoint marital therapy, based on a social-learning model, for the marital pair. Although the mix of the two therapies varies, depending upon the needs of the individual case, the developers usually used twelve sessions for cognitive therapy and eight for marital therapy. In the first two weeks, four sessions of individual cognitive therapy were targeted at the identified patient's depression and one session was devoted to the couple. The third marital session was a roundtable, where the goals of the marital therapy were outlined and the couple (particularly the nondepressed partner) was asked to commit to conjoint (couple) therapy. The researchers found a lower rate of refusal to engage in this kind of couple therapy than in the more conventional conjoint treatment (Coffman and Jacobson 1990:141). Individual and conjoint work followed for a total of twenty sessions, sometimes extended in extreme cases. Engaging the depressed individual and the spouse or partner in therapy focusing on relationship problems facilitated the treatment of the depression, which lessened after this conjoint treatment took place.

The Marital Discord Treatment Model

Beach, Sandeen, and O'Leary (1990) have formulated a model for understanding and intervening in the treatment of depression in couple/marital relationships. The authors think that these relationships may be influential in the genesis and the persistence of depression but that these same relationships may also be a source of strength (1990:53). They believe that there are six elements in relationships that provide support and help the depressed individual cope: couple cohesion, acceptance of emotional expression, actual and perceived coping assistance, self-esteem support, spousal dependability, and intimacy (1990:54).

The factors that worsen interaction and depression are verbal and physical aggression; threats of separation and divorce; severe spousal denigration, criticism, and blame; severe disruption of scripted (automatic and repetitive) routines; and major idiosyncratic marital stressors (1990). Although each of these factors may result from couple discord, and thus either heighten or lower the depressive reaction, each can also result from depression, which, in their view, lowers the ability of both the depressed person and his or her partner to cope and may produce patterns of avoidance by the couple and an increase in frustration (Beach, Sandeen, and O'Leary 1990:82).

Each of these areas provides a focus for intervention, and the authors propose a structured, fifteen-session course of therapy with provisions made for follow-up booster sessions. The approach is a form of behavioral marital therapy with elements from a number of other orientations. There is an assessment prior to beginning treatment, as the authors are highly empirical in their approach and evaluate the efficacy of intervention. Therapy is viewed in three general phases: The first phase is, as quickly as possible, to lessen and eliminate stressors and heighten couple cohesion, caring, and companionship. The second phase is to change a couple's communication and the way each interacts to shape a more stable, functional relationship. The third stage is to work with the couple to maintain gains and to prevent future relapses (Beach, Sandeen, and O'Leary 1990:88).

The therapy is structured, but it is flexible enough to provide for individual and couple differences. The authors include suggestions, exercises (such as the "caring-days" exercise [Stuart 1980]), and sample courses of therapy. We feel that the approach is of value not only as a way to intervene with the couple aspects of depression but because the concepts of the approach can be integrated with a variety of other theoretical treatments.

Psychoeducational Family Intervention

Another innovative approach is the application of *psychoeducational family intervention*, originally designed for families with a schizophrenic patient, to families of depressives (Holder and Anderson 1990:159–184). The work is based on the principle that increasing the sense of self-worth and control of both the patient and family members will ease the depressive condition and that family and individual functioning will be improved. There is active work on changing the interactions of the client and family, thus relieving tensions and self-defeating patterns of behavior by all members of the family system.

Intervention is viewed as consisting of the following phases: Phase 1, *connecting*, where strengths are identified and, in the identifying of patterns and perceptions, the hope of change is enhanced. A product of this phase is a "contract" that redefines the problem(s) and spells out the goals of therapy. Phase 2 is the *workshop*, lasting four to six hours, where information is presented didactically and there is discussion and questioning. Methods of treatment are discussed, along with a frank discussion of their effectiveness. There is ventilation of feelings, particularly about previously unsuccessful attempts to resolve problems. This is followed by detailed information about the mutual interaction of depression and family life and ways the family can cope. Phase 3 is *application and maintenance*, where the principles and procedures discussed in the workshop are applied. The patient, and the family, may also be receiving other kinds of therapy during this time.

The psychoeducational approach may well suffice as an approach by itself, or it may be conducted concurrently with other treatments, including medication and other forms of psychotherapy. The number of sessions, as well as the emphasis of the intervention, may vary. A long list of topics may be included in this process, although there is no theoretical or practical limitation on what might be covered (Holder and Anderson 1990:170–171). Although the approach seems to have been designed initially for middle-aged married patients, we believe that it can also be applied to nonmarried couples, children, adolescents, and the elderly—all situations where family factors, and the nature of family interactions with the depressed person, are central.

In one study, thirty-six marital pairs, each with a depressed wife, were randomly assigned to behavioral marital therapy, individual cognitive therapy, or a waiting list that was considered a control condition (O'Leary and Beach 1990). These were all volunteer clients who were highly motivated to improve their lives. Both marital and individual therapy lasted fifteen to sixteen weeks, including emergency telephone contacts; control subjects were kept on the waiting list for fifteen weeks.

Both therapies reduced depressive symptoms significantly more than the control condition, but they did not differ significantly from each other. However, the women in the marital therapy group scored significantly higher in marital satisfaction—an indication that the depressions seem to have been lowered by improving the marital situations. The marital therapy focused not on cognitions but on relationship factors. The experimenters point out that it is often more difficult to do marriage therapy, because one is working on change in two people and they must *both* change. They conclude (we believe rightfully so) that marital therapy may not be indicated for all depressed married clients (sometimes, for example, divorce may be a legitimate outcome), but it is important to assess the couple relationship as a factor in planning treatment for people involved in relationships (O'Leary and Beach 1990:185).

Conclusion

■■ Much of the rationale for recommending couple and family
■■ therapy for some depressives is based on "clinical wisdom." These modalities seem a promising area for exploration and development, not only for married couples but for unmarried couples, whether following traditional or nontraditional roles and life-styles. We agree that "at present, very little is known about the appropriateness of combining individual and marital therapy sessions in the treatment of depression" (Dobson, Jacobson, and Victor 1988:82). We also agree that these modalities should be explored and developed, as still another factor in a multifaceted approach to multifaceted problems: the depressions.

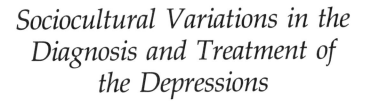

Sociocultural Variations in the Diagnosis and Treatment of the Depressions

The Biopsychosocial Approach to Diagnosis and Assessment

Advocates of a biopsychosocial model hold that to understand the determinants of a condition such as depression and to treat the condition effectively, one must consider the social context of patients as well as their dysfunctions (Engel 1977:1333).

Increasingly, we have become aware that different cultures approach psychiatric problems differently. For example, a multinational study comparing care of depressed patients in Japan, Italy, and the United States has shown that the care of depressives in Japan is clearly biological; in Italy the stress is on social psychiatry, with less emphasis on the medical model (particularly in northern Italy); and in the United States the care varies to the degree that therapists combine biological and social models (Trainor 1991).

As cross-cultural studies of depression have increased, some problems have become apparent (Kleinman and Good 1985; Marsella, Hirschfeld, and Katz 1987). One of the difficulties in making comparisons from culture to culture is that there are cultural variations in defining when a fluctuation in mood changes from normal to abnormal (Marsella, DeVos, and Hsu 1985). The diagnostic categories vary in different epidemiological studies, as do the procedures for identifying cases and for sampling populations. Thus diagnoses of depression or affective disorder vary widely; in addition their reliability is low (Marsella 1985:303). Furthermore, diagnostic categories—especially those based on observation of Western patients, such as the system in the D.S.M.-III-R—often either do not detect or they hide cultural differences in the expression of depression. In particular, there are many cultural differences in the expression of "guilt, existential despair, self-denigration, and suicidal ideation" (Marsella 1985:303). Because of these differences in cultural norms and expressions of affective disturbances, many of the cross-cultural studies we reviewed for this chapter tend to downplay the more psychological symptoms and focus on the somatic aspects of depression.

Although we can speak with ease of the cultural differences among allegedly disparate countries such as Japan, Italy, and the United States, we must remember that even within a country such as the United States, cultural and social differences may be as large as those among different countries. These variations within our country must be considered in assessing and treating all psychiatric problems, although we shall limit our discussion to the affective disorders.

We discuss two broad, interrelated topics in this chapter. The first is the importance of understanding cultural variables as they affect the therapist's understanding of clients' symptoms of depression and response to treatment. This, of course, includes therapists' awareness of their own cultural orientation and values. The primary, although certainly not the only, cultural and social factors that impact upon our views of the diagnosis and treatment of depression are such differences as how the "self" is viewed; the expression of depression; systems of beliefs about health and mental illness; religious and spiritual beliefs; and the importance of family/community/social support. We shall address each of these factors later.

We then discuss some sociocultural factors, particularly those that are known to increase vulnerability to such conditions as depression. These include race and racism; age, gender and sexuality, including minority sexual orientation; and socioeconomic status, particularly poverty, unemployment, and homelessness.

A number of social and ethnic groups will then be described, focusing on aspects relative to the incidence and expression of the affective disorders as well as some indicators for treatment. Although there are many groups in this category, we have included the following: African-Americans (blacks); Hispanic-Americans (Latinos, "La Raza"); Asian and Pacific Americans; and Native-Americans (American Indians, Alaskan Natives).

These categories follow the typical groupings in cross-cultural studies, although this approach encompasses a number of problems. One is the overlapping of topics, because cross-cultural studies often compare these very groups, and the findings of individual studies are usually relevant to several groups. Another problem is the tremendous variation found within groups. Most cross-cultural studies compare different *ethnic groups* ("a type of group contained within the national boundaries of America and defined or set off by race, religion or national origin" [Gordon (1985) quoted in Devore and Schlesinger 1987:10–11]). They label individuals as members of ethnic groups, but do not take into account the individual's degree of identity with a group or its cultural tradition (Marsella 1987:393). For example, "Some Puerto Rican people may be more 'Anglo' than a Vermont farmer in their behavior patterns, values and way of life" (Marsella 1987:393). Young (1983:19) cautions that it can be hard to tell the "extent to which . . . [one's] legacy from the past affects . . . [one's] current beliefs and behavior." Teaching often occurs indirectly, through current entertainment, the use of "verbal platitudes," the words used when consoling and encouraging others, and so on. Individuals (e.g., Chinese people reared in Hong Kong in a Western educational system) are often unaware of the degree to which their beliefs and values are based on their cultural traditions. Even when they appear to be in step with contemporary (i.e., Western) norms and standards, these individuals may revert to deeply ingrained beliefs and responses during stressful situations. A good example was provided by Young (1972), who described how Chinese-Americans in Hawaii, when interviewed, were highly critical of the idealized extended family. At the same time, many lived very close to their parents and grandparents, who also assumed an important role in rearing their children.

Entire volumes, in several disciplines, have been written about each of the topics and subtopics we address in this chapter. We can only hope to sensitize the reader to some of the important issues and components, giving an occasional example or two to illustrate or emphasize a point and indicating the direction for seeking further information. We must also speak very broadly, and generally, although we are certainly aware that when we mention an ethnic group (e.g., the Japanese) and speak of certain characteristics of this group, there are actually many variations within the group.

The Relationship of Culture to Depression

■■ As we cross the boundary from psychology and psychiatry
■■ to anthropology, we find that the concept of depression takes on different meanings. As Kleinman and Good (1985:14) point out, depression, defined as an emotion in current psychology, is a Western viewpoint. Lutz (1985:63) defines emotion not as a "psychobiological process" but as culture-bound ways that people use to define their situations and relationships. Some cultures view emotion as a "system of social behavior" (Kleinman and Good 1985:15).

An expert on ethnocultural differences, Anthony J. Marsella, Professor of Psychology at The University of Hawaii, states that the way individuals behave is largely determined by the outer and inner representations of their culture: family, religion and education, political and economic institutions; how the world is viewed, value and belief systems, and more (1985:288). Definitions of mental disorders are based on deviance from what is considered "acceptable" behavior. As Marsella (1985:303) points out, these cultural differences in mental disorders (e.g., depression) are not simply in how they are expressed or displayed, but "the entire phenomenon is different." Based on this view, Marsella believes that understanding culture is so essential for understanding mental disorders that it should be a part of both psychiatry and the behavioral sciences (Marsella 1985:281–282).

How the Self Is Viewed

Essential to the understanding of cultural variables is how the self is viewed. *Self* is defined as the "universal features of being a person" (Marsella 1985:285). The self is a central concept explaining behavior; it is different from "ego structure." Marsella argues that cultural traditions of thought influence how the self perceives itself; in turn, this perception interacts with, rather than is determined by, the operation of underlying coping mechanisms (the ego) or "personality structure" (DeVos, Marsella, and Hsu 1985:6–7).

The nature and the goals of self are defined quite differently in Eastern and Western cultures. In the West, self-identity is based on individuality; but self-identity may be the least important goal for a Hindu whose identify depends on "lineage, family, house, and personal name." Similarly, for the Chinese, the idea of developing self-identity "alone," without experiencing the support of a community, "is inconceivable" (DeVos, Marsella, and Hsu 1985:17). In fact, in many Eastern cultural groups (e.g., Japanese, Balinese, and Filipino) the concept of self actually includes significant others—a concept known by various names, such as *collateral, diffuse,* or *undifferentiated* self. Marsella points out that the "unindividuated self" is the norm in some Eastern cultures, but Western cultures often view this state as pathological (Marsella 1985:290). Of course, as we have emphasized, each cultural group includes considerable variations. As Lebra (1976:156) points out, the Japanese display individuality, although it is not the dominant ethos. Some take some pride in exhibiting a certain amount of autonomy within the groups they belong to. However, individuality (even when desired) is usually attained at the cost of social involvement in the group (Lebra 1976:158).

These differences in the cultural views of self are often the basis of the variations in how mental illnesses are expressed in different cultures.

The Expression of Depression

Marsella (1980:261) has stated that depression has very different meanings and consequences, depending on the culture. For example, the Chinese display somatic symptoms, the Japanese show interpersonal strain, and the Caucasians exhibit existential problems (Marsella 1985:299). One basic difference that seems consistent in all these ethno-cultural studies is that in Western cultures psychological symptoms are stressed—for example, "depressed mood, feelings of inadequacy, guilt, and isolation and detachment." In Eastern cultures symptoms are often expressed somatically, but individuals rarely feel isolated or alone, because they do not lose their group identity (Marsella 1985:300). In free association to the term *depression* (or the Eastern equivalent of the term), Westerners responded with individual, personal feelings of internalized mood using words such as *sadness, despair, dejection;* Japanese subjects responded with references to external events such as *storm, clouds, mountain*—words that depersonalized the experience (Marsella 1985:301).

Belief Systems: Health and Mental Illness

The way mental health is viewed is another important cultural difference. In the Western view of self as "object," health and mental health are often expressed in disease metaphors or analogies, whereas Eastern cultures view the self as " 'process.' . . . considering the many levels of human functioning as a harmonious blend" (Marsella 1985:299). Of course there are many variations within each of these polarized views.

Among the causes of mental illness, Chinese-Americans include "organic disorders, supernatural intervention, genetic vulnerability or hereditary weakness, physical or emotional exhaustion caused by situational factors, metaphysical factors such as the imbalance between yin and yang (negative and positive sides of energy; [*yang*, "day," *yin*, "night," *yang*, "birth," *yin*, "death," and so on—Lau 1979:15–16]), fatalism, and character weakness (Wong 1982:192). Wong indicates that Chinese-Americans, Japanese-Americans, and Filipino-Americans believe they can control their mental illness through will power (1982:192).

The type of care one seeks for what is called depression is also closely associated with cultural beliefs about mental health and illness. Whereas Westerners seek mental health practitioners trained to examine intrapsychic factors, some cultural groups seek folk healers (e.g., *curanderos*) and spiritual healers, or they look for help within their family and community support systems (Mokuau 1988:51–52). Barberra (1982:122) points out that in current society, when healers such as *curanderos* are consulted, they may be seen in conjunction with Western mental health services: "these *curanderos* [often] make referrals to community mental health centers."

Religious and Spiritual Beliefs

Although Western cultures tend to look at mood and pain from an illness perspective, other cultures view these same experiences within the context of religion (Keyes 1985:154). Some theorists view religious beliefs, among other cultural factors, as ways of providing a safe outlet for emotions (Shweder 1985:191–192). Since a population may include more than one religious group, it is more useful to look at the religious beliefs of a particular group and to examine what these beliefs mean in terms of the experience of depression. For example, Shweder points out that some religions incorporate a belief in the existence of a soul (1985:191– 192). These groups tend to speak of loss in terms of loss of soul—often associated with death—which is described as feeling empty, dispirited, or often, depressed; other groups express loss as existential despair (Shweder, quoted by Kleinman and Good 1985:177).

Wong (1985:195) indicates that there are religions in which some priestly functions and roles, of a self-disclosing confessional quality, are similar to psychotherapy. In some Eastern religions endurance, self-sacrifice, and personal suffering are emphasized—qualities completely different from the "verbal expressiveness of Western modes of treatment."

Some studies have shown that involvement in a religion has a "buffering" effect on depression (e.g., in African-Americans) (Brown and Gary 1988). This is a factor in Western cultures, where depression is considered undesirable; these findings would not hold across all cultures. Kleinman and Good (1985:3) point out that for Buddhists, experiencing a "willful dysphoria is . . . the first step on the road to salvation." Similarly, experiencing dysphoria fully is valued by Iranian Shi'ite Muslims, who also view grief as a religious experience.

Cultural groups such as Native-Americans and Pacific Islanders are closely tied to their land, both spiritually and emotionally. Mokuau (1988:57) describes the Hawaiian myth of the creation of man as the union of the sky (*Papa*) and the earth (*Wakea*). Since for many of these cultural groups, this spiritual union has been disrupted by political and environmental changes, a kind of rootlessness has developed, which has led to feelings of hopelessness and despair. Observers of these cultural groups believe that this kind of depression cannot be treated on an interpersonal level. To treat this depression, the land must be restored; "to restore the lands is to restore their identity; to restore their identity is to restore their sense of pride; and to return their pride is to rebuild their confidence" (Kanahele 1982:21, quoted in Mokuau 1988:57).

Although members of a religious group may ascribe to the same set of beliefs about certain phenomena and issues, they may have widely divergent beliefs as members of different cultural groups or as a result of the degree of assimilation into a particular culture. For example, Jews, among other religious groups in America, come from families who lived for generations in many countries in Europe, Asia, and other parts of the world.

Importance of the Social Network: Family, Community, and Social Support

Social support, broadly defined, is "support accessible to an individual through social ties to other individuals, groups, and the larger community" (Lin et al. 1979:109, quoted in Marsella, Hirschfeld, and Katz 1987:350). It seems to be generally agreed that social support—or a support system—is important in mediating stress and even illness. Gerald Caplan (1974:7), an early advocate of this theory, described the support system as playing an important role in preserving the person's psychological and physical integrity. Another positive effect of social support, as delineated by Maguire (1991:xv) is a sense of self. Social support provides an environment that allows a person who is having "difficulty with individuality. . . . to develop an awareness of his or her own autonomous and unique existence" (Maguire 1991). The absence of a supportive relationship (intimate, confiding) has been identified as a strong risk factor for developing affective disorders (John and Weissman 1987:351). Social support is also a positive indicator for success in treating depression.

Social support is often mentioned in relation to depression in different racial and ethnic groups. However, the definitions of *support* and *support system* vary, as do the expectations and goals of support. For example, the definitions given earlier emphasizing integrity of the individual and the development of an awareness of one's autonomous, unique existence are clearly goals of Western cultures. Liu and Cheung (1985:505) have stated that the American norms of kinship relations cannot be applied to support systems for refugees from Indochina; there are strong and binding obligations found outside of the boundary-clear group of relatives seen in America as kin ties. Maguire (1991:ix) offers a broad definition, pointing out that *family* can be defined as "any collection of individuals who define themselves as a family and who take on the responsibilities and functions generally considered necessary for healthy family life."

The research on social support and depression, which we shall mention later in reference to particular racial and cultural groups, shows mixed results. On the one hand, social support has usually been shown to have a positive effect. For example, certain family and community-oriented cultural groups (e.g., the Native-American Oglala Sioux group, described by Maguire [1991:1–2]) generally turn to their support systems and receive a great deal of help from them. But there can also be negative or mixed effects. In many of these network-oriented groups (e.g., the Chinese), seeking mental health services outside their groups brings stigma and shame, which results in the withdrawal of support; therefore outside help is sought only as a last resort (Wong 1982:192–193).

Suicide and Loss of Face

In those cultures where the family and extended community are valued above the individual, seeking outside help, and thus exposing one's behavior "for all to see" is considered shameful—not only for the individual but for the family group (Wong 1982:192–193). Ryan (1985:338) states that this is very serious, involving loss of face; and in these groups, loss of face and shame are very strong motivators for suicide. Within this view, suicide is seen as a "noble death," the voluntary relinquishing of one's life to show how deeply an action (e.g., personal failure for shaming the family and group) is regretted—and the community supports such an action.

As explained by Ryan (1985:338), the Chinese-American considers suicide a "personal matter that society is not supposed to intervene in. . . . one kills oneself because of others or for others, and not only because of oneself." This is opposite to the Western view, in which a suicide is seen as an indication of mental illness, and families experience guilt and, to some degree, dishonor if a member commits suicide. Conversely, in Asian cultures, a family is dishonored by a mental illness, and suicide is viewed as a selfless act—"an honorable solution to problems" (Ryan 1985:338).

Sometimes the person who threatens suicide or actually carries through with it is not the one whose actions shamed the group, but one of the group members who lost face. For example, a parent might threaten suicide, or carry out this threat, if a child acts (or even intends to act) in a way that is considered to be shameful. Suicide may also be an act of retaliation; a way of taking revenge on another by upsetting him or causing him to lose face (Kambe 1972:43, quoted in Lebra 1976:194). However, in Western, as in Eastern cultures, the threat of suicide may be a self-punishing form of blackmail (Lebra 1976:194).

In summary, these diverse beliefs impact upon the treatment of depression. Later in this chapter we discuss how they may be assessed and handled in treatment.

Racism, Low Socioeconomic Status, and Other Social Factors That Increase Vulnerability to Depression

■■ As we discuss in the following sections, individuals in cer-
■■ tain groups are particularly vulnerable to depression, as well
as other devastating conditions. These groups have often been under-
serviced, for a number of reasons. Frequently, it is because of economics—the poor (as well as the young, old, women, ethnic minorities, and
so on) often lack the money to pay for services. One consequence of
long-term institutionalized racism is that rates of unemployment are
higher (e.g., among blacks and Hispanics, compared with whites), with
accompanying inequities in health insurance and levels of medical care
received ("Health Insurance Gaps" 1991). Underservice has long been
rationalized by stereotyping various groups as "untreatable" (Snowden
1982:11). These views are not supported by research, as we shall see,
and increasingly they are being challenged.

Racism

Racism has been defined as a "belief that race is the primary
determinant of human traits and capacities and that racial differences
produce an inherent superiority of a particular race" (*Webster's* 1989:969).
Racism is often (but not always) associated with other kinds of societal
oppression, such as fewer opportunities for education and for jobs that
provide adequate salaries and status. Thus racial minorities are often
poor; have low-status, low-salaried jobs; or are unemployed and/or
homeless. All these factors contribute to low self-esteem and increase
vulnerability to depression (Kessler and Neighbors 1986:107). However,
even when these other factors are not present, the effects of racism
alone produce serious effects and these are also connected to higher
rates of depression (Kessler and Neighbors 1986:113).

The Economically Disadvantaged: Low Socioeconomic Status, Poverty, and Depression

According to McGrath and colleagues (1990:xii), "poverty is a
pathway to depression." Among other consequences, poverty has a
demoralizing effect, which lowers self-esteem and is numbing (Schwartz
1986:132). The poor frequently lose hope and become demoralized (Frank
1974). This is partly due to the many life stresses associated with poverty, not the least of which is malnutrition.

We described in chapter 8 the importance of many vitamins and minerals in transmitting the neurochemicals associated with mood. As Kanarek and Marks-Kaufman (1991:22) explain, malnutrition (which involves the lack of these essential substances) results in "apathy, lethargy, social isolation, and impairment in memory." Studies of the effects of malnutrition also reveal other effects, such as a general slowing down in all activities, but especially in mental alertness, self-discipline, motivation, and sex drive. Often these are accompanied by corresponding increases in moodiness, irritability, and apathy (1991:23). These are clearly symptomatic of depression. Poverty is the breeding ground for many other conditions that can result in depression, such as under- or unemployment and, increasingly, homelessness.

DEPRESSION AND UNEMPLOYMENT

As a number of studies have shown, the unemployed are frequently depressed. The reasons are obvious, considering the relationship of work to self-esteem in our society, where "what you do" often is interpreted as "what you are." Certainly, for blacks, unemployment is one of the more obvious and vicious effects of racism. The relationship of work to self-esteem and mental health (particularly lack of depression and the presence of feelings of well-being) is obvious and needs no further discussion. Unemployed individuals and their families, lacking money and health insurance, are often undertreated for physical and mental health problems.

DEPRESSION AND THE HOMELESS

An increasingly visible problem in many American cities is the homeless—a large, unfortunately growing, and far from uniform group. (The homeless Vietnam veterans in Washington, D.C., for example, differ from homeless people in Baltimore or in New York City.)

Bassuk (1991:66) points out that "houselessness" is only one part of homelessness. Homeless people are often without friends, family, and other kinds of support systems. Homelessness is a vicious cycle, made worse by both chronic and acute medical problems and by malnutrition. Worse still, homelessness is often seen as the fault of the individual, a reflection of his inability to cope because of moral shortcomings (Bassuk 1991:74). The trend to condemn, rather than to understand or help, the homeless seems to be growing.

A perceptive study of the homeless in Baltimore showed that 51 percent were female, 54 percent were black, only 5 percent were married at the time of the study, and only 29 percent were over the age of forty-one (Belcher and DiBlasio 1990). In this group, 75 percent were considered to have a problem with depression, and of this depressed group, 37 percent had problems serious enough to need immediate clinical attention. As might be expected, depression was associated with low self-esteem, disturbed family relations, poor health, drug abuse, and other conditions, but the main two factors contributing to depression were low self-esteem and food deprivation. The authors point out that although "causation" is hard to establish and it is impossible to determine if hunger or depression came first, hunger certainly did not help raise low self-esteem or lessen depression. They make the very sensible suggestion that feeding the homeless should be part of intervention and may be as important as (if not more important than) psychotherapy.

Depression is but one of the mental and physical ailments troubling the homeless. The true extent of mental health problems among the homeless has long been controversial. In the increasingly judgmental view taken of the homeless (i.e., blaming them for their condition), the importance of mental illness tends to be understated. We lack accurate data, but in New York City (the largest city in the country), the estimates of the number of homeless range from 50,000 to 100,000, 40 percent of whom are seriously mentally ill (Cody 1991). Estimates nationwide run from 250,000 to over 3 million people (Rossi et al. 1987). Other studies have estimated that the rate of chronic mental illness ranges from 10 to 40 percent. From 20 to 30 percent of this number presently abuse drugs and/or alcohol (in addition, more than 50 percent have abused these substances at some time in their past), and from 10 to 20 percent exhibit signs of psychosis ("Mental Illness and Homelessness: Part I" 1990). Within the homeless who are identified as suffering from a mental disorder, the rates of affective disorder run from over 5 percent to more than 50 percent (Goodwin and Jamison 1990:177). Even accounting for errors in reporting, and lacking information on the exact number of the homeless, these rates of depression are higher than those in the population as a whole. Furthermore, as observed by Goodwin and Jamison (1990:177), substance abuse may mask other mental illnesses, such as depression. Thus the actual rates of affective disorder among the homeless may be much greater.

The homeless population also includes a large number of former psychiatric patients discharged from hospitals under policies of deinstitutionalization. The extent to which these former patients cause, exacerbate, or are the victims of the current problem of homelessness is hotly debated (Belcher and DiBlasio 1990:264).

Accompanying depression, and impossible to isolate as to which is cause and which is effect, is substance abuse, including all the drugs of abuse but particularly alcohol. In New York City, although traumatic injury was the main reason for the use of hospital emergency rooms by homeless people, substance abuse and mental disorder (including depression) were seen as major factors (Padgett and Struening 1991). Homeless people, when interviewed, frequently reported feelings of lack of self-worth, with very little control over their lives, resulting in depression and often physical illness (Kinzel 1991). These people engaged in little, and often ineffectual, "health-seeking behaviors." They were isolated from families and health agencies and often felt that nobody really cared (Kinzel 1991). This feeling of isolation further decreased any sense of trust, which further lessened seeking help (Kinzel 1991). Kinzel called for both physical and psychological help to be made more available by bringing the health care personnel into the streets, shelters, and other places where homeless people are found (1991).

Vulnerability Based on Sexual Orientation: Depression in Female and Male Homosexuals

Reliable data on the mental health of homosexual women and men are difficult to obtain. Homophobia ("abnormal fear of homosexuals" [Thomas 1989:839]) is comparable in its effects on people to sexism and racism. The stress of being "gay" in a "straight" world directly affects self-image. The frequently self-cited emotion of shame—a cousin to guilt—is fertile breeding ground for depression. Many homosexuals, of both genders, report strains in maintaining secrecy, as they often fear disclosure (Markowitz 1991b:29). This constant repression must certainly limit options and produce feelings of helplessness, which engender hopelessness—all hallmarks of depression.

Among the problems of being gay in a straight world are the problems of same-sex couples who have decided to live together in a relationship that is presently not legally recognized in any state (Macsherry 1991). Same-sex couples almost always lack the legal status and protection of the legally married couple, which is no small consideration when it comes to such matters as health insurance, inheritance rights, and custody of children being raised by the pair. There is also the strain of experiencing rejections by two families, who often do not understand, and do not accept their children's partners. Most families, for example, have "no constructive language to deal with [their children coming out]" (Hersch 1991:41). Social support is lessened, which increases the potential for depressive responses and affective disorders.

The suicide rates for homosexual women and men are higher than those for their heterosexual counterparts. White lesbians attempt suicide two and one-half times more often than heterosexual women

(Saunders and Valente 1987, reported in McGrath et al. 1990:88). Similar data hold for homosexual men.

SOME TREATMENT ISSUES

Although homosexuality is no longer considered an illness by the psychiatric establishment, a high percentage of today's therapists received their training when homosexuality and "ego-dystonic homosexuality" *were* considered illnesses (McGrath et al. 1990:89). Furthermore, as sensitively put by Markowitz (1991b:28) "straight therapists . . . [assume] it is less than normal or less preferable to be homosexual." Straight therapists may frequently experience countertransference reactions: uncertainty of their own sexual identity, or fear that they may be gay or have latent homosexual tendencies. These reactions must certainly interfere with therapy, either through avoidance of a central issue of sexual preference and identity or, reported frequently by homosexual clients, through seemingly positive attempts by the therapist to refer them elsewhere—allegedly, on the basis that a gay therapist would understand them better (Markowitz 1991b:30).

Being heterosexual is not an impediment to working with homosexual clients of either gender; therapists must be aware of their own attitudes and prejudices and must make sure these do not interfere with good treatment. The assumption of the superiority of a heterosexual way of life is probably the greatest barrier to full therapeutic understanding. The argument that only gays can understand gays is not, in our opinion, valid. If put into practice, it would mean referring all homosexual clients to homosexual therapists, depriving this group of needed help. Many gays—like many straights—do not make an overt pronouncement of their sexual preference when they go for therapy. The "admission tickets" for the therapy might be any one of a number of reasons: phobias, work problems, depression, and so forth. In the course of working with clients, it often happens that sexual preference issues emerge. We believe it is unethical to interrupt a good therapeutic relationship to refer the client.

Many gay women seek psychiatric treatment. In a study of lesbian women in San Francisco, two-thirds of white lesbians and more than 50 percent of black lesbians had been in therapy (Markowitz 1991b:29). Another estimate was that about 80 percent of lesbians had seen a counselor or therapist (Albro and Tulley, 1979, cited in McGrath et al. 1990:89).

Self-help groups have been increasingly used by homosexuals, not only for issues involving couples but for substance abuse and other problems (Macsherry 1991). Although less of a problem in urban areas than in rural ones, these self-help groups (e.g., Alcoholics Anonymous) may be dominated by males and by homophobic males and females. Although these groups may provide enormous help, they may also facilitate further discrimination (McGrath et al. 1990:89).

One final note: AIDS, no longer strictly a gay disease, has become epidemic. There is increasing research on AIDS, particularly its psychological aspects, including depression. Several studies have shown that depression in AIDS patients is a function of the physical symptoms; as the disease worsens, the degree of affective disorder also increases (Rabkin et al. 1991; Gorman et al. 1991). Thus treatment of the depression often accompanying the AIDS infections should be considered along with the treatment of the disease.

Needless to say, we need more research on AIDS. We also need more research on the interactions of sexual preference with all mental health issues, including depression.

Depression in African-Americans/Blacks

DO AFRICAN-AMERICANS SUFFER FROM DEPRESSION?

In the United States, race and social class are often interrelated to such an extent that it is difficult to separate the two. In particular it was long thought that African-Americans (or blacks; we shall use both terms) did not suffer from depression. This was partly because African-Americans represented only a very small portion of those treated in public clinics, in hospitals, and by private practitioners. Another factor was the perpetuation of the stereotypes about African-Americans as happy (i.e., nondepressed) individuals—their good humor, ready smiles, and so forth. As later research proved, these stereotypes were very far from the truth. Blacks do suffer from depression and, in certain age and status categories (to be discussed later), in rates that surpass those of both whites and other minority groups.

Fellin (1989) did a very comprehensive and thoughtful review of depression among African-Americans. It considered epidemiology (prevalence and incidence counts), assessment (diagnosis), help-seeking behaviors (utilization), treatment, and rehabilitation (Fellin 1989:245). In considering studies of the rates of treatment, Fellin points out that African-Americans underutilize treatment—or perhaps more accurately, do not receive it at rates comparable to those of whites. We discuss these and other relevant issues next.

Less availability of treatment. One reason for the low number of African-Americans seen in treatment facilities is that there was—and continues to be—obvious racial discrimination. Blacks were denied access to these facilities, as they have been denied access to schools, public accommodations, and the like. As the laws segregating the races were overturned and as behavior changed (admittedly, at a slower rate) more blacks have had access to and have used these facilities, resulting in greater awareness of the true prevalence of depression among African-Americans.

A second factor is that blacks lived primarily in rural Southern areas, where there were few treatment facilities. Consequently, they had little opportunity for treatment and therefore had low recorded rates of depression. As blacks migrated to urban, often Northern areas, treatment facilities were more available and recorded rates of depression increased.

Invisibility. Another reason for the low rate of utilization of mental health facilities by blacks lies in the nature of depression itself. In other mental illnesses the person suffering from the condition is more likely to be visible. For example, the schizophrenic hallucinates and often disturbs other people. (It has been said that many people are in mental hospitals not because they are disturbed but because they are disturbing!) Depressives of all races usually withdraw, not disturbing other people, and thus may escape the attention of authorities as well as of potential helpers. This quality of the "invisible man" also applies to African-American depressives.

Less help sought for treatment. Most depressed people do not receive treatment from professional therapists, and African-Americans look for help even less than white Americans (Sussman, Robins, and Earls 1987:190). In particular, "those at highest risk of not seeking care were the young (35 years old or younger) those with few symptoms in a single episode, those who had experienced few episodes in their lifetimes, and those without long episodes" (Sussman, Robins, and Earls 1987:190). Blacks were quoted as saying, much more frequently than whites, that they were afraid of being put into the hospital; that they did not have the time and were really frightened of therapy. African-Americans may also view the treatment systems as more alien and intimidating than whites do (Sussman, Robins, and Earls 1987: 190).

Underdiagnosis because of culturally biased criteria. A number of studies indicate that the rate of depression in African-Americans is understated because of deficiencies in clinical practices and procedures. Jones and Gray (1986) specify that "psychiatry relies primarily on signs, symptoms, behaviors . . . [which] may be similar for different illnesses and may be culturally related . . . [or which may] differ from one ethnic group to another." Schizophrenia is often overdiagnosed and depression is frequently underdiagnosed, because of divergences in language and mannerisms and because of problems black clients have in relating to white therapists (and vice versa). These are all distorted by the general, and untrue, belief—still fairly widely held—that blacks do not suffer from depression (Jones and Gray 1986:61).

A previous study (Jones et al. 1982) theorized that depression in African-Americans may be difficult to assess (and, by implication, even more difficult for nonblack clinicians) because it is presented differently and that blacks have unusual coping devices. They cite the case of a person who has an intensely pessimistic view of the future who may very well engage in such actions as robbing banks or attacking police officers, which are labeled sociopathic but which are actually suicide attempts, although not always conscious ones.

In discussing what he called "depression and nonwhiteness," Claudewell S. Thomas, then (1975) professor of psychiatry at Rutgers University, observed that depression and depressive equivalents were increasing, particularly in the visible minority person who is especially vulnerable to feelings of low self-esteem and desperation and who has a gloomy view of the future, because the needs of the minority person were often overlooked, deliberately or otherwise, by the dominant social order. (In other words, discrimination causes what Thomas called a lack of reciprocity between the social order and the minority person.) The low self-esteem of the often depressed minority person may result in escapist behavior in an attempt to ease the pain of depression. This includes self-medication—anesthetizing oneself with drugs or alcohol or with fantasies of great achievements, such as winning large amounts of money by gambling. All these factors, which had the effect of isolating an individual from his or her pain, often seemed "to have a life of their own" (Thomas 1975:21).

These attempts to ease the pain of depression, isolation, and discrimination are self-defeating and increase depression, poor self-image, and so forth. Furthermore, these behaviors, according to Thomas, often fit into the stereotype of the minority person as a "spaced-out, drunken, irresponsible and shiftless human being" (Thomas 1975:21).

Alcohol and drugs often lower inhibitions and heighten the chances that the depressed person will "act in an *extra-punitive manner*" (Thomas 1975:21, emphasis in the original).

> Thus, in an effort to make his own candle burn brighter, the depressed minority person may be forced to put out that of his neighbor and frequently does so with violence. . . . for example, homicides . . . [by] blacks and whites differ. . . . alcohol has been found to be involved in over two-thirds of black homicides . . . [with] white homicides the rate of alcohol usage was less than half that of black[s]. . . . compared with white homicides, black homicide tends to be alcohol-induced, sudden,

unpremeditated and takes place in familiar surroundings [Thomas 1975: 21–22].

Bell (1988) points out that head trauma may be an organic etiological factor that may be a complication of the diagnosis of depression in blacks, minorities, and lower socioeconomic groups; this trauma may be followed by mania (Bell 1988:135). He strongly recommends that when clients, especially blacks, show with hostile and/or aggressive behavior, a "history of central nervous system insult should not be overlooked" (Bell 1988:136).

Bell, commenting on the work of Jones, Gray, and Parson, reiterated that overcrowded, understaffed, and underbudgeted inner-city institutions, where careful assessments and diagnoses are impossible, add to the social distance between staff and clients and are compounded by "culturally biased diagnostic criteria, such as standardized psychological tests" that do not accurately probe the depth of black psychic functioning (Bell 1988:135). Furthermore, as we have pointed out, the majority of professionals are white, and the whole process of screening and diagnosis may not have been "validated for black populations" (Bell 1988:246).

In summary, although the preceding comments were made in reference to African-Americans, particularly the empirical studies showing that blacks experience high rates of schizophrenia and low rates of depression, they could be made for *all* minority groups. Misdiagnoses seem to be based on two conflicting assumptions made by researchers and mental health personnel: "(1) Blacks and whites exhibit symptomatology similarly but diagnosticians mistakenly assume that they are different; (2) blacks and whites display psychopathology in different ways but diagnosticians are unaware of or insensitive to such cultural differences" (Neighbors et al. 1989). It seems apparent that these two conflicting and unresolved assumptions underlie much of the contemporary confusion on minority group status and the diagnosis of affective disorders.

BIOLOGICAL DIFFERENCES IN THE EXPRESSION OF DEPRESSION AMONG AFRICAN-AMERICANS AND OTHER RACIAL GROUPS

Vernon and Roberts (1982), in applying the Schedule for Affective Disorders–Research Diagnostic Criteria (SAD–RDC), detected no significant differences in the incidence (current rate) of major or minor depression among whites, blacks, and Mexican-Americans. However, the lifetime rates for whites and Mexican-Americans were similar to each other, and both were higher than the rate for black Americans. One interesting finding of their study was that both blacks and Mexican-Americans had rates for bipolar II disorder ("a diagnosis of lower reliability and questionable validity") that were double those for whites (Vernon and Roberts 1982).

Jones, Gray, and Parson (1988:134), in stating that depression among blacks and whites may manifest itself differently, point out that frequently there may be both paranoid and grandiose delusions. In addition, there may be hallucinations and thought disorders, especially in bipolar disturbances with both whites and blacks, including "flight of ideas, incoherence, loosening of association and illogical thinking . . . [and] the diagnostic picture may be further complicated by alcohol and/ or drug abuse and hostile and/or aggressive behavior"; these latter factors are also seen in whites, but the authors state that they may be found more frequently among black Americans (Jones, Gray, and Parson 1988:134).

These and similar findings led to questions about the possibility of biological differences in the expression of depression among different racial groups.

First (1988:138) states that these differing rates of major affective disorder among separate ethnic groups may be due to "biologically intrinsic differences, . . . environmentally associated differences [e.g., poverty] . . . or bias during diagnosis." He makes the meaningful observation that these biases are not necessarily overcome by the use of criteria (by implication, those of the D.S.M.-III-R) because there may still be cultural bias on the part of the investigator, who may be more familiar with one group (usually, the one he or she belongs to) than with others. First discusses the issue of *false positives* (mistakenly stating a condition exists when it does not), which he states is responsible for the mistaken identification of more bipolar II in blacks and Latinos than in whites. Similarly, *false negatives* (overlooking a condition when it does exist) occur when depressive equivalent behavior is overlooked. For example, there is a higher incidence of somatic symptoms in blacks than in whites (also a higher occurrence among Asians) and these are often incorrectly identified as somatic or physical illness rather than as depression. According to First (1988:138), these false negatives also account for the underreporting among blacks, and we believe that the same is true for Asians.

At the end of a three-year study of 147 patients, Curtis (1988:140) and his colleagues concluded that there was nothing unusual about how blacks experienced either bipolar or unipolar disorders. He does not rule out genetic inheritance within particular family groups and feels that there should be more studies of this topic. However, as for genetic inheritance on the basis of race, he points out that most racial groups, such as American blacks, are not genetically pure, for there has been an infusion of genes from American whites and Native-Americans (Curtis 1988:140).

German (1988:137) adds that the D.S.M.-III and the D.S.M.-III-R are culture-bound, that "persecutory delusions, irritability and aggression, and grosser degrees of thought disorder," which appear in bipolar disorder, also occur much more frequently in African blacks, in Asians, and in Latin Americans. Although these symptoms were first seen among European whites, their incidence is probably underdescribed among white Americans (German 1988:137). German comments that he is "a little saddened" by the failure of American psychiatry to utilize the international literature and, by implication, accuses American clinicians of being culture-bound.

When discussing depression among minorities in the United States, and especially among American blacks, it becomes fairly obvious that we are not talking about a biological problem. More important is the impact of *social* factors. With African-Americans, a number of these confounding social factors are relevant and must be considered. For example, Fellin (1989:246) indicated that risk factors associated with depression, in addition to race, were social class, employment status, gender, age, marital status, household income, and household composition.

In short, there seem to be many determinants of the alleged low rate of depression among blacks (and other racial and ethnic minority groups in this country, for the preceding factors certainly apply to Native-Americans, Americans of Asian descent, and others). These seem to be social factors, with psychological consequences, rather than factors based in biology, neurology, and so forth. As social conditions such as racial discrimination change, one side effect should be increasing and more equal access to treatment facilities.

SOCIOECONOMIC STATUS AND DEPRESSION AMONG AFRICAN-AMERICANS

As many professionals have observed, there is no shortage of psychiatric problems among African-Americans. In the National Survey of Black Americans (NSBA; 2,107 interviews of a representative sample of adult blacks eighteen years of age and older), in responses to standardized scales, 30 percent of the sample exhibited "high levels of psychiatric symptomatology," a slightly higher proportion than that in other studies of similar populations (E. H. Johnson 1989:1221). This sample is believed to be truly representative, since previously studied populations underrepresented blacks (E. H. Johnson 1989:1221). Not surprisingly, the NSBA showed that blacks with higher levels of symptoms tended to be from the lower socioeconomic groups. It was hypothesized that lack of money and/or health insurance stood in the way of seeking help until conditions became very serious (E. H. Johnson 1989:1221).

Most studies of the rates of treatment reveal no significant differences in rates of depression between blacks and whites when social class was controlled (Wahrheit, Holzer, and Arey 1975; Gary 1985:21). One variation on this theme is the study of Cockerham (1990), whose research did not support the belief that poorer blacks suffer greater distress than poorer whites. He found "no significant differences . . . at the lowest income levels but . . . as income increases among blacks and whites, psychological distress decreases . . . [especially] for blacks" (Cockerham 1990).

SUICIDE AMONG AFRICAN-AMERICANS

The rate of suicide has increased among both blacks and whites, but there are differences by age and gender. Suicide among blacks tends not to rise—or to rise less dramatically—by age. The rates among blacks are the highest, for both men and women, between the ages of twenty-five and forty-four, and they decline after age forty-five (Baker 1990:504). In 1981, the rate for white men was 30.3 per 100,000 for ages sixty-five to seventy-four, rising to 43.8 for ages seventy-five to eighty-four and 53.6 for those over eighty-five. The comparable figures, for the same age groups among black men, are 9.7, 18.0, and 12.7 percent (Baker 1990:497). For white women ages sixty-five to seventy-four the rate is 7.3, dropping to 5.5 for ages seventy-five to eighty-four and to 3.7 for those over eighty-five. The comparable figures for black women are 3.0, 1.0, and 1.8 (Baker 1990). The suicide rate for black women was, and remains, low among all age groups.

In 1981 the suicide rate for young males fifteen to twenty-four years old was higher among whites than among blacks (21.2 percent compared to 11.1 percent). For ages twenty-five to thirty-four it was 26.2 percent for white males compared to 21.8 percent for black males, but in 1950 the figures for the fifteen- to twenty-four age group were 6.6 percent (for whites) versus 4.9 percent (for blacks) and for ages twenty-five to thirty-four they were 13.8 percent versus 9.3 percent. What these data reveal is that the rates for older blacks are low compared to those of older whites; however, the rates for young blacks and whites, both male and female, have risen dramatically between 1950 and 1981 (Baker 1990:495)!

These figures are even more upsetting when we consider that the 1980 census showed that 41 percent of all blacks were between the ages of sixteen and thirty-nine—the age group with the highest rate for black suicide (Baker 1990:495). There are problems with census data, including underrepresentation of blacks, which would inflate these rates, especially compared to whites. However, even granting underrepresentation of blacks, particularly black males fifteen to thirty-nine, these data are distressing.

Data relating to the comparative morbidity (extent) of depression and affective illness between blacks and whites are contradictory. We shall not expand upon them here, except to say that individuals suffering from emotional problems, particularly affective disorders and schizophrenia, who also abuse chemical substances, particularly alcohol, are at higher risk for attempted and successful suicides (Baker 1990:505). Preventive strategies outlined by Baker are interventions that deal with "in-group" stress (e.g., family problems, friendships, personal relationships) and with the "extra-group" stresses (e.g., work problems and financial difficulties).

The *urban stress* theory holds that the high suicide rate among young black males is actually a way of dealing with the "compounded urban stresses . . . of poverty, unemployment, racism, poor housing, . . . poor education" to which we add a view of the future as being without hope or promise (Baker 1990:503–504). As stated by Chunn (1981), the increasing opportunities for blacks have resulted in their adopting values of the larger culture; however, in the transition, they have left behind more traditional values and support systems, such as the church, the black community, and the black family, both nuclear and extended. The need for these supports continues, and one result of their not being available might be lessened ability to cope and, in desperation, suicide.

In short, one of the main elements in the suicide of young blacks, both male and female, is depression. The dehumanizing effects of such adverse social situations as discrimination and lack of job opportunities are among the high-risk factors for developing depression.

DEPRESSION IN AFRICAN-AMERICAN MEN AND WOMEN

Both black and white psychiatrists have said that depression was the problem most commonly seen in both black men and women; furthermore, there were many similarities, but few differences attributable to gender, in the psychotherapy of black men and black women (Jones and Gray 1984:21).

Unfortunately, most studies comparing rates of depression between blacks and whites do not go further and make cross-comparisons of gender, by race. However, even though the data sometimes present a confusing picture, Fellin (1989:247) concludes that black women are more likely to suffer from depression than white women, because of "two second-class citizenship positions . . . being black and being female."

In comparing the rates of depression of black women and black men, there is a great deal of inconsistency in the data. Several studies reviewed by Gary (1985) revealed that black women showed lower depression scores than black men. Other studies did not find differences in rates between black women and black men. He made the interesting point that researchers have used "comparative research paradigms . . . [and] have tended not to study depression *within the context of the black community.* . . . [failing] to ask whether the same variables are useful for predicting depressive symptoms both in the black . . . and white community" (Gary 1985:22, emphasis added). Complicating these comparative studies is the small size of the sample of blacks, particularly when the percentage of black men included in the studies has often been lower than the ratio of black men to black women in the population.

Gary (1985) found that demographic factors, such as age, marital status, and so on, and stressful life events, such as change in job, unemployment, change in residence, physical illness, and arrests, were better predictors of depression than sociocultural patterns, such as social ties, family relationships, religious involvement, friendship ties, and social support. Gary (1985:23) states that blacks are more likely to be involved in religious activities than whites. Furthermore, the black church serves eight functions: economic development, education development, group identity and values, leadership development, social support, protest and political development, psychological support and social intercourse and amusement.

Several of Gary's findings are contrary to expectations and contrary to those for white males. Younger black men were more depressed than older black men; the opposite is true of white men. Also contrary to the data on whites, separated or divorced black men were less depressed than married black men. Unemployment was among the stressful life events, and although the data are not statistically significant, black males with no arrests or illness had lower depression scores than those with arrests or illness (Gary 1985:27). Of the men in the study, "the depressed men were young, never married, high school graduates who lived in large households with an annual income of less than $8,000, had a high rate of residential mobility and were unemployed. . . . [those] less likely to be depressed were 45 years or older, married, and employed with a family income of $20,000 or more; had some college education or were college graduates; and lived in a household with two or three persons. These characteristics are not found frequently in the black male community" (Gary 1985:27).

Interestingly, the rate of depression among black men identified as being very conscious of race appeared to be higher than those black men who were not very racially conscious; this finding was identified as one needing further research, with the author stating that "perhaps a more refined racial consciousness measure is needed" (Gary 1985:27). Furthermore, involvement with an extended family did not lower depression scores; those more likely to be depressed lived in "extended family units . . . [with] few friends, . . . [were] inactive in community activities, . . . [with] low involvement in religious activities, and . . . very conscious of racial issues," whereas those "less likely to be depressed lived in nuclear families, participated in both community and religious activities, had an extensive network of friends, and were not too conscious of race" (Gary 1985:27). The author urges caution in the interpretation of these profiles, for the scores on these sociocultural variables and the depression scores were not statistically significant; these relationships may be better described as trends. Furthermore, and this is Gary's editorial comment, "useful measures of socio-cultural variables have not been developed for the Black community" (Gary 1985:27).

We have reviewed Gary's study at length, for it was one of the first to examine depression among black men. It was not a probability sample (randomly or systematically chosen), and some of the instruments were admittedly either not specifically designed for use with blacks or had to be adapted for use in this particular study. We agree with Gary that what is needed is a further development of these measures for use with blacks, a point that could be made when discussing assessment of depression with other minority groups.

Depression in poor black single mothers. A useful article, entitled "Depression, Danger, Dependency, Denial: Work with Poor, Black, Single Parents," was written by Richard Wortman (1981:662), who describes himself as a middle-class white male clinician, as are most of the workers with poor black single mothers. Wortman paints a vivid picture of a group of poor women, often subsisting on inadequate welfare payments or inadequate remittances from absent men, who were burdened by poverty and discrimination and were living under the real threat of violence. Frequently without assistance of any kind, they were responsible for caring for children who were often very sick and disturbed. These women were frequently depressed, although they did not know it. They "*needed strenuously to deny dependency needs and the* *impact of severe losses and traumas.* The motto of these women was 'be strong' " (Wortman 1981:664, emphasis in the original). Wortman made a number of excellent suggestions for treating these poor, depressed, single black mothers that are a model for empathic understanding. We shall discuss these later, in the final section on treatment, as they apply to other, similar minority groups.

SOME TREATMENT ISSUES

Broman (1987) has pointed out that previous studies on the relationship of race to help-seeking have been inconsistent. In his reanalysis of the results of two national studies, Broman found that blacks and whites sought help in almost equal proportions, but there were differences in the *sources* of help sought. Blacks, more than whites, asked for help from mental health professionals, but particularly for economic and health problems. Another possibility is that economic and physical problems may affect blacks much more than whites (Broman 1987:480). Similarly, blacks more than whites sought help from teachers, lawyers, social workers, and emergency rooms. Whites more frequently sought help from doctors and—not consistent with previous studies—from the clergy. Broman states that the previous findings of blacks not using mental health services are based on faulty inference that because the poor do not use mental health services and because more blacks are poor, blacks do not use mental health services (1987:480). Income seems to have lessened in importance as a variable in using professional help. Broman quotes Veroff, Douvan, and Kulka (1981) as showing that one important element in seeking help from professionals is whether or not the person thinks that professionals can help solve their problems.

The social distance between patient and therapist may be a problem. Sometimes a social class difference exists between a black middle-class therapist and a black lower-class client, who might also have difficulty relating to each other (Thomas 1975:22).

When asked if there were indications that nonwhites would require significantly different forms of treatment, Thomas (1975:22) said that "the forms of treatment available were essentially the same for black or white, that . . . response[s] to . . . drugs are biological responses *that should not vary on the basis of whiteness or non-whiteness*" (emphasis in the original).

Studies have consistently shown that the presence of social participation and social support was linked to lower levels of depression (Fellin 1989:248). For example, those elderly blacks who felt that they had supportive relationships experienced less depression than those who did not report such support (Smith-Ruiz 1985:1017). Older blacks who were married had lower rates of depressive symptoms (Smith-Ruiz 1985:1017). Several studies have shown that blacks who participate in community events tend to show low rates of depression. One particular study showed that social support did not seem to affect the mental health of black men, either positively or negatively, but it had a positive effect on the mental health of black women (Brown and Gary 1987).

Participation in social activities, as well as the availability of social supports, seems essential for the mental health of blacks and should be built into intervention. The mental health needs of depressed blacks and of other minority groups, are probably best served with a "combination of primary group help and professional mental health services" (Fellin 1989:249). (Treatment for *all* racial and ethnic minority groups is discussed at the end of this chapter.)

Depression Among Asian- and Pacific-Americans

The category *Asian- and Pacific-American* includes more than thirty-two discrete groups and many subgroups that are markedly different from each other (Wong 1982:186). For example, people from Asia—particularly Southeast Asia, the source of much recent immigration to the United States—are often referred to as a group, but the term *Southeast Asia* covers a great number of cultures, languages, and societies. It has been pointed out that within the groups from Southeast Asia there are common factors that are very relevant to health and mental health matters. Although some of the concerns are unique to that group of nations, there are some general trends that also apply to a number of the different Asian and Pacific cultures.

Tung (1985) has pointed out that among these Southeast Asian people "feelings and emotional problems are rarely considered proper reasons for seeking professional assistance." Psychological explanations are not accepted as reasons for not fulfilling one's duties. Illnesses of a psychological nature, or with psychological causes, are seen as "extraordinary, supernatural, or magical phenomena" (Tung 1985). For these reasons, newly arrived immigrants from this area are often unwilling to seek help from professional mental health services and do so only when life situations seem unsolvable (Owan 1985:2). This reluctance to seek help outside of the family and community is typical of many Asian and Pacific-American groups (Wong 1982:189). Any intervention must be culturally relevant, and useful to the individual; the helper should be aware of cultural taboos (Wong 1982:3).

Many peoples identified as Asian (in particular the Chinese, Japanese, and Koreans) concentrate on physical symptoms, which heightens the relevance and effectiveness of a "medical approach" to problems (Kinzie 1985). Interestingly enough, several investigators have reported that the dosages of psychotropic medication used with southeast Asians, as well as with other Asians, should often be much lower than those used with whites (Wong 1982:122–123). One consequence of this phenomenon is that many Asians (probably overmedicated) do not take their medication, possibly because of severe reaction to the excessive dosages prescribed (Wong 1982:125).

Tung (1985:10–11) states that people from Southeast Asia may very well be troubled with depression, and guilt—particularly about leaving home, and possibly about relatives left behind—but these are considered private matters not to be discussed in public or with strangers. In some of these cultures, misfortunes and suffering (distress) are seen as the constants of life. Since everyone experiences them, complaining will do no good and is often seen as a sign of weakness and a lack of character (Tung 1985). If one needs comfort, it should be sought from the family or from friends, because they can empathize and understand. This cannot be expected from a stranger (e.g., a professional). As explained by Tung, in many of these countries of origin (in Asia) there are either no mental health professionals, or the professionals themselves are few and/or not seen as a source of help (1985).

Char (1980:68–69) indicates that among the Chinese in Hawaii, there are several groups that are inclined to depression. One group is made up of students who come with high aspirations yet must adjust to differences in language and culture, all made worse by loneliness. Another group is middle-aged women who have dutifully fulfilled their traditional roles as wives, daughters-in-law, and mothers, with the expectation of a "seat of reverence" as elders. When this does not happen, they become very depressed.

Eastern attitudes on suicide often differ markedly from Western views, where suicide is seen as a result of illness or pathology and is condemned. It is seen as a personal decision that stems from motives considered more "normal" in these cultures. Suicide may be committed for the honor of self or of the group (saving face), for political purposes (such as the incidents of political protestors dousing themselves with gasoline and setting themselves afire), or—a throwback to the Samurai warrior's Code of Bushido—it may be an honor-saving path from a moral problem or situation (Seward 1968). Outsiders are considered to lack knowledge of the person's motives and thus cannot interfere. Only intimate friends and the family, not society, can comment on or judge the rightness or wrongness of the act (Tung 1985:11). (Ryan [1985] provides a cogent discussion of suicide among Chinese-Americans, as well as appropriate approaches to treating Chinese-Americans.)

Anxiety and depression are the most frequent nonpsychotic conditions for which Indochinese patients most readily seek help. Other complaints are headache, tension in the neck and back, thoracic oppression, palpitations, dizziness, flatulence, poor appetite, lassitude, fatigue, aches and pains in the limbs, and sleep disorder (Tung 1985:19). One factor complicating treatment that is often overlooked when dealing with Asian-Americans is that in these groups there may be marked problems with drugs, often the drugs of abuse but increasingly alcohol (Trimble, Padilla, and Bell 1987:7–8). We have already stressed the interrelatedness of drug abuse, alcohol abuse, and depression (see chapter 10).

SOME TREATMENT ISSUES

The stress from life in a new land has made recent Asian and Pacific-American immigrants vulnerable to mental and emotional disorders. According to Wong (1982:189), they attempt to handle this stress by themselves, avoiding established mental health services. If they do use these services, they often drop out after a few contacts. They may reestablish contact only when there is an acute crisis. They often feel that these services do not help them and do not understand them (Wong 1982:190). Wong stresses that just the presence of Asian-American workers does not seem to increase utilization very much (1982:190). However, if these services are designed specifically for Asian- and Pacific-Americans—including "community outreach, community participation in decision making and bilingual workers" aware of and sensitive to their culture—then they are more likely to be used.

A number of large cities have many recent immigrants from Southeast Asia. Their inability to communicate well in English hampers their access to mental health treatment, especially when we consider the extent to which psychotherapeutic intervention in the United States depends upon verbal skills. Moreover, because of their problems with English, many people new to this country are unaware of the services available (Tung 1985:6).

Although mental health providers who know the culture and the language of the Asian people are in short supply, this may not always be a negative. Tung (1985) has reported that some Asian clients prefer non-Asian therapists because they are afraid that counselors from their own communities and groups will not maintain confidentiality. The use of an interpreter presents similar problems; with three people involved, the likelihood of keeping confidentiality decreases (Ishisake, Nguyen, and Okimoto 1985:44–45). As Tung (1985:8) also points out, in his experience not many "Southeast Asian auxiliaries" can assume the detached stance of the professional translator. They often become caught up with the client's problems, insert themselves into the situation, offer their opinions, and propose solutions. (The senior author of this book has had the same experience while working in New York City with Puerto Rican interpreters, who interposed not only their views but their extreme and often punitive value judgments on their countrymen who could not "stand on their own two feet." There was an unspoken but implied comparison with the interpreter, who *could* do so.) Clients usually do not welcome these opinions but may not be able to protest or may be too intimidated. Unfortunately, bilingual and bicultural workers—especially Asians—are scarce (Tung 1985:9).

Tung (1985:25–27) believes that psychotherapy must be brief (to avoid "imposing" upon strangers); limited to the presenting problem and to the identified patient; goal directed (to a goal determined by the client); and usually restricted to alleviating the symptoms or the crisis that provoked the visit. Furthermore, the therapist should take an active role, assuming that the patient complies with therapeutic suggestions. Role modeling, persuasion, pressure, and advice are some techniques suggested by Tung. The therapist may also use many other techniques, including placebos and environmental manipulation, material assistance, advocacy, bolstering of the client's coping abilities "at the conscious level," and focus on the present and immediate future. Little attention should be paid to the past, consistent with the client's value system, which—in Southeast Asia—emphasizes a continual search for "peace and harmony with others and with the world in general." This philosophy promotes "accommodation, appeasement, submission and acceptance, rather than . . . confrontation, aggression, impatience and rebellion" (Tung 1985:25–27).

Some Western therapies have been adapted very well to help Asian clients in the United States. Kim (1985) has proposed a form of family therapy, based on strategic-structural principles. For example, speaking to clients in a way that takes into account their rank and status within the family hierarchy (as defined by their culture) is suggested as a good way to start a family session. Many Asian cultures (as reflected in their languages) do not lend themselves to family therapy carried on in an "egalitarian, open, direct and conjoint fashion" (Kim 1985:345). Kim's use of the structural-strategic principles emphasizes goal-setting, use of the family, emphasis on the present, and other adaptations that are in accord with Asian cultural norms.

Hispanics/Latinos/La Raza and Depression

The terms *Latino* and *Hispanic* cover a number of groups. Snowden (1982:17–18) uses the term *La Raza*, which is explained as a "term applied to a large diverse group of people linked by the Spanish language and the Hispanic culture." It may include people of Mexican descent (Mexican-Americans), which includes Mexican-Americans born in the United States (some here for several generations) and those who are either newcomers to the United States or may go back and forth between the two countries. This breaks down even further: Some Mexican-Americans are either partly or fully Indian, and some proudly trace an unbroken racial line to Spain. Needless to say, within Mexico discriminations exist based on skin color, racial background, economics, and other factors. Add to this the discrimination in the United States—particularly in the Southwest, California, and Texas—and it becomes even more complicated.

There are many other kinds of Latinos with similar divisions: Puerto Ricans and refugees from El Salvador and immigrants from the Dominican Republic, Central and South America, various Caribbean islands, and elsewhere.

Reviewing only a few of the many studies on the various La Raza groups shows the same confusion and conflicting results as do studies on African-Americans, and many of the same precautions should be taken in interpreting these data. Studies have shown more depressed mood, negative affect, and somatic disturbance among Mexican-Americans than among non-Hispanic whites, but these have been associated with lower socioeconomic status and lower education rather than with ethnic differences (Golding and Lipton 1990).

Several studies showed that immigrant status was correlated with greater stress and depression. A study comparing 258 immigrants from Central America and Mexico with both native-born Mexican-Americans and Anglo-Americans showed that over half the immigrants who escaped war or political turmoil reported symptoms of posttraumatic stress syndrome (PTSD); those diagnosed with PTSD showed high levels of depression, anxiety, and other psychiatric disturbances (Cervantes, Salgado-de-Snyder, and Padilla 1989). Similarly, a study of over three thousand Mexican-Americans between the ages twenty and seventy-four showed a higher level of hopelessness about the future, self-depreciation, and lack of enjoyment of life as compared to Anglo-Americans (Garcia and Marks 1989).

The stresses of discrimination, sex-role conflicts (between Mexican definitions of women's roles and Anglo definitions), and family concerns put Mexican-American women immigrants especially at risk of developing psychological problems, particularly depression (Salgado-de-Snyder 1987a;1987b).

SOME TREATMENT ISSUES

Barberra (1982:122) investigated a number of beliefs about Mexican-Americans—that there is less psychological disorder because of such natural support groups as the family, that they underutilize services because they have a negative attitude toward these services and the professionals who run them, and that they tend to use *curanderos* (folk healers). He points out that the role of support groups is not unique to this cultural group; that services are utilized—even overutilized when they meet the needs of this group, particularly if there is a bilingual staff; and that *curanderos* are consulted, but not necessarily instead of usual mental health services. An earlier study showed that missed appointments usually resulted not from culture-related causes but from economics, specifically the lack of transportation (Lindstrom 1975).

When language is *not* a problem (i.e., when the client can speak English or the therapist can speak Spanish), Barberra (1982:133) states that the therapist need not be a member of the same group. What is important is that the therapist speaks the language and is obviously motivated to treat Latinos.

A study of expectations of length of treatment revealed shorter times for Mexican-Americans (seventeen sessions) than Euro-Americans (twenty-three sessions), suggesting that this aspect of therapy should be clarified (Acosta 1979, quoted in Barberra 1982:130). Crisis intervention has been suggested for treating Mexican-Americans, with back-up treatment that includes the range of individual, family, and group treatment. Mental health can also be improved by "providing basic resources such as education, housing, employment" (Barberra 1982:139).

Depression Among Puerto Ricans in the Mainland United States

People from Puerto Rico are also considered Hispanic or Latino. Mexican-Americans and Puerto Ricans suffer from some of the same effects of discrimination based on language, culture, and race. They also experience the same possibility of misdiagnosis as do African-Americans, particularly those with bipolar depression, who often are diagnosed as schizophrenic, especially if they are young and their affective disorders are combined with auditory hallucinations (Mukherjee 1983).

Since most Puerto Ricans live in heavily urbanized areas, there is the expected co-relationship of addiction (drugs and alcohol) with depression (Kosten, Rounsaville, and Kieber 1985). In fact, one report stated that, "Puerto Ricans in New York consider drug abuse to be the most important health problem faced by their community" (Trimble, Padilla, and Bell 1987:28). Among Puerto Ricans aged fifteen to forty-four, drugs were the second-highest cause of death (37.9 per 100,000, as compared with 23.2 for the population as a whole [Trimble, Padilla, and Bell 1987:28]). Puerto Rican women are considered particularly vulnerable to drug abuse and depression, because of the clash of cultural values between the traditional role of a Latino woman as homemaker and the conflicting role of principal wage earner that is often thrust on her in New York (Trimble, Padilla, and Bell 1987:31). Puerto Rican children are also at great risk for affective disorders (Bird et al. 1989).

A number of studies have found that Puerto Rican clients living on the United States mainland suffer from a high rate of depression, which is higher for women than for men. Somatic disorders are high on the list of symptoms. In an interesting application of cultural concepts to the understanding of depression, Comas-Dias (1984) attributed much of the women's problems to the concept of *personalismo*. Puerto Rican culture places considerable emphasis on the interpersonal aspects of any interaction, and because women are more affectively oriented than men, they experience more stress (Comas-Dias 1984:81). Paralleling the concept of *personalismo* was the concept of *marianismo*. This is a reflection of the predominantly Roman Catholic orientation, related to the "cult of the Virgin Mary," which emphasized that women are to be "self-sacrificing toward children and [must] endure the sufferings inflicted by men" (Comas-Dias 1984:81).

Culture shock affected both Puerto Rican women and men. The effects of a strange language, culture, and climate were devastating. (The authors vividly recall meeting recent Puerto Rican migrants to New York City who came from this tropical island feeling prepared for the rigors of a New York winter because they had "brought a sweater.") However, previous research found that Puerto Rican clients who were acculturated often evidenced more psychopathology than those who clung to more traditional values.

SOME TREATMENT ISSUES

Comas-Dias (1984) found that cognitive-behavioral group intervention was effective for poor, depressed Puerto Rican women. Recurring themes centered around interpersonal relations, children, spouses and lovers, mental symptoms, and issues of family of origin.

Therapists who treat Puerto Rican clients need to be aware of cultural variations in the expression of emotions, particularly depression and affective disorders. Many Puerto Rican clients are quite verbal and often are not reticent; consequently, their outward appearances can be deceptive. The therapist must understand that the external behavior may be hiding serious affective disorder. Again, the social distances between helper and client, as well as language and cultural differences, make communication difficult and increase the possibility of misdiagnosis and mistreatment or lack of treatment.

Puerto Rican clients may also use informal neighborhood spiritual healers called *curanderos*. Their importance has been described in data from an early community-based epidemiological study (Hohmann et al. 1990). People who consulted these healers often worked outside the home, were poor, had generally sought help previously for emotional and psychiatric problems, and were frequently depressed.

Depression in Native-Americans: American Indians and Alaskan Natives

In several books on ethnicity (e.g., Hraba 1979) the experiences of Native-Americans are discussed simultaneously with those of Mexican-Americans. The link between the two groups (besides the fact that many Mexicans and Mexican-Americans have Indian ancestry) is that both groups came under the influence and the domination of the "Anglos." Although we do not usually think of the two groups together, many of the generalizations about Mexican-Americans are true for Native-Americans. The conditions of the latter, of course, have been complicated by their being isolated socially and being forced to live in designated areas, called reservations. About half of all Native-Americans live on reservations, usually rural; the other half live in cities, primarily in the West and Midwest (Trimble, Padilla, and Bell 1987:2). In 1980 there were about 1.5 million Native-Americans comprising approximately 253 recognized tribal entities (an additional 85 are unrecognized), currently speaking almost 150 major languages with "hundreds of dialectical variations" (Manson and Trimble 1982:144).

Poverty, alcoholism, illegitimate births, drug addiction, unemployment, racism (second-class status and reservation living), and child abuse all may cause or occur in conjunction with depression and affective disorders (Berlin 1987). There is much delinquency, out-of-home placement, dropping out from school, and intergenerational conflict (Yates 1987). Again, much of the discussion of Native-American life today stresses the destructive role of alcohol abuse (Trimble, Padilla, and Bell 1987:2–3).

One study of depression among Native-Americans identified three distinct patterns: (1) uncomplicated major depression, (2) depression with a history of alcoholism (there is a "chicken-and-egg" question here), and (3) "complicated depression superimposed on an underlying chronic depression or personality disorder" (Shore et al. 1987). The marginal status of residence (many young Native-Americans experience on and off reservation living) results in a variation of dysthymic disorder. Shore and colleagues call this "synergistic dual anomic depression," which features frustration at not being able to make it in the Anglo or Westernized town near where they live and discontent with the reservation, particularly with its poverty and barrenness (Topper and Curtis 1987). A study of adolescents living in American Indian boarding schools revealed that 58 percent were classified as clinically depressed (Manson et al. 1990). Other studies have replicated these findings (Ackerson et al. 1990).

The suicide rate among Native-Americans is high, although (unlike that among whites and more like that of African-Americans), it peaks young, in the twenties and thirties, the ages when members of the majority culture are preparing for occupations, marrying, and so forth (McIntosh and Santos 1981). One author declares that Native-Americans are the "most severely disadvantaged of any population in the United States" (Yates 1987).

Native-Americans receive markedly inferior education, not only on the reservations but in the Indian boarding schools. Those with high school diplomas often find they are functioning on a seventh- or eighth-grade level and cannot compete for jobs. This often results in depression (sometimes suicide) and retreat back to the reservation, an abdication from participating in the majority culture (Devore and Schlesinger 1987:59).

Byler provided a profile of the Native-American who was at high risk for suicide, based on experiences during a childhood of living off the reservation: "He has lived with a number of ineffective or inappropriate parental substitutes because of family disruption. . . . He has spent time in boarding schools and moved from one to another (Byler 1978:9, quoted in Devore 1987:60).

SOME TREATMENT ISSUES

Snowden (1982:17) points out that the federal government has a great deal of responsibility for both the Alaskan Natives and American Indians but has failed to provide effective, appropriate care. A review of available evidence revealed many "service delivery" problems, and many obstacles to using existing services.

Some characteristics of these groups related to treatment and treatment delivery are a culturally based attitude of passivity when dealing with outsiders, the importance of collaborating with family and clan members and involving them in the treatment process, the need to collaborate with traditional healers, and the need for increased control of services by the community (Zane et al. 1982:230). Many Indian clients are fearful, confused, and upset at psychotherapies and interventions directed at changing their traditional behavior. Often the value systems and the goals of the therapist and the Indian client differ, so that the Indian client, who disagrees with these psychotherapeutic goals, may be seen as unmotivated to change (Manson and Trimble 1982:149–150).

Manson and Trimble (1982:149) state that there are serious problems in treating Indian and Native clients with psychotherapy. These frequently lead to unfavorable outcomes. In particular, therapist and client are "most likely to evidence discrepancies in their shared assumptions, experiences, beliefs, values, expectations, and goals." The patient may take a passive, dependent stance in the therapy, and resist the efforts of the therapist, particularly with regard to attempts at clarifying his feelings, exploring his self, developing insight, and so forth. Part of these problems relate to long-held attitudes of "fatalism, mistrust, superstition, externalization of control and submission to authority figures" which often result in feelings of powerlessness (Manson and Trimble 1982:149). Manson and Trimble recommend that therapists (especially therapists who are not Native-Americans) carefully define both expectations and goals of treatment from the viewpoint of the *client* and investigate both traditional and nontraditional (folk-healing) forms of treatment (Manson and Trimble 1982:148).

Intervention

Research on Intervention

It is hard to generalize from the research on intervention with racial and ethnic minority groups for a number of reasons. For instance, much of this research on racial differences has been done in analogue studies ("Research . . . [conducted] under conditions that only resemble or approximate the . . . [real-life] situation"), which consistently show greater effect of racial differences than do studies of real treatment (Kazdin 1986:32).

Furthermore, not many studies systematically included and controlled for ethnicity and race. In addition, the number of minority clients and therapists has usually been small, and many of these studies were "correlational" studies, which adds to the difficulty in generalizing about cause and effect.

Although some studies indicate that race and ethnicity have no effect, others show that they do. As stated by Sue (1988:304), the only agreement among authorities is that there has not been enough research and that which has been published "suffers from methodological and conceptual limitations."

Sue advances the idea that in our pluralistic society clients should be able to choose therapists, and if they wish, to select those with characteristics that match their own (e.g., race, gender, sexual orientation, and so on). There is an obvious dearth of therapists from minority and ethnic groups, so that matching is difficult and often impossible. However, Sue further states that ethnicity, by itself, reveals little about the "attitudes, values, experiences, and behaviors of *individuals,* therapists or clients, who interact in a therapy session. . . . *groups* exhibit cultural differences, [but] considerable individual differences may exist within groups" (Sue 1988:306, emphasis in the original). Individuals from the same ethnic and cultural group but different social classes can be a worse mismatch than those from different ethnic groups but the same class, with the same life-style and other values. Despite its limitations, current research does not reveal differences in outcomes related to well-being, which is not the same as therapist or client preferences. Sue (1988:307) states that "ethnic or racial match is a moral or ethical issue, . . . cultural match is an empirical issue; we must study actual behaviors in therapy and then relate these factors to outcome measures." He concludes his important reviews by stating, "Ethnicity is important, but what is more important is its meaning" (1988:307).

In discussing the effects of cultural and social factors in depression in the United States, it is generally hypothesized that roles and stress (often related to discrimination) are the main reasons for the higher rates of depression among minorities. Stress over roles, functions, and lack of opportunities in many areas of their lives probably heighten feelings of helplessness and inadequacy (DeVos, Marsella, and Hsu 1985:3).

If the stress of poverty, racism, hunger and malnutrition, and forms of social disintegration heightens the probability of depression (and evidence suggests that this is so), then we need to see if we can link specific affective disorders to specific stresses and/or ascertain if the depressions are really a "generalized response to any major stressor among vulnerable individuals" (Marsella et al. 1985:313). There are hypothesized connections for the relationship of sociocultural factors and the depressions, but we must be careful to differentiate between hypotheses and facts that have been established through research (Marsella et al. 1985:313).

Treating Clients from Different Cultural, Socioeconomic, and Minority Groups

Health care professionals, especially those involved in any form of counseling or therapy, must *always* be sensitive to the differences that exist between themselves and their clients. These differences may include culturally based values (e.g., the role of family and significant others), how problems are interpreted and presented, expectations of treatment, and so on.

In this section we focus on how to evaluate clients from these different groups and treat them with sensitivity.

TREATING ETHNIC MINORITY CLIENTS WITH SENSITIVITY

Experts now tend to agree that therapists need not be of the same ethnic, minority, or socioeconomic group as the clients they treat as long as they recognize and overcome certain barriers (Devore and Schlesinger 1987; Mokuau 1988).

The first and most obvious barrier is language: It is best if the therapist and client can communicate directly. As we have discussed, the use of interpreters often introduces additional problems for the client. The therapist who is not from the same ethnic group as a client should also be aware that differences in how we express ourselves may cause misunderstandings. For example, if a Japanese client (e.g., one born in Japan who speaks English) tells you someone died, the usual Western response "I'm sorry" would be inappropriate and confusing, because it would be understood as an apology rather than as an expression of regret (Sikkema and Niyekawa-Howard 1977:15). One should be alert to any response of confusion, which is a cue that clarification may be needed.

Mokuau (1988) reminds us that the therapist and client may have different views of the world. To overcome this barrier, the therapist should understand both his or her own cultural values (including taboos) and those of the client. Some of the values mentioned earlier in the chapter as relevant to treating depressed clients are how the self is viewed; beliefs about health and mental health, including how depression is defined and expressed; religious and spiritual beliefs, including the use of spiritual healers; and the importance of family and community support. It is important not to stereotype clients but to investigate how each client defines these values. The therapist who plans to work with a particular ethnic group should attempt to learn in advance as much as possible about their culture.

Culturally proscribed behavior or affect in the presence of the thera-pist must also be considered. We have mentioned the passivity of the Native-American, the tendency of Puerto Rican women to be very talk-ative, and the reserve of the Asian client, who might be reluctant to impose upon the therapist, who is a stranger. These behaviors must be evaluated and should not be taken at face value as symptoms of depres-sion.

We have discussed the importance of trying to understand the client's degree of acculturation, which is often difficult to assess. The client may be unaware of deeply ingrained values, sometimes revealed by such remarks as, "I sounded like my mother [or father] when I said that to my child." Exploring clients' roles and relationships provides many valuable clues; for example: what the clients' parents expected of them, what they expect of their parents and children, how disagreements and conflicts are handled between different generations, the role of grand-parents, and the role of community groups (Sikkema and Niyekawa-Howard 1977:29). It has also been suggested that the therapist evaluate the "family's understanding or misunderstanding of mainstream Amer-ican values" (Spiegel 1982).

The Assessment Guide in chapter 16 is flexible enough to be used to assess both cultural difference and degree of acculturation, bearing in mind that the D.S.M-III-R criteria for making a formal diagnosis may not apply equally to all ethnic and minority groups. We shall note some of the areas of this guide where these factors may be revealed, which should be emphasized when questioning a client from a different ethnic or cultural group, such as the ones we have addressed in this chapter. We shall also note some areas that should be deemphasized. (The numbers of these items correlate with those in the assessment guide.)

I. *Therapist inquiry on the nature of the problem.*

1. *What is the problem?*

Client describes his or her problems in impersonal terms—for ex-ample, with references to external events (storms, clouds, etc.); prob-lem(s) described primarily as disrupting family or group harmony; may state reason for coming as wanting to restore harmony to group.

2. *What brought the client in at this time?*

Primarily, pressure from family or group; denial of help needed for self.

3. *How the client has been coping with the specified problem.*

Tried will power; sought help from family or community, from spiri-tual healer.

4. *Further specification of the presenting problem.*

Client might state causes such as organic reasons, supernatural intervention, inherited weakness, situational factors, metaphysical factors (imbalance of some sort, such as negative or positive energy, fatalism, or character weakness).

II. *Assessing the depression.*

A. *Evaluating the symptoms.*

Symptoms described are somatic, with no or very little mention of mood.

C. *Differentiation of the symptoms.*

Therapist should not ask questions at this time about affective symptoms that emphasize mood, but may focus on other questions pinpointing when and where symptoms occur; how this differs from normal; when symptoms do or do not occur.

3. *Attitude toward self and environment.*

Self is described in undifferentiated manner (e.g., in terms of lineage, family, community).

4. *Physiological changes and body complaints.*

What gives you pleasure? Client answers in terms of fulfilling expectations of family or community group.

D.1. *Assessing losses.*

If client is an immigrant, there may be many losses, including country, home, familiar way of life, family and friends; even change in climate may be extreme and impose difficulties. These may not be understood by client as losses; clarification needed.

E.2. *Assessment of suicide risk.*

Among other factors, client talks of shame and loss of face.

G.1. *Indicators of physical illness.*

What kind of doctor does client see when ill? Does he or she (or family members) ever consult a nontraditional doctor or healer?

IV. *Short, personal history.*

3. *Marital and family status.*

In answer to questions about response of significant others, client may indicate their disapproval, including shame, and loss of face.

4. Family of origin.

Lineage may be given, rather than or in addition to location.

5. Exploration of family roles.

Client will speak of obligation, duty, honor; elders have authority; family obligations may be more important than those of individuals.

6. Significant others.

May include immediate as well as extensive extended family; family- or community-based clubs or other organizations should be explored, if not mentioned.

7. Religious background.

Mention of belief in fate or the supernatural.

V. Information on psychological treatment.

2. Expectations of current therapy.

Goals stated in objective terms (e.g., return to harmony) rather than subjective feelings; or in terms of group (e.g., fulfillment of duties).

VII. Provision of information about the therapist.

Although this information may be very important to the client (especially the therapist's education and training), there may be cultural restraints against asking; the therapist should volunteer this information.

VIII. Feedback about assessment and treatment.

When the client is not oriented toward psychological causes of mental problems, providing this kind of information may indicate that the therapist does not understand the client's problem or needs.

IX. Closing the interview.

3. Assessment of client's mood.

Asking "How do you feel?" at the end of the interview might draw a response similar to that for question VIII—that the therapist does not understand the client's problem or need.

SOME TREATMENT CONSIDERATIONS

Therapists must "convey a sense of acceptance and willingness to help" (Wong 1982:196). They must be aware that a client from a minority cultural group might find the treatment system alien and may anticipate prejudice. They should also understand what is important in establishing a relationship with a client in a particular ethnic group. For example, in some cultures (e.g., La Raza groups and Hawaiians), initial contacts should be relaxed and informal; in some Asian groups, an authoritative stance is expected.

Therapists should realize that clients may not understand the treatment process, as practiced by a Western therapist, including the therapeutic relationship and the roles of both therapist and client. Expectations of outcome (goals) might also be different. Discrepancies should be explored, and goals should be set that are both realistic for the client and based on what the client wants. Length of treatment is another factor. The client may expect that problems will be resolved in a few sessions, but the therapist may expect to work with him or her longer. Cultural differences also may arise with regard to the need to keep appointments, be on time, and so on. These factors should be discussed and clarified early in the treatment process.

Devore and Schlesinger (1987:163) caution therapists to try to guard against being "paternal." In particular, they should not assume that the way they define the client's problem is more valid than the way the client defines it.

Treatment should fit the needs of the client and should *usually* be given in ways that are harmonious with the cultural values or world view of the client. It should also be given with an awareness of the client's support systems (as defined by the client) and their importance to the client's mental health and well-being. We stress *usually*, because it is sometimes in a client's best interest to challenge these values from the viewpoint of the predominant culture and even within the cultural group. For example, when these authors were conducting a treatment seminar in Hong Kong, a Chinese social worker presented the case of a young mother overburdened by multiple problems who threatened to kill her infant daughter if they did not take the child from her. Since infanticide (especially of girls) was not unknown in this culture, the group agreed that this child should be removed. The suggestion was made (from the Western point of view) that this threat might actually be a "cry for help" and that it should be explored further. This assessment proved correct, and the situation was resolved by helping the client to reconnect with her alienated family, who then provided the needed support to both the mother and child.

TREATING ECONOMICALLY AND SOCIALLY DISADVANTAGED CLIENTS

A third barrier that therapists must be aware of is that of class-bound values, which usually refers to socioeconomic class, particularly therapists of a higher socioeconomic status working with clients of a lower socioeconomic status. Because the issues when working with other vulnerable populations (e.g., those discriminated against on the basis of race or sexual preference) are similar, we have included them as well. The impact of poverty, prejudice, and other factors contributing to the vulnerability of these groups, especially their vulnerability to depression, should be understood. It is also highly probable that clients in these groups have had bad experiences with the treatment system that leads them to expect prejudice and discrimination, as well as poor treatment and poor results.

The Assessment Guide in chapter 16 is well suited for use with the economically and socially disadvantaged. We have highlighted certain areas of particular importance, emphasizing the questions that help to diagnose problems and areas of inquiry to be focused on or avoided. (The numbers of these items correspond with those in the guide.)

I. *Therapist inquiry on the nature of the problem.*

Client may emphasize societal reasons; feelings of anger, powerlessness, helplessness and hopelessness may be revealed.

3. *How the client has been coping.*

At this point, the therapist should attempt to assess the client's experiences with the health care system, and if his or her attitudes are positive or negative.

II. *Assessing the depression.*

C.3. *Attitude toward the self and the environment.*

When low self-esteem is very obvious, these questions might be postponed; focus instead on factual information.

C.4. *Physiological changes and body complaints (including changes in appetite).*

It is important to evaluate demands on time and energy, as well as physical condition (see later).

D.1. *Assessing losses.*

There may be many losses connected with changes in role, employment, residence, loss of family and friends, and so on.

D.2. *Assessment of other life stresses, including those in section D.3.*

D.3. *Physical or sexual abuse and/or exploitation.*

Disadvantaged clients are usually vulnerable to multiple severe stresses, including victimization.

E.2. *Assessment of suicide risk.*

Look for "equivalent" behavior, such as lack of caution or taking dangerous risks, violent behavior, and so on.

G.1. *Indicators of physical illness.*

Evaluate the availability and use of health care, when needed. Also get information about diet and nutrition.

IV. *Short personal history.*

Emphasis should be on significant others and the availability of a support network.

V. *Information on psychological treatment.*

2. *Expectations of current therapy.*

Since treatment will probably be short, it is important to arrive at mutual specification of hierarchy of goals that are realistic in terms of client's resources.

SOME TREATMENT ISSUES

Wortman (1981:669–671) made some eminently sensible suggestions for treating poor black women who were single parents that could serve as a model of empathic understanding of all poor and disadvantaged clients. He makes the following points: Their resources, in terms of energy, are limited; therefore a therapist must be careful not to ask more of clients than they want from the contacts. Stretching out the intervention may foster unrealistic expectations (e.g., of "magical results"). Contacts must be short (five or six sessions, or less), focusing on what the client needs within the time, effort, and resources available to the therapist. These are usually in very short supply but this assessment of what is possible is essential (Wortman 1981:670).

If appointments are missed, and they will be, follow up immediately. The therapist should let the clients know that they will not be rejected, as they may imagine. Allowing missed appointments shows flexibility, but it is good to let the clients know that you care about their attendance. The therapist should discuss missed appointments as a way of showing that he or she cares but is not "laying a guilt trip" on them. Referrals are to be avoided, for they often result in clients dropping out or "falling between the cracks." Many of these clients have been referred before and may feel "shoved around."

Wortman suggests keeping the contacts direct and focused on the main problems, not wasting time, and (very important) showing the basic courtesies that will help facilitate a relationship so that the client may be helped. Depressed people can be especially sensitive to either real or imagined slights.

Appropriate medication should be used if clients are very depressed, for many have family responsibilities, and they resist hospitalization because of personal and financial reasons. The medication should be accompanied by supportive therapy. Cases should be divided from the beginning, or the work should begin with families and then divided, rather than starting with individuals and then involving others, for this sharing might be met with jealousy, resistance, and a feeling of loss.

Other experts have indicated that in working with disadvantaged clients, particularly the poor, there must also be an emphasis on the provision of services to meet such basic needs as food, clothing, and shelter; health care; and employment—because lack of basic needs is certainly depressiogenic. It is also very important to pay attention to the realities of these clients' lives. The therapist should not assume that clients in these groups are resistant to help: Practitioners should be flexible and ready to make adaptations in the therapy. Above all, clients must be treated as individuals.

Summary

■■ In short, although the phenomenon of depression may vary
■■ from group to group and from individual to individual within these groups, it is well to remember that regardless of ethnicity, social class, bias, and poverty, it is possible to view all depressed individuals within a biopsychosocial framework and, with a multitude of approaches and techniques, to help them. The depressions today are very treatable. They can be overcome, and people can be helped to lead happier and fuller lives.

NOTES

1. Defining Clinical Depression

1. A disease is considered a "pathological state of the body . . . [with] clinical signs and symptoms and laboratory findings. . . . [It] is usually tangible and . . . [sometimes] measurable . . . [unlike] illness [which is] . . . highly individual and personal" (Thomas 1989:513). Disease is usually considered to have an etiology, to run a course, and to have certain outcomes.

2. For further information on bipolar disorders, the reader is referred to Goodwin and Jamison (1990). In an extraordinary work of more than nine hundred pages, the authors have included the research and theory—to date—on the bipolar disorders and have included much relevant material on other forms of the depressions.

3. A good discussion summarizing the issues of psychosomatic medicine may be found in Rogers and Reich (1988:387–417).

2. The Symptoms of Depression

1. The symptoms of mental illness, particularly the mood disorders, vary from one culture to another. We agree with the American Psychiatric Association's statement that great caution should be used in applying these criteria to people from other cultures, especially to those from "non-Western" cultures (D.S.M-III-R:xxvi). (We discuss cross-cultural aspects of depression further in chapter 21.)

2. Although the danger of suicide is present at all phases in the depressive cycle, the greatest danger is when the patient is on an upswing. One source states that the highest suicidal mortality occurs in the six to nine months after symptomatic improvement (Klerman 1988:313). In short, even though there may be symptomatic improvement, and the patient seems to be getting better, the therapist cannot relax and must be constantly aware of this threat to the client.

3. The Formal Diagnosis of Depression

1. So many of the Research Diagnostic Criteria (R.D.C.) have been absorbed into the D.S.M.-III-R that we shall not elaborate upon them in this book. Since the diagnostic system most used in agencies and hospitals is the D.S.M.-III-R,

we shall stress the diagnostic criteria of this manual. (The D.S.M.-III-R is currently being revised, with a tentative publication date for the D.S.M.-IV planned for the early 1990s.)

For those who are interested, the Research Diagnostic Criteria may be found in Spitzer, Endicott, and Robins (1978).

2. We are indebted to Professor Fred DiBlasio, of the School of Social Work, the University of Maryland at Baltimore, for his help in clarifying these concepts.

3. The validity of the distinction between major depression and organic mood disorder has been questioned by Fogel (1990), who states that, among other factors, there is often confusion between causal and contributory organic factors. The suggestion is that the axis I diagnoses be "strictly phenomenological" and that any organic factors that might be germane be listed on axis III.

4. A more detailed list of other conditions, including infectious diseases, neurological problems, endocrine disorders, immunological diseases, metabolic and other disorders, and drug reactions may be found in Fava (1986).

4. Heredity and the Genetic Basis of Depression

1. The National Center for Human Genome Research of the National Institutes for Health has recently begun a fifteen-year project aimed at identifying the exact location of every human gene and uncoding its protein instructions. The budget for this Human Genome Project is $3 billion.

2. A description of the techniques used in this research may be found in Whatley and Owen (1991:11–24).

3. "If a trait is 100 percent genetically determined and one partner . . . develops [it], then the other twin will also develop it . . . [then] the concordance rate is 100%" (Papolos and Papolos 1987:44–45).

4. All the original reports appeared in *Nature*, February 26, 1987.

5. The Biological Systems Associated with Depression: A Brief Review

1. For a more complete explanation of the structure and functioning of the brain, we highly recommend Andreasen (1984) *The Broken Brain*, especially chapter 5—"The Revolution in Neuroscience: What Is the Brain?" pp. 83–138).

2. Some (e.g., Thomas 1989) categorize these differently, into parts and subdivisions. We are following Andreasen's outline and have drawn from her descriptions as well as from Thomas and other sources.

6. The Neurological System and Depression

1. Melatonin, which will be discussed in chapter 9, is also an indoleamine (Whybrow, Askiskal, and McKinney 1984:126).

2. Further coverage of this very technical topic is beyond the scope of this book; the interested reader is referred to Thase, Frank, and Kupfer (1985).

3. Those who want more detailed and technical information should see Schatzberg and Cole (1991).

4. Fluoxetine (Prozac) has been proclaimed a wonder drug. See, for example, the article by Schumer (1989) in *New York Magazine.* However, as often is the case with new psychotropic drugs, such side effects as intense agitation, tremors, and sometimes mania and preoccupation with suicide (Teicher, Glod, and Cole 1990; Wolfe 1991) begin to be reported, as well as sexual (orgasmic) dysfunctions (Herman et al. 1990). Furthermore, since at least 15 percent of patients do not respond to Prozac, the early euphoria has been replaced with more careful and conservative evaluations (Angier 1990a, 1990c; Markowitz 1991a).

5. The question of whether there *are* such serious differences between American and British depressives that justify such marked differences in practice in the use of these drugs in combination has not been answered. Widely divergent practices can also be found within this country.

6. Developments in noninvasive technologies, like the positron emission tomographic (PET) scan, magnetic resonance imaging (MRI), and others are increasingly enabling us to observe and understand these processes.

7. Lieber (1987) states that recent research cannot substantiate some of the claims for this form of data gathering. The procedures for obtaining and measuring these metabolites are expensive, cumbersome, and (since the processing is often done by distant commercial laboratories) often slow (a minimum of seven to ten days). Because of the expense, delays, and "limited clinical yield," Lieber no longer performs these tests routinely but recommends that they "may have some value in cases with medico-legal implications."

8. There are a number of second messenger systems (different neurotransmitters activate different systems), and these systems exist presynaptically as well as postsynaptically (Koslow and Gaist 1987:118). One is thought to be the location of the remedial actions of lithium, which we discuss at greater length in chapter 10 (Hyman 1988d:374).

7. The Neuroendocrine System and Depression

1. The interested reader may find lengthier and more technical discussions in the following: Carroll (1987); Hirschfeld, Koslow, and Kupfer (1985); Lieber (1987); Pohl (1987); and Ritchie et al. (1990), among others. Arana and Mossman (1988) present a good literature review (109 references) in addition to the history and the theoretical basis of the test.

2. Nonsuppression is also associated with such conditions as schizophrenia, alcohol abuse, depressed schizoaffective disorder, mania, panic disorder, anorexia, organic brain syndrome, and pseudodementia. High rates of false positives are associated with many other conditions, including age (over sixty), pregnancy, certain illnesses (including Cushing's disease, organic brain disease, temporal lobe epilepsy, and diabetes), active drinking, withdrawal from barbiturates, and the use of birth control pills and certain other drugs (e.g., Valium) (Pohl 1987:16).

8. The Circulatory System and Depression

1. Wurtman (1987:235) points out that the term *lecithin* is used in two different but acceptable ways: "To the psychiatrist and scientist . . . it is a particular
set of choline-containing phospholipids, the PCs. . . . To the food industry . . .
it is a mixture. . . . [with] 20% or less authentic PC."Furthermore, there are
different kinds (or "pools") of PCs, as distinguished by either their composition
or their function. Each kind may serve a different function. It is the pure lecithin
that is recommended for therapeutic use.

2. Interestingly, three antidepressant medications—imipramine, amitriptyline, and doxepin—were recently found to trigger carbohydrate craving and
increased appetite in patients suffering from major depressions (Yeragani et al.
1988). The meaning of this interaction is still not understood.

9. The Chronobiology of Depression: Our Biological Clocks

1. Self-reports of insomnia can be very misleading. Dement (1974:81) reported that about 50 percent of the individuals seen in a sleep clinic, who stated
that they suffered from severe sleeplessness, actually slept much longer than
they thought they did. Individuals who suffer from pseudo-insomnia seem to
experience all the symptoms of real insomnia, including feeling exhausted.

2. For example, alcohol is metabolized during sleep, so the person experiences withdrawal and often wakes up. Similarly, when one withdraws from
nicotine, depression, headaches, difficulties with concentration, nervousness,
agitation, and anxiety ensue. With smoking, of course, there is also the danger
of falling asleep with a lighted cigarette and causing a fire (Lamberg 1984:127).
Both substances carry the additional risk of habituation or addiction. Caffeine—
found in coffee, tea, chocolate, many soft drinks, and other foods—also interferes with falling asleep, although this is more commonly known.

Other sleep disrupters are foods high in sugar and fat, as they trigger the
production of insulin, which accelerates hormonal activity. Very salty foods also
disrupt sleep, as they may stimulate activity of the adrenal glands. The person
who goes to sleep hungry may also have difficulty sleeping, as the blood sugar
level will be low, which leads to an increase in hormone secretion and glandular
activity.

3. Sometimes studies are conducted over two and three nights to offset an
"adaptational or first-night effect" that could confound the results. Depressives
often display these increases in certain measurements after the first night. Even
though it is often important to extend the time to two or more nights, because
of costs and other factors such as shortages of facilities, the usual time for a
clinical study is one night (Fawcett and Kravitz 1985:479).

4. The American Medical Association in 1974 warned that barbiturates should
be avoided except for very serious symptoms. They also advised, in *The New
England Journal of Medicine,* that these drugs are out of date and should not be
used. However, barbiturates are still being prescribed (Schwartz and Aaron,
1979:152). The chloral derivatives and piperidineodionide derivatives are not
frequently prescribed but are sometimes selected for specific reasons.

Nonprescription medications receive mixed reviews in the literature. On the one hand, they *do* help to induce and to maintain sleep. On the other hand, they have many negative effects, such as "disorientation and confusion . . . dizziness, ringing in the ears [tinnitus], lassitude, poor coordination, blurred or double vision and irritability." The researcher further questions whether their utility is not exceeded by their dangers (Lamberg 1984:148). Bassuk, Schoonover, and Gelenberg (1983:217) think that these nonprescription sleeping pills are no better than placebos.

5. In November 1989 the Center for Disease Control identified a link between ingesting L-tryptophan and a serious, in some cases fatal, blood disorder, eosinophilia-myalgia syndrome. More than 1,500 individuals were affected by this illness and there were twenty-seven fatalities. The F.D.A. ordered a recall of all the L-tryptophan on the market. The illnesses were eventually shown to be caused by the products of a particular manufacturer who was using a new strain of the bacteria employed to ferment the L-tryptophan and was not adequately filtering impurities (*Baltimore Sun* August 9, 1990).

6. Because of the mechanics of the process, the full committee charged with revising the affective disorders never discussed SAD; the committee met early in the revision process, in 1984 and 1985, before the increasing importance of SAD was apparent (Spitzer and Williams 1989:82). The term *regular temporal relationship*, in the opinion of Spitzer and Williams, covers the case of summer SAD (1989:83).

7. Researchers recently reported success in actually *resetting* the body clocks of a group of subjects by exposing them to bright lights, of the magnitude of daylight, for approximately five hours per day for two to three days. Exposure to ordinary room light was also found effective, but the phase shifts were not as large (Czeisler et al. 1989). This particular study did not include depressed patients; nevertheless the findings are significant, and it is hoped that future studies will explore the use of this technique with SAD patients.

8. According to Rosenthal (1989a), there are currently a number of distributors whose products have been adequately tested. Names of these distributors may be obtained by contacting Dr. Rosenthal's office at the Clinical Psychobiology Branch, National Institute of Mental Health in Bethesda, Maryland (301–496–2141 or 301–496–0500). These devices are not yet regulated by the F.D.A., and there are no regulations regarding qualifications for giving light therapy or for reimbursement by insurance companies.

9. Interestingly, three antidepressant medications—imipramine, amitriptyline, and doxepin—were recently found to trigger carbohydrate craving and increased appetite in patients suffering from major depressions (Yeragani et al. 1988). The meaning of this interaction is still not understood.

10. Other Biological Factors and Treatments

1. A psychopharmacologist is a physician who specializes in the "science of drugs having an effect on psychomotor behavior and emotional states" (Thomas 1989:1516).

2. In using drugs to treat depression, a problem that is encountered far too

often is that "antidepressants probably are not used as often as they should be *or in high enough doses.* For example, the required amount can be predicted (*for some tricyclic antidepressants*) by testing the blood level of the drug twenty-four hours after a single small, safe test dose; this is not done as often as it could be. *When moderate amounts do not work, the dose should be raised aggressively, especially if the blood level of the drug is low"* (Baldessarini 1990:5, emphasis added).

3. The value of generic drugs has been very controversial. Early in 1990, the state of Maryland removed a number of generic drugs from the list that could be substituted without a physician's order on the ground that they were not absorbed rapidly enough (Bor 1990).

4. There are many variables, including ethnic group. Recent studies have shown, for example, that patients in Japan and Taiwan require less lithium than Caucasians (Holden 1991).

5. On November 13, 1991, the F.D.A. announced that it planned to work toward speeding the process for the approval of new drugs by "using outside experts to review new drugs and cooperating with other nations to standardize testing and regulation." They feel that these new procedures will cut the present ten-year approval period (from laboratory tests to availability to the public) to about three or four years (Leary 1991).

6. Patient advocacy groups can be very effective at getting the attention of Congress. For example, patients and their advocates have rebelled against the high cost of Clozaril, a drug used in the treatment of schizophrenia (Goleman 1990), and patients who have had bad reactions to Prozac have initiated multi-million-dollar lawsuits (Angier 1990b).

7. Carbamazepine, similar to lithium, is a drug that must be administered carefully, with the dosage increased until the patient experiences side effects and with constant monitoring (Wise 1989:124). It is still considered by some to be an experimental drug. It is being tested with a number of conditions, including pain (Fromm 1990), Alzheimer's disease (Gleason and Schneider 1990), and others. Carbamazepine may be therapeutic for the mood disorders because it changes both serotonin and dopamine actions (Elphick, Yang, and Cowen 1990). At the present time, the generic form of carbamazepine (oral tablets, 200 milligrams) has been removed from the list of generic drugs to be dispensed without a prescription because of slow rate of absorption into the bloodstream (Bor 1990).

8. A recent report indicated that "The Newcastle ECT Predictor Scale" successfully predicted both immediate and six-month success rates in a sample of twenty-six patients suffering from a major depressive episode. The dexamethasone suppression test was unsuccessful in prediction (Katona et al. 1987).

9. At the present time, the report of the Task Force has not been subjected to intense scrutiny.

10. Marilyn Rice, a former ECT patient, heads the Committee for Truth in Psychiatry, a national group opposed to ECT. Other opposition groups include the Coalition to Stop Electroshock and the Network Against Psychiatric Assault. The latter group publishes a newspaper called "Madness Network News: All the Fits That's News to Print" (*Washington Post,* December 12, 1989).

11. For information about the actions of specific drugs, the reader is referred

to Cohen, S. (1989) *The Chemical Brain: The Neurochemistry of Addictive Disorders.* Irvine, CA, CareInstitute Press.

12. The major evidence supporting this conclusion is that only dopamine receptor blockers interfere with self-administration of cocaine (Kuhar, Ritz, and Boja 1991:300).

13. The federal government has increased financial support for this research through the Alcohol, Drug Abuse and Mental Health Administration. Fifty-three million dollars has been allocated for 1991 (Goleman 1990).

14. Carbohydrate craving obesity, an eating disorder clarified by the bidirectional component of Wurtman's precursor theory, is related to seasonal affective disorder, and discussed in chapter 9.

11. The Biopsychiatric Approach to Treating Patients

1. These observations were reported by a number of clinicians including Stanley McCracken of the Anxiety/Depression Clinic, University of Chicago.

2. We are grateful to Stanley McCracken, LCSW, PhD, for the description of the clinic at the University of Chicago.

12. Psychodynamic Approaches to Depression

1. A full review of personality and depression may be found in Millon and Kotik (1985).

2. The interested reader is referred to Arieti and Bemporad (1978:315–343) for an extended discussion of the case of "Fred," who received three years of treatment for mild depression. For several case vignettes of serious depression, see Arieti and Bemporad (1978:230–252).

3. Transference is the "process whereby the patient displaces onto the therapist feelings, attitudes and attributes which properly belong to a significant attachment figure of the past, usually a parent, and responds to the therapist accordingly" (Walrond-Skinner 1986:364).

14. Behavioral Approaches to Depression

1. Obviously, there are serious ethical questions about doing this kind of research with animals, and many people object on humane grounds. The defenders, such as Harlow, maintained that the knowledge obtained by experimenting on animals produced usable knowledge for the treatment of humans and outweighed the admittedly aversive impact on the animals. Such research with humans is, of course, unthinkable.

2. Lack of social support is another "life context factor" that has always been stressed most by therapists with a behavioral orientation. It has been increasingly recognized as crucial in therapy. In fact, one of the functions, and consequences of, therapy is to provide temporary support to compensate for deficiencies in the client's environment (Moos 1990).

3. Lengthier, albeit concise, discussions of this "reformulation" may be found in Williams (1984:12–16) and in Peterson and Seligman (1985:922–932).

4. These are brief and oversimplified explanations. For further explication of these techniques see Schwartz (1982; 1983).

5. Elaboration of these factors is beyond the scope of this book and may be found, in detail, in Schwartz (1982), especially chapter 6, "Differential Approaches to Behavioral Intervention: Depression as an Illustration" (1982:165–216).

6. There are a number of additional possible operant explanations, which become too involved to discuss here (see Schwartz 1982:165–215).

15. Cognitive and Cognitive-Behavioral Approaches to Depression

1. As we discussed in chapter 12, "Psychodynamic Approaches to Depression," this view has been challenged by Arieti and Bemporad (1978:45–46.)

2. For a good discussion of these commonalities, see Williams (1984:24–25.)

3. A discussion of a negative view of the future as a part of depression may be found in Rush and Giles (1982:157–158).

4. Beck's views have reached the general reading public, for his research has provided the basis of a best-selling self-help book on depression called *Feeling Good: The New Mood Therapy* (Burns 1980) and a self-help book specifically designed for women who are depressed: *Getting Undepressed: How a Woman Can Change Her Life Through Cognitive Therapy* (Emery 1988).

5. These examples were modeled after the "Sample Rational Self-Help Form (1976)" printed by the Institute for Rational Emotive Therapy; 45 East 65th Street; New York, NY 10021.

6. Ellis's views have been incorporated into an excellent self-help book by Hauck (1973) entitled *Overcoming Depression*.

7. Beck also uses the Minnesota Multiphasic Personality Inventory (MMPI) and the Lazarus Life History Questionnaire (Beck et al. 1979:106). Since these two instruments are used primarily for research purposes, the therapist in this case illustration decided—as do many cognitive therapists—that, along with his clinical observations, the Beck Depression Inventory (BDI) was valid, accurate, and sufficient to chart the results of therapy.

8. This is not intended to downplay the utility of case studies or of single-subject research designs. In many ways, these case-by-case efforts (particularly single-subject research) may eventually have more utility for psychotherapy research than the traditional classical "experimental-control group" paradigm adopted from the "harder" sciences. For a fuller discussion of single-subject design see Sidman (1960) or Bloom and Fischer (1982).

9. This literature is summarized in Hollon and Beck (1986), Hollon and Najavits (1988), and Hollon (1990).

10. A meta-analysis is a methodology that summarizes and equates, statistically, intervention outcomes of different studies. A study is then done of these summarizing statistics. It is an "analysis of analyses, or meta-analysis," that makes it possible to compare these different studies (see Smith, Glass, and Miller 1980:39).

11. There are a number of good reviews of research on behavioral and cognitive-behavioral approaches. This overview draws from Lewinsohn and

Hoberman (1985), Hollon and Beck (1986), Emmelkamp (1986), Hollon and Najavits (1988), and Hollon (1990).

16. Assessing and Treating the Depressions: A Unified Approach

1. Whybrow, Akiskal, and McKinney (1984) suggest taking both a thorough genetic-family history and a detailed developmental history. We do not recommend this. However, if this is to be part of the assessment procedure, then collateral interviews with relatives may be helpful in obtaining and corroborating this information. Of course, very seriously depressed clients may be unable to give this information, and these significant others may be the only source for this information, at least for the present.

2. There are a number of standardized interview guides in the literature, many of which are reproduced in the appendix of Beckham and Leber (1985:980–1025).

3. We have not reproduced the Mental Status Examination. The interested reader should consult one of the standard textbooks in psychiatry or either of the following references: Nicholi (1988b) or chapter 12 ("The Psychiatric Examination") in Goodwin and Guze (1989).

4. There are other classification systems, such as the International Classification of Disease (I.C.D.-9) or the Research Diagnostic Criteria (R.D.C.) (Spitzer, Endicott, and Robins 1978), but the D.S.M. is the one most widely used.

5. For a fuller, more detailed description of these conditions, see Gold (1987a:74–119).

6. Another definition of *mild* is a score under 24 on the Beck Depression Inventory, a scale used often by contemporary clinicians (Beck et al. 1979:398–399).

7. For another view of the indicators for choosing among psychodynamic, cognitive, and IPT therapies, see Karasu (1990b:274–278).

8. In a survey of 123 psychologists, Starker (1988) found that 36 percent regularly gave books to clients and 60 percent said they did occasionally. Scogin and colleagues (1989) found that older (average age, sixty-eight) men and women raised their mood by two-thirds: half read *Feeling Good* (Burns 1980) and half read *Control Your Depression* (Lewinsohn et al. 1986). Gains were maintained at follow-up six months later. (There was no difference between the response obtained with the two books. The former takes a cognitive approach; the latter is primarily behavioral.)

9. One organization, the Depression and Related Affective Disorders Association (DRADA), concerned with both bipolar and major depression, helps people form and conduct support groups and has a training program for leaders, many of whom suffer from mood disorders. DRADA is associated with Johns Hopkins Hospital. Its address is DRADA, Meyer 4–181; Johns Hopkins; 600 North Wolfe Street; Baltimore, MD 21205. Telephone: 410-955-4647.

Another is the Manic-Depressive Illness Foundation, which may be contacted through Dr. Kay R. Jamison, President; the Manic-Depressive Illness Foundation; 2723 P Street, NW; Washington, DC 20007.

There are others. A more complete listing may be found in DePaulo and Ablow (1989:171–174).

17. Gender and Depression

1. We are not including in this section the woman whose baby has died during or just after delivery. This is obviously a realistic, tragic source of anguish to the mother. Similarly, the loss of a child through sudden infant death (SIDS) is not included.

2. Unfortunately, some migraine sufferers who are free of headaches in the last six months of pregnancy have a serious recurrence during the third to the seventh day after childbirth (Dalton 1980:12).

3. Earlier psychoanalytic theory held that the mother with postpartum psychiatric difficulties allegedly displays insufficient maternal feelings toward her child and becomes "masculine." Most psychoanalysts now reject this notion, along with the observation that "dormant homosexual tendencies" are "rekindled" after childbirth (Arieti and Bemporad 1978:254). Furthermore, a number of recent psychoanalytic writers have stated that the phenomenon of depression and other psychiatric disturbances after childbirth is more complicated than these early theories assumed. We mention this to recognize that within our professional lifetimes these assumptions were held to be true and interventions were based on them. Certainly, most of these early theorists, whose views (in our opinion) are still maintained to a distressing degree, understated the social, psychological, and physiological stress of the birth experience to mothers.

One cannot help but sympathize with mothers who developed depression after childbirth, who were treated by therapists with such notions, most of which centered on blaming the woman for somehow being either inadequate or, the old standby, ill at ease in and rejecting of her feminine role. The "blaming" approach of past therapies seems today almost inhuman.

4. Pitt (1973) recounted that 84 percent of his sample cited a specific cause for their blues. These included worry about their babies (who were sometimes not doing well) and worry about themselves. Mothers were often homesick or experiencing varying kinds of physical difficulties. Only 14 percent of his sample experienced these blues for more than three days, and although more of the women who felt blue eventually were diagnosed with puerperal depression than controls, the differences were statistically insignificant.

5. Lists of these groups, by states, may be found in Dix (1985:225–241). (In Great Britain the leading support group is called MAMA, for Meet-A-Mum-Association [Dalton 1980:110].)

6. For a detailed account of the complex and multifactor nature of the relationship of hormones and mood changes, which is beyond the scope of this book, see the review article by Halbreich, Holtz, and Paul (1988).

7. The diagnosis requires five of the following ten symptoms: (1) marked affective lability (e.g., feeling suddenly sad, tearful, irritable or angry); (2) persistent and marked anger or irritability; (3) marked anxiety, tension, feelings of being "keyed up" or "on edge"; (4) markedly depressed mood, feelings of hopelessness, or self-deprecating thoughts; (5) decreased interest in usual activ-

ities (e.g., work, friends, hobbies); (6) marked lack of energy or a tendency to be easily fatigued; (7) subjective sense of difficulty in concentrating; (8) marked change in appetite, overeating, or specific food cravings; (9) hypersomnia or insomnia; (10) other physical symptoms, such as breast tenderness or swelling, headaches, joint or muscle pain, a sensation of bloating, weight gain.

There are other criteria, which we shall not present here, except for the statement that the "disturbance is not merely an exacerbation of the symptoms of another disorder, such as Major Depression, Panic Disorder, Dysthymia" (D.S.M.-III-R 1987:369).

8. In a study of alcoholic and nonalcoholic women, four factors were isolated that accounted for much of the variance: current mood, low self-esteem, negative perceptions of childhood, and somatic symptoms. It was hypothesized that there were no basic differences between alcohol-induced depression in women and depression in the control group, who were depressed nonalcoholic women (Turnbull and Gomberg 1990).

9. For additional information on depression in women, summarizing the empirical literature on topics such as risk factors, treatment, and special populations, the reader is directed to E. McGrath et al., *Women and Depression: Risk Factors and Treatment Issues* (Washington, DC: The American Psychological Association, 1990). This is the final report of the American Psychological Association's National Task Force on Women and Depression.

18. Depression and Aging

1. Erikson (1963), in his classic work admittedly focusing on youth, described adulthood and maturity (old age) as the last two stages of life; he did not assign years to these states. In a more recent view, Levinson spoke of the era of late adulthood as 60–? (Sic) (1986:8). Levinson says that the ages of fifty-five to sixty are the "culminating life structure for middle adulthood," and those from sixty to sixty-five are "late adult transitions" linking middle and late adulthood. The last stage, "late, late adulthood" begins at approximately age eighty (Levinson et al. 1978:38). Sheehy (1981:64–66) speaks of "older age" by decades: the "Freestyle Fifties," the "Selective Sixties," the "Thoughtful Seventies," and the "Proud Eighties." This is as far as she carries it. Other researchers have formulated additional classifications.

2. For a description of the Global Deterioration Scale devised by Reisberg and associates, which specifies "seven major clinically distinguishable stages [of Alzheimer's disease] from normality to most severe," see Kaplan and Sadock (1990:212–215).

3. A very useful guide for the professional, as well as the family member involved with an Alzheimer's patient, is by Mace and Rabins, *The 36–Hour Day: A Family Guide to Caring for Persons with Alzheimer's Disease* (Baltimore: Johns Hopkins Press, 1991).

4. Memory is a much more complicated topic than originally thought, and its loss is not an inevitable part of the aging process. Although it is true that depressed older people may speak of memory loss more often than nondepressed people, there is often a confounded relationship between reports of

memory loss and performance on memory tasks. Depressed older people often feel they have more memory loss than they display on memory tasks in test situations (O'Connor et al. 1990).

5. A detailed description of the "aggressive assessment" procedures at Emory Hospital in Atlanta, including sequences of medication usage, can be found in Stoudemire (1987:3, 10).

6. The statistics for all ages show that the most common way to commit suicide is by shooting. However, the elderly tend to use "covert techniques" including starvation, not taking medication, and taking overdoses of prescribed medicines (Kobren 1989).

7. A book on assisted suicide, *Final Exit*, advising people with terminal illnesses on how they could commit suicide, was published in August 1991. Written by Derek Humphry, the executive director of The Hemlock Society (an organization dedicated to the advancement of "rational suicide"), the book was an immediate best-seller. Arthur Caplan, an expert on bioethics, found this popularity "frightening. . . . the loudest statement of protest of how medicine is dealing with terminal illness and dying" (Altman 1991a).

8. Further detailed discussion of drugs for the elderly depressed is beyond the scope of this book. We recommend Tobias and Lippman (1988) and Schatzberg and Cole (1991).

19. Depression in Children, Adolescents, and College Students

1. The literature agrees overwhelmingly that both physical abuse and mental abuse of children cause marked depressive symptoms, lower self-esteem, and feelings of lack of control over their lives (much lower than age appropriate) that are accompanied by "heightened externality" (i.e., the feeling that things are controlled from without rather than from within). These findings hold across gender, race, socioeconomic status, and age (Allen and Tarnowski 1989).

2. Bowlby (1960) felt that infants separated from their mothers went through three stages: (1) crying, screaming, and thrashing in an attempt to reunite with the mother; (2) despair, where there is less and quieter crying and less thrashing but where the infant still is looking for the mother and appears acutely depressed; (3) defense or detachment, where the infant may seem to have overcome the loss of mother, responding to other adults and no longer looking for mother; in fact, the infant may ignore her if she comes back into the picture.

Is this second stage of Bowlby's formulation—where the infant, after protesting, may become unhappy, withdrawn, and apathetic—depression, mourning, or a deprivation reaction?

3. Poznanski is one of the developers of the widely used Children's Depression Rating Scale (CDRS) (Poznanski, Cook, and Carroll 1979). (For further validation of its use, see Shanahan and colleagues [1987].) A number of other scales for children are useful both for screening and for use in combination with clinical interviews, observations, and other sources of information. For a good listing see Hodges and Siegel (1985:530–536).

4. These data are available in a number of sources; they are summarized in Pfeffer (1986:24–25) and in Brent and Kolko (1990).

5. Self-destructive behavior might also be a feature of mental retardation and several rare genetic and metabolic diseases.

6. The literature on the use of MAO inhibitors in children is still experimental and highly anecdotal. There seems to have been little work with children, especially because of the necessity of dietary restrictions.

7. A number of good books on adolescent suicide exist. We recommend Curran (1987) and Pfeffer (1986) for the professional and, McCoy (1982), Klagsbrun (1976), Jacobs (1980), Chiles (1986), and Hafen and Frandsen (1986) for the nonprofessional.

8. There were numerous newspaper accounts of this "epidemic." A good account, especially relevant for the nonprofessional reader, may be found in Loren Coleman's book *Suicide Clusters* (1987).

REFERENCES

Ablow, K. R. (1990a). "Exploring Mazes of the Mind: Chemical Imbalances or Disordered Lives?" *Washington Post* (*Health* magazine), August 7, p. 14.

Ablow, K. R. (1990b). "Electroshock Reconsidered: Controversial Treatment Is Effective but Discomforting." *Washington Post*, September 4, p. 10.

Ackerson, L. M., Dick, R. H., Manson, S. M., and Baron, A. E. (1990). "Properties of the Inventory to Diagnose Depression in American Indian Adolescents." *Journal of the American Academy of Child and Adolescent Psychiatry* 29(4): 601–607.

Acosta, F. X. (1979). "Barriers Between Mental Health Services and Mexican-Americans: An Examination of a Paradox." *American Journal of Community Psychology* 7: 503–520.

Agras, W. S. (1978). "The Token Economy." In W. S. Agras, ed., *Behavior Modification: Principles and Clinical Applications*. Second Edition. Boston: Little, Brown, pp. 64–85.

Akiskal, H. S. and Simmons, R. C. (1985). "Chronic and Refractory Depressions: Evaluation and Management." In E. E. Beckham and W. R. Leber, eds., *Handbook of Depression: Treatment, Assessment, and Research*. Homewood, IL: Dorsey Press, pp. 587–605.

Albro, J. C. and Tulley, C. (1979). "A Study of Lesbian Lifestyles in the Homosexual Micro-culture and the Heterosexual Macro-culture." *Journal of Homosexuality* 4: 331–344.

Alda, M. (1988). "Method for Prediction of Serum Lithium Levels." *Biological Psychiatry* 24(2): 218–224.

Alder, E. and Bancroft, J. (1988). "The Relationship Between Breast Feeding Persistence, Sexuality, and Mood in Postpartum Women." *Psychological Medicine* 18(2): 389–396.

Allen, D. M. and Tarnowski, K. J. (1989). "Depressive Characteristics of Physically Abused Children." *Journal of Abnormal Child Psychology* 17(1): 1–11.

Altman, L. K. (1989). "How Medical Detectives Identified the Culprit Behind a Rare Disorder." *New York Times*, November 28, p. C-3.

Altman, L. K. (1991a). "A How to Book on Suicide Surges to Top of Best-seller List in Week." *New York Times*, August 9, pp. A-1, A-10.

Altman, L. K. (1991b). "Cell Channel Finding Earns Nobel Prize." *New York Times*, October 8, pp. C-1, C-3.

Altmann, E. O. and Gotlib, I. H. (1988). "The Social Behavior of Depressed Children: An Observational Study." *Journal of Abnormal Child Psychology* 16(1): 29–44.

Alzheimer's Disease: Report of the Secretary's Task Force on Alzheimer's Disease (1984). Washington, D.C.: U.S. Department of Health and Human Services, September.

American Psychiatric Association (1987). *Diagnostic and Statistical Manual of Mental Disorders,* Third Edition, Revised. Washington, D.C.: American Psychiatric Association.

American Psychiatric Association, Task Force on ECT (1990). "The Practice of ECT: Recommendations for Treatment, Training and Privileging." *Convulsive Therapy* 6(2): 85–120.

Andreasen, N. C. (1984). *The Broken Brain: The Biological Revolution in Psychiatry.* New York: Harper & Row.

Andrews, E. I. (1990). "The Intriguing Potential of Molecular Switches." *New York Times,* February 4, p. F-8.

Angier, N. (1990a). "Eli Lilly Facing Million-Dollar Suits on Its Antidepressant Drug Prozac." *New York Times,* August 16, p. B-13.

Angier, N. (1990b). "Environmental Illness May Be Mental." *New York Times,* December 26, p. A-24.

Angier, N. (1990c). "New Anti-depressant Drug Is Acclaimed but Not Perfect. " *New York Times,* March 29, p. B-9.

Angier, N. (1991). "Erroneous Triple Helping of DNA Is Implicated in Disease." *New York Times,* August 6, p. C-3.

Angst, J. ed. (1983). *The Origins of Depression: Current Concepts and Approaches.* Berlin: Springer-Verlag.

Anthony, E. J. (1975). "Two Contrasting Types of Adolescent Depression and Their Treatment." In E. J. Anthony and T. Benedek, eds., *"Depression and Human Existence."* Boston: Little, Brown, pp. 445–460.

Arana, G. and Mossman, D. (1988). "The Dexamethasone Suppression Test and Depression: Approaches to the Use of a Laboratory Test in Psychiatry." *Neurologic Clinics* 6(1): 21–39.

Arieti, S. (1977). "Psychotherapy of Severe Depression." *American Journal of Psychiatry* 134: 864–868.

Arieti, S. (1982). "Individual Psychotherapy." In E. S. Paykel, ed., *Handbook of Affective Disorders.* New York: Guilford Press.

Arieti, S. and Bemporad, J. (1978). *Severe and Mild Depression: The Psychotherapeutic Approach.* New York: Basic Books.

Asarnow, J. R., Goldstein, M. J., Carlson, G. A., Perdue, S., Bates, S., and Keller, J. (1988). "Childhood-Onset Depressive Disorders: A Follow-up of Rates of Rehospitalization and Out-of-Home Placement Among Child Psychiatric Inpatients." *Journal of Affective Disorders* 15(3): 245–253.

Askmark, H. and Wiholm, B. E. (1990). "Epidemiology of Adverse Reactions to Carbamazepine as Seen in a Spontaneous Reporting System." *Acta Neurologica Scandinavica* 81(2): 131–140.

Avery, D. (1987). "Alcoholism and Depression: Cause and Effect." *Clinical Advances in the Treatment of Depression* 1(1): 1–3.

Azrin, N. H. and Foxx, R. M. (1974). *Toilet Training in Less Than a Day.* New York: Simon and Schuster.

Baker, F. M. (1990). "Black Youth Suicide: Literature Review with a Focus on Prevention." *Journal of the National Medical Association* 82(7): 495–507.

Baldessarini, R. J. (1985). *Chemotherapy in Psychiatry: Principles and Practice*. Revised and Enlarged Edition. Cambridge, Mass.: Harvard University Press.

Baldessarini, R. J. (1986). "Clinical Pharmacology of Antidepressant and Mood-Stabilizing Agents: Summary." Paper presented at NIMH Conference on Depression: Awareness, Recognition, Treatment, Bethesda, Md., June 9.

Baldessarini, R. J. (1990). "Update on Antidepressants." *The Harvard Medical School Mental Health Letter* 6(7): 4–6.

Baldessarini, R. J. and Cole, J. O. (1988). "Chemotherapy." In A. M. Nicholi, Jr., ed., *The New Harvard Guide to Psychiatry*. Cambridge, Mass.: Belknap/Harvard University Press, pp. 481–533.

Bandura, A. (1986). *Social Foundations of Thought and Action: A Social Cognitive Theory*. Englewood Cliffs, NJ: Prentice-Hall.

Barberra, M., Jr. (1982). "Raza Populations." In L. R. Snowden, ed., *Reaching the Underserved: Mental Health Needs of Neglected Populations*. Vol. 3: Sage Annual Reviews of Community Mental Health. Beverly Hills, Cal.: Sage Publications, pp. 119–142.

Barrington, W. H. (1991). "The NIMH Genetic Studies of Affective Disorders." Paper presented at the *Fifth Annual Mood Disorders Research/Education Symposium*, April 17. Baltimore: Johns Hopkins University.

Bart, P. B. (1971). "Depression in Middle-Aged Women." In V. Gornick and B. K. Moran, eds., *Woman in Sexist Society*. New York: Basic Books, pp. 99–117.

Bart, P. B. (1985). "Emotional and Social Status of the Older Woman." In *No Longer Young: The Older Woman in America*. Proceedings of the 26th Annual Conference on Aging. The Institute of Gerontology: The University of Michigan and Wayne State University, pp. 3–21.

Basch, M. F. (1980). *Doing Psychotherapy*. New York: Basic Books.

Basch, M. F. (1988). *Understanding Psychotherapy: The Science Behind the Art*. New York: Basic Books.

Bassuk, E. L. (1991). "Homeless Families." *Scientific American* 265 (December): 66–74.

Bassuk, E. L., Schoonover, S. C., and Gelenberg, A. J. (1983). *The Practitioner's Guide to Psychoactive Drugs*. Second Edition. New York: Plenum Medical Book Company.

Bauer, M. S. and Whybrow, P. C. (1991). "Rapid Cycling Bipolar Disorder: Clinical Features, Treatment, and Etiology." In J. D. Amsterdam, ed., *Refractory Depression*. New York: Raven Press, pp. 191–208.

Bays, J. (1990). "Substance Abuse and Child Abuse: Impact of Addiction on the Child." *Pediatric Clinics of North America* 37(4): 881–904.

Beach, S. R. H., Sandeen, E. E., and O'Leary, K. D. (1990). *Depression in Marriage: A Model for Etiology and Treatment*. New York: Guilford Press.

Beck, A. T. (1967). *Depression: Clinical, Experimental, and Theoretical Aspects*. Philadelphia: University of Pennsylvania Press.

Beck, A. T. (1972). *Depression: Causes and Treatment*. Philadelphia: University of Pennsylvania Press.

Beck, A. T. (1976). *Cognitive Therapy and the Emotional Disorders.* New York: International Universities Press.

Beck, A. T. (1986). "Cognitive Therapy: A Sign of Retrogression or Progress." *Behavior Therapist* 9(1): 2–3.

Beck, A. T., Rush, A. J., Shaw, B. F., and Emery, G. (1979). *Cognitive Therapy of Depression.* New York: Guilford Press.

Beck, A. T. and Wright, J. H. (1983). "Cognitive Therapy of Depression: Theory and Practice." *Hospital and Community Psychiatry* 34:1119–1127.

Beck, A. T. and Young, J. E. (1978). "College Blues." *Psychology Today,* September, pp. 80–92.

Becker, R. E., Heimberg, R. G., and Bellack, A. S. (1987). *Social Skills Training Treatment for Depression.* New York: Pergamon Press.

Beckham, E. E. (1990). "Psychotherapy of Depression Research at a Crossroads: Directions for the 1990s." *Clinical Psychology Review* 10: 207–228.

Beckham, E. E. and Leber, W. R., eds. (1985). *Handbook of Depression: Treatment, Assessment, and Research.* Homewood, Ill.: Dorsey Press.

Belcher, J. R. and DiBlasio, F. A. (1990). "The Needs of Depressed Homeless Persons: Designing Appropriate Services." *Community Mental Health Journal* 26(3): 255–266.

Bell, C. C. (1988). "Commentary" [on Jones, Gray, and Parson, 1988]. *Integrative Psychiatry* 6: 135–136.

Bellack, A. S. (1985). "Psychotherapy Research in Depression: An Overview." In E. E. Beckham and W. R. Leber, eds., *Handbook of Depression: Treatment, Assessment, and Research.* Homewood, Ill.: Dorsey Press, pp. 204–219.

Bellack, A. S., Hersen, M., and Kazdin, A. E. (1990). *International Handbook of Behavior Modification and Therapy.* Second Edition. New York: Plenum Press.

Bemporad, J. (1985). "Long-Term Analytic Treatment of Depression." In E. E. Beckham and W. R. Leber, eds., *Handbook of Depression: Treatment, Assessment, and Research,* Homewood, Ill.: Dorsey Press, pp. 82–99.

Bemporad, J. (1988). "Psychodynamic Treatment of Depressed Adolescents." *Journal of Clinical Psychiatry* 49(9)(Suppl): 26–31.

Bennett, W. I., ed. (1990). "Tryptophan: National Disaster." *Harvard Medical School Health Letter* 15(4): 1–2.

Benson, H. (1975). *The Relaxation Response.* New York: William Morrow. .

Benson, H. with W. Proctor (1984). *Beyond the Relaxation Response.* New York: Times Books.

Berlin, I. N. (1987). "Effects of Changing Native American Cultures on Child Development." *Journal of Community Psychology* 15(3): 299–306.

Berman, A. L. (1988). "Playing the Suicide Game." In *Readings: A Journal of Reviews and Commentary in Mental Health* 3(2): 20–23.

Bernardi, E., Jones, M., and Tennant, C. (1989). "Quality of Parenting in Alcoholics and Narcotic Addicts." *British Journal of Psychiatry* 154: 677–682.

Bertelsen, A. (1988). "Genetic Aspects in Affective Disorders." In T. Helgason and R. J. Daly, eds., *Depressive Illness: Prediction of Course and Outcome.* Heidelberg: Springer-Verlag.

Bibring, E. (1953). "The Mechanism of Depression." In P. Greenacre, ed., *Affective Disorders: Psychoanalytic Contributions to Their Study.* New York: International Universities Press.

References   459

Billig, N. (1987). *To Be Old and Sad: Understanding Depression in the Elderly.* Lexington, Mass.: Lexington Books.

Bird, H. R., Gould, M. S., Yager, T., Staghezza, B., and Canino, G. (1989). "Risk Factors for Maladjustment in Puerto Rican Children." *Journal of the American Academy of Child and Adolescent Psychiatry* 28(6): 847–850.

Black, D. A. (1987). "Treating Depression with Electroconvulsive Therapy." *Clinical Advances in the Treatment of Depression* 1(5): 6–7, 11.

Black, D. W., Rathe, A., and Goldstein, R. B. (1990). "Environmental Illness: A Controlled Study of 26 Subjects with '20th Century Disease.' " *Journal of the American Medical Association* 264(24): 3166–3170.

Blackwell, B. (1979). "Treatment Adherence: A Contemporary Overview." *Psychosomatics* 20: 27–35.

Blakeslee, S. (1989). "New Research Links Depression with Asthma Deaths in Children." *New York Times*, May 30, p. C-3.

Blaney, P. H. (1981). "The Effectiveness of Cognitive and Behavioral Therapies." In L. Rehm, ed., *Behavior Therapy for Depression: Present Status and Future Directions.* New York: Academic Press, pp. 1–32.

Blazer, D. (1982). *Depression in Late Life.* St. Louis: C. V. Mosby.

Blazer, D. (1987). "Diagnosis and Management of the Suicidal Older Adult." *Clinical Advances in the Treatment of Depression* 1(4): 4–5.

Blehar, M. C. and Rosenthal, N. E (1989). "Introduction and Overview." In N. E. Rosenthal and M. C. Blehar, eds., *Seasonal Affective Disorders and Phototherapy.* New York: Guilford Press.

Bloom, M. and Fischer, J. (1982). *Evaluating Practice: Guidelines for the Accountable Professional.* Englewood Cliffs, N.J.: Prentice-Hall.

Blouin, J., Blouin, A., Perez, E., and Barlow, J. (1989). "Bulimia: Independence of Antibulimic and Antidepressant Properties of Desipramine." *Canadian Journal of Psychiatry* 34(1): 24–29.

Blum, K., Noble, E. P., Sheridan, P. J., Montgomery, A., Ritchie, T., Jagadeeswaran, P., Nogami, H., Briggs, A. H., and Cohn, J. B. (1990). "Allelic Association of Human Dopamine D2 Receptor Gene in Alcoholism." *Journal of the American Medical Association* 262(15): 2055–2060.

Blum, K. and Trachtenberg, M. C. (1988). "Alcoholism: Scientific Basis of a Neuropsychogenetic Disease." *International Journal of Addiction* 23(8): 781–796.

Bohm, P. E. (1984). "Drug Addiction." In F. J. Turner, ed., *Adult Psychopathology: A Social Work Perspective.* New York: The Free Press, pp. 438–465.

Bonime, W. (1966). "The Psychodynamics of Neurotic Depression." In S. R. Arieti, ed., *American Handbook of Psychiatry.* Vol. 3. New York: Basic Books.

Boodman, S. G. (1989). "Treating Cocaine Addicts: Why It's So Tough." *Washington Post*, November 28, pp. 12–15.

Boodman, S. G. (1990a)."Hooked on Drugs and Alcohol: Multiple Addictions Make Treatment Difficult." *Washington Post*, January 30, p. 7.

Boodman, S. G. (1990b). "A History of Electroshock Treatment." *Washington Post*, September 4, p. 11.

Bootzin, R. J., Loftus, E. F., and Zajonc, R. B. (1983). *Psychology Today: An Introduction.* Fifth Edition. New York: Random House.

Bor, J. (1989). "Electroshock Regains Acceptance Where Other Treatment Has Failed." *Baltimore Sun,* October 22, pp. 1–A, 6–A.

Bor, J. (1990). "State Removes Six Generic Drugs from List of Allowed Substitutes." *Baltimore Sun,* January 14, p. 5–B.

The Boston Woman's Health Book Collective (1984). *The New Our Bodies Ourselves.* Revised Edition. New York: Touchstone/Simon and Schuster.

Bower, B. (1989). "Growing Up Sad: Depression in Children Attracts Scrutiny." *Science News* 136(August 5): 90–91.

Bowlby, J. (1960). "Separation Anxiety." *International Journal of Psychoanalysis* 41: 89–113.

Boyce, P. and Parker, G. (1988). "Seasonal Affective Disorder in the Southern Hemisphere." *American Journal of Psychiatry* 145: 96—-99.

Boyd, J. H. and Weissman, M. M. (1981). "Epidemiology of Affective Disorders: A Reexamination and Future Directions." *Archives of General Psychiatry* 38: 1039–1046.

Boyd, J. H. and Weissman, M. M. (1982). "Epidemiology." In E. S. Paykel, ed., *Handbook of Affective Disorders.* New York: Guilford Press, pp. 109–125.

Boyer J. L. and Guthrie, L. (1985). "Assessment and Treatment of the Suicidal Patient." In E. E. Beckham and W. R. Leber, eds., *Handbook of Depression: Treatment, Assessment, and Research,* pp. 606–633.

Breggin, P. R. (1991). *Toxic Psychiatry: Why Therapy, Empathy, and Love Must Replace the Drugs, Electroshock, and Biochemical Theories of the "New Psychiatry."* New York: St. Martin's Press.

Brent, D. A. and Kolko, D. J. (1990). "Suicide and Suicidal Behavior in Children and Adolescents." In B. D. Garfinkel, G. A. Carlson, and E. B. Weller, eds., *Psychiatric Disorders in Children and Adolescents,* pp. 372–391.

Breier, A., Kelsoe, J. R., Kirwin, P. D., Beller, S. A., Wolkowitz, O. M., and Pickar, D. (1988). "Early Parental Loss and Development of Adult Psychopathology." *Archives of General Psychiatry* 45: 987–993.

Brent, D. A. and Kolko, D. J. (1990). In B. D. Garfinkel, G. A. Carlson, and E. B. Weller, eds., *Psychiatric Disorders in Children and Adults.* Third Edition. New York: John Wiley, pp. 372—-391.

Broman, C. L. (1987). "Race Differences in Professional Help-seeking." *American Journal of Community Psychology* 15(4): 473—-489.

Brown, D. and Gary, L. (1987). "Stressful Life Events, Social Support Networks, and the Physical and Mental Health of Urban Black Males." *Journal of Human Stress* 13: 165–174.

Brown, D. and Gary, L. (1988). "Unemployment and Psychological Distress Among Black American Women." *Sociological Focus* 21: 209–221.

Brown, G. W. and Bifulco, A. (1990). "Motherhood, Employment, and the Development of Depression: A Replication of a Finding?" *British Journal of Psychiatry* 156(1): 169–179.

Brown, G. W. and Harris, T. O. (1978). *Social Origins of Depression: A Study of Psychiatric Discord in Women.* London: Tavistock.

Brown, G. W., Harris, T. O., and Bifulco, A. (1986)."Long-Term Effects of Early Loss of Parent." In M. Rutter, C. E. Izard, and P. B. Read, eds., *Depression in Young People: Developmental and Clinical Perspectives.* New York: Guilford Press, pp. 251–296.

Brown, R. A. and Lewinsohn, P. M. (1984). *Participant Workbook for the Coping with Depression Course.* Eugene, Ore.: Castalia.

Brown, S. A. and Schuckit, M. A. (1988). "Changes in Depression Among Abstinent Alcoholics." *Journal of Studies on Alcohol* 49(5): 412–417.

Brozan, N. (1988). "Finally, Doctors Ask if Brutal Falls Need Be a Fact of Life for the Elderly." *New York Times*, December 29, p. B-9.

Bruch, H. (1978). *The Golden Cage: The Enigma of Anorexia Nervosa.* Cambridge: Harvard University Press.

Bruch, H. (1988). *Conversations with Anorexics.* New York: Basic Books.

Brush, M. G., Bennett, T., and Hansen, K. (1988). "Pyridoxine in the Treatment of Premenstrual Syndrome: A Retrospective Survey in 630 Patients." *British Journal of Clinical Practice* 42(11): 448—452.

Bruun, R. D. and Bruun, B. (1982). *The Human Body.* New York: Random House.

Bulmahn, L. (1990). "Better Understanding of Alzheimer's Raises Hopes of Cure." *Baltimore Sun* (*Health* magazine), September 18, p. 7.

Burns, D. D. (1980). *Feeling Good: The New Mood Therapy.* New York: Signet (New American Library). .

Burns, D. D. (1989). *The Feeling Good Handbook: Using the New Mood Therapy in Everyday Life.* New York: William Morrow.

Burros, M. (1991). "Dietary Supplements: Let The Buyer Beware." *New York Times*, October 16, pp. C-1, C-6.

Campbell, J. L. and Winokur, G. (1985)."Postpartum Affective Disorders: Selected Biological Aspects." In D. G. Inwood, ed., *Recent Advances in Postpartum Psychiatric Disorders.* Washington, D.C.: American Psychiatric Press, pp. 20–39.

Caplan, G. (1974). *Support Systems and Community Mental Health: Lectures on Concept Development.* New York: Behavioral Publications.

Carlson, G. A. (1990). "Bipolar Disorders in Children and Adolescents." In B. D. Garfinkel, G. A. Carlson, and E. B. Weller, eds., *Psychiatric Disorders in Children and Adults.* Third Edition. New York: John Wiley, pp. 21–36.

Carlsson, A. (1987). "Commentary" [on Wurtman, 1987]. *Integrative Psychiatry* 5: 238–239.

Carroll, B. J. (1987). "The Controversial DST: Two Sides to the Issue; Pro." *Clinical Advances in the Treatment of Depression* 1(2): 16, 13–14.

Casado-Flores, J., Bano-Rodrigo, A., and Romero, E. (1990). "Social and Medical Problems in Children of Heroin-Addicted Parents: A Study of 75 Patients." *American Journal of Diseases of Children* 144(9): 977–979.

Cervantes, R. C., Salgado-de-Snyder, V. N., and Padilla, A. M. (1989). "Post-traumatic Stress in Immigrants from Central America and Mexico." *Hospital and Community Psychiatry* 40(6): 615–619.

Chang, G., Warner, V., and Weissman, M. M. (1988). "Physicians's Recognition of Psychiatric Disorders in Children and Adolescents." *American Journal of Diseases of Children* 142(7): 736–739.

Char, W. F., Tseng, W.-S., Lum, K.Y., and Hsu, J. (1980). "The Chinese." In McDermott, J. F., Jr., Tseng, W.S., and Maretski, T. W., eds., *People and Cultures of Hawaii: A Psychocultural Profile.* Honolulu: The University of Hawaii Press, pp. 53–72.

Charatan, F. B. (1987). "Psychodynamic Aspects of Treating the Elderly." *Clinical Advances in the Treatment of Depression* 1(3): 4–5.

Cheifetz, P. N., Posener, J. A., LaHaye, A., Zajdman, M., and Benierakis, C. E. (1987). "An Epidemiologic Study of Adolescent Suicide." *Canadian Journal of Psychiatry* 32(8): 656–659.

Chesler, P. (1972). *Women and Madness.* Garden City, N.Y.: Doubleday.

Chiles, J. (1986). *Teenage Depression and Suicide.* New York: Chelsea House.

Christensen, L. and Burrows, R. (1990). "Dietary Treatment of Depression." *Behavior Therapy* 21: 183–193.

Christie, K. A., Burke, J. D., Regier, D. A., Rae, D. S., Boyd, J. H., and Locke, B. Z. (1988). "Epidemiologic Evidence for Early Onset of Mental Disorders and Higher Risk of Drug Abuse in Young Adults." *American Journal of Psychiatry* 145: 971–975.

Chunn, J. (1981). "Suicide Taking Its Toll on Blacks." *Crisis* 88: 401 (cited in Devore and Schlesinger, 1987).

Clarkin, J. F., Haas, G. L., and Glick, I. D., eds. (1988). *Affective Disorders and the Family: Assessment and Treatment.* New York: Guilford Press.

Clayman, C. B. and Kunz, J. R., eds. (1986). *Women: How to Understand Your Symptoms.* New York: Random House.

Clayton, P. J. (1983). "The Prevalence and Course of the Affective Disorders." In J. M. Davis and J. W. Maas, eds., *The Affective Disorders.* Washington, D.C.: American Psychiatric Press, pp. 193–202.

Cockerham, W. C. (1990). "A Test of the Relationship Between Race, Socioeconomic Status, and Psychological Distress." *Social Science and Medicine* 31(12): 1321–1326.

Cody, P. (1991, December 20). "N.Y. Psychiatrists Help Homeless Through Innovative Outreach Program." *Psychiatric News* 26(24): 1, 21.

Coffman, S. J. and Jacobson, N. S. (1990). "Social Learning-Based Marital Therapy and Cognitive Therapy as a Combined Treatment for Depression." In G. I. Keitner, ed., *Depression and Families: Impact and Treatment.* Washington, D.C.: American Psychiatric Association Press, pp. 137–155.

Cohen, S. (1988). *The Chemical Brain: The Neurochemistry of Addictive Disorders.* Irvine, Cal.: CareInstitute (CompCare Publishers).

Cohen, S. Z. and Gans, B. M. (1988). *The Other Generation Gap: The Middle-Aged and Their Aging Parents.* Revised Edition. New York: Dodd, Mead.

Coleman, L. (1987). *Suicide Clusters.* Boston: Faber and Faber.

Collins, G. (1985a). "Elderly Alcoholics: Finding the Causes and Cures." *New York Times,* June 17, p. C-13.

Collins, G. (1985b). "For Aged, Problem Drinking Is on the Rise." *New York Times,* June 17, p. C-13.

Collins, J. L., Rickman, L. E., Mathura, C. B. (1980). "Frequency of Schizophrenia and Depression in a Black Inpatient Population." *Journal of the National Medical Association* 72(9): 851–856.

Comas-Dias, L. (1984). "Content Themes in Group Treatment with Puerto Rican Women." *Social Work with Groups* 7(3): 75–84.

Comfort, A. (1990). *Say Yes to Old Age: Developing a Positive Attitude Toward Aging.* New York: Crown.

Consumer Reports (1990). "The Telltale Gene." *Consumer Reports* 55(7): 483–488.

Conway, P. (1988). "Losses and Grief in Old Age." *Social Casework* 69(9): 541–549.

Cooper, T. B., Bergnor, P. E. E., and Simpson, G. M. (1973). "The 24–Hour Serum Lithium Level as a Prognosticator of Dosage Requirements." *American Journal of Psychiatry* 130: 601–603.

Cooper, T. B. and Simpson, G. M. (1976). "The 24-Hour Serum Lithium Level as a Prognosticator of Dosage Requirements: A 2-Year Follow-up Study." *American Journal of Psychiatry* 133: 440–442.

Costello, C. G. (1972). "Depression: Loss of Reinforcers or Loss of Reinforcer Effectiveness?" *Behavior Therapy* 3: 240–247.

Coyne, J. C. (1987). "Depression, Biology, Marriage, and Marital Therapy." *Journal of Marital and Family Therapy* 13(4): 393–407.

Coyne, J. C. (1988). "Strategic Therapy." In J. F. Clarkin, G. L. Haas, and I. D. Glick, eds., *Affective Disorders and the Family: Assessment and Treatment*. New York: Guilford Press, pp. 89–113.

Craighead, W. E. (1990). "There's a Place for Us: All of Us." *Behavior Therapy* 21: 3–23.

Csikszentmihalyi, M. and Larson, R. (1984). *Being Adolescent: Conflict and Growth in the Teen-age Years*. New York: Basic Books.

Curran, D. K. (1987). *Adolescent Suicidal Behavior*. Washington, D.C.: Hemisphere.

Curtis, J. L. (1988). "Commentary" [on Jones, Gray, and Parsons, 1988]. *Integrative Psychiatry* 6: 139–140.

Cutrona, C. E. and Troutman, B. R. (1986). "Social Support, Infant Temperament, and Parenting Self-efficacy: A Mediational Model of Postpartum Depression." *Child Development* 57(6): 1507–1518.

Cytryn, L., McKnew, D. H., and Bunney, W. E. (1980). "Diagnosis of Depression in Children: A Reassessment." *American Journal of Psychiatry* 137(1): 22–25.

Czeisler, C. A., Kronauer, R. E., Allan, J. S., Duffy, J. F., Jewett, M. E., Brown, E. N., and Ronda, J. M. (1989). "Bright Light Induction of Strong Type O) Resetting of the Human Circadian Pacemaker." *Science* 244: 1328–1333.

D'Agostino, A. M. (1975). "Depression: Schism in Contemporary Psychiatry." *American Journal of Psychiatry* 132(6): 629–640.

Dalton, K. (1980). *Depression After Childbirth: How to Recognize and Treat Postnatal Illness*. Oxford: Oxford University Press.

Dalton, K. (1984). *The Premenstrual Syndrome and Progesterone Therapy*. Second Edition. London: William Heinemann Medical Books.

Dalton, K. (1987). *Once a Month: The Original Premenstrual Syndrome Handbook*. Third Revised Edition. Claremont, Cal.: Hunter House.

Davidson, J. R. T., Miller, R. D., Turnbull, C. D., and Sullivan, J. L. (1982). "Atypical Depression." *Archives of General Psychiatry* 39(5): 527–534.

Davis, J. M., Dyksen, M. W., Matuzas, M. D., and Nasr, S. J. (1982)."Use of the Laboratory in Depression." Unpublished manuscript. Illinois State Psychiatric Institute, University of Illinois, and University of Chicago.

Davis, J. M and Maas, J. W., eds. (1983). *The Affective Disorders*. Washington, D.C.: American Psychiatric Press.

Dean, A., ed.(1985). *Depression in Multidisciplinary Perspective*. New York: Brunner/Mazell.

Dement, W. C. (1974). *Some Must Watch While Some Must Sleep*. San Francisco: W. H. Freeman.

DePaulo, J. R. and Ablow, K. R. (1989). *How to Cope with Depression: A Complete Guide for You and Your Family*. New York: McGraw-Hill.

DePaulo, J. R., Simpson, S. G., Folstein, S., and Folstein, M. F. (1989). "The New Genetics of Bipolar Affective Disorder: Clinical Implications." *Clinical Chemistry* 35: B28–B32.

Derogatis, L. R., ed. (1986). *Clinical Psychopharmacology*. Menlo Park, Cal.: Addison-Wesley.

Derogatis, L. R. and Cleary, P. A. (1977). "Confirmation of the Dimension Structure of the SCL-90: A Study in Construct Validation." *Journal of Clinical Psychology* 33: 981–989.

Devore, W. and Schlesinger, E. G. (1987). *Ethnic-Sensitive Social Work Practice*. Second Edition. Columbus, Ohio: Merrill.

DeVos, G., Marsella, A. J., and Hsu, F. L. K. (1985). "Introduction: Approaches to Culture and Self." In A. J. Marsella, G. DeVos, and F. L. K. Hsu, eds., *Culture and Self: Asian and Western Perspectives*. New York: Tavistock, pp. 2–23.

The Diagram Group (1987). *The Brain: A User's Manual*. New York: Perigree Books/G. P. Putnam.

Dietch, J. T. and Fine, M. (1990). "The Effect of Nortriptyline in Elderly Patients with Cardiac Conduction Disease." *Journal of Clinical Psychiatry* 51(2): 65–67.

Dix, C. (1985). *The New Mother Syndrome: Coping with Postpartum Stress and Depression*. Garden City, N.Y.: Doubleday.

Dobson, K. S. (1989). "A Meta-analysis of the Efficacy of Cognitive Therapy for Depression." *Journal of Consulting and Clinical Psychology* 57(3): 414–419.

Dobson, K. S., Jacobson, N. S., and Victor, J. (1988). "Integration of Cognitive Therapy and Behavioral Marital Therapy." In J. F. Clarkin, G. L. Haas, and I. D. Glick, eds., *Affective Disorders and the Family: Assessment and Treatment*. New York: Guilford Press, pp. 53–88.

Doghramji, K. (1989). "Sleep Disorders: A Selective Update." *Hospital and Community Psychiatry* 40(1): 29–40.

Dorus, W., Ostrow, D. G., Anton, R., Cushman, P., Collins, J. F., Schaefer, M., Charles, H. L., Desai, P., Hayashida, M., Malkerneker, U., Willenbring, M., Fiscella, R., and Sather, M. R. (1989). "Lithium Treatment of Depressed and Nondepressed Alcoholics." *Journal of the American Medical Association* 262: 1646–1652.

Duke, P. and Turan, K. (1987). *Call Me Anna: The Autobiography of Patty Duke*. Toronto: Bantam Books.

Dulbecco, R. (1987). *The Design of Life*. New Haven: Yale University Press.

Dunne, E. J., McIntosh, J. L, and Dunne-Maxim, K., eds. (1987). *Suicide and Its Aftermath: Understanding and Counseling the Survivors*. New York: W. W. Norton.

Dyer, C. (1991). "Halcion Daze." *British Medical Journal* 303(6805): 740.

Edelson, E. (1988). *Nutrition and the Brain.* New York: Chelsea House.

Egeland, J. A., and Hostetter, A. M. (1983). "Amish Study, I: Affective Disorders Among the Amish, 1976–1980." *American Journal of Psychiatry* 140: 56–61.

Egeland, J. A., Hostetter, A. M., and Eshleman, S. K. (1983). "Amish Study, III: The Impact of Cultural Factors on Diagnosis of Bipolar Illness." *American Journal of Psychiatry* 140: 67–71.

Egeland, J. A., Gerhard, D. S., Pauls, D. L., Suxxex, J. N., Kidd, K. K., Allen, C. R., Hostetter, A. M., and Housman, D. E. (1987). "Bipolar Affective Disorders Linked to DNA Markers on Chromosome 11." *Nature* 325(6107): 783–787.

Elkin, I., Parloff, M. B., Hadley, S. W., and Autry, J. H. (1985). "NIMH Treatment of Depression Collaborative Research Program." *Archives of General Psychiatry* 42(3): 305–316.

Elkin, I., Shea, T., Watkins, J. T., Imber, S. D., Sotsky, S. M., Collins, J. F., Glass, D. R., Pilkonis, P. A., Leber, W. R., Docherty, J. P., Fiester, S. J., and Parloff, M. B. (1989). "National Institute of Mental Health Treatment of Depression Collaborative Research Program: General Effectiveness of Treatments." *Archives of General Psychiatry* 46(11): 971–982.

Ellis, A. (1962). *Reason and Emotion in Psychotherapy.* New York: Lyle Stuart.

Ellis, A. and Geiger, R., eds. (1977). *Handbook of Rational-Emotive Therapy.* New York: Springer.

Elphick, M., Yang, J. D., and Cowen, P. J. (1990). "Effects of Carbamazepine on Dopamine- and Serotonin-Mediated Neuroendocrine Responses." *Archives of General Psychiatry* 47(2): 135–140.

Emery, G. (1988). *Getting Undepressed: How a Woman Can Change Her Life Through Cognitive Therapy.* New York: Touchstone/Simon and Schuster. .

Emmelkamp, P. M. G. (1986). "Behavior Therapy with Adults." In S. L. Garfield and A. E. Bergin, eds., *Handbook of Psychotherapy and Behavior Change.* Third Edition. New York: John Wiley, pp. 385–442.

Emslie, G. J. (1987). "Sleep EEG Findings in Depressed Children and Adolescents." *American Journal of Psychiatry* 144(5): 668—670.

Emslie, G. J., Rush, A. J., Weinberg, W. A., Rintelmann, J. W., and Roffward, H. P. (1990). "Children with Major Depression Show Reduced Rapid Eye Movement Latencies." *Archives of General Psychiatry* 47(2): 119–124.

Endicott, J. and Spitzer, R. L. (1978). "A Diagnostic Interview: The Schedule for Affective Disorders and Schizophrenia." *Archives of General Psychiatry* 35: 837–844.

Engel, G. L. (1977). "The Need for a New Medical Model: A Challenge for Biomedicine." *Science* 196: 129–136.

Epstein, N. B., Keitner, G. I., Bishop, D. S., and Miller, I. W. (1988). "Combined Use of Pharmacological and Family Therapy." In J. F. Clarkin, G. L. Haas, and I. D. Glick, eds., *Affective Disorders and the Family: Assessment and Treatment.* New York: Guilford Press, pp. 153–172.

Erikson, E. H. (1963). "Eight Ages of Man." In *Childhood and Society.* Revised Edition. New York: W. W. Norton, pp. 247–274.

Erlanger, S. (1987). "A Scholar's Suicide: Trying to Spare a Family Anguish." *New York Times*, October 26, pp. B-1, B-12.

Falloon, I. R. H., Hole, V., Mulroy, L., Norris, L. J., and Pembleton, T. (1988)."Behavioral Family Therapy." In J. F. Clarkin, G. L. Haas, and I. D. Glick, eds., *Affective Disorders and the Family: Assessment and Treatment*. New York: Guilford Press, pp. 117–133.

Fava, G. A. (1986). "Diagnosis and Treatment of Depression in the Medically Ill." *Progress in Neuro-psychopharmacology and Biological Psychiatry* 10: 1–9.

Fawcett, J. and Kravitz, H. M. (1985)."New Medical Diagnostic Procedures for Depression." In E. E. Beckham and W. R. Leber, eds., *Handbook of Depression: Treatment, Assessment, and Research*. Homewood, Ill.: Dorsey Press, pp. 445–513.

Feinson, M. C. (1985). "Aging and Mental Health: Distinguishing Myth from Reality." *Research on Aging* 7(2): 155–174.

Feinson, M. C. (1986). "Aging Widows and Widowers: Are There Mental Health Differences?" *International Journal of Aging and Human Development* 23(4): 241–255.

Feinson, M. C. (1987). "Mental Health and Aging: Are There Gender Differences?" *The Gerontologist* 27(6): 703–711.

Fellin, P. (1989). "Perspective on Depression Among Black Americans." *Health and Social Work* 14(4): 225–304.

Ferster, C. B. (1973). "A Functional Analysis of Depression." *American Psychologist* 28: 857–870.

Fingarette, H. (1990). "We Should Reject the Disease Concept of Alcoholism." *Harvard Medical School Mental Health Letter* 6(8): 4–6. .

Fink, M. (1990a). "Continuation of ECT." *The Harvard Medical School Mental Health Letter* 6(10): 8.

Fink, M. (1990b). "The 1990 APA Task Force Report: A Quiet Revolution." *Convulsive Therapy* 6(2): 75–78.

Fink, M. and Nemeroff, C. B. (1989). "A Neuroendocrine View of ECT." *Convulsive Therapy* 5(3): 296–304.

Fink, P. J. (1988). "Depressive-Illness Stigma Insults Millions." *New York Times*, August 14, p. E-22.

First, M. B. (1988). "Commentary" [on Jones, Gray, and Parson, 1988]. *Integrative Psychiatry* 6: 138–139.

Fisch, R. Z. (1987). "Masked Depression: Its Interrelations with Somatization." *International Journal of Psychiatry in Medicine* 17(4): 367–379.

Fisher, L. M. (1991). "Breaching the Brain's Wall to Deliver Drugs." *New York Times*, September 4, p. D-7.

Fitzgerald, R. V. (1973). *Conjoint Family Therapy*. New York: Jason Aronson.

Foa, E. B and Emmelkamp, P. M. G., eds. (1983). *Failures in Behavior Therapy*. New York: John Wiley.

Fogel, B. S. (1990). "Major Depression Versus Organic Mood Disorder: A Questionable Distinction." *Journal of Clinical Psychiatry* 51(2): 53–56.

Foley, S. H., O'Malley, S., Rounsaville, B., Prusoff, B. A., and Weissman, M. M. (1987). "The Relationship of Patient Difficulty to Therapist Performance in Interpersonal Psychotherapy of Depression." *Journal of Affective Disorders* 12(3): 207–217.

Folkenberg, J. and Spritzer, C. (1989). "The Heat Is On: How Much Does Hot Weather of Summer Lead to Depression and Crime?" *Baltimore Sun*, July 4, pp. 5–6.

Fotuhi M. (1988). "One More Cup of Coffee." *Baltimore Sun (To Your Health)*, December 6, p. 10.

Fowles, D. G. (1988). *A Profile of Older Americans: 1988*. Washington, D.C.: American Association of Retired Persons.

Fox, H. A., Rosen, A., and Campbell, R. J. (1989). "Are Brief Pulse and Sine Wave ECT Equally Efficient?" *Journal of Clinical Psychiatry* 50(11): 432–435.

Frances, A. J. (1989). *Depression: Diagnosis and Treatment*. New York: Guilford. (Audio program.)

Frances, A. and Popkin, M. K. (1988). "Managing Depressive Symptoms After the Onset of Leukemia." *Hospital and Community Psychiatry* 39(6): 610–611.

Frances, A., Weiner, R. D., and Coffey, C. E. (1989). "ECT for an Elderly Man with Psychotic Depression and Concurrent Dementia." *Hospital and Community Psychiatry* 40(3): 237–242.

Frank, J. D. (1961). *Persuasion and Healing: A Comparative Study of Psychotherapy*. New York: Schocken Books.

Frank, J. D. (1974). "Psychotherapy: The Restoration of Morale." *American Journal of Psychiatry* 131: 271–272.

Frankel, F. H. (1988). "Electroconvulsive Therapy." In A. M. Nicholi, Jr., ed., *The New Harvard Guide to Psychiatry*. Revised Edition. Cambridge: Belknap/ Harvard University Press, pp. 580–588.

Frankel, F. H. (1990). "Editorial: The 1978 and 1990 APA Task Force Reports." *Convulsive Therapy* 6(2): 79–81.

Freedman, A. D. (1987). "Nutrients, Neurotransmitters, and Behavior." *Integrative Psychiatry* 5: 225.

Freedman, D. X. (1989). "Editorial Note (Especially for the Media)." *Archives of General Psychiatry* 46: 983.

Freeman, A. and Davis, D. D. (1990). "Cognitive Therapy of Depression." In A. S. Bellack, M. Hersen, and A. E. Kazdin, eds., *International Handbook of Behavior Modification and Therapy*. Second Edition. New York: Plenum Press, pp. 333–352.

Freud, Sigmund (1917). "Mourning and Melancholia." In Philip Rieff, ed., *Sigmund Freud: General Psychological Theory; Papers on Metapsychology*. New York: Collier Books, pp. 164–179.

Fromm, G. H. (1990). "Clinical Pharmacology of Drugs Used to Treat Head and Face Pain." *Neurological Clinics* 8(1): 143–151.

Gadpaille, W. J., Sanborn, C. F., and Wagner, W. W., Jr. (1987). "Athletic Amenorrhea, Major Affective Disorders, and Eating Disorders." *American Journal of Psychiatry* 144(7): 939–942.

Gallagher, D. E. and Thompson, L. W. (1982). "Treatment of Major Depressive Disorder in Older Adult Outpatients with Brief Psychotherapies." *Psychotherapy: Theory, Research, and Practice* 19(4): 482–490.

Gallo, J. J. (1990). "The Effect of Social Support on Depression in Caregivers of the Elderly." *Journal of Family Practice* 30(4): 430–440.

Garattini, S. (1989). "Further Comments" [on Wurtman, 1987]. *Integrative Psychiatry* 6: 235–238.

Garcia, M. and Marks, G. (1989). "Depressive Symptomatology Among Mexican-American Adults: An Examination with the CES-D Scale." *Psychiatry Research* 27(2): 137–148.

Garfield, S. L and Bergin, A. E., eds. (1986). *Handbook of Psychotherapy and Behavior Change*. Third Edition. New York: John Wiley.

Garfinkel, B. D., Carlson, G. A., and Weller, E. B., eds. (1990). *Psychiatric Disorders in Children and Adolescents*. Philadelphia: W. B. Saunders.

Gary, L. E. (1985). "Depressive Symptoms and Black Men." *Social Work Research and Abstracts* 21(4): 21–29.

Gawin, F. H. (1991). "Cocaine Addiction: Psychology and Neurophysiology." *Science* 251: 1580–1586.

Gelenberg, A. J., Bassuk, E. L., and Schoonover, S. C., eds. (1991). *The Practitioner's Guide to Psychoactive Drugs*. Third Edition. New York: Plenum Press.

Gelfand, D. M. and Teti, D. M. (1990). "The Effects of Maternal Depression on Children." *Clinical Psychology Review* 10: 329–353.

Gennaro, S. (1988). "Postpartal Anxiety and Depression in Mothers of Term and Preterm Infants." *Nursing Research* 37(2): 82–85.

German, G. A. (1988). "Commentary" [on Jones, Gray, and Parson, 1988] *Integrative Psychiatry* 6: 136–138.

Giannini, A. J. (1988). "Drug Abuse and Depression: Possible Models for Geriatric Anorexia." *Neurobiology of Aging* 9(1): 26–27.

Gibbs, J. T. (1984). "Black Adolescents and Youth: An Endangered Species." *American Journal of Orthopsychiatry* 54(1): 6–21.

Gillin, J. C. (1990). "Sleeping Pills." *Harvard Medical School Health Letter* 15(7): 2–7.

Gittleman-Klein, R. (1977). "Definitional and Methodological Issues Concerning Depressive Illness in Children." In J. G. Schulterbrandt and A. Raskin, eds., *Depression in Childhood: Diagnosis, Treatment, and Conceptual Models*. Rockville, Md.: National Institute of Mental Health.

Gleason, R. P. and Schneider, L. S. (1990). "Carbamazepine Treatment of Agitation in Alzheimer's Outpatients Refractory to Neuroleptics." *Journal of Clinical Psychiatry* 51(3): 115–118.

Gochros, H. L., Gochros, J. S., and Fischer, J., eds. (1986). *Helping the Sexually Oppressed*. Englewood Cliffs, N.J.: Prentice-Hall.

Goebel, M., Spalthoff, G., Schulze, C., and Florin, I. (1989). "Dysfunctional Cognitions, Attributional Style and Depression in Bulimia." *Journal of Psychosomatic Research* 33(6): 747–752.

Gold, M. S. (1987a). *The Good News About Depression: Cures and Treatments in the New Age of Psychiatry*. New York: Villard Books.

Gold, M. S. (1987b). "Women's Disease? Depression Research Marred by Bias." *Alcoholism and Addiction* 7(5): 11.

Gold, M. S., and Pearsall, H. R. (1983). "Hypothyroidism—Or Is It Depression?" *Psychosomatics* 24(7): 646–657.

Goldberg, H. (1976). *The Hazards of Being Male: Surviving the Myth of Masculine Privilege*. New York: New American Library.

Golding, J. M. and Burnam, M. A. (1990). "Stress and Social Support as Predictors of Depressive Symptoms in Mexican Americans and Non-Hispanic Whites." *Journal of Social and Clinical Psychology* 9(2): 268–287.

Golding, J. M. and Lipton, R. I. (1990). "Depressed Mood and Major Depressive Disorder in Two Ethnic Groups." *Journal of Psychiatric Research* 24(1): 65–82.

Goleman, D. (1986). "What Colleges Have Learned About Suicide." *New York Times,* February 23, p. 4–22.

Goleman, D. (1988a). "Depression Among Elderly Patients Is Often Undetected, Study Finds." *New York Times,* December 22.

Goleman, D. (1988b). "Food and Brain: Psychiatrists Explore the Use of Nutrients in Treating Disorders." *New York Times,* March 1, pp. C-1, C-10.

Goleman, D. (1989a)."Feeling Gloomy? A Good Self-help Book May Actually Help." *New York Times,* July 6, p. B-6.

Goleman, D. (1989b). "Pioneering Studies Find Surprisingly High Rate of Mental Ills in Young." *New York Times,* January 10, pp. C-1, C-9.

Goleman, D. (1990). "Outcry Grows over Method of Selling New Drug." *New York Times,* September 27, p. B-1.

Goodwin, D. W. and Guze, S. B. (1989). *Psychiatric Diagnosis.* Fourth Edition. New York: Oxford University Press.

Goodwin, F. K. and Jamison, K. R. (1990). *Manic-Depressive Illness.* New York: Oxford University Press.

Gordon, D., Burg, D, Hammen, C., Adrian, C., Jaenicke, C., and Hiroto, D. (1989). "Observations of Interactions of Depressed Women with Their Children." *American Journal of Psychiatry* 146(1): 50–55.

Gordon, M. M. (1985). Foreword to R. D. Alba, *Italian-Americans: Into the Twilight of Ethnicity.* Englewood Cliffs, N.J.: Prentice-Hall, p. v.

Gorman, J. M., Kertzner, R., Cooper, T., Goetz, R. R., Lagomasino, I., Novacenko, H., Williams, J. B., Stern, Y., Mayeux, R., and Ehrhardt, A. A. (1991). "Glucocorticoid Level and Neuropsychiatric Symptoms in Homosexual Men with HIV Infection." *American Journal of Psychiatry* 148: 41–45.

Gotlib, I. H. and Whiffen, V. E. (1989). "Depression and Marital Functioning: An Examination of Specificity and Gender Differences." *Journal of Abnormal Psychology* 98(1): 23–30.

Gould, R. L. (1978). *Transformations: Growth and Change in Adult Life.* New York: Simon and Schuster.

Grant, B. F., Hasin, D. S., and Harford, T. C. (1989). "Screening for Major Depression Among Alcoholics: An Application of Receiver Operating Characteristic Analysis." *Drug and Alcohol Dependence* 23(2): 123–131.

Graze, K. K., Nee, J., and Endicott, J. (1990). "Premenstrual Depression Predicts Future Major Depressive Disorder." *Acta Psychiatrica Scandinavica* 81(2): 201–205.

Green, A. I., Mooney, J. J., and Schildkraut, J. J. (1988). "The Biochemistry of Affective Disorders: An Overview." In A. M. Nicholi, Jr., ed., *The New Harvard Guide to Psychiatry.* Revised Edition. Cambridge: Belknap/Harvard University Press, pp. 129–138.

Greenberg, B. R., and Harvey, P. D. (1987). "Affective Lability Versus Depression as Determinants of Binge Eating." *Addictive Behavior* 12(4): 357–361.

Greenberg, D. S. (1990). "Decade of the Brain." *Baltimore Sun,* July 30, p. 5–A.

Greist, J. H. and Jefferson, J. W. (1984). *Depression and Its Treatment: Help for the Nation's No. 1 Mental Problem.* Washington, D.C.: American Psychiatric Press.

Grinspoon, L., ed. (1990a). "Atypical Depression." *Harvard Medical School Mental Health Letter* 6(12): 1–3.

Grinspoon, L., ed. (1990b). "Psychedelic Drugs." *Harvard Medical School Mental Health Letter* 6(8): 1–4.

Grinspoon, L. and Bakalar, J. B. (1988). "Substance Use Disorders." In A. M. Nicholi, Jr., ed., *The New Harvard Guide to Psychiatry.* Revised Edition. Cambridge: Belknap/Harvard University Press, pp. 418–433.

Grinspoon, L. and Bakalar, J. B. (1990). "Depression and Other Mood Disorders." *The Harvard Medical School Mental Health Review* No. 4.

Guntrip, H. (1971). *Psychoanalytic Theory, Therapy, and the Self.* New York: Basic Books.

Gutstein, S. E. and Rudd, M. D. (1988). *Adolescents and Suicide: Restoring the Kin Network.* Austin: Hogg Foundation for Mental Health (The University of Texas).

Guttmacher, L. B. and Cretella, H. (1988). "Electroconvulsive Therapy in One Child and Three Adolescents." *Journal of Clinical Psychiatry* 49(1): 20–23.

Guttmacher, L. B., Cretella, H., and Houghtalen, R. (1989). "Dr. Guttmacher and Colleagues Reply" [to McGough et al., 1989]. *Journal of Clinical Psychiatry* 50(3): 106–107.

Haas, G. L. and Clarkin, J. F. (1988). "Affective Disorders and the Family Context." In J. F. Clarkin, G. J. Haas, and I. D. Glick, eds., *Affective Disorders and the Family: Assessment and Treatment.* New York: Guilford Press, pp. 3–28.

Haas, G. L., Clarkin, J. F., and Glick, I. D. (1985). "Marital and Family Treatment of Depression." In E. E. Beckham and W. R. Leber, eds., *Handbook of Depression: Treatment, Assessment, and Research.* Homewood, Ill.: Dorsey Press, pp. 151–183.

Hafen, B. Q. and Frandsen, K. J. (1986). *Youth Suicide: Depression and Loneliness.* Evergreen, Colo.: Cordillera Press.

Halbreich, U., Holtz, I., and Paul, L. (1988)."Premenstrual Changes: Impaired Hormonal Homeostasis." *Neurologic Clinics* 6(1): 173–194.

Hall, R. C. W., ed. (1980). *Psychiatric Presentations of Medical Illness: Somatopsychic Disorders.* New York: SP Medical and Scientific Books.

Hamilton-Obaid, B. (1989). "Helping Adolescents in Crisis: A Case Study." *Adolescence* 24(93): 59–63.

Harper, R. G., Kotik-Harper, D., and Kirby, H. (1990). "Psychometric Assessment of Depression in an Elderly General Medical Population: Over- or Underassessment?" *Journal of Nervous and Mental Disease* 178(2): 113–119.

Harrington, R. C. (1990). "Depressive Disorder in Children and Adolescents." *British Journal of Hospital Medicine* 43(2): 108, 110, 112.

Harris, B. (1981). " 'Maternity Blues' in East African Clinic Attenders." *Archives of General Psychiatry* 38(11): 1293–1295.

Harrison, M. (1985). *Self-help for Premenstrual Syndrome.* New and Revised Edition. New York: Random House.

Hartmann, E. (1988). "Sleep." In A. M. Nicholi, Jr., ed., *The New Harvard Guide to Psychiatry*. Cambridge: Belknap/Harvard University Press, pp. 152–170.

Hauck, P. A. (1973). *Overcoming Depression*. Philadelphia: Westminster Press.

Hawton, K. (1986). *Suicide and Attempted Suicide Among Children and Adolescents*. Beverly Hills, Cal.: Sage Publications.

Hayashida, M., Alterman, A. I., McLellan, A. T., O'Brien, C. P., Purtill, J. J., Volpicelli, J. R., Raphelson, A. H., and Hall, C. P. (1989). "Comparative Effectiveness and Costs of Inpatient and Outpatient Detoxification of Patients with Mild-to-Moderate Alcohol Withdrawal Syndrome." *New England Journal of Medicine* 320(6): 358–365.

"Health Insurance Gaps Laid to Racial Bias" (1991). *New York Times*, May 14, C-2.

Hellekson, C. (1989). "Phenomenology of Seasonal Affective Disorder: An Alaskan Perspective." In N. E. Rosenthal and M. C. Blehar, eds., *Seasonal Affective Disorders and Phototherapy*. New York: Guilford Press, pp. 33–45.

Hendrie, H. C., Clair, D. K., Brittain, H. M., and Fadul, P. E. (1990). "A Study of Anxiety/Depressive Symptoms of Medical Students, House Staff, and Their Spouses/Partners." *Journal of Nervous and Mental Disorders* 178(3): 204–207.

Henn, F. A., Edwards, E., and Anderson, D. (1986). "Receptor Regulation as a Function of Experience." National Institute on Drug Abuse Research Monograph Series, Monograph 74. Bethesda, Md.: National Institute on Drug Abuse.

Herman, J. B., Brotman, A. W., Pollack, M. H., Falk, W. E., Biederman, J. M., and Rosenbaum, J. F. (1990). "Fluoxetine-Induced Sexual Dysfunction." *Journal of Clinical Psychiatry* 51(1): 25–27.

Hersch, P. (1991). "Secret Lives." *The Family Therapy Networker* 15(1): 36–43.

Herzog, D. B. (1988). "Eating Disorders." In A. M. Nicholi, Jr., ed., *The New Harvard Guide to Psychiatry*. Cambridge: Belknap/Harvard University Press, pp. 434–448.

Hinchcliffe, M. K., Hooper, D., and Roberts, F. J. (1978). *The Melancholy Marriage: Depression in Marriage and Psychosocial Approaches to Therapy*. Chichester, England: John Wiley.

Hinrichsen, G. A., Lieberman, J. A., Pollack, S., and Steinberg, H. (1989). "Depression in Hemodialysis Patients." *Psychosomatics* 30(3): 284–289.

Hirschfeld, R. M. A., Koslow, S. H., and Kupfer, D. J., eds. (1985). *Clinical Utility of the Dexamethasone Suppression Test*. Rockville, Md.: National Institute of Public Health DHHS Pub. No. (ADM) 85–1318.

Hoberman, H. M. and Lewinsohn, P. M. (1985). "The Behavioral Treatment of Depression." In E. E. Beckham and W. R. Leber, eds., *Handbook of Depression: Treatment, Assessment, and Research*. Homewood, Ill.: Dorsey Press, pp. 39–81.

Hochschild, A. (1989). *Second Shift*. New York: Viking.

Hodges, K. K. and Siegel, L. J. (1985). "Depression in Children and Adolescents." In E. E. Beckham and W. R. Leber, eds., *Handbook of Depression: Treatment, Assessment, and Research*. Homewood, Ill.: Dorsey Press, pp. 517–555.

Hodgkinson, S., Mullan, M., and Murray, R. M. (1991). "The Genetics of Vulnerability to Alcoholism." In P. McGuffin and R. Murray, eds., *The New Genetics of Mental Illness*. Oxford, England: Butterworth-Heinemann, pp. 182–197.

Hohmann, A. A., Richport, M., Marriott, B. M., Canino, G. J., Rubio-Stipec, M., and Bird, H. (1990). "Spiritism in Puerto Rico: Results of an Island-wide Community Study." *British Journal of Psychiatry* 156: 328–335.

Holden, C. (1986). "Youth Suicide: New Research Focuses on a Growing Social Problem." *Science* 233: 839–841.

Holden, C. (1991). "New Center to Study Therapies and Ethnicity." *Science* 251: 748.

Holder, D. and Anderson, C. M. (1990). "Psychoeducational Family Intervention for Depressed Patients and Their Families." In G. I. Keitner, ed., *Depression and Families: Impact and Treatment*. Washington, D.C.: American Psychiatric Press, pp. 157–184.

Hollon, S. D. (1981). "Comparisons and Combination with Alternative Approaches." In L. P. Rehm, ed., *Behavior Therapy for Depression: Present Status and Future Directions*. New York: Academic Press, pp. 33–71.

Hollon, S. D. (1990). "Cognitive Therapy and Pharmacotherapy for Depression." *Psychiatric Annals* 20(5): 249–251, 255–256, 258.

Hollon, S. D. and Beck, A. T. (1986). "Cognitive and Cognitive-behavioral Therapies." In S. L. Garfield and A. E. Bergin, eds., *Handbook of Psychotherapy and Behavior Change*. Third Edition. New York: John Wiley, pp. 443–482.

Hollon, S. D. and Najavits, L. (1988). "Review of Empirical Studies on Cognitive Therapy." In A. J. Frances and R. E. Hales, eds., *American Psychiatric Press Review of Psychiatry*. Vol. 7. Washington, D.C.: American Psychiatric Press, pp. 643–666.

Hoover, C. F. and Fitzgerald, R. G. (1981). "Marital Conflict of Manic-Depressive Patients." *Archives of General Psychiatry* 38(1): 65–67.

Horney, K. (1950). *Neurosis and Human Growth: The Struggle Toward Self-realization*. New York: W. W. Norton.

Hraba, J. (1979). *American Ethnicity*. Itasca, Ill.: F. E. Peacock.

Hudson, J. I., Pope, H. G., Jr., Yurgelun-Todd, D., Jona, J. M., and Frankenburg, F. R. (1987). "A Controlled Study of Lifetime Prevalence of Affective and Other Psychiatric Disorders in Bulimic Outpatients." *American Journal of Psychiatry* 144(10): 1283–1287.

Humphry, D. (1991). *Final Exit: The Practicalities of Self-deliverance and Assisted Suicide for the Dying*. Secaucus, N.J.: Hemlock Society.

Hussian, R. A. and Davis, R. L. (1985). *Responsive Care: Behavioral Interventions with Elderly Persons*. Champaign, Ill.: Research Press.

Hyman, S. E. (1988a). "Recent Developments in Neurobiology: Part I. Synaptic Transmission." *Psychosomatics* 29(2): 157–165.

Hyman, S. E. (1988b). "Recent Developments in Neurobiology: Part II. Neurotransmitter Receptors and Psychopharmacology." *Psychosomatics* 29(3): 254–263.

Hyman, S. E. (1988c). "The Role of Molecular Biology in Psychiatry." *Psychosomatics* 29(3): 328–332.

Hyman, S. E. (1988d). "Recent Developments in Neurobiology: Part III. Effectors of Transmitter Action." *Psychosomatics* 29(4): 373–378.

Hyman, S. E. (1991a). "The Biology of Depressive Disorders." Paper presented at Symposium on the Biology and Treatment of Depressive Disorders, Philadelphia, July 27.

Hyman, S. E. (1991b). "Neuropharmacology of Mood Disorder." In *Biology and Treatment of Depressive Disorders*. Proceedings of the 1991 U.S. Depressive Disorders Update, pp. 23–39.

Isaacs, G., Stainer, D. S., Sensky, T. E., Moor, S., Thompson, C. (1988). "Phototherapy and Its Mechanisms of Action in Seasonal Affective Disorder." *Journal of Affective Disorders* 14(1): 13–19.

Ishisake, H. A., Nguyen, Q. T., and Okimoto, J. T. (1985). "The Role of Culture in the Mental Health Treatment of Indochinese Refugees." In T. C. Owan, ed., *Southeast Asian Mental Health: Treatment, Prevention, Services, Training, and Research.* Bethesda, Md.: National Institute of Mental Health, pp. 41–63.

Isikoff, M. (1990). "Fighting Drugs with Drugs: Remedies Sought for Addiction." *Washington Post*, August 20, pp. A-1, A-4–5.

Jacobs, D. and Brown, H. N., eds. (1989). *Suicide: Understanding and Responding.* Madison, Conn.: International Universities Press.

Jacobs, J. (1980). *Adolescent Suicide.* Revised Edition. New York: Irvington.

Jacobsen, F. M., Murphy, D. L., and Rosenthal, N. E. (1989). "The Role of Serotonin in Seasonal Affective Disorder and the Antidepressant Response to Phototherapy." In N. E. Rosenthal and M. C. Blaher, eds., *Seasonal Affective Disorders and Phototherapy.* New York: Guilford Press, pp. 333–341.

Jacobson, B., Nyberg, K., Gronbladh, L., Bygdeman, M., and Rydberg, U. (1990). "Opiate Addiction in Adult Offspring Through Possible Imprinting After Obstetric Treatment." *British Medical Journal* 301(6760): 1067–1070.

Jacobson, E. (1938). *Progressive Relaxation.* Chicago: University of Chicago Press.

Jacobson, E. (1971). *Depression: Comparative Studies of Normal, Neurotic, and Psychotic Conditions.* New York: International Universities Press.

Jarrett, R. B. and Rush, A. J. (1991). "Psychotherapeutic Approaches for Depression." In R. Michels, ed., *Psychiatry.* Vol 2. Revised Edition (Looseleaf). Philadelphia: J. B. Lippincott, pp. 1–35.

Jobe, P. C., Ko, K. H., and Daily, J. W. (1984). "Abnormalities in Norepinephrine Turnover Rate in the Central Nervous System of the Genetically Epilepsy-Prone Rat." *Brain Research* 290: 357–360.

Joffee, R. T., Offord, D. R., and Boyle, M. H. (1988). "Ontario Child Health Study: Suicidal Behavior in Youth Age 12–16 Years." *American Journal of Psychiatry* 145(11): 1420–1423.

John, K. and Weissman, M. M. (1987). "The Familial and Psychosocial Measurement of Depression." In A. J. Marsella, R. M. A. Hirschfeld, and M. M. Katz, eds., *The Measurement of Depression.* New York: Guilford Press, pp. 344–375.

Johnson, E. H. (1989). "Psychiatric Morbidity and Health Problems Among Black Americans: A National Survey." *Journal of the National Medical Association* 81(12): 1217–1223.

Johnson, J. (1989). "Childhood Is Not Safe, Congress Study Warns." *New York Times*, October 2, p. A-12.

Johnson, S. R., McChesney, C., and Bean, J. A. (1988). "Epidemiology of Premenstrual Symptoms in a Nonclinical Sample. I. Prevalence, Natural History and Help-seeking Behavior." *Journal of Reproductive Medicine* 33(4): 340–346.

Jones, B. E. and Gray, B. A. (1986). "Problems in Diagnosing Schizophrenia and Affective Disorders Among Blacks." *Hospital and Community Psychiatry* 37: 61–65.

Jones, B. E., Gray, B. A., and Parson, E. B. (1988). "Major Affective Disorders in Blacks: A Preliminary Report." *Integrative Psychiatry* 6: 131–140.

Jones, B. E., Robinson, W. M., Parson, E. B., and Gray, B. A. (1982). "The Clinical Picture of Mania in Manic-Depressive Black Patients." *Journal of the National Medical Association* 74(6): 553–560.

Joyce, P. R. and Paykel, E. S. (1989). "Predictors of Drug Response to Depression." *Archives of General Psychiatry* 46(1): 89–99.

Kahn, A. (1991). "Menstrual Cycle Important Factor When Prescribing Psychotropic Drugs." *Psychiatric News*, October 4, p. 24.

Kambe, T. (1972). "Suicide Among Japanese Adolescents." *Scientific Reports of Kyoto Prefectural University: The Humanities* 24: 41–46 (quoted in Lebra, 1976, p. 194).

Kanahele, G. (1982). "The New Hawaiians." *Social Process in Hawaii* 29: 1–31 (cited in Mokuau, 1988, p. 57).

Kanarek, R. B. and Marks-Kaufman, R. (1991). *Nutrition and Behavior: New Perspectives.* New York: Van Nostrand Reinhold.

Kanfer, F. H. and Gaelick, L. (1986). "Self-management Methods." In F. H. Kanfer and A. P. Goldstein, eds., *Helping People Change: A Textbook of Methods.* Third Edition. New York: Pergamon Press, pp. 283–345.

Kanfer, F. H. and Haagerman, S. (1981). "The Role of Self-regulation." In L. P. Rehm, ed., *Behavior Therapy for Depression: Present Status and Future Directions.* New York: Academic Press, pp. 143–179.

Kantak, K. M., Lawley, S. I., Wasserman, S. J., and Bourg, J. F. (1991). "Magnesium-maintained Self-administration Responding in Cocaine-Trained Rats." *Psychopharmacology* 104(4): 527–535.

Kaplan, H. I. and Sadock, B. I. (1990). *Pocket Handbook of Clinical Psychiatry.* Baltimore: Williams and Wilkins.

Karasu, T. B. (1990a). "Toward a Clinical Model of Psychotherapy for Depression, I: Systematic Comparison of Three Psychotherapies." *American Journal of Psychiatry* 147(2): 133–147.

Karasu, T. B. (1990b). "Toward a Clinical Model of Psychotherapy for Depression, II: An Integrative and Selective Treatment Approach." *American Journal of Psychiatry* 147(3): 269–278.

Kashani, J. H., Beck, N. C., and Burk, J. P. (1987). "Predictors of Psychopathology in Children of Patients with Major Affective Disorders." *Canadian Journal of Psychiatry* 32(4): 287–290.

Kashani, J. H., Carlson, G. A., Beck, N. C., Hoeper, E. W., Corcoran, C. M., McAllister, J. A., Fallahi, C., Rosenberg, T. K., and Reid, J. C. (1987).

"Depression, Depressive Symptoms, and Depressed Mood Among a Community Sample of Adolescents." *American Journal of Psychiatry* 144(7): 931–934.

Kashani, J. H. and Orvaschel, H. (1988). "Anxiety Disorders in Mid-adolescence: A Community Sample." *American Journal of Psychiatry* 145(8): 960–964.

Kashani, J. H. and Sherman, D. D. (1988). "Childhood Depression: Epidemiology, Etiological Models, and Treatment Implications." *Integrative Psychiatry* 6: 1–21.

Kasper, J. A. (1982). "Prescribed Medicines: Use, Expenditures, and Sources of Payment." In *Prescribed Medicines.* Bethesda, Md.: U.S. Department of Health and Human Services.

Kasper, S., Rogers, S. L. B., Yancey, A., Skwerer, R. G., Schulz, P. M., and Rosenthal, N. E. (1989). In N. E. Rosenthal and M. C. Blehar, eds., *Seasonal Affective Disorders and Phototherapy.* New York: Guilford Press, pp. 260–270.

Kathol, R. G. (1985). "Depression Associated with Physical Disease." In E. E. Beckham and W. R. Leber, eds., *Handbook of Depression: Treatment, Assessment, and Research.* Homewood, Ill.: Dorsey Press, pp. 745–762.

Katon, W. (1987). "Treating Patients Who Present with Somatic Symptoms." *Clinical Advances in the Treatment of Depression.* 1(4): 7, 11.

Katona, C. L., Aldridge, C. R., Roth, M., and Hyde, J. (1987). "The Dexamethasone Suppression Test and Prediction of Outcome in Patients Receiving ECT." *British Journal of Psychiatry* 150: 315–318.

Kaye, W. H. (1987). "Commentary" [on Wurtman, 1987] *Integrative Psychiatry* 5: 255–257.

Kaye W. H., Gwirtsman, H. E., Brewerton, T. D., George, D. T., and Wurtman, R. J. (1988). "Bingeing Behavior and Plasma Amino Acids: A Possible Involvement of Brain Serotonin in Bulimia Nervosa." *Psychiatry Research* 23(1): 31–43.

Kazdin, A. E. (1986). "Research Designs and Methodology." In S. L. Garfield and A. E. Bergin, eds., *Handbook of Psychotherapy and Behavior Change.* Third Edition. New York: John Wiley, pp. 23–68.

Kazdin, A. E. (1990). "Childhood Depression." *Journal of Child Psychology and Psychiatry* 31(1): 121–160.

Keane, S. M. and Sells, S. (1990). "Recognizing Depression in the Elderly." *Journal of Gerontological Nursing* 16(1): 21–25.

Keddie, K. M. (1987). "Severe Depressive Illness in the Context of Hypervitaminosis D." *British Journal of Psychiatry* 150: 394–396.

Keitner, G. I., ed. (1990). *Depression and Families: Impact and Treatment.* Washington, D.C.: American Psychiatric Press.

Keller, M. B. and Shapiro, R. W. (1982). " 'Double Depression': Superimposition of Acute Depressive Episodes on Chronic Depressive Disorders." *American Journal of Psychiatry* 139(4): 438–442.

Kennedy, S. H., Garfinkel, P. E., Parienti, V., Costa, D., and Brown, G. M. (1989). "Changes in Melatonin Levels but Not Cortisol Levels Are Associated with Depression in Patients with Eating Disorders." *Archives of General Psychiatry* 46(1): 73–78.

Kessler, R. and Neighbors, H. (1986). "A New Perspective on the Relationships

Among Race, Social Class, and Psychological Distress." *Journal of Health and Social Behavior* 27: 107–115.

Keyes, C. F. (1985)."The Interpretive Basis of Depression." In A. Kleinman and B. Good, eds., *Culture and Depression: Studies in the Anthropology and Cross-cultural Psychiatry of Affect and Disorder.* Berkeley: University of California Press, pp. 153–174.

Khantzian, E. J. (1986). "A Contemporary Psychodynamic Approach to Drug Abuse Treatment." *American Journal of Drug and Alcohol Abuse* 12(3): 213–222.

Khantzian, E. J. (1987). "A Clinical Perspective of the Cause-Consequence Controversy in Alcoholic and Addictive Suffering." *Journal of the American Academy of Psychoanalysis* 15(4): 521—537.

Khantzian, E. J. (1989). "From Theory to Practice: The Planned Treatment of Drug Users." *International Journal of Addiction* 24(4): 351–383.

Killern, J. D., Taylor, C. B., Telch, M. J., Robinson, T. N., Maron, D. J., and Saylor, K. E. (1987). "Depressive Symptoms and Substance Use Among Adolescent Binge Eaters and Purgers: A Defined Population Study." *American Journal of Public Health* 77(12): 1539–1541.

Kiloh, L. G. (1982). "Electroconvulsive Therapy." In E. S. Paykel, ed., *Handbook of Affective Disorders.* New York: Guilford Press, pp. 262–275.

Kim, S. C. (1985). "Family Therapy for Asian Americans: A Strategic-Structural Framework." *Psychotherapy* 22: 342–348.

Kim, H. R., Delva, N. J., and Lawson, J. S. (1990). "Prophylactic Medication for Unipolar Depressive Illness: The Place of Lithium Carbonate in Combination with Antidepressant Medication." *Canadian Journal of Psychiatry* 35(2): 107–114.

Kingsbury, S. J. (1992). "What Is the Value of Self-help Books for Patients and Psychotherapists?" *The Harvard Mental Health Letter.* 8(7): 8.

Kinzel, D. (1991). "Self-identified Health Concerns of Two Homeless Groups." *Western Journal of Nursing Research* 13(2): 181–190. (Abstract.)

Kinzie, J. D. (1985). "Overview of Clinical Issues in the Treatment of Southeast Asian Refugees." In T. C. Owan, ed., *Southeast Asian Mental Health: Treatment, Prevention, Services, Training, and Research.* Bethesda, Md.: National Institute of Mental Health, pp. 113–135.

Klagsbrun, F. (1976). *Youth and Suicide: Too Young to Die.* New York: Pocket Books.

Klein, D. F and Wender, P. H. (1988). *Do You Have a Depressive Illness? How to Tell, What to Do.* New York: New American Library.

Kleinman, A. and Good, B. (1985). *Culture and Depression: Studies in the Anthropology and Cross-cultural Psychiatry of Affect and Disorder.* Berkeley: University of California Press.

Klerman, G. L. (1978). "Affective Disorders." In A. M. Nicholi, Jr., ed., *The Harvard Guide to Modern Psychiatry.* Cambridge: Belknap/Harvard University Press, pp. 253–281.

Klerman, G. L. (1985). "Birth-cohort Trends in Rates of Major Depressive Disorders Among Relatives of Patients with Affective Disorder." *Archives of General Psychiatry* 42: 689–693.

Klerman, G. L. (1986). "Drugs and Psychotherapy." In S. L. Garfield and A. E.

Bergin, eds., *Handbook of Psychotherapy and Behavior Change*. Third Edition. New York: John Wiley, pp. 777–820.

Klerman, G. L. (1987). " The Nature of Depression: Mood, Symptom, Disorder." In A. J. Marsella, R. M. A. Hirschfeld, and M. M. Katz, eds., *The Measurement of Depression*. New York: Guilford Press, pp. 3–19.

Klerman, G. L. (1988). "Depression and Related Disorders of Mood (Affective Disorders)." In A. M. Nicholi, Jr., ed., *The New Harvard Guide to Psychiatry*. Cambridge: Belknap/Harvard University Press, pp. 309–336.

Klerman, G. L. (1989). "Evaluating the Efficacy of Psychotherapy for Depression: The USA Experience." *European Archives of Psychiatry and Neurological Sciences* 238(5–6): 240–246.

Klerman, G. L. (1990). "NIMH Collaborative Research on Treatment of Depression." *Archives of General Psychiatry* 47: 686–688.

Klerman, G. L., Weissman, M. M., Rounsaville, B. J., and Chevron, E. S. (1984). *Interpersonal Psychotherapy of Depression*. New York: Basic Books.

Knight, C. (1990). "Use of Support Groups with Adult Female Survivors of Child Sexual Abuse." *Social Work* 35(3): 202–206.

Kobren, G. (1989). "The Theft of One's Self." *The Baltimore Sun*, June 27, pp. 4–6.

Koenig, H. G. and Breitner, J. C. (1990). "Use of Antidepressants in Medically Ill Older Patients." *Psychosomatics* 31(1): 22–32.

Kolata, G. (1982). "Food Affects Human Behavior." *Science* 218: 1209–1210.

Kolata, G. (1986). "Manic-Depression: Is It Inherited?" *Science* 232: 575–576.

Kolata, G. (1987). "Manic-Depression Gene Tied to Chromosome 11." *Science* 235: 1139–1140.

Kolata, G. (1990). "Researchers Cannot Confirm a Genetic Link to Alcoholism." *New York Times*, December 26, p. A-1.

Koplan, C. R.(1983). "Pediatric Psychopharmacology." In E. L. Bassuk, S. C. Schoonover, and A. J. Gelenberg, eds., *The Practitioner's Guide to Psychoactive Drugs*. Second Edition. New York: Plenum Medical Book Company, pp. 313–352.

Koslow, S. H. and Gaist, P. A. (1987). "The Measurement of Neurotransmitters in Depression." In A. J. Marsella, R. M. A. Hirschfeld, and M. M. Katz, eds., *The Measurement of Depression*. New York: Guilford Press, pp. 109–152.

Kosten, T. R., Rounsaville, B. J., and Kieber, H. D. (1985). "Ethnic and Gender Differences Among Opiate Addicts." *International Journal of the Addictions* 20(8): 1143–1162.

Kovacs, M. (1989). "Affective Disorders in Children and Adolescents." *American Psychologist* 44(2): 209–215.

Kovacs, M. and Beck, A. T. (1977). "An Empirical-Clinical Approach Toward a Definition of Childhood Depression." In J. G. Schulterbrandt and A. Raskin, eds., *Depression in Childhood: Diagnosis, Treatment, and Conceptual Models*. Rockville, Md.: National Institute of Mental Health, pp. 1–26.

Kovacs, M., Paulauskas, S., Gatsonic, C., and Richards, C. (1988). "Depressive Disorders in Childhood: III. A Longitudinal Study of Comorbidity with and Risk for Conduct Disorders." *Journal of Affective Disorders* 15(3): 205–217.

Kramlinger, K. G., and Post, R. M. (1990). "Addition of Lithium Carbonate to

Carbamazepine: Hematological and Thyroid Effects." *American Journal of Psychiatry* 147(5): 615–620.

Kripke, D. F., Mullaney, D. J., Savides, T. J., and Gillin, J. C. (1989). "Phototherapy for Nonseasonal Major Depressive Disorders." In N. E. Rosenthal and M. C. Blehar, eds., *Seasonal Affective Disorders and Phototherapy*. New York: Guilford Press, pp. 342–356.

Krucoff, C. (1989). "From Diet to Jobs to Sex: How Seasons Affect Mood and Behavior." *Washington Post*, February 28, pp. 12–14.

Kuhar, M. J., Ritz, M. C., and Boja, J. W. (1991). "The Dopamine Hypothesis of the Reinforcing Properties of Cocaine." *Trends in Neuroscience* 14(7): 299–302.

Kupfer, D. J., Targ, E., and Stack, J. (1982). "EEG Sleep in Unipolar Depressive Subtypes: Support for a Biologic and Familial Classification." *Journal of Nervous and Mental Disease* 170: 494–498.

Lacoste, V. and Wirz-Justice, A. (1989). "Seasonal Variation in Normal Subjects: An Update of Variables Current in Depression Research." In N. E. Rosenthal and M. C. Blehar, eds., *Seasonal Affective Disorders and Phototherapy*. New York: Guilford Press, pp. 167–229.

Laessle, R. G., Schweiger, U., and Pirke, K. M. (1988). "Depression as a Correlate of Starvation in Patients with Eating Disorders." *Biological Psychiatry* 23(7): 719–725.

Laird, L. K. and Lydiard, R. B. (1989). "Imipramine-Related Tinnitus," *Journal of Clinical Psychiatry* 50(4): 146.

Lalinec-Michaud, M., Engelsmann, F., and Marino, J. (1988). "Depression After Hysterectomy: A Comparative Study." *Psychosomatics* 29(3): 307–314.

Lamberg, L. (1984). *The American Medical Association Guide to Better Sleep*. Revised and Updated Edition. New York: Random House.

Lamberg, L. (1988). *Drugs and Sleep*. The Encyclopedia of Psychoactive Drugs, Series 2. New York: Chelsea House.

Lansky, M. R. (1988). "Common Clinical Predicaments." In J. F. Clarkin, G. L. Haas, and I. D. Glick, eds., *Affective Disorders and the Family: Assessment and Treatment*. New York: Guilford Press, pp. 213–238.

Larson, R. W., Raffaelli, M., Richardson, M. H., Ham, M., and Jewell, L. (1990). "Ecology of Depression in Late Childhood and Early Adolescence: A Profile of Daily States and Activities." *Journal of Abnormal Psychology* 99(1): 92–102.

Lau, T. (1979). *The Handbook of Chinese Horoscopes*. New York: Harper/Colophon Books.

Lazarus, A. A. (1968). "Learning Theory and the Treatment of Depression." *Behaviour Research and Therapy* 6: 83–89.

Lazarus, A. A. (1971). *Behavior Therapy and Beyond*. New York: McGraw-Hill.

Leary, W. E. (1991). "F. D. A. Says It Plans to Quicken Process for Approving New Drugs." *New York Times*, November 14, p. B-14.

Leber. W. R., Beckham, E. E., and Danker-Brown, P. (1985). "Diagnostic Criteria for Depression." E. E. Beckham and W. R. Leber, eds., *Handbook of Depression: Treatment, Assessment, and Research*. Homewood Ill.: Dorsey Press, pp. 343–371.

Lebra, T. S. (1976). *Japanese Patterns of Behavior*. Honolulu: University of Hawaii Press.

Lee, C. M. and Gotlib, I. H. (1989). "Clinical Status and Emotional Adjustment of Children of Depressed Mothers." *American Journal of Psychiatry* 146(4): 478–483.

Lehmann, L. (1985). "The Relationship of Depression to Other DSM-III Axis I Disorders." In E. E. Beckham and W. R. Leber, eds., *Handbook of Depression: Treatment, Assessment, and Research.* Homewood, Ill.: Dorsey Press, pp. 669–699.

Lehrer, P. M and Woolfolk, R. L. (1985)."The Relaxation Therapies." In R. M. Turner and L. M. Ascher, eds., *Evaluating Behavior Therapy Outcome.* New York: Springer, pp. 95–121.

Lentz, R. D. (1990). "When a Depressed Patient Fails to Improve." *Postgraduate Medicine* 87(4): 251–258.

Lepkifker, E., Horesh, N., and Floru, S. (1985). "Long-Term Lithium Prophylaxis in Recurrent Unipolar Depression: A Controversial Indication?" *Acta Psychiatrica Belgica* 85(3): 434–443.

Lepkifker, F., Horesh, N., and Floru, S. (1988). "Life Satisfaction and Adjustment in Lithium-Treated Affective Patients in Remission." *Acta Psychiatrica Scandinavica* 78(3): 391–395.

Lesnoff-Caravaglia, G. (1988). "Predetermined Death: Suicide in Old Age." *Social Casework* 69(9): 584–587.

Lesse, S., ed. (1974). *Masked Depression.* New York: Jason Aronson.

Levey, A. B., Dixon, K. N., and Stern, S. L. (1989). "How Are Depression and Bulimia Related?" *American Journal of Psychiatry* 146(2): 162–169.

Levinson, D. (1986). "A Conception of Adult Development." *American Psychologist* 41(1): 3–13.

Levinson, D., with Darrow, E. B., Klein, E. B., Levinson, M. H., and McKee, B. (1978). *The Seasons of a Man's Life.* New York: Alfred A. Knopf.

Levitt, E. E. (1971). "Research on Psychotherapy with Children." In A. E. Bergin and S. L. Garfield, eds., *Handbook of Psychotherapy and Behavior Change.* New York: John Wiley, pp. 474–494.

Levy, A. B., Dixon, K. N., and Stern, S. L. (1989). "How Are Depression and Bulimia Related?" *American Journal of Psychiatry* 146(2): 162–169.

Lewinsohn, P. M., Antonuccio, D. O., Breckenridge, J. S., and Teri, L. (1984). *The Coping with Depression Course: A Psycho-educational Intervention for Unipolar Depression.* Eugene, Ore.: Castalia.

Lewinsohn, P. M., and Hoberman, H. M. (1985). "Depression." In M. Hersen and A. E. Kazdin., eds., *International Handbook of Behavior Modification and Therapy.* Student Edition. New York: Plenum Press, pp. 173–207.

Lewinsohn, P. M., Munoz, R. F., Youngren, M. A., and Zeiss, A. M. (1986). *Control Your Depression.* Revised and Updated. Englewood Cliffs, N.J.: Prentice-Hall.

Lewy, A. J., Sack, R. L., Miller, S., and Hoban, T. M. (1987). "Antidepressant and Circadian Phase-Shifting Effects of Light." *Science* 235: 352–354.

Lewy, A. J., Sack, R. L., Singer, C. M., White, D. M., and Hoban, T. M. (1989). "Winter Depression and the Phase-Shift Hypothesis for Bright Light's Therapeutic Effects: History, Theory, and Experimental Evidence." In N. E. Rosenthal and M. C. Blehar, eds., *Seasonal Affective Disorders and Phototherapy.* New York: Guilford Press, pp. 295–310.

Liberman, R. P. and Raskin, D. E. (1971)."Depression: A Behavioral Formulation." *Archives of General Psychiatry* 24: 515–523.

Lidz, T. (1968). *The Person: His Development Throughout the Life Cycle.* New York: Basic Books.

Lieber, A. L. (1987). "The Use of Biological Markers in Diagnosing Depression." *Clinical Advances in the Treatment of Depression* 1(3): 6–8.

Lieberman, H. R., Cabbalero, B., and Finer, N. J. (1986). "The Composition of Lunch Determines Afternoon Plasma Tryptophan Ratios in Humans." *Journal of Neural Transmission* 65: 211–217.

Lieberman, H. R., Wurtman, R. J., Emde, G. G., Roberts, C., and Coviella, I. L. (1987). "The Effects of Low Dose of Caffeine on Human Performance and Mood." *Psychopharmacology* 92(3): 308–312.

Liebowitz, M. R., Quitkin, F. M., Stewart, J. W., McGrath, P. J., Harrison, W. M., Markowitz, J. S., Rabkin, J. G., Tricamo, E., Goetz, D. M., and Klein, D. F. (1988). "Antidepressant Specificity in Atypical Depression." *Archives of General Psychiatry* 45(2): 129–137.

Lin, N., Simeone, R. S., Ensel, W. M., and Kuo, W. (1979). "Social Support, Stressful Life Events and Illness: A Model and an Empirical Test." *Journal of Health and Social Behavior* 20: 108—119 (cited in John and Weissman, 1987, p. 350].

Lindstrom, C. J. (1975). "No-Shows: A Problem in Health Care." *Nursing Outlook* 23: 755–759.

Liu, W. T. and Cheung, F. (1985). "Research Concerns Associated with the Study of Southeast Asian Refugees." In T. C. Owan, ed. *Southeast Asian Mental Health: Treatment, Prevention, Services, Training, and Research.* Bethesda, Md.: National Institute of Mental Health, pp. 487—516.

Lobel, B. and Hirschfeld, R. M. A. (1984). *Depression: What We Know.* Rockville, Md.: National Institute of Mental Health DHHS Pub. No. (ADM) 84–1318.

Loebel, J. P., Loebel, J. S., Dager, S. R., Centerwall, B. S., and Reay, R. T. (1991). "Anticipation of Nursing Home Placement May Be a Precipitant of Suicide Among the Elderly." *Journal of the American Geriatrics Society* 39: 407–408.

Loffelholz, K. (1987). "Commentary" [on Wurtman, 1987]. *Integrative Psychiatry* 5: 242–244.

Logan, J. (1978). *Movie Stars, Real People, and Me.* New York: Delacorte Press.

Logue, C. M., Crowe, R. R., and Bean, J. A. (1989). "A Family Study of Anorexia Nervosa and Bulimia." *Comprehensive Psychiatry* 30(2): 179–188.

Lukas, C. and Seiden, H. M. (1987). *Silent Grief: Living in the Wake of Suicide.* New York: Charles Scribner's Sons.

Lutz, C. (1985). "Depression and the Translation of Emotional Worlds." In A. Kleinman and B. Good, eds., *Culture and Depression: Studies in the Anthropology and Cross-cultural Psychiatry of Affect and Disorder.* Berkeley: University of California Press, pp. 63–100.

Mace, N. L. and Rabins, P. V. (1991). *The 36–Hour Day: A Family Guide to Caring for Persons with Alzheimer's Disease.* Revised Edition. Baltimore, Md.: Johns Hopkins University Press.

Mack, J. E. (1989). "Adolescent Suicide: An Architectural Model." In D. Jacobs and H. N. Brown, eds., *Suicide: Understanding and Responding.* Madison, Conn.: International Universities Press, pp. 221–238.

Mackenzie, T. B., Robiner, W. N., and Knopman, D. S. (1989). "Differences Between Patient and Family Assessments of Depression in Alzheimer's Disease." *American Journal of Psychiatry* 146: 1174–1178.

Macsherry, C. (1991). "Lifetime Companions: Gay and Lesbian Couples Fight for Recognition and Rights." *City Paper*, December 6, pp. 11–19.

Maguire, L. (1991). *Social Support Systems in Practice: A Generalist Approach.* Silver Spring, Md.: National Association of Social Workers.

Majumdar, S. K., Shaw, G. K., and Bridges, P. K. (1988). "The Dexamethasone Suppression Test in Chronic Alcoholics with and without Depression and Its Relationship to the Hepatic Status." *Drug and Alcohol Dependence* 21(3): 231–235.

Makanjuola, J. O. and Olaifa, E. A. (1987). "Masked Depression in Nigerians Treated at the Neuropsychiatric Hospital at Abeokuta." *Acta Psychiatrica Scandinavica* 76(5): 480–485.

Malan, D. (1976). *Individual Psychotherapy and the Science of Psychodynamics.* London: Butterworths.

Maldonado, D., Jr. (1987). "(The) Aged." *Encyclopedia of Social Work* Eighteenth Edition. Silver Spring, Md.: National Association of Social Workers, pp. 95–106.

Malmquist, C. P. (1977). "Childhood Depression: A Clinical and Behavioral Perspective." In J. G. Schulterbrandt and A. Raskin, eds., *Depression in Childhood: Diagnosis, Treatment, and Conceptual Models.* Rockville, Md.: National Institute of Mental Health, pp. 31–56.

Mann, J. (1973). *Time-Limited Psychotherapy.* Cambridge: Harvard University Press.

Manson, S. M., Ackerson, L. M., Dick, R. W., Baron, A. E., et al. (1990). "Depressive Symptoms Among American Indian Adolescents: Psychometric Characteristics of the Center for Epidemiologic Studies Depression Scale (CES-D). *Psychological Assessment* 2(3): 231–237.

Manson, S. M. and Trimble, J. E. (1982). "American Indian and Alaska Native Communities: Past Efforts, Future Inquiries." In L. R. Snowden, ed., *Reaching the Underserved: Mental Health Needs of Neglected Populations.* Vol. 3: Sage Annual Reviews of Community Mental Health. Beverly Hills, Cal.: Sage Publications, pp. 143—163.

Marieb, E. N. (1984). *Essentials of Human Anatomy and Physiology.* Menlo Park, Cal.: Addison-Wesley.

Markowitz, J., Brown, R., Sweeney, J., and Mann, J. J. (1987). "Reduced Length and Cost of Hospital Stay for Major Depression in Patients Treated with ECT." *American Journal of Psychiatry* 144(8): 1025–1029.

Markowitz, L. M. (1991a). "Better Therapy Through Chemistry?" *The Family Therapy Networker* 15(3): 22–31.

Markowitz, L. M. (1991b). "Homosexuality: Are We Still in the Dark?" *The Family Therapy Networker* 15(1): 26–35.

Marsella, A. J. (1980). "Depressive Experience and Disorder Across Cultures."

In H. C. Triandis and J. G. Draguns, eds., *Handbook of Cross-cultural Psychology*. Vol. 6: Psychopathology. Boston: Allyn and Bacon, pp. 237–290.

Marsella, A. J. (1985). "Culture, Self, and Mental Disorder." In A. J. Marsella, G. Devos, and F. L. K. Hsu, eds., *Culture and Self: Asian and Western Perspectives*. New York: Tavistock, pp. 281–307.

Marsella, A. J. (1987)."The Measurement of Depressive Experience and Disorder Across Cultures." In A. J. Marsella, R. M. A. Hirschfeld, and M. M. Katz, eds., *The Measurement of Depression*, pp. 376–397.

Marsella, A. J., Devos, G., and Hsu, F. L. K., eds. (1985). *Culture and Self: Asian and Western Perspectives*. New York: Tavistock.

Marsella, A. J., Hirschfeld, R. M. A., and Katz, M. M., eds. (1987). *The Measurement of Depression*. New York: Guilford Press.

Marsella, A. J., Sartorius, N., Jablensky, A., and Fenton, F. R. (1985). "Cross-cultural Studies of Depressive Disorders: An Overview." In A. Kleinman and B. Good, eds., *Culture and Depression*. Berkeley: University of California Press, pp. 299–324.

Marshall, W. L. and Segal, Z. V. (1990). "Drugs Combined with Behavioral Psychotherapy." In A. S. Bellack, M. Hersen, and A. E. Kazdin, eds., *International Handbook of Behavior Modification and Therapy*. Second Edition. New York: Plenum Press, pp. 267–279.

Maslow, A. H. (1969). *The Psychology of Science: A Reconnaissance*. Chicago: Gateway/Henry Regnery Company.

Matson, J. L., Barrett, R. P., and Helsel, W. J. (1988). "Depression in Mentally Retarded Children." *Research in Developmental Disabilities* 9(1): 39–46.

Matussek, N. (1988). "Biological Aspects of Course and Outcome in Depressive Illness." In T. Helgason and R. J. Daly, eds., *Depressive Illness: Prediction of Course and Outcome*. Berlin: Springer-Verlag.

Maugh, T. H. II (1991). "Alzheimer's Advance Reported." *Baltimore Sun*, August 15, p. A-1.

Maxmen, J. S. (1986). *Essential Psychopathology*. New York: W. W. Norton.

McCabe, B. and Tsuang, M. T. (1982). "Dietary Considerations in MAO Inhibitor Regimes." *Journal of Clinical Psychiatry* 43: 178—181.

McCoy, K. (1982). *Coping with Teenage Depression: A Parent's Guide*. New York: Signet/New American Library.

McGough, J. J., McCall, W. V., and Shelp, F. E. (1989). "ECT in Children and Adolescents." *Journal of Clinical Psychiatry* 50(3): 106.

McGrath, E., Keita, G. P., Strickland, B. R., and Russo, N. F., eds. (1990). *Women and Depression: Risk Factors and Treatment Issues*. Final Report of the American Psychological Association's National Task Force on Women and Depression. Washington, D.C.: American Psychological Association.

McGuffin, P. and Sargeant, M. P. (1991). "Genetic Markers and Affective Disorder." In P. McGuffin and R. Murray, eds., *The New Genetics of Mental Illness*. Oxford: Butterworth-Heinemann, pp. 165–181.

McGuffin, P. and Murray, R., eds. (1991). *The New Genetics of Mental Illness*. Oxford: Butterworth-Heinemann.

McIntire, A., Angle, C., and Schlicht, M. L. (1980). "Suicide and Self-poisoning in Pediatrics." *Resident and Staff Physician* February, pp. 72–85.

McIntosh, J. L. and Santos, J. F. (1981). "Suicide Among Native Americans: A Compilation of Findings." *Omega* 11: 303–316.

McKinney, W. T., Suomi, S. J., and Harlow, H. F. (1971). "Depression in Primates." *American Journal of Psychiatry* 127: 1313–1320.

Mead, G. H. (1934). *Mind, Self, and Society.* Chicago: University of Chicago Press.

Meeks, J. E. (1980). *The Fragile Alliance: An Orientation to the Outpatient Psychotherapy of the Adolescent.* Second Edition. Huntington, N.Y.: Robert E. Krieger.

Mendlewicz, J. (1985). "Genetic Research in Depressive Disorders." In E. E. Beckham and W. R. Leber, eds., *Handbook of Depression: Treatment, Assessment, and Research.* Homewood, Ill.: Dorsey Press, pp. 795–811.

Meichenbaum, D. (1977). *Cognitive-Behavior Modification: An Integrative Approach.* New York: Plenum Press.

Menninger, K. (1938). *Man Against Himself.* New York: Harcourt, Brace and World.

Menolascino, F. J. (1987). "Commentary" [on Wurtman, 1987], *Integrative Psychiatry* 5: 254–255.

"Mental Illness and Homelessness: Part I" (1990). *Harvard Mental Health Newsletter* 7(1): 1–4.

Merikangas, K. R., Weissman, M. M., and Prusoff, B. A. (1990). "Psychopathology in Offspring of Parents with Affective Disorders." In G. I. Keitner, ed., *Depression and Families: Impact and Treatment.* Washington, D.C.: American Psychiatric Press, pp. 85–100.

Mesulam, M. M. (1988). "Neural Substrates of Behavior: The Effects of Brain Lesions upon Mental State." In A. M. Nicholi, Jr. ed., *The New Harvard Guide to Psychiatry.* Cambridge: Belknap/Harvard University Press, pp. 91–128.

Millon, T. and Kotik, D. (1985). "The Relationship of Depression to Disorders of Personality." In E. E. Beckham and W. R. Leber, eds., *Handbook of Depression: Treatment, Research, and Assessment.* Homewood, Ill.: Dorsey Press, pp. 700–744.

Mirin, S. M. and Weiss, R. D. (1983). "Substance Abuse." In E. L. Bassuk, S. C. Schoonover, and A. J. Gelenberg, eds., *The Practitioner's Guide to Psychoactive Drugs.* Second Edition. New York: Plenum Medical Book Company, pp. 221–291.

Mokros, H. B., Poznanski, E., Grossman, J. A., and Freeman, L. N. (1987). "A Comparison of Child and Parent Ratings of Depression for Normal and Clinically Referred Children." *Journal of Child Psychology and Psychiatry and Allied Disciplines* 28(4): 613–624.

Mokuau, N. (1986). "Ethnic Minorities." In H. L. Gochros, J. S. Gochros, and J. Fischer, eds., *Helping the Sexually Oppressed.* Englewood Cliffs, N.J.: Prentice-Hall, pp. 141–161.

Mokuau, N. (1988). "Social Work Practice with Individuals and Families in a Cross-cultural Perspective." In D. S. Sanders and J. Fischer, eds., *Visions for the Future: Social Work and Pacific-Asian Perspectives.* Honolulu: University of Hawaii Press, pp. 46—61.

Moller, S. E. and Kirk, L. (1987). "Commentary" [on Wurtman, 1987]. *Integrative Psychiatry* 5: 249–254.

Monk, M. and Warshauer, M. E. (1974)."Completed and Attempted Suicide in Three Ethnic Groups." *American Journal of Epidemiology* 100: 333–345.

Moore, P. (1986). *Useful Information on Suicide.* Rockville, Md.: NIMH, DHHS Publication No. (ADM) 86–1289.

Moos, R. H. (1990). "Depressed Outpatient's Life Contexts, Amount of Treatment, and Treatment Outcome." *Journal of Nervous and Mental Disease* 178(2): 105–112.

Moreau, D. L., Weissman, M. M., and Warner, V. (1989). "Panic Disorder in Children at High Risk for Depression." *American Journal of Psychiatry* 146(8): 1059–1060.

Morley, J. E. (1989). "An Approach to the Development of Drugs for Appetite Disorders." *Neuropsychobiology* 21(1): 22–30.

Morgan, A. (1989). "Special Issues of Assessment and Treatment of Suicide Risk in the Elderly." In D. Jacobs and H. N. Brown, eds., *Suicide: Understanding and Responding.* Madison, Conn.: International Universities Press, pp. 239–256.

Moss, H. B., Yao, J. K., Burns, M., Maddock, J., and Tarter, R. E. (1990). "Plasma GABA-like Activity in Response to Ethanol Challenge in Men at High Risk for Alcoholism." *Biological Psychiatry* 27(6): 617–625.

Mukherjee, S., Shukla, S., Woodle, J., Rosen, A. M., and Olarte, S. (1983). "Misdiagnosis of Schizophrenia in Bipolar Patients: A Multiethnic Comparison." *American Journal of Psychiatry* 140(12): 1571–1574.

Murphy, J. M. (1986). "Trends in Depression and Anxiety: Men and Women." *Acta Psychiatrica Scandinavica* 73: 113–127.

Murray, J. B. (1990)."New Applications of Lithium Therapy." *Journal of Psychology* 124(1): 55–73.

Nakajima, T., Post, R. M., Pert, A., Ketter, T. A., and Weiss, S. R. B. (1989). "Perspectives on the Mechanism of Action of Electroconvulsive Therapy: Anticonvulsant, Peptidergic, and c-fos Proto-oncogene Effects." *Convulsive Therapy* 5(3): 274–295.

Nakamura, M. M., Overall, J. E., Hollister, L. E., and Radcliffe, E. (1983). "Factors Affecting Outcome of Depressive Symptoms in Alcoholics." *Alcoholism: Clinical and Experimental Research* 7(2): 188–193.

Naylor, M. W., Greden, J. F., and Alessi, N. E. (1990). "Plasma Dexamethasone Levels in Children Given the Dexamethasone Suppression Test." *Biological Psychiatry* 27(6): 592–600.

Neighbors, H. W., Jackson, J. S., Campbell, L., and Williams, D. (1989). "The Influence of Racial Factors on Psychiatric Diagnosis: A Review and Suggestions for Research." *Community Mental Health Journal* 25(4): 301–311.

Neill, J. C. and Cooper, S. J. (1989)."Evidence that D-Fenfluramine Anorexia Is Mediated by 5–HT1 Receptors." *Psychopharmacology (Berlin)* 97(2): 213–218. (Abstract.)

Nelson, B. (1983). "The Biology of Depression Makes Physicians Anxious." *New York Times,* September 11, D-8.

"New Defects that Cause Alzheimer's Discovered" (1991). *Baltimore Sun,* October 4, p. 3–A.

Newman, M. (1990). "Crack Tied to Eating Disorders." *Baltimore Sun* (*Health* magazine), August 7, p. 5.

Nezu, A. M, Nezu, C. M., and Perri, M. G. (1989). *Problem-Solving Therapy for Depression: Theory, Research, and Clinical Guidelines.* New York: John Wiley.

Nguyen, T. V., Kobierski, L., Comb, M., and Hyman, S. E. (1990). "The Effect of Depolarization on Expression of the Human Proenkephalin Gene Is Synergistic with cAMP and Dependent upon a cAMP-Inducible Enhancer." *The Journal of Neuroscience* 10(8): 2825–2833.

Nicholi, A. M., Jr. (1988a). "The Adolescent." In A. M. Nicholi, Jr., ed., *The New Harvard Guide to Psychiatry.* Cambridge: Belknap/Harvard University Press, pp. 637–664.

Nicholi, A. M., Jr., ed. (1988b). *The New Harvard Guide to Psychiatry.* Cambridge: Belknap/Harvard University Press.

Nichols, W. C. (1988). *Marital Therapy: An Integrative Approach.* New York: Guilford Press.

Nies, A. and Robinson, D. S. (1982). "Monoamine Oxidase Inhibitors." In E. S. Paykel, ed., *Handbook of Affective Disorders.* New York: Guilford Press, pp. 246–261.

NIH/NIMH (1985). "Electro-convulsive Therapy." *Consensus Development Conference Statement* 5(11): 7–7.

Noll, K. M., Davis, J. M., and DeLeon-Jones, F. (1985). "Medication and Somatic Therapies in the Treatment of Depression." In E. E. Beckham and W. R. Leber, eds., *Handbook of Depression: Treatment, Assessment, and Research.* Homewood, Ill.: Dorsey Press, pp. 220–315.

Norris, R. V., with C. Sullivan (1983). *PMS: Premenstrual Syndrome.* New York: Berkeley Books.

Notman, M. T. (1989). "Depression in Women: Psychoanalytic Concepts." *Psychiatric Clinics of North America* 12(1): 221–230.

O'Connor, C. (1985). "ElectroShock." *Washington Post Magazine,* December 1, pp. 11, 13, 18–21.

O'Connor, D. W., Pollitt, P. A., Roth, M., Brook, P. B., and Reiss, B. B. (1990). "Memory Complaints and Impairment in Normal, Depressed, and Demented Elderly Persons Identified in a Community Survey." *Archives of General Psychiatry* 47(3): 224–227.

O'Hara, M. W., Zekoski, E. M., Philipps, L. H., and Wright, E. J. (1990). "Controlled Prospective Study of Postpartum Mood Disorders: Comparison of Childbearing and Non-childbearing Women." *Journal of Abnormal Psychology* 99(1): 3–15.

O'Leary, K. D. and Beach, S. R. H. (1990). "Marital Therapy: A Viable Treatment for Depression and Marital Discord." *American Journal of Psychiatry* 147: 183–186.

O'Leary, K. D. and Wilson, G. T. (1987). *Behavior Therapy: Application and Outcome.* Second Edition. Englewood Cliffs, N.J.: Prentice-Hall.

Ornstein, R. and Thompson, R. F. (1984). *The Amazing Brain.* Boston: Houghton Mifflin.

Owan, T. C., ed. (1985). *Southeast Asian Mental Health: Treatment, Prevention, Services, Training, and Research.* Bethesda, Md.: NIMH, with the Office of Refugee Resettlement, Social Security Administration.

Padgett, D. K. and Struening, E. L. (1991). "Influence of Substance Abuse and Mental Disorders on Emergency Room Use by Homeless Adults." *Hospital and Community Psychiatry* 42: 834–838.

Page, C., Benaim, S., and Lappin, F. (1987). "A Long-Term Retrospective Follow-up Study of Patients Treated with Prophylactic Lithium Carbonate." *British Journal of Psychiatry* 150: 175–179.

Palca, J. (1989). "Sleep Researchers Awake to Possibilities." *Science* 245: 351–352.

Palinkas, L. A., Wingard, D. L., and Barrett-Connor, E. (1990). "The Biocultural Context of Social Networks and Depression Among the Elderly." *Social Science and Medicine* 30(4): 441–447.

Papolos, D. F. and Papolos, J. (1987). *Overcoming Depression.* New York: Harper & Row.

Pardridge, W. M. (1987). "Commentary" [on Wurtman, 1987]. *Integrative Psychiatry* 5: 248–249.

Parry, B. L. (1989). "Reproductive Factors Affecting the Course of Affective Illness in Women." *Psychiatric Clinics of North America* 12(1): 207–20.

Parry, B. L., Berga, S. L., Kripke, D. F., Klauber, M. R., Laughlin, G. A., Yen, S. S., and Gillin, J. C. (1990). "Altered Waveform of Plasma Nocturnal Melatonin Secretion in Premenstrual Depression." *Archives of General Psychiatry* 47(12): 1139–1146.

Parsons, B., Quitkin, F. M., McGrath, P. J., Stewart, J. W., Tricamo, E., Ocepek-Welikson, K., Harrison, W., Rabkin, J. G., Wager, S. G., and Nunes, E. (1989). "Phenelzine, Imipramine, and Placebo in Borderline Patients Meeting Criteria for Atypical Depression." *Psychopharmacology Bulletin* 25(4): 524–534.

Pary, R. and Lippmann, S. B. (1989). "Evaluating Dysphoria in the Alcoholic Patient." *Clinical Advances in the Treatment of Psychiatric Disorders* 3(1): 8–9.

Pary, R., Lippmann, S. B., and Tobias, C. R. (1988). "Depression and Alcoholism: Clinical Considerations in Management." *Southern Medical Journal* 81(12): 1529–1533.

Paykel, E. S., ed. (1982). *Handbook of Affective Disorders.* New York: Guilford Press.

Peele, S. (1991). "What We Now Know About Treating Alcoholism and Other Addictions." *Harvard Mental Health Letter* 8(6): 5–7.

Pekkanen, J. (1983). "Beating the Winter Blues." *The Washingtonian*, December, pp. 61–62.

Peterson. C. and Seligman, M. E. P. (1985). "The Learned Helplessness Model of Depression: Current Status of Theory and Research." In E. E. Beckham and W. R. Leber, eds., *Handbook of Depression: Research, Treatment, and Assessment.* Homewood, Ill.: Dorsey Press, pp. 914–939.

Pfeffer, C. R. (1986). *The Suicidal Child.* New York: Guilford Press.

Pfeffer, C. R. and Trad, P. V. (1988). "Sadness and Suicidal Tendencies in Preschool Children." *Journal of Developmental and Behavioral Pediatrics* 9(2): 86–88.

Pirke, K. M. and Ploog, D. W. (1987). "Commentary" [on Wurtman, 1987]. *Integrative Psychiatry* 5: 40–241.

Pitt, B. (1973)."Maternity Blues." *British Journal of Psychiatry* 122: 431–433.

Pitt, B. (1982). "Depression and Childbirth." In E. S. Paykel, ed., *Handbook of Affective Disorders*. New York: Guilford Press, pp. 361–378.

Plomin, R. (1990). "Behavioral Genetics: Nature and Nurture." *Harvard Medical School Mental Health Letter* 6(11): 4–6.

"PMS After Menstruation." *Harvard Mental Health Letter* 8(7): 5.

Pohl, R. (1987). "The Controversial DST: Two Sides to the Issue (Con)." *Clinical Advances in the Treatment of Depression* 1(2): 16, 12, and 14.

Pope, H. G., Jr., Hudson, J. I., and Yurgelun-Todd, D. (1989). "Depressive Symptoms in Bulimic, Depressed, and Nonpsychiatric Control Subjects." *Journal of Affective Disorders* 16(1): 93—99.

Popper, C., ed. (1987). *Psychiatric Pharmacosciences of Children and Adolescents.* Washington, D.C.: American Psychiatric Press.

"Postpartum Disorders" (1989). *The Harvard Medical School Mental Health Letter* 5(11): 1–3.

Poznanski, E. O. (1982). "The Clinical Phenomenology of Childhood Depression." *American Journal of Orthopsychiatry* 52(2): 308—313.

Poznanski, E. O., Cook, S. C., and Carroll, B. J (1979). "A Depression Rating Scale for Children." *Pediatrics* 64: 442–450.

Preskorn, S. H. (1990). "The Future and Psychopharmacology: Potentials and Needs." *Psychiatric Annals* 20(11): 625–633.

Price, L. H., Charney, D. S., Delgado, P. L., and Heninger, G. R. (1990)."Lithium and Serotonin Function: Implications for the Serotonin Hypothesis of Depression." *Psychopharmacology* 100: 3—12.

Puig-Antich, J. (1986). "Psychobiological Markers: Effects of Age and Puberty." In I. Rutter, C. E. Izzard, and P. B. Read, eds., *Depression in Young People: Developmental and Clinical Perspectives.* New York: Guilford Press, pp. 341–381.

Rabkin, J. G., Williams, J. B., Remien, R. H., Goetz, R., Kertzner, R., and Gorman, J. M. (1991). "Depression, Distress, Lymphocyte Subsets, and Human Immunodeficiency Virus Symptoms on Two Occasions in HIV-Positive Homosexual Men." *Archives of General Psychiatry* 48: 11–119.

Rado, S. (1928). "The Problem of Melancholia." *International Journal of Psychoanalysis* 9: 420–438.

Railton, R., Fisher, J, Sinclair, A., and Shrigmankar, J. M. (1987). "Comparison of Electrical Measurements on Constant Voltage and Constant Current ECT Machines." *British Journal of Psychiatry* 151(August): 244–247.

Raju, U., Koumenis, C., Nunez-Regueiro, M., and Eskin, A. (1991). "Alteration of the Phase and Period of a Circadian Oscillator by a Reversible Transcription Inhibitor." *Science* 253: 673–677.

Rauch, J. B. (1988). "Social Work and the Genetics Revolution: Genetic Services." *Social Work* 33(5): 389–395.

Ray, O. S. (1972). *Drugs, Society, and Behavior*. St. Louis: C. V. Mosby.

Raymond, C. (1989). "Researchers Link Manic-Depressive Illness and Artistic Creativity." *Chronicle of Higher Education* 21(June): A4–A6.

Reese, E. P, Howard, J., and Reese, T. W. (1978). *Human Behavior: Analysis and Application.* Second Edition. Dubuque, Iowa: Wm. C. Brown.

Rehm, L. P. (1977). "A Self-control Model of Depression." *Behavior Therapy* 8(5): 787–804.

Rehm, L. P., ed. (1981). *Behavior Therapy for Depression: Present Status and Future Directions.* New York: Academic Press.

Reid, W. J. and Shyne, A. (1969). *Brief and Extended Casework.* New York: Columbia University Press.

Reiss, S. and Bootzin, R. R., eds. (1985). *Theoretical Issues in Behavior Therapy.* Orlando, Fla.: Academic Press.

Rifkin, A. (1988). "ECT Versus Tricyclic Antidepressants in Depression: A Review of the Evidence." *Journal of Clinical Psychiatry* 49(1): 3–7.

Rippere, V. and Williams, R., eds. (1985). *Wounded Healers: Mentals Health Workers' Experience of Depression.* Chichester: John Wiley.

Riskind, J. H., Beck, A. T., and Steer, P. A. (1985). "Cognitive-Behavioral Therapy in Geriatric Depression." *Journal of Consulting and Clinical Psychology* 53: 944–945.

Ritchie, J. C., Belkin, B. M., Krishnan, K. R., Nemeroff, C. B., and Carroll, B. J. (1990). "Plasma Dexamethasone Concentrations and the Dexamethasone Suppression Test." *Biological Psychiatry* 27(2): 159–173.

Rodin, G., Craven, J., and Littlefield, C. (1991). *Depression in the Medically Ill: An Integrated Approach.* New York: Brunner/Mazel.

Roffman, R. A. (1987). "Drug Use and Abuse" In A. Minehan, ed., *Encyclopedia of Social Work.* Eighteenth Edition. Silver Spring, Md.: National Association of Social Workers, pp. 477–487.

Rogers, M. and Reich, P. (1988). "Psychosomatic Medicine and Consultation-Liaison Psychiatry." In A. M. Nicholi, Jr., ed., *The New Harvard Guide to Psychiatry.* Cambridge: Belknap/Harvard University Press, pp. 387–417.

Rose, K. J. (1988). *The Body in Time.* New York: John Wiley.

Rose, S. (1977). *Group Therapy: A Behavioral Approach.* Englewood Cliffs, N.J.: Prentice-Hall.

Rosenberg, S. E. (1985). "Brief Dynamic Psychotherapy for Depression." In E. E. Beckham and W. R. Leber, eds., *Handbook of Depression: Treatment, Assessment, and Research.* Homewood, Ill.: Dorsey Press, pp. 100–123.

Rosenthal, N. E. (1989a). *Seasons of the Mind: Why You Get the Winter Blues and What You Can Do About It.* New York: Bantam Books.

Rosenthal, N. E. (1989b). Paper presented at Conference on Seasonal Affective Disorders, The Education Center of Sheppard-Pratt Hospital, Baltimore, MD, June 28.

Rosenthal, N. E. and Blehar, M. C., eds. (1989). *Seasonal Affective Disorders and Phototherapy.* New York: Guilford Press.

Rosenthal, N. E., Sack, D. A., Gillin, J. C., Lewy, A. J., Goodwin, F. K., Davenport, Y., Mueller, P. S., Newsome, D. A., and Wehr, T. A. (1984). "Seasonal Affective Disorder: A Description of the Syndrome and Prelimi-nary Findings with Light Treatment." *Archives of General Psychiatry* 41: 72–80.

Rosenthal, N. E., Sack, D. A., Skwerer, R. G., Jacobsen, F. M., and Wehr, T. A. (1989). "Phototherapy for Seasonal Affective Disorders." In N. E. Rosenthal and M. C. Blehar, eds., *Seasonal Affective Disorders and Phototherapy.* New York: Guilford Press, pp. 273–294.

Rosenthal, P. A. and Rosenthal S. (1984)."Suicidal Behavior by Preschool Children." *American Journal of Psychiatry* 141: 520—525.

Ross, H. M. (1975). *Fighting Depression.* Atlanta: Larchmont Books.

Ross, M. H. and Roth, J. (1990). *The Mood-Control Diet: 21 Days to Conquering Depression and Fatigue.* Englewood Cliffs, N.J.: Prentice-Hall.

Rossi, P. H., Wright, J. D., Fisher, G. A., and Willis, G. (1987). "The Urban Homeless: Estimating Composition and Size." *Science* 235: 1336–1341.

Rothenberg, A. (1988). "Differential Diagnosis of Anorexia Nervosa and Depressive Illness: A Review of 11 Studies." *Comprehensive Psychiatry* 29(4): 427–432.

Rounsaville, B. J., Klerman, G. L., Weissman, M. M., and Chevron, E. S. (1985)."Short-Term Interpersonal Psychotherapy (IPT) for Depression." In E. E. Beckham and W. R. Leber, eds., *Handbook of Depression: Treatment, Assessment, and Research.* Homewood, Ill.: Dorsey Press, pp. 124–150.

Rounsaville, B. J., O'Malley, S., Foley, S., and Weissman, M. M. (1988). "Role of Manual-Guided Training in the Conduct and Efficacy of Interpersonal Psychotherapy for Depression." *Journal of Consulting and Clinical Psychology* 56(5): 681–688.

Rounsaville, B. J., Weissman, M. M., Prusoff, B. A., and Herceg-Baron, R. (1979). "Marital Disputes and Treatment Outcome in Depressed Women." *Comprehensive Psychiatry* 20: 473–490.

Rovner, S. (1989). "Illuminating the Mystery of Shorter Days, Longer Faces." *Washington Post (Health* magazine), September 12, p. 9.

Roy, R., Thomas, M., and Matas, M. (1984). "Chronic Pain and Depression: A Review." *Comprehensive Psychiatry* 25(1): 96–105.

Royce, J. E. (1989). *Alcohol Problems and Alcoholism: A Comprehensive Survey.* Revised Edition. New York: The Free Press.

Rubin, E., Zorumski, C. F., and Burke, W. J. (1988). "Overlapping Symptoms of Geriatric Depression and Alzheimer-Type Dementia." *Hospital and Community Psychiatry* 39(10): 1074–1079.

Rush, A. J., ed. (1982). *Short-Term Psychotherapies for Depression: Behavioral, Interpersonal, Cognitive, and Psychodynamic Approaches.* New York: Guilford Press.

Rush, A. J. (1983). "Cognitive Therapy of Depression: Rationale, Techniques, and Efficacy." *Psychiatric Clinics of North America* 6(1): 105–127.

Rush, A. J. (1986, June 10)."Psychosocial Treatment of Depression." NIMH Conference on Depression: Awareness, Recognition, and Treatment, Bethesda, MD.

Rush, A. J. and Giles, D. G.(1982). "Cognitive Therapy: Theory and Research." In A. J. Rush, ed., *Short-Term Therapies for Depression.* New York: Guilford Press, pp. 143–181.

Rutter, M. (1988). "Commentary" [on Kashani and Sherman, 1988]. *Integrative Psychiatry* 6: 8–11. .

Rutter, M., Izard, C. E., and Read, P. B., eds. (1986). *Depression in Young People: Developmental and Clinical Perspectives.* New York: Guilford Press.

Ryan, A. S. (1985). "Cultural Factors in Casework with Chinese-Americans." *Social Casework: The Journal of Contemporary Social Work* 66: 333–340.

Sacco, W. P. and Beck, A. T. (1985). "Cognitive Therapy of Depression." In

E. E. Beckham and W. R. Leber, eds., *Handbook of Depression: Treatment, Assessment, and Research.* Homewood, Ill.: Dorsey Press, pp. 3–38.

Salgado-de-Snyder, V. N. (1987a). "Factors Associated with Acculturative Stress and Depressive Symptomatology Among Married Mexican Immigrant Women." *Psychology of Women Quarterly* 11(4): 475–488.

Salgado-de-Snyder, V. N. (1987b). "Mexican Immigrant Women: The Relationship of Ethnic Loyalty and Social Support to Acculturative Stress and Depressive Symptomatology." *Spanish Speaking Mental Health Research Center Occasional Papers* No. 22, 73 pp.

Salzman, C. (1990). "Practical Considerations in the Pharmacologic Treatment of Depression and Anxiety in the Elderly." *Journal of Clinical Psychiatry* 51(Suppl.): 40–43.

Santos, J. F., Hubbard, R. W., and McIntosh, J. L. (1983). "Mental Health and the Minority Elderly." In L. D. Breslau and M. R. Haug, eds., *Depression and Aging: Causes, Care, and Consequences.* New York: Springer, pp. 51–70.

Sargent, M. (1989). *Depressive Illnesses: Treatments Bring New Hope.* Revised Edition. Rockville, Md.: National Institute of Mental Health DHHS Pub. No. (ADM) 89–1491.

Saunders, J. M. and Valente, S. M. (1987). "Suicide Risk Among Gay Men and Lesbians: A Review." *Death Studies* 11: 1–23 (cited in McGrath et al., 1990, p. 88).

Scarf, M. (1980). *Unfinished Business: Pressure Points in the Lives of Women.* Garden City, N.Y.: Doubleday.

Schatzberg, A. F. and Cole, J. O. (1991). *Manual of Clinical Psychopharmacology.* Second Edition. Washington, D.C.: American Psychiatric Press.

Schleifer, S. J., Macari-Hinson, M. M., Coyle, D. A., Slater, W. R., Kahn, M., Gorlin, R., and Zucker, H. D. (1989). "The Nature and Course of Depression Following Myocardial Infarction." *Archives of Internal Medicine* 149: 1785–1789.

Schlesier-Carter, B., Hamilton, S. A., O'Neil, P. M., Lydiard, R. B., and Malcolm, R. (1989). "Depression and Bulimia: The Link Between Depression and Bulimic Cognitions." *Journal of Abnormal Psychology* 98(3): 322–325.

Schmeck, H. M. (1987). "Defective Gene Tied to Form of Manic-Depressive Illness." *New York Times,* February 26, pp. B-1, B-7.

Schmeck, H. M. (1988). "Depression in Alcoholics Transitory, Study Finds." *New York Times,* September 8, p. B-3.

Schmeck, H. M. (1989). "Scientists Now Doubt They Found Faulty Gene Linked to Mental Illness: New Data Challenge Earlier Report on Manic Depression." *New York Times,* November 7, p. C-3.

Schoen, D. A. (1983). *The Reflective Practitioner: How Professionals Think in Action.* New York: Basic Books.

Scogin, F., Jamison, C., and Gochneaur, K. (1989). "Comparative Efficacy of Cognitive and Behavioral Bibliotherapy for Mildly and Moderately Depressed Older Adults." *Journal of Consulting and Clinical Psychology* 57: 403–407.

Schoonover, S. C. (1983a). "Depression." In E. L. Bassuk, S. C. Schoonover, and A. J. Gelenberg, eds., *The Practitioner's Guide to Psychoactive Drugs.* Second Edition. New York: Plenum Medical Book Company, pp. 19–78.

Schoonover, S. C. (1983b). "Introduction: The Practice of Pharmacotherapy." In E. L. Bassuk, S. C. Schoonover, and A. J. Gelenberg, eds., *The Practitioner's Guide to Psychoactive Drugs*. Second Edition. New York: Plenum Medical Book Company, pp. 1–18.

Schuckit, M. A. (1983a). "Alcoholic Patients with Secondary Depression." *American Journal of Psychiatry* 140: 711–714.

Schuckit, M. A. (1983b). "Alcoholism and Other Psychiatric Disorders." *Hospital and Community Psychiatry* 34: 1022–1027.

Schuckit, M. A. (1986). "Why Are Children of Alcoholics at High Risk for Alcoholism?" *Harvard Medical School Mental Health Letter* 3(5): 8.

Schulterbrandt, J. G. and Raskin, A., eds. (1977). *Depression in Childhood: Diagnosis, Treatment, and Conceptual Models*. Rockville, Md.: ADMAHA, NIMH, DHEW Pub. No. (ADM) 77–476.

Schumer, F. (1989). "Bye-Bye, Blues: A New Wonder Drug for Depression." *New York Magazine*, December 18, pp. 47–53.

Schvehla, T. J., Faust, L. J., Herjanic, M., and Muniz, C. E. (1987)."Lithium Therapy for Affective Disorders." *American Family Physician* 36(1): 169–175.

Schwartz, A. (1982). *The Behavior Therapies: Theories and Applications*. New York: The Free Press.

Schwartz, A. (1983). "Behavioral Principles and Approaches." In A. Rosenblatt and D. Waldfogel, eds., *Handbook of Clinical Social Work*. San Francisco: Jossey-Bass, pp. 202–228.

Schwartz, A. (1986). "The Poor." In H. L. Gochros, J. S. Gochros, and J. Fischer, eds., *Helping the Sexually Oppressed*. Englewood Cliffs, N.J.: Prentice-Hall, pp. 132–140.

Schwartz, A. K. and Aaron, N. S. (1979). *Somniquest: The Five Types of Sleeplessness and How to Overcome Them*. New York: Harmony Books.

Scogin, F., Jamison, C., and Gochneaur, K. (1989). "Comparative Efficacy of Cognitive and Behavioral Bibliotherapy for Mildly and Moderately Depressed Older Adults." *Journal of Consulting and Clinical Psychology* 57(3): 403–407.

Segal, H. (1979). *Melanie Klein*. New York: Viking Press.

Seligman, M. E. P. (1975). *Helplessness: On Depression, Development, and Death*. San Francisco: W. H. Freeman.

Seligman, M. E. P. (1981). "A Learned Helplessness Point of View." In L. P. Rehm, ed., *Behavior Therapy for Depression: Present Status and Future Directions*. New York: Academic Press, pp. 123–141.

Seward, J. (1968). *Hara-Kiri: Japanese Ritual Suicide*. Rutland, Vt.: Charles E. Tuttle.

Shaffer, D. (1986). "Developmental Factors in Child and Adolescent Suicide." In M. Rutter, C. E. Izard, and P. B. Read, eds., *Depression in Young People: Developmental and Clinical Perspectives*. New York: Guilford Press, pp. 383–398.

Shaffi, M., Steltz-Lenarsky, J., Derrick, A. M., Beckner, C., and Whittinghill, J. R. (1988). "Co-morbidity of Mental Disorders in the Postmortem Diagnosis of Completed Suicide in Children and Adolescents." *Journal of Affective Disorders* 15(3): 227–233.

Shaltout, T. and Lippman, S. B. (1988). "Depression and Drug Dependence: A

Correlation?" *Clinical Advances in the Treatment of Psychiatric Disorders* 2(5): 7, 10.

Shanahan, K. M., Zolkowski-Wynne, J., Coury, D. L., Collins, E. W., and O'Shea, J. S. (1987). "The Children's Depression Rating Scale for Normal and Depressed Outpatients." *Clinical Pediatrics* 26(5): 245–247.

Sheehy, G. (1974). *Passages: Predictable Crises of Adult Life*. New York: E. P. Dutton.

Sheehy, G. (1981). *Pathfinders*. Toronto: Bantam Books.

Sherman, I. W. and Sherman, V. G. (1983). *Biology: A Human Approach*. New York: Oxford University Press.

Shintoub, S. A. and Soulairac, A. (1961). "L'Enfant Auto-mutilateur." *Psychiatrie de l'Enfant* 3: 119 (cited in Pfeffer, 1986, p. 13).

Sholomskas, A. J., Chevron, E. S., Prusoff, B. A., and Berry, C. (1983). "Short-Term Interpersonal Therapy (IPT) with the Depressed Elderly: Case Discussion." *American Journal of Psychotherapy* 37(4): 552–566.

Shore, J. H., Manson, S. M., Bloom, J. D., Keepers, G. A., et al. (1987). "A Pilot Study of Depression Among American Indian Patients with Research Diagnostic Criteria." *American Indian and Alaska Native Mental Health Research* (2): 4–15. (Abstract.)

Shuchman, M. (1991). "Psychiatric Drugs Used to Treat Children." *Washington Post* (*Health* magazine), August 13, p. 9.

Shweder, R. A. (1985). "Menstrual Pollution, Soul Loss, and the Comparative Study of Emotions." In A. Kleinman and B. Good, eds., *Culture and Depression: Studies in the Anthropology and Cross-cultural Psychiatry of Affect and Disorder*. Berkeley: University of California Press, pp. 182–215.

Sidman, M. (1960). *Tactics of Scientific Research: Evaluating Experimental Data in Psychology*. New York: Basic Books.

Sikkema, M. and Niyekawa-Howard, A. M. (1977). *Cross-cultural Learning and Self-growth: Getting to Know Ourselves and Others*. New York: International Association of Schools of Social Work.

Silverman, M. M., Lalley, T. L., Rosenberg, M. L., Smith, J. C., Parron, D., and Jacobs, J. (1988). "Control of Stress and Violent Behavior: Mid-course Review of the 1990 Health Objectives." *Public Health Reports* 103(1): 38–49.

Silverstone, B. (1989). "Mainstay Families." *New York Times*, August 7, p. A-14.

Skinner, B. F. (1953). *Science and Human Behavior*. New York: The Free Press.

Skinner, B. F. and Vaughn, M. E. (1983). *Enjoy Old Age: A Program of Self-Management*. New York: W. W. Norton.

Skwerer, R. G., Jacobsen, F. M., Duncan, C. C., Kelly, K. A., Sack, D. A., Tamarkin, L., Gaist, P. A., Kasper, S., and Rosenthal, N. E. (1989). "Neurobiology of Seasonal Affective Disorder and Phototherapy." In N. E. Rosenthal and M. C. Blehar, eds., *Seasonal Affective Disorders and Phototherapy*. New York: Guilford Press, pp. 311–332.

Slagle, P. (1987). *The Way Up from Down*. New York: Random House.

Smeraldi, E. (1988). "Genetic Aspects in the Course and Outcome of Affective Disorders." In T. Helgason and R. J. Daly, eds., *Depressive Illness: Prediction of Course and Outcome*. Heidelberg: Springer-Verlag, pp. 49–55.

Smith, M. L., Glass, G. V., and Miller, T. I. (1980) .*The Benefits of Psychotherapy.* Baltimore: Johns Hopkins University Press.

Smith, M. A., Kling, M. A., Whitfield, H. J., Brand, H. A., Demitrack, M. A., Geracioti, Y. D., Chrousos, G. P., and Gold, P. W. (1989). "Corticotropin-Releasing Hormone: From Endocrinology to Psychobiology." *Hormone Research* 31(1–2): 66–71.

Smith-Ruiz,D. (1985). "Relationship Between Depression, Social Support, and Physical Illness Among Elderly Blacks: Research Notes." *Journal of the National Medical Association* 77: 1017—1019.

Snowden, L. R., ed. (1982). *Reaching the Underserved: Mental Health Needs of Neglected Populations.* Vol. 3: Sage Annual Reviews of Community Mental Health. Beverly Hills: Sage Publications.

Sonis, W. A. (1989). "Seasonal Affective Disorder of Childhood and Adolescence: A Review." In N. E. Rosenthal and M. C. Blehar, eds., *Seasonal Affective Disorders and Phototherapy.* New York: Guilford Press, pp. 46–54.

Spiegel, J. (1982). "An Ecological Model of Ethnic Families." In M. McGoldrick, J. Pearce, and J. Giordano, eds., *Ethnicity and Family Therapy.* New York: Guilford Press, pp. 31–51.

Spirito, A., Overholser, J., and Stark, L. J. (1989). "Common Problems and Coping Strategies. Ill.: Findings with Adolescent Suicide Attempters." *Journal of Abnormal Child Psychology* 17(2): 213–221.

Spitz, R. A. (1946). "Anaclitic Depression: An Inquiry into the Genesis of Psychiatric Conditions in Early Childhood, II." *Psychoanalytic Study of the Child* 2: 313–347.

Spitz, R. A. (1965). *The First Year of Life.* New York: International Universities Press.

Spitzer, R. L., Endicott, J., and Robins, E. (1978). "Research Diagnostic Criteria: Rationale and Reliability." *Archives of General Psychiatry* 35(6): 773–782.

Spitzer, R. L. and Williams, J. B. (1989). "The Validity of Seasonal Affective Disorder." In N. E. Rosenthal and M. C. Blehar, eds., *Seasonal Affective Disorders and Phototherapy.* New York: Guilford Press, pp. 79–84.

Spitzer, R. L., Williams, J. B. W., Gibbon, M., and First, M. (1990). *Structured Clinical Interview for DSM-III-R (SCID): User's Guide.* Washington, D.C.: American Psychiatric Press.

Squires, S. (1987). "Shock Therapy's Return to Respectability." *New York Times Magazine,* November 22, pp. 78–79, 85, 88–89.

Squires, S. (1990a)."In the Maze of the Mind, New Complexities: A Combination of Chemistry and Psychotherapy Offers Fresh Promise." *Washington Post* (*Health* magazine), January 30, p. 16.

Squires, S. (1990b). "Ethnic Groups May Differ in Metabolizing Drugs." *Washington Post* (*Health* magazine), February 13, p. 5.

Srole, L., Langner, T. S., Michael, S. T., Opler, M. K., and Rennie, T. A. C. (1962). *Mental Health in the Metropolis: The Midtown Manhattan Study.* New York: McGraw-Hill.

Starker, S. (1988). "Psychologists and Self-help Books: Attitudes and Prescriptive Practices of Clinicians." *American Journal of Psychotherapy* 42(3): 448–455.

Steiner, M. (1990). "Postpartum Psychiatric Disorders." *Canadian Journal of Psychiatry* 35(1): 89–95.

Stern, S. L. and Mendels, J. (1986). "The Psychopharmacologic Treatment of Depressive Disorders." In L. R. Derogatis, ed., *Clinical Psychopharmacology*. Menlo Park, Cal.: Addison-Wesley, pp. 69–82.

Steuer, J. (1982). "Psychotherapy with the Elderly." *Psychiatric Clinics of North America* 5(1): 199–213.

Stoudemire, A. (1987). "Differentiating Between Depression and Dementia." *Clinical Advances in the Treatment of Depression* 1(2): 1–3, 10.

Stoudemire, A. and Blazer, D. (1985)."Depression in the Elderly." In E. E. Beckham and W. R. Leber, eds., *Handbook of Depression: Treatment, Assessment, and Research*. Homewood, Ill.: Dorsey Press, pp. 556–566.

Stoudemire, A. Frank, R., Hedemark, N., Kamlet, M., and Blazer, D. (1986). "The Economic Burden of Depression." *General Hospital Psychiatry* 8: 387–394.

Strand, F. L. (1983). *Physiology*. New York: Macmillan.

Strauss, C. C., Last, C. G., Hersen, M., and Kazdin, A. E. (1988). "Association Between Anxiety and Depression in Children and Adolescents with Anxiety Disorders." *Journal of Abnormal Child Psychology* 16(1): 57–68.

Strupp, H. H., Sandell, J. A., Waterhouse, G. J., O'Malley, S. S., and Anderson, J. L. (1982). "Psychodynamic Therapy: Theory and Research." In A. J. Rush, ed., *Short-Term Psychotherapies for Depression: Behavioral, Interpersonal, Cognitive, and Psychodynamic Approaches*. New York: Guilford Press, pp. 215–250.

Stuart, R. B. (1980). *Helping Couples Change: A Social Learning Approach to Marital Therapy*. New York: Guilford Press.

Stunkard, A. J., Grace, W. J., and Wolff, H. G. (1955). "The Night-Eating Syndrome." *American Journal of Medicine* 19: 78–86.

Stunkard, A. J., and Mahoney, M. J. (1976). "Behavioral Treatment of the Eating Disorders." In H. Leitenberg, ed., *Handbook of Behavior Modification and Behavior Therapy*. Englewood Cliffs, N.J.: Prentice-Hall, pp. 45–73.

Stuppaeck, C., Barnas, C., Miller, C., Schwitzer, J., and Fleischhacker, W. W. (1990). "Carbamazepine in the Prophylaxis of Mood Disorders." *Journal of Clinical Psychopharmacology* 10(1):39–42.

Styron, W. (1990). *Darkness Visible: A Memoir of Madness*. New York: Random House.

Sue, S. (1988). "Psychotherapeutic Services for Ethnic Minorities: Two Decades of Research Findings." *American Psychologist* 43(4): 301–308.

Suomi, S. J. and Harlow, H. F. (1977). "Production and Alleviation of Depressive Behaviors in Monkeys." In J. D. Maser and M. E. P. Seligman, eds., *Psychopathology: Experimental Models*. San Francisco: W. H. Freeman, pp. 131–173.

Susman, V. L. and Katz, J. L. (1988). "Weaning and Depression: Another Postpartum Complication." *American Journal of Psychiatry* 145(4): 498–501.

Sussman, L. K., Robins, L. N., and Earls, F. (1987). "Treatment-Seeking for Depression by Black and White Americans." *Social Science and Medicine* 24(3): 187–196.

Teicher, M. H. and Baldessarini, R. (1987). "Developmental Pharmacodynamics." In C. Popper, ed., *Psychiatric Pharmacosciences of Children and Adolescents.* Washington, D.C.: American Psychiatric Press.

Teicher, M. H., Glod, C., and Cole, J. O. (1990). "Emergence of Intense Suicidal Preoccupation During Fluoxetine Treatment." *American Journal of Psychiatry* 147(2): 207–210.

Tennant, C. (1988). "Parental Loss in Childhood: Its Effect in Adult Life." *Archives of General Psychiatry* 45(11): 1045–1050.

Terman, M. (1988). "On the Question of Mechanism in Phototherapy for Seasonal Affect Disorder: Considerations of Clinical Efficacy and Epidemiology." *Journal of Biological Rhythms* 3(2): 155–172.

Terman, M. (1989). "On The Question of Mechanism in Phototherapy for Seasonal Affective Disorder: Considerations of Clinical Efficacy and Epidemiology." In N. E. Rosenthal and M. C. Blaher, eds., *Seasonal Affective Disorders and Phototherapy.* New York: Guilford Press, pp. 357–376.

Terman, M., Terman, J. S., Quitkin, F. M., Cooper, T. B., Lo, E. S., Gorman, J. M., Stewart, J. W., McGrath, P. J. (1988). "Response of the Melatonin Cycle to Phototherapy for Seasonal Affective Disorder: Short Note." *Journal of Neural Transmission* 72(2): 147—165.

Thase, M. E. (1989). "Comparison Between Seasonal Affective Disorder and Other Forms of Recurrent Depression." In N. E. Rosenthal and M. C. Blaher, eds., *Seasonal Affective Disorders and Phototherapy.* New York: Guilford Press, pp. 64–78.

Thase, M. E., Frank, E., and Kupfer, D. J. (1985). "Biological Processes in Major Depression." In E. E. Beckham and W. R. Leber, eds., *Handbook of Depression: Treatment, Assessment, and Research.* Homewood, Ill.: Dorsey Press, pp. 816–913.

Thienhaus, O. J., Margletta, S., and Bennett, J. A. (1990). "A Study of the Clinical Efficacy of Maintenance ECT." *Journal of Clinical Psychiatry* 51(4): 141–144.

Thomas, C. L., ed. (1977). *Taber's Cyclopedic Medical Dictionary.* Thirteenth Edition. Philadelphia: F. A. Davis.

Thomas, C. L., ed. (1989). *Taber's Cyclopedic Medical Dictionary.* Sixteenth Edition. Philadelphia: F. A. Davis.

Thomas, C. S. (1975). "Depression and Nonwhiteness." In *On Understanding Depression: A Report of the 1975 National Conference on Depressive Disorders.* Arlington, Va.: National Association for Mental Health, pp. 21–22.

Thomas, P. (1991). "Prozac: Sad Attack." *Harvard Health Letter* 16(12): 1–4.

Thompson, L. (1989). "Unlocking the Brain." *Washington Post,* June 27, pp. 12–17.

Thompson, L. W. and Gallagher, D. (1984). "Efficacy of Psychotherapy in the Treatment of Late-Life Depression. *Advances in Behaviour Research and Therapy* 6(2): 127–139.

Thompson, L. W., Gallagher, D., and Breckenridge, J. S. (1987). "Comparative Effectiveness of Psychotherapies for Depressed Elders." *Journal of Consulting and Clinical Psychology* 55(3): 385–390.

Thompson, C. and Isaacs, G. (1988). "Seasonal Affective Disorder: A British

Sample: Symptomatology in Relation to Mode of Referral and Diagnostic Subtype." *Journal of Affective Disorders* 14: 1—11.

Tobias, C. R., and Lippman, S. B. (1988). "How to Manage Depression in the Elderly Patient." *Clinical Advances in the Treatment of Psychiatric Disorders* 2(3): 8–10.

Tolchin, M. (1989). "When Long Life Is Too Much: Suicide Rises Among Elderly." *New York Times*, July 19, pp. 1, 15.

Toner, B. B., Garfinkel, P. E., and Garner, D. M. (1988). "Affective and Anxiety Disorders in the Long-Term Follow-up of Anorexia Nervosa." *International Journal of Psychiatry in Medicine* 18(4): 357–364.

Topper, M. D., and Curtis, J. (1987). "Extended Family Therapy: A Clinical Approach to the Treatment of Synergistic Dual Anomic Depression Among Navajo Agency-Town Adolescents." *Journal of Community Psychology* 15(3): 334–348.

Trachtenberg, M. C. and Blum, K. (1987). "Alcohol and Opioid Peptides: Neuropharmacological Rationale for Physical Craving of Alcohol." *American Journal of Drug and Alcohol Abuse* 13(3): 365–372.

Trainor, D. (1991). "Different Approaches to Psychiatric Care Uncovered by Cross-national Study." *Psychiatric News* 26(7): 15, 19.

Treasure, J. L. and Holland, A. J. (1991). "Genes and the Etiology of Eating Disorders." In P. McGuffin and R. Murray, eds., *The New Genetics of Mental Illness*. Oxford, England: Butterworth-Heinemann, pp. 198–211.

Trimble, J. E., Padilla, A. M., and Bell, C. S., eds. (1987). *Drug Abuse Among Ethnic Minorities*. Rockville, Md.: National Institute on Drug Abuse.

Tung, T. M. (1985). "Psychiatric Care for Southeast Asians: How Different Is Different?" In T. C. Owan, *Southeast Asian Mental Health: Treatment, Prevention, Services, Training, and Research*. Bethesda, Md.: National Institute of Mental Health, pp. 5–40.

Turnbull, J. E., and Gomberg, E. S. (1990). "The Structure of Depression in Alcoholic Women." *Journal of Studies on Alcohol* 51(2): 148–155.

Turner, R. M. and Ascher, L. M., eds. (1985). *Evaluating Behavior Therapy Outcome*. New York: Springer.

Turner, R. M., DiTomasso, R. A., Deluty, M. (1985). "Systematic Desensitization." In R. M. Turner and L. M. Ascher, eds., *Evaluating Behavior Therapy Outcome*. New York: Springer, pp. 15–55.

"Two Treatments for Cocaine Addiction" (1990). *New York Times*, July 21, p. A-30.

Vaillant, G. E. (1977). *Adaptation to Life*. Boston: Little, Brown.

Vaillant, G. E. (1988). "The Alcohol-Dependent and Drug-Dependent Person." In A. M. Nicholi, Jr., ed., *The New Harvard Guide to Psychiatry*. Cambridge: Belknap/Harvard University Press, pp. 700–713.

Van, J. (1982). "Depressed Children: Hidden Corner of the Generation Gap." *Chicago Tribune*, March 28, pp. 1–16.

Van Gent, E. M., Vida, S. L., and Zwart, F. M. (1988). "Group Therapy in Addition to Lithium Therapy in Patients with Bipolar Disorders." *Acta Psychiatric Belgica* 88(5–6): 405–418. (Abstract.)

Van Praag, H. M. (1987). "Commentary" [on Wurtman, 1987]." *Integrative Psychiatry* 5: 246–248.

Van Praag, H. M., and Lemus, C. (1986). "Monoamine Precursors in the Treatment of Psychiatric Disorders." In R. J. Wurtman and J. J. Wurtman, eds., *Nutrition and the Brain*. New York: Raven Press, pp. 89–138.

Vernon, S. W. and Roberts, S. E. (1982). "Use of the SADS-RDC in a Tri-Ethnic Community Survery." *Archives of General Psychiatry* 39: 47–52.

Veroff, J., Douvan, E., and Kulka, R. (1981). *The Inner American: A Self-portrait from 1957 to 1976*. New York: Basic Books.

Vogel, G. W. (1983). "Evidence for REM Sleep Deprivation as the Mechanism of Action of Antidepressant Drugs." *Progress in Neuro-Psychopharmacology and Biological Psychiatry* 7: 343–349.

Vogel, G. W., Vogel, F., McAbee, R. S., and Thurmond, A. J. (1980). "Improvement of Depression by REM Sleep Deprivation: New Findings and a Theory." *Archives of General Psychiatry* 37: 247–253.

Wahrheit, G., Holzer, C., and Arey, S. (1975). "Race and Mental Illness: An Epidemiological Update." *Journal of Health and Social Behavior* 16: 243–256.

Wallerstein, J. S. (1985). "Children of Divorce: Emerging Trends." *Psychiatric Clinics of North America* 8: 837–855.

Wallerstein, J. S. and Blakeslee, S. (1989). *Second Chances: Men, Women, and Children a Decade After Divorce*. New York: Ticknor and Fields.

Walrond-Skinner, S. (1986). *A Dictionary of Psychotherapy*. London: Routledge and Kegan Paul.

Walter, C. A. (1986). *The Timing of Motherhood*. Lexington, Mass.: Lexington Books.

Webster's Ninth New Collegiate Dictionary (1989). Springfield, Mass.: Merriam-Webster.

Wehr, T. A. (1989). "Seasonal Affective Disorders: A Historical Overview." In N. E. Rosenthal and M. C. Blehar, eds., *Seasonal Affective Disorders and Phototherapy*. New York: Guilford Press, pp. 11–32.

Wehr, T. A., Giesen, H., Schulz, P. M., Joseph-Vanderpool, J. R., Kasper, S., Kelly, K. A., and Rosenthal, N. E. (1989). "Summer Depression: Description of the Syndrome and Comparison with Winter Depression." In N. E. Rosenthal and M. C. Blehar, eds., *Seasonal Affective Disorder and Phototherapy*. New York: Guilford Press, pp. 55–63.

Wehr, T. A., Sack, D. A., and Rosenthal, N. E. (1987). "Seasonal Affective Disorder with Summer Depression and Winter Hypomania." *American Journal of Psychiatry* 144: 1602–1603.

Wehr, T. A. and Wirz-Justice, A. (1982). "Circadian Rhythm Mechanisms in Affective Illness and in Antidepressant Drug Actions." *Pharmacopsychiatry* 15: 31–39.

Wehr, T. A., Wirz-Justice, A., Goodwin, F. K., Duncan, F. K., and Gillin, J. (1979). "Phase Advance of the Circadian Sleep-Awake Cycle as an Antidepressant." *Science* 296: 710–713.

Wehr T. A., Jacobsen, F. M., Sack, D. A., Arendt, J., Tamarkin, L., and Rosenthal, N. E. (1986). "Phototherapy of Seasonal Affective Disorder: Time of Day and Suppression of Melatonin Are Not Critical for Antidepressant Effects." *Archives of General Psychiatry* 43: 870–875.

Weiss, R. L. and Heyman, R. E. (1990). "Marital Distress." In A. S. Bellack, M.

Hersen, and A. E. Kazdin, eds., *International Handbook of Behavior Modification and Therapy*. Second Edition. New York: Plenum Press, pp. 475–501.

Weissman, M. M. (1986). "Epidemiology of Depression: Frequency, Risk Groups, and Risk Factors." Unpublished paper, Symposium on Depression: Awareness, Recognition, Treatment. Bethesda, Md., June 8–10

Weissman, M. M. (1990). "Depression and Families: A Comment." In G. I. Keitner, ed., *Depression and Families: Impact and Treatment*. Washington, D.C.: American Psychiatric Association Press, pp. 185–190.

Weissman, M. M. and Boyd, J. H. (1983). "The Epidemiology of Bipolar and Nonbipolar Depression: Rates and Risks." In J. Angst, ed., *The Origins of Depression: Current Concepts and Approaches*. Berlin: Springer-Verlag, pp. 27–37.

Weissman, M. M., Gammon, G. D., John, K., Merinkas, G. G., Warner, V., Prusoff, B. A., and Sholomskas, D. (1987). "Children of Depressed Parents: Increased Psychopathology and Early Onset of Major Depression." *Archives of General Psychiatry* 44: 847–853.

Weissman, M. M. and Klerman, G. L. (1977). "Sex Differences and the Epidemiology of Depression." *Archives of General Psychiatry* 34(1): 98–111.

Weissman, M. M. and Klerman, G. L. (1985). "Gender and Depression." *Trends in Neuroscience* 8(9): 416–20 .

Weissman, M. M., Leaf, P. J., Bruce, M. L., and Florio, L. (1988). "The Epidemiology of Dysthymia in Five Communities: Rates, Risks, Comorbidity, and Treatment." *American Journal of Psychiatry* 145(7): 815–819.

Weissman, M. M. and Paykel, E. S. (1974). *The Depressed Woman: A Study of Social Relationships*. Chicago: University of Chicago Press.

Weissman, M. M., Wickramartne, P., Warner, V., John, K., Prusoff, B. A., Merikangas, K. R., and Gammon, G. D. (1987). "Assessing Psychiatric Disorders in Children: Discrepancies Between Mothers's and Children's Reports." *Archives of General Psychiatry* 44(8): 747–753.

Weller, E. B. (1988). "Further Comments" [on Kashani and Sherman, 1988]. *Integrative Psychiatry* 6: 141–142.

Weller, E. B. and Weller, R. A. (1990a). "Depressive Disorders in Children and Adolescents." In B. D. Garfinkel, G. A. Carlson, and E. B. Weller, eds., *Psychiatric Disorders in Children and Adolescents*. Philadelphia: W. B. Saunders, pp. 3–20.

Weller, E. B. and Weller, R. A. (1990b). "Grief in Children and Adolescents." In B. D. Garfinkel, G. A. Carlson, and E. B. Weller, eds., *Psychiatric Disorders in Children and Adolescents*. Philadelphia: W. B. Saunders, pp. 37–47.

Wender, P. H. and Klein, D. F. (1981). *Mind, Mood, and Medicine: A Guide to the New Biopsychiatry*. New York. Farrar, Straus and Giroux.

Wetzel, J. W. (1984). *Clinical Handbook of Depression*. New York: Gardner Press.

Whatley, S. A. and Owen, M. J. (1991). "The Cell, Molecular Biology, and the New Genetics." In P. McGuffin and R. Murray, eds., *The New Genetics of Mental Illness*. Oxford: Butterworth-Heinnemann, pp. 1—26.

White-Bowden, S. (1987). *Everything to Live For: A Mother's Story of Her Teenage Son's Suicide*. New York: Pocket Books.

Whybrow, P. C., Akiskal, H. S., and McKinney, W. T. (1984). *Mood Disorders: Toward a New Psychobiology*. New York: Plenum Press.

Williams, J. M. G. (1984). *The Psychological Treatment of Depression: A Guide to the Theory and Practice of Cognitive-Behavior Therapy.* New York: The Free Press.

Willner, P. (1985). *Depression: A Psychobiological Synthesis.* New York: Wiley-Interscience.

Wing, J. K. and Bebbington, P. (1985). "Epidemiology of Depression." In E. E. Beckham and W. R. Leber, eds., *Handbook of Depression: Treatment, Assessment, and Research.* Homewood, Ill.: Dorsey Press, pp. 765–794.

Wise, S. S. (1989). "Carbamazepine: Treatment Option for Bipolar Patients." *Hospital and Community Psychiatry* 40(2): 123–124.

Wolfe, S. M., ed. (1991). "Update: The Dangers of Prozac." *Public Citizen Health: Research Group Health Letter* 7(5): 8–9.

Wolpe, J. (1976). *Theme and Variations: A Behavior Therapy Casebook.* New York: Pergamon Press.

Wolpe, J. (1982). *The Practice of Behavior Therapy.* Third Edition. New York: Pergamon Press.

Wolpe, J. (1990). *The Practice of Behavior Therapy.* Fourth Edition. New York: Pergamon Press.

Wong, H. Z. (1982). "Asian and Pacific Americans." In L. R. Snowden, ed., *Reaching the Underserved: Mental Health Needs of Neglected Populations.* Vol. 3: Sage Annual Reviews of Community Mental Health. Beverly Hills, Cal.: Sage Publications, pp. 185–204.

Wong, H. Z. (1985). "Training for Mental Health Service Providers to Southeast Asian Refugees: Models, Strategies, and Curricula." In T. C. Owan, ed., *Southeast Asian Mental Health: Treatment, Prevention, Services, Training, and Research.* Bethesda, Md.: National Institute of Mental Health, pp. 345–390.

Woods, N. F. (1987). "Premenstrual Symptoms: Another Look." *Public Health Reports* 102(4, suppl.): 106–112.

Woody, G. E., O'Brien, C. P., and Rickels, K. (1975). "Depression and Anxiety in Heroin Addicts: Placebo Controlled Study of Doxepin in Combination with Methadone." *American Journal of Psychiatry* 132: 447–450.

World Health Organization (1978). *Mental Disorders: Glossary and Guide to Their Classification in Accordance with the Ninth Revision of the International Classification of Diseases.* Geneva: World Health Organization.

Wortman, R. A. (1981). "Depression, Danger, Dependency, Denial: Work with Poor, Black, Single Parents." *American Journal of Orthopsychiatry* 51(4): 662–671.

Wright, A. F. (1991). "The Genetics of the Common Forms of Dementia." In P. McGuffin and R. Murray, eds., *The New Genetics of Mental Illness.* Oxford: Butterworth-Heinemann, pp. 259–273.

Wright, J. H. and Beck, A. T. (1983). "Cognitive Therapy of Depression: Theory and Practice." *Hospital and Community Psychiatry* 34(12): 1119–1127.

Wurtman, R. J. (1985). "Aspartame: Possible Effect on Seizure Susceptibility [letter]." *Lancet* 2(8463): 1060.

Wurtman, R. J. (1987). "Nutrients Affecting Brain Composition and Behavior." *Integrative Psychiatry* 5: 226–257.

Wurtman, J. J., Brzezinski, A., Wurtman, R. J., and LaFerrere, B. (1989). "Effect of Nutrient Intake on Premenstrual Depression." *American Journal of Obstetrics and Gynecology* 161(5): 1228–1234.

Wurtman, R. J. and Wurtman, J. J. (1989). "Carbohydrates and Depression." *Scientific American* 260(1): 68–75.

Yalom, I. D., Lunde, D. T., Moos, R. H., and Hamburg, D. A. (1968). "Postpartum Blues' Syndrome." *Archives of General Psychiatry* 18(1): 16–27.

Yates, A. (1987). "Current Status and Future Directions of Research on the American Indian Child." *American Journal of Psychiatry* 144(9): 1135–1142.

Yates, W. R. (1988). "Depression and Cocaine Abuse: An Undesirable Link." *Clinical Advances in the Treatment of Psychiatric Disorders* 2(5): 4, 10.

Yeragani, V. K., Pohl, R., Aleem, A., Balon, R., Sherwood, P., and Lycaki, H. (1988). "Carbohydrate Craving and Increased Appetite Associated with Antidepressant Therapy." *Canadian Journal of Psychiatry* 33(7): 606–610.

Young, N. F. (1972). "Changes in Values and Strategies Among Chinese in Hawaii." *Sociology and Social Research* 56: 228–241.

Young, J. E., and Beck, A. T. (1982). "Cognitive Therapy: Clinical Applications." In A. J. Rush, ed., *Short-Term Psychotherapies for Depression*. New York: Guilford Press, pp. 182–214.

Young, K. P. H. (1983). *Coping in Crisis*. Hong Kong: Hong Kong University Press.

Young, M. A., Fogg, L. F., Scheftner, W. A., Keller, M. B., and Fawcett, J. A. (1990). "Sex Differences in the Lifetime Prevalence of Depression: Does Varying the Diagnostic Criteria Reduce the Female/Male Ratio?" *Journal of Affective Disorders* 18(3): 187–192.

Young, M. A., Scheftner, W. A., Fawcett, J. and Klerman, G. L. (1990). "Gender Differences in the Clinical Features of Unipolar Major Depressive Disorder." *Journal of Nervous and Mental Disease* 178(3): 200–203.

Youssef, F. A. (1990). "The Impact of Group Reminiscence Counseling on a Depressed Elderly Population." *Nurse Practitioner* 15(4): 35–38.

Zane, N., Sue, S., Castro, F. G., and George, W. (1982). "Service Models for Ethnic Minorities." In L. R. Snowden, ed., *Reaching the Underserved: Mental Health Needs of Neglected Populations*, vol. 3: Sage Annual Reviews of Community Mental Health. Beverly Hills, Cal.: Sage Publications, pp. 229–258.

Zinberg, N. E. (1990). "From Theory to Practice: The Planned Treatment of Drug Users." *International Journal of the Addictions* 25(2): 195–235.

Zisook, S. (1989). "Diagnosis and Treatment of Late-Life Depression." *Clinical Advances in the Treatment of Psychiatric Disorders* 3(1): 1–3, 10.

Zucker, I. (1989). "Seasonal Affective Disorders: Animal Models Non Fingo (sic)." In N. E. Rosenthal and M. C. Blehar, eds., *Seasonal Affective Disorders and Phototherapy*. New York: Guilford Press, pp. 149–164.

NAME INDEX

Johnson, S. R., 327
Jones, B. E., 413, 414–15, 418
Jones, M., 392
Joyce, P. P., 296

Kahn, A., 120
Kambe, T., 405
Kanahele, G., 403
Kanarek, R. B., 92, 94, 95–96, 117, 144–45, 154–55, 156, 315, 407
Kanfer, F. H., 239
Kantak, K. M., 143
Kaplan, H. I., 15, 312, 338–39, 340, 341, 349
Karasu, T. B., 175–76, 179, 290, 293, 295, 301, 302
Kashani, J. H., 362, 368, 370, 371
Kasper, J. A., 335
Kasper, S., 108, 116
Kathol, R. G., 15
Katon, W., 2
Katona, C. L., 446n8
Katz, J. L., 323–24
Katz, M. M., 3, 398, 404
Kaye, W. H., 93, 153
Kazdin, A. E., 368, 431
Keane, S. M., 337
Keitner, G. I., 390
Keller, M. B., 31
Kennedy, S. H., 157
Kessler, R., 406
Keyes, C. F., 3, 403
Khantzian, E. J., 138, 148
Kieber, H. D., 428
Killern, J. D., 154
Kim, H. R., 122
Kim, S. C., 425
Kingsbury, S. J., 305
Kinzel, D., 409
Kinzie, J. D., 423
Kirby, H., 337
Kirk, L., 93
Klein, D. F., 6, 10–11, 15, 17, 62, 63, 94, 126, 158, 169, 271, 290, 295–96
Klein, M., 356
Kleinman, A., 3, 398, 400, 403
Klerman, G. L., 1, 5, 18–20, 22, 187–93, 196, 198, 200, 204, 208, 264, 306, 312, 313, 314, 316, 330–31, 388, 441n2
Knight, C., 307
Kobren, G., 339, 340, 452n6
Koenig, H. G., 349

Kolata, G., 46, 47, 145
Kolko, D. J., 366
Koplan, C. R., 361, 367, 368
Koslow, S. H., 65, 72, 74, 75, 83, 443n8
Kosten, T. R., 428
Kotik, D., 175
Kotik-Harper, D., 337
Kovacs, M., 315, 356, 357, 358, 361, 362, 365, 372
Kraepelin, E., 8, 35, 160
Kramlinger, K. G., 125
Kravitz, H. M., 70, 86, 103, 444n3
Kripke, D. F., 114
Krucoff, C., 110
Kuhar, M. J., 138, 447n12
Kulka, R., 421
Kupfer, D. J., 35, 60, 65, 70, 71, 83, 103, 104, 109, 114, 313, 314, 315
Kunz, J. R., 317, 329

Lacoste, V., 107, 111, 115, 116, 118
Laessle, R. G., 154
Laird, L. K., 68
Lamberg, L., 98, 102, 105, 107, 444n2, 445n4
Lansky, M. R., 393
Larson, R., 370
Larson, R. W., 359
Lasagna, L., 121
Lau, T., 402
Lawson, J. S., 122
Lazarus, A. A., 233
Leary, W. E., 446n5
Leber, W. R., 9, 269, 272, 312
Lebra, T. S., 401, 405
Lee, C. M., 391
Lehmann, L., 135, 141, 145, 146, 147, 148, 149
Lehrer, P. M., 220
Lemus, C., 92
Lentz, R. D., 13, 15
Lepkifker, F., 122, 124
Lesnoff-Caravaglia, G., 346
Lesse, S., 16
Levy, A. B., 156
Lewinsohn, P. M., 219, 233–35, 240, 242, 260, 261
Lewy, A. J., 113, 115
Liberman, R. P., 243
Lidz, T., 317
Lieber, A., 71, 83, 443n7
Liebowitz, M. R., 30

SUBJECT INDEX